The Sources of Labour Law

Studies in Employment and Social Policy

VOLUME 54

Editors

Professor Alan Neal (founding editor of the *International Journal of Labour Law and Industrial Relations*, and Convenor of the European Association of Labour Law Judges); Professor Manfred Weiss (past president of the International Industrial Relations Association); and Professor Birgitta Nyström (professor of private law at the Law Faculty, University of Lund, Sweden, and member of the European Committee of Social Rights).

Objective

Studies in Employment and Social Policy series seeks to provide a forum for highlighting international and comparative research on contemporary areas of significance for evaluation and regulation of the world of work.

Introduction

Launched in 1997, the Studies in Employment and Social Policy Series now boasts over fifty titles, addressing key policy and development issues in the fields of industrial relations, labour law, social security, and international labour regulation.

Content

With contributions from leading figures in the field, the series brings together key policymakers, academics, and regulators, providing a unique context in which to analyse and evaluate the rapid and dramatic work and social policy developments taking place around the globe.

The titles published in this series are listed at the end of this volume.

The Sources of Labour Law

Edited by

Tamás Gyulavári
Emanuele Menegatti

Wolters Kluwer

Published by:
Kluwer Law International B.V.
PO Box 316
2400 AH Alphen aan den Rijn
The Netherlands
E-mail: international-sales@wolterskluwer.com
Website: lrus.wolterskluwer.com

Sold and distributed in North, Central and South America by:
Wolters Kluwer Legal & Regulatory U.S.
7201 McKinney Circle
Frederick, MD 21704
United States of America
Email: customer.service@wolterskluwer.com

Sold and distributed in all other countries by:
Air Business Subscriptions
Rockwood House
Haywards Heath
West Sussex
RH16 3DH
United Kingdom
Email: international-customerservice@wolterskluwer.com

ISBN 978-94-035-0284-7

e-Book: ISBN 978-94-035-0204-5
web-PDF: ISBN 978-94-035-0235-9

Editors

Tamás Gyulavári is a professor of Labour Law and Chair of the Labour Law Department at Pázmány Péter Catholic University in Budapest, Hungary. He studied and did research at the Universities of Budapest, Warwick, Groningen and Aix-Marseilles and was also a visiting fellow at the European University Institute in Florence in 2013. He has been a regular lecturer at the Academy of European Law in Trier, and lectured at several universities, including Porto, Bologna, Vienna, Quito, Jakarta and Chicago. He is the founding editor of the *Hungarian Labour Law E-Journal*. He has been engaged in a dozen of European projects with several international organisations and institutions, including the ILO and ETUI. He is the member of the European Labour Law Network and the Academic Network of Experts on Disability.

Emanuele Menegatti is Professor of Labour Law and Dean of the School of Economics and Management at the University of Bologna. He has been a visiting professor at many Universities, including the University of Illinois, Monash University (Melbourne), Curtin University (Perth), Pázmány Péter Catholic University (Budapest, Hungary). He is the editor-in-chief of the *Italian Labour Law E-Journal*. His main fields of specialisation are Comparative and EU Labour Law. His main current research interests include the balance between social rights and economic freedoms in European Union law, minimum wage regulation, new forms of work in the gig-economy. He is the author of two books and a broad number of scientific publications on high-ranking Italian and international journals.

Contributors

Edoardo Ales is Full Professor of Labour and Social Security Law at the Department of Law of the University of Naples 'Parthenope' (Italy). He also teaches European Labour Law at the LUISS – G. Carli in Rome (Italy) and the Vienna University of Economics and Business (Austria). He is an invited professor of International and European Labour Law at the Pontifical Lateran University (Vatican State). He is Member of the Board of Directors of the *Giornale del Diritto del Lavoro e delle Relazioni Industriali*, of *Rivista del Diritto della Sicurezza Sociale*, of the *Italian Labour Law E-Journal*. He is Member of the Scientific Committee of the Marco Biagi Foundation of the University of Modena and Reggio Emilia (Italy). He is the National Expert for Italy in the ICF-ECE and MoveS Network supporting the EU Commission in the field of Labour Law and Free Movement of Workers.

Mark Bray holds the Foundation Chair in Employment Studies at the University of Newcastle, Australia. He is a lead author (with Peter Waring, Rachel Cooper and Johanna Macneil) on the widely adopted university textbook, *Employment Relations: Theory and Practice* (4th Edition, 2018, McGraw-Hill, Sydney) and has recently authored (with Johanna Macneil and Andrew Stewart) the research monograph *Cooperation at Work: How Tribunals Can Help Transform Workplaces* (Federation Press, Sydney, 2017). His current research projects include studies of cooperation in the workplace and the roles of different regulatory instruments, like awards and collective agreements.

Alan C. Neal is Professor of Law in the University of Warwick, United Kingdom, and an employment judge in the Central London Employment Tribunals. He is the Convenor of the European Association of Labour Court Judges. He is a lifetime professor in the Zhejiang University (PRC) and Visiting Professor in the Beijing Jiao Tong University (PRC), as well as in the University of Paris II (Pantheon) and USEK (Beirut). He was the founding editor and is now Scientific

Director of the *International Journal of Comparative Labour Law and Industrial Relations*. He is the General Editor of the monograph series 'Studies in Employment and Social Policy' (published by Kluwer Law International).

Isabelle Daugareilh is a CNRS research director in the Center for Comparative Labour and Social Security Law, at Bordeaux University. She is a specialist in international and comparative labour law and has been teaching in several master's programmes at Bordeaux University and Bordeaux Institute for Political Studies. She is an associate researcher at Interuniversity Research Centre on Globalization and Work (CRIMT) in Canada.

Michael Doherty is Professor of Law, and Head of the Department of Law, at Maynooth University (Ireland), with particular expertise in the areas of Irish and EU employment and labour law, industrial relations and social dialogue. He has published widely in national and international outlets on these topics and presented his work at numerous domestic and international conferences. He is a frequent media contributor on labour relations issues and a member of a number of pan-European research networks.

Jedidiah Kroncke is an Associate Professor of Law at the University of Hong Kong. His work centres on the relationship of law to economic and political development, with a focus on alternative forms of labour and property institutions. As a comparative and historical scholar, his writing has focused on the political economy of the American, Chinese and Brazilian legal systems as well as the general development of comparative law as a global discipline.

Rochelle Le Roux is Professor in the Faculty of Law at the University of Cape Town. She currently serves as a non-executive director of the South African Reserve Bank. Some of her publications include *Harassment in the Workplace: Law, Policies and Processes*, *Reinventing Labour Law*, both with Alan Rycroft; *Laws Against Strikes* with the late Prof Sir Bob Hepple and Prof Silvana Sciarra; and *Retrenchment Law in South Africa*.

David Mangan is Assistant Professor at the Department of Law, Maynooth University. His research in labour, common law obligations and information technology has been published internationally. Prior to moving to Ireland, David completed his doctorate and subsequently held academic positions in the United Kingdom.

José María Miranda Boto is Lecturer in Labour Law at the University of Santiago de Compostela in Spain. He is the author of over 100 papers on Spanish and European Labour Law. He is the member of several funded research projects on Spanish and European Labour Law for the European Commission, the Spanish Government, regional authorities and trade unions. He is also the member of the

Experts' Group designated by the Ministry of Employment of Spain to study the consequences of *the De Diego Porras* ECJ's ruling; Spanish expert for the Conseil d'orientation pour l'emploi of the French Government; Secretary-General of the Spanish Association of Labour and Social Security Law.

Łukasz Pisarczyk is Professor at the University of Warsaw, Department of Labour Law and Social Policy; Visiting Professor at the University of Silesia in Katowice; from 2016 to 2018, Member of the Codification Committee of Labour Law; Head of Postgraduate Studies (Labour Law) at the Faculty of Law, Warsaw University; General Secretary of the Polish Section of the International Society for Labour and Social Security Law; Member of Editorial Board of the journal *Monitor Prawa Pracy* (Monitor Labour Law); Associate Editor of the journal *Studia Iuridica*; and Author of numerous scholar publications.

Joellen Riley Munton is a professor of Law at the University of Technology Sydney. She has been teaching and researching in the field of labour law since 1998. Her academic career includes time on the law faculties of the University of New South Wales and the University of Sydney (where she served as Dean and Professor of Labour Law from 2013 till 2018). She is also admitted as a legal practitioner in New South Wales.

Martin Risak is Associate Professor in the Department of Labour Law and Law of Social Security at the University of Vienna (Austria) and the chairperson of Senate II of the Austrian Equal Treatment Commission. He was an associate with the international law firm CMS Reich-Rohrwig Hainz, Professor of Labour Law and Civil Law at the University of Passau (Germany) and a Marie Curie-Fellow at the University of Otago (New Zealand). He is the national expert for Austria of the European Centre of Expertise ('ECE') in the field of labour law, employment and labour market policies that advises the European Commission.

Olga Rymkevich is a senior researcher in labour law and industrial relations at the Marco Biagi Foundation, University of Modena and Reggio Emilia, Modena (Italy). She graduated in St. Petersburg State University, Russia, in foreign languages and international relations and in Economics in the University of Modena, Italy, and Reggio Emilia and has a degree of PhD in Labour Law (University of St. Petersburg, Russia). Her research interests include international and comparative labour law. She also serves as a managing editor of *The International Journal of Comparative Labour Law and Industrial Relations* (Kluwer Law International).

Christian Højer Schjøler is Associate Professor in the Department of Law at the University of Southern Denmark and specialises in labour law and employment law and European Labour Law. He publishes internationally as well as in

Danish. He wrote a comprehensive doctoral thesis on the topic of age discrimination and publishes independently as well as a co-author. Prior to his career in Academia, he worked as a solicitor in an employer organisation and in law firms representing both employers and employees.

Paul Secunda is a professor of Law at Marquette University Law School in Milwaukee, Wisconsin. In his eighteenth year of teaching, he focuses on workplace, benefits and education law, often taking an international and comparative law focus. He is a senior Fulbright Scholar, member of the American Law Institute, and his research concerns the labour, civil and retirement rights of employees and students. He has written dozens of articles, books and chapters on these topics.

Iacopo Senatori is Researcher of Labour Law at the Marco Biagi Foundation, University of Modena and Reggio Emilia. He received a PhD in Labour Law and Industrial Relations at the University of Bologna. He is Coordinator of the Labour Law Area in the PhD Programme of Labour, Development and Innovation at the University of Modena and Reggio Emilia; Managing Editor of the *Italian Labour Law E-Journal.* His research interests include EU Labour Law, freedom of association and collective bargaining, workers' well-being and the regulation of new forms of work. He is the author of a book and several articles and essays written in Italian and English, published on high-ranking national and international journals. He has coordinated several international research projects co-funded by the European Commission.

Andrew Stewart is the John Bray Professor of Law at the University of Adelaide, a Legal Consultant to the law firm Piper Alderman and an editor of the *Australian Journal of Labour Law*. His books include *Stewart's Guide to Employment Law, Creighton & Stewart's Labour Law, Cooperation at Work: How Tribunals Can Help Transform Workplaces* (with Mark Bray and Johanna Macneil) and *The Wages Crisis in Australia* (co-edited with Jim Stanford and Tess Hardy). His current research projects include studies of the prevalence and regulation of internships, and of work organised through digital platforms.

Jenny Julén Votinius, Professor in private law at the Faculty of Law, Lund University, has wide experience of labour law research in comparative and international settings. She has been a visiting researcher at the University of California in Berkeley. Her works regularly appear in high-impact journals and international publications. Her research is characterised by an interdisciplinary approach, integrating perspectives from social science and political philosophy in the legal analysis. Julén Votinius serves in the European Commission Expert Legal Network in Gender Equality, and she has repeatedly served as an expert to the ILO, *inter alia,* within a project on the prevention and resolution of individual labour disputes.

Manfred Weiss has been a full professor for labour law and civil law (first at the University of Hamburg and since 1977 at the Goethe University in Frankfurt); Professor emeritus since 2008; 2000–2003 President of ILERA; 1998–2002 Deputy President of German Lawyers' Association (DJT); for many years, Consultant to the International Labour Organisation since 1980 and to the Commission of the EU. He received Honorary Doctorates in Budapest (2005), Lima (2006), Bordeaux (2011), Northwest University (NWU) / South Africa (2015); Award of the Labour Law Research Network (LLRN) for outstanding contribution to Labour Law (2015).

Dong Yan received his doctoral degree from the University of Warwick and currently acts as the associate professor in the Law School of Beijing Foreign Study University. He is a standing member of China Social Law Society and has chaired a number of labour law research projects since 2011. He has been a member of the Chinese Bar Association since 2016 and part-time labour arbitrator in Beijing since 2018.

Summary of Contents

Table of Contents

Foreword

Labour law in the past thirty years has suffered from an Alice in Wonderland syndrome where perceptions are distorted leading to disorientation. Those who wish to have a certain labour standard abolished often do not attack it directly but instead proclaim some noble-sounding goal, such as flexibility, and declare that working people do not want protectionism but prefer choice. Those who oppose the abandonment of the endangered labour standard find themselves portrayed as opposing 'flexibility' and by implication, as favouring rigidity and protectionism. Media coverage is brief, with little or no examination of the potential result of dismantling labour standards. Today we see books and articles about rising inequality in society, a result which surely could have been predicted thirty years ago by anyone seriously considering the impact of lowering labour standards.

This movement to deregulate must be seen in a wider context. Sir Otto Kahn-Freund once observed that economics is the primary force in industrial relations, with labour law a secondary force that seeks to restrain the power of management and support workers. This undoubtedly is correct, but the focus should not be on management but on capital. Managers are merely the agents of the company. What has changed greatly since the early 1980s are the expectations of the owners of the company. There has been acceptance of shareholder value theory, which states that the most important measure of a company's performance is the extent to which it brings value to shareholders, that is, whether the price of the company's stock increases and dividends increase. Once those who invest in stocks embraced this theory, managers were compelled to increase earnings. Modifying Kahn-Freund's framework for today's reality, we see that labour law is seeking to restrain the power of investors as they seek the highest return on their investments.

The easiest way for capital/management to reduce the cost of producing a product or service is to reduce the cost of labour. While some efficiencies can be achieved by improved organisation of work and upgrading the skills of workers, more significant cost reductions can be gained, and gained more quickly, by the employer/capital moving work from regular to 'temporary' employees, by categorising workers as independent contractors rather than employees, and by offering work as needed rather than on a set schedule. In this way, various items can be avoided, such as redundancy pay and payments for health or accident insurance, as only employees are covered. By the time individuals realise the effect the insecurity of work has on their standard of living, they are often powerless. As individuals they have no bargaining power. Moreover, unions traditionally have relied on the ability to engage in industrial action as the basis of bargaining power, but these workers often cannot go on strike because they are neither viewed as employed nor are they working on any regular basis for the same company.

This phenomenon, labelled the fissuring of work by Professor David Weill, is found in many countries, but the labour laws of these countries are quite different. How has labour law, once thought robust become so weakened in setting standards for those who work? This volume explores how companies circumvented existing labour regulation by devising new patterns of engaging individuals to undertake work such that labour costs are lowered with work for many individuals insecure. This analysis can be done only by those who possess a deep understanding not only of labour law but also of industrial relations systems, collective bargaining and social history. In particular, the scholar must understand how the law responds to and supports the industrial relations system and how it regulates the labour market.

Tamás Gyulavári and Emanuele Menegatti have assembled a group of eminent scholars who engage in a careful and most thoughtful analysis of these issues. Comparative labour lawyers will especially appreciate the unusual attention paid to the sources of change (e.g., the legislature, the courts (and at what level) and the social partners through collective bargaining). Not only is this a volume to read, but one to keep as an invaluable reference source.

Janice Bellace
University of Pennsylvania

Acknowledgements

The editors would like to express their acknowledgements above all to the authors of this volume and everyone at Kluwer Law International, in particular Suzanne Leppen and Christine Robben for their helpful and friendly editorship. Professor Alan C. Neal has also given precious help at all stages of the publication process, starting from the very beginning. We are also grateful to Gábor Kártyás, Sylvaine Laulom and Jeremias Prassl for their help, comments and advice. Finally, a special thanks goes to Leonardo Battista for his remarkable support through all the editorial process.

Budapest and Bologna, September 2019
Tamás Gyulavári and Emanuele Menegatti

CHAPTER 1

Introduction: Recent Trends in the Hierarchy of Labour Law Sources

Tamás Gyulavári & Emanuele Menegatti

A remarkable building stands in the heart of Cordoba, the so-called Mosque-Cathedral. The Mosque was constructed from 784 AD and the result is a fantastic forest of columns. In 1523, the transformation of the central part of the Mosque to a Cathedral was decided by the Bishop. When partial demolition of the Mosque started, the Town Council appealed all the way to Emperor Charles V. When the Emperor saw the demolition in 1526, he reportedly said:

> Had I known what this was, I would not have allowed it to reach the ancient part, because you have done what could be done anywhere; and you have undone that which is unique in the world.

The editors of this book perceive labour law as a 'unique' achievement of modern civilised societies, which should be protected like the great monuments of world architecture. However, in the last decade, a gradual 'demolition' of labour standards can be seen all over the world. Recently labour law institutions, just like ancient buildings in recent history, have been under pressure of change and 'modernisation', whatever this latter is supposed to mean.

In employment regulation, 'flexibility' has become the new incantation, which new policy inevitably leads to degrading protection of employees, 're-structuring' of labour law regulation. Flexibilisation of labour law is pursued not only by amendments of existing labour provisions but also by reshuffling the sources and structure of labour regulation. The aim of the book is to focus on this second trend, namely the changing structure of regulating employment relations.

1.1 OBJECTIVES AND STRUCTURE OF THE BOOK

The challenge of flexibilisation has been anatomised by a large number of books and articles in recent years. Our venture in this book goes beyond the details of flexibilised labour laws, and rather watches the field of regulation from a distance above, like from an aircraft. The structure of labour law sources is a distinctive feature of labour law regulation, since there is a historically elaborated set of sources and also a traditional hierarchy of statutory law, collective agreements at various levels and the employment contract.

Thus, the fundamental objective of the book is to outline the relevant sources of labour regulation, starting from statutory law, down to collective bargaining and individual agreements, not forgetting judicial and unilateral sources (e.g., company statutes and by-laws). The main sources of labour law will be highlighted both from a comparative/horizontal perspective and also from the prospect of national labour law. Therefore, the book may contribute to a deeper understanding of labour regulation in the different corners of the planet. It may also help the reader to understand the labour regulation of the examined countries.

Beyond enumerating and analysing the sources of labour law, the hierarchy of these sources is our second main topic. The relationships between these fundamental pillars of labour law have traditionally been built on the concept of favourability, which considers the interest of the employee above all the basis of regulation. The principle of employee's 'favour' makes statutory law the legal minimum, which may be improved by collective agreements, making the employment contracts the last layer of obligatory norms.

The idea of this book was inspired by our experience from many countries all over the world, which drew attention to cracks and fissures on the above characterised classical 'pyramid' of labour law sources. We had the impression that the traditional hierarchy of labour law, built on the principle of favour, had been endangered by massive flexibilisation tendencies regarding both collective agreements and individual employment contracts. So, our hypothesis was that the structure of labour law sources and their hierarchy have recently been challenged by endeavours of legislation, politicians, economists and of course employers' lobbies.

Therefore, the underlying aim of this book is to map tendencies tangible all over the world in relation to recent transformations of labour law sources and their hierarchical order. First, the authors of the national chapters will describe the structure of labour law regulations in the examined legal systems. Second, the hierarchy of these sources, its historical development and recent reforms will be highlighted.

What is the central pillar of labour regulation in the given legal system? Is there an effective collective bargaining and at what level(s)? What is the role for contractual freedom of the parties? How is the traditional hierarchy between these sources and has it been changed recently? These questions and many related ones will be answered by the authors of the book, who are all distinguished labour law scholars from the five continents. As a result, the reader will gain a thorough and comprehensive knowledge of labour law regulation and recent tendencies in national labour laws in various corners of the globe.

Thus, the book is addressed to the changing hierarchy of labour law sources in a selection of countries. We will focus on the elaboration of the traditional hierarchy of these sources, such as between the law, different levels of collective agreements and the agreements of the parties of the employment contract, in the light of recent trends. The book will be divided into two parts. The first part will consist of five chapters on horizontal issues. The second part of the volume contains fifteen national reports from all continents, however, with a strong focus on Europe (representing ten countries of the fifteen reports). In the following sections we will outline the contents of the horizontal and the national chapters.

1.2 HORIZONTAL CHAPTERS

The book contains five horizontal chapters.

In Chapter 2, Alan Neal provides a historical reconstruction of the roots of the current regulation of work. He considers in the first place the centrality of the contract of employment, giving account of the traditional division between the common law approach and the civil law tradition, adding on the side an insight on the progressive adoption of the principles of 'contract' in the Chinese system. The historical distinction between western market economies and socialist systems as for the increasing dominant role of states normative intervention and the consideration given to collective agreements is at the basis of the Author's subsequent considerations. Neal's comparative analysis eventually leads to the conclusion that the current regulatory framework should be urgently revised, being no longer able to reflect modern employment relations and labour markets.

In Chapter 3, Edoardo Ales analyses the regulatory function of collective agreements in the light of its relationship with statutory instruments and individual workers' rights, adopting a multilevel approach that involves international and supranational provisions of collective and individual labour law. In this regard, he takes into close scrutiny the large recognition – and its limits – of regulatory (and derogatory) functions of collective agreements made by the International Labour Organisation, the European Union (EU) and the Council of Europe primary and secondary statutory instruments. As Ales interestingly argues, the extensive role attributed to collective bargaining has eventually produced a 'downscaling' of the individual employment contract regulatory capacity.

In following Chapters 4 and 5, Joellen Riley Munton and Martin Risak consider the role played by case law, respectively, in common law and civil law countries in the framework of the labour law sources. They show how, despite the well-known distinct function assigned to the judges in the legal systems belonging to the two families – making the law through their decisions versus application of the law given by legal codes – the role they eventually played in the development of labour law is remarkably similar.

More in detail, Riley gives account of the way common law jurisprudence has developed many central concepts of labour law, first and foremost the definition of 'employment', and adapted them to the challenges arising from the constant transformation of work; while, at the same time, courts have had to face the considerable complexity created by the increasing presence of statutory law in the field of labour relations.

On the side of civil law countries, Risak explains as the courts ended up playing an important law-creating role, particularly when they have to fill the gap in statutory legislation. This function carried on by labour courts and tribunals has been permitting the same adaptation, as in common law systems, of labour rules to the changing world of work, taking care of the 'protective' function of labour law.

In Chapter 6, Emanuele Menegatti investigates the impact that the European Economic Governance has had on the hierarchy of labour law sources of many Member States. He explains how the EU, clearly supporting the trend promoted by neo-liberal market mechanisms, challenged that model of employment regulation, built on a rigid floor of mandatory statutory protections and a centralised system of collective bargaining, endorsing a completely different and more flexible one. Menegatti then analyses the results achieved by the EU economic governance in a selection of countries, working out some conclusive considerations on its effectiveness.

1.3 THE CIRCLE AND ISSUES OF NATIONAL REPORTS

The second part of the book describes the developments in a wide range of countries, from five continents. In the selection process, the editors tried to ensure a colourful set of examples, representing different regions, legal traditions, social developments. Two-thirds of the examined countries are found in Europe, which are all EU Member States, except for Russia. This may be explained by the important role the European countries and also the EU plays in the regulation of labour standards. At the same time, countries from global North and global South are also involved in our analysis. Mentioning another possible aspect of clustering, continental legal systems and common law countries are also widely represented. Overall, the editors tried to include a large number of national laws representing different continents, regions, integrations and legal systems.

The national reports have a similar structure with the following main issues; however, the emphasis will always be put on the most crucial topics in the given country:

- the most important sources of labour law and their historical development;
- the relationship between law and collective agreements;
- the relationship between various levels of collective agreements, including decentralisation of collective bargaining;
- the relationship between employment contract and mandatory rules coming from statutory law and collective agreements; and finally
- the role of case law.

In the following parts of this introduction, we will provide a brief comparative analysis of the fundamental features of national labour regulations and the recent changes in the relationship between national labour law sources. First, we will touch upon the constitutional dimension of labour rights, which is followed by the relationship between statutory law and collective bargaining, collective bargaining decentralisation and the role of individual contracting.

1.3.1 The Constitutional Dimension of Labour Regulation

In the classical pyramid of statutory regulation, the Constitution plays a fundamental role, representing the top of the pyramid in many countries. At the same time, the constitutional traditions of the various countries and legal systems are quite diverse. Fundamentally, we have to make a distinction between continental legal systems, where a written Constitution compulsorily enlists, among others, the fundamental employment rights, and some common law countries without a written Constitution and a similar constitutional system.

The Constitution is self-evidently placed at the highest rank in the hierarchy of the sources in the countries with a continental legal system. This outstanding role in labour regulation is clearly reflected by the chapters on Denmark, France, Italy, Spain and Sweden. In South Africa, as explained by Rochelle Le Roux (Chapter 19), despite the common law roots, the 1996 Constitution is now the supreme source of law, which contains a Bill of Rights, including employment rights.

Germany is one of the best examples for the constitutional tradition and practice of European countries with a continental legal system. Manfred Weiss (Chapter 12) explains that in Germany, the Constitution is at the top of the hierarchy of sources of labour law. The first and most important chapter of the Constitution contains a catalogue of fundamental rights. These fundamental rights are the strongest pillar on which Germany is built. It has also a gap-filling function, as problems not regulated by the legislator have to be solved by recourse to the Constitution.

The German constitutional tradition has had a strong influence in Central and Eastern Europe, which is reflected by the chapters on Hungary and Poland. As a contrast, the Russian Constitution is also the supreme juridical source, defining the system of legal acts regulating labour relations, their scope and competence. However, from the point of view of labour law, the current provisions are characterised by a strong path dependency in relation to the previous Soviet Constitutions.

Common law countries are rather different in this respect from the above-mentioned tradition of continental legal systems. Andrew Stewart and Mark Bray (Chapter 7) report that Australia's Constitution, unlike its counterparts in some other countries, has nothing directly to say about labour standards. Nor does it formally enshrine human rights that might be asserted in an employment context. Moreover, the United States (US) Supreme Court, as highlighted by Paul Secunda (Chapter 21), even struck down many state workplace-protective legislation under the guise of a constitutional form of 'liberty of contract' between employer and employee. Finally, with regard to the United Kingdom (UK), Michael Doherty and David Mangan (Chapter 20) report that it does not operate under a written constitutional system. Rather, it employs an unwritten Constitution which places the government in a pivotal role of directing the sources of national labour law.

Besides the presence of a (written) Constitution, the Constitutional Court may also play an important role in elaborating labour standards. Some chapters provided excellent examples when the Constitutional Court remarkably influenced the elaboration of the system of labour law sources. For instance, in France, as explained by Isabelle Daugareilh (Chapter 11), legislation has been engaged in a process of decentralising collective bargaining towards the enterprise level since the 1980s. This movement has been supported by the Constitutional Court, as it established this relationship between law and collective bargaining in a ruling of 29 December 2004. Similarly, the Italian, Spanish, Polish and Hungarian chapters also provide many examples, when these Constitutional Courts have also played a fundamental role in the regulation of labour law sources.

1.3.2 The Relationship Between Statutory Law and Collective Bargaining

The classical relationship between statutory law and collective agreements (at any level) has been based on the 'principle of favour'. Namely, the collective agreement may derogate from the provisions of statutory law, if the derogation is allowed (formally not prohibited) by the law and the derogation is more favourable for the employee. This principle of favour has widely been used in national labour laws throughout the world. Based on the reports in this volume, we can state that this is the usual, widely accepted relationship between law and collective agreements in the examined countries.

The theoretical consideration behind this legal relationship is that statutory law establishes the minimum protection and these standards are partly *ius cogent*, which do not allow any deviation for other sources, but mostly dispositive rules, which may be improved by collective agreements and also by agreements of the parties (employment contract). Consequently, the collective agreement is considered as the main, but not the only, source of improving labour standards. And this improvement may be tailored by the contracting parties of the collective agreement to the special conditions and situation of the employer(s) or sector, depending on the level of the given collective agreement.

However, this easily understandable, simple relationship between law and collective bargaining has been slowly but constantly changing in several countries. Probably Hungary has introduced the most radical reform in 2012, by allowing free deviation even to the detriment of employees from most of the statutory minimum rules (of the Labour Code). The reason behind this radical reform was to stimulate hardly existing collective bargaining by incenting employers' interests to get more flexible employment conditions. In several countries, this legislative change has been more moderate (e.g., Australia, France, Italy and Poland), since the principle of favour remained the main rule; however, the number of exceptions giving way to *in peius* derogations have increased, particularly in the field of working time. In France, legislation has undermined the 'most favourable' principle that governed the hierarchy of sources by multiplying the opportunities for collective agreements to establish derogations *in peius*.

In Italy, collective agreements may introduce flexible arrangements on working time or on the use of atypical forms of employment, in such a way that it would be complicated to identify which regulatory solution fits better with the interest of the employees. The best description of the Italian relationship between the two sources is probably the image of a competition disguised as hierarchy, where the law, claiming its formal prominence, attempts to exert an influence on collective bargaining, whereas the latter, as an expression of contractual autonomy, tends to circumvent any external interference and conform to it only as long as it matches the social partners' will.

In Australia, legislative attention has been devoted to the circumstances in which registered collective agreements can breach the minimum standards set by either legislation or awards. These have involved a series of 'tests' administered by tribunals or other statutory agencies to determine whether agreements (individual or collective) are approved, and thereby gain legal standing. They have been variously called a no-disadvantage test, a fairness test and – the current nomenclature – a better off overall test. Their operation has often been controversial.

At the same time, many legal systems (e.g., Brazil, China, Germany, Russia and Spain) have kept the principle of favour (almost) unchanged. In these legal systems, the possibility of *in peius* derogations hardly exists and there is no increase in the number of exceptions from the general rule of *in melius* derogations. In Germany, the relationships are made somewhat complicated by the fact that if the law does not set a minimum standard but only contains non-binding regulations, the collective agreement may disregard these regulations. The problem is that it is often not clear whether the legislature intended to set binding or non-binding standards, and it is left to the courts to decide these cases by interpreting the legislative intent.

The Danish model is unique, as the passive role of the Parliament in relation to the formation of labour norms naturally adds to the perceived primacy of collective agreements, but it is not as such a strict rule resulting in a hierarchical primacy whereby collective agreements cannot be set aside by statutory legislation. It is rather a token of a high degree of voluntarism leaving rights and obligations on the labour market to the social partners to agree upon. Collective agreements are still the preferred way of regulating pay and working conditions, which meant that legislation has been sporadic and piecemeal. More so, when the legislature has seen fit to legislate on labour conditions, the purpose has not been to deregulate collective agreements, but rather to extend the well-proven principles and worker protection found in collective agreements to persons not covered by them.

Evidently, the relationship between statutory law and collective agreements is quite colourful around the world and it often exists in a quite complex system (*see* for instance Australia or France). Therefore, there is not one single trend in this respect, but rather a set of changes reflecting different legal and social realities. However, in a growing number of countries, it is a decisive trend to allow collective agreements to lower labour standards by *in pejus* derogations from statutory rules.

1.3.3 Decentralisation of Collective Bargaining

As for the internal hierarchy of collective bargaining, it is possible to work out from the national reports a general distinction between, on the one side, centralised collective bargaining systems, where sectoral-level agreements play normally the most important role, on the other side, largely or completely decentralised systems, based almost exclusively on single-employer agreements. Excluding China, Russia and the US, where collective bargaining, for the reasons explained by Dong Yan (Chapter 9), Olga Rymkevich (Chapter 16) and Paul Secunda (Chapter 21), does not have any significant role, to the first group belong the Nordic, Central and Southern European countries, plus South Africa and Brazil, to the second the Anglo-Saxon and Central-Eastern European countries.

In the decentralised system of collective bargaining, no significant change towards a different model of industrial relations has taken place in the last couple of decades, neither in the law nor in the industrial relations practices. Despite some legislative support – sometimes real, sometimes only apparent – collective bargaining coverage is not very significant in many of the countries considered, and steadily declining in all of them.

In the UK, as reported by Michael Doherty and David Mangan (Chapter 20), company collective agreements have always been the main and almost only level of collective bargaining, across the different political seasons, from the post-war period to the present. What has instead changed is the relevance of collective autonomy, marked by the switch away from collective labour law carried out by the Conservative government during the 1980s and never seriously reversed by its successors.

Similarly based almost only on company-level agreements is collective bargaining in the Central-Eastern European countries considered in this book. Here a free system of collective bargaining was developed only at the end of the 1990s, after the collapse of the communist system. However, coverage of collective bargaining has remained very low, even decreasing over the last years, notwithstanding the attempt of the Hungarian legislator, described by Tamás Gyulavári (Chapter 13), to incentivise the conclusion of collective agreements by increasing their ability to worsen most of the Labour Code provisions.

A very peculiar position of enterprise agreements is reported by Andrew Stewart and Mark Bray (Chapter 7), in the context of the layered system of Australian labour regulation. Company agreements have always had an extensive role in Australia, becoming at some points the main rule-making process. The primacy of company collective agreements is still supported by the current framework, set out by the Fair Work Act of 2009, even though falling coverage of collective bargaining is compromising their importance compared to other sources (legislation and awards). Multi-employer agreements, unlike company-level agreements, do not receive any statutory support. They are a rarity, and even when they apply, one employer can lawfully get rid of them by simply making his own firm-level agreement.

The relative stability of decentralised systems contrasts with the ongoing great transformation which centralised systems are facing. Multi-employer bargaining and, in particular, sectoral agreements have here traditionally served the purpose of taking wages and employment conditions out of competition. The combination between central governance of collective bargaining and statutory mandatory working conditions has, on the one side, compensated the asymmetry of bargaining power between the parties of the employment contract, preventing a deterioration of working conditions by individual negotiations and company-level agreements and, on the other side, created a levelled playfield for competition between companies (and workers) within the domestic markets.

However, the change of the economic paradigm brought by the neo-liberal globalisation has vanished the benefits this set-up of labour law sources granted to companies, which instead turned out to be rather undesirable for those employers having to compete on the global market. In the framework of global competition, especially for export-driven companies, wages and other employment conditions could no longer be excluded from competition; on the contrary, they have become key components of competitive strategies. Moreover, the volatility of globalised markets does not affect to the same extent companies belonging to the same sector; therefore, some of them might need to go beyond the uniformity of industry-level agreements and statutory protections.

In order to meet the request for more flexible and 'dynamic' working conditions prompted by the new economic setting, international and supranational institutions have started promoting a sort of neo-liberal agenda, which included the dogma of 'decentralisation', involving ample room for a flexible adaptation of working conditions at the firm level, beyond the uniformity of 'centralised' regulation.

This pressure towards decentralisation has achieved tangible results in many of the considered countries. Not so far as to overthrow the primary role of sectoral agreements, which is nevertheless under continual challenge. Indeed, the topics dealt with by company agreements have increased, now even related to crucial areas of employment regulation. Above all, the articulation and coordination of collective bargaining have been significantly altered, following two different processes of decentralisation. 'Organised' decentralisation, which has been mostly governed by the social partners (i.e., Denmark, Sweden, Germany and Italy) and in some cases by the legislator (i.e., France), and a parallel process of 'disorganised' decentralisation, affecting countries presenting high public debts and major macroeconomic imbalances, are carried out by the legislators under the pressure of international and supranational institutions, mostly the EU Commission (Chapter 6).

France is a very representative example. As described by Daugareilh (Chapter 11), competences, functions and overall relevance of company-level collective bargaining have constantly increased, starting from the *Auroux* reform of 1982. The Macron reform of 2017 has then taken the process of decentralisation to the next level, involving an unprecedented, and partly unconditional, primacy of company agreements over the declining regulatory capacity of sectoral agreements. In this respect, 'Disorganised' decentralisation reaches its climax in 'competitiveness collective agreements' (*accords de performance collective*), which may worsen working conditions, including salaries, provided by sectoral agreements, out of any union involvement and even out of any negotiation. In small companies, the employer can even propose a draft agreement made by himself, which, if approved by a qualified majority of the employees, automatically replaces any contrary and incompatible clause of the employment contract.

Another significant example is Spain, where Royal decree 3/2012, in the framework of the huge reform of the Spanish labour market aimed at tackling the great recession through a set of neo-liberal policies, has reversed the internal hierarchy of collective bargaining. As Miranda Boto explains (Chapter 17), in some areas – such as working time, job classification and wages – firm-level agreements prevail over industry-level agreements, out of any principle of favour and with no possibility for collective autonomy to overturn this rule. Furthermore, the same 2012 reform has also introduced the possibility for companies, facing an adverse situation, to suspend the application of certain conditions provided by collective agreements, consulting unions and/or employees' representatives.

Even Germany, despite having a strong surplus economy and being internationally considered as an example of 'controlled' decentralisation, has experimented some kind of 'disorganised' decentralisation, especially in the retail sector, achieved by companies simply withdrawing from the sectoral collective agreement.

The considered examples testify as the new economic paradigm has eclipsed the traditional function of collective bargaining in 'centralised' system. By allowing a customisation of employment conditions to companies' needs, which might involve a detrimental impact on working conditions set by statutes and sectoral agreements, collective bargaining has been diminishing the traditional protection afforded to workers and losing the capacity of regulating competition between companies.

Apparently, the instances of decentralisation have not affected Brazil and South Africa yet, still presenting a strongly centralised system of collective bargaining. As reported by Jedidiah Kroncke (Chapter 8), in Brazil firm-level agreements are not very common. A recent reform introduced in 2017, looking for more individualisation in labour regulation, will probably encourage company-level bargaining, but it is still to see. South Africa, explains Le Roux (Chapter 19), seems still moving on the opposite trend of centralisation of collective bargaining, due to its peculiar social, political and economic history.

Despite these two last cases, at the end of the day, the picture of the global trend we can work out from the national reports included in this book is that of a neo-liberal convergence between collective bargaining systems, mostly guided by the state legislative intervention.

1.3.4 The Role of the Employment Contract

The prevalence of mandatory minimum working conditions set out in statutory law and collective agreements over those agreed by the parties in the employment contract has traditionally granted the development of labour law. It would be otherwise easy for the employer imposing, thanks to her normally higher bargaining power, worse working conditions by means of individual negotiations. For this reason, in almost all the considered jurisdictions, as a general rule, only more favourable employment conditions expressly agreed in the employment contract can prevail over those established by the statutory and collective sources of employment regulation.

There are, however, some considerable exceptions. In Australia, as Stewart and Bray explain (Chapter 7), some individual agreements could have, under certain statutory conditions, the force of legislation, prevailing over working conditions established by awards and collective agreements. This is no longer the case, even if under the Fair Work Act 2009, there is still room for individual negotiation to introduce 'flexibility agreements' which can derogate to certain awards or collective agreement provisions.

A similar situation, where the employment contract has some room for derogating, even *in peius*, to certain statutory provisions is reported by Gyulavári for Hungary (Chapter 13) as a consequence of the Labour Code enacted in 2012. Also, in Brazil, according to Kroncke (Chapter 8), a dramatic increase of the role of the individual contracting has been put forward by a 2017 reform, where for high-income employees, individual agreements can replace the application of collective agreements.

The 'liberty of contract' was and is still held in the highest regard by the US legal system. Secunda (Chapter 21) argues that, notwithstanding the introduction of increasing common law and statutory law (federal and state) employment protection, a new 'Lochner era' – where workers' rights were abused without consequences – is probably shaping up. This is mostly caused by pre-dispute compulsory arbitration agreements which concern more than half of non-unionised workers. By signing these agreements, employees renounce to their right to settle disputes in courts and are also quite often prevented from participating in class-action lawsuits. This situation, for the reasons explained by Secunda, eventually makes it difficult for workers to enforce their rights.

Another recent example of statutory scheme allowing employees to sign away their rights is that provided by the UK legislation. A 2013 amendment to the Employment Rights Act 1996 has permitted a trade-off between shares and employment rights: if the worker accepts to become a shareholder of the employing company, he must surrender some important statutory protections.

On the opposite side are located the Nordic countries, where the space for individual contracting still remains limited. Jenny Julén Votinius (Chapter 18) details that in Sweden employees who are member of the signatory Trade Unions are entitled to the application of the collective agreements over the individual agreement, which cannot contradict the former. Employers, in their turn, because of the normative function of the collective agreements, are obliged to apply them to union and non-union members. In Denmark, the room for individual contracting seems even more restricted. Christian Højer Schjøler (Chapter 10) explains that the application of the agreement is effectively granted by the labour court, both for unionised and non-unionised workers, by a peculiar financial penalty, involving a punitive sanction. Furthermore, in the non-frequent cases in which collective agreements are not applicable, if the terms of the individual agreement are unreasonable, they can be modified by the court, notwithstanding the respect of statutory provisions.

The freedom of the parties to agree conditions different from those provided by the statutes and, above all, collective agreements, looks even narrower in South Africa, involving here any kind of derogation. As pointed out by Le Roux (Chapter 19), when collective agreements provide actual working conditions (and not just minimum), they are incorporated into the employment contracts with precedence even over more favourable working terms agreed by the parties.

Notwithstanding these exceptions to the favour principle, it does not look like there is an overall ongoing trend of enhancement of the individual autonomy over the minimum working conditions established by collective agreements and statutory law. National labour laws are still keen on compensating of the asymmetry of bargaining power between the parties of the employment contract. However, as considered above, the same cannot be said with regard to the asymmetry inherent collective bargaining at the firm level. Here the increasing precedence given to firm-level collective agreement over branch agreements and sometimes above statutes, out of any coordination with sectoral agreements, and, in some countries, even outside a real negotiation, can make totally useless the limitations still surrounding individual contracting. In other words, restrictions to the parties' freedom of contract could reveal to be useless if the employer can worsen employment condition by means of the full control granted him on company-level bargaining by legislations.

Part I Horizontal Issues

CHAPTER 2

Recalling Some of the Historical Roots for Twenty-First Century Approaches to Regulation of the World of Work

Alan C. Neal

2.1 INTRODUCTION

The juxtaposition of instruments designed to regulate individual employment relationships, collective-level agreements, and State-imposed legislation in the world of work has presented a variety of complex challenges to labour law scholars across generations. Thus, for example, when endeavouring to evaluate the relative standing or significance of the instruments developed to provide discipline for working life arrangements, focus has been placed upon the nature of individual relationships - for example, a claimed trend from 'status' to 'contract'.[1] So, too, has there been concern to test the legitimacy of the content and the legal standing of the 'agreements' entered into by parties commonly characterised as displaying a dramatic differential in bargaining power.[2] Meanwhile, when considering the implications of 'collectivisation' - whether on the labour side, in the shape of trade unions, or in relation to employing enterprises, through employers' associations or the like - importance has been placed upon 'the product of collective bargaining', in the shape of 'collective agreements' between the representatives of the often opposing interests of enterprises and

1. *See* the discourse in relation to this since the work of H. Maine, *Ancient Law: Its Connection with the Early History of Society and Its Relation to Modern Ideas* (London 1861).
2. *See*, for example, the five-volume work by S. Anderman, A. Neal, T. Sigeman & A. Victorin (eds), *Law and the Weaker Party: An Anglo-Swedish Comparative Study* (London 1981-1992) ['Anderman et al.'].

their workforces.[3] Always in the background (and, some would argue, increasingly at the forefront in modern regulatory arrangements) for the development of both individual and collective work relations has lurked 'the legislator' – setting the boundaries of the scope permitted by the State for freedom of action between the industrial parties, sometimes undertaking the dual role of actor (in the form of State-owned or controlled enterprises or undertakings) and regulator in the name of 'the public interest', and consistently defining the politico-economic direction desired for the national economy, of which industrial relationships constitute a fundamental component.

From today's perspectives, when addressing the development of regulatory techniques for the twenty-first-century world of work, what can be seen to be well-established instruments that have evolved over the preceding century-and-a-half are now approached through the optic of more recently developed forms of normative standard-setting. They are also seen against a backdrop of what has come to be described as 'globalisation', with all of its associated social, economic, and political challenges.

In consequence, a number of relatively recent phenomena have markedly affected the analysis of those working relationships. For those national systems which are subject to the regulatory arrangements of the European Union (EU), this would include the instruments elaborated within the 'social dialogue' developed in the context of EU social policy and law by reference to what are now Articles 151-156 of the Treaty on the Functioning of the European Union.[4] Of importance, too, has been the sharpened impact achieved by 'international labour standards' – particularly those enshrined in Recommendations and Conventions developed at the level of the International Labour Organisation (ILO).[5] That line of development at the supranational level has now shown itself to constitute an influential frame of reference for a wide range of modern trade agreements and international labour accords around the world.[6] By the same

3. *See* F. Schmidt & A. Neal, *Collective Agreements and Collective Bargaining* (Tübingen 1984), republished in *International Encyclopedia of Comparative Law*, Volume XV, Labour Law, Chapter 12 (Tübingen 2014) ['Schmidt & Neal']. *See also* L. Nagy, *The Socialist Collective Agreement* (Budapest 1984).
4. Originally introduced as Article 118b of the Treaty Establishing the European Community (TEC) (inserted by the Single European Act 1986), and thereafter developed as Articles 136-139 of the TEC. This EU notion of 'social dialogue', which can lead to agreements, differs from use of the same terminology by the ILO, which regards its 'social dialogue' as having a main aim to 'promote consensus building and democratic involvement among the main stakeholders in the world of work'.
5. *See* the ILO's *Declaration on Fundamental Principles and Rights at Work* (1998) and its 'Follow-up procedure', with concentration upon the 'Core Conventions' No. 29 (Forced Labour), No. 87 (Freedom of Association and Protection of the Right to Organise), No. 98 (Right to Organise and Collective Bargaining), No. 100 (Equal Remuneration), No. 105 (Abolition of Forced Labour), No. 111 (Discrimination Employment and Occupation), No. 138 (Minimum Age) and No. 182 (Worst Forms of Child Labour).
6. *See inter alia* the expression of those values – and direct textual incorporation of the language of the ILO 'Core Conventions' – in draft or final versions of the *Comprehensive Economic and Trade*

token, the increasing significance of 'Codes of Conduct' (including 'International Framework Agreements') which have developed during the past quarter of a century reflects a reality that the values encompassed by such 'international labour standards' are not confined to State or supranational diplomatic bodies, but also constitute an important consideration for both State-owned and private multinational enterprises. Whether articulated within the rhetoric of 'corporate social responsibility' or otherwise as part of initiatives designed to promote 'good corporate governance' (including respect for human rights and fundamental labour standards), the very existence of such instruments underlines the extent to which there has been an impact achieved by 'soft-law' initiatives designed to facilitate the underpinning of acceptable labour standards by both national and transnational employing organisations.[7] Indeed, there is evidence that the transformation of 'corporate social responsibility' from a 'corporate fig leaf' into a driver for improving governance and accountability standards in enterprises operating in the globalised economy has been accompanied by a variety of initiatives designed to provide 'soft-law' undertakings with the 'teeth' necessary to give them credibility in a globalised corporate environment.

Historically, however, it is only in the past century and a half that these interrelationships have come to the fore – principally in response to the development of a regulatory normative mechanism for collective labour representation, in the shape of the collective agreement – while modern evaluation of new forms of work, technology-driven relationships in the workplace, and tendencies towards de-collectivisation in employment relationships have moved us to a new era in which that triumvirate of normative instruments has itself been placed under challenge.

One problem with addressing issues concerning these regulatory instruments from a 'modern' perspective is that the thinking and assumptions of today are retroactively infused into evaluation of the historical roots from which the regulatory journey has developed. With that in mind, therefore, the following endeavours to offer a brief reminder of a more traditional era in which phenomena such as globalisation, collective bargaining, or individual employment relations were not necessarily approached in the same way as can now be seen. A time, too, when features such as 'platform working' or the ever-closer supervision of (and intrusion into) the personal space of workers in the digital

---

Agreement between Canada and the European Union (Chapter 23); the *Comprehensive and Progressive Agreement for Trans-Pacific Partnership*, replacing the previous draft proposed for a *Trans-Pacific Partnership*; and the *United States–Mexico–Canada Agreement* designed to replace the 1993 North American Free Trade Agreement arrangements between those three countries.

7. *See, inter alia*, European Commission, *Corporate social responsibility: A business contribution to sustainable development* (COM(2002) 347 final); A. Neal, 'Corporate Social Responsibility: Governance Gain or Laissez-Faire Figleaf?' (2008) 29 *Comparative Labor Law and Policy Journal* 459; European Commission, *A renewed EU strategy 2011-14 for Corporate Social Responsibility* (COM (2011) final); I. Chiu, 'An Institutional Theory of Corporate Regulation' (2018) 71 *Current Legal Problems* 279.

economy facilitated by modern technology were, for most observers and for those involved, scarcely matters for concern.

2.2 THE FOUNDATION STONE OF SOMETHING KNOWN AS THE 'CONTRACT OF EMPLOYMENT'

The historical centrality of the individual employment contract in national systems has been described at length by leading authors.[8] Generally, the historical trajectory reflects a development from traditional notions of servitude (in particular, the notion of 'master and servant' law) in the direction of an economic relationship governed by law, in the context of which fundamental questions are raised as to whether a 'contractual' frame of reference imposed by the law should draw upon the normal principles applicable to arm's-length commercial relations or should be infused with some degree of modification in the interest of the protection of 'the weaker party' (generally regarded as the worker).[9]

In passing, a sometimes overlooked feature of modern scholarship should be mentioned. Much of the scholarship upon which analytical reliance is placed in modern debate derives from experience under common law systems - including the United Kingdom, the United States of America, and various former colonial possessions spread around the globe. Partly on account of the dominance of the English language as the medium of communication for that scholarship in this field, that experience may be regarded as holding an over-exaggerated position of influence for the discourse engendered. While European Continental experience is well represented in scholarly writings utilising the French, German, Italian, or Spanish languages, the pragmatic reality - especially since the emergence of the World Wide Web - has been that material produced in English has touched a wider audience, with the consequence that some of the significant experiences in those contexts is underestimated in popular presentations. This, of course, is not a new phenomenon - as the predominance of German-language scholarly writing in the field confirms in the first half of the twentieth century, just as French-language contributions had earlier held particular sway around the turn of that century.

Systems which have developed under the umbrella of the civil law tradition include those which have drawn directly and heavily upon either Romanist or Germanic traditions of labour regulation - and, indeed, Supiot has

8. Each national system has given rise to major detailed treatises on the subject. For a comparative 'European' perspective *see*, for example, the contributions in B. Hepple (ed.), *The Making of Labour Law in Europe: A Comparative Study of Nine Countries up to 1945* (London & New York 1986) and the broader canvas painted by the subsequent B. Hepple & B. Veneziani (eds), *The Transformation of Labour Law in Europe: A Comparative Study of 15 Countries 1945-2004* (London 2009) - in particular the respective chapters by Bruno Veneziani.
9. *See* Anderman et al., *supra*.

gone so far as to suggest that, at least so far as the conception of the employment relationship is concerned, all European systems have drawn inspiration from one or other of those roots.[10] While this proposition may invite a raised eyebrow when applied, without reservation, to the socialist systems of labour regulation developed after the Bolshevik Revolution of 1917,[11] the position outside Europe is more variegated - with a variety of 'borrowings',[12] imposition of foreign models under colonialisation[13] and some (limited) attempts to develop 'virgin soil' frameworks.[14]

Even as recently as in the last half-century, organisational analyses of working relationships have attracted attention through various attempts to develop a frame of reference within which to evaluate the relationship between individual workers and their employing organisations from sociological, political, or economic viewpoints. By way of example, consideration of the notion of 'status and contract' from an 'industrial relations' perspective advanced by Streeck in the mid-1980s[15] offers an interesting contrast between that author's thesis and the 'legal perspective' use of the same terms by labour law commentators such as Kahn-Freund.[16] The point for present purposes is that both of these approaches derive their terminology of 'status to contract' from much more deep-rooted sources - in this case, more than a century earlier, in the work of Henry Maine.[17]

A sharp contrast is to be found as between the approaches adopted in different national systems to this crucial issue. For example, the English Common Law has consistently refused to treat the contract of employment as a species of 'special contract'. Thus, applicability of rules on 'duress', or the consequences of 'illegality' in relation to any element in the relationship, can

10. *See* A. Supiot, *Au-delà de l'emploi – Le rapport Supiot* (Paris 1999), at p. 18.
11. Including the USSR and the Post-Second World War group of East European socialist countries, as well as the People's Republic of China after its foundation in 1949.
12. Including 'legal transplants' as well as wholesale adoption of non-native models. *See*, for an oft-cited discussion of such phenomena (not confined to the field of labour regulation), O. Kahn-Freund, 'On Uses and Misuses of Comparative Law' (1974) 37 *Modern Law Review* 1.
13. As with French influence in North Africa, Spanish (and some German) inspiration in Latin America, and the wide-ranging legacy of the British Empire.
14. With the creation of a regulatory framework for the PRC 'with Chinese characteristics' perhaps being one of the most fascinating over the last quarter of a century.
15. *See* W. Streeck, 'The Uncertainties of Management in the Management of Uncertainty: Employers, Labor Relations and Industrial Adjustment in the 1980s' (1987) 1 *Work, Employment & Society* 281, especially at pp. 291 ff.
16. *See*, for example, O. Kahn-Freund, 'A Note on Status and Contract in British Labour Law' (1967) 30 *Modern Law Review* 635.
17. H. Maine, *Ancient Law: Its Connection with the Early History of Society and Its Relation to Modern Ideas* (London 1861).

give rise to especially harsh consequences in terms of deprivation of employment protections when exercised in the context of the individual work relationship.[18]

That consequence may also follow from overly strict adherence to traditional principles governing relationships of 'personal service'.[19] Indeed, while judicial concerns have been expressed in recent years at the widespread practice of 'importing armies of lawyers' to draft terms in individual employment contracts whose intent is explicitly to circumvent established notions of the scope of employment protection by reference to 'employee status' or the like, little has been achieved in terms of restoring any sense of balance between the parties when the 'negotiation' of such terms is left essentially to some ideological notion of 'freedom of contract' without any account being made of the inherent weakness suffered by 'the weaker party' to that relationship.

This has had significant consequences in terms of the ability (especially in systems which have drawn largely upon the English Common Law) to deliver meaningful 'employment protection' to individual workers. Indeed, it was such problems that led this author a decade-and-a-half ago to suggest that labour law lacks the necessary sensitivity for its subject matter and is ill-equipped to respond effectively to challenges arising in a labour market which, in the space of a few years, has changed out of all recognition.[20]

Thus, it is maintained, the foundations of individual labour law relationships in the early years of the twenty-first century have remained constrained by traditional concepts – the 'employee'/'worker'; the fiction of 'equality of bargaining power'; the undesirability of restrictive covenants on grounds of 'public policy' – a notion developed to deal with commercial transactions at the turn of the twentieth century; inappropriately applied doctrines relating to 'duress' and to 'illegal contracts'; and a whole host of other issues.

Meanwhile, in a number of countries reflecting the civil law tradition, there has been substantial focus upon how to classify the work relationship – with some marked divergence between particular national models. Thus, the protective umbrella of 'social law' has been utilised to separate the employment relationship from otherwise harsh consequences as a result of the contractual frame of analytical reference. Despite this, however, various groups (e.g., travelling salesmen) have been considered undeserving of the 'social' protective cloak and have been consigned to a regime reflecting more 'commercial'

18. European Commission, *The Evolution of Labour Law (1992–2003), Volume 2, National Reports* (Luxembourg 2005), at 520, and the elaboration of that position in A. Neal, 'The Protection of Working Relationships under United Kingdom Law', in F. Pennings & C. Bosse (eds), *The Protection of Working Relationships: A Comparative Study* (Alphen aan den Rijn 2011).
19. An issue in relation to which the work of the British scholar Mark Freedland over half a century has proved particularly illuminating.
20. The comment was made specifically by reference to experience at the time in the United Kingdom but has resonance much more broadly.

considerations. The result which can follow from such an approach is illustrated by Hasselbalch et al.,[21] when commenting on the stark divide between the 'protected' worker, the less favoured 'independent contractor', and the 'mighty and hardened' employer of staff – a process which, in the view of those authors, 'contributes towards creating the very polarisation whose consequences the system of labour law ought to be remedying'.

The conceptual approaches to the individual contract of employment also give rise to interesting variations from a comparative perspective. In particular, the civil law system obsession with seeking to classify work relationships as commercial, social, or even 'special' forms of contract leads to rigidities which may run the risk of depriving vulnerable workers of protections through a contract of employment or the like. Similarly, the Common Law's refusal to regard the contract of employment as anything other than 'a contract at large' leaves, as has been seen, major lacunae in the protective coverage of English Labour Law for individual workers.

Other examples of 'incomplete protective coverage' for individual workers can be found in systems such as the Swedish, where non-unionised workers are deprived of the specialist enforcement mechanisms available through the Swedish Labour Court.[22] Yet, even where attempts have been made to provide thoroughgoing protection for individual workers, these have not necessarily succeeded in achieving universal protective coverage – as can be seen with experience in the People's Republic of China under the framework Labour Law 1994 and the subsequent Labour Contract Law 2007.[23]

2.3 A NOTE ON EXPERIENCE IN SOCIALIST SYSTEMS OF LABOUR REGULATION

Mention of recent Chinese experience offers the opportunity briefly to note the approach to regulation of individual employment relationships in socialist systems – particularly by reference to the experience in the USSR and the former socialist countries of Eastern Europe between 1917 and 1989. In this context, the

21. Hasselbalch et al., at p. 49.
22. This – at first glance somewhat 'strange' – situation has its origins in the purposes envisaged for the Labour Court (*Arbetsdomstolen*) when it was established in 1929, with the primary task of dealing with disputes over the interpretation and application of collective agreements and associated matters concerning non-strike regulations under statute. The current rules governing procedure in the Court derive from the 1974 Labour Disputes (Judicial Procedure) Act (1974:371) which maintained the position whereby claims falling outside the ('collectivised') jurisdiction of the Labour Court must be brought in the District Court, although any subsequent appeal will be heard before the Labour Court. In any event, the decision of the Labour Court is final.
23. For analysis of those statutory provisions and a presentation of the context surrounding Chinese labour law developments at the turn of the century, *see* the contributions in A. Neal (ed.), *Cross-Currents in Modern Chinese Labour Law* (Alphen aan den Rijn 2014).

experience of the People's Republic of China since its foundation in 1949 provides a further line of development to compare with the evolution in Western market economies and in systems where 'freedom of contract' extends to the formation of working relationships subject to law.

As regards the historical developments in Eastern Europe before the fall of the Berlin Wall in 1989, the point should be made that 'comparative' studies across the European socialist systems were sparse and were essentially conducted by and through the Institute of the State and Law of the USSR Academy of Sciences in Moscow.[24] Nevertheless, from the available studies it is clear that the model for regulation of individual working relationships established after the Bolshevik Revolution in Russia can be seen to have inspired most, if not all, of the countries which eventually introduced socialist values and forms of regulation in the years which followed the ending of the Second World War in 1945.[25] What has been said to characterise the legal status of the individual in the Soviet Union was:[26]

> that the rights and freedoms of citizens in all spheres of State and social life are guaranteed by the Soviet State. Such guarantees ensure, first, the reality of effectuating, and the actual possibility of exercising, those rights which have been granted to each Soviet person by the USSR Constitution, by labour legislation, and by other normative acts. ... Second, such guarantees ensure that labour in the USSR is a major factor in the comprehensive development of the individual and the formation of his vocational capacities. Finally, socially-useful labour and its results determine the status of a person in society in the Soviet Union (Article 14, USSR Constitution). This important constitutional principle is the legal basis of State and social life under socialism.

The overriding approach of normative imposition emerges starkly from that observation and makes for significant challenges when attempting to compare regulatory experiences in non-socialist systems which provide more scope for 'contractual freedom' between the parties to the employment relationship – notwithstanding the recognition that in many instances, that relationship may reflect dramatic differences in bargaining power between the actors involved. Certainly, when addressing the much remarked upon function of labour

---

24. The position is described by Semion Ivanov in his contribution to W. Butler, B. Hepple & A. Neal, *Comparative Labour Law: Anglo-Soviet Perspectives* (Aldershot 1987) ['Butler et al.'], where he makes reference to collaboration between the Institute and the Law Faculty of the Moscow State University. *See* S. Ivanov, 'Methodological Problems of Comparative Legal Research in Labour Law', in Butler et al., *supra*, at p. 12.
25. *See*, in particular, the material presented in S. Ivanov (ed.), **Кодоификация законодатель'ства о труде социалистических стран** [Codification of Labour Legislation of the Socialist Countries] (Moscow 1979), and S. Ivanov, M. Slavin & A. Chepin (eds), **Социалистическое трудовое право в условиях научно-технического прогресса** [Socialist Labour Law in the Conditions of Scientific and Technological Progress] (Moscow 1981).
26. A. Stavtseva, 'Protection of the Labour Rights and Interests of Workers and Employees', in Butler et al., *supra*, at p. 79.

law as 'to protect the weaker party', the point of protective intervention contrasts sharply across the differing systems.

Meanwhile, the experience of the PRC since the end of the Cultural Revolution and the death of Chairman Mao Zedong in 1976 has provided a different example of the shift to 'contractualisation' of the labour relationship. That development also offers an interesting example of the ability of a system based upon socialist principles to learn from (as opposed to borrowing from) foreign experience in the development of a national regulatory framework 'with Chinese characteristics'.

Thus, from a situation whereby 'contracts', in any Western legal sense, had all but disappeared, the emergence of tentative trends in the direction of the establishment of 'Chinese Labour Law' from 1978 onwards eventually gave rise to a situation in which a conscious choice was made by the Chinese regulator to found working relationships upon principles of 'contract' – within a development of acknowledgement of 'Rule of Law' within the Chinese system as a whole.[27] The development of modern PRC 'Labour Law' is generally taken to have sent on its way with tentative instruments from 1978 – and thereafter the first 'modern' labour law regulatory instruments gradually emerged in the late 1980s. Of particular significance for the contractualisation of working relationships was the publication in 1986 of the *Interim Regulations on the Practice of the Labour Contract System in State-Owned Enterprises*.[28]

As the sociopolitical development of the post-1978 'Open Door' era developed further,[29] the broader acceptance of notions of a 'labour market' for the PRC added to the impetus provided by these early instruments for regulatory arrangements reflecting ideas of 'employment contracting'. Undoubtedly the most significant push in this direction came with the enactment of the Labour Law 1994,[30] and by the time the innovatory Labour Contract Law 2007 had come into force at the beginning of 2008 the modern development was complete.[31]

One particularly interesting feature of the developing Chinese landscape has been the expansion of the regulatory activity beyond merely the arrangements provided for in normative form by the Labour Law 1994. Thus, litigation

27. *See* A. Neal, 'Towards a Functioning Framework for Individual Labour Law Rights: Challenges for China in a Changing World of Work' (2011) 27 *The International Journal of Comparative Labour Law and Industrial Relations* 365, and the contributions to A. Neal (ed.), *Cross-Currents in Modern Chinese Labour Law* (Alphen aan den Rijn 2014).
28. GUOFA (1986) No. 77.
29. The so-called open door policy was launched in December 1978 with an announcement by Deng Xiaoping. *See inter alia* G. Huan, 'China's Open Door Policy 1978-1984' (1986) 39(2) *Journal of International Affairs* 1.
30. Labour Law of the People's Republic of China, adopted at the 8th Meeting of the Standing Committee of the 8th National People's Congress of the People's Republic of China on 5 July 1994.
31. Labour Contract Law of the People's Republic of China, adopted at the 28th Session of the Standing Committee of the 10th National People's Congress on 29 June 2007.

before the first-instance and intermediate People's Courts has seen disputes over payments to workers for 'overtime' work performed come under consideration alongside the (in this respect narrower) jurisdiction of Labour Arbitration Committees (LACs) in relation to the payment of wages. Such developments have not been without criticism from commentators who question the justifiability of opening up such new causes of action and redress and enabling claims to be handled judicially in the People's Courts. However, even within the long-established arrangements set up through the LACs, it should be noted that it is not difficult to find examples of 'contractual analysis' being brought to bear in the course of determining disputes over non-payment of, or deductions from, wages.[32]

Here, too, there is evidence of the impact which a rapidly expanding body of specialised labour law litigators in the PRC is having upon the enjoyment by workers of 'access to justice' and the facilitation of effective remedies in relation to disputes touching employment security, payment of wages, and compliance with statutory provisions introduced by the Labour Law 1994 and subsequently built upon by the Labour Contract Law 2007.

2.4 EMERGENCE OF THE COLLECTIVE AGREEMENT AS AN INSTRUMENT OF (QUASI-AUTONOMOUS) REGULATION

The treatment of the collective agreement in a comparative perspective can be seen to reflect not only the relative balance of power between industrial partners who may enter into such arrangements, but also the extent to which the political system is prepared to concede space for those industrial actors to exercise some degree of autonomy in the establishment of regulatory norms for their field of activity.

Historically, the analysis of this phenomenon has given rise to a variety of legal characterisations, but what emerges clearly from the developments in (particularly) the latter years of the nineteenth century and the beginning of the twentieth century is that the emergence of this regulatory instrument was closely linked to the history of the trade union movement.[33] This immediately raises problems when comparisons have been made between political systems which base their economic activities upon 'market' approaches to business – most notably, the countries of Western Europe and North America – and those which seek to reflect 'socialist' values such as those found in Eastern Europe prior to

32. This can particularly be seen in the activities of a special 'pilot' forum for labour dispute resolution in Shenzhen (Guangdong Province), as a self-standing part of the intermediate level of the People's Court in that city zone.
33. *See* A. Adlercreutz, *Kollektivavtalet. Studier över dess tilkomsthistoria* (Lund 1954), some of the material in which is to be found in the same author's 'The Rise and Development of the Collective Agreement' (1958) 2 *Scandinavian Studies in Law* 11.

1989 or in the PRC since its foundation in 1949. Thus, differing notions of what should be described as a 'collective agreement' are to be found in Western market economies as compared with socialist (or former socialist) regimes.

In the former, the collective agreement has classically been treated as 'the product of collective bargaining', entered into by autonomous parties who regard the product of their bargaining as 'binding' upon themselves. That 'binding' quality may be underpinned by legal sanctions and processes, or may (as was classically the case in the United Kingdom) result from the relative de facto balance of power between the actors on the industrial relations stage (employers, or associations of employers, in respect of trade unions).[34]

Meanwhile, the socialist approach has tended to prescribe mechanisms for the regulation of the terms and conditions of multiple workers through a single normative instrument. Such agreements (generally described as 'collective contracts') had existed under the Tsarist regime, although they then went into abeyance in the wake of the 1917 revolution until their reintroduction by Articles 15-26 of the 1922 Labour Code of the RSFSR. Thus, Article 15 of the 1922 Code provided for the conclusion of collective contracts, which were defined as: 'an agreement concluded between a trade union, as representative of the workers, on the one hand, and an employer, on the other hand, laying down the conditions of work and employment for individual undertakings, institutions, and businesses or groups thereof, and specifying the contents of future individual contracts of employment'.

In a comparative perspective, one has only to contrast the 1984 theoretical frame of reference for 'the collective agreement' put forward by Schmidt & Neal[35] with that presented in relation to the socialist collective agreement by László Nagy,[36] published in the same year, to see fundamentally differing starting points for analysing phenomena described by the same terminology.[37]

Thus, for example, even an attempt to offer a 'functional' analysis of the role of the collective agreement results in remarkable diversity. The role and function of the modern Chinese collective agreement, as provided for in the

34. The notion of the collective agreement constituting a 'gentlemen's agreement' in English Law has been well documented and contrasts markedly with legal regimes which regard the product of bargaining as some variety of binding legal instrument underpinned by judicially or similarly imposed enforcement mechanisms. *See* B. Hepple, 'Intention to Create Legal Relations' (1970) *Cambridge Law Journal* 122; A. Neal, 'The Collective Agreement as a Public Law Instrument', in E. Banakas, *United Kingdom Law in the 1980s* (London 1988).
35. Schmidt & Neal, *supra.*
36. Nagy, *supra.*
37. For discussion of the institution of the 'collective agreement' in the former socialist legal systems of Eastern Europe, *see* Schmidt & Neal, *supra.* and, in particular, the material derived from memoranda prepared by Professor Karel Witz and Professor Marie Kalenska (University of Prague, Czechoslovakia), at pp. 84 ff. An early post-war presentation of the phenomenon in a specific USSR setting (with historical references) is to be found in 'Reports and Inquiries: Collective Agreements in the U.S.S.R.' (1952) 66 *International Labour Review* 477.

PRC's Labour Law 1994,[38] thus contrasts sharply with the purportedly universal so-called Schmidt/Neal model,[39] and even displays variation from the former Soviet approach (as eventually manifested in the 1922 RSFSR Labour Code) from which it was derived.[40]

Even within the functional framework spelled out by the 1984 'Schmidt/Neal model' there has been a dramatic shift in the prioritisation of the functions listed over the thirty-five years which have passed since that model was first presented. The model identifies, in particular, five 'basic functions' of the collective agreement as the product of collective bargaining: namely (1) a cease-fire agreement, or a treaty securing industrial peace; (2) an instrument for the employees to control the supply of labour, and to protect the individual employee, as the weaker party to the contract of employment, against pressures from the employer; (3) a form of standard conditions: rather like a form for an insurance policy, or a bill of lading; (4) an instrument of co-operation between the *Sozialpartner*; and (5) an industrial code, i.e., a method of regulating wages and other conditions of employment, comparable with a statutory enactment. In particular, the fourth of the five functions identified by those authors – 'an instrument of "co-operation" between the *Sozialpartner*' – has come dramatically to the fore with the development of the notion of 'social dialogue' at the level of the EU.[41]

Closely intertwined with regulatory mechanisms designed to facilitate collaborative standard-setting through collective bargaining or some variant thereof, the primary function of the collective agreement – to establish 'a cease-fire agreement, or a treaty securing industrial peace' – has been the most controversial aspect attracting attention. Indeed, if one merely looks at recent activity within the sphere of activity of the ILO, the vexed issue of 'the right to strike' continues to command centre stage.[42] While normative provisions for the establishment of 'peace obligations' continue to deliver relative legal stability in national systems such as Germany and the Nordic countries, the introduction of approaches more familiar to practitioners in 'conflictual' systems of industrial relations has undoubtedly served to destabilise the received orthodoxy at the level of international standard-setting.

38. *See* Chapter 3, esp. Articles 33-35.
39. For comment on the significance of that 'model', *see* N. Bruun, *The Autonomy of Collective Agreement*, General Report Presented to the VII European Regional Congress: Stockholm (Sweden) 4-6 September 2002.
40. *See*, for example, A. Shebanova, 'The Collective Contract in the USSR', in Butler et al., at 71ff.
41. *See*, A. Neal, 'We Love You Social Dialogue – But Who Exactly Are You?', in Fondazione Giulio Pastore, *La contrattazione collettive europea: Profili giuridici ed economici* (2001), 113.
42. *See*, for example, J. Bellace, 'The ILO and the Right to Strike' (2014) 153 *International Labour Review* 29.

Once again, some of the old 'underlying certainties' of former times have found themselves under increasing pressure, with unforeseeable potential consequences for the institutions and regulatory mechanisms of labour law. Coupled with a weakening of 'collective solidarity' in many parts of the world, and an increasing encouragement of decentralisation and individualisation of labour relationships, this leaves many of the tried and tested approaches to labour market regulation in desperate need of critical revisiting.

2.5 THE RISE AND RISE OF NORMATIVE INTERVENTION BY THE STATE

Underlying all of the trends alluded to above, perhaps the most remarkable matter of consistency wherever one looks has been the dominance of normative regulation – usually through initiatives at the level of the State legislator – in late twentieth century and post-Millennium industrial relationships. The role of 'the Law' in this field of socio-economic activity has become steadily more intrusive, and many of the most notable examples of collective autonomy – such as that experienced in Sweden since 1938,[43] or the fabled 'collective laissez-faire'[44] said to have characterised British industrial relations – can no longer be seen in the same light as was the case half a century ago.

In countries with well-established Constitutions (and associated 'Constitutional Courts' or their equivalent), the legitimacy of this normative intervention into the field of industrial relationships has rarely been an issue. Even where a broad scope of autonomy has historically been granted to the industrial actors, the pre-eminence of the State – as the guardian of 'the public interest', with responsibility for ensuring industrial peace and the economic well-being of the citizenry, and as the legitimised power to regulate in the name of *vox populis* – has taken precedence over 'party autonomy' in the industrial economic sphere.

It has also to be recognised that, in an increasingly globalised economy, the influence of international labour standards – whether in their own right or through the medium of international trade arrangements – has enhanced the trend towards normative frameworks for regulating the world of work. Even where politico-legal arrangements such as those established for the EU of

43. As revered through the 'Spirit of Saltsjöbaden' ushered in with the so-called Basic Agreement of 1938. For a recent critique of the orthodox presentation of this process, *see* A. Hedin, 'Before the Breakdown of the Saltsjöbaden Spirit of Labour Market Co-operation: The Swedish Employers' Confederation and Workplace Democracy in the 1960s' (2019) 44 *Scandinavian Journal of History* 591. As regards individual employment protection through normative legislation, the introduction of an Employment Protection Law in 1974 (SFS 1974:12) arguably marked the break with the previous abstentionist approach. *See* A. Neal, 'Employment Protection Laws: The Swedish Model' (1984) 33 *International and Comparative Law Quarterly* 634.
44. The epithet attributed by Kahn-Freund to what was perceived as an approach of 'legal abstentionism' on the part of the legislator and (with exceptions) the judges.

twenty-eight nations have endeavoured to limit the extent of intrusion into the regulation of industrial relationships, there has been a marked seepage of normative intervention which appears to find acquiescence among a large number of Member State governments.[45]

2.6 ADJUSTMENT FOR THE REGULATION OF LABOUR LAW IN A GLOBAL SETTING

In one of his final contributions to scholarship in this field, delivered in a series of lectures to the British Academy at the end of 1978, the late Sir Otto Kahn-Freund wrote of 'heritage and adjustment' in labour relations – recognising the increasing pace of change in the fields of industrial relations and labour law regulation, and seeking to indicate ways in which traditional paradigms (reflected in the 'heritage' of the field) might develop (the need for 'adjustment') in order to make them better 'fit for purpose'. The recognition of the regulatory challenge posed by dramatic change for the institutions and attitudes of the actors in the world of work was not universally shared four decades ago. However, with experience well into the first quarter of the twenty-first century, there are nowadays few who would deny that the rapid pace of change, as well as the nature of that change, for modern labour markets makes reconsideration of traditional approaches and regulatory tools a matter of pressing urgency.

A decade-and-a-half ago this author lamented (in a comment of applicability to the Common Law system in general) that: 'Labour law in the United Kingdom currently stands ill equipped to respond effectively to the swiftly-changing phenomena emerging in a labour market which has changed out of all recognition in the course of a quarter of a century.'[46] That lack of fitness for purpose encompassed both the judicial analytical approach to the contract of employment and the framework for regulating collective labour relations in a rapidly changing labour market. It also extended to a failure to develop institutional arrangements within which labour disputes might be effectively and sensitively resolved, breaking away from the shadow of traditional civil law commercial dispute resolution frameworks.

45. As with the gradual move through light touch measures to facilitate rudimentary 'information and consultation', in the direction of increasing regulation for 'participation' and varieties of 'joint regulation' in the context of novel institutions such as 'European Works Councils' and ever more detailed procedures to formalise the arrangements for discharging obligations to inform and consult. Contrast, for example, the scope of European Union social policy at the time of the *Communication from the Commission concerning its Action Programme relating to the Implementation of the Community Charter of Basic Social Rights for Workers* (COM(89) 568 final), of 29 November 1989, with the approaches reflected in Directive 2002/14/EC establishing a general framework for informing and consulting employees, or the recast Directive 2009/38/EC on European Works Councils.

46. European Commission, *The Evolution of Labour Law (1992–2003), Volume 2, National Reports* (Luxembourg 2005), at 520.

Also taking as his primary frame of reference the British experience – but infusing it with examples drawn from a variety of European national systems of law and industrial relations – Kahn-Freund observed in his 1978 analysis that 'We carry the heavy burden of an old tradition.'[47] While Kahn-Freund's insistence upon clinging to 'voluntary bargaining methods' as the foundation for future adjustment – reflecting a broader refusal by industrial relations commentators of the time to acknowledge the inexorable incursion of normative statute law into 'the plains of free collective bargaining'[48] – has, with the benefit of hindsight, proved misplaced, his particular insight four decades ago was that 'conservatism, the cult of tradition, is our worst enemy' and that what was required amounted to a transformation of existing tripartite arrangements 'into something more regular and more regulated'. What that 'something more regular and more regulated' might be, however, was not elaborated upon!

More recently, continental European scholars such as Alain Supiot have taken the critique further,[49] to the extent of declaring that 'you would have to be blind to deny the need for fundamental reform of labour laws'.[50]

Notwithstanding occasional attempts to suggest otherwise, the overwhelming sense is of a regulatory framework which no longer reflects the realities of modern labour markets and the relations between the parties to them. Indeed, so dramatic have the changes been, that it is hard to relate to the claim made by a senior member of the United Kingdom judiciary at the turn of the Millennium that: '... over the last 30 years or so, the nature of the contract of employment has been transformed. It has been recognised that a person's employment is usually one of the most important things in his or her life. It gives not only a livelihood but an occupation, an identity and a sense of self-esteem. The law has changed to recognize this social reality'.[51]

Of more concern, however, is the associated sense that the available 'toolkit' for achieving effective regulation in the modern world of work is no longer up to the tasks being demanded of it. The individual contract of employment lacks the sensitivity, flexibility, and robustness needed to strike a balance between inherently 'weaker party' performers of work and whatever nowadays may constitute their 'employing' counterpart. Collective agreements

47. O. Kahn-Freund, *Labour Relations: Heritage and Adjustment* (London 1979), at p. 88.
48. *See* B. Weekes, M. Mellish, L. Dickens & J. Lloyd, *Industrial Relations and the Limits of Law: The Industrial Effects of the Industrial Relations Act, 1971* (Oxford 1975) for a contemptuous dismissal of the British experience with the Industrial Relations Act 1971 as a 'failed intervention', demonstrating 'the limits of law' in labour market regulation.
49. A. Supiot, *Au-delà de l'emploi – Le rapport Supiot* (Paris 1999), published in English as *Beyond Employment – Changes in Work and the Future of Labour Law in Europe* (Oxford 2001).
50. A. Supiot, 'Et si l'on refondait le droit du travail ...', *Le Monde diplomatique* (October 2017), translated into English as 'A Labour Code for the 21st century', *Le Monde diplomatique* (May 2018).
51. *See* the Opinion of Lord Hoffmann in *Johnson v. Unisys Limited* [2001] UKHL 13, at paragraph 35.

no longer appear apt to serve the functions identified by Schmidt & Neal, while the socialist version of the collective agreement envisaged by Nagy belongs firmly to a bygone era. This would seem to be the case, whether those 'collective agreements' conform to the theoretical models envisaged by Philipp Lotmar,[52] Barthélemy Raynaud,[53] Hugo Sinzheimer,[54] Östen Undén,[55] or the drafters of the 1922 RSFSR Labour Code or the architects of the Labour Law 1994 of the People's Republic of China. Nor do instruments evolving in some 'social dialogue' or other 'soft-law' guise appear to constitute anything more substantial than 'Emperor's new clothes'. Meanwhile, the power of the State wields the blunt statutory weapon, introducing ever more detailed new measures, or removing vestiges of the old order, with meaningful participation in the regulatory process through 'employee voice' or old familiar channels of collective representation increasingly drowned in the tidal wave of normative intervention.

In consequence, the temptation to tear down the old edifices and replace them with shiny new 'pleasure domes' becomes ever more appealing. Yet, as has always been the case, there remain pragmatic demands upon any would-be regulator operating in the field of working relationships. There remains a pressing need to reconsider the instruments which we continue to refer to as employment contracts, collective agreements, and legislation, and to question whether they possess continued utility – with or without significant 'tweaking'.

As that reconsideration is undertaken, in a world of work where ever-looser legal-liability linkages are the goal, in which 'platform workers' float in a haze of digital isolation, and where lawyerly constructs such as 'triangular relationships' are created to defy the paradigm of bilateral contractual obligations, let us remind ourselves of what has gone before. To what extent our historical regulatory roots have something to offer towards meeting the needs of the fast-moving and ever more challenging modern world of work has to be carefully explored before yielding to the temptation to 'throw out the bathwater – baby and all'. For it might just turn out that, even if we are with Supiot in his assertion that 'you would have to be blind to deny the need for fundamental reform of labour laws', the achievement of appropriate and effective 'fundamental reform' may well derive from that wealth of experience built up over decades of wrestling with precisely the 'old-established toolkit'.

52. P. Lotmar, *Die Tarifverträge zwischen Arbeitgebern und Arbeitnehmern* (BraunsArch 1900).
53. B. Raynaud, *Le contrat collectif de travail* (Paris 1901).
54. H. Sinzheimer, *Der korporative Arbeitsnormenvertrag I* (Leipzig 1907) and *Der korporative Arbeitsnormenvertrag II* (Leipzig 1908).
55. Ö. Undén, *Kollektivavtalet enligt gällande svensk rätt* (Lund 1912).

BIBLIOGRAPHY

A. Adlercreutz, *Kollektivavtalet. Studier över dess tilkomsthistoria* (Lund 1954).

S. Anderman, A. Neal, T. Sigeman & A. Victorin (eds), *Law and the Weaker Party: An Anglo-Swedish Comparative Study* (London 1981-1992).

J. Bellace, *'The ILO and the Right to Strike'* (2014) 153 *International Labour Review* 29.

N. Bruun, *The Autonomy of Collective Agreement*, General Report Presented to the VII European Regional Congress: Stockholm (Sweden) 4-6 September 2002.

W. Butler, B. Hepple & A. Neal, *Comparative Labour Law: Anglo-Soviet Perspectives* (Aldershot 1987).

I. Chiu, *'An Institutional Theory of Corporate Regulation'* (2018) 71 *Current Legal Problems* 279.

European Commission, *A renewed EU strategy 2011-14 for Corporate Social Responsibility* (COM (2011) final).

European Commission, *Corporate social responsibility: A business contribution to sustainable development* (COM(2002) 347 final).

European Commission, *The Evolution of Labour Law (1992–2003)*, Volume 2, National Reports (Luxembourg 2005).

European Commission, *The Evolution of Labour Law* (1992–2003), Volume 2, National Reports (Luxembourg 2005), 520.

A. Hedin, *'Before the Breakdown of the Saltsjöbaden Spirit of Labour Market Co-operation: The Swedish Employers'*, Confederation and Workplace Democracy in the 1960s' (2019) 44 *Scandinavian Journal of History* 591.

B. Hepple & B. Veneziani (eds), *The Transformation of Labour Law in Europe: A Comparative Study of 15 Countries* 1945-2004 (London 2009).

B. Hepple (ed.), *The Making of Labour Law in Europe: A Comparative Study of Nine Countries up to 1945* (London & New York 1986).

B. Hepple, *'Intention to Create Legal Relations'* (1970) *Cambridge Law Journal* 122.

G. Huan, *'China's Open Door Policy 1978-1984'* (1986) 39(2) *Journal of International Affairs* 1.

S. Ivanov (ed.), ***Кодоификация законодатель'ства о труде социалистических стран*** [Codification of Labour Legislation of the Socialist Countries] (Moscow 1979).

S. Ivanov, *'Methodological Problems of Comparative Legal Research in Labour Law'*, in Butler et al., *Comparative Labour Law: Anglo-Soviet Perspectives*, (Aldershot 1987).

S. Ivanov, M. Slavin & A. Chepin (eds), *Социалистическое трудовое право в условиях научно-технического прогресса* [Socialist Labour Law in the Conditions of Scientific and Technological Progress] (Moscow 1981).

O. Kahn-Freund, *'A Note on Status and Contract in British Labour Law'* (1967) 30 *Modern Law Review* 635.

O. Kahn-Freund, *'On Uses and Misuses of Comparative Law'* (1974) 37 *Modern Law Review* 1.

O. Kahn-Freund, *Labour Relations: Heritage and Adjustment* (London 1979), 88.

P. Lotmar, *Die Tarifverträge zwischen Arbeitgebern und Arbeitnehmern* (BraunsArch 1900).

H. Maine, *Ancient Law: Its Connection with the Early History of Society and Its Relation to Modern Ideas* (London 1861).

L. Nagy, *The Socialist Collective Agreement* (Budapest 1984).

A. Neal (ed.), *Cross-Currents in Modern Chinese Labour Law* (Alphen aan den Rijn 2014).

A. Neal, *'Corporate Social Responsibility: Governance Gain or Laissez-Faire Figleaf?'* (2008) 29 *Comparative Labor Law and Policy Journal* 459.

A. Neal, *'Employment Protection Laws: The Swedish Model'* (1984) 33 *International and Comparative Law Quarterly* 634.

A. Neal, *'The Collective Agreement as a Public Law Instrument'*, in E. Banakas, *United Kingdom Law in the 1980s* (London 1988).

A. Neal, *'The Protection of Working Relationships under United Kingdom Law'*, in F. Pennings & C. Bosse (eds), *The Protection of Working Relationships: A Comparative Study* (Alphen aan den Rijn 2011).

A. Neal, *'Towards a Functioning Framework for Individual Labour Law Rights: Challenges for China in a Changing World of Work'* (2011) 27 *The International Journal of Comparative Labour Law and Industrial Relations* 365.

A. Neal, *'We Love You Social Dialogue – But Who Exactly Are You?'*, in Fondazione Giulio Pastore, *La contrattazione collettive europea: Profili giuridici ed economici* (2001), 113.

B. Raynaud, *Le contrat collectif de travail* (Paris 1901).

F. Schmidt & A. *Neal, Collective Agreements and Collective Bargaining* (Tübingen 1984), republished in *International Encyclopedia of Comparative Law*, Volume XV, Labour Law, Chapter 12 (Tübingen 2014) ['Schmidt & Neal'].

A. Shebanova, *'The Collective Contract in the USSR'*, in Butler et al., *Comparative Labour Law: Anglo-Soviet Perspectives* (Aldershot 1987), 71.

H. Sinzheimer, *Der korporative Arbeitsnormenvertrag I* (Leipzig 1907).

H. Sinzheimer, *Der korporative Arbeitsnormenvertrag II* (Leipzig 1908).

A. Stavtseva, *'Protection of the Labour Rights and Interests of Workers and Employees'*, in Butler et al., *Comparative Labour Law: Anglo-Soviet Perspectives* (Aldershot 1987).

W. Streeck, '*The Uncertainties of Management in the Management of Uncertainty: Employers, Labor Relations and Industrial Adjustment in the 1980s*' (1987) 1 *Work, Employment & Society* 281.A. Supiot, '*Et si l'on refondait le droit du travail …*', *Le Monde diplomatique* (October 2017).

A. Supiot, *Au-delà de l'emploi – Le rapport Supiot* (Paris 1999), 18.

Ö. Undén, *Kollektivavtalet enligt gällande svensk rätt* (Lund 1912).

B. Weekes, M. Mellish, L. Dickens & J. Lloyd, *Industrial Relations and the Limits of Law: The Industrial Effects of the Industrial Relations Act*, 1971 (Oxford 1975).

CHAPTER 3

The Regulatory Function of Collective Agreements in the Light of Its Relationship with Statutory Instruments and Individual Rights: A Multilevel Approach

Edoardo Ales

3.1 THE RECOGNITION OF THE REGULATORY FUNCTION

3.1.1 The International Labour Organisation

If one looks at International Labour Law as provided by the International Labour Organisation (ILO) in its binding instruments, one finds out that since the very beginning of such a legislative action, attention has been paid to the regulatory function of collective bargaining.

In fact, already the Hours of Work (Industry) Convention 1 of 1919[1] contemplated exceptions to the maximum daily working time '(b) where by law, custom, or *agreement between employers' and workers' organisations, or, where no such organisations exist, between employers' and workers' representatives*, the hours of work on one or more days of the week are less than eight, the limit of eight hours may be exceeded on the remaining days of the week by the sanction of the competent public authority, or *by agreement between such organisations or representatives* (...)' (Article 2).[2]

1. *See* Carla Spinelli, *ILO Convention 1* (Edoardo Ales, Mark Bell, Olaf Deinert & Sophie Robin-Olivier, eds) *International and European Labour Law*, 1321 (Nomos, 2018). Among the Countries taken into account in this book, only Spain has ratified that Convention.
2. Emphasis always added.

In that simple statement, the parties of the Convention highlight almost all the elements that matter in our analysis, such as the existence of (different) actors (‘*employers’ and workers’ organisations, or, where no such organisations exist, between employers’ and workers’ representatives*’); the fact that agreements signed among them may have the same value and effect of the law; the prevalence of those agreements on the individual employment contract to which no reference is made.

The regulatory function of collective agreements is mentioned also in the Minimum Wage-Fixing Machinery Convention 26 of 1928,[3] according to which ‘minimum rates of wages which have been fixed [through the machinery] *shall be binding on the employers and workers concerned so as not to be subject to abatement by them by individual agreement, nor, except with general or particular authorisation of the competent authority, by collective agreement*’ (Article 3(2) n. 3). Once again, what is not allowed to the individual contract is permitted, although under general or particular authorisation, to collective bargaining.

Finally yet importantly, a direct recognition of the regulatory function of collective bargaining is provided by the Holidays with Pay Convention 52 of 1936.[4] Within it, the ‘remuneration determined by *collective agreements*’ is understood as an alternative to the ‘usual remuneration, calculated in a manner which shall be prescribed by *national laws or regulations*’ every person taking a holiday shall receive during the full period of it. In this case, too, the Convention does not mention the individual agreement among the instruments that can define the pay due to the worker.

To sum up, the references made by the just mentioned Conventions to collective bargaining and agreements confirm that, already at its earliest stage of existence, the ILO has recognised the presence of a source of regulation of working conditions other than the law, which can produce the same effects of the latter thus prevailing on the individual employment contract.

In a more comprehensive perspective, the relevance of collective bargaining finds its definitive acknowledgement in the Declaration of Philadelphia 1944

3. Among the Countries taken into account in this book, ratified by Australia, Brazil, China, France, Germany, Hungary, Italy, Poland and Spain. *See also*, on this point the Minimum Wage Fixing Convention 131 of 1970 according to which ‘Minimum wages shall have the force of law and shall not be subject to abatement, and failure to apply them shall make the person or persons concerned liable to appropriate penal or other sanctions’ (Article 2(1)). ‘Subject to the provisions of paragraph 1 of this Article, the freedom of collective bargaining shall be fully respected’ (Article 2(2)). On this Convention *see* Claire La Hovary, *ILO Convention* 131 (Edoardo Ales, Mark Bell, Olaf Deinert & Sophie Robin-Olivier, eds) *International and European Labour Law*, 1120 (Nomos, 2018).
4. As substituted by Convention 132 of 1970. Among the Countries taken into account in this book, ratified by Brazil, France, Hungary and Italy. *See*, Carla Spinelli, *ILO Convention 132* (Edoardo Ales, Mark Bell, Olaf Deinert & Sophie Robin-Olivier, eds) *International and European Labour Law*, 1370 (Nomos, 2018).

(Part III), which 'recognizes the solemn obligation of the ILO to further among the nations of the world programmes which will achieve: (e) *the effective recognition of the right of collective bargaining* (...)'.[5]

That one contained in the Declaration of Philadelphia is the first recognition, at least at international level, of collective bargaining as a *right*. The meaning of that 'right', however, is everything but clear. In the view of the regulatory function of collective bargaining, having recourse to the words of the Court of Justice of the European Union (CJEU), it could be understood as the right to '*exercise (...) their legal autonomy by associations or organizations which do not come under public law*'.[6] That of *legal autonomy of the parties involved* seems to be the proper way to conceive that right, since it emphasises the *immanent 'dual' nature* of the regulatory function of collective bargaining, being it inherently *common to management and labour* if they want to define working conditions *further* to those provided by the legislator, to be applied to the relevant individual employment relationship. Therefore, the exercise of the right to collective bargaining presupposes the shared determination of the parties to negotiate, with the end of signing a collective agreement.

Despite its very nature of binding instrument, while in line with the Declaration of Philadelphia, the Right to Organise and Collective Bargaining Convention 98 of 1949[7] does only contain a 'promotional' provision. According to it, 'measures appropriate to national conditions shall be taken, where necessary, to encourage and promote the full development and utilisation of machinery for voluntary negotiation between employers or employers' organisations and workers' organisations, with a view to the regulation of terms and conditions of employment by means of collective agreements (Article 4)'.

This seemed to confirm that the ILO aims at recognising the regulatory function of collective bargaining as already exists within the national systems of the Members more than at setting a common regulation of collective bargaining at international level.

However, a more dubitative conclusion could be drawn looking at the approach adopted by the (promotion of) Collective Bargaining Convention 154

---

5. As well as 'the cooperation of management and labour in the continuous improvement of productive efficiency, and the collaboration of workers and employers in the preparation and application of social and economic measures'. *See* Adalberto Perulli, *The Declaration of Philadelphia (DoP)* (Edoardo Ales, Mark Bell, Olaf Deinert & Sophie Robin-Olivier, eds) *International and European Labour Law*, 361 (Nomos, 2018).
6. CJEU, 12 December 1974, C-36/74, *Walrave*, ECLI:EU:C:1974:140, paragraph 18; CJEU, 18 December 2007, C-341/05, *Laval un Partneri*, ECLI:EU:C:2007:809, paragraph 98.
7. Among the Countries taken into account in this book, ratified by Australia, Brazil, France, Germany, Hungary, Italy, Poland, Spain and United Kingdom. *See* Anne Trebilcock, *ILO Conventions 87, 98, 154* (Edoardo Ales, Mark Bell, Olaf Deinert & Sophie Robin-Olivier, eds) *International and European Labour Law*, 1492 (Nomos, 2018).

of 1981.[8] Although for its limited purpose, it provides a definition of collective bargaining that 'extends to all negotiations which take place between an employer, a group of employers or one or more employers' organisations, on the one hand, and one or more workers' organisations, on the other'. Negotiations fall within the scope of collective bargaining if they aim at: (a) determining working conditions and terms of employment; and/or (b) regulating relations between employers and workers; and/or (c) regulating relations between employers or their organisations and a workers' organisation or workers' organisations (Article 2).

Yet, where national law or practice recognises the existence of workers' representatives as defined in Article 3(b) of the Workers' Representatives Convention 135 of 1971,[9] the former may determine the extent to which the term collective bargaining shall also extend, for the purpose of Convention 154, to negotiations with these representatives.

While determining the objective scope of application of ILO promotional activity towards collective bargaining, Convention 154 provides also a comprehensive definition of its purposes and actors, whose nature is decisive, from the workers' side, in order to verify if collective bargaining is really at stake. In fact, a negotiation between the employer and non-union agents as workers representatives could be, even if carried out on issues recalled under letts (a) and (b) could not, in some countries, be equalised to collective bargaining, being non-union workers representatives not entitled to the right to collective action, strike included.[10] This does not mean that those negotiations and the agreements they eventually have resulted into could not be regarded as regulatory sources of working conditions, above all if they have been carried out without prejudice of the workers' organisations concerned (Article 3(2)).

Once identified as collective bargaining, measures *adapted to national conditions* shall be taken to promote it (Article 5(1)). Aims of those measures should be:

- making collective bargaining possible for all employers and all groups of workers in the branches of activity covered by the Convention (Article 5(2)(a));
- progressively extending collective bargaining to all matters mentioned in the above (Article 5(2)(b));
- encouraging the establishment of rules of procedure agreed between employers' and workers' organisations (Article 5(2)(c));

8. Among the Countries taken into account in this book, ratified by Brazil, Hungary and Spain. *See* Trebilcock (n. 7) 1492.
9. *See* section 3.2.
10. *See* section 3.2.

- avoiding that collective bargaining could be hampered by the absence of rules governing the procedure to be used or by the inadequacy or inappropriateness of such rules (Article 5(2)(d));
- conceiving bodies and procedures for the settlement of labour disputes as to contribute to the promotion of collective bargaining (Article 5(2)(e)).

As it happens in other fields,[11] ILO's approach to collective bargaining is mainly that one of promoting, all over the world, the development of its regulatory functions of working conditions as already exists in many Members. ILO's approach is therefore respectful of the legislation and the tradition of the Members in which a collective bargaining system is at stake. Nevertheless, Convention 154 emphasises the relevance of 'bodies and procedures for the settlement of labour disputes', not to be seen, as it happens in some Members, in contrast with the right to collective bargaining as intrinsically linked to that one to collective action. The relationship between the right to collective bargaining and the right to collective action is obviously a crucial point[12] on which the ILO has adopted a clear orientation in favour of disputes resolution systems, which aim at avoiding the (unreflective) recourse to collective action, strike included. On the other hand, as also recently and dramatically confirmed,[13] the recognition of the right to collective bargaining by the ILO binding instruments does not entail the recognition of the right to collective action.

3.1.2 The European Union

The 'respectful' recognition of the right to collective bargaining characterises also the European Union (EU) Law approach. Already the Community Charter of Fundamental Social Rights for Workers of 1989,[14] under the Freedom of association and collective bargaining Title provides that 'Employers or employers' organizations, on the one hand, and workers' organizations, on the other, shall have the right to negotiate and conclude collective agreements *under the conditions laid down by national legislation and practice.*' (paragraph 12).

Typical of the supranational dimension of the EU is, conversely, the recognition of 'contractual relations in particular at inter-occupational and

11. *See*, as paramount example Safety and Health: Edoardo Ales, *ILO Convention 187* (Edoardo Ales, Mark Bell, Olaf Deinert & Sophie Robin-Olivier, eds) *International and European Labour Law*, 1437 (Nomos, 2018).
12. *See* section 3.3.
13. K. D. Ewing, *Myth and Reality of the Right to Strike as a 'Fundamental Labour Right'*, 29 *International Journal of Comparative Labour Law and Industrial Relations* 145-166 (2013); L. Swepston, *Crisis in the ILO Supervisory System: Dispute over the Right to Strike*, 29 *International Journal of Comparative Labour Law and Industrial Relations* 199-218 (2013).
14. *See* B. Bercusson, *The European Community's Charter of Fundamental Social Rights for Workers*, 53 *Modern Law Review* 624-642 (1990).

sectoral level' 'the dialogue between the two sides of industry at European level, which must be developed' may result in 'if the parties deem it desirable' (paragraph 12).[15]

Contrary to the abstentionist ILO's approach, although in a separate point (paragraph 13), the Community Charter recognises 'the right to resort to collective action', even if with the limited scope of conflicts of interests, that 'shall include the right to strike, subject to the obligations arising under national regulations and collective agreements'. The reference to collective agreements is of high relevance in our perspective, since it includes in their regulatory function the relationships between management and labour in case of disputes on interests, i.e. (mainly if not exclusively) during the negotiation of collective agreements. Similar to ILO's approach, 'in order to facilitate the settlement of industrial disputes', the Community Charter emphasises the need to encourage 'the establishment and utilization at the appropriate levels of conciliation, mediation and arbitration procedures', thus sharing ILO's auspice of a reflected resort to collective action, strike included. The limitation of the right to strike to conflicts of interests leads to the recognition of disputes resolution procedures as unavoidable, at least under the Community Charter in case of disputes on rights deriving from the application of the collective agreement to the individual employment relationship.

A cumulative view of the right to collective bargaining and of the right to collective action, strike included, resulting into the 'Right of collective bargaining *and* action', is adopted, on the contrary, by Article 28 of the Charter of Fundamental Rights of the European Union (CFREU).[16] On the other hand, the 'respectful' recognition of characterises also Article 28, which, further to 'national laws and practices', makes 'the right to negotiate and conclude collective agreements at the appropriate levels and, in cases of conflicts of interest, to take collective action to defend their interests, including strike action' conditional upon 'Community Law'.

From the perspective of the regulatory function of collective bargaining and agreements, Article 28 adds some important elements to our reflection:

- that one of the cumulative view, resulting into the 'Right of collective bargaining *and* action', completed by the lack of reference to disputes resolution systems, which contradicts the 'last resort attitude' towards

15. *See* section 3.2.
16. *See* Catharine Barnard, *Article 28* (Steve Peers, Tamara Hervey, Jeff Kenner & Angela Ward, eds) *The EU Charter of Fundamental Rights: A Commentary*, 773 (Hart Publishing, 2014); Daniel Ulber, *Article 28 CFREU* (Edoardo Ales, Mark Bell, Olaf Deinert & Sophie Robin-Olivier, eds) *International and European Labour Law*, 1457 (Nomos, 2018); Filip Dorssemont & Marco Rocca, *Article 28 – Right of Collective Bargaining and Action* (Filip Dorssemont, Klaus Lörcher, Stefan Clauwaert & Mélanie Schmitt, eds) *The Charter of Fundamental Rights of the European Union and the Employment Relationship*, 465 (Hart Publishing, 2019).

collective action typical of the partnership approach to the relationship between management and labour dominant in 'Community Law' and in the 'national laws and practices' of many Member States;[17]

- that one of 'Community Law' as legislative framework 'in accordance' to which the right has to be conceived, further to 'national laws and practices', which makes the approach even more 'respectful' and the very notion of the right extremely complex to be decrypted, being it linked to a bottom-up process of 'deductive constitutionalisation'[18] of both national and Community Laws;[19]
- that one of highlighting the distinction between the *right to negotiate* and the *right to conclude* collective agreements, which emphasises, on the one hand, the relevance of having taken part to the negotiation, even if it has not resulted into an agreement, for instance for the purpose of recognising the labour contracting party as workers representatives at undertaking level. On the other hand, the importance of reaching an agreement as natural conclusion of any negotiation process;
- that one of referring explicitly to the 'appropriate levels' at which the right to negotiate and conclude collective agreements can be exercised, ranging, therefore, from the micro, i.e., establishment and undertaking,[20] to the macro, i.e., up to the European Social Dialogue.

Indeed, from the point of view of the regulatory function of collective bargaining and agreements, with particular reference to their relationship with the law, the establishment of the European Social Dialogue represents a *unicum* within EU Law sources.[21] As a matter of fact, in the view of 'promoting the consultation of management and labour at Union level' and to 'take any relevant measure to facilitate their dialogue by ensuring balanced support for the parties', the European Commission, 'before submitting proposals in the social policy field (...) shall consult [them] on the possible direction of Union action' (Article 154 Treaty on the functioning of the European Union (TFEU)). 'On the occasion of

---

17. Edoardo Ales, *EU Collective Labour Law: A Vertically and Horizontally Combined (National and Supranational) Embedded Jurisdiction* (Beryl ter Haar & Attila Kun, eds) *European Collective Labour Law* (forthcoming).
18. Edoardo Ales, *Article 27 CFREU* (Edoardo Ales, Mark Bell, Olaf Deinert & Sophie Robin-Olivier, eds) *International and European Labour Law*, 214 (Nomos, 2018). On that provision *see* also Filip Dorssemont, *Article 27* (Steve Peers, Tamara Hervey, Jeff Kenner & Angela Ward, eds) *The EU Charter of Fundamental Rights: A Commentary*, 749 (Hart, 2014); Bruno Veneziani, *Article 27 – Worker's Right to Information and Consultation within the Undertaking* (Filip Dorssemont, Klaus Lörcher, Stefan Clauwaert & Mélanie Schmitt, eds) *The Charter of Fundamental Rights of the European Union and the Employment Relationship*, 429 (Hart Publishing, 2019).
19. *See* section 3.3.
20. *See* section 3.5.
21. Edoardo Ales, *The State, Industrial Relations and Freedom of Association: A History of Functional Embeddedness* (Adalberto Perulli & Tiziano Treu, eds) *The Role of the State and Industrial Relations* (Wolters Kluwer, 2019).

that consultation, management and labour may inform the Commission of their wish to initiate the process provided for in Article 155,' i.e., 'the dialogue between them at Union level may lead to contractual relations, including agreements'. They 'shall be implemented either in accordance with the procedures and practices specific to management and labour and the Member States or, in matters covered by Article 153,[22] at the joint request of the signatory parties, by a Council decision on a proposal from the Commission' (Article 155 TFEU).

What is clearly at stake is the provision of a *decision-making process alternative to the ordinary one* that recognises to management and labour[23] a regulatory function the product of which, if they so require, may have the same effect of EU statutory instruments. Alternatively, agreements concluded at European level (so-called autonomous European Social Dialogue)[24] shall (or better *may*) be implemented 'in accordance with the procedures and practices specific to management and labour and the Member States'.

Main products of the European Social Dialogue implemented through EU Law statutory instruments are the Framework Agreement on part-time work concluded by UNICE, CEEP and the ETUC;[25] the framework agreement on fixed-term work concluded by ETUC, UNICE and CEEP;[26] and the revised Framework Agreement on parental leave concluded by BusinessEurope, UEAPME, CEEP and ETUC and repealing Directive 96/34/EC.[27]

Main products of the autonomous European Social Dialogue[28] are the Framework Agreement on Telework of 16 July 2002 concluded by UNICE, CEEP and the ETUC; the Framework Agreement on work-related stress of 8 October

22. Edoardo Ales, *Article 153 TFEU* (Edoardo Ales, Mark Bell, Olaf Deinert & Sophie Robin-Olivier, eds) *International and European Labour Law*, 155 (Nomos, 2018).
23. *See* section 3.4.
24. Stefano Giubboni, *The EU and the Industrial Relations Systems: A Critical Assessment* (Adalberto Perulli & Tiziano Treu, eds) *The Role of the State and Industrial Relations* (Wolters Kluwer, 2019).
25. Implemented by Council Directive 97/81/EC of 15 December 1997 concerning the Framework Agreement on part-time work concluded by UNICE, CEEP and the ETUC (OJ L 14, 20.1.1998, pp. 9-14). *See* Jean-Philippe Lhernould, *Directive 97/81/EC* (Edoardo Ales, Mark Bell, Olaf Deinert & Sophie Robin-Olivier, eds) *International and European Labour Law*, 872 (Nomos, 2018).
26. Implemented by Council Directive 1999/70/EC of 28 June 1999 concerning the framework agreement on fixed-term work concluded by ETUC, UNICE and CEEP (OJ L 175, 10.7.1999, pp. 43-48). *See* Alexia Gardin, *Directive 1999/70/EC* (Edoardo Ales, Mark Bell, Olaf Deinert & Sophie Robin-Olivier, eds) *International and European Labour Law*, 882 (Nomos, 2018).
27. Implemented by Council Directive 2010/18/EU of 8 March 2010 implementing the revised Framework Agreement on parental leave concluded by BusinessEurope, UEAPME, CEEP and ETUC and repealing Directive 96/34/EC (OJ L 68, 18.3.2010, pp. 13-20) (*see* Sudabeh Kamanabrou & Anne Christin Wietfeld, *Directive 2010/18/EU* (Edoardo Ales, Mark Bell, Olaf Deinert & Sophie Robin-Olivier, eds) *International and European Labour Law*, 1026 (Nomos, 2018)), to be repealed by Directive (EU) 2019/1158 of the European Parliament and of the Council of 20 June 2019 on work-life balance for parents and carers and repealing Council Directive 2010/18/EU (OJ L 188, 12.7.2019, pp. 79-93).
28. Marco Peruzzi, *L'autonomia nel dialogo sociale europeo* (Il Mulino 2011).

2004 concluded by UNICE, CEEP, EUAPME and the ETUC; Framework Agreement on harassment and violence at work of 26 April 2007 concluded by BusinessEurope, UEAPME, CEEP and ETUC; the Framework Agreement on inclusive labour markets of 25 March 2010 concluded by BusinessEurope, UEAPME, CEEP and ETUC; and Framework Agreement on Active Ageing and an Inter-generational Approach of 8 March 2017 concluded by BusinessEurope, UEAPME, CEEP and ETUC.

The debate remains open whether the products of the European Social Dialogue can be regarded as collective agreements. In my view, they can surely be seen as an expression of the *legal autonomy* of the European Social Partners as recognised by EU or national law, therefore provided with a regulatory function that cannot be ignored in the present contribution.

However, the regulatory function of collective bargaining and agreements is widely recognised also by secondary EU Law.

Just to mention some relevant examples, one can start from the Transfer of Undertaking Directive,[29] according to which 'following the transfer, the transferee shall continue to observe the terms and conditions agreed in any *collective agreement on the same terms applicable to the transferor under that agreement, until the date of termination or expiry of the collective agreement or the entry into force or application of another collective agreement.* (...)' (Article 3, paragraph 3).[30]

Another paramount example is that one of the Posting of Workers Directive,[31] according to which Member States shall ensure to workers who are posted to their territory the terms and conditions of employment which are laid down in the Member State where the work is carried out '*by collective agreements or arbitration awards which have been declared universally applicable or otherwise apply in accordance with paragraph 8*'.

The same concept of remuneration, for the purpose of the Directive, means all the 'constituent elements' of it 'rendered mandatory by national law,

29. Council Directive 2001/23/EC of 12 March 2001 on the approximation of the laws of the Member States relating to the safeguarding of employees' rights in the event of transfers of undertakings, businesses or parts of undertakings or businesses (OJ L 82, 22.3.2001, pp. 16-20). *See* Sylvaine Laulom, *Directive 2001/23/EC* (Edoardo Ales, Mark Bell, Olaf Deinert & Sophie Robin-Olivier, eds) *International and European Labour Law*, 996 (Nomos, 2018); Edoardo Ales, *The Transfer of Undertaking Directive: A Puzzling Piece of Legislation* (Erika Kovács & Martin Winner, eds) *Stakeholder Protection in Restructuring: Selected Company and Labour Law Issues*, 185 (Nomos, 2019).
30. On the problematic relationship between Article 3(1) and (3) Directive 2001/23/EC *see* section 3.5.
31. Directive 96/71/EC of the European Parliament and of the Council of 16 December 1996 concerning the posting of workers in the framework of the provision of services (OJ L 18, 21.1.1997, pp. 1-6). *See* Alexandre Defossez, *Directive 96/71/EC* (Edoardo Ales, Mark Bell, Olaf Deinert & Sophie Robin-Olivier, eds) *International and European Labour Law*, 643 (Nomos, 2018); Marco Rocca, *Posting of Workers and Collective Labour Law: There and Back Again: Between Internal Market and Fundamental Rights* (Intersentia, 2015).

regulation or administrative provision, or *by collective agreements or arbitration awards which, in that Member State, have been declared universally applicable or otherwise apply in accordance with paragraph 8'* (Article 3(1)).

Furthermore, if the effective duration of a posting exceeds twelve months, Member States shall ensure to workers who are posted to their territory all the applicable terms and conditions that are laid down *'by collective agreements or arbitration awards which have been declared universally applicable or otherwise apply in accordance with paragraph 8'* (Article 3(1a)).

Paragraph 8 (of Article 3) provides with a very interesting overview of the solution that has been adopted by Member States in relation to the personal scope of application of collective agreements. In particular, it makes clear that '"collective agreements or arbitration awards which have been declared universally applicable" means collective agreements or arbitration awards which must be observed by all undertakings in the geographical area and in the profession or industry concerned'.

Moreover, it explains that 'in the absence of, or in addition to, a system for declaring collective agreements or arbitration awards to be of universal application, Member States may base themselves on: collective agreements or arbitration awards which are generally applicable to all similar undertakings in the geographical area and in the profession or industry concerned'. Member States can also rely on 'collective agreements which have been concluded by the most representative employers' and labour organisations at national level and which are applied throughout national territory' if their application ensures equality of treatment between to undertakings posting the workers and national undertakings that are in a similar position.

What is clear from the reference made by the Posting of Workers Directive to the regulatory function of collective agreements is that, whatever the solution adopted by the Member States, the result should be the universal (*erga omnes*) application of the same working conditions in order to guarantee the equal treatment of all the undertakings providing the service at stake.

The CJEU has adopted a strict interpretation of the concept of *universal application of collective agreements* in the view of ensuring equal treatment to all the service providers. In fact, in Rüffert it has excluded from it a collective agreement covering only a part of the sector falling within its geographical area of application, 'since, first, the law which gives it such an effect applies only to public contracts and not to private contracts and, second, the collective agreement has not been declared universally applicable'.[32]

Furthermore, in Laval, the CJEU has drawn a clear distinction between the recognition of the regulatory function of already existing collective agreements

32. CJEU, 3 April 2008, C-346/06, *Rüffert*, ECLI:EU:C:2008:189, paragraph 29, as confirmed by CJEU, 17 November 2015, C-115/14, *RegioPost*, ECLI:EU:C:2015:760, paragraph 74.

and that one of collective bargaining, deciding that the Posting of Workers Directive is 'to be interpreted as precluding a trade union, from attempting, by means of collective action in the form of a blockade (...) *to force a provider of services established in another Member State to enter into negotiations with it on the rates of pay for posted workers and to sign a collective agreement*'.[33]

For the Posting of Workers Directive and the free provisions of services within the EU,[34] the *universal application of collective agreements in the view of ensuring equal treatment to all the service providers* has to be regarded, therefore, as one of the major problematic aspect for the recognition of their regulatory function in relation to both statutory instruments and the individual employment contract. The universal application of collective agreement (*erga omnes*) is, of course, one of the hottest issues also as far as national Collective Labour Law is concerned.

On the contrary, the principle of *universal application* seems to be less relevant when it comes to the Working Time Directive,[35] which allows various derogations to some of its basic provisions[36] for some specific groups of workers[37] or in general[38] by way of collective agreements as an alternative to statutory provisions[39] or as exclusive means.[40] In doing so, Articles 17(2) and 19(2) generically refer to 'collective agreements or agreements between the two sides of industry'. Article 18, more specifically, recalls 'collective agreements or agreements concluded between the two sides of industry at national or regional level or, in conformity with the rules laid down by them, by means of collective agreements or agreements concluded between the two sides of industry at a lower level'.

If in case of Article 17(2), the fact that collective bargaining is put in alternative to 'laws, regulations or administrative provisions' can lead to the conclusion that collective agreements shall be of universal application. On the contrary, as for Articles 18 and 19(2), in which no alternative is at stake, this consideration does not help. However, at least as far as collective agreements recalled under Article 18 are concerned, the last paragraph of the latter seems to exclude the *universal application* as their necessary feature. In fact, it allows Member States to lay down rules '(b) for the extension of the provisions of

33. *Laval un Partneri* (n. 6) paragraph 111.
34. *See* section 3.3.
35. Directive 2003/88/EC of the European Parliament and of the Council of 4 November 2003 concerning certain aspects of the organisation of working time (OJ L 299, 18.11.2003, pp. 9-19) *see* Vito Leccese, *Directive 2003/88/EC* (Edoardo Ales, Mark Bell, Olaf Deinert & Sophie Robin-Olivier, eds) *International and European Labour Law*, 1285 (Nomos, 2018).
36. Daily rest (Article 3), breaks (Article 4), weekly rest period (Article 5), length of night work (Article 8) and reference periods (Article 16).
37. Article 17(2)(3)(4)(5).
38. Articles 18 and 19(2).
39. Article 17(2).
40. Articles 18 and 19(2).

collective agreements or agreements concluded in conformity with this Article to other workers in accordance with national legislation and/ or practice'.

Of no help as well, seems to be the distinction made by Article 18(2) between Member States in which there is no statutory system ensuring the conclusion of collective agreements or agreements concluded between the two sides of industry at national or regional level and Member States in which there is a specific legislative framework for this purpose. In fact, statutory systems do not necessarily grant the *universal application* of collective agreements concluded within their framework. However, the application to members of the signatory parties of collective agreements is an intrinsic feature of them. However, it can be decisive only in case of a single collective branch or undertaking agreements, which is not always the case.

If the Working Time Directive does not add much to the reflection on the *universal application* of collective agreements, it is extremely significant with regard to the tendency to decentralisation collective bargaining is increasingly facing since the end of the nineties. The reference made within Article 18 to 'collective agreements or agreements concluded between the two sides of industry *at a lower level*', even if concluded in conformity with the rules laid down by collective agreements or agreements signed between the two sides of industry at national or regional level, confirms the relevance of that tendency.

However, as already illustrated in the above, the same Article 28 CFREU does recognise 'the right to negotiate and conclude collective agreements *at the appropriate levels*', allowing management and labour to choose them. It is however noteworthy that Article 18 explicitly permits a derogation to the basic provisions of the Working Time Directive by collective agreements signed at a level lower the national and the regional, without specifying that they should have *universal application* and without requiring the Member States to make a clear choice in favour of the derogation, as necessary under Articles 17(2) and 19(2).[41]

This seems to be a rather unlimited recognition of the regulatory function of collective bargaining at any level, which has pushed to the limit, in the working time domain, more than one national industrial relations system. In *Accardo and Others*, for instance, a clause of a collective agreement derogating the weekly rest provision (Article 5) has been deemed by some workers, falling within its scope of application, as being contrary to national constitutional and statutory provisions. The national judge called to decide the case has asked to the Court of Justice whether that clause could be compatible with the objectives of the Working Time Directive. According to the Court, the compatibility of derogations finds its limit in the *principle of legal certainty* as a general principle of EU Law, requiring precision and clarity in the derogating provisions, whatever

41. CJEU, 21 October 2010, C-227/09, *Accardo and Others*, ECLI:EU:C:2010:624, paragraphs 50-54.

its kind. However, in the specific case, even recalling that it is up to the national court to decide whether derogations are against national law, the Court of Justice has directly stated that a derogation to weekly rest provided by a collective agreement in conflict with national law 'cannot be relied on against individuals'.[42]

The Information and Consultation Framework Directive,[43] too, although in a different perspective, does recognise the regulatory function of collective agreements *whatever the level at which they have been bargained and concluded*. More precisely, according to Article 5(1), 'Member States may entrust management and labour *at the appropriate level, including at undertaking or establishment level*, with defining freely and at any time through negotiated agreement the practical arrangements for informing and consulting employees' (Article 5(1)).

Moreover, such agreements 'and agreements existing on the date [fixed for the transposition], as well as any subsequent renewals of such agreements, may establish, while respecting the principles set out in Article 1 and subject to conditions and limitations laid down by the Member States, provisions which are different from those referred to in Article 4 [Practical arrangements for information and consultation]'.[44]

In this case, the specific reference to the *undertaking and the establishment level* at which agreements on practical arrangements for information and consultation can be concluded has to do with the fact that the Directive aims at developing workers involvement the closest possible to where the relevant decisions are taken by management.

Such an intent of the EU legislator is also confirmed by the principle affirmed by Article 1(3) which highlights the role of 'the employer and the employees' representatives' as well as that they 'shall work in a spirit of cooperation (...) taking into account the interests both of the *undertaking or establishment and of the employees*', 'when defining or implementing practical arrangements for information and consultation'.

The closeness of the bargaining level to the decision-making power in the view of realising workers' involvement is also a topical feature of the European Works Council (EWC) Directive.[45] In fact, according to Article 1(3), 'information

42. *Accardo and Others* (n. 41) paragraphs 55-59.
43. Directive 2002/14/EC of the European Parliament and of the Council of 11 March 2002 establishing a general framework for informing and consulting employees in the European Community (OJ L 80, 23.3.2002, pp. 29-34). *See* Pascale Lorber, *Directive 2002/14/EC* (Edoardo Ales, Mark Bell, Olaf Deinert & Sophie Robin-Olivier, eds) *International and European Labour Law*, 1551 (Nomos, 2018); Edoardo Ales, *2002/14/EC: Framework Information and Consultation* (Monika Schlachter, ed.) *EU Labour Law. A Commentary*, 519 (Wolters Kluwer, 2014).
44. On the derogatory function, *see* section 3.4.
45. Directive 2009/38/EC of the European Parliament and of the Council of 6 May 2009 on the establishment of an EWC or a procedure in Community-scale undertakings and Community-scale groups of undertakings for the purposes of informing and consulting employees (Recast)

and consultation of employees must occur at the relevant level of management and representation, according to the subject under discussion', in this case that one of Community-scale undertaking and Community-scale group of undertakings.

For this purpose, the Directive recognises the regulatory function of collective bargaining at Community-scale undertaking/group level as primary means to establish an EWC or and information and consultation procedure (section II). Only a subsidiary role is attributed to the legislative provisions contained in Annex I of the Directive. The establishment of EWCs has stimulated the conclusion of the so-called Transnational Company Agreements (TCA). Although the juridical basis of their regulatory function is still disputed, the effectiveness of TCA in regulating workers' rights and duties within multinational companies cannot be denied or disregarded.

In a very different perspective, the General Framework for Equal Treatment in Employment and Occupation Directive[46] and the Equal Opportunities and Equal Treatment of Men and Women in Matters of Employment and Occupation (Recast) Directive,[47] do recognise the regulatory function of collective agreements *without any reference either to universal application or to the bargaining level.*

Both Directives focus on the fact that, having a crucial regulatory function, collective agreements shall comply with EU Antidiscrimination Law, whatever their scope of application and their level. In fact, with an identical working, Article 16(b) General Framework Directive and Article 23(b) Equal Opportunities and Treatment Directive require Member States to 'take all necessary measures to ensure that (...) provisions contrary to the principle of equal treatment *in individual or collective contracts or agreements, internal rules of undertakings or rules governing the independent occupations and professions and workers' and employers' organisations or any other arrangements* shall be, or may be, declared null and void or are amended'.

The Court of Justice, already in *Defrenne II*, has made the application of EU Antidiscrimination Law (in particular Article 119 TEC) to collective agreements

(OJ L 122, 16.5.2009, pp. 28-44). *See* Iacopo Senatori, *Directive 2009/38/EC* (Edoardo Ales, Mark Bell, Olaf Deinert & Sophie Robin-Olivier, eds) *International and European Labour Law*, 1601 (Nomos, 2018); Filip Dorssemont & Thomas Blanke, eds, *The Recast of the European Works Council Directive* (Intersentia 2010).

46. Council Directive 2000/78/EC of 27 November 2000 establishing a general framework for equal treatment in employment and occupation (OJ L 303, 2.12.2000, pp. 16-22). *See* Elise Muir & Lisa Waddington, *Directive 2000/78/EC* (Edoardo Ales, Mark Bell, Olaf Deinert & Sophie Robin-Olivier, eds) *International and European Labour Law*, 520 (Nomos, 2018).

47. Directive 2006/54/EC of the European Parliament and of the Council of 5 July 2006 on the implementation of the principle of equal opportunities and equal treatment of men and women in matters of employment and occupation (recast) (OJ L 204, 26.7.2006, pp. 23-36). *See* Jule Mulder, *Directive 2006/54/EC* (Edoardo Ales, Mark Bell, Olaf Deinert & Sophie Robin-Olivier, eds) *International and European Labour Law*, 547 (Nomos, 2018).

clear.[48] In that decision, the Court stated that 'it is not possible to sustain any objection that the application by national courts of the principle of equal pay would amount to modifying *independent agreements concluded privately or in the sphere of industrial relations such as individual contracts and collective labour agreements*'.[49] In fact, 'since Article 119 is mandatory in nature, the prohibition on discrimination between men and women applies not only to the action of public authorities, but also extends to *all agreements which are intended to regulate paid labour collectively, as well as to contracts between individuals*'.[50]

The Court of Justice has confirmed and even taken its position to the extreme in Enderby,[51] stating that '(...) the fact that the respective rates of pay of two jobs of equal value, one carried out almost exclusively by women and the other predominantly by men, were arrived at by collective bargaining processes which, although carried out by the same parties, are distinct, and, taken separately, have in themselves no discriminatory effect, is not sufficient objective justification for the difference in pay between those two jobs'.

In *Royal Copenhagen*, however, the Court, while recalling the *Defrenne II* doctrine, has highlighted that 'the fact that the rates of pay have been determined by *collective bargaining or by negotiation at local level* may be taken into account by the national court as a factor in its assessment of whether differences between the average pay of two groups of workers are due to objective factors unrelated to any discrimination on grounds of sex'.[52] In *Kenny and Others*, the Court has developed its argument in terms of '*interests of good industrial relations*' that 'may be taken into consideration by the national court as one factor among others in its assessment of whether differences between the pay of two groups of workers are due to objective factors unrelated to any discrimination on grounds of sex and are compatible with the principle of proportionality'.[53]

The *interests of good industrial relations* underpinned the regulatory function of collective bargaining and agreements has, therefore, become part of the reasoning of the Court of Justice even in one of the fields in which, as discrimination on the ground of sex, EU Antidiscrimination Law is stricter.

In the same vein, while confirming the Defrenne II doctrine, the Court of Justice has emphasised the importance of the regulatory function of collective

48. CJEU, 4 April 1976, C-43/75, *Defrenne II*, ECLI:EU:C:1976:56.
49. *Ibid.*, paragraph 38.
50. *Ibid.*, paragraph 39.
51. CJEU, 27 October 1993, C-127/92, *Enderby*, ECLI:EU:C:1993:859, paragraph 23.
52. CJEU, 31 May 1995, C-400/93, *Royal Copenhagen*, ECLI:EU:C:1995:155, paragraph 50.
53. CJEU, 28 February 2013, C-427/11, *Kenny and Others*, ECLI:EU:C:2013:122, paragraphs 48 and 50.

agreements also with reference to the General Framework Directive.[54] Indeed, Article 13(2) of the Directive as well as, with a similar working, Article 21(2) of the Equal Opportunities and Treatment Directive, calls Member States on encouraging 'the social partners, *without prejudice to their autonomy*, to conclude at the appropriate level agreements laying down anti-discrimination rules in the fields referred to in [the Directive] which fall within the scope of collective bargaining. These agreements shall respect the minimum requirements laid down by [the] Directive and by the relevant national implementing measures'. Furthermore, as also recalled by the Court of Justice,[55] according to Article 18, Member States 'may entrust the social partners, at their joint request, with the implementation of [the] Directive as regards provisions concerning collective agreements'.

Also on this ground, the Court of Justice has recognised, further to Member States also, 'where appropriate, *to social partners at national level* (...) a broad discretion in their choice, not only to pursue a particular aim in the field of social and employment policy, but also in the definition of measures capable of achieving it',[56] when it comes to 'differences of treatment on grounds of age [that] shall not constitute discrimination, if, within the context of national law, they are objectively and reasonably justified by a legitimate aim, including legitimate employment policy, labour market and vocational training objectives, and if the means of achieving that aim are appropriate and necessary' (Article 6 General Framework Directive).

However, relying once again on the *Defrenne II* doctrine, the Court of Justice affirms that despite the 'broad discretion in their choice, not only to pursue a particular aim in the field of social and employment policy, but also in the definition of measures capable of achieving it', social partner enjoy no immunities from EU Antidiscrimination Law.

That happens, for instance, when at stake is 'a measure laid down by a collective agreement (...) which provides that, within each salary group, the basic pay step of a public sector contractual employee is determined on appointment by reference to the employee's age'.[57] Or when, 'in fixing at 60 the age-limit from which airline pilots (...) are considered as no longer possessing

54. *See*, with reference to age, CJEU, 8 September 2011, C-297/10 and C-298/10, *Hennigs and May*, ECLI:EU:C:2011:560, paragraph 63; CJEU, 13 September 2011, C-447/09, *Prigge and Others*, ECLI:EU:C:2011:573, paragraph 48; CJEU, 7 June 2012, C-132/11, *Tyrolean Airways Tiroler Luftfahrt*, ECLI:EU:C:2012:329, paragraph 22; CJEU, 21 December 2016, C-539/15, *Bowman*, ECLI:EU:C:2016:977, paragraph 19; CJEU, 19 September 2018, C-312/17, *Bedi*, ECLI:EU:C:2018:734, paragraph 70. With reference to sexual orientation, CJEU, 12 December 2013, C-267/12, *Hay*, ECLI:EU:C:2013:823, paragraph 22.
55. *Hennigs and May* (n. 54) paragraph 64.
56. CJEU, 16 October 2007, C-411/05, *Palacios de la Villa*, ECLI:EU:C:2007:604, paragraph 68; CJEU, 12 October 2010, C-45/09, *Rosenbladt*, ECLI:EU:C:2010:601, paragraph 41; *Hennigs and May* (n. 54) paragraph 64.
57. *Hennigs and May* (n. 54) paragraph 78.

the physical capabilities to carry out their occupational activity, *while national and international legislation authorize the carrying out of that activity, under certain conditions, until the age of 65*, the social partners imposed on those pilots a disproportionate requirement'.[58]

If in the first case, the choice of social partners seems to be irreparably against the principle of non-discrimination on the ground of age, in the second the Court of Justice has heavily interfered with the same 'broad discretion' recognised in the above. It even went beyond the reasonable assumption that 'the fact that the task of striking a balance between their respective interests is entrusted to the social partners offers *considerable flexibility*, as each of the parties may, where appropriate, opt not to adopt the agreement'.[59] As happened in Accardo, this has been decided in order to protect the interest of single employees against the regulation adopted by the collective agreement applying to them, in the name of their right to work longer as guaranteed by national and international law.

An important exception to the prevalence of the non-discrimination principle in terms of equal treatment on collective bargaining and agreements is that one allowed by the Temporary Agency Work Directive.[60] According to Article 5(3), 'Member States may, after consulting the social partners, give them, at the appropriate level and subject to the conditions laid down by the Member States, the option of upholding or concluding collective agreements which, while respecting the overall protection of temporary agency workers, may establish arrangements concerning the working and employment conditions of temporary agency workers which may differ from those referred to in paragraph 1.' That is, 'the basic working and employment conditions of temporary agency workers shall be, for the duration of their assignment at a user undertaking, at least those that would apply if they had been recruited directly by that undertaking to occupy the same job'.

However, the Temporary Agency Work Directive provides food for thought as far as the *universal application* of such derogatory agreements is concerned. In fact, Article 5(4) allows 'Member States in which there is either *no system in law for declaring collective agreements universally applicable* or *no such system in law or practice for extending their provisions to all similar undertakings in a certain sector or geographical area* (...) after consulting the social partners at

58. *Prigge and Others* (n. 54) paragraph 75.
59. *Rosenbladt* (n. 56) paragraph 67.
60. Directive 2008/104/EC of the European Parliament and of the Council of 19 November 2008 on temporary agency work (OJ L 327, 5.12.2008, pp. 9-14). *See* Jean-Philippe Lhernould, *Directive 2008/104/EC* (Edoardo Ales, Mark Bell, Olaf Deinert & Sophie Robin-Olivier, eds) *International and European Labour Law*, 894 (Nomos, 2018).

national level and on the basis of an agreement concluded by them, establish-[ing] arrangements concerning the basic working and employment conditions which derogate from the principle established in paragraph 1.'

By doing so, Article 5(4) indirectly argues for the *universal application* of collective agreements concluded under Article 5(3) and, more in general, of collective agreements derogating EU Law principles or statutory provisions.

3.1.3 The Council of Europe

At last but not at least for certain European Countries,[61] one has to remind that the Council of Europe (CoE) too has recognised the 'Right to bargain collectively' in the European Social Charter (ESC)[62] at Article 6.[63] In the view of ensuring the effective exercise of that right, its recognition is accompanied by the commitment of the parties (States) to promote:

> 'joint consultation between workers and employers;' (1)
>
> 'where necessary and appropriate, machinery for voluntary negotiations between employers or employers' organisations and workers' organisations, with a view to the regulation of terms and conditions of employment by means of collective agreements;' (2)
>
> 'the establishment and use of appropriate machinery for conciliation and voluntary arbitration for the settlement of labour disputes (...);' (3)
>
> and also to recognise 'the right of workers and employers to collective action in cases of conflicts of interest, including the right to strike, subject to obligations that might arise out of collective agreements previously entered into.' (4).

Without prejudice of the weakness affecting the ESC because of the lack of a jurisdictional body guaranteeing its application to the Signatory Parties, one has to admit that Article 6 can be regarded as providing the most comprehensive recognition of the right to collective bargaining encompassing *joint consultation, machinery for negotiation and labour disputes settlement* and the *right to collective action*.

That weakness, on the other hand, does not affect the European Convention on Human Rights, the respect of which is guaranteed by the European Court of Human Rights. This Court has adopted since 2008 an "augmented" interpretation of Article 11 of the Convention on 'Freedom of Assembly and Association', in the view of guaranteeing not only 'the right to form and to join trade unions

61. *See* Teun Jaspers, *Collective Action in the Netherlands* (Edoardo Ales & Tonia Novitz, eds) *Collective Action and Fundamental Freedoms in Europe: Striking the Balance*, 135 (Intersentia, 2010).
62. *See* Niklas Bruun, Klaus Lörcher, Isabelle Schömann & Stefan Clauwaert, *The European Social Charter and the Employment Relation* (Hart Publishing, 2017).
63. *See* Filip Dorssemont, *The Right to Collective Bargaining: A Matrix for Industrial Relations* (Niklas Bruun, Klaus Lörcher, Isabelle Schömann & Stefan Clauwaert, eds) *The European Social Charter and the Employment Relation*, 249 (Hart Publishing, 2017).

for the protection of [everyone's] interests' but also the right to collective bargaining and action.[64] That interpretation relies on and has triggered a noteworthy debate among labour law scholars on the relationship between workers' rights and human rights that risks to be a deadly embrace for the former if not handled with the due care by the latter.[65]

3.2 ACTORS AND INSTRUMENTS

Any discourse on the regulatory function of collective bargaining will be incomplete without a mention to its actors and the instruments at their disposal. Actually, in some legal orders, the reference to actors is crucial as for *the very notion of collective bargaining and agreements* when it comes to the relationship with regulatory instruments negotiated and adopted outside the (trade) union realm, as it happens with *workers' representation by works councils at the undertaking or establishment level.*

The main difference is that one between *freedom of association*, leading to the establishment of workers' and employers' organisations, and the *individual right of the worker to be represented by a specific body provided by the law*. The ILO and the CoE explicitly acknowledge such a difference, whereas the EU has taken a rather ambiguous stance on it.

As for the ILO, the Freedom of Association and Protection of the Right to Organise Convention 87 of 1948[66] recognises the right of 'workers and employers, without distinction whatsoever, to establish and, subject only to the rules of the organisation concerned, to join *organisations* of their own choosing without previous authorization' (Article 2). For the purpose of Convention 87, 'the term *organisation* means any *organisation of workers or of employers for furthering and defending the interests of workers or of employers*' (Article 10). At turn, 'workers' and employers' organisations shall have the right to establish and join

64. *See* Klaus Lörcher, *The New Social Dimension in the Jurisprudence of the European Court of Human Rights (ECtHR): The Demir an Baykara Judgement, Its Methodology and Follow-up* (Filip Dorssemont, Klaus Lörcher, & Isabelle Schömann, eds) *The European Convention on Human Rights and the Employment Relationship*, 3 (Hart Publishing, 2013); Isabelle Van Hiel, *The Right to Form and Join Trade Unions Protected by Article 11 ECHR*, *ibid.*, 287; Antoine Jacobs, *Article 11 ECHR: The Right to Bargain Collectively*, *ibid.*, 309; Filip Dorssemont, *The Right to Take Collective Action under Article 11 ECHR*, *ibid.*, 333; Filip Dorssemont, *The European Convention on Human Rights as Fountain of Labour Rights* (Janice R. Bellace & Beryl ter Haar, eds) *Research Handobbok on Labour, Business and Human Rights Law*, 314 (Edward Elgar, 2019); Tonia Novitz, *Freedom of Association: its Emergence and the Case for Prevention of its Decline*, *ibid.*, 231; Vania Brino, *La giurisprudenza della Corte europea dei diritti dell'uomo* (Antonio Baylos Grau & Lorenzo Zoppoli a cura di) *La libertà sindacale nel mondo: nuovi profile e vecchi problemi*, 77 (Editoriale Scientifica, 2019).
65. Janice R. Bellace & Beryl ter Haar, *Perspectives on Labour and Human Rights* (Janice R. Bellace & Beryl ter Haar, eds) *Research Handbook on Labour Business and Human Rights Law*, 2 (Edward Elgar, 2019).
66. *See* Trebilcock (n. 7) 1492.

federations and confederations and any such organisation, federation or confederation shall have the right to affiliate with international organisations of workers and employers' (Article 5).

The only limit to the right to organise admitted by Convention 87 is the respect, by 'workers and employers and their respective organisations, like other persons or organised collectivities' of the law of the land, which 'shall not be such as to impair, nor shall it be so applied as to impair, the guarantees provided for in [the] Convention' (Article 8).

The reference to the respect of the law of the land confirms that freedom of association, i.e., the right to organise are embedded into the national legislation of each Member, which, at turn, shall respect the principles laid down by Convention 87.

It is clear that, although never mentioning it explicitly, what is at stake from the workers' side is the (Trade) Union Model, organised at its traditional levels, not necessarily entailing the undertaking or the establishment.

However, the same ILO has adopted the Workers' Representatives (in the Undertaking) Convention 135 of 1971.[67] For its purpose, the term '*workers' representatives* means persons who are recognised as such *under national law or practice*, whether they are:

(a) trade union representatives, namely, representatives designated or elected by trade unions or by members of such unions; or
(b) '*elected representatives, namely, representatives who are freely elected by the workers of the undertaking in accordance with provisions of national laws or regulations or of collective agreements* and *whose functions do not include activities which are recognised as the exclusive prerogative of trade unions in the country concerned.*' (Article 3).

In the case of representatives under lett. (b), among the activities that can be recognised 'as the *exclusive prerogative of trade unions*', there is surely *collective bargaining* as defined by Article 2 Convention 154 already mentioned in the above. In fact, according to Article 3(1) of the latter, 'national law or practice may determine the extent to which the term *collective bargaining* shall also extend, for the purpose of this Convention, to negotiations with these representatives'.

Moreover, as already highlighted, one has also to remind that, in any case, where the term collective bargaining also includes negotiations with the workers' representatives under Article 3 lett. (b) Convention 135, 'appropriate measures shall be taken, wherever necessary, to ensure that the existence of these representatives is not used to undermine the position of the workers' organisations concerned' (Article 3(2) Convention 154).

67. Among the Countries taken into account within this book, ratified by Australia, Brazil, France, Germany, Hungary, Italy, Poland, Spain and United Kingdom.

One can conclude, therefore, that without prejudice of the possibility for national legislators to entrust workers' representatives with the right to collective bargaining, which shall include the right to collective action, the ILO recognises the former and, by consequence, although indirectly, also the latter, as a Trade Union and Employer Organisation prerogative. This does not mean, however, that agreements concluded between an employer and workers' representatives in the undertaking, outside collective bargaining, may not have a regulatory function *if so provided by the national legislation*. In this case, the crucial point is the relationship between those agreements and collective agreements. In the ILO perspective, the latter should have priority on working conditions the regulation of which the law does not explicitly entrust to workers' representatives as confirmed by the already mentioned Convention 1, according to which agreements between employers' and workers' representatives on working time may be concluded only where employers' and workers' organisations do not exist (Article 2(b)).

A less clear-cut distinction between freedom of association and workers' representation (mainly) established by the law is that one drawn by the CoE. In fact, on the one hand, also the Revised Social Charta provides for a separate recognition of the Right to Organise[68] (Article 5) from 'The right of workers' representatives to protection in the undertaking and facilities to be accorded to them' (Article 28). On the other hand, however, neither Article 5 nor Article 28 ESC requires the intervention of national legislation in order to entrust workers' representative with the right to collective bargaining and action (Article 6 ESC). Indeed, as already emphasised in its heading, Article 28 aims rather at 'ensuring the effective exercise of the right of workers' representatives to carry out their functions', than at affirming an exclusive trade unions prerogative on collective bargaining and action.

Highly controversial is the distinction between freedom of association and workers' representation (workers' involvement) in EU Law, above all if one looks at it from the transnational perspective already highlighted with reference to EWC. In fact, although rather frequently signatory parties of TCAs, EWCs are deemed by many scholars and by the same European Trade Union Federation[69] as not entitled to the right to collective bargaining, being the expression of *workers' involvement*, not of *freedom of association*.

However, as correctly highlighted, 'The Directive on EWC (...) manifested its potentials in many directions, allowing a diffused practice of transnational

68. Actually the '*freedom* of workers and employers to form local, national or international *organisations* for the protection of their economic and social interests and to join those organisations'. In this case, too, no direct reference is made to the undertaking and the establishment.
69. *See* E. Ales, *EU Betriebsräte und transnationale Festlegung der Arbeitsbedingungen: Auf der Suche nach einem Kompromiss zwischen Tarifautonomie und Mitwirkung*, 9 *Soziales Recht*, 258 - 266 (2019).

bargaining',[70] even if it 'does not explicitly empower them with bargaining rights'.[71]

As already touched upon, this is a very challenging point since, in some Member States, *workers involvement* and *freedom of association* are looked at as two separate issues, in the sense that the former is referred, at least formally, to works councils, the latter to trade unions only. This idea has been embraced by Article 153 TFEU that clearly distinguishes between 'information and consultation of workers' (lett. e) as well as 'representation and collective defence of the interests of workers and employers, including co-determination' (lett. f), on the one hand, from freedom of association (and collective action) on the other.[72]

Such a perspective is typical of the *double channel approach* to workers representation and to the way in which employers and employees interact in terms of necessitate *cooperation* (works councils) or of *conflict* where appropriate, the latter to be exercised by trade unions only, in the light of freedom of association. This has also to do with the fact that, in those Member States, the law regulates the establishment, the structure and the prerogatives of works councils.

As a relevant consequence of this approach, collective bargaining and collective action result as the exclusive prerogative of trade unions with EWC playing the role of mere *facilitators* of the negotiating process. In my view, this is not acceptable, since it presupposes to look at EWC only through the lens of the double channel approach. A conclusion that, at least at EU level, is contradictory in itself. On the one hand, in fact, Article 28 CFREU recognises to workers and employers (or their respective organisations) 'the right to negotiate and conclude collective agreements at the appropriate levels and, in cases of conflicts of interest, to take collective action to defend their interests, including strike action'.

On the other hand, EU Law, to be regarded as a benchmark of that right according to Article 28 CFREU, and namely the EWC Directive (as any other directive dealing with workers involvement), leaves Member States free to determine whom workers representatives are. Therefore, EU Law does not exclude the possibility that EWC's could be the direct expression of trade unions in Member States that have adopted the single-channel model/approach. In the same vein, the EWC Directive does not explicitly deny to EWC's 'the right to negotiate and conclude collective agreements at the appropriate levels and, in

70. Silvana Sciarra, *Solidarity and Conflict: European Social Law in Crisis*, 68 (CUP 2018).
71. Sciarra *ibid.*, 67.
72. One has to stress that if, on the one hand, freedom of association is excluded from EU legislative competences (Article 153(5) TFEU), on the other, it is recognised by Article 12 CFREU that echoes Article 11 ECHR. *See* Iacopo Senatori, *Rappresentanza collettiva dei lavoratori e ordinamento europeo. La prospettiva dei diritti fondamentali* (Giappichelli 2018).

cases of conflicts of interest, to take collective action to defend their interests, including strike action'.

The exclusion of EWC's from the right to collective bargaining seems even more problematic taking into account that multinational companies look at them as reliable negotiating partners, as confirmed by the rather high number of transnational 'texts' signed with them since the nineties.[73] On purpose, I have used the word 'text' instead of 'agreement' since the latter recalls collective bargaining and its regulatory function. Indeed, an empirical analysis shows that in many cases documents currently named as Transnational Collective Agreements (TCA) have neither the form nor the structure of a collective agreement, even if EWC and trade unions have signed it jointly.

If, on the one hand, this can sound as a confirmation of the lack of legitimacy of EWC's to collective bargaining, on the other, the fact that Multinational Companies could have signed those documents just because they do not consider them collective agreements should not be underestimated.

Concluding on this point, one may argue that EU Law does not preclude workers' representatives, within the framework of the so-called involvement, signing agreements with regulatory function without the need to qualify them as collective agreements in the meaning of the double channel approach.[74]

The absence of a constant wording in EU Secondary Law as for the definition of actors of collective negotiation seems to confirm such a conclusion. In fact, it ranges from the mere reference to collective agreements, without any mention to their signatory parties in the Transfer of Undertaking,[75] the General Framework[76] as well as the Equal Opportunities and Treatment[77] Directives, to the reference to the '*most representative employers' and labour organisations at national level*' in the Posting of Workers Directive.[78] From the '*two sides of industries* at national or regional level' or 'at the appropriate level' used within the Working Time Directive,[79] to '*management and labour* at the appropriate level, including at undertaking or establishment level' as well as '*employer and the employees' representatives*' in the Information and Consultation Directive.[80]

73. http://ec.europa.eu/social/main.jsp?catId=978 (last accessed 30 July 2019).
74. *See* CJEU, 4 April 2019, C-699/17, *Allianz Vorsorgekasse*, ECLI:EU:C:2019:290, paragraph 55.
75. Article 3.
76. Article 16.
77. Article 23.
78. As signatory parties of collective agreements in 'absence of, or in addition to, a system for declaring collective agreements or arbitration awards to be of universal application' (Article 3(8)).
79. Articles 17 and 18 in the view of signing collective agreements or agreements that derogate to some basic provisions of the Working Time Directive.
80. Respectively, Article 5, in order to define 'freely and at any time through negotiated agreement the practical arrangements for informing and consulting employees', and Article 1(3), when defining and implementing those agreements 'in a spirit of cooperation and with due regard for their reciprocal rights and obligations, taking into account the interests both of the undertaking or establishment and of the employees'.

Not to mention the '*special negotiating body*' that shall negotiate with the central management on the establishment of an EWC or a procedure for informing and consulting employees referred to by the European Workers Council Directive.[81]

3.3 LIMITS TO THE REGULATORY FUNCTION OF COLLECTIVE BARGAINING AND AGREEMENTS

As already stressed in the above, Article 28 CFREU provides the recognition of the right to collective bargaining and action 'in accordance with Community Law and national laws and practices'. That wording is a clear example of *deductive constitutionalisation* that takes into account not only the differences that characterise the legal order and the industrial relations system of each Member State but also the limits that can derive to that right from EU Law.

This is a long and well-known history of the problematic relationship between the individual and the collective dimension of the regulation of economic and social interests, which involves Competition Law and exercise of the Economic Freedoms.[82] A relationship that has been regulated by the Court of Justice in some of its leading cases in the field of Collective Labour Law. In fact, after the failure of the so-called Monti II Regulation,[83] what is left of the EU legislative action on the issue at stake is the commitment to be found in the Services in the Internal Market Directive[84] and in the Amendment to the Posting of Workers Directive.[85] Both shall not 'affect the right to negotiate, conclude and enforce collective agreements and to take industrial action in accordance with national law and practices'. In the most recent Amendment Directive, the condition, foreseen by the Service Directive, according to which national law and practices are not affected if they respect 'Community Law', has disappeared.

Already in the late eighties, National Competition Authorities and private undertakings have put the regulatory function of collective agreements into question with reference to their application, by way of legislative extension, to economic actors not belonging to the signatory parties. As the Court of Justice

81. Articles 1(i) and 5(2).
82. *See* Edoardo Ales, Teun Jaspers, Pascale Lorber, Corinne Sachs-Durand & Ulrike Wendeling-Schröder, eds, *Fundamental Social Rights in Europe: Challenges and Opportunities* (Intersentia, 2009); Marc De Vos, *European Union Internal Market and Labour Law: Friends or Foes* (Intersentia, 2009); Mark Freedland & Jeremias Prassl, *Viking, Laval and Beyond* (Hart, 2014).
83. M. Rocca, *The Proposal for a (So-Called) 'Monti II' Regulation on the Exercise of the Right to Take Collective Action Within the Context of the Freedom of Establishment and the Freedom to Provide Services: Changing Without Reversing, Regulating Without Affecting*, 3 *European Labour Law Journal* 19-34 (2012).
84. Article 1(7) Directive 2006/123/EC of the European Parliament and of the Council of 12 December 2006 on services in the internal market (OJ L 376, 27.12.2006, pp. 36-68).
85. Recital - 1a. Directive (EU) 2018/957 of the European Parliament and of the Council of 28 June 2018 amending Directive 96/71/EC concerning the posting of workers in the framework of the provision of services (OJ L 173, 9.7.2018, pp. 16-24).

has stated in *Albany* and some related decisions,[86] 'it is beyond question that certain restrictions of competition are inherent in collective agreements between organisations representing employers and workers. However, the social policy objectives pursued by such agreements would be seriously undermined if management and labour were subject to [EU Competition Law] when seeking jointly to adopt measures to improve conditions of work and employment'.

The Court has reached this conclusion taking into account the EU commitment towards the improvement of working conditions as recognised by the Treaties.[87] In *van der Woude*[88] it has furthered the *Albany* doctrine by referring to the fact that the contested agreement 'was concluded in the *form of a collective agreement and constitutes the result of collective bargaining between organisations representing employers and those representing employees*'. Moreover, the Court has stressed that as for its *purpose*, the agreement 'contributes to improving the working conditions of the employees, not only by ensuring that they have the necessary means to meet [certain social needs] but also by reducing the costs, which, in the absence of a collective agreement, would have to be borne by the employees'.[89]

More recently, the *Albany* doctrine has been confronted with the problem of a collective agreement regulating working conditions not only for employee but also for self-employed.[90] Indeed, already in the past the Court of Justice had the occasion to take a (very radical) stance on the issue, stating that the that doctrine 'cannot be applied to an agreement which, whilst being intended (...) to guarantee a certain level of pension to all the members of a profession and thus to improve one aspect of their working conditions, namely their remuneration, is not concluded in the context of collective bargaining between employers and employees'.[91] The Court had reached such a conclusion on the ground that 'the Treaty contains no provisions (...) encouraging the members of the liberal professions to conclude collective agreements with a view to improving their terms of employment and working conditions and providing that, at the request

86. CJEU, 21 September 1999, C-67/96, *Albany*, ECLI:EU:C:1999:430, paragraph 59.
87. *Ibid.*, paragraph 67; CJEU, 21 September 1999, Joined Cases C-115/97, C-116/97 and C-117/97, *Brentjens and Others*, ECLI:EU:C:1999:434, paragraphs 51-57; CJEU, 21 September 1999, C-219/97, *Drijvende Bokken*, ECLI:EU:C:1999:437, paragraphs 41-47; CJEU, 3 March 2011, C-437/09, *AG2R Prévoyance*, ECLI:EU:C:2011:112, paragraphs 31-33, 35 and 38.
88. CJEU, 21 September 2000, C-222/98, *van der Woude*, ECLI:EU:C:2000:475, paragraphs 24 and 25; CJEU, 9 July 2009, C-319/07 P, *3F*, ECLI:EU:C:2009:435, paragraph 51.
89. *Ibid.*, paragraph 25.
90. A different case *should be* that one of a decision of a liberal profession to set up a pension fund responsible for managing a supplementary pension scheme and to request the public authorities to make membership of that fund compulsory for all the members of that profession: CJEU, 12 September 2000, C-180/98 to C-184/98, *Pavlov and Others*, ECLI:EU:C:2000:428, paragraphs 68-70. *See*, however, further in the text.
91. *Ibid.*, paragraph 68.

of members of the professions, such agreements be made compulsory by the public authorities, for all the members of the profession in question'.[92]

In *FNV Kunsten*[93] the Court has confirmed its restrictive approach to the collective regulation by self-employed of their economic and social interests *when they act as undertakings for the purpose of EU Competition Law.*[94] According to the Court 'a provision of a collective labour agreement (...) in so far as it was concluded by an employees' organisation in the name, and on behalf, of the self-employed services providers who are its members, does not constitute the result of a collective negotiation between employers and employees, and cannot be excluded, by reason of its nature, from the scope of [EU Competition Law]'. However, this cannot prevent 'such a provision of a collective labour agreement from being regarded also as *the result of dialogue between management and labour if the service providers, in the name and on behalf of whom the trade union negotiated, are in fact "false self-employed", that is to say, service providers in a situation comparable to that of employees*'.[95] In fact, as the Court admits, 'in today's economy it is not always easy to establish the status of some self-employed contractors as "undertakings".'[96] Therefore, collective bargaining can explicate its regulatory function 'in so far as it sets minimum fees for service providers who are "false self-employed".'[97]

By doing so, the Court of Justice has adopted a teleological approach to the regulatory function of collective agreements that allows going beyond the formal aspects related to the qualification of the work relationship and to avoid the automatic prevalence of the reasons of Competition Law on those ones of Labour Law.

Such a teleological approach characterises also the solutions adopted by the Court when the regulatory function of collective bargaining and agreements, instead of directly referring to the setting of working conditions (normative part), has to do with the establishment of bodies or machineries functional to it (obligatory part). In this view, the Court has recognised that 'both sides of industry (...), when they enter into an agreement concerning a particular aspect of working conditions, must also be able to agree to the creation of a separate body for the purpose of implementing the agreement and this body must be able to have recourse to another insurer'. By consequence, a worker cannot invoke Competition Law in order to choose a different insurer than that one designated by the body established by the collective agreement.[98]

92. *Ibid.*, paragraph 69.
93. CJEU, 4 December 2014, *FNV Kunsten Informatie en Media*, Case C-413/13, ECLI:EU:C:2014:2411.
94. *Pavlov and Others* (n. 90) paragraph 82.
95. *FNV Kunsten Informatie en Media* (n. 93) paragraph 31.
96. *Ibid.*, paragraph 32.
97. *Ibid.*, paragraph 41.
98. *van der Woude* (n. 88) paragraph 26.

However, in the view of the Court, such reasoning does not affect the separate question of compliance with EU rules on freedom of establishment and freedom to provide services in the field of public procurement when designating pension bodies entrusted with implementing a clause of a collective agreement.[99] In fact, 'it cannot be considered that it is inherent in the very exercise of the freedom of management and labour and of the right to bargain collectively that the directives which implement freedom of establishment and the freedom to provide services in the field of public procurement will be prejudiced'.[100] Indeed, 'unlike the objective, agreed between management and labour, of enhancing the level of the pensions of (...) employees, the designation of bodies and undertakings in a collective agreement does not affect the *essence of the right to bargain collectively*'.

The same applies if the decision to designate such a body or undertaking is made conditional upon the exercise of a right of co-decision by a works council or of a right of opposition of one-third of the staff if a works council does not exist.[101] In fact, according to the Court, *both constitute two expressions of the fundamental right of collective bargaining.*[102]

A final, highly controversial issue is the combination of a collective agreement, the terms of which are liable to deter an undertaking from exercising its freedom of establishment under Article 49 TFEU, and a collective action aimed at inducing the same undertaking to enter that agreement. In *International Transport Workers' Federation,*[103] the Court has deemed such an action as constituting a restriction to freedom of establishment within the meaning of Article 49 TFEU the justification of which could be regarded as doubtful. In fact, the action was part of a strategy under which it would have been called even if the exercise of the freedom of establishment and the change of working conditions there attached were not likely to produce harmful consequences on the employees at stake. In this case, according to the Court, the choice in favour of the collective agreement the undertaking should have entered into would have been based on protectionism of national trade unions instead of on workers' protection as an overriding reason of public interest.

Concluding on this point, one can argue that if pursuing a genuine objective of workers' protection, collective bargaining and agreements as well as their regulatory function will not find any limit in EU Competition and Free Movement Law, as interpreted by the Court of Justice. Protectionist behaviours, although disguised as protection of workers through collective bargaining will,

99. CJEU, 15 July 2010, C-271/08, *Commission v. Germany*, ECLI:EU:C:2010:426, paragraph 46.
100. *Ibid.*, paragraph 47.
101. *Allianz Vorsorgekasse* (n. 74) paragraph 58.
102. *Ibid.*, paragraph 55.
103. CJEU, 11 December 2007, C-438/05, *International Transport Workers' Federation (Viking Line)*, ECLI:EU:C:2007:772 and, although under other circumstances, *Laval un Partneri* (n. 6).

on the contrary, find the fierce opposition of the Court in the view of guaranteeing 'improved living and working conditions, so as to make possible their harmonisation while the improvement is being maintained' (Article 151 TFEU).

3.4 DELEGATED DEROGATORY AND REGULATORY FUNCTIONS

As already highlighted in the above, the relationship between the law and collective bargaining may also be that one of the delegations of the regulatory function of the former to the latter, sometimes also in the view of derogating the statutory provision through a collective agreement.

This is the case, for instance, in International Labour Law. In fact, the Hours of Work (Industry) Convention 1 of 1919 allows derogations to the eight hours in the day and forty-eight hours in the week limit by way of 'agreement between employers' and workers' organisations, or, where no such organisations exist, between employers' and workers' representatives'. If 'the hours of work on one or more days of the week are less than eight', that 'limit of eight hours may be exceeded on the remaining days of the week' (Article 2). In a different perspective, although in the same vein, according to the Minimum Wage-Fixing Machinery Convention 26 of 1928, the competent authority may allow collective agreement to derogate minimum rates wages that have been fixed through that machinery (Article 3(1)(1)).

As already mentioned in the above, derogations are allowed, in EU Law, to some basic provisions of the Working Time Directive either upon decision of a Member State 'by means of collective agreements or agreements between the two sides of industry' with reference to some specific groups of workers (Article 17) or upon direct determination of the same Directive. In this case, they may occur 'by means of collective agreements or agreements concluded between the two sides of industry at national or regional level or, in conformity with the rules laid down by them, by means of collective agreements or agreements concluded between the two sides of industry at a lower level' (Article 18(1)). On top of that, 'Member States in which there is no statutory system ensuring the conclusion of collective agreements or agreements concluded between the two sides of industry at national or regional level (...) or those Member States in which there is a specific legislative framework for this purpose and within the limits thereof, may, in accordance with national legislation and/or practice, allow derogations (...) by way of collective agreements or agreements concluded between the two sides of industry at the appropriate collective level' (Article 18(2)).

Derogation by collective agreement may be foreseen even to the *non-discrimination/equal treatment principle*. As for the former, we have already mentioned in the above that, according to the interpretation of the Court of

Justice,[104] social partner at the national level 'may provide that differences of treatment on grounds of age shall not constitute discrimination, if (...) they are objectively and reasonably justified by a legitimate aim, including legitimate employment policy, labour market and vocational training objectives, and if the means of achieving that aim are appropriate and necessary'(Article 6(1) General Framework Directive). As for the equal treatment principle, of high relevance in such a perspective is the derogation foreseen by the Temporary Agency Work Directive. In fact, Member States may after consulting the social partners, give them, at the appropriate level, the option of upholding or concluding collective agreements that, while respecting the overall protection of temporary agency workers, may establish working and employment conditions that derogate that principle (Article 5(3)).

In the same derogatory perspective, the Information and Consultation Framework Directive, allows Member States entrusting management and labour at the appropriate level, including at undertaking or establishment, with defining freely and at any time through agreements the practical arrangements for informing and consulting employees. These agreements may establish, while respecting the general principles set out by the Directive and subject to conditions and limitations laid down by the Member States, provisions that are different from those referred to in the Directive (Article 5).

However, delegation to collective bargaining and agreements can be foreseen with a *regulatory function* as an alternative to statutory instruments. That can be found in International Labour Law as in the (promotion of) Collective Bargaining Convention 154 of 1981, the provisions of which 'can be made effective by means of collective agreements, arbitration awards' (Article 4).

More systematically, under EU Law, 'a Member State may entrust management and labour, at their joint request, with the implementation of directives' adopted within the framework of Article 153 or 155 TFEU. In this case, the Member State shall ensure that, no later than the transposition date, management and labour introduce the necessary measures by agreement. The Member State concerned is required to take any necessary measure, at any time, to be in a position to guarantee the results imposed by that directive (Article 153(3) TFEU).

As already emphasised in the above, both *derogatory and regulatory delegations* entail problems in relation to the level at which the agreement has been concluded, its universal application and the representativeness of the signatory parties.[105] However, as highlighted by the same Court of Justice with

104. *See* decisions in n. 56.

105. A paramount example as for the European Social Dialogue in Court of First Instance, 17 June 1998, T-135/96, *UEAPME*, ECLI:EU:T:1998:128.

reference to national legislation, *derogatory and regulatory delegation* to collective bargaining and agreements has the advantage of a 'considerable flexibility'. Therefore, due account may be taken not only of the overall situation in the labour market concerned but also of the specific features of the job in question.[106]

3.5 THE INDIVIDUAL RIGHTS

The reference to the single job as the *final object* of the regulatory function of collective bargaining and agreements allows us to deal, last but not at least, with the individual employment relationship. Actually, looking at International and European Labour Law, the employment contract does not seem to play any relevant regulatory role, since they take for granted that the work relationship is regulated either by the law or by collective agreement, most of the time of universal application. A more relevant issue is the protection of rights the individual has acquired through a collective agreement, put at risk because of a change in employment conditions.

A paramount example is represented by the change of employer and its consequences on the workforce as regulated by the Transfer of Undertaking Directive, not without some relevant tensions between the individual and the collective dimension of workers' protection. In fact, on the one hand, 'transferor's rights and obligations *arising from a contract of employment or from an employment relationship* existing on the date of a transfer shall, by reason of such transfer, be transferred to the transferee' (Article 3(1)). On the other, 'following the transfer, the transferee *shall continue to observe the terms and conditions agreed in any collective agreement* on the same terms applicable to the transferor under that agreement, until the date of termination or expiry of the collective agreement or the entry into force or application of another collective agreement' (Article 3(3)).

As illustrated by the case law of the Court of Justice, in many circumstances a provision that seems to be plain is likely to produce big uncertainties for the transferee and for the transferred worker. This happens, for instance, in a situation in which the transferee neither is a member of any employers' association nor is bound by any collective agreement. Therefore, the rights and obligations of that agreement do not apply to it according to the principle of freedom of the parties to arrange their own affairs and to be free to enter into obligations with each other.[107] However, in respect of the transfer of an undertaking and its consequences on employment relationships, unconditional

106. *Palacios de la Villa* (n. 56) paragraph 74; *Rosenbladt* (n. 56) paragraph 67; *Hennigs and May* (n. 56) paragraph 92.
107. CJEU, 9 March 2006, C-499/04, *Werhof*, ECLI:EU:C:2006:168, paragraph 23.

application of the above-mentioned principle could result in erosion of the rights, which the employee has under his contract of employment and the collective agreement to which the employer transferring the undertaking was party, but not the transferee.[108]

Nevertheless, 'the wording of the Directive does not in any way indicate that the Community legislature intended that the transferee be bound by collective agreements other than the one in force at the time of the transfer and, consequently, that the terms and conditions be subsequently amended through the application of a new collective agreement concluded after the transfer'.[109]

Furthermore, 'although in accordance with the objective of the Directive the interests of the employees concerned by the transfer must be protected, those of the transferee, who must be in a position to make the adjustments and changes necessary to carry on his operations, cannot be disregarded'.[110] In fact, according to the Court, the interpretation of Article 3 'must in any event comply with Article 16 [CFERU], laying down the freedom to conduct a business, which covers, among the others, the freedom of contract'.[111]

By consequence, a clause of the *individual contract* referring to the collective agreement applied by the transferor shall be subject to a *'static' interpretation*, the one that 'makes it possible to avoid a situation in which the transferee of a business who is not party to a collective agreement is bound by future changes to that agreement'.[112] Indeed, a *'dynamic' interpretation* of the contractual reference clause would mean that 'future collective agreements apply to a transferee who is not party to a collective agreement and that his fundamental right not to join an association could be affected'.[113]

More in general, according to the Court, 'it is lawful for the transferee to apply, from the date of the transfer, the working conditions *laid down by the*

108. *Ibid.*, paragraph 24.
109. *Ibid.*, paragraph 29.
110. *Ibid.*, paragraph 31.
111. CJEU, 18 July 2013, C-426/11, *Alemo-Herron and Others*, ECLI:EU:C:2013:521, paragraphs 31-33. On Article 16 CFREU *see* Bruno Veneziani, *Article 16 – Freedom to Conduct a Business* (Filip Dorssemont, Klaus Lörcher, Stefan Clauwaert & Melanie Schmitt) *The Charter of Fundamental Rights of the European Union and the Employment Relation*, 351 (Hart Publishing, 2019).
112. *Werhof* (n. 107) paragraph 35.
113. *Ibid.*, paragraph 34. However, *see* CJEU, 27 April 2017, Joined Cases C-680/15 and C-681/15, *Asklepios Kliniken*, paragraph 29, according to which 'Article 3 of Directive 2001/23, read together with Article 16 of the Charter, must be interpreted as meaning that, in the case of a transfer of a business, the continued observance of the rights and obligations of the transferor arising from a contract of employment, extends to the clause which the transferor and the worker agreed pursuant to the principle of freedom of contract, pursuant to which their employment relationship is governed not only by the collective agreement in force on the date of the transfer, but also by agreements subsequent to the transfer and which supplement it, amend it or replace it, if the national law provides for the possibility for the transferee to make adjustments both consensually and unilaterally.'

collective agreement in force with him, including those concerning remuneration'.[114] However, the 'implementation of the option to replace, with immediate effect, the conditions which the transferred workers enjoy under the collective agreement with the transferor with those laid down by the collective agreement in force with the transferee *cannot (…) have the aim or effect of imposing on those workers conditions which are, overall, less favourable than those applicable before the transfer*'.[115] On the other hand, the Directive '*cannot usefully be invoked in order to obtain an improvement of remuneration or other working conditions on the occasion of a transfer of an undertaking*'.[116] Being confronted with such an aporia, the Court has decided that it would be contrary to the objective of Directive not to take account any possibility of preventing the transferred workers from suffering a substantial reduction in salary compared with their situation immediately before the transfer.[117]

Put in these terms, the issue of the working conditions to be guaranteed to the transferred worker by the transferee ends up to be a matter of conditions provided by the *applicable collective agreement instead of contents of the individual employment contract*. Such an impression is not contradicted by the statement of the Court according to which 'Article 3(3) of Directive 2001/23 is intended to maintain not the application of a collective agreement as such but *the "terms and conditions" put into place by such an agreement*.'[118] In fact, as specified further by the Court, 'Article 3(3) of the directive requires *the terms and conditions put in place by a collective agreement to continue to be observed, without the specific origin of their application being decisive*.'[119]

3.6 CONCLUSIONS

As it results from the analysis carried out in this essay, both International and EU Labour Laws extensively recognise the regulatory function of collective agreements as a product of the right to collective bargaining and action. Such a right is primarily recognised to workers (trade unions) and employers *organisations*, at the different levels at which they are established within the framework of the principle of freedom of association, as recognised as well at international and

114. CJEU, 6 September 2011, C-108/10, *Scattolon*, ECLI:EU:C:2011:542, paragraph 74.
115. *Ibid.*, paragraph 76.
116. *Ibid.*, paragraph 77.
117. *Ibid.*, paragraph 81. In the circumstances of the case, 'by means of at least partial recognition of the length of service of the transferred workers'.
118. CJEU, 11 September 2014, C-328/13, *Österreichischer Gewerkschaftsbund*, ECLI:EU:C:2014:2197, paragraph 23.
119. *Ibid.*, paragraph 24. In the circumstances of the case, 'terms and conditions laid down in a collective agreement, which, pursuant to the law of a Member State, despite the rescission of that agreement, continue to produce their effects as regards the employment relationship which was governed by them before the agreement was terminated' (paragraph 31).

supranational level. However, as recently affirmed by the Court of Justice,[120] also workers representatives outside the trade union realm (works councils) are entitled to that right even if, from a formal point of view, they do not sign collective agreements. Whoever the actors of collective bargaining, a crucial point about their regulatory function is linked to the universal application of collective agreements, whatever the level at which they have been signed, undertaking and establishment included. In this perspective, one can say that both International and EU Laws seem to take for granted that collective agreements do have that quality, necessary to guarantee to workers and employers the same legal certainty as offered by the law. The capacity to provide regulations that can apply with the same value and effect of the statutory instruments has highlighted the capacity of collective bargaining and agreements to interfere with Competition Law and with the exercise of economic freedoms as recognised by the EU Treaties. In such a view, EU Law as interpreted by the Court of Justice limits collective bargaining and action when they exceed the aim of protecting workers and tend to realise protectionist conditions in favour of national labour. The universal application is also likely to stimulate International, EU and national legislator to delegate to management and labour derogatory or regulatory functions that can exercise as complement or substitute of statutory instruments. The legal autonomy recognised by the law to collective bargaining and agreements assumed to be of universal application has produced the downscaling of the individual employment contract regulatory tool of the working conditions and as a source of individual rights. Therefore, the conclusion that can be drawn is that, at least looked at through the lens of International and EU Labour Law, the regulatory function of collective bargaining and agreements is in very good health, above all in case it is able to guarantee the same effect of the law offering, however, a considerable flexibility.

BIBLIOGRAPHY

Edoardo Ales, *2002/14/EC: Framework Information and Consultation* (Monika Schlachter, ed) *EU Labour Law: A Commentary*, 519 (Wolters Kluwer, 2014).

Edoardo Ales, *Article 153 TFEU* (Edoardo Ales, Mark Bell, Olaf Deinert & Sophie Robin-Olivier, eds) *International and European Labour Law*, 155 (Nomos, 2018).

Edoardo Ales, *Article 27 CFREU* (Edoardo Ales, Mark Bell, Olaf Deinert & Sophie Robin-Olivier, eds) *International and European Labour Law*, 214 (Nomos, 2018).

120. *Allianz Vorsorgekasse* (n. 74) paragraph 55.

Edoardo Ales, et al., *Fundamental Social Rights in Europe: Challenges and Opportunities* (Intersentia, 2009).

Edoardo Ales, *EU Betriebsräte und transnationale Festlegung der Arbeitsbedingungen: auf der Suche nach einem Kompromiss zwischen Tarifautonomie und Mitwirkung*, 9 *Soziales Recht* 258-266 (2019).

Edoardo Ales, *EU Collective Labour Law: A Vertically and Horizontally Combined (National and Supranational) Embedded Jurisdiction* (Beryl ter Haar & Attila Kun, eds) *European Collective Labour Law* (forthcoming).

Edoardo Ales, *ILO Convention 187* (Edoardo Ales, Mark Bell, Olaf Deinert & Sophie Robin-Olivier, eds) *International and European Labour Law*, 1437 (Nomos, 2018).

Edoardo Ales, *The State, Industrial Relations and Freedom of Association: A History of Functional Embeddedness* (Adalberto Perulli & Tiziano Treu, eds) *The Role of the State and Industrial Relations* (Wolters Kluwer, 2019).

Edoardo Ales, *The Transfer of Undertaking Directive: A Puzzling Piece of Legislation* (Erika Kovács & Martin Winner, eds) *Stakeholder Protection in Restructuring: Selected Company and Labour Law Issues*, 185 (Nomos, 2019).

Catharine Barnard, *Article 28* (Steve Peers, Tamara Hervey, Jeff Kenner & Angela Ward, eds) *The EU Charter of Fundamental Rights: A Commentary* (Hart, 2014).

Brian Bercusson, *The European Community's Charter of Fundamental Social Rights for Workers*, 53 *Modern Law Review* 624-642 (1990).

Vania Brino, *La giurisprudenza della Corte europea dei diritti dell'uomo* (Antonio Baylos Grau & Lorenzo Zoppoli a cura di) *La libertà sindacale nel mondo: nuovi profile e vecchi problemi*, 77 (Editoriale Scientifica, 2019).

Niklas Bruun, Klaus Lörcher, Isabelle Schömann & Stefan Clauwaert, *The European Social Charter and the Employment Relation* (Hart Publishing, 2017).

Marc De Vos, *European Union Internal Market and Labour Law: Friends or Foes* (Intersentia 2009).

Alexandre Defossez, *Directive 96/71/EC* (Edoardo Ales, Mark Bell, Olaf Deinert & Sophie Robin-Olivier, eds) *International and European Labour Law*, 643 (Nomos, 2018).

Filip Dorssemont & Marco Rocca, *Article 28 – Right of Collective Bargaining and Action* (Filip Dorssemont, Klaus Lörcher, Stefan Clauwaert & Mélanie Schmitt, eds) *The Charter of Fundamental Rights of the European Union and the Employment Relationship*, 465 (Hart Publishing, 2019).

Filip Dorssemont, *Article 27* (Steve Peers, Tamara Hervey, Jeff Kenner & Angela Ward, eds) *The EU Charter of Fundamental Rights: A Commentary*, 749 (Hart Publishing, 2014)

Filip Dorssemont, Klaus Lörcher & Isabelle Schömann, eds, *The European Convention on Human Rights and the Employment Relation* (Hart, 2013).
Filip Dorssemont, *The European Convention on Human Rights as Fountain of Labour Rights* (Janice R. Bellace & Beryl ter Haar, eds) *Research Handobbok on Labour, Business and Human Rights Law*, 314 (Edward Elgar, 2019)
Filip Dorssemont, *The Right to Collective Bargaining: A Matrix for Industrial Relations* (Niklas Bruun, Klaus Lörcher, Isabelle Schömann & Stefan Clauwaert, eds) *The European Social Charter and the Employment Relation*, 249 (Hart Publishing, 2017).
Filip Dorssemont, *The Right to Take Collective Action under Article 11 ECHR* (Filip Dorssemont, Klaus Lörcher, & Isabelle Schömann, eds) *The European Convention on Human Rights and the Employment Relationship*, 333 (Hart Publishing, 2013)
Keith D. Ewing, *Myth and Reality of the Right to Strike as a 'Fundamental Labour Right'*, 29 *International Journal of Comparative Labour Law and Industrial Relations* 145-166 (2013).
Mark Freedland & Jeremias Prassl, *Viking, Laval and Beyond* (Hart, 2014).
Alexia Gardin, *Directive 1999/70/EC* (Edoardo Ales, Mark Bell, Olaf Deinert & Sophie Robin-Olivier, eds) *International and European Labour Law*, 882 (Nomos, 2018).
Stefano Giubboni, *The EU and the Industrial Relations Systems: A Critical Assessment* (Adalberto Perulli & Tiziano Treu, eds) *The Role of the State and Industrial Relations* (Wolters Kluwer, 2019).
Antoine Jacobs, *Article 11 ECHR: The Right to Bargain Collectively* (Filip Dorssemont, Klaus Lörcher, & Isabelle Schömann, eds) *The European Convention on Human Rights and the Employment Relationship*, 309 (Hart Publishing, 2013).
Teun Jaspers, *Collective Action in the Netherlands* (Edoardo Ales & Tonia Novitz, eds) *Collective Action and Fundamental Freedoms in Europe: Striking the Balance*, 135 (Intersentia, 2010).
Sudabeh Kamanabrou & Anne Christin Wietfeld, *Directive 2010/18/EU* (Edoardo Ales, Mark Bell, Olaf Deinert & Sophie Robin-Olivier, eds) *International and European Labour Law*, 1026 (Nomos, 2018).
Claire La Hovary, *ILO Convention* 131 (Edoardo Ales, Mark Bell, Olaf Deinert & Sophie Robin-Olivier, eds) *International and European Labour Law*, 1120 (Nomos, 2018).
Sylvaine Laulom, *Directive 2001/23/EC* (Edoardo Ales, Mark Bell, Olaf Deinert & Sophie Robin-Olivier, eds) *International and European Labour Law*, 996 (Nomos, 2018).
Vito Leccese, *Directive 2003/88/EC* (Edoardo Ales, Mark Bell, Olaf Deinert & Sophie Robin-Olivier, eds) *International and European Labour Law*, 1285 (Nomos, 2018).

Jean-Philippe Lhernould, *Directive 2008/104/EC* (Edoardo Ales, Mark Bell, Olaf Deinert & Sophie Robin-Olivier, eds) *International and European Labour Law*, 894 (Nomos, 2018).

Jean-Philippe Lhernould, *Directive 97/81/EC* (Edoardo Ales, Mark Bell, Olaf Deinert & Sophie Robin-Olivier, eds) *International and European Labour Law*, 872 (Nomos, 2018).

Pascale Lorber, *Directive 2002/14/EC* (Edoardo Ales, Mark Bell, Olaf Deinert & Sophie Robin-Olivier, eds) *International and European Labour Law*, 1551 (Nomos, 2018).

Klaus Lörcher, *The New Social Dimension in the Jurisprudence of the European Court of Human Rights (ECtHR): The Demir an Baykara Judgement, its Methodology and Follow-up* (Filip Dorssemont, Klaus Lörcher, & Isabelle Schömann, eds) *The European Convention on Human Rights and the Employment Relationship*, 3 (Hart Publishing, 2013)

Elise Muir & Lisa Waddington, *Directive 2000/78/EC* (Edoardo Ales, Mark Bell, Olaf Deinert & Sophie Robin-Olivier, eds) *International and European Labour Law*, 520 (Nomos, 2019).

Jule Mulder, *Directive 2006/54/EC* (Edoardo Ales, Mark Bell, Olaf Deinert & Sophie Robin-Olivier, eds) *International and European Labour Law*, 547 (Nomos, 2018).

Tonia Novitz, *Freedom of Association: Its Emergence and the Case for Prevention of its Decline* (Janice R. Bellace & Beryl ter Haar, eds) *Research Handobbok on Labour, Business and Human Rights Law*, 231 (Edward Elgar, 2019).

Adalberto Perulli, *The Declaration of Philadelphia (DoP)* (Edoardo Ales, Mark Bell, Olaf Deinert & Sophie Robin-Olivier, eds) *International and European Labour Law*, 361 (Nomos, 2018).

Marco Peruzzi, *L'autonomia nel dialogo sociale europeo* (Il Mulino, 2011).

Janice R. Bellace & Beryl ter Haar, *Perspectives on labour and human rights* (Janice R. Bellace & Beryl ter Haar, eds) *Research Handbook on Labour Business and Human Rights Law*, 2 (Edward Elgar, 2019)

Marco Rocca, *Posting of Workers and Collective Labour Law: There and Back Again – Between Internal Market and Fundamental Rights* (Intersentia, 2015).

Marco Rocca, *The Proposal for a (So-Called) 'Monti II' Regulation on the Exercise of the Right to Take Collective Action Within the Context of the Freedom of Establishment and the Freedom to Provide Services: Changing Without Reversing, Regulating Without Affecting, 3 European Labour Law Journal*, 19-34 (2012).

Silvana Sciarra, *Solidarity and Conflict: European Social Law in Crisis*, 68 (CUP, 2018).

Iacopo Senatori, *Directive 2009/38/EC* (Edoardo Ales, Mark Bell, Olaf Deinert & Sophie Robin-Olivier, eds) *International and European Labour Law*, 1601 (Nomos, 2018).

Iacopo Senatori, *Rappresentanza collettiva dei lavoratori e ordinamento europeo. La prospettiva dei diritti fondamentali* (Giappichelli, 2018).

Carla Spinelli, *ILO Convention 1* (Edoardo Ales, Mark Bell, Olaf Deinert & Sophie Robin-Olivier, eds) *International and European Labour Law*, 1321 (Nomos, 2018).

Carla Spinelli, *ILO Convention 132* (Edoardo Ales, Mark Bell, Olaf Deinert & Sophie Robin-Olivier, eds) *International and European Labour Law*, 1370 (Nomos, 2018).

L. Swepston, *Crisis in the ILO Supervisory System: Dispute over the Right to Strike*, 29 *International Journal of Comparative Labour Law and Industrial Relations* 199-218 (2013).

Anne Trebilcock, *ILO Conventions 87* (Edoardo Ales, Mark Bell, Olaf Deinert & Sophie Robin-Olivier, eds) *International and European Labour Law*, 98, 154, 1492 (Nomos, 2018).

Daniel Ulber, *Article 28 CFREU* (Edoardo Ales, Mark Bell, Olaf Deinert & Sophie Robin-Olivier, eds) *International and European Labour Law*, 1457 (Nomos, 2018).

Isabelle Van Hiel, *The Right to Form and Join Trade Unions Protected by Article 11 ECHR* (Filip Dorssemont, Klaus Lörcher, & Isabelle Schömann, eds) *The European Convention on Human Rights and the Employment Relationship*, 287 (Hart Publishing, 2013)

Bruno Veneziani, *Article 16 – Freedom to Conduct a Business* (Filip Dorssemont, Klaus Lörcher, Stefan Clauwaert & Melanie Schmitt) *The Charter of Fundamental Rights of the European Union and the Employment Relation*, 351 (Hart Publishing, 2019).

Bruno Veneziani, *Article 27 – Worker's Right to Information and Consultation within the Undertaking* (Filip Dorssemont, Klaus Lörcher, Stefan Clauwaert & Mélanie Schmitt, eds) *The Charter of Fundamental Rights of the European Union and the Employment Relationship*, 429 (Hart Publishing, 2019).

CHAPTER 4

Judge-Made Law in the Common Law World: A Conservative Influence on the Transformation of Labour Law by Statute

Joellen Riley Munton

4.1 INTRODUCTION

In common law jurisdictions, judge-made law has long been an important source of labour law, notwithstanding the antiquity of many statutes regulating labour market relationships.[1] 'Common law' means (in at least one of its several meanings) the 'law based on cases, or law evolved through adjudication in particular cases, as opposed to law derived from the analysis and exposition of authoritative texts'.[2] As such, the common law is 'a living system of law, reacting to new events and new ideas, and so capable of providing ... a system of practical justice, relevant to the times in which [citizens] live'.[3] So in theory at least, the common law, or judge-made law, ought to be capable of maintaining a system of labour laws suitable for the needs of contemporary society. In practice, the common law's inherent conservatism, and its embedded individualism and commitment to the protection of property interests, has meant that labour law systems in common law jurisdictions have depended upon the enactment of statutory schemes to achieve many social objectives. This means that any consideration of the role of case law as a source of labour law needs to

1. *See* for example the Statute of Labourers of 1349 and 1350. *See* generally James Macken, Carolyn Moloney & Greg McCarry, *The Common Law of Employment*, 1-6 (Law Book Co Ltd 1978).
2. A.W. Brian Simpson, *Common Law* (Peter Cane & Joanna Conaghan, eds) *The New Oxford Companion to Law*, 166 (Oxford University Press 2008).
3. Lord Goff of Chieveley, in *Kleinwort Benson Ltd v. Lincoln CC* (1998) 2 AC 349, 377.

recognise several characteristics of the relationship between common law and statute.

First, the doctrine of precedent (obliging judges to follow the principles determined in earlier cases decided by courts higher up in the court hierarchy[4]) means that the evolution of common law principle is gradual, whereas statutory law can disrupt the trajectory of legal developments quite violently, especially in highly politicised fields of law, such as labour law.

Second, while common law doctrine gives way to any contrary rule determined by a valid and applicable statute, a principle of statutory interpretation in the common law world presumes that statutes do not intend to overturn fundamental common law principles without 'unmistakable and unambiguous language'.[5] 'It is in the last degree improbable that the legislature would overthrow fundamental principles, infringe rights, or depart from the general system of law, without expressing its intention with irresistible clearness.'[6]

Third, statutes which use words and phrases developed through judicial reasoning in the common law intend to adopt those common law meanings, so that past jurisprudence around those concepts remains relevant. 'There is abundant authority for the proposition that where the Parliament repeats words which have been judicially construed, it is taken to have intended the words to bear the meaning already judicially attributed to them.'[7]

Finally, there is a tendency, in recent times, for courts considering principled development of the common law to look to statutory law for guidance,[8] or at least, to be mindful not to permit any common law principle to develop that would be incoherent with statutory law. Professor Douglas Brodie describes this as the propensity for statute to act as either a 'catalyst' or a 'constraint' on common law development.[9] A statute is a catalyst when it prompts judicial development of the common law in line with the underpinning policy of the statute. It is a constraint when such development is restrained on the assumption that the statute intended to cover the field.

4. *See* A.W. Brian Simpson, *The Ratio Decidendi of a Case and the Doctrine of Binding Precedent* (Anthony Gordon Guest, ed.) *Oxford Essays in Jurisprudence (First Series)* (Clarendon Press 1961).
5. *Electrolux Home Products Pty Limited v. Australian Workers Union* (2004) 221 CLR 309, [118] per McHugh J, citing *Coco v. The Queen* (1994) 179 CLR 427, 437 per Mason CJ, Brennan, Gaudron and McHugh JJ; *Plaintiff S157/2002 v. The Commonwealth* (2003) 211 CLR 476, 492 [30] per Gleeson CJ.
6. O'Connor J in *Potter v. Minahan* (1908) 7 CLR 277, [21], cited in Michelle Sanson, *Statutory Interpretation*, 247 (2nd ed., Oxford University Press 2016). *See also R v. Home Secretary; Ex parte Pierson* [1998] AC 539, 587, 589 per Lord Steyn.
7. *Re Alcan Australia Ltd; Ex parte Federation of Industrial, Manufacturing & Engineering Employees* (1994) 181 CLR 96, [20].
8. R. Pound, *Common Law and Legislation*, 21 Harvard Law Review, 383, 385-386 (1908) identified this as the first of four ways that common law judges may deal with new legislation.
9. *See* D. Brodie, *Mutual Trust and Confidence: Catalysts, Constraints and Commonality*, 37 Industrial Law Journal, 329 (2008); D. Brodie, *The Dynamics of Common Law Development*, 32 (1) The International Journal of Comparative Labour Law and Industrial Relations, 45, 47 (2016).

It is generally accepted that the development of an implied obligation not to destroy mutual trust and confidence in English employment law arose from the perceived need to ensure that new statutory protections were not undermined by perverse employer conduct.[10] (This is statute acting as a catalyst for common law development.) The propensity for judges to show deference to the underpinning policy or philosophy of statutory schemes in dealing with related but distinct common law questions has been apparent in a number of significant employment law cases in recent years. For example, in *Johnson v. Unisys Ltd*,[11] the English House of Lords decided to limit the availability of common law damages for termination of an employment contract in a case where the plaintiff employee was also entitled to compensation under a statutory scheme. (This demonstrates a constraint.) Johnson effectively curtailed the development of common law damages for breach of the emergent obligation not to destroy mutual trust and confidence in the employment relationship out of concern that such development might cause common law remedies to outstrip the statutory cap on damages for an unfair termination of employment. *Johnson* was clarified in *Eastwood v. Magnox Electric plc*,[12] which drew a distinction between mutual trust breaches constituted by termination of employment (within the *Johnson* 'exclusion zone'), and mutual trust breaches arising during the course of employment, entitled to common law compensation. This pair of decisions has justified other courts in other jurisdictions (e.g., in *State of NSW v. Paige*[13] and *Commonwealth Bank of Australia v. Barker*[14]) in refusing to recognise or develop a common law duty where statutory provisions operate.

Similarly, in *Edwards v. Chesterfield Royal Hospital NHS Foundation Trust* and *Botham (FC) v. Ministry of Defence*,[15] some members of the court construed the express terms of an employment contract in a way that assumed the employer had intended to operate within the parameters of a statutory scheme imposing obligations of procedural fairness in disciplining staff. It was assumed that disciplinary procedures included in the employment contract were intended to do no more than ensure compliance with statutory requirements, so breach of these procedures should therefore attract no more than statutory sanctions. The Australian Federal Court adopted similar reasoning in finding that a statutory obligation to prevent workplace harassment justified a finding that an employer's undertaking (in a workplace policy manual) to prevent harassment at work was seriously made and was therefore contractually binding on both parties.[16]

10. Mark Freedland, *The Personal Employment Contract*, 155 (Oxford University Press 2003).
11. [2003] 1 AC 518.
12. [2005] 1 AC 503.
13. (2002) 60 NSWLR 371.
14. (2014) 253 CLR 169.
15. [2011] UKSC 58 (14 December 2011).
16. *See Romero v. Farstad Shipping (Indian Pacific) Pty Ltd* [2104] FCAFC 177.

With these characteristics of the common law's relationship with statute in mind, this chapter will consider the role of common law jurisprudence in developing some central notions of labour law in common law jurisdictions: the definition of 'employment' as a form of labour engagement; the existence of implied terms in employment contracts; the employer's common law duty of care towards employees; the employer's duty (such as it is) to provide the employee with appropriate work; and the common law constraints on taking industrial action. A final section will also consider the relationship between collective agreements, made under the authority of statute, and common law employment contracts.

4.2 EMPLOYMENT

In many common law jurisdictions, the important business of defining the category of worker entitled to many standard employment protections is left to the common law, notwithstanding that this definition developed in the context of determining a master's vicarious responsibility for the actions of servants and that a great deal of scholarly analysis has found this common law definition problematic.[17]

The problem of distinguishing a contract 'of service' (employment) from other contracts 'for services' has become especially acute as the accretion of new statutory protections (such as unfair dismissal protection) has tempted some employers to seek forms of labour engagement that avoid those liabilities. Employers' attempts to retain their common law entitlement to hire and fire at will, now constrained by statute in many jurisdictions, has produced a volume of case law in recent times.[18] Employment status is, however, not susceptible to

17. *See* for example Kenneth William Wedderburn & Jon Clark, *Modern Law: Problems, Functions and Policies* (Kenneth William Wedderburn, Roy Lewis & Jon Clark, eds) *Labour Law and Industrial Relations* (Oxford Clarendon Press 1983); H. Collins, *Independent Contractors and the Challenge of Vertical Disintegration*, 10 Oxford Journal of Legal Studies, 353 (1990); Freedland (n. 10); M. Freedland, *From the Contract of Employment to the Personal Work Nexus*, 35 Industrial Law Journal, 1 (2006); M. Freedland, *Application of Labour and Employment Law Beyond the Contract of Employment*, 146 International Labour Review, 3 (2007); Mark Freedland & Nicola Kountouris, *The Legal Construction of Personal Work Relations* (Oxford University Press 2011); Guy Davidov & Brian Langille, *Boundaries and Frontiers of Labour Law* (Hart Publishing 2006); Guy Davidov & Brian Langille, *The Idea of Labour Law* (Oxford University Press 2011); O. Razzolini, *The Need to Go Beyond the Contract: 'Economic' and 'Bureaucratic' Dependence in Personal Work Relations*, 31 Comparative Labour Law and Policy Journal, 267 (2010); Giuseppe Casale, *The Employment Relationship: A Comparative Overview* (Hart Publishing, International Labour Organisation 2011); Joellen Riley, *The Definition of the Contract of Employment and Its Differentiation from Other Contracts and Other Work Relations* (Mark Freedland, ed.) *The Contract of Employment* (Oxford University Press 2016).
18. *See* for example *Consistent Group Ltd v. Kalwak and Ors* [2008] EWCA 430; [2008] IRLR 505; *Protectacoat Firthglow Ltd v. Szilagyi* [2009] EWCA Civ 98; *Autoclenz Ltd v. Belcher* [2011] UKSC 41.

destruction by misdescription. The common law tests for distinguishing employment from independent contracting look to the 'true' or 'real relationship' between the parties[19] and are not distracted by any 'cloud of words'[20] used by employers to obfuscate the relationship.[21]

The courts have evolved several tests over time to identify a 'true' employment relationship, although none of them has proven entirely satisfactory for all purposes.[22] Deakin and Wilkinson have identified four tests developed by the English courts at different times in history: control, integration, economic reality, and mutuality of obligation.[23] With the exception of 'mutuality of obligation', these tests comprise the 'multi-indicia' test used by Australian courts and tribunals, in weighing many factors to form an overall view of the 'real' character of the relationship.[24]

4.2.1 Control

The earliest case law concerned the vicarious liability of masters for wrongs committed by their servants. The common law concept of vicarious liability derives from the mediaeval notion that the master of the house should be held legally responsible for the actions of subservient household members (including wives, children, and domestic servants).[25] The rationale for vicarious liability – now extended also to relationships of principal/agent and employer/employee – is that masters/principals/employers exert ultimate control over their subordinates, and benefit from their actions, so ought also to bear any risks created by servants or agents undertaking business activities on their behalf.[26] In early cases, the employer's control was manifested in the ability to dictate the manner in which work was to be performed,[27] and when masters were expert instructors, very likely to be participating in the work themselves.[28] The emergence of highly skilled employment, undertaken in the service of impersonal corporate

19. *Protectacoat Firthglow Ltd v. Szilagyi* [2009] EWCA Civ 98, [60].
20. *Cam & Sons Pty Ltd v. Sargent* (1940) 14 ALJ 162, 163 per Dixon J; *Massey v. Crown Life Insurance* [1977] EWCA Civ 12; [1978] 2 All ER 576.
21. *See also Application by DJ Porter for an Inquiry into an Election in the Transport Workers' Union of Australia* (1989) 34 IR 179, 184.
22. Freedland (n. 17) 20.
23. Simon Deakin & Frank Wilkinson, *The Law of the Labour Market: Industrialization, Employment and Legal Evolution*, 306-307 (Oxford University Press 2005); David Cabrelli, *Employment Law in Context*, 80-81 (Oxford University Press 2014).
24. *Stevens v. Brodribb Sawmilling Co Pty Ltd* (1986) 160 CLR 13; *Hollis v. Vabu Pty Ltd* (2001) 207 CLR 21.
25. *Scott v. Davis* (2000) 204 CLR 333, [230] per Gummow J. *See also* O.W. Holmes, *Agency*, 4 Harvard Law Review, 345, 364 (1891).
26. *See Hollis v. Vabu Pty Ltd* (2001) 207 CLR 21, [90] per McHugh J.
27. *See Performing Rights Society Ltd v. Mitchell & Brooker Ltd (Palais de Danse)* [1924] 1 KB 762, 767-8.
28. *See* O. Kahn-Freund, *Servants and Independent Contractors*, 14 Modern Law Review, 504, 505-506 (1951).

employers, has seen this test evolve from actual control into a residual right to dictate the terms and conditions of work and monitor performance.[29]

Collins has criticised this 'diffuse' form of the control test as 'indeterminate' because it is potentially both under-inclusive and overinclusive.[30] Entrepreneurial professionals running their own businesses may also agree to accept certain terms of work, including subjection to regular monitoring, without surrendering their autonomy as independent business people. Nevertheless, the control test has continued to serve well in many recent cases where low-skilled workers have been engaged on 'sham' independent contracts.[31]

4.2.2 Integration

According to Deakin and Wilkinson, the organisational integration test emerged when judges were called upon to adjudicate disputes over the application of social insurance and workers' compensation legislation to managerial and professional labour.[32] The integration test asks whether the worker is undertaking work that is an integral part of the employer's business or working in a business of his or her own,[33] providing services that are merely 'accessory' to the employer's enterprise.[34] According to this test, managerial workers who provide strategic direction to an enterprise are also employees, even though they are ostensibly in control of the organisation themselves. Courts applying the integration test ask questions such as does the worker wear the employer's uniform or carry the employer's trademarks? Who supplies the equipment needed to perform the work?[35]

4.2.3 Economic Reality

The advent, following the Second World War, of advanced social insurance legislation and income taxation regimes prompted the development in some jurisdictions of a test based on the economic reality of working relationships, principally to ensure that enterprises could not strategise to avoid these imposts

29. *See Zuijs v. Wirth Bros Pty Ltd* (1955) 83 CLR 561, 571.
30. *See* H. Collins, *Independent Contractors and the Challenge of Vertical Disintegration to Employment Protection Laws*, 10 Oxford Journal of Legal Studies, 353, 370 (1990).
31. *See* for example *Protectacoat Firthglow Ltd v. Szilagyi* [2009] EWCA Civ 98 at [69]; *Autoclenz Ltd v. Belcher* [2011] UKSC 41; *Country Metropolitan Agency Contracting Services Pty Ltd v. Slater* (2003) 124 IR 293; *Fair Work Ombudsman v. Quest South Perth Holdings Pty Ltd* [2015] HCA 45 (2 December 2015); *Joshua Klooger v. Foodora Australia Pty Ltd* [2018] FWC 6836 (16 November 2018).
32. Deakin & Wilkinson (n. 23), table 3.1.
33. *Market Investigations Ltd v. Minister of Social Security* [1969] 2 QB 173, 184 per Cooke J.
34. *See Stevenson, Jordan and Harrison Ltd v. MacDonald & Evans* [1952] 1 TLR 101, 111 per Lord Denning.
35. The integration test has also been criticised for its indeterminacy: *see* Collins (n. 30) 370-371.

by artificial arrangements for engaging staff. The decision of the Supreme Court of the United States (US) in *National Labour Relations Board v. Hearst Publications*[36] provides a useful illustration. In Hearst, the employer had refused to recognise that their newspaper sellers enjoyed any right to collective bargaining under the National Labour Relations Act 1935 (US). The paper sellers won the case because the 'economic facts' of their engagement showed that their earnings were effectively dictated by the employer, who dictated prices, volume of supply of newspapers, and their sales territories. The court interpreted the term 'employee' in the Act in the light of the purpose of the statute and the economic reality of the relationship rather than from any 'technical legal classification [of the relationship] for purposes unrelated to the statute's objective'.[37]

Courts in England and Australia have been prepared to look past the documentation to the economic reality of the relationship in finding that workers purportedly engaged as independent contractors are really employees.[38] In this respect, the case law method has proven to be adept at detecting new stratagems to avoid employment obligations. It must be said, however, that many of these cases arise in the context of determining whether a particular statutory benefit (minimum wage rates, worker's compensation insurance, unfair dismissal protection, for instance) are available to a worker who has been engaged by way of some ingenious form of contract.[39] The purpose of a protective statute often provides the catalyst for judicial development of the boundary of the category of 'employment'.

4.2.4 Mutuality of Obligation

In the 1970s, statutory protections against capricious dismissal emerged, and courts were called upon to determine whether casual staff, employed from time to time with no commitment to ongoing engagement, should be included within these protections. Stephenson LJ in *Nethermere (St Neots) Ltd v. Gardiner* said that there must be 'an irreducible minimum of obligation on each side to create a contract of service'.[40] This mutuality of obligation test ensures that parties who never intended any continuous employment obligations fall outside of the statutory protections.[41] This test makes it all the more important that courts be

36. 322 US 111 (1943).
37. 322 US 128 (1943).
38. *See Autoclenz Ltd v. Belcher* [2011] UKSC 41; *Boss Projects LLP v. Bragg* [2013] WL 6536645; *Country Metropolitan Agency Contracting Services Pty Ltd v. Slater* (2003) 124 IR 293.
39. *See* for example *Damevski v. Giudice* (2003) 133 FCR 438.
40. [1984] ICR 612, 623.
41. *See* for example *Carmichael v. National Power plc* [1999] UKHL J1118-2; [1999] 1 WLR 2042 considering eligibility to benefits under the *Employment Protection (Consolidation) Act* 1978.

prepared to look past sham arrangements, in which employers disguise continuing employees as casuals.

4.2.5 Multi-Indicia or Multifactorial Test

Nowadays, the above tests tend to be considered in combination. In *Ready Mixed Concrete (South East) Ltd v. Minister of Pensions and National Insurance*,[42] MacKenna J. identified three conditions for finding a contract of employment: the worker agrees to provide his or her own work and skill in exchange for remuneration (the 'personal service' requirement); the worker agrees to be subject to the employer's control (the control test); and 'other provisions of the contract are consistent with its being a contract of service'.[43] These 'other provisions' include those factors generally associated with the integration test and the economic reality of the relationship.

The ultimate question for the court is: does the worker serve the employer's business interests or her own? Who provides capital to the enterprise, and who has the capacity to profit from the effective management of a capital contribution is an influential factor in classifying the worker.[44] Courts are becoming increasingly astute at seeing through the stratagems of employers and the 'armies of lawyers' who advise them and have found that employees who have been made to look like business partners, or even incorporated businesses themselves, are in truth employees.[45] It has nevertheless taken statutory intervention to widen the net of many statutory protections to capture the kinds of vulnerable workers sometimes described as 'dependent contractors'. In *Aslam & Ors v. Uber BV & Ors*,[46] the United Kingdom Employment Tribunal decided that rideshare drivers engaged by Uber were in fact 'workers' as defined by the Employment Rights Act 1996 section 230(3)(b), the Working Time Regulation 1998 regulation 36(1), and the National Minimum Wage Act section 54(3). These provisions extended coverage of basic working conditions in respect of wages and hours to a category of workers who, while not strictly 'employees' according to the common law, were nevertheless providing personal services, but not to 'clients' or 'customers'

42. [1968] 2 QB 497, 515C.
43. *Ibid.*
44. Compare, for example, *Vabu Pty Ltd v. Federal Commissioner of Taxation* (1996) 33 ATR 537 with *Hollis v. Vabu Pty Ltd* (2001) 207 CLR 21, [58].
45. *See Consistent Group Ltd v. Kalwak* [2007] IRLR 560; *Protectacoat Firthglow Ltd v. Szilagyi* [2009] EWCA Civ 98; *Autoclenz Ltd v. Belcher* [2011] UKSC 41; *Massey v. Crown Life Insurance* [1978] ICR 590, 594.

    For commentary on 'sham' contract arrangements, *see* J. McClelland, *A Purposive Approach to Employment Protection or a Missed Opportunity?*, 75 (3) Modern Law Review, 387 (2012); A.L. Bogg, *Sham Self-Employment in the Supreme Court*, 41 (3) Industrial Law Journal, 328 (2012); A.C.L. Davies, *Sensible Thinking about Sham Transactions: Protectacoat Firthglow Ltd v. Szilagyi* [2009] EWCA Civ 98; [2009] IRLR 365', 38 (3) Industrial Law Journal, 318-328 (2009).
46. [2016] UKET 2202551/2015 (28 October 2016).

of their own professional business undertakings. In a jurisdiction that does not (presently) enjoy this wider statutory definition of 'worker', an Uber driver working under essentially the same contract terms was held not to be an employee, and hence ineligible to claim statutory employment rights.[47] For radical and rapid solutions to new forms of engagement in the contemporary economy, employee advocates cannot afford to wait for incremental evolution of the common law but must lobby for legislative change.

4.3 IMPLIED TERMS

Case law has also made highly important contributions to basic principles of labour law by the formulation of implied terms in employment contracts. The employment contract is, in historical terms, a relatively recent construct.[48] Before the early twentieth century, the engagement of workers was largely governed by status-based master and servant law, and extensive 'factories and shops' legislation. As employment began to be treated as a contractual relationship, courts were called upon to fill gaps in the express agreements made between employers and employees in order to resolve disputes over the respective obligations of the parties.[49] The earliest principles of employment contract law adopted the assumption of servitude embedded in the earlier master and servant law. Hence, the employee's duties of obedience to lawful and reasonable commands and of fidelity and loyalty to the employer's interests developed as 'terms implied by law' into the common law employment contract.[50] These duties have remained relatively constant over time, although courts have been required to consider the implication of duties to obey and be loyal in the context of many new social circumstances. For example, the proliferation of social media platforms and the surveillance technologies now available to track employees have tested the limits of the employer's right to command obedience from employees in matters affecting the employer's business interests.[51] On the whole, however, the weight of authority suggests that the implied duties of obedience and loyalty have proven to be robust in ensuring that the courts

47. *See Kaseris v. Rasier Pacific VOF* [2017] FWC 6610.
48. *See* A. Merritt, *The Historical Role of the Law in the Regulation of Employment: Abstentionist or Interventionist?*, 1 Australian Journal of Law & Society, 56 (1982); Simon Deakin, *The Many Futures of the Employment Contract* (Joanne Conaghan, Michael Fischel & Karl Klare, eds) *Labour Law in an Era of Globalisation: Transformative Practices and Possibilities*, 193 (Oxford University Press 2002); J. Howe & R. Mitchell, *The Evolution of the Contract of Employment in Australia: A Discussion*, 12 Australian Journal of Labour Law, 113 (1999).
49. For a full analysis of implied terms in employment contracts *see* Hugh Collins, *Implied Terms in the Contract of Employment* (Mark Freedland, ed.) *The Contract of Employment*, Chapter 22 (Oxford University Press 2016).
50. *See Turner v. Mason* (1845) 14 M & W 112, 117-118.
51. *See* Gordon Anderson, Douglas Brodie & Joellen Riley, *The Common Law Employment Relations: A Comparative Study*, 142-165 (Edward Elgar 2017).

remain vigilant in prioritising employers' interests in such contests, often even in the face of statutory protections for human rights.[52]

In more recent times, the development of new implied terms to accommodate contemporary expectations of the employment relationship have proved more problematic. Since the 1970s, the common law in the United Kingdom (UK) has developed an implied term in employment contracts, binding upon both employers and employees, that parties to an employment contract will not act in a manner calculated or likely to destroy mutual trust and confidence in the employment relationship.[53] This obligation is said to recognise that in contemporary society, employment 'gives not only a livelihood but an occupation, an identity and a sense of self-esteem' to working citizens.[54] It arose very much as a response to employer tactics to avoid paying statutory compensation to employees upon unfair termination of employment.[55] As the statute applied only to termination at the initiative of the employer, some employers engaged in behaviours designed to frustrate and annoy employees into resignation. Examples of such behaviour included carping criticism,[56] capricious withdrawal of benefits,[57] and unreasonable investigations and disciplinary procedures.[58]

While this implied term has been cemented into the common law as an important incident of the employment relationship in the UK, it has received a mixed reception by courts in other parts of the common law world. New Zealand embraced the concept, and it was definitively accepted as part of the canon of New Zealand law in *Auckland Electric Power Board v. Auckland Provincial District Local Authorities Officers IUOW*.[59] It has also been embedded in New Zealand's labour laws by inclusion in the Employment Relations Act 2000 (NZ). The objects in section 3(a)(i) of this Act state 'that employment relationships must be built not only on the implied mutual obligations of trust and confidence,

52. *See* V. Mantouvalou, *Human Rights and Unfair Dismissal: Private Acts in Public Spaces*, 71 (6) Modern Law Review, 912 (2008).
53. The English case law is extensive. The implied term first appeared in *Western Excavating v. Sharp* [1978] QB 761. Its existence was affirmed by the House of Lords decision in *Malik v. Bank of Credit and Commerce International SA (in liq)* [1998] AC 20. For early commentary on this development, *see* D. Brodie, *The Heart of the Matter: Mutual Trust and Confidence*, 25 Industrial Law Journal, 121 (1996); D. Brodie, *Beyond Exchange: The New Contract of Employment*, 27 Industrial Law Journal, 79 (1998); D. Brodie, *A Fair Deal at Work*, 19 Oxford Journal of Legal Studies, 83 (1999). *See also* M. Freedland, *Constructing Fairness in Employment Contracts*, 36 Industrial Law Journal, 136 (2007); D. Cabrelli, *The Implied Duty of Mutual Trust and Confidence: An Emerging Overarching Principle*, 34 Industrial Law Journal, 284 (2005) and D. Brodie, *Fair Dealing and the World of Work*, 43 (1) Industrial Law Journal, 29 (2014).
54. Anderson, Brodie & Riley (n. 51) 119.
55. Employment Rights Act 1996 (UK) clause 18.
56. *See Lewis v. Motorworld Garages Ltd* [1986] ICR 157.
57. *See Clark v. Nomura International plc* [2000] IRLR 766; *Horkulak v. Cantor Fizgerald International* [2005] ICR 402, 419-420, [48].
58. *See Bliss v. South East Thames Regional Health Authority* [1987] ICR 700 *Eastwood v. Magnox Electric plc* [2005] 1 AC 503.
59. [1994] 2 NZLR 415. For commentary *see* G. Anderson, *Good Faith in the Individual Employment Relations in New Zealand*, 32 Comparative Labor Law and Policy Journal, 685 (2000).

but also on a legislative requirement for good faith behaviour' which is set out in section 4.[60] In Australia, however, the notion that the employment relationship, by its very nature, must involve a mutual obligation of trust and confidence was treated with scepticism by all but a few courts.[61] Ultimately, it was rejected by the Australian High Court in *Commonwealth Bank of Australia v. Barker*, as a 'foreign' doctrine that ought not to be accommodated into Australian law.[62] A key argument for the Australian High Court was that the putative implied term did not meet the usual test of 'necessity' required in general commercial contract law before a new term implied by law can be accepted. Another key argument was that employment rights in Australia are now extensively governed by statute, leaving little room for innovation by the courts. These findings are likely to curb the development of any new terms implied by the common law in Australian employment contract law.

However, Canadian employment law has been more willing to experiment with the concept of an obligation of mutual trust and confidence and hence an obligation of good faith between the parties to an employment contract.[63] Claire Mummé has explained that Canada's more robust common law development is due to the absence of any general development of statutory unfair dismissal laws in Canada. The common law continues to play a central role in determining wrongful termination disputes in Canada.[64]

Of course, all common law implied terms surrender to any express stipulation binding the parties in a statute, an applicable collective bargain, or in the express terms of an individual employment contract. Given the propensity in the modern world to require all staff (even those occupying the most lowly positions) to sign detailed contract documents upon recruitment, opportunities for arguments over implied terms are limited.

4.4 COMMON LAW DUTY OF CARE

Another (and generally less contentious) term implied by law into the employment contract, as a consequence of common law development, is the employer's duty to take reasonable care to avoid exposing employees to unnecessary risk of foreseeable harm.[65] This contractual implied term is said to be coextensive with

60. *See* G. Anderson, *Transplanting Good Faith into New Zealand Labour Law: The Experience under the Employment Relations Act 2000*, 9 Murdoch University Electronic Journal of Law, 40 (2002).
61. *See* J. Riley, *Siblings but Not Twins: 'Mutual Trust' and 'Good Faith' in Employment Contracts*, 36 Melbourne University Law Review, 521, 530-536 (2012).
62. (2014) 253 CLR 169, [18].
63. *See* C. Mummé, *Bhasin v. Hrynew: A New Era for Good Faith in Canadian Employment Law, or Just Tinkering at the Margins?*, 32 (1) International Journal of Comparative Labour Relations Law and Industrial Relations, 117 (2016).
64. *See* Claire Mummé, *A Comparative Reflection from Canada – A Good Faith Perspective* (Mark Freedland, ed.) *The Contract of Employment*, Chapter 14, 295 (Oxford University Press 2016).
65. *See Lister v. Romford Ice and Cold Storage Co Ltd* [1957] AC 555.

the employer's common law duty of care in tort. Courts have explained this implied duty as the natural consequence of the employer's prerogative to command obedience from employees. The duty 'arises from the degree of control that the employer exercises over the lives of the employees'.[66] Courts have differed, however, on the question of whether this implied duty can be cut down by express terms in the contract, limiting the employer's obligations. In *Johnstone v. Bloomsbury Health Authority*,[67] for example, a majority of the English Court of Appeal held that express terms in a young doctor's employment contract permitting him to be rostered on for excessively long hours must be read down, in the light of an overarching obligation to take reasonable care for his physical health. However, the Australian High Court has held that the extent of an employer's common law duty of care cannot be determined 'without taking account of the obligations that the parties owe one another under the [express terms of] the contract of employment'.[68]

In recent times, courts have come under pressure to extend this common law duty of care to an obligation upon employers to take appropriate steps to protect the psychiatric well-being of staff. As contemporary society begins to recognise the debilitating effects of mental distress (even absent any physical injury), common law courts have been called upon to adjudicate claims for compensation by, for example, police officers suffering post-traumatic stress and victims of workplace bullying or incompetently managed disciplinary processes.[69] In this field too, common law developments have varied between jurisdictions.[70]

4.5 DUTY TO PROVIDE WORK

The evolution of the common law's attitude to whether employers owe an obligation to provide actual work to their employees illuminates the way in which common law developments follow (with sticky feet) the 'new events and new ideas'[71] in an evolving society. Employees tend to argue for such a duty when they wish to resign to take up other gainful employment, but the employer is seeking to enforce a long notice period to keep them out of the labour market.

66. *See Patrick Stevedores (No 1) Pty Ltd v. Vaughan* [2002] NSWCA 275, [16].
67. [1992] 2 All ER 293.
68. *Koehler v. Cerebos Pty Ltd* (2005) 222 CLR 44, 53-54. *See* too the statement by Gordon J in *Govier v. The Uniting Church in Australia Property Trust (Q)*, [2018] HCATrans 65 (13 April 2018) that: '[O]ne does not look at the tort in terms of the duty and scope without understanding what the contractual framework is'. The Australian position has not been favoured by English courts: *see* D. Brodie & J. Riley, *A Duty of Good Management? Protected Interests and the Employment Contract*, 50 (2) Victoria University of Wellington Law Review (forthcoming 2019).
69. *See* for example *Hatton v. Sutherland* [2002] 2 All ER 1; *Barber v. Somerset* [2004] 2 All ER 385; *State of New South Wales v. Briggs* [2016] NSWCA 344; *Bau v. State of Victoria* [2009] VSCA 107.
70. Brodie & Riley (n. 68).
71. *See* n. 3.

As is often the case, the orthodox common law doctrine favours the interests of employers in such cases, although some important exceptions have been established to ensure that this principle cannot cause the starvation of those workers who are paid by commission,[72] or ruin the careers of performers who work as much for fame as remuneration.[73] Perhaps the most often cited statement of the orthodoxy that employers are not generally obliged to provide duties comes from *Collier v. Sunday Referee Publishing Co Ltd*:[74] 'provided I pay my cook her wages regularly she cannot complain if I choose to take any or all of my meals out'. Even in *Collier*, this already antiquated stereotype of employment as service to an individual master was inept to determine the result of the case. Mr Collier, a newspaper editor, was ultimately permitted to escape his contract because the publisher had sold the newspaper and made it impossible for Collier ever to serve as editor again.

Over time, the rigour of this orthodox principle has been ameliorated, as courts have recognised the reality of working life, particularly in skilled professions. Lord Denning recognised this need in *Langston v. Amalgamated Union of Engineering Workers*, where he held that the employee 'should be given the opportunity of doing ... work when it is available'.[75] And in *William Hill Organisation Ltd v. Tucker*,[76] the English Court of Appeal was prepared to imply a duty to provide work in a 'specific and unique post', requiring regular exercise of special skills. In *Potter v. New Brunswick*,[77] the Supreme Court of Canada held that an employer 'may not withhold work in bad faith, or without justification'.[78] Nevertheless, it has taken statutory intervention to establish a clear entitlement for wrongfully dismissed workers to be reinstated to duties, and such statutory intervention is rare in common law jurisdictions.[79]

In *Blackadder v. Ramsay Butchering Services Pty Ltd*,[80] the High Court of Australia was asked to consider whether a right to reinstatement under a statutory unfair dismissal regime afforded the worker a right to return to actual duties, or just an entitlement to reinstatement of his contract. The Federal Court, from which this case had been appealed, followed the orthodox common law doctrine expressed in *Collier* to deny the worker an entitlement to return to actual duties.[81] The High Court bench, however, interpreted the statutory provisions in a manner that permitted the tribunal to reinstate the employee to

72. *Turner v. Sawdon & Co* [1901] 2 KB 653, 656.
73. *Marbe v. George Edwards (Daly's Theatre) Ltd* [1928] 1 KB 269.
74. [1940] 2 KB 647, 60 per Asquith J.
75. [1974] 1 WLR 185, 192.
76. [1999] ICR 291.
77. [2015] 1 SCR 500.
78. *See* Brodie & Riley (n. 68), 46.
79. Australia is an exception, in providing the remedy of reinstatement and not just compensation for unfair dismissal: *See* Fair Work Act 2009 (Cth) Pt 3-3.
80. [2005] HCA 22.
81. (2003) 127 FCR 381.

actual duties. In so finding, two members of the court cast some doubt on the relevance of older authorities (such as *Collier*) today. They said:

> One might question the current relevance of judicial pronouncements made more than 60 years ago in the United Kingdom as to the extent to which an employer might be obliged to dine at home in order to provide work for his cook. It may be that in modern times, a desire for what has been called 'job satisfaction', and a need for employees of various kinds, to keep and to be seen to have kept their hands in by actual work have a role to play in determining whether work in fact should be provided.[82]

This obiter has not yet been followed in other cases to establish any new general principle, and many relatively recent decisions continue to refuse to recognise a professional person's entitlement to be given meaningful work.[83] The common law can be particularly slow in responding to 'new events and new ideas',[84] even when those ideas are decades old.

4.6 COMMON LAW CONSTRAINTS ON INDUSTRIAL ACTION

Under the common law, most forms of industrial action (including strikes and other work bans) constitute a serious breach of the employment contract, in respect of individual employees,[85] and an 'economic' or 'industrial tort', of conspiring to injure the employer in their trade or business, in respect of the collective actors in industrial disputation. The common law recognises no right to strike, nor any immunity from suit for those engaging in industrial action.[86] Indeed, some of the earliest convicts transported from Britain to the Australian colonies in 1834 were guilty of no worse a crime than taking an illegal oath to combine to bargain collectively with their masters to retain their wage rates in the face of a threatened pay cut.[87] In the common law world, the rights of trade unions to conduct industrial campaigns to agitate for better working conditions are entirely due to statutory immunities from suit for such action, usually contained in specific legislation permitting the formation and registration of

82. (2005) 215 ALR 87, [80].
83. *See* for example *BearingPoint Australia Pty Ltd v. Hillard* [2008] VSC 115, concerning a managing director.
84. *See* n. 3.
85. *See Rookes v. Barnard* [1963] 1 QB 623, 682, per Donovan LJ. *See also* Keith Ewing, *The Right to Strike*, Chapter 2 (Clarendon Press 1991).
86. *See* S. Deakin & J. Randall, *Rethinking the Economic Torts*, 72 (4) Modern Law Review, 519-553 (2009). *See* Carolyn Sappideen, Paul O'Grady & Joellen Riley, *Macken's Law of Employment*, Chapter 14 (8th ed., Thomson Reuters 2016) for a compete explanation of the industrial torts. Significant cases include: *Allen v. Flood* [1898] AC 1; *Quinn v. Leathem* [1901] AC 495; *Sorrell v. Smith* [1925] AC 700; *Crofter Hand Woven Harris Tweed v. Veitch* [1942] AC 435; *D C Thomson & Co Ltd v. Deakin* [1952] Ch. 646; *Rookes v. Barnard* [1964] AC 1129; *Ansett Transport Industries (Operations) Pty Ltd v. Australian Federation of Air Pilots* (1989) 95 ALR 211.
87. *See R v. Loveless* (1834) 174 ER 119, and the account of the case given by Herbert Vere Evatt, *The Tolpuddle Martyrs: Injustice Within the Law* (Sydney University Press 2009).

trade unions, and authorising forms of collective bargaining. Generally these statutory immunities are limited. For example, the statutory immunities from liability for economic torts and other legal sanctions in the Australian Fair Work Act 2009 (Cth) extend only to industrial action that conforms to highly prescriptive bargaining protocols.[88] And even those statutory immunities have been narrowly construed to preserve a so-called common law 'right to sue'.[89] For example, in *Electrolux Home Products Pty Ltd v. Australian Workers' Union,*[90] the Australian High Court, by majority, narrowly construed statutory provisions concerning the extent of the matters that a union could include in its log of claims, while taking protected industrial action. The court's justification for this narrow construction was explained as a concern to preserve the employer's common law right to access the courts to protect contract and property rights. This is an illustration of the principle of statutory interpretation (noted above) that presumes that statutory provisions do not intend to limit 'fundamental' common law rights unless they are explicit in doing so. That an employer's right to sue a collective of workers should be treated as such a fundamental right illustrates the underpinning conservatism of the common law and its preoccupation with private rights derived from the law of property.

4.7 COLLECTIVE AGREEMENTS MADE UNDER STATUTE AND COMMON LAW CONTRACTS

A matter that regularly causes confusion in common law jurisdictions which permit the making of collective industrial agreements according to rules and procedures set out in a statute is the status of those collective agreements under the common law of contract. Are these agreements also enforceable as common law contracts? Do these agreements have any role to play in supplying terms, by incorporation or implication, in individual employees' common law employment contracts? These arguments may arise because there has been some flaw in the registration process for the collective agreement, meaning it cannot be enforced under the statute, or because an old agreement has expired and is no longer enforceable under the statute.

Generally, a collective agreement made under statutory provisions will not be enforceable as a common law contract, because collective agreements rarely comply with the usual principles of common law contract doctrine. The common law of contract is inherently individualistic in its focus. The doctrine of privity of contract, which holds that only those parties who have voluntarily agreed to the

88. *See* Fair Work Act 2009 (Cth) Part 3-3. For a treatise on this law, *see* Shae McCrystal, *The Right to Strike in Australia* (Federation Press 2010).
89. *See* S. McCrystal, *The Right to Strike and the 'Deadweight' of the Common Law*, 50 (2) Victoria University of Wellington Law Review (2019 forthcoming).
90. (2004) 221 CLR 309.

terms of contract will be bound by it, means that contract law is unsuited to the enforcement of collective agreements. Collective agreements are often made after seeking the approval of a majority of employees, but will nevertheless purport to bind all employees, including employees who did not agree, and even those who had not yet been engaged at the time the collective agreement came into force.[91] Collective agreements will nevertheless be binding according to the terms of the statute enabling their making, so long as they comply with any formalities dictated by the statute. Breach of a statutory collective instrument will attract statutory remedies, if not common law damages for breach of contract.

Sometimes parties to collective industrial instruments will nevertheless seek to argue that some or all of the terms of that instrument have become incorporated into a common law employment contract, possibly because the parties are seeking the more generous remedy of contractual damages for breach. (Sometimes the statute affords more parsimonious remedies than the expectation-based damages available under the common law of contract.) If parties to an individual employment contract expressly agree to incorporate the terms of a collective instrument, then it will become binding in contract also. Without express incorporation, parties will sometimes seek to argue that the terms of a collective agreement should be implied, in fact, or by law, or by custom and usage, into an employment contract. Such an argument failed, comprehensively, in a leading Australian High Court decision on the status of a 'termination, change and redundancy' (TCR) clause in a collective industrial award made under an industrial statute.[92] (A TCR clause requires an employer who wishes to dismiss staff to comply with certain procedures.) Essentially, the court held that the terms in the collective instrument could not be implied into the individual employment contracts because it could not be presumed that the parties had agreed to undertake these obligations as a matter of contract law. The collective instrument was an arbitrated award made by a tribunal and was not the fruit of voluntary agreement between the parties. Neither did the clause meet the usual necessity test for implying terms at law. It was not necessary for the effective operation of the employment contract that the employer should be bound to follow the TCR procedures before dismissing staff. Indeed, since the employer would already be bound to follow the procedures on pain of prosecution for breach of the statute, there was no need at all to make them part of the common law contract. Remedies for breach of the procedures must be limited to

91. *See Ryan v. Textile Clothing & Footwear Union Australia* [1996] 2 VR 235 for an example of a case in which a union tried, but failed, to enforce an unregistered statutory collective agreement as a common law contract.
92. *See Byrne v. Australian Airlines Limited* (1995) 185 CLR 410.

the remedies dictated by the statute, and there were no grounds for extending those remedies to include contractual damages.[93]

4.8 CONCLUSIONS

As we have seen, the common law, developed incrementally by the courts on a case-by-case basis, has contributed many fundamental concepts to labour law and has shown a capacity to adapt principles to the emerging challenges of new times. This is the great strength of the common law tradition. Even without the benefit of guidance from statute, the common law method is capable of resolving new conflicts. The development of the concept of employment over many decades, and in response to social developments, is a clear example of the adaptability of the common law. Nevertheless, the great accretion of statutory law in the field of labour relations has created considerable complexity for the courts. Must the statute be construed narrowly, leaving room for the continuation of old precedent? Must the statute be observed as a guidepost to the direction for any further development? Or is the statute a warning sign, forbidding trespass into the field by new common law developments? If Parliament has been silent on a particular issue, should the courts assume that the territory is open for exploration, or must they read Parliament's silence as a decision to permit no development in that space? This latter interpretation encourages courts to abdicate their customary and indeed constitutional role in developing the common law to address new problems with just solutions. In any event, the courts will continue to play a vital role in the development of labour law, if only through their role in interpreting an evergrowing corpus of legislation and statutory instruments.

BIBLIOGRAPHY

Gordon Anderson, Douglas Brodie & Joellen Riley, *The Common Law Employment Relations: A Comparative Study*, (Edward Elgar 2017).

G. Anderson, *Good Faith in the Individual Employment Relations in New Zealand*, 32 Comparative Labor Law and Policy Journal, 685 (2000).

G. Anderson, *Transplanting Good Faith into New Zealand Labour Law: The Experience under the Employment Relations Act 2000*, 9 Murdoch University Electronic Journal of Law, 40 (2002).

A.W. Brian Simpson, *Common Law* (Peter Cane & Joanne Conaghan, eds) *The New Oxford Companion to Law*, 166 (Oxford University Press 2008).

93. *See* Joellen Riley, *Developments in Contract of Employment Jurisprudence in Other Common-Law Jurisdictions: A Study of Australia* (Mark Freedland, ed.) *The Contract of Employment*, 277-279 (Oxford University Press 2016).

A.W. Brian Simpson, *The Ratio Decidendi of a Case and the Doctrine of Binding Precedent* (Anthony Gordon Guest, ed.) *Oxford Essays in Jurisprudence (First Series)* (Clarendon Press 1961).

D. Brodie & J. Riley, *A Duty of Good Management? Protected Interests and the Employment Contract*, 50 (2) Victoria University of Wellington Law Review (forthcoming 2019).

D. Brodie, *A Fair Deal at Work*, 19 Oxford Journal of Legal Studies, 83 (1999).

D. Brodie, *Beyond Exchange: The New Contract of Employment*, 27 Industrial Law Journal, 79 (1998).

D. Brodie, *Fair Dealing and the World of Work*, 43 (1) Industrial Law Journal, 29 (2014).

D. Brodie, *Mutual Trust and Confidence: Catalysts, Constraints and Commonality*, 37 Industrial Law Journal, 329 (2008).

D. Brodie, *The Dynamics of Common Law Development*, 32 (1) The International Journal of Comparative Labour Law and Industrial Relations, 45, (2016).

D. Brodie, *The Heart of the Matter: Mutual Trust and Confidence*, 25 Industrial Law Journal, 121 (1996).

David Cabrelli, *Employment Law in Context*, 80-1 (Oxford University Press 2014).

D. Cabrelli, *The Implied Duty of Mutual Trust and Confidence: An Emerging Overarching Principle*, 34 Industrial Law Journal, 284 (2005).

Giuseppe Casale, *The Employment Relationship: A Comparative Overview* (Hart Publishing, International Labour Organisation 2011).

Hugh Collins, *Implied Terms in the Contract of Employment* (Mark Freedland, ed.) *The Contract of Employment*, Chapter 22 (Oxford University Press 2016).

H. Collins, *Independent Contractors and the Challenge of Vertical Disintegration*, 10 Oxford Journal of Legal Studies, 353 (1990).

H. Collins, *Independent Contractors and the Challenge of Vertical Disintegration to Employment Protection Laws*, 10 Oxford Journal of Legal Studies, 353, (1990).

Guy Davidov & Brian Langille, *Boundaries and Frontiers of Labour Law* (Hart Publishing 2006).

Guy Davidov & Brian Langille, *The Idea of Labour Law* (Oxford University Press 2011).

A.C.L. Davies, *Sensible Thinking about Sham Transactions: Protectacoat Firthglow Ltd v. Szilagyi* [2009] EWCA Civ 98; [2009] IRLR 365', 38 (3) Industrial Law Journal, 318-328 (2009).

Simon Deakin & Frank Wilkinson, *The Law of the Labour Market: Industrialization, Employment and Legal Evolution*, 306-307 (Oxford University Press 2005)

Simon Deakin, *The Many Futures of the Employment Contract* (Joanne Conaghan, Michael Fischel & Karl Klare, eds) *Labour Law in an Era of Globalisation: Transformative Practices and Possibilities*, 193 (Oxford University Press 2002).

Keith Ewing, *The Right to Strike*, Chapter 2 (Clarendon Press 1991).

Mark Freedland & Nicola Kountouris, *The Legal Construction of Personal Work Relations* (Oxford University Press 2011).

M. Freedland, *Application of Labour and Employment Law Beyond the Contract of Employment*, 146 International Labour Review, 3 (2007).

M. Freedland, *Constructing Fairness in Employment Contracts*, 36 Industrial Law Journal, 136 (2007).

M. Freedland, *From the Contract of Employment to the Personal Work Nexus*, 35 Industrial Law Journal, 1 (2006).

Mark Freedland, *The Personal Employment Contract*, 155 (Oxford University Press 2003).

O.W. Holmes, *Agency*, 4 Harvard Law Review, 345, (1891).

J. Howe & R. Mitchell, *The Evolution of the Contract of Employment in Australia: A Discussion*, 12 Australian Journal of Labour Law 113 (1999).

O. Kahn-Freund, *Servants and Independent Contractors*, 14 Modern Law Review, 504, (1951).

James Macken, Carolyn Moloney & Greg McCarry, *The Common Law of Employment*, 1-6 (Law Book Co Ltd 1978).

V. Mantouvalou, *Human Rights and Unfair Dismissal: Private Acts in Public Spaces*, 71 (6) Modern Law Review, 912 (2008).

S. McCrystal, *The Right to Strike and the 'Deadweight' of the Common Law*, 50 (2) Victoria University of Wellington Law Review (2019 forthcoming).

Shae McCrystal, *The Right to Strike in Australia* (Federation Press 2010).

A. Merritt, *The Historical Role of the Law in the Regulation of Employment: Abstentionist or Interventionist?*, 1 Australian Journal of Law & Society 56 (1982).

Claire Mummé, *A Comparative Reflection from Canada: A Good Faith Perspective* (Mark Freedland, ed.) *The Contract of Employment*, Chapter 14, 295 (Oxford University Press 2016).

C. Mummé, *Bhasin v. Hrynew: A New Era for Good Faith in Canadian Employment Law, or Just Tinkering at the Margins?* 32 (1) International Journal of Comparative Labour Relations Law and Industrial Relations, 117 (2016).

O. Razzolini, *The Need to Go Beyond the Contract: 'Economic' and 'Bureaucratic' Dependence in Personal Work Relations*, 31 Comparative Labour Law and Policy Journal, 267 (2010).

Joellen Riley, *Developments in Contract of Employment Jurisprudence in Other Common-Law Jurisdictions: A Study of Australia* (Mark Freedland, ed.) *The Contract of Employment*, 277-279 (Oxford University Press 2016).

J. Riley, *Siblings but Not Twins: 'Mutual Trust' and 'Good Faith' in Employment Contracts*, 36 Melbourne University Law Review, 521, (2012).

Joellen Riley, *The Definition of the Contract of Employment and Its Differentiation for Other Contracts and Other Work Relations* (Mark Freedland, ed.) *The Contract of Employment* (Oxford University Press 2016).

Michelle Sanson, *Statutory Interpretation*, 247 (2nd ed., Oxford University Press 2016)

Carolyn Sappideen, Paul O'Grady & Joellen Riley, *Macken's Law of Employment*, Chapter 14 (8th ed., Thomson Reuters 2016).

Herbert Vere Evatt, *The Tolpuddle Martyrs: Injustice Within the Law* (Sydney University Press 2009).

Kenneth William Wedderburn & Jon Clark, *Modern Law: Problems, Functions and Policies* (Kenneth William Wedderburn, Roy Lewis & Jon Clark, eds) *Labour Law and Industrial Relations* (Oxford Clarendon Press 1983).

CHAPTER 5

Filling the (Increasing) Gaps: The Role of Judges as Substitute Legislators in Labour Law in the Civil Law Countries

Martin Risak

5.1 INTRODUCTION

In the so-called civil law tradition, the legal system is based on the idea that its core principles are codified in a referable system, usually some kind of general Civil Code. In pre-republican times such codes were passed as a statute by emperors; nowadays they are statutory laws passed by Parliament. These codes are usually based on the framework of Roman law rooted in a historical tradition that originated with the fact that since the eleventh century Roman law was the basis of the academic training of lawyers at the universities that were founded all over Europe originating from Northern Italy. Despite all the local differences, the teaching of the law was therefore strongly Roman all over Europe. Although its actual practice varied from place to place, it was nevertheless held together by a common tradition as well as a common stock of learning and a common terminology. Although Roman law, as such, was never in effect nowhere, but still constituted the basis of study, training and discourse everywhere in Europe over centuries. In spite of all local variety, the then so-called civil law also conveyed a sense of unity.

However, this unity was undermined by the religious divisions of the Reformation and Counter-Reformation in the sixteenth and seventeenth centuries and by the rise of nationalism. In the field of law, the expression of this divergence found its expression in the national codifications especially in the field of private law. Through these projects the law was unified within each nascent nation, and at the same time, it was simultaneously set apart from that of all others. The most important and influential of these civil codes were the French Code Napoleon of 1804 and the German Bürgerliches Gesetzbuch (BGB) of 1900. The concept of codification was originally the product of the Enlightenment and the move away from natural law although earlier codes like the Austrian Allgemeines Bürgerliches Gesetzbuch (ABGB) of 1812 were still rooted in this concept. Later they were also important results of the democratisation of the lawmaking process and the idea that laws are man-made. Interestingly the civil codes still referred not only to statutory law as a source of law but also to customary rules (e.g., in Italy in Article I of its Introductory Provisions) – they played a major role in the beginning but lost their relevance with the intensification of the parliamentary lawmaking process and the increasingly closely knitted net of statutory laws. It is now accepted that in a complex pluralistic post-industrial society the development of spontaneous practices based on the belief that they are carried out as a legal obligation (*opinio juris sive necessitatis*) is not possible anymore.[1]

In a way the civil codes were an important part of the civil ('bourgeoise') revolution that significantly changed the way societies organised themselves – away from status towards contract. Citizens were seen as equals who organised themselves by way of negotiations and concluding contracts. Also, in the world of work the idea of the employer–employee relationship is now promoted as one of an exchange of free and equal contracting parties. Here two drivers for change play an important role: the industrialisation sweeping over Europe combined with the liberalisation of the labour markets and the abolishment of police and penal laws enforcing the state direction of labour. 'The individual worker, released from the spider's web of police regulation on the Continent (...) was now subject to the employer's power to regulate his working life under the guise of a contract.'[2] This guise becomes the most evident in the phenomenon Karl Marx describes as the 'double-freedom' requirement necessary for capitalist production: Workers must be (at least in the legal sense formally) 'free' to sell their labour-power and they must also be 'free' from the means of production.[3] This 'double-freedom' describes the fact that the workers in general had (and still have) no other choice than selling their labour-power as they have no means of production with which to produce their own means of subsistence. If they

1. Ernst A. Kramer, *Juristische Methodenlehre*, 212 (3rd ed., Stämpfli Verlag, 2010).
2. Bruno Veneziani, *The Evolution of the Contract of Employment* (Bob Hepple, ed.), *The Making of Labour Law in Europe*, 54 (Hart Publishing 1986).
3. Karl Marx, *Capital*, Vol. I, 120 (2015): 'For the conversion of his money into capital, therefore, the owner of money must meet in the market with the free labourer, free in the double sense, that as a free man he can dispose of his labour-power as his own commodity, and that on the other hand he has no other commodity for sale, is short of everything necessary for the realisation of his labour-power.'

could produce their own means of subsistence, they would not be compelled to sell their labour-power to their employers.

The civil law system is based on the concept of the separation of powers mirrored in all European Constitutions of the twentieth century (e.g., Article 20 in the German Grundgesetz). The legislative power is vested in the democratically elected Parliament and the judicative power with independent courts. Case law is therefore not given the rank of a formal source of law, but the courts have the role to apply the given legislation by way of interpretation but not to create it. This is well mirrored in Article 1.6. of the Spanish Civil Code where it is stated that 'case law shall complement the legal system by means of the jurisprudence of the Supreme Court in its interpretation and application of statutes, customs and general principles'.

Therefore, the courts – at least conceptionally – only apply the given law by way of interpretation but do not create new legal rules. Formally therefore they are not given any lawmaking power. Thus, precedent does not have any formally binding effect in the way of the stare decisis-principle known in common law systems.[4] But on the other side, nobody believes anymore that the law knows everything (*lex semper loquitur*) like it was argued by the legal positivists in the nineteenth century. It is now generally accepted that the law is never perfect and that statutory gaps or loopholes are inherent. § 7 of the Austrian ABGB as well as Article 12 paragraph 2 of the Disposizioni Preliminari of the Italian Codice Civile or Article 4 paragraph 1 of the Spanish Código Civil explicitly refer to this problem. According to Claus-Wilhelm Canaris,[5] such a gap that may be filled by the courts exists where the legislature has not regulated a case which it would have clearly regulated if it had recognised the need for regulation. A statutory gap is 'an unplanned incompleteness within the positive law, measured by the standard of the entire applicable legal order' (translation by the author). In such cases, the courts may go beyond the mere wording of statutory law by either restricting its application (*contra verba legis*) as the law is overinclusive or going beyond it (*praeter verba legis*) usually by applying a provision by way of analogy (*per analogiam*). The latter is mentioned explicitly for example in § 7 of the Austrian ABGB, Article 12 paragraph 2 of the Disposizioni Preliminari of the Italian Codice Civile or Article 4 paragraph 1 of the Spanish Código Civil. In the country chapters on Hungary and Germany, the relevance of case law in filling the gaps left by labour regulation has been especially stressed.

As reference is made to the purpose of the law (the *telos*), this is also called a teleological restriction or extension. Important is that this law-creating exercise is still based on the idea that the statutory gap was not intended by the lawmaker

4. Ernst A. Kramer (n. 1) 273.
5. Claus-Wilhelm Canaris, *Die Feststellung von Lücken im Gesetz*, 39 (2nd ed., Duncker and Humblot, 1983).

and therefore the mentioned techniques are applied to actually fulfil its intention in the light of the wording that is too far-reaching or incomplete. The courts then actually follow the *telos* applying the general rule of equality to treat similar cases in a similar way according to the legal saying '*ubi eadem ratio, ibi eadem iuris dispositio*' (where there is the same underlying value there should be the same rule). In labour law often the rationales underlying its existence, the inequality of bargaining powers as well as the duty to work in person lead to courts construing implied rights and obligations to honour the general notion that labour law first has to protect the weaker party of the employment contract.

And, of course, civil codes also include general clauses like *bones mores*, the general duty to take into account the interests of the other party to a contract or the concept of 'employee' that need to be substantiated by case law. They are called gaps *intra legem* or *intra verba legis*. Formally statutory law exists, but the resolution of the underlying social problem has been delegated deliberately to the courts. This phenomenon therefore has been also been referred to as 'complementary lawmaking by the courts'.[6] It is important to point out that although a decision has to be found that shall apply to the singularities of each case, the courts have to justify their ruling taking into account especially existing jurisprudence. Although not formally binding, this orientation on previous decisions can be explained by the general principles of equal treatment and the protection of legitimate expectations. This has been called the presumption of precedent[7] in the civil law system, meaning that if following established case law the *rationes decedendi* do not have to be laid out again fully - only if not following precedent the arguments why the judge deviates from it have to be developed fully. Therefore, although no formal doctrine of precedent obliging judges to follow the principles determined in earlier cases decided by courts higher up in the court hierarchy exists, in practice – where the law leaves space to develop it further *intra legem* or even *contra legem* – established jurisprudence is followed and future decisions are foreseeable to a certain extent.

Another significant factor of civil law jurisprudence is the reference to individual constitutional rights that are usually oriented towards the state but that are applied nevertheless also *inter privatos* where apt. This so-called indirect or horizontal effect is the result of interpreting general clauses like *bones mores* or general personal rights that have to be respected by all parties in the light of the relevant Constitution. As constitutional law is higher up the legislative hierarchy than 'ordinary' statutory law the latter has to be interpreted

6. Ernst A. Kramer (n. 1) 76.
7. Martin Kriele, *Theorie der Rechtsgewinnung*, 243 (2nd ed., Duncker and Humblot, 1976).

in conformity with the Constitution giving it relevance also in private relationships. Especially in Germany that has led to the effect of the so-called constitutionalisation of labour law and to courts often arguing based on constitutional arguments.

With these characteristics of the role of case law in civil law countries in mind,[8] this chapter will explore the role of jurisprudence in developing some central notions of labour law in civil law jurisdictions: the definition of 'employment' as a form of labour engagement; the existence of implied terms in employment contracts; the employer's duty of care towards employees; the employer's duty (such as it is) to provide the employee with appropriate work; and the possible judicial constraints on the right enshrined in many Constitutions and international treaties to take industrial action. In the following subchapters, reference will be made to the country chapters in this book and the jurisdictions treated in them as well as additionally to the Austrian legal order as another example of a civil law system.

5.2 EMPLOYMENT

The definition of the notion of the employee and/or of the 'contract of employment' is of major significance as it draws the line between those persons that are protected by the full scope of the labour laws including collective agreements as well as workplace representation and those who are not. In not all of the civil law jurisdictions treated in this volume (Germany, France, Poland) a statutory definition exists.[9] In Hungary section 42 of the Labour Code provides that an employment relationship is deemed to have been established by entering into an employment contract. Under an employment contract, the employee is required to work as instructed by the employer; the employer is required to provide work for the employee and to pay wages.[10] In Spain, Article 1.1 of the Labour Code states that it is applicable to those workers who voluntarily provide paid service for someone else, under the management and within the organisational sphere of another natural person or legal entity, called the employer.[11] In Italy, Article 2094 of the Italian Codice Civile defines the employee as an individual working under the control and instructions of the employer and who receives a salary to

---

8. For the development of labour law in these countries Bruno Veneziani, *The Employment Relationship* (Bob Hepple & Bruno Veneziani, eds), *The Transformation of Labour Law in Europe*, 99 (Hart Publishing 2009).
9. Comparative Overview, in Bernd Waas & Guus Herrma van Voss, *Restatement of Labour Law in Europe, Volume I: The Concept of Employee* (1st, Hart Publishing, 2017).
10. György Kiss, *The Concept of 'Employee': The Position in Hungary* (Bernd Waas & Guus Herrma van Voss, eds), *Restatement of Labour Law in Europe, Volume I: The Concept of Employee*, 293 (1st, Hart Publishing 2017).
11. Joaquín García Murcia & Iván Rodríguez Cardo, *The Concept of 'Employee': The Position in Spain* (Bernd Waas & Guus Herrma van Voss, eds), *Restatement of Labour Law in Europe, Volume I: The Concept of Employee*, 659 (1st, Hart Publishing 2017).

perform his or her duties.[12] Under Polish law Article 22 paragraph 1 of the Polish Labour Code stipulates that by establishing an employment relationship, an employee undertakes to carry out specific work for the benefit und under the guidance of an employer, and an employer undertakes to employ an employee in return for remuneration.[13]

In all other countries, it was on the courts to develop this concept and interestingly the results reached are very similar. In Germany, there is a judge-made definition based on doctrine, and accordingly an employee is a person 'who on the basis of a contract of private law is obliged to perform work in the service of another person'.[14] In France, the Court de Cassation case law concludes that the existence of an employment contract is characterised by a legal relationship of subordination between the employee and the employer.[15] And, of course, also in the countries with legal definitions, they are defined in a rather open and often indistinct way and are therefore in need of interpretation by the courts.

In the end, at the core of all these definitions provided either by statute and interpreted by the courts or solely developed by case law is the notion of subordination, i.e., the subjection of the employee to the directive, control and disciplinary powers of the employer.[16] This is very much an element that is referred to be the control test in English law (*see* J. Riley, section 4.2.1).

This element is interesting though as the most frequently cited underlying rationales of labour law is the already mentioned twofold economic dependence of the employee. This refers, first, to the fact that resources (e.g., materials, machines or an organisation) are typically needed to perform the work and that employees have, at least historically, depended on the employer to provide them. Second, it implies dependence of the employee on 'selling' his or her labour in exchange for remuneration from the employment relationship to sustain his or her living. This leads to the inequality of bargaining power and the need of legislator intervention and/or to the acceptance of collective representation as well as collective bargaining in order to negotiate for fair pay and working conditions on an equal basis.[17] The legal orders of the civil law tradition

12. Edoardo Ales, *The Concept of 'Employee': The Position in Italy* (Bernd Waas & Guus Herrma van Voss, eds), *Restatement of Labour Law in Europe, Volume I: The Concept of Employee*, 352 (1st, Hart Publishing 2017).
13. Leszek Mitrus, *The Concept of 'Employee': The Position in Poland* (Bernd Waas & Guus Herrma van Voss, eds), *Restatement of Labour Law in Europe, Volume I: The Concept of Employee*, 526 (1st, Hart Publishing 2017).
14. Bernd Waas, *The Concept of 'Employee': The Position in Germany* (Bernd Waas & Guus Herrma van Voss, eds), *Restatement of Labour Law in Europe, Volume I: The Concept of Employee*, 659 (1st, Hart Publishing 2017).
15. Francis Kessler, *The Concept of 'Employee': The Position in France* (Bernd Waas & Guus Herrma van Voss, eds), *Restatement of Labour Law in Europe, Volume I: The Concept of Employee*, 197 (1st, Hart Publishing 2017).
16. Waas & van Voss (n. 10).
17. Martin Risak & Thomas Dullinger, *The Concept of 'Worker' in EU Law*, 10 (ETUI, 2018).

treated to in this volume, however, do not refer to these economic arguments, focusing instead on the way the work is actually performed. Especially the second aspect (dependence on the salary to earn a living) is usually considered impractical, as employers often have no means to ascertain whether their contractual partners actually have other sources of income or their reasons for working more generally.[18]

As the examples treated above show that most jurisdictions have followed an organisational approach focusing on the notion of restricted self-determination when working, as this, on the one hand, delivered satisfactory results and, on the other, was practical and relatively easy to apply. This was based on the fact that only those having enough resources were able to become self-employed and that they were able to negotiate for pay that satisfied their needs. However, those working under the close supervision of another person often did not have enough bargaining power when negotiating pay and conditions of work. In those circumstances, it was rather unproblematic to equal organisational and economic dependency in the past.[19]

This is not true anymore as one of the key features of the early twenty-first century is not only the flexibilisation of the employment relationship but also the emergence of a growing number of self-employed. This can be attributed to a number of different factors: Advances in digital technologies, the widespread availability of handheld devices and ever-increasing high-speed connectivity combined with the realities presented by several cycles of economic downturn, shifts in lifestyle and generational preferences have all led to this increase in the number of self-employed workers. However, these new 'solo-entrepreneurs' and freelancers are very different from those of the past, where 'liberal professions' such as lawyers, architects and other high-skilled professionals had the power to bargain for high remuneration and controlled their own working conditions. The 'new' self-employed, especially those active in the virtual realms of the gig-economy today (known as 'platform workers'), resemble more the workers of the early twentieth century who did not have any other alternatives than to sell their labour in a highly competitive market. They compete with a large reserve army of labour unlike those self-employed in liberal professions. They are also similar to traditional employees, as they carry out the work in person and, in so doing, sell their labour and not an end product. Finally, they are also vulnerable, as they earn their livelihood by doing this for only one or a very limited number of immediate contractual partners. The only difference between them and traditional employees is the fact that they are formally free to work doing

18. This economic criterion is only applied when extending the scope of some labour law legislation like it is the case in Germany with the so-called employee-like persons (*arbeitnehmerähnliche Personen*) to whom in particular the Federal Annual Leave Act as well as the Labour Court Act applies. Also, collective bargaining agreements can cover this group.
19. Martin Risak, Thomas Dullinger (n. 17) 12.

whatever they choose whenever they choose – however, it may often be the case that this freedom is in name only owing to an economic situation which leaves them few alternatives to selling their labour in a certain way to a limited number of contractual partners.[20]

This challenge has already been addressed in 2006 by the European Commission in its Green Paper 'Modernising labour law to meet the challenges of the 21st century':[21] 'The emergence of diverse forms of non-standard work has made the boundaries between labour law and commercial law less clear. The traditional binary distinction between "employees" and the independent "self-employed" is no longer an adequate depiction of the economic and social reality of work. Disputes concerning the legal nature of the employment relationship can arise where that relationship has either been disguised or where a genuine difficulty arises in seeking to fit new and dynamic work arrangements within the traditional framework of the employment relationship.' And it goes on to state: 'The concept of "economically dependent work" covers situations which fall between the two established concepts of subordinate employment and independent self-employment. These workers do not have a contract of employment. They may not be covered by labour law since they occupy a "grey area" between labour law and commercial law. Although formally "self-employed," they remain economically dependent on a single principal or client/employer for their source of income. This phenomenon should be clearly distinguished from the deliberate misclassification of self-employment.'

These changes in the world of work described by the European Commission in 2006 are now being accelerated by the digital transformation, making it very timely to consider again the fundamental question of labour law: Who is protected and why? The Commission Staff Working Document accompanying the consultation on the European Pillar of Social Rights[22] likewise emphasises that the distinction between 'worker' and 'self-employed' and that between 'self-employed' and 'entrepreneur' the boundaries are sometimes blurred. The case of the collaborative economy (or more appropriate: the platform economy) is considered particularly illustrative, as it is based on a business model which allows individuals to capitalise on their own assets such as cars or houses, while these companies provide tasks rather than fully fledged services, making it hard to account for work and workers under current standards.

If such a need to extend the protective scope of labour law, or at least that of certain parts of it, is found to exist, in civil law countries – especially those with explicit definitions of the concept of employee stressing the organisational element of subordination – the primary option would be to redefine the concept

20. Martin Risak, Thomas Dullinger (n. 17), 12. *See also* M. Risak & T. Dullinger, *The Concept of Worker in EU-Labour Law – Still Fit for Purpose?*, Kutafin Law Review, 21 (2018).
21. COM(2006) 708 final.
22. SWD(2016) 51 final; *see also* SWD(2017) 206 final.

of 'employee' by the way of legislation or to introduce specific legislative initiatives aimed at giving the vulnerable self-employed access to a range of employment rights. If such a legal definition does not exist (e.g., like in Germany) the change may also be achieved by courts interpreting the traditional concept of 'employee' differently. If the economic situation of the employee is the reason why these rights and entitlements have been developed in the first place, it is difficult to argue why the scope of their application should not be extended to persons in the same situation based merely on the premise that they are not formally integrated enough into the business of their contractual partners. This would be an example of a purposive (teleological) approach to the concept of employee – it can be applied by way of interpretation by the courts where no statutory definition exists that refers to the element of subordination or personal dependency. If on the other hand the relevant statutory definition explicitly refers to the element of subordination only legislation will be able to change this element that was considered to be crucial for defining the protective scope of labour law in the past.

The complicated interplay between legislation and jurisprudence can be well demonstrated by the mixed reactions to the proposal of the European Commission for a Directive on Transparent and Predictable Working Conditions in the European Union (EU) in 2017.[23] The European Commission suggested clarifying the personal scope of this Directive in line with the parameters set out by the European Court of Justice since decades to identify an employment relationship by including criteria which would help achieve more consistency in the personal scope of application of this Directive. It intended to make clear that the proposed Directive applies to every type of person that, for a certain period of time, performs services for and under the direction of another person in return for remuneration (Article 2(1)(a) of the proposed Directive),[24] including domestic workers, temporary agency workers, on-demand workers, intermittent workers, voucher-based workers and platform workers (recital 7 of the proposed Directive, now recital 8). Although this clarification that certain types of contractual arrangements do not exclude persons per se from the scope of protection of the Directive, it was clear that the proposed 'new' definition did not go beyond the received concept of 'employee', as it uses the 'classic' Lawrie-Blum formula very much based on the concept of subordination. If one sees a necessity to go beyond this traditional concept, the proposal might also prove counterproductive, as it would have closed the door to interpret the concept of 'employee' in an expansive way and to substitute, where appropriate, a lack of subordination with economic arguments. This could also have influenced the interpretation of the concept of 'employee' in other contexts. In the end, no such

23. COM(2017) 797 final.
24. This formula is based on the leading judgment of the European Court of Justice of 3 July 1986, *Deborah Lawrie-Blum v. Land Baden-Württemberg*, C-66/85, ECLI:EU:C:1986:284.

definition was included in the final text of the Directive (EU) 2019/1152 of the European Parliament and of the Council of 20 June 2019 on transparent and predictable working conditions in the EU as the employer side did not want any definition at all and the employee side feared that a narrow definition would hinder the development of case law that interprets the concept extensively. This example clearly demonstrates the advantages and pitfalls of a statutory definition of the concept of 'employee' that has been undertaken in several civil law countries but not in all of them.

It seems that a lack of a legal definition of 'employee' or a wide one at least methodologically enables the jurisprudence to adapt the personal scope of labour law in a political arena where there is no consensus between the two sides of the industry (employees and employers) which direction to take. A change in statutory law is therefore not realistic due to the lack of majorities in the national parliaments to achieve this.

The more likely avenue actually taken is often not a redefinition of the concept of 'employee' but the introduction of a third, intermediary category. This way at least some of the legislation protecting employees could be extended to this group of vulnerable self-employed. A number of countries have introduced legislative measures to safeguard the legal status of economically dependent and vulnerable self-employed workers. For example, in Germany and Austria, some employment regulations are also applicable to 'employee-like persons' (*arbeitnehmerähnliche Personen*). In Austria, these individuals are defined as persons who perform work/services by order of and on account of another person without being in an employment relationship, but who may be considered employee-like owing to their economic dependence. Only some provisions of labour law apply to these employee-like persons, e.g., those on the competence of the labour courts, temporary agency work, employee liability and anti-discrimination. In Germany, this intermediate category is similarly defined and is also covered by the Collective Agreements Act (Tarifvertragsgesetz); persons belonging to this category may therefore conclude collective agreements with normative effect. In the already mentioned 2006 Green Paper, the European Commission also cites as examples the notion of 'para-subordinate' in Italy and the Self-Employed Workers' Statute in Spain on the rights and benefits of the self-employed, including economically dependent workers. Such legislative action, of course, also has effects on the interpretation of the concept of 'employee' by the courts – if some elements are constitutive for the intermediary category it cannot be argued anymore that there is statutory gap in the received definition of employee unintended by the legislator. In fact, the opposite is the case: This group must not be included in the employee-category as the law intentionally created a third category and thereby blocked the full application of labour legislation for this group of workers.

5.3 IMPLIED TERMS

Also, in civil law countries case law has made important contributions to basic principles of labour law by the formulation of implied terms in employment contracts. Methodologically this is achieved by interpreting the individual employment contracts and by accepting that they will always be incomplete and will not be able to cover all the possible issues that may arise when fulfilling it. This means that the contract has to be not only interpreted but also developed further to cover these issues that have not been foreseen by the parties when concluding the contract. The technique applied is the 'supplementary interpretation of contract according to hypothetical intention of the parties' by asking what the parties would have agreed upon if they would have anticipated a given problem in the light of the existing terms and conditions of the contract. In a way thereby the courts further develop the contract by taking into account the existing agreement.

Some implied terms are derived from the general idea that all contracts – not only the employment contract – include a duty of the parties to protect the interests of the other in a reasonable way. The duties of the employee to follow lawful and reasonable commands by the employer as well as a general duty of fidelity and loyalty to the employer's interests can be derived this way. However, the employer has to protect the person of the employee due to the fact that he/she has to work in person. This means that the employer has to provide a safe and healthy workplace and to respect the employees' privacy. This is an example of the indirect application of constitutional laws concerning human rights like, especially, the right to privacy as enshrined in Article 8 of the European Convention of Human Rights.

These examples show that although written employment contracts become more prevalent and detailed, there is still not only the space but also the need for supplementary interpretation of the employment contract for the purpose of filling the gaps by the courts.

5.4 THE GENERAL DUTY OF CARE

As already mentioned above, a very important implied term is the duty of the parties to a contract to reasonably protect each other's interests. Especially in the case of new phenomena like mobbing by colleagues or the use of information and communication technologies (ICT), such general notions become of relevance again as the lawmaker may be too slow to react. The courts still have to find solutions to new problems brought before them though. The general duty of care has been the basis for the argument that the employer has to protect the employee from mobbing by his/her colleagues.[25] This is also the case when such mobbing cannot be qualified as harassment under equal treatment legislation as it is not connected to the relevant criteria like gender and sex, age, sexual orientation, race and ethnic origin.

Another example is the issues connected with the use of ICT that now enables not only the employee to often work anytime and anywhere but also the employer to reach the employee twenty-four hours a day and seven days a week. This concerns not only telephone calls but also communication via e-mails and messenger services. It is therefore interesting whether this being on call 24/7 is seen as a problem by the courts and what strategies have been developed to counter the negative effects of these developments. This is considered necessary as employees often not only enjoy flexibility in when and how they work but also may be under constant stress that they may be called to work around the clock and due to this work overlong hours and do not observe the required rest periods. This is where the right to disconnect comes in that has been established in the French so-called El Khomri Law,[26] in Belgium[27] or recently also in Italy.[28] In those countries where such explicit statutory provisions do not exist, it seems very likely that courts will use the idea of the general duty of care for the other party's interests to construe an obligation of the employer to establish some right to disconnect to facilitate the actual use of rest periods for the employee.

5.5 DUTY TO (ACTUALLY) PROVIDE WORK

In an employment relationship, the question can arise if the employer actually has to provide the employee with work or if it is enough to pay remuneration. In

25. (Austrian) Supreme Court of 19.12.2014, 8 Ob A 45/14x.
26. The so-called El Khomri Law added a new paragraph to Article 55 of the French Labour Code (Code du travail) introducing a provision concerning the right to disconnect (in force since 1 January 2017): '(7) The procedures for the full exercise by the employee of his right to disconnect and the establishment by the company of mechanisms for regulating the use of digital tools, with a view to ensuring respect for rest periods and leave as well as personal and family life. Failing agreement, the employer shall draw up a charter, after consultation with the works council or, failing that, with the staff delegates. This charter defines these procedures for the exercise of the right to disconnect and furthermore provides for the implementation, for employees and management and management personnel, of training and awareness-raising activities on the reasonable use of digital tools.' (unofficial translation as provided for at https://en.wikipedia.org/wiki/Right_to_disconnect, last accessed on 30 August 2019).
27. Articles 15-17 loi belge du 26 mars 2018 relative au renforcement de la croissance économique de la cohesion sociale.
28. Senate Act No. 2233-B 'Measures to safeguard non-entrepreneurial self-employment and measures to facilitate flexible articulation in times and places of subordinate employment.' Article 19(1) of the Act governs the implementation for an Agreement on Aggregate Work and includes some form of the right to disconnect by stating that 'The agreement also identifies the worker's rest periods as well as the technical and organisational measures necessary to ensure that the worker is disconnected from the technological equipment.' (unofficial translation as provided for at https://en.wikipedia.org/wiki/Right_to_disconnect, last accessed on 30 August 2019).

the case of a lack of explicit statutory legislation,[29] this issue has to be resolved by the courts. The solutions reached show well the different value a legal system attributes to work and to its actual fulfilment – and that this can change over time.

A good example is Germany, where in the past, the Federal Labour Court was of the opinion that it was sufficient for the employee to receive his/her remuneration. The employment contract was seen as a means to earn a living, and if remuneration was paid, all interests of the employee were fulfilled. In the case of non-employment he/she was even relieved of the burden to work. This approach has changed due to a landmark case in 1955,[30] and since then, the courts grant the employee the right to be actually employed by the employer, irrespective of the remuneration. This right to be provided with work is based on the employee's general constitutional right to be respected as a person as well as with the respect and the appreciation of the employee that comes with it is an important component of the development of mental and physical abilities and thus the development of the employee's personality. Therefore, according to German case law, the employee is generally entitled to be provided with work during the employment relationship. This is not the case though if the employee has waived this right (e.g., often during the notice period a 'garden leave' is agreed upon in the employment contract) or if there is good cause for suspending the employment contract like in case of the threat to operational safety if the employees show up drunk for work.

In Austria, a country with a similar labour law tradition as in Germany, the jurisprudence has taken a different turn. Here the right to be actually provided with work is only granted in exceptional cases, i.e., if the employee will lose qualifications due to the lack of the opportunity to work like in the case of airline pilots, surgeons and professional soccer players. The latter though only have the right to train with the first team but not to be actually used in a game.[31] This right to employment is construed as an implied term as the employee has a special interest in the work beyond earning his/her living. This right to be provided with work does not go very far though as, for example, a university professor has been refused such a right without a provision in the contract.[32]

Again, these examples show that courts have to resolve the same problems all over Europe in cases of a lack of statutory provisions. They also highlight though that the results reached may differ due to the emphasis the courts in different countries put on different arguments. It is of relevance if they hold the

29. For example section 18 Austrian Act on Working in Theatres (*Theaterarbeitsgesetz – TAG*) that provides a right to be actually employed but does not make it enforceable as the legal consequence for a breach are (only) damages.
30. (German) Federal Labour Court of 10.11.1955, 2 AZR 591/54.
31. (Austrian) Supreme Court of 1.2.2007, 9 Ob A 121/06v.
32. (Austrian) Supreme Court of 18.8.2016, 9 Ob A 51/16i.

view that an employment contract has mainly the function to provide for the living or if working also contributes to the self-fulfilment of a person. Although the courts from time to time use the comparative method, i.e., they look towards other, usually similar legal orders for inspiration.[33] Legal diversity is still recognisable over Europe even in such fundamental questions like the right of the employee to be actually provided with work.

5.6 CONSTRAINTS ON INDUSTRIAL ACTION

In the nineteenth century when the labour movement in Europe gradually gained importance, the first obstacle to overcome was the sanctions of criminal law. Only when they were removed from the arena of industrial conflict, restraints on the freedom to strike stemming from civil law doctrines emerged. Most forms of industrial action (especially strikes) were considered a serious breach of the employment contract that gave reason to dismiss the employee participating in a strike with immediate effect. In a way industrial action was tolerated but not recognised as a legitimate way to ameliorate working conditions and to counter the inequality of bargaining power on the individual level.[34] Such recognition sometimes took quite long as the lawmaker often refrained from regulating the much-disputed field of industrial action. Neither employer organisations nor unions were interested in hard regulations as one side feared that thereby strike would become socially acceptable, while the other clearly saw the risks of restrictive regulation especially concerning the liabilities of unions towards economic losses of employers due to a strike that they organised.

This complicated situation was also mirrored by the relevant international treaties: While some explicitly recognise a right to strike like Article 6 of the Revised European Social Charter or Article 28 of the Charter of Fundamental Rights of the EU, others like Article 11 of the European Convention of Human Rights only mention the right to form and to join trade unions for the protection of employees' interests. In the past the latter was interpreted restrictively by the European Court of Human Rights, but in its newer jurisprudence it has been interpreted to also include an individual right to strike, i.e., a right of the employee to participate in a strike without being disciplined by the employer.[35]

The right or freedom to take collective action is in most civil law countries treated in this volume (France, Germany, Hungary, Italy, Poland, Spain) guaranteed in the Constitution. The right or freedom to take collective action is in most civil law countries treated in this volume (France, Germany, Hungary,

33. Ernst A. Kramer (n. 1) 252.
34. *See* Antoine Jacobs, *Collective Self Regulation* (Bob Hepple, ed.), *The Making of Labour Law in Europe*, 240 (Hart Publishing 1986).
35. European Court of Human Rights [2009] ECHR 2251 – *Enerji Yapi-Yol Sen v. Turkey*; [2014] ECHR 366 – *RMT v. UK*.

Italy, Poland, Spain) guaranteed in the Constitution, though sometimes (i.e., Germany – *see* below), it is not expressly mentioned in the Constitutional text. In any case it is an area of law which in many countries (France, Germany, Italy) has been mainly developed through the courts as no detailed legislation exists on the topic.

Probably the most interesting example for the relevance of case law in this field is Germany. As already mentioned, the freedom to strike is not explicitly mentioned in the German Constitution but is derived from the constitutional freedom of association (Article 9 paragraph 3). This freedom of association is interpreted to include a right to collective bargaining, and this again is seen as to include to take industrial action as – to use the wording of the German Federal Labour Court – without such a right collective bargaining is reduced to 'collective begging'.[36] German labour dispute regulations are almost entirely based on case law, the main issue being whether or not a particular labour dispute is legal. Pursuant to the line of argument above a strike in Germany is only legal if it is linked to a collective agreement and must be initiated by a trade union. In general secondary actions, i.e., solidarity strikes, are considered unlawful as are political strikes.[37] There exists a finely differentiated jurisprudence on the criteria when secondary strikes are considered legal the idea behind it being that the employer of the secondary dispute shall have the possibility to influence the employer of the primary dispute. Only then the link to collective bargaining is considered to be close enough.

In France, although the basic right to strike is guaranteed by the French Constitution, the details – except for the public service (Act of 31 July 1963) – are also mainly shaped by case law. Also in France, the aim of the strike must be lawful, and strikes conducted for political reasons and solidarity strikes are considered to be abusive. As the purpose of political strikes is not to improve wages or working conditions, courts have ruled that they no longer possess the character of an act in support of professional or occupational demands but are intended as criticism of government policy. This is considered an abuse of the right to strike and a major offence by strikers.[38]

Hungary may serve as the example where not only the right to strike is explicitly granted in the Constitution (Article 70/C) but also where detailed legislation exists about the exercise of this right. As the Constitution provides that it may be exercised within the limits determined by the Act regulating that right an act exists that regulates the right to strike (Act No. VII, adopted in April 1989).[39]

36. (German) Federal Labour Court of 10. 6. 80-1 AZR 168/79.
37. Wiebke Warneck, *Strike Rules in EU27 and Beyond – A Comparative View*, 32 (ETUI, 2007).
38. Wiebke Warneck, *Ibid.*, 30.
39. Wiebke Warneck, *Ibid.*, 36.

The examples show that disputed areas of labour law, like the exercise of the right to strike, may often lack explicit statutory legislation. If it is guaranteed by the Constitution, courts have to accept its existence in general but have to fill the gap that is left by the lack of legislation regulating the details of its practice. They then have to develop a line of ruling that provides guidance to the parties of the employment relationship and may act as something like a substitute legislator.

5.7 COLLECTIVE AGREEMENTS: LEGAL EFFECTS AND THE RELATIONSHIP BETWEEN DIFFERENT AGREEMENTS

Collective self-regulation in the form of collective agreements has been present in industrial relations since the very beginning of the modern employment relationship. It especially emerged where public authorities, intentionally or unintentionally, abstained from direct regulation of labour relations. In the absence of state regulation, the freedom of contract combined with the strong bargaining position of the employers led to the deterioration of working conditions and induced employees to find counter-strategies. It led to them joining forces (in the form of trade unions) in order to build a countervailing power strong enough to extract better working conditions. This process of collective bargaining and the conclusion of collective agreements was first repressed and later tolerated and finally not only recognised but also protected on different levels.[40] The 'collective laissez-faire'[41] was later often substituted by a more or less elaborate statutory legal framework for collective bargaining and the effects of the agreements reached during this process. Such regulation usually includes provisions on who has the power to collectively bargain (a recognition procedure), on the process of collective bargaining and mechanisms to resolve conflicts like mediation and arbitration and on the legal effects of collective agreements. When it comes to the latter the double nature of collective agreements often becomes evident; on the one hand, they are created like a contract by consensus of unions and employers or employer organisations and, on the other, collective agreements have a so-called normative effect on the employment relationship of those persons who are members of the concluding parties although they are not part of the negotiations. And sometimes this effect is even extended to non-members either directly by way of law (so-called erga omnes-effect like in Austria, Hungary or Poland) or by an extension procedure (like in Germany). The density and the detail of the regulation of collective bargaining differs a lot in civil law countries depending on the very different industrial

40. Antoine Jacobs (n. 34), 223.
41. Otto Kahn-Freund, *Labour Law* (Morris Ginsberg, ed.), *Law and Opinion in England in the Twentieth Century*, 224 (Praeger 1959).

relation traditions and resulting path trajectories. The diversity is significant ranging from a lack of a general framework beyond a constitutional right to collective bargaining in Italy[42] to detailed specific regulation like in Germany.

The role of case law concerning collective agreements therefore differs also in the different civil law countries: It is of major importance where the important questions like the legal effect of this autonomous source of law are not regulated at all like in Italy where the Constitution in Article 39 envisages the possibility that unions may, through a special registration procedure, acquire legal personality and that collective agreements concluded by such unions have a binding effect on all members to which the agreement refers. The legislation necessary to implement this provision was never passed, and therefore collective agreements have not been able to acquire erga omnes-effect like in Poland where this is provided for by legislation. This gap has been closed though by the Italian courts to a certain extent: For pay a quasi-erga omnes-effect is construed based on Article 36 of the Italian Constitution that gives an employee the right to receive pay commensurate with the quality and quantity of the work performed and, in any event, sufficient to ensure a free and dignified existence for him-/herself and his/her family. In applying this provision, the Italian courts use the parameter of 'fair' pay set by collective agreements declaring individual contractual arrangements which provide for lower pay null and void. This is not because they do not comply with the collective agreement, but because of the conflict with Article 36 of the Italian Constitution.[43]

As pointed out in the country chapters, collective agreements are considered to be a source of law in their own right and do not get incorporated into the individual employment contract but have a legal effect on them comparable to that of a mandatory provision of law. The contract therefore can usually only derogate *in melius*, i.e., in favour of the employee.[44] To actually evaluate what is more favourable in a given case is not an easy exercise though and court practice often plays an important role in applying this general notion. What is to be compared: each item in an isolated way resulting in cherry-picking or those clauses that are dealing with the same problem in some kind of group comparison or the collective agreement and the employment contract as a whole? In Germany, for example, the Federal Labour Court has opted for the solution in between, the group comparison comparing items belonging closely to each

42. *See* M. Magnani, *The Role of Collective Bargaining in Italian Labour Law*, 7 E-Journal of International and Comparative Labour Studies, 2 (2018).
43. Mariella Magnani, *Ibid.*, 6; (Italian) Supreme Court of 4 July 2018, No. 17421; of 23 December 2016, No. 26953.
44. This principle is now very much under stress as the country chapters like the one on France show.

other.[45] The same solution was followed by the Hungarian Supreme Court[46] for the situation before the 2012 Labour Code went into force. Now, this issue is explicitly addressed in Article 277(5) of the Hungarian Labour Code by stating that derogations for the benefit of the employee shall be adjudged by a comparative assessment of related regulations. The legal literature still sees a need for court decisions though to decide on how to interpret this provision.

The relationship between statutory law and collective agreements is sometimes not that clear either. This situation often exists in Germany where it is not clear whether the legislature intends to set binding or non-binding standards, and it is left to the courts to decide these cases be interpreting legislative intent. In Italy, the Constitutional Court made it clear on several occasions that there is no reservation of competence in favour of collective agreements and that therefore the law is able to restrict the regulatory action of the social partners.[47]

Another issue where case law plays an important role is the relationship between different collective agreements (usually a conflict between a sectoral and a company agreement). As this problem is often not resolved by legislation, the courts have no other choice than to fill this gap left by legislative inertia if cases are brought before them. And interestingly they have found different solutions: In Germany, for example, the judiciary has developed the principle of specialty, meaning that the company collective agreement replaces the sectoral collective agreement.[48] Sometimes the legislation has intervened though in this politically very disputed area as this is the case in France where the recent Macron orders made it clear that enterprise-level agreements take precedence when they offer 'equivalent guarantees'. In Spain a legislative reform in 2012 made it possible to opt out of sectoral collective agreements in times of economic difficulties, and the company level-workers' representatives can agree to change *in peius* provisions in sectoral agreements. In Russia however Article 48(6) of the Labour Code states that any conflicts between higher- and lower-level agreements should be decided on the *in favorem* principle.

In summary, it can be noted that as far as collective bargaining is concerned the role of case law differs much more between the different civil law countries than concerning individual employment law. This is due to the diversity of the industrial relation systems in Europe and the different approaches taken. Case law plays the most significant role in that field in those countries where there are obvious gaps in statutory law that have to be filled by jurisprudence like in Italy. In other countries, the courts have to interpret the existing legislation often concerning important issues like the favourability principle.

45. For example (German) Federal Labour Court of 4 July 2001, 2 AZR 469/00 concerning notice periods.
46. (Hungarian) Supreme Court of 1991, Resolution No. 147.
47. (Italian) Constitutional Court of 19 December 1962, No. 106 and of 7 February 1985, No. 34.
48. (German) Federal Labour Court of 26 January 1994, 10 AZR 611/92.

5.8 CONCLUSIONS

Case law is not considered a formal source of law in the civil law tradition, and in all countries treated in this volume (France, Germany, Hungary, Italy, Poland, Russia, Spain) it is not considered to have binding force beyond the single case that has been decided. Still, it plays an important role not only in interpreting the law, especially general clauses like *bones mores* as well as open concepts like 'employee', but also in filling gaps in statutory legislation. The most telling example for the latter is the restrictions on the constitutionally guaranteed right or freedom to strike that are not regulated by statute but left to the courts to be developed when cases are brought before them. Here the case law – especially in Germany – has developed incrementally on a case-by-case basis making it similar to the common law system.

The gap-filling function of case law also becomes very evident when facing challenges of new times like digitalisation and new forms of employment like platform work. Here on the one hand the open concept of 'employee' shows its benefit being able to adapt to new circumstances by way of interpretation. The difference between the civil law and the common law system is then not so big nowadays as in common law systems statutory law has gained increased importance and in civil law systems flexibility is provided not only by general clauses and open legal concepts that inherently provide flexibility to adapt to a changing environment. And in many instances, the courts just have to develop the legal order forward as gaps exist in the statutory legislation that require judicial activity in order not to come to unfair and inequitable solutions. This is especially stressed in the country chapter on Germany where Manfred Weiss points out that given the legislative inertia or the frequent inability to generate the necessary votes on specific issues, the courts have little choice but to act on behalf of the legislation.

In any event, it seems that in times of profound and at the same time rapid changes in the way work is organised, the role of the courts will increase as the political situation in many countries has developed in a way that majorities cannot be easily reached in Parliament to resolve these issues balancing the interests of both employees and employers. This is seen as being especially the case when Member States of the EU have to transpose European legislation as well as decisions of the European Court of Justice in particular into national law. Due to the lack of activity of the legislator, the courts have to act and to develop the law further in order to bring it into line with the European legal requirements. It is therefore likely that even in civil law countries, courts will not only interpret the law but also develop it further increasingly. They then act often out of necessity as a kind of 'substitute legislator' in those fields where legislative gaps become evident. And it seems that these gaps are increasing due to the manifold reasons just mentioned.

BIBLIOGRAPHY

Edoardo Ales, *The Concept of 'Employee': The Position in Italy* (Bernd Waas & Guus Herrma van Voss, eds), *Restatement of Labour Law in Europe, Volume I: The Concept of Employee*, 352 (1st, Hart Publishing 2017).

Claus-Wilhelm Canaris, *Die Feststellung von Lücken im Gesetz*, 39 (2nd ed., Duncker and Humblot, 1983).

Antoine Jacobs, *Collective Self Regulation* (Bob Hepple, ed.), *The Making of Labour Law in Europe*, 240 (Hart Publishing 1986).

Ernst A. Kramer, *Juristische Methodenlehre*, 212 (3rd ed., Stämpfli Verlag, 2010).

Martin Kriele, *Theorie der Rechtsgewinnung*, 243 (2nd ed., Duncker and Humblot, 1976).

M. Magnani, *The Role of Collective Bargaining in Italian Labour Law*, 7 E-Journal of International and Comparative Labour Studies, 2 (2018).

Martin Risak & Thomas Dullinger, *The Concept of 'Worker' in EU Law*, 10 (ETUC, 2018).

Bruno Veneziani, *The Employment Relationship* (Bob Hepple & Bruno Veneziani, eds), *The Transformation of Labour Law in Europe*, 99 (Hart Publishing 2009).

Bruno Veneziani, *The Evolution of the Contract of Employment* (Bob Hepple, ed.), *The Making of Labour Law in Europe*, 54 (Bloombsbury Professional 1986).

Bernd Waas & Guus Herrma van Voss, *Restatement of Labour Law in Europe, Volume I: The Concept of Employee* (1st, Hart Publishing, 2017).

Wiebke Warneck, *Strike Rules in EU27 and Beyond: A Comparative View*, 32 (ETUI 2007).

CHAPTER 6

The Impact of the European Union Economic Governance on the Hierarchy of National Labour Law Sources

Emanuele Menegatti

6.1 INTRODUCTION

In coordinating national economic policies within the framework of the European Economic Governance (EEG), the Institutions of the European Union (EU) have interfered with the hierarchy of labour law sources of some Member States. In this respect, the EU has challenged the traditional European model of employment regulation, built on a rigid floor of mandatory statutory protections and a centralised system of collective bargaining, endorsing a completely different and more flexible one, that is to say, a model based on decentralised collective bargaining and on a loose application of one of the founding principles of labour law, the so-called favour (or favourability) principle.

The results are tangible. According to a recent report,[1] twelve countries have presented decentralisation tendencies since 2008, from the cross-sector towards the sector or company levels, and/or from the sector towards the company level, most of them under the influence of the EU institutions.

In investigating the impact of the EU economic governance on the hierarchy of national labour law sources, this chapter will provide a preliminary brief description of the functioning of the EEG (section 6.2), followed by a consideration of the economic arguments underpinning the revision of the hierarchy of

1. Paul Marginson & Christian Welz, *Changes to Wage-Setting Mechanisms in the Context of the Crisis and the EU's New Economic Governance Regime*, 24 (Eurofound 2014).

labour law sources promoted by the EU institutions (section 6.3). It will then consider the recommendations addressed to a selection of countries within the framework of the EEG (section 6.4), analysing the results generated by them (section 6.5). Finally, it will focus on a possible and desirable change of course compared to the trend promoted by the EEG so far (section 6.6).

6.2 THE 'ORDINARY' AND 'EXTRAORDINARY' CHANNELS OF THE EU ECONOMIC GOVERNANCE

In the broad context of EU economic coordination, we have witnessed two main channels of the Union intervention which have affected in general work regulations and their sources.

The first, and more dramatic, concerned those countries that received financial assistance under the so-called bailout plans. The assistance came alternatively from the so-called Troika (the European Commission acting in liaison with the European Central Bank and the International Monetary Fund (IMF)), bilateral loans, but mostly from the European Financial Stabilization Mechanism and its successor, the European Stability Mechanism.[2] These programmes concerned both Eurozone countries (Ireland, Portugal, Greece and Cyprus) and non-Eurozone countries (Hungary, Latvia and Romania) and even though the money came from various sources, they all shared a same relevant characteristic: the financial assistance was conditioned by satisfactory implementation of reforms formally agreed to by Member States under (binding) memoranda of understanding (MoUs). These reforms, we will see (section 6.4.3), have sometimes involved the set-up of labour law sources.

Semi-bailout received by Spain and Italy in 2011 and 2012 can be included in this first channel of intervention. For both countries, the European Central Bank purchase of government bonds was conditional on policy reforms.

The second and 'ordinary' channel of intervention is that referring to the new version of the EEG, widely reformed in response to the financial and economic crisis of 2008. The present system is a stronger revamped version of the weak and ineffective 'multilateral surveillance', set up under Article 121 TFEU and implemented in the late 1990s through the original Stability and Growth Pact (SGP).[3] The most significant amendments to the original system came from the so-called Six-Pack (five regulations and one directive), providing: (i) stricter oversight over annual stability and convergence programmes; (ii)

2. The European Stability Mechanism was designed to become the main and stable way for managing Eurozone Member States financial crisis. Unlike its predecessor, it works outside the EU institutional context, bases on an Intergovernmental Organisation created by the Eurozone countries, similarly to the IMF.
3. Under the former (pre-2008) SGP, Member States could not be compelled to implement responsible fiscal policies, so much so that departures from such policies were never subject to penalty.

semi-automatic sanctions for Eurozone countries in excessive deficit position, not following the direction provided by the Council;[4] (iii) a brand-new procedure aimed at correcting and preventing excessive macroeconomic imbalances;[5] and (iv) a single process, the so-called European Semester, merging together the surveillance over budgetary positions, coordination of economic policies, prevention of excessive macroeconomic imbalances and integrated guidelines for growth and employment coming from the Europe 2020 strategy in just one process.[6]

Despite its name, the European Semester basically consists in a yearly cycle where each Member State receives Country-Specific Recommendations (CSRs) drawn up by the Commission on the basis of a detailed analysis of national budgetary and structural policies and macroeconomic imbalances. Once endorsed by the heads of state and governments within the European Council and formally adopted by the Council of the EU, these recommendations are to be transformed into national 'reform programmes' whose effectiveness will again be assessed by the Commission.

Quite often, the recommendations addressing the sources of work regulation, in particular wage-setting mechanisms, have been generated by the procedure for macroeconomic surveillance. This starts with the alert mechanism report, through which the Commission analyses the economic situation of every country using a scoreboard with ten indicators covering the major sources of macroeconomic imbalance. The current scoreboard includes the unemployment rate and the variation of the unit labour cost (ULC).

The ULC has played a central role in the topic we are dealing with. As the European Commission has repeatedly stressed, the increase in nominal ULC corresponds to a rise in labour costs exceeding the increase in labour productivity, which might erode competitiveness.[7] This has become a problem of major concern after the creation of the monetary union. The increasing differences in competitiveness between EU countries (between so-called surplus and deficit countries) are mainly owed to the divergent trends in wages and ULCs. Many

4. According to Article 6 of Regulation (EU) No. 1173/2011 of the European Parliament and of the Council of 16 November 2011 on the effective enforcement of budgetary surveillance in the euro area, a fine amounting to 0.2% of the Member State's Gross Domestic Product (GDP) in the preceding year can be imposed by the Council on the basis of a Commission recommendation, unless a qualified majority of Member States should vote against such a fine (under the so-called reverse qualified majority voting procedure).
5. Regulation (EU) No. 1176/2011 of the European Parliament and of the Council of 16 November 2011 on the prevention and correction of macroeconomic imbalances, and Regulation (EU) No. 1174/2011 of the European Parliament and of the Council of 16 November 2011 on enforcement measures to correct excessive macroeconomic imbalances in the euro area.
6. Regulation (EU) No. 1175/2011 of the European Parliament and of the Council of 16 November 2011 amending Council Regulation (EC) No. 1466/97 on the strengthening of the surveillance of budgetary positions and the surveillance and coordination of economic policies.
7. *See* European Commission, '*Scoreboard for the Surveillance on Macroeconomic Imbalances*,' European Economy Occasional Papers 92, 14 (2012).

countries in the past have been able to circumvent this problem by devaluating their national currencies, but this is obviously no longer possible under the single currency. Nowadays, according to the EU institutions, the same result can be achieved by policies of 'internal devaluation', meaning a reduction of labour costs able to increase the competitiveness of deficit countries.[8]

An economic reading of the scoreboard indicators does not lead to any automatic conclusions.[9] They are just symptoms of probable macroeconomic imbalances subject to a further in-depth Commission review. If on the basis of the in-depth review the situation cannot be considered dramatic, it will be dealt with under the preventive arm of the procedure, leading to recommendations requiring countries to take actions to correct the identified imbalances, which become part of the CSRs. Otherwise, when macroeconomic imbalances are deemed excessive and in need of corrective actions, the Commission may ask the Council to place the country in question under the corrective arm (the excessive imbalance procedure). Here the Council issues a set of policy recommendations to be followed within a deadline. Non-compliant Eurozone Member States will face financial sanctions designed with a high level of automatism.

Sanctions against Eurozone Member States are provided not only for macroeconomic imbalances but also for failure to meet the deficit target set in the SGP under the excessive deficit procedure (EDP) set forth in Article 126 TFEU.[10]

6.3 THE ECONOMIC PARADIGM UNDERPINNING THE EEG INTERVENTION ON LABOUR LAW SOURCES

The economic argument promoting a reduction of labour costs and an increase in employment flexibility has played a pivotal role in the framework of the EEG.[11] With regard to the sources of employment regulation, it provided the basis for all the recommendations promoting flexible working conditions,

8. K. Armingeon & L. Baccaro, *Political Economy of the Sovereign Debt Crisis: The Limits of Internal Devaluation*, 41 *Industrial Law Journal*, 254-256 (2012).
9. As literally expressed in Article 3(2) of Regulation No. 1176/2011: The Commission's 'conclusions shall not be drawn from a mechanical reading of the scoreboard indicators'.
10. The EDP has been revised by Regulation No. 1175/2011 and Council Regulation (EU) No. 1177/2011 of 8 November 2011 amending Regulation (EC) No. 1467/97 on speeding up and clarifying the implementation of the excessive deficit procedure; it was subsequently reinforced by the Treaty on Stability, Coordination and Governance in the Economic and Monetary Union (the so-called Fiscal Compact), providing the golden rule on balanced budgets; and most recently it was amended by the so-called Two-Pack (Regulation Nos 472 2013 and 473 2013).
11. T. Schulten & T. Müller, *A new European interventionism? The impact of the new European economic governance on wages and collective bargaining* (David Natali & Bart Vanhercke, eds), *Social developments in the European Union*, 186 (ETUI 2012).

adaptable to firms' contingent or permanent needs and to the specific characteristics of individual employment relations, such as to enable differentiation across sectors, firms and workers.

In the light of this argument, not surprisingly, a radical change of the relations between the various layers of labour law regulation has been promoted for those European countries experiencing excessive deficits and/or macroeconomic imbalances (i.e., France, Belgium, Italy, Spain and Portugal) and presenting the following common pattern: traditionally quite strict employment protection, largely predominant multi-employer collective bargaining, and, on the top of that, the (explicit or implicit) recognition of the principle of favour. This principle, as is well known, covers the relationship between statutory law, collective bargaining and individual contracting and, less often, the relationship between the different levels of collective bargaining. It stipulates that derogation to the mandatory rules provided by higher-ranking sources is possible only improving them, precisely, in employees' favour.

That model of labour law sources hierarchy has been considered by the EU institutions outmoded with regard to the current economic paradigm.[12] Multi-employer collective bargaining and, in particular, industry-level agreements have traditionally served the purpose of taking wages and employment conditions out of competition. Uniformity of working conditions within the different sectors has limited competitive pricing among entrepreneurs and competition among workers in the labour market. Moreover, the combination with the favour principle has traditionally supported the traditional functions of labour law as a floor of mandatory protections aimed at compensating the asymmetry of bargaining power between the parties of the employment contract, so preventing any derogation to the detriment of working conditions at the firm level, both by individual negotiations and by collective agreements.[13]

Multi-employer bargaining, combined with statutory mandatory protection, provided therefore a common floor of protection and a levelled playfield, based on stable and predictable labour cost, for competition between companies (and workers) within the domestic market. However, when the playfield has started becoming bigger, crossing national borders, 'stability' (and rigidity) of employment conditions, granted by the traditional set-up of labour law sources, turned out to be rather undesirable for companies having to compete on the global market.

---

12. *See* the analysis of Isabelle Schömann, *Collective Labour Law under Attack: How Anti-crisis Measures Dismantle Workers' Collective Rights*, 2 *ETUI Policy Brief* (2014), https://www.etui.org/Publications2/Policy-Briefs/European-Economic-Employment-and-Social-Policy/Collective-labour-law-under-attack-how-anti-crisis-measures-dismantle-workers-collective-rights (accessed 23 April 2019).
13. M. Pallini, *Italian Industrial Relations: Toward a Strongly Decentralized Collective Bargaining*, 38 *Comparative Labor Law & Policy Journal*, 1, 2 (2016).

In the context of global competition, especially for export-driven companies, wages and other employment conditions could no longer be excluded from competition; on the contrary, they have become key components of competitive strategies.[14] Moreover, the volatility of globalised markets does not affect to the same extent companies belonging to the same sector; therefore, some of them might need to go beyond the uniformity of industry-level agreements and statutory protections. Last but not least, financialisation of the economy has led to short-term strategies, which hardly fit in with changes negotiated only when an expiring contract is to be replaced, every three or four years or so.[15]

The 'stability' provided by industry-level bargaining combined with strong statutory protections and the favour principle has, in the opinion of many, become at odds with flexible and 'dynamic' working conditions requested by the new economic setting. This apparent mismatch has put pressure on models based on centralised collective bargaining. Where social partners have not been able to quickly react, in particular by promoting a process of 'organised' decentralisation of working conditions, the system of industrial relations got into a crisis.[16] The outcome varied across countries, leading to: collective bargaining coverage and trade union density decline; proliferation of collective agreements signed by scarcely representative trade unions promoting a race to the bottom of wage and working conditions; the switch to single-employer bargaining by some big companies.

Very often, the absence of any reaction from social partners has been compensated by the interventionism of national legislators. The autonomy of collective bargaining has been frequently invaded by statutory 'opt-out' clauses, allowing derogation to the sectoral standards by company-level agreements and even individual negotiations or unliteral regulations.[17] An increasing number of employers decided to move towards single-employer agreements and to get completely rid of employment protection by subcontracting and more in general by replacing employment contracts with civil law and commercial law contracts.

Some economists have welcomed these changes to the traditional model of employment regulation, which has been accused of charging unionised companies with high transaction costs. In their view, the constraints normally posed to managerial discretion by multi-employer agreements represent a sort of union tax on company earnings, leading to slow response to economic shocks and then

14. *See* J. Visser, *Wage Bargaining Institutions-From Crisis to Crisis*, 488 *European Economy-Economic Papers* (2013), https://ec.europa.eu/economy_finance/publications/economic_paper/2013/pdf/ecp488_en.pdf(accessed 22 October 2019).
15. T. Darcillon, *How Does Finance Affect Labor Market Institutions? An Empirical Analysis in 16 OECD Countries*, 13 *Socio-Economic Review*, 477 (2015).
16. P. Marginson, *Coordinated Bargaining in Europe: From Incremental Corrosion to Frontal Assault?*, 21 *European Journal of Industrial Relations*, 97, 99 (2015).
17. *See* the analysis of Maarten Keune, *Wage Flexibilisation and the Minimum Wage*, in *Industrial Relations in Europe*, 127 (Publications Office of the European Union 2010).

poor performance[18]; something difficult to accept in the current competitive and dynamic economic environments.

Similar arguments have been shared also by the EU institutions, clearly supporting, in the framework of the EEG, the trend promoted by market mechanisms.[19] In this respect, we are going to see into detail how the European Semester has, in a selection of countries (France, Italy and Portugal), implicitly and sometimes rather explicitly, forced national legislators towards the promotion of decentralised collective bargaining – especially 'uncoordinated' decentralisation – and towards the overcoming of the principle of favour.[20]

6.4 ECONOMIC GOVERNANCE VERSUS NATIONAL SYSTEM OF EMPLOYMENT REGULATION

6.4.1 The Case of France

The French case is a very good example of the effective vertical relationship between the EU and Member States created by the reinforced EEG. France was under EDP since the launch of the European Semester until 2018, systematically failing to meet the SGP requirements. In the same period, it presented macroeconomic imbalances, which became excessive from 2015 to 2107. The country has therefore been constantly under the Commission specific monitoring, just one step away from the corrective arms of the EEG.

As far as labour regulation is concerned, the issue of main concern for the union has constantly been the exaggerated level and pace of the minimum wage, not in line with productivity gains, and the excessive labour market rigidity. It is exactly on this latter point that the European Commission has challenged the French hierarchy of labour law sources and in particular that 'internal' to collective bargaining.

France belongs to the group of the above-mentioned countries, where: the relationship between statutory law – namely the *Code du Travail* (Labour Code)

18. B.T. Hirsch, *Sluggish Institutions in a Dynamic World: Can Unions and Industrial Competition Coexist?*, 22 *Journal of Economic Perspectives*, 153, 154 (2008); 'In dynamic economic settings, the high transaction costs of union governance result in sluggish response to shocks, placing union companies at a competitive disadvantage.'
19. L. Bordogna & R. Pedersini, *What Kind of Europeanization? How EMU Is Changing National Industrial Relations in Europe*, 146 *Giornale di Diritto del Lavoro e di Relazioni Industriali*, 184-187 (2015).
20. J. Cruces, I.A. Francisco Trillo & S. Leonardi, *Impact of the euro crisis on wages and collective bargaining in southern Europe – A comparison of Italy, Portugal and Spain* (Guy Van Gyes & Thorsten Schulten, eds), *Wage bargaining under the new European economic governance*, 93, 100 (ETUI 2015); F. Bergamante & M. Marocco, *New European Economic Governance and Decentralisation of the Collective Bargaining Structure in Italy: Did It Work Out?*, 4 (2018), https://ssrn.com/abstract=3228590 (accessed 23 April 2019).

– collective agreements, individual contracting, as well as the collective bargaining 'internal' hierarchy used to be based on the application of the favour principle; sectoral agreements represented the core level of employment regulation and they can be provided of universal application throughout the whole sector by the Ministry of Labour.

Things started changing from Auroux reform of 1982. From this point on, the relevance and spread of company-level collective bargaining have been increasing, currently covering more than half of the workforce.[21] This growth has been achieved mainly thanks to the obligation to negotiate at the company level certain items: initially just referred to wages, working time and work organisation, then extended during the 2000s to many other subjects such as gender equality, employees' participation in company profits and employment of senior workers.

The process of overcoming the traditional relations between the various layers of regulation was then accelerated in 2004 by the loi Fillon. It introduced consistent room for company collective bargaining to derogate to working conditions established at the sectoral level, with the only exception of some protected areas (i.e., minimum wage and classification). However, it was not a disruptive change in the hierarchy of sources yet. Social partners had the power to 'lock up' conditions provided at the sectoral level, so preventing company derogations or cancelling it *ex post*, as they often did.[22] In any case, the 1982 and 2004 reforms paved the way to further and more radical changes.

Since the inception of the EEG, the EU institutions immediately noticed that the level of decentralisation of employment regulation achieved by France was not enough. Starting from 2015, the Commission has insisted that more flexibility for the employers to depart from industry-level agreement should have been granted.[23] To this end, the favourability principle should have been repealed for topics such as minimum wages, job classifications, supplementary social protection and multi-company and cross-sector vocational training funds[24]; furthermore, a priority should have been given to company-level agreements in establishing the rules governing working time, wages, working conditions and

21. On the development of decentralised bargaining in France *see* U. Rehfeldt & C. Vincent, *The decentralisation of collective bargaining in France: an escalating process* (Salvo Leonardi & Roberto Pedersini, eds), *Multi-employer bargaining under pressure – Decentralisation trends in five European countries*, 151 (ETUI 2018).
22. Rehfeldt & Vincent (n. 21) 155. Jean-Marie Pernot, *France and the European Agenda: an Ambiguous Impact on Industrial Relations*, in *The New EU Economic Governance and Its Impact on the National Collective Bargaining Systems: Final Report* 100 (2014), https://www.fondazionedivittorio.it/sites/default/files/content-attachment/GOCOBA_Final%20report.pdf (accessed 23 April 2019).
23. European Commission, *Country Report France 2015. Including an In-Depth Review on the prevention and correction of macroeconomic imbalances* 16, https://ec.europa.eu/info/sites/info/files/file_import/cr2015_france_en_0.pdf (accessed 23 April 2019).
24. *Ibid.*

employment.[25] The Commission's view was completely endorsed by the Council of the EU in the 2015 CSRs: 'recent reforms have created only limited scope for employers to depart from branch-level agreements through company-level agreements', therefore, recommending accordingly to 'facilitate take-up of derogations at company and branch level from general legal provisions'.[26] The same recommendation was then repeated in 2016.[27]

The reaction of France to the stimulus coming from the EU has been quite fast, prompted by the so-called Combrexelle Report of 2015.[28] It proposed to prioritise the regulative role of collective bargaining, over that of the Labour Code, and in particular to give to company-specific collective agreements a larger role, according to a desirable 'proximity regulation'. The subsequent El Khomri reform of 2016 drove forward the project of reversing the hierarchy of sources.[29] In this respect, it has created a new shared competence between statutory law and collective agreements in specific areas, such as working time, overtime pay, paid holidays and weekly rest. Without prejudice of the fundamental principles of labour law provided by peremptory statutory norms, related to constitutional principles, sectoral or company agreements can freely regulate the working conditions in the mentioned areas. Company agreements have a priority over sectoral regulation, apart from matters not open to derogation established by the latter. Statutory protections beyond and above the 'minimum legal framework' apply only in the absence of collective agreements.

One year later, the process of reform made another significant step forward. The so-called Enabling Act, adopted by the French Parliament on 2 August 2017, allowed the Government to pass the legislation by decrees (so-called ordonnances), giving birth to the so-called Macron reform of the Labour Code.

The Macron reform was aimed, among other things, at enlarging the field of collective bargaining and reinforcing sectoral agreements. To this purpose, it has reserved to industry-level collective bargaining thirteen topics, including jobs classification and appropriate minimum wages, probation period, some

25. European Commission, *Country Report France 2016. Including an In-Depth Review on the prevention and correction of macroeconomic imbalances* 58, https://ec.europa.eu/info/sites/info/files/cr_france_2016_en.pdf (accessed 23 April 2019).
26. Council Recommendation on the 2015 National Reform Programme of France and delivering a Council opinion on the 2015 Stability Programme of France (2015/C 272/14), https://eur-lex.europa.eu/legal-content/EN/TXT/?uri=CELEX%3A32015H0818%2815%29 (accessed 23 April 2019).
27. Council Recommendation on the 2016 National Reform Programme of France and delivering a Council opinion on the 2016 Stability Programme of France (2016/C 299/27), https://eur-lex.europa.eu/legal-content/EN/TXT/?uri=uriserv%3AOJ.C_.2016.299.01.0114.01.ENG&toc=OJ%3AC%3A2016%3A299%3ATOC (accessed 23 April 2019).
28. Jean-Denise Combrexelle, *La négociation collective le travail et l'emploi* (2015), https://www.ladocumentationfrancaise.fr/rapports-publics/154000638/index.shtml (accessed 23 April 2019).
29. Rehfeldt & Vincent (n. 21) 161.

aspects concerning working time and restrictions to temporary employment. Company agreements are not allowed to regulate this reserved area unless they provide 'at least equivalent guarantees'.

At a closer scrutiny, according to some commentators, the reinforcement of sectoral agreements turns out to be only at the expense of statutory law, which can now be changed *in peius* for employees by collective agreements.[30] In a matter of fact, the Macron reform has taken the priority given until then to company agreements to the next level. In this connection, the sectoral 'lock-up' – unlimited under the 2004 law – has been reduced to only four specific areas (i.e., disabled workers). Company agreements, for their part, have acquired a competence on everything that does not fall into the sectoral agreements and legislative ones. This has created a considerable room for negotiating at the company level worse working conditions concerning, for example, remuneration, without prejudice to the minimum wage.[31]

The outcome has been a significant and unprecedented primacy of company agreements, the parallel decline of the regulatory capacity of sectoral agreements, and the restriction of the favourability principle, even with regard to the relationship between statutory law and collective bargaining.

Obviously, less favourable employment conditions should be collectively negotiated and accepted by bargaining actors representing employees. However, this has been facilitated by the Macron reform itself in workplaces where trade unions are not present. Thus, in small companies employing less than twenty employees, the employer can propose a draft agreement made by himself, which should be approved by 2/3 of the staff. In non-unionised bigger companies, elected representatives or employees delegated by trade unions can be the signatory parties of the agreement. By these rules, the French Government clearly wanted to give access to company-level collective bargaining to all employers as a means to achieve more flexibility (that is to say, weaker employment conditions, including lower wages).

As anticipated, all the considered changes in the hierarchy of labour law sources have been recommended in the framework of the EEG. It is therefore not surprising that these actions have been finally well received by the European Commission, which in the 2018 Country Report highlighted that 'recent reforms are expected to improve the functioning of the labour market over time' and contributing to 'the competitiveness of the French economy'.[32]

30. Rehfeldt & Vincent (n. 21) 163.
31. *Ibid.*
32. European Commission, *Country Report France 2018. Including an In-Depth Review on the prevention and correction of macroeconomic imbalances* 11, https://ec.europa.eu/info/sites/info/files/2018-european-semester-country-report-france-en.pdf (accessed 23 April 2019).

6.4.2 The Case of Italy

Similar targets – in particular, decentralisation of collective bargaining – but in a rather different context of industrial relations have been pursued by the EU with regard to Italy. Differently from France and from other Mediterranean countries, Italian industrial relations, with the exception of the Fascist period, have always been scarcely institutionalised, mostly based on voluntarism. A statutory regulation of collective bargaining process, structure and efficacy is completely missing. Nonetheless, despite the absence of a mechanism for the extension of collective agreements to non-members, coverage of industry-level collective bargaining has constantly been quite high – around 80% according to Organisation for Economic Co-operation and Development (OECD) data[33] – mainly because labour courts and some legislative prescriptions have managed to force employers towards the application of sectoral agreements.[34]

As for the hierarchy between the different levels of collective bargaining, the current framework has been moving from that established by a 1993 tripartite economy-wide collective agreement.[35] This was based on a two-tier bargaining structure providing a strict subordination of company and territorial-level agreements (second level) to sectoral agreements (first level). Second-level agreements were not only prevented from *in peius* modifications, but also from any regulation of employment other than those expressly allowed by industry-level. According to the ne bis in idem principle, the former cannot deal with topics already regulated by the latter. As a matter of fact, company collective bargaining was almost exclusively entrusted of setting additional wages related to productivity gains. This framework has remained pretty untouched for nearly two decades, even if it turned out to be sometimes unstable: being not supported by statute, it could only rely on voluntary compliance of bargaining players at the firm and territorial level.[36]

The change of economic paradigm and eventually the 'Great Recession' jeopardised the functioning of the 1993 framework. In particular, the employers' side challenged the centrality of industry-level collective bargaining, deemed to be inappropriate. Export-driven companies advocated more room for adapting the rules negotiated at the industry level to their specific needs. That was, in particular, the case of FIAT-FCA, one of the most important and iconic Italian company. FIAT-FCA set up in 2010 its own single-employer collective agreement

33. OECD, Collective Bargaining Coverage, https://stats.oecd.org/Index.aspx?DataSetCode=CBC (accessed 19 April 2019).
34. *See* Gaetano Zilio Grandi, *Collective barganiing* (Franco Carinci, Emanuele Menegatti, eds), *Labour law and industrial relations in Italy*, Chapter XV (Wolters Kluwer 2015); Pallini (n. 13) 16-17.
35. Zilio Grandi (n. 34) 309-310.
36. G.A. Recchia, *The Future of Collective Bargaining in Italy Between Legislative Reforms and Social Partners' Responses*, 23 *Transfer: European Review of Labour and Research*, 457, 458 (2017).

with a view to achieve more flexibility with regard to working time and shift work than that allowed by the sectoral metal workers agreement.

The pressure towards decentralisation managed to be successful for the first time in 2009, when a new tripartite agreement, not signed by the largest Italian trade union, opened up a breach in the centralisation of the system of collective bargaining. Industry-level remained the central level of negotiation, but, differently from the 1993 rules, company-level agreements were allowed to derogate *in peius* to sectoral agreements, only under sectoral agreements permission (opening clauses). A subsequent economy-wide agreement, signed in June 2011 by all the major trade unions, went further, increasing the room for derogation in favour of company-level agreements, which can now worsen the working conditions provided by sectoral agreements even in the absence of opening clauses, if justified by a situation of crisis or in order to improve companies economic performances.[37]

When the EU institutions decided in 2011 to step in and influence the way Italy was addressing the crisis, they found therefore a fertile sole, already prepared by internal players. The first intervention was that of the European Central Bank, which told in a 'secret' letter sent to the Italian Government on 5 August 2011 that, among other things, the system of industrial relations had to be reformed, in order to 'allow enterprise-level agreements to cut wages and working conditions to the specific needs of companies and make these agreements more relevant than other negotiating levels'.[38]

The purchase of hundred millions of Italian Government bond was at stake. Therefore, not surprisingly, the Government reacted very quickly, approving in August 2011 a law decree entitled 'support for proximity collective bargaining'. By this act, company or territorial-level agreements can derogate not only from industry-level agreements but also from statutory law, outside of any principle of favour, on most of the employment matters. The deviation should respect the constraints deriving from constitutional provisions, international conventions and EU law. It shall also be justified on the ground of company objective needs, such as managing crisis, increasing employment or productivity and new investments. Differently from the just considered economy-wide agreement of a couple of months before (June 2011), here company agreements are totally disconnected from any delegation and control of industry-level agreement and statutes. A form of 'disorganised decentralisation' has made its appearance in Italy for the first time in recent decades.[39]

37. *See* the detailed reconstruction by Pallini (n. 13) 3-5.
38. Recchia (n. 36) 459.
39. S. Leonardi, M. Concetta Ambra & A. Ciarini, *Italian collective bargaining at a turning point* (Salvo Leonardi & Roberto Pedersini, eds), *Multi-employer bargaining under pressure – Decentralisation trends in five European countries*, 185, 193 (ETUI 2018).

The European Semester moved in this same direction since its inception. In 2012 the Council addressed to Italy the recommendation, similarly repeated also in 2013, of reinforcing 'the new wage setting framework [that provided by mentioned economy wide agreement of 2011] in order to contribute to the alignment of wage growth and productivity at sector and company level'.[40] This implicitly included the request for further decentralisation of collective bargaining, as it turned out in the subsequent 2013 country report: 'The dominant level of collective bargaining in Italy remains the national level ... This hampers a better alignment of wages to firms or local economic and competitiveness conditions.'[41]

The 2014 Commission Country Report on Italy complained about the fact that company-level agreements still covered a minority of workers and firms.[42] The 2015 Council CSRs required explicitly to Italy to 'promote, in consultation with the social partners and in accordance with national practices, an effective framework for second-level contractual bargaining'.[43] Again the 2016[44] and 2017[45] CSRs reported the insufficient use of second-level bargaining which, in the opinion of the Council, made it difficult to develop innovative solutions at firm level that could improve productivity and foster the response of wages to labour market conditions.

A response from the Italian Government came in the framework of a major reform of Italian labour law, the so-called Jobs Act. Legislative decree No. 81 of 2015 specified that anytime statutory law delegates the regulation of employment relations to collective bargaining, and the reference shall be intended to any level of it (industry, local, company level). Even if this rule does not directly deal with the relationship between different levels of collective agreements and to its contents, it contributes to an alteration of it, conferring company-level

40. Council Recommendation on the National Reform Programme 2013 of Italy and delivering a Council opinion on the Stability Programme of Italy 2012-2017 (2013/C 217/11), https://eur-lex.europa.eu/LexUriServ/LexUriServ.do?uri=OJ:C:2013:217:0042:0046:EN:PDF(accessed 22 October 2019).
41. European Commission, *Assessment of the 2013 national reform programme and stability programme for ITALY* 10, https://ec.europa.eu/info/sites/info/files/file_import/swd2013_italy_en_0.pdf (accessed 23 April 2019).
42. European Commission, *Assessment of the 2014 national reform programme and stability programme for ITALY* 20, https://ec.europa.eu/info/sites/info/files/file_import/swd2014_italy_en_0.pdf (accessed 23 April 2019).
43. Council Recommendation of 14 July 2015 on the 2015 National Reform Programme of Italy and delivering a Council opinion on the 2015 Stability Programme of Italy, https://eur-lex.europa.eu/legal-content/EN/TXT/?uri=CELEX%3A32015H0818%2817%29 (accessed 23 April 2019).
44. Council Recommendation of 12 July 2016 on the 2016 National Reform Programme of Italy and delivering a Council opinion on the 2016 Stability Programme of Italy, https://eur-lex.europa.eu/legal-content/EN/TXT/?uri=uriserv%3AOJ.C_.2016.299.01.0001.01.ENG&toc=OJ%3AC%3A2016%3A299%3ATOC (accessed 23 April 2019).
45. Council Recommendation on the 2017 National Reform Programme of Italy and delivering a Council opinion on the 2017 Stability Programme of Italy (2017/C 261/11), https://eur-lex.europa.eu/legal-content/EN/TXT/PDF/?uri=CELEX%3A32017H0809%2811%29 (accessed 23 April 2019).

agreements the same regulative power which used to be of industry-level agreements, outside of any principle of favour. Thus, it is a significant step towards equalisation of the different levels.[46]

Social partners, for their part, have confirmed the importance of second-level bargaining in 2018, by a new economy-wide framework agreement.

At the end of the day, the internal pressure coupled with the external coming from the EU has been able to achieve a certain degree of decentralisation, along two parallel tracks: one drafted by the legislator, heading towards uncoordinated decentralisation; the other governed by collective autonomy, where industry-level collective bargaining still keeps the control over territorial and company-level agreements.

6.4.3 The Case of Portugal

Portugal used to have a centralised system of collective bargaining, mostly at the industry-level. Differently from France and Italy or even from the Spanish neighbours, company-level agreements have historically been very rare in Portugal since very rare have always been the workers' representatives presence at workplace level. Not surprisingly, given the peculiarity of the Portuguese productive fabric, which presents an overwhelming prevalence of very small companies. In this context, mechanisms to articulate collective bargaining have remained very weak, since they never received particular attention by the social partners and the legislator.[47] Nevertheless, coverage of collective bargaining used to be quite high. It was the result of two main factors: the legal extensions of the scope of industry-level agreements, which was almost automatically granted by the Ministry of Labour; and the 'after-effect' rules, allowing expired collective agreements to remain valid until renegotiated.[48]

The Portuguese collective bargaining system has been criticised because it did not grant the necessary flexibility to companies. Moreover, the after-effect rule attracted a great deal of disapproval. It was accused of being a major factor of rigidity, because it took away from trade unions the pressure normally caused by expiring collective agreements, making them less prone to make concession to employers.[49]

46. M. Magnani, *The Role of Collective Bargaining in Italian Labour Law*, 7 *Labour Studies*, 13 (2018); Recchia (n. 36) 466.
47. *See* L. Fulton, *Worker Representation in Europe* (2015), http://www.worker-participation.eu/National-Industrial-Relations (accessed 23 April 2019).
48. M. do Rosário Palma Ramalho, *Portuguese Labour Law and Industrial Relations During the Crisis*, ILO Working Paper 54 (2013), https://www.ilo.org/wcmsp5/groups/public/---ed_dialogue/---dialogue/documents/publication/wcms_232798.pdf (accessed 24 April 2019).
49. I. Távora & P. González Tabora, *Labour Market Regulation and Collective Bargaining in Portugal During the Crisis: Continuity and Change*, 22 *European Journal of Industrial Relations*, 251, 256 (2016).

Things started changing when an important process of reform was undertaken during the first decade of the 2000s. The 2003 revision of the Labour Code eliminated the favour principle related to the relations between statutory law and collective agreements, then partially reinstated by a subsequent 2009 revision of the Labour Code for some 'core' areas like non-discrimination, wage, working time limitations, protection of worker's 'personality'. The same 2009 Labour Code revision set an eighteen months ceiling to the after-effect rule, provided that any of the bargaining parties have requested the expiration of the agreement.

Following the bailout, Portugal entered the Economic Adjustment Programme, which covered the period 2011-2014. The MoU of 17 May 2011 proposed the usual target of promoting 'coordinated decentralised bargaining'. This led to a couple of changes by the 2012 revision of the Labour Code: reduction of the threshold required for non-union workers' representatives to conclude collective agreements – from company employing at least 500 employees to 150 – and the introduction of the possibility for sectoral agreements to provide opening clauses admitting the derogation by company agreements on some topics.

These were just marginal adjustments.[50] The real target of the MoU was instead the mechanism for the extension of collective agreements. The definition of 'clear criteria to be followed for the extension of collective agreements', taking into close consideration not only 'the representativeness of the negotiating organisations' but also 'the implications of the extension for the competitive position of non-affiliated firms' deemed necessary by the Troika.[51]

As a result, the extension of collective agreements was first suspended in 2011 and 2012, waiting for the definition of the new criteria, then approved by the Government in October 2012. According to these, only collective agreements signed by an association representing 50% or more of the employees in the respective sector could be extended. The outcome was a sharp restriction of the extension mechanism and, of course, a huge reduction of extended agreements.[52] However, because of the protests of social partners, the rule has been relaxed in 2014, admitting as an alternative to it, the possibility of extension if at least 30% of the members of the signatory employers' association were small

50. Since the overwhelming majority of Portuguese corporations is very small, the reduction of the threshold from 500 to 150 had a very limited impact. As for the opening clauses, they were already enabled by former legislation. *See* Cruces, Álvarez, Trillo & Leonardi (n. 20) 108-109.
51. Memorandum of Understanding on specific economic policy conditionality, Portugal, 17 May 2011, 23-24, § 4.7.
52. According to the data provided by União Geral de Trabalhadores (UGT), Relatório Anual da Negociação Coletiva – 2014, https://www.ugt.pt/NC_relatorioanual2014.pdf (accessed 24 April 2019) the number of extended agreements collapsed from 296 in 2008 to 85 in 2012, slowly recovering to 94 in 2013.

and medium enterprises. Which is a very likely condition, given that 99.9% of Portuguese companies belong to this category.[53]

Still, the 2012 reform of the Labour Code led to the erosion of the application of the favourability principle, covering the relations between statutory law and collective and individual contracting, for the purpose of reducing labour costs. Some examples are the statutory reduction of overtime payments and abolition of paid compensatory time off, with the neutralisation of better regimes provided by collective agreements. Overtime payment higher than that provided by collective agreements was suspended and clauses on compensatory time off declared null and void. Provisions have then be declared unconstitutional.[54] Another significant example is the 'time bank' scheme, allowing some work after normal working time not to be considered as overtime, and then paid the regular hourly wage. This working scheme, which worsens statutory conditions, used to be permitted only if regulated by collective agreements. After the 2012 reform, it can be adopted by individual negotiation, which will therefore prevail over statutory regulation.

Once the bailout programme was concluded in 2014, Portugal entered the ordinary cycle of economic governance. The European Commission noted immediately the significant decline of collective bargaining under the bailout programme.[55] The number of sectoral agreements reached the lowest point ever in 2012,[56] as well as that of firm-level agreements, but in a measure proportionally less adverse.[57] Measures to 'foster collective bargaining' were then considered necessary.[58] This had nothing to do with the traditional 'equity' and 'stability' provided by sectoral agreements. On the contrary, the target the Commission had in mind was that of inducing 'greater dynamism and make wages more flexible' passing through the promotion of 'a more effective decentralisation of wage bargaining'.[59] Here it comes again, the switch from the old economic model based on patient capital and the new one based on shareholder value and short-term profits (*see supra* section 6.3).

53. Távora & González Tabora (n. 49) 256.
54. Decision of the Portuguese Constitutional Court No. 602 of 2013, https://dre.pt/pesquisa/-/search/502979/details/maximized (accessed 24 April 2019).
55. European Commission, *Assessment of the 2014 national reform programme and stability programme for PORTUGAL* 18, https://ec.europa.eu/info/sites/info/files/file_import/swd2014_portugal_en_0.pdf (accessed 23 April 2019).
56. *See* above (n. 52).
57. Above (n. 52). *See also* Maria da Paz Campos Lima, *EUROFOUND in Portugal: Decline in Collective Bargaining Reaches Critical Point* (2014), https://www.eurofound.europa.eu/publications/article/2014/portugal-decline-in-collective-bargaining-reaches-critical-point (accessed 24 April 2019).
58. European Commission (n. 55).
59. *Ibid.*

Still in the 2014 Country Report, the Commission went on to propose 'the introduction of a mutually agreed temporary opt-out from the collective agreement, when a firm is facing economic difficulties'.[60] This policy was considered so important that it was included in the CSRs for 2014, connected to a specific deadline: 'By September 2014, present proposals on mutually agreed firm-level temporary suspension of collective agreements and on a revision of the survival of collective agreements.'[61] One year later, in the 2015 CSRs, the Council decided to put forward the 'classic theme' of wage bargaining decentralisation, for the usual purpose of promoting 'the alignment of wages and productivity ... taking into account differences in skills and local labour market conditions as well as divergences in economic performance across regions, sectors and companies'.[62]

Portugal has been extremely reactive to all the above-mentioned recommendations. The 2014 Act (No. 55/2014) has made it possible to suspend collective agreements when companies are in crisis. The request for a 'greater dynamism' has been addressed by reducing the after-effect period from eighteen to twelve months and the validity of successive renewal clauses from five to three years.

As for the results of the reform process undertaken, when collective bargaining recovered from the decline recorded during the adjustment programme, it presented nearly half of the number of sectoral agreements in force in 2008, and almost the same small number level of firm-level agreements (not exceeding a hundred).[63] At the end of the day, the degree of decentralisation of collective bargaining, achieved by the extraordinary measures put in place under the bailout programme and then the ordinary cycle of EEG, has not been as pronounced as the growth of individual arrangements of working conditions.[64] In practice, rather than just simply prompting a decentralisation of collective bargaining – probably an unrealistic target considered the limited capacity of Portuguese firms to engage in collective bargaining[65] – the unstated objective, or

60. *Ibid.*, 28.
61. Council Recommendation on the National Reform Programme 2014 of Portugal and delivering a Council opinion on the Stability Programme of Portugal, 2014 (2014/C 247/20), https://eur-lex.europa.eu/legal-content/EN/TXT/?uri=CELEX%3A52014DC0423 (accessed 22 October 2019).
62. Council Recommendation on the 2015 National Reform Programme of Portugal and delivering a Council opinion on the 2015 Stability Programme of Portugal (2015/C 272/25), https://eur-lex.europa.eu/legal-content/EN/TXT/?uri=CELEX%3A32015H0818%2826%29 (accessed 24 April 2019).
63. Compare data included in UGT, Relatório Anual da Negociação Coletiva – 2014 above (n. 52) and UGT, Relatório Anual da Negociação Coletiva – 2018, https://www.crlaborais.pt/documents/10182/13326/CRL+-+Relatório+Anual+NC+-+2017+ +%28versão+atualizada+em+08.08.2018%29/2f65f793-0178-4a7a-8bed-2a01d01e0b85 (accessed 24 April 2019). In 2008, 173 industry-level and 95 company-level collective agreements were concluded, whereas in 2018 only 98 industry-level and 96 at the firm-level agreements.
64. Távora & González Tabora (n. 49) 262.
65. Fernando Rocha & Alan Stoleroff, *The Challenges of the Crisis and the External Intervention in Portugal*, in *The New EU Economic Governance and Its Impact on the National Collective*

maybe just unintentional, of the State intervention under the auspices of the EEG has been that of jeopardising collective autonomy and its regulatory capacity in favour of managerial unilateralism.[66]

6.5 THE ACHIEVEMENTS OF THE EEG

6.5.1 The Legal Changes under the 'Implicit' Conditionality

The description of the reforms undertaken by France, Italy and Portugal in response to the recommendations coming from the EU has shown a high commitment of national governments and legislations to the EEG. Under the EU guidance, national legislations have intervened to steer collective bargaining and more in general the hierarchy of sources towards a more desirable, in the opinion of the EU, configuration. This has given rise to 'uncoordinated' priority to the company-level agreement, out of any principle of favour, for the purpose of providing companies with the ability to deviate from general standard of employment protection provided by higher-level agreements and even by the statutes.[67] The switch to a new institutional set-up of the sources of employment regulation took place even where the system of industrial relations was historically based on strong voluntarism, like in Italy.

The system of 'ordinary' economic governance has therefore proven to be very effective. Its reinforcement undertaken with the so-called 2011 Six-Pack has worked, thanks, probably, to the spectre of sanctions for the case Member States under the 'corrective arms' persistently departed from the course indicated by the EU institutions.

A mechanism, therefore, based on 'implicit' conditionality.[68] Whereas 'explicit' conditionality is related to the case of bailout countries, for which expected behaviours and related sanctions for non-compliance were expressly formalised in the MoUs, 'implicit' conditionality is otherwise based on the understanding that in case of non-compliance with certain expected behaviours there may be consequences. The precondition is an underlying asymmetry of power, created by the mentioned threat of sanctions or by the promise of financial support, in order to avoid the strict 'explicit' conditionality which the

Bargaining Systems: Final Report 158 (2014), https://www.fondazionedivittorio.it/sites/default/files/content-attachment/GOCOBA_Final%20report.pdf (accessed 24 April 2019).

66. Cruces, Álvarez, Trillo & Leonardi (n. 20) 107-108.
67. R. Perdersini, *Conclusions and outlook. More challenges and some opportunities for industrial relations in the European Union* (Salvo Leonardi, Roberto Pedersini, eds), *Multi-employer bargaining under pressure – Decentralisation trends in five European countries* 291 (ETUI 2018).
68. S. Sacchi, *Conditionality by Other Means: EU Involvement in Italy's Structural Reforms in the Sovereign Debt Crisis*, 13 *Comparative European Politics*, 77 (2015).

IMF (or Troika) assistance would require.[69] This has made the EEG a sort of 'hybrid' legal system, 'a step away from ... a purely soft law mechanism'.[70]

6.5.2 The Changes in Actual Practice: The Resistance of Social Partners

While is true that the economic governance has permitted to the EU institutions to achieve the desired change of national institutional frameworks, nonetheless it has not always been able to achieve the desired results in practice, because of the resistance of national social partners. In the wake of the mentioned shifting economic paradigms (above section 6.3), social partners, to a different extent in the different countries, have tried to govern the stream of change. In doing so, they sometimes opposed their solutions to that put forward by the legislation under the control of the EEG.

That was the case of the recent legislative reforms in France, aimed at stimulating company-level derogation to standards established by sectoral agreements, negotiable even without the involvement of trade unions. They have not produced the expected results. Trade unions kept being involved in negotiations at the firm level, and the worsening of employment standards provided by industry-level agreements, including a reduction of labour costs, has not normally taken place.[71] So far, the actors of collective bargaining, including employers, have decided not to take advantage of the tools made available by the new legislative framework, probably because they do not really need them.[72]

This is clearly confirmed by data collected by the French Ministry of Labour.[73] The large majority of company agreements are still signed by union delegates or employees mandated by trade unions. As for the number of company agreements, after the significant increase between the 1980s and the 2010s, boosted by the Auroux Law of 1982, imposing for the first time mandatory company negotiation in unionised companies, and by the Aubry laws of 1998 and 2000, allowing company bargaining on working time reductions, the

69. *Ibid.*, 83. *See also* A. Steinbach, *EU Economic Governance after the Crisis: Revisiting the Accountability Shift in EU Economic Governance*, A Gwilym Gibbon Centre for Public Policy Working Paper (2018), https://www.nuffield.ox.ac.uk/media/2664/2018-07-eu-economic-governance-after-the-crisis.pdf (accessed 24 April 2019).
70. P. Pecinovsky, *EU Economic Governance and the Right to Collective Bargaining. Part 1. Standard and Extreme Governance and the Indicators and Limits of the Right to Collective Bargaining*, 9 *European Labour Law Journal*, 274, 388 (2018). On the de fact binding nature of CSRs *see also* E. Menegatti, *Challenging the EU Downward Pressure on National Wage Policy*, 33 *International Journal of Comparative Labour Law and Industrial Relations*, 195, 210-213 (2017).
71. Rehfeldt & Vincent (n. 21) 182-184.
72. That is the assumption of Jean-Marie Pernot (n. 22) 101.
73. *See* the report produced by the Ministère du Travail – Direction de l'animation de la recherche, des études et des statistiques, *Bilans de la négociation collective par la Commission nationale de la négociation collective* (2018), https://travail-emploi.gouv.fr/IMG/pdf/bnc_2018-hd-web.pdf (accessed 24 April 2019).

number of collective agreements signed from 2012 to 2017 is similar to that of 2000.

National legislation has opened up to 'uncoordinated' decentralisation also in Italy, fostering 'proximity' collective bargaining as an open alternative to statutory and industry-level regulation outside of any delegation and favour principle. However, the (most representative) social partners have managed to resist the pressure coming from the EEG, still keeping a certain degree of coordination over company-level bargaining.[74] To this end, they expressly and quite successfully committed all their structures, at any level, not to take advantage of the potentially disruptive 'proximity' agreements.[75] The industry-level agreements signed after 2011 respected this instruction when they regulated the opening clauses, maintaining a coordination over decentralised collective bargaining.[76]

The action of the social partners, embracing their own decentralisation process parallel to that of the legislator, has therefore helped to reduce the impact of the mentioned and unprecedented legislative intrusions in industrial relations. Since the model of coordinated collective bargaining provided by social partners has been able to grant to companies a fair degree of flexibility, company-level collective agreements have rarely resorted to the harsh flexibility admitted by legislations.

However, the main current problem regarding the layers of employment regulations in Italy does not concern the process of decentralisation of collective bargaining. If we look at the figures provided by a recent survey,[77] the coverage of the second-level agreement has actually decreased from around 34% in 2005 to 27% in 2015, whereas the coverage of industry-level agreements is around 93%, higher than that usually estimated by OECD.[78] Behind this apparently reassuring figures is hidden the most striking problem for the Italian framework of employment regulation sources: the increasing number of industry-level collective agreements signed by scarcely representative organisations (so-called pirate agreements), aiming at making available to companies wages lower and employment conditions weaker than those provided by 'mainstream' collective

74. Leonardi, Ambra & Ciarini (n. 39) 200-201.
75. This clause has been included in an amendment to the Economy-Wide agreement of June 2011. Apparently they have been of their words, since il ricorso alle deroghe ex Article 8 risulterebbe finora molto contenuto (Cisl 2013; Toma- setti 2015; Banca d'Italia 2013.
76. Leonardi, Ambra & Ciarini (n. 39) 197. However, Massimo Pallini, cit., 4 has a totally different opinion, believing that despite the efforts, the 'chaos reigns'.
77. *See* INAPP (National Institute for Public Policy Analysis) – RIL (Longitudinal Detection on Labour and Enterprises) survey, https://inapp.org/it/dati/ril (accessed 24 April 2019), analysed by Bergamante, Marocco (n. 20).
78. OECD, *Collective Bargaining in OECD and accession countries*, http://www.oecd.org/employment/collective-bargaining.htm (accessed 24 April 2019).

agreements.[79] A very effective instrument for achieving cost competitiveness, even more disruptive for the industrial relations system than uncoordinated company-level collective bargaining.

Even in Portugal, despite the legislative reforms undertaken under the extraordinary adjustment programme and the ordinary cycle of economic governance, company-level agreements have not much increased their presence. They were really rare before the crisis and they are still very rare in 2018.[80] In a productive fabric where very small companies are hugely overrepresented, the activation of firm-level bargaining is just unrealistic. But even the number of sectoral collective agreements signed in 2018, after reaching their historic lows in 2003, has been only around one-third of that it used to be before the crisis. As for their coverage, estimates are rather conflicting.[81] Anyway, it looks like the drop in the number of sectoral collective agreements has not affected by the same proportion the share of workers covered. That probably because those workers not covered by new agreements are still covered by existing agreements, relying on the mentioned after-effect rule. Even if after the 2009 reform the expiration of agreements is an option that one of the parties of collective agreements may trigger, this has not happened very frequently because also employers are normally reluctant to let agreements expire.[82]

As anticipated, rather than promoting any sort of decentralisation of collective bargaining, the real effect of the changes in Portugal has been that of weakening collective bargaining at any level. This probably might depend on the already highlighted lack of a clear articulation between the different levels of collective bargaining and, more in general, on the characteristic of the Portuguese industrial relations system too reliant on institutional protections. Differently from France and Italy, social partners have not been able to control the centrifugal pressures, gradually moving the main source of employment regulation, from centralised collective bargaining and statutory law to individual contracting and managerial unilateralism.

79. Magnani (n. 46) 13, quotes the CNEL (National Council for Economics and Labour) census, which reports that in September 2017 there were 868 national level collective agreements, whereas in 2013 there were 561 and 396 in 2008. Not surprisingly, the increasing number of 'pirate' agreements goes hand in hand with the that of companies withdrawing from employers' associations, as confirmed by the survey quote above in n. 77. This has been made possible by the continued absence in Italy of a mechanism for the selection of bargaining players, notwithstanding the effort recently made by the most representative social partners.

80. *See* n. 63.

81. According to UGT, Relatório Anual da Negociação Coletiva – 2018, cit. above nt. 65, the number of workers covered by valid agreements had a slight decline during the crisis: from 83.5% to around 80%. OECD, Collective Bargaining in OECD and accession countries, http://www.oecd.org/employment/collective-bargaining.htm, embraces a more pessimist view, reporting that coverage dropped from 86% in 2008 until reaching 72% in 2015.

82. Távora & González Tabora (n. 49) 258.

6.6 CONCLUSIONS

Changing economic models have put the traditional hierarchy of labour law sources under stress. This is particularly true for those countries where employment regulation used to rely on strong centralised collective bargaining and the favour principle providing little room for derogation at the company level and even less for individual contracting and managerial unilateral decision.

Against this background, in some countries social partners have completely or partially lost the control of the undergoing transformation. National governments, supported (or forced) by the EEG, big companies and even 'non-mainstream' trade unions have successfully achieved disorganised decentralisation and invidualisation of employment regulation.

This is clearly placing in jeopardy the purpose of labour law and even its very existence. The increasing room for derogation to protections afforded by statutes and multi-employer collective bargaining might lead to the end of labour law itself, replaced with a general freedom of contract regime. We are not there yet, and probably not even close. National systems of industrial relations have demonstrated to be rather resistant to the external pressure, especially in France and Italy. By and large, the traditional set-up of the hierarchy of labour law sources has not been disrupted hitherto. In particular, industry-level collective bargaining seems still barycentric and many companies, especially small, seem willing to rely on the 'stability' which sectoral agreements are able to provide.

However, if we look at the overall trend, we can appreciate that the medium long-term trajectory is a neo-liberal convergence between the different systems. Industrial relations are reducing 'the constraints – in the form of labor law or collective regulation – acting on employers ... increas[ing] their ability to manage the workplace and their relationship with their employees as they please'.[83] This trend of 'marketisation' is inevitably leading to negative externalities: i.e., market forces are very keen on getting rid of Employment Protection Legislation and public pension schemes, not considering that these create workers anxiety about the future and people failing to acquire pensions, eventually leading to reduced consumptions and a lot of old people in extreme poverty situation.[84]

Collective bargaining has the capacity to mitigate these negative externalities by establishing arrangements which are able to provide substantive and procedural certainty for both workers and employers, and in particular greater

83. L. Baccaro, C. Howell, *A Common Neoliberal Trajectory: The Transformation of Industrial Relations in Advanced Capitalism*, 39 *Politics & Society* 521, 549 (2011) who gave particular emphasis to the decentralisation of collective bargaining, concluding that the resilience of national institutions to common challenges and trend is just surface.

84. C. Crouch, *Introduction: Labour Markets and Social Policy after the Crisis*, 20 *Transfer: European Review of Labour and Research*, 7, 9 (2014).

security for workers.[85] However, in order to ensure the sound functioning of collective bargaining, and more in general the maintenance of the traditional hierarchy of labour law sources based on the principle of favour, the social partners should be capable of a quick response to shifting economic paradigms, by governing the change, rather than opposing a counterproductive defence.

The best way of doing so is probably that of pursuing the trend, opened in the 1990s by the collective autonomy in many countries, towards 'organised' decentralisation.[86] According to empirical analysis, where the relationship between the different levels is coordinated by well-defined articulation mechanism, the labour market is more efficient[87] and the outcomes of collective bargaining are also consistent with the EU target of cost competitiveness.[88] This might require the intervention of the legislature, especially where systems based on strong voluntarism are no longer able to work properly, as in the case of Italy, in order to support the social partners' choices. Or where, again in the case of Italy, but also Portugal, mechanisms for stimulating second-level collective bargaining (at the territorial or firm-level) under trade unions' control are required in order to avoid managerial unilateralism.

BIBLIOGRAPHY

K. Armingeon &, L. Baccaro, *Political Economy of the Sovereign Debt Crisis: The Limits of Internal Devaluation*, 41 *Industrial Law Journal*, 254-256 (2012).

L. Baccaro &, C. Howell, *A Common Neoliberal Trajectory: The Transformation of Industrial Relations in Advanced Capitalism*, 39 *Politics & Society*, 521, 549 (2011).

F. Bergamante &, M. Marocco, *New European Economic Governance and Decentralisation of the Collective Bargaining Structure in Italy: Did It Work Out?*, 4 (2018), https://ssrn.com/abstract=3228590 (accessed 23 April 2019).

---

85. P. Marginson, M. Keune & D. Bohle, *Negotiating the Effects of Uncertainty? The Governance Capacity of Collective Bargaining under Pressure*, 20 *Transfer: European Review of Labour and Research*, 37, 39 (2014).
86. G.P. Cella, *Quale futuro per la contrattazione collettiva?*, 150 *Giornale di diritto del lavoro e di relazioni industriali*, 217, 226-229 (2016). For a recognition of the models of industrial relations based either on organised decentralisation or unorganised: *See* the analysis of F. Traxler, *Two logics of collective action in industrial relations* (Colin Crouch, Franz Traxler, eds), *Organized industrial relations in Europe: What future?* (Avebur 1995).
87. This is the conclusion of the OECD, *Employment Outlook 2018*, OECD Publishing, Paris, 73-122, showing that the employment rate is higher in system where collective bargaining is coordinated than in system entirely based on firm-level bargaining, or even centralised collective bargaining but weekly coordinated. Same conclusions are reached with specific regard to the weaker segments of the labour market: youth, women and low-skilled unemployment rates are much lower in coordinated bargaining systems.
88. These are the findings of the research conducted by F. Traxler & B. Brandl, *Collective Bargaining, Inter-Sectoral Heterogeneity and Competitiveness: A Cross-National Comparison of Macroeconomic Performance*, 50 *British Journal of Industrial Relations*, 73-98 (2012).

L. Bordogna &, R. Pedersini, *What Kind of Europeanization? How EMU Is Changing National Industrial Relations in Europe*, 146 *Giornale di Diritto del Lavoro e di Relazioni Industriali*, 184-187 (2015).

G.P. Cella, *Quale futuro per la contrattazione collettiva?*, 150 *Giornale di diritto del lavoro e di relazioni industriali*, 217, 226-229 (2016).

C. Crouch, *Introduction: Labour Markets and Social Policy after the Ccrisis*, 20 *Transfer: European Review of Labour and Research*, 7, 9 (2014).

J. Cruces, I. A., Francisco Trillo &, S. Leonardi, *Impact of the euro crisis on wages and collective bargaining in southern Europe: A comparison of Italy, Portugal and Spain* (Guy Van Gyes & Thorsten Schulten, eds), *Wage bargaining under the new European economic governance*, 93, 100 (ETUI 2015).

Maria da Paz Campos Lima, *EUROFOUND in Portugal: Decline in Collective Bargaining Reaches Critical Point* (2014), https://www.eurofound.europa.eu/publications/article/2014/portugal-decline-in-collective-bargaining-reaches-critical-point (accessed 24 April 2019).

T. Darcillon, *How Does Finance Affect Labor Market Institutions? An Empirical Analysis in 16 OECD Countries*, 13 *Socio-Economic Review*, 477 (2015).

M. do Rosário Palma Ramalho, *Portuguese Labour Law and Industrial Relations During the Crisis*, ILO Working Paper 54 (2013), https://www.ilo.org/wcmsp5/groups/public/---ed_dialogue/---dialogue/documents/publication/wcms_232798.pdf (accessed 24 April 2019).

European Commission, '*Scoreboard for the Surveillance on Macroeconomic Imbalances*,' European Economy Occasional Papers 92, 14 (2012).

B.T. Hirsch, *Sluggish Institutions in a Dynamic World: Can Unions and Industrial Competition Coexist?*, 22 *Journal of Economic Perspectives*, 153, 154 (2008).

Maarten Keune, *Wage Flexibilisation and the Minimum Wage*, in *Industrial Relations in Europe*, 127 (Publications Office of the European Union 2010).

Salvo Leonardi, Maria Concetta Ambra &, Andrea Ciarini, *Italian Collective Bargaining at a Turning Point* (Salvo Leonardi & Roberto Pedersini, eds), *Multi-Employer Bargaining under Pressure: Decentralisation Trends in Five European Countries*, 185, 193 (ETUI 2018).

M. Magnani, *The Role of Collective Bargaining in Italian Labour Law*, 7 *Labour Studies*, 13 (2018).

Paul Marginson &, Christian Welz, *Changes to Wage-Setting Mechanisms in the Context of the Crisis and the EU's New Economic Governance Regime*, 24 (Eurofound 2014).

P. Marginson, *Coordinated Bargaining in Europe: From Incremental Corrosion to Frontal Assault?*, 21 *European Journal of Industrial Relations* 97, 99 (2015).

P. Marginson, M. Keune &, D. Bohle, *Negotiating the Effects of Uncertainty? The Governance Capacity of Collective Bargaining under Pressure*, 20 *Transfer: European Review of Labour and Research*, 37, 39 (2014).

M. Pallini, *Italian Industrial Relations: Toward a Strongly Decentralized Collective Bargaining*, 38 *Comparative Labor Law & Policy Journal*, 1, 2 (2016).

P. Pecinovsky, *EU Economic Governance and the Right to Collective Bargaining: Part 1. Standard and Extreme Governance and the Indicators and Limits of the Right to Collective Bargaining*, 9 *European Labour Law Journal*, 274, 388 (2018).

Roberto Perdersini, *Conclusions and Outlook. More Challenges and Some Opportunities for Industrial Relations in the European Union* (Salvo Leonardi & Roberto Pedersini, eds), *Multi-Employer Bargaining under Pressure: Decentralisation Trends in Five European Countries*, 291 (ETUI 2018).

Jean-Marie Pernot, *France and the European Agenda: An Ambiguous Impact on Industrial Relations*, in *The New EU Economic Governance and Its Impact on the National Collective Bargaining Systems: Final Report* 100 (2014), https://www.fondazionedivittorio.it/sites/default/files/content-attachment/GOCOBA_Final%20report.pdf (accessed 23 April 2019).

G.A. Recchia, *The Future of Collective Bargaining in Italy Between Legislative Reforms and Social Partners' Responses*, 23 *Transfer: European Review of Labour and Research*, 457, 458 (2017).

Udo Rehfeldt &, Catherine Vincent, *The Decentralisation of Collective Bargaining in France: An Escalating Process* (Salvo Leonardi & Roberto Pedersini, eds), *Multi-Employer Bargaining under Pressure: Decentralisation Trends in Five European Countries*, 151 (ETUI 2018).

Fernando Rocha &, Alan Stoleroff, *The Challenges of the Crisis and the External Intervention in Portugal*, in *The New EU Economic Governance and Its Impact on the National Collective Bargaining Systems: Final Report* 158 (2014), https://www.fondazionedivittorio.it/sites/default/files/content-attachment/GOCOBA_Final%20report.pdf (accessed 24 April 2019).

S. Sacchi, *Conditionality by Other Means: EU Involvement in Italy's Structural Reforms in the Sovereign Debt Crisis*, 13 *Comparative European Politics*, 77 (2015).

Isabelle Schömann, *Collective Labour Law under Attack: How Anti-crisis Measures Dismantle Workers' Collective Rights*, 2 ETUI Policy Brief (2014), https://www.etui.org/Publications2/Policy-Briefs/European-Economic-Employment-and-Social-Policy/Collective-labour-law-under-attack-how-anti-crisis-measures-dismantle-workers-collective-rights (accessed 23 April 2019).

T. Schulten &, T. Müller, *A New European Interventionism? The Impact of the New European Economic Governance on Wages and Collective Bargaining*

(David Natali & Bart Vanhercke, eds), *Social developments in the European Union*, 186 (ETUI 2012).

A. Steinbach, *EU Economic Governance after the Crisis: Rrevisiting the Accountability Shift in EU Economic Governance*, A Gwilym Gibbon Centre for Public Policy Working Paper (2018), https://www.nuffield.ox.ac.uk/media/2664/2018-07-eu-economic-governance-after-the-crisis.pdf (accessed 24 April 2019).

I. Távora &, P. González Tabora, *Labour Market Regulation and Collective Bargaining in Portugal During the Crisis: Continuity and Cchange*, 22 *European Journal of Industrial Relations*, 251, 256 (2016).

F. Traxler &, B. Brandl, *Collective Bargaining, Inter-Sectoral Heterogeneity and Competitiveness: A Cross-National Comparison of Macroeconomic Performance*, 50 *British Journal of Industrial Relations*, 73-98 (2012).

Franz Traxler, *Two Logics of Collective Action in Industrial Relations* (Colin Crouch & Franz Traxler, eds), *Organized Industrial Relations in Europe: What Future?* (Avebur 1995).

J. Visser, *Wage Bargaining Institutions-From Crisis to Crisis*, 488 *European Economy-Economic Papers* (2013), https://ec.europa.eu/economy_finance/publications/economic_paper/2013/pdf/ecp488_en.pdf (accessed 23 April 2019).

Gaetano Zilio Grandi, *Collective Bargaining* (Franco Carinci & Emanuele Menegatti, eds), *Labour Law and Industrial Relations in Italy*, Chapter. XV (Wolters Kluwer 2015).

Part II National Reports

CHAPTER 7

Australia's Layered and Evolving System of Labour Regulation

Andrew Stewart & Mark Bray

7.1 INTRODUCTION

Australia has long been recognised for its distinctive approach to labour regulation – in particular, its use of compulsory arbitration by public tribunals during the twentieth century to resolve interests disputes over wages and working conditions.[1] Even after a shift in the 1990s to more autonomous collective bargaining, tribunals have continued to set minimum standards. Where other countries have predominantly relied on legislation and collective bargaining to establish minimum employment standards, Australia has had a third major source: a network of awards governing particular industries, occupations or enterprises. Many countries have delegated the power to set minimum wages to officials or agencies. But the sheer scale and depth of the regulation embodied in Australian awards, including thousands of different minimum wage rates that depend on the nature of the work and when it is performed, have little if any parallel elsewhere.[2]

The coexistence of awards with legislation, collective bargaining, employment contracts and other sources has made for an extremely complex system. It has also gone through much change over the past thirty years, as the political pendulum has swung between two major forces: the pro-worker Australian

1. *See*, e.g., R. Freeman, *Learning from Other Economies: The Unique Institutional and Policy Experiments Down Under*, 82 Econ. Record, 195 (2006).
2. New Zealand used to have a similar system of labour arbitration but has not had awards since 1991: *see*, e.g., M. Bray & E. Rasmussen, *Developments in Comparative Employment Relations in Australia and New Zealand: Reflecting on 'Accord and Discord'*, 28 Lab. & Indus., 31 (2018).

Labor Party, with strong links to the country's trade union movement; and the pro-business coalition of two conservative parties, the Liberal and National Parties (LNP). These parties have initiated a number of waves of labour law reform.

One consistent trend over this period has been a progressive centralisation of legislative authority.[3] Australia is a federation, comprising the Commonwealth of Australia, six States and a number of Territories. Its Constitution has no clear demarcation of legislative authority over labour matters, other than to ensure that valid federal (Commonwealth) laws take precedence over State or Territory laws in the event of inconsistency. For much of the twentieth century, the States had their own arbitration and award systems that coexisted with those of the Commonwealth. But more creative use of federal powers and an intergovernmental agreement reached in 2009 have altered that. The main federal labour statute, the Fair Work Act 2009 (FW Act), now regulates employment conditions and labour relations for all private sector (i.e., non-governmental) employers. The only exception is in Western Australia, although even there all companies (and most employees) are covered by the federal statute. Of the four other States that have retained arbitration systems, these apply only to State (and in some cases local) government workers. That said, there are important exceptions to the pattern of federal dominance. The regulation of work health and safety, workers compensation, training and child labour, for instance, are all matters that, even under the FW Act, are primarily left to the States and Territories. Discrimination is another matter on which federal, State and Territory laws can and do coexist.

In the remainder of the chapter, we start by providing a broad overview in section 7.2 of the role played in Australia by the following sources of labour regulation:

- constitutional norms;
- legislation;
- delegated legislation, including awards;
- collective agreements;
- statutory individual agreements;
- the common law (judge-made law);
- soft law (non-binding, quasi-legal instruments).

We also outline some of the key 'interaction rules' governing the relationship of these sources. Section 7.3 then explains how the use of those sources has varied over time, by reference to what in previous work we have identified as

3. As to what follows, *see* generally Andrew Stewart et al., *Creighton & Stewart's Labour Law*, Chapters. 5-6 (6th ed., Federation Press 2016).

five distinct periods (or 'regimes') of federal labour regulation.[4] From there, section 7.4 highlights important trends in the evolution of Australian labour law, before section 7.5 explores in more detail three distinctive features of the Australian model. Besides awards, these are the availability and use of what in most other countries would be regarded as an oxymoron, a non-union collective agreement, and the complexity created by the layering of so many different types of regulatory instrument. Section 7.6 contains a brief conclusion.

We should clarify that our main focus is on the regulation of employment relationships, rather than other forms of labour (such as independent contracting or voluntary work). Nor do we consider some of the issues that bear on the broader question of labour market regulation, such as migration controls, occupational licensing, taxation and so on. We also generally concentrate on federal regulation, given the broad coverage of the FW Act.

7.2 SOURCES OF AUSTRALIAN LABOUR LAW: AN OVERVIEW

7.2.1 Constitutional Norms

Australia's Constitution, unlike its counterparts in some other countries, has nothing directly to say about labour standards.[5] Nor does it formally enshrine human rights that might be asserted in an employment context. The High Court of Australia has recognised a freedom of communication on political matters that is said to be implicit in the Constitution's establishment of a system of representative and democratic government. This has been invoked to invalidate overly broad legislative restrictions on, among other things, the disclosure of information by public servants, the conduct of workplace protests or the funding of political campaigns by trade unions.[6] But the 'freedom' operates purely as a restraint on legislative power: it is not a 'personal right' that individuals or corporations can claim or assert in resolving private disputes.[7]

4. *See* M. Bray & A. Stewart, *What Is Distinctive about the Fair Work Regime?*, 26 Aust. J. Lab. L., 20 (2013).
5. Section 51(xxxv) does authorise the Commonwealth legislature to establish a system for the conciliation and arbitration of labour disputes that cross State boundaries. But while this provision provided the primary basis during the twentieth century for federal labour law, other constitutional powers have since been used to expand the federal system. Today, no part of the FW Act depends on section 51(xxxv) for its validity: *see* Stewart et al. (n. 3) 100-104.
6. *See*, respectively, *Bennett v. President, Human Rights and Equal Opportunity Commission* (2003) 204 ALR 119; *Brown v. Tasmania* (2017) 261 CLR 328; *Unions NSW v. New South Wales* (2019) 93 ALJR 166.
7. *Comcare v. Banerji* (2019) 93 ALJR 900. The same is true of section 116 of the Constitution, which seeks to ensure both freedom of and from religion.

7.2.2 Legislation

Besides delegating authority to create or adjust rights, as discussed in the next section, there are many different ways in which Australian legislation acts as a source of labour regulation. In substantive terms, these include:

- imposing minimum terms and conditions for the employment of workers;
- prohibiting employers, workers or unions from engaging in certain types of conduct, such as discriminating against a person because of their race, gender and union membership;
- permitting conduct that might otherwise be unlawful: for example, to take or organise certain forms of industrial action;
- laying down detailed rules as to the conduct expected of government employees;[8] and
- regulating the formation and internal affairs of unions or employer associations that choose to register under industrial statutes and thereby gain certain privileges.

Legislation is also an important source of procedural regulation, for example, by mandating or otherwise regulating the processes for the making of a collective agreement, or for the conduct of court or tribunal proceedings

Since federal legislation operates with overriding force, subject to the limits imposed by the Constitution, it will generally prevail over any of the types of legal instrument discussed below, including awards, collective agreements and individual employment contracts. In principle, awards and collective agreements made or given effect under federal law are capable of ousting State or Territory statutes, to the extent of any inconsistency. But as noted earlier, the FW Act makes the operation of federal awards and agreements subject to the pre-emptive effect of State and Territory laws on matters such as discrimination, workers compensation or health and safety.

7.2.3 Delegated Legislation

It is common in Australia for legislation to delegate to the executive government the power to make detailed rules and regulations that supplement the main statutory provisions. These are typically subject to disallowance by one or other of the legislative chambers (usually in practice the upper one, since the

8. As to the differences between public and private sector regulation, *see* Stewart et al. (n. 3) 269-273. Where not otherwise indicated, the rules and processes described in this chapter generally apply to private and public sector employment alike.

government of the day usually controls the lower or popularly elected one).[9] The Fair Work Regulations 2009 (Cth), for instance, prescribe the matters on which employers must keep records or the forms that must be used for various processes stipulated by the FW Act.

What is perhaps more notable in relation to labour law, however, is the extent to which industrial tribunals such as the federal Fair Work Commission (FWC) are given delegated powers not just to control their own procedures, but to set or adjust rights and obligations for employers and workers. The FW Act empowers the FWC, for instance, to:

- set and annually review a minimum wage for award/agreement-free employees (s. 285);
- determine that an ex-employee has been dismissed harshly, unjust or unreasonably and, to ensure 'a fair go all round', order that they be either reinstated or compensated (Pt 3-2);
- issue a bargaining order to regulate the process for negotiating an 'enterprise agreement' (a registered collective agreement), in particular to ensure that bargaining takes place in good faith (ss 229-233); or
- suspend or terminate what is otherwise 'protected' (lawful) industrial action (ss 423-428).

The most far-reaching power delegated to the FWC, however, is the one already mentioned: to make or vary awards.[10] These instruments, which in practice almost exclusively impose obligations on employers, are sometimes framed to cover a single enterprise. But more commonly today, they operate on a 'common rule' basis, applying to specified types of employer when hiring employees in categories or 'classifications' set out in the award. Although there are no definitive statistics, it is likely that between 70 and 80% of current employees are covered by an award. Most of those excluded are managerial or professional workers.

Awards operate with the force of legislation. Any failure to comply can result in a court imposing a monetary penalty, and/or (among other things) ordering the rectification of any underpayment. An award can be overridden by the terms of a registered collective agreement, of the type discussed below. But that bare statement masks what has been a changing pattern of interaction between the two types of instrument. More is said about that in section 7.3.

7.2.4 Collective Agreements

The changing role and significance of collective agreements in Australia are also explained in more detail in section 7.3. For now, it suffices to say that such

9. *See*, e.g., Legislation Act 2003 (Cth) Chapter 3 Pt 2.
10. Part 2-5 of the FW Act also allows the FWC to make 'workplace determinations' to resolve bargaining disputes, but only in very limited situations.

agreements may take one of two forms. The great majority today are made in accordance with a statutory process and formally registered with an industrial tribunal. Registration requires the tribunal to be satisfied that various criteria are met, concerning both the negotiation and content of the agreement. An agreement may cover one or more employers, although for reasons explained below most current agreements cover all or part of a single enterprise. As with awards, their operation is usually confined to non-managerial employees. Even when negotiated by a trade union, they will typically cover union members and non-members alike.

A registered agreement operates with statutory force, rather than as a contract[11] and can be enforced in the same way as an award. It sets wages and conditions not just for existing employees, but workers hired in the future who fall within its classifications. Registered agreements must have a nominal duration. When an agreement reaches its 'expiry date', it continues in force but becomes easier to terminate or replace. In recent years, registered agreements have covered up to 40% of the workforce, though there has been a recent fall-off in coverage, due to factors that include falling union membership and employer resistance.[12]

Collective agreements can also be, and sometimes are, made outside the type of statutory framework just described. In principle, such unregistered agreements can take effect at common law as contracts. But it is far from clear that they satisfy the ordinary requirements for a binding contract.[13] Nor can they override an award or alter the operation of either a labour statute or the registered agreements made under it.[14] There have been instances in which, just as in the United Kingdom (UK), the terms of an unregistered collective agreement have been found to be impliedly incorporated into (and enforceable as part of) the employment contracts of affected workers.[15] But this does not appear to be common in practice.

7.2.5 Statutory Individual Agreements

Since 1996, federal labour law has provided for some form of individual agreement which, when made in accordance with statutory procedures, operates with the force of legislation. The most notorious example of these,

11. *Toyota Motor Corp Australia Ltd v. Marmara* (2014) 222 FCR 152 at [89]-[90].
12. Alison Pennington, *On the Brink: The Erosion of Enterprise Agreement Coverage in Australia's Private Sector* (Centre for Future Work 2018). As to the general impact of the FW Act on collective bargaining, *see* Shae McCrystal, Breen Creighton & Anthony Forsyth (eds), *Collective Bargaining under the Fair Work Act* (Federation Press 2018).
13. *See*, e.g., *Ryan v. Textile, Clothing & Footwear Union of Australia* [1996] 2 VR 235.
14. *See*, e.g., *John Holland Group Pty Ltd v. Automotive, Food, Metals, Engineering, Printing and Kindred Industries Union* (2011) 34 VR 635.
15. Stewart et al. (n. 3) 293-294.

Australian Workplace Agreements (AWAs), is discussed in section 7.3. At their height, they covered 7% of employees and could override both awards and registered collective agreements. The FW Act no longer provides for such agreements. But it does require both awards and enterprise agreements to permit the making of 'individual flexibility arrangements', which can vary the operation of selected provisions in the main instrument, as they apply to a particular worker. In practice, not many of these are made. When they are used, research indicates that they are often imposed by employers as a condition of employment, despite this being forbidden by the legislation.[16]

7.2.6 The Common Law

To the extent that it is not displaced by legislation or industrial instruments, the common law plays an important role in regulating employment relations in Australia. For example, almost all forms of collective action are unlawful as a matter of common law. While statutory rights to form trade unions and take 'protected' (lawful) industrial action have helped overcome that, it is still possible for unprotected strikes or work bans to attract civil liability under what are called the 'industrial torts'. These are actions that seek to protect people and (more especially) businesses from the intentional and wrongful infliction of economic loss.[17] A range of other common law principles or causes of action may also impact on employment relations. These include the doctrine of restraint of trade, which (among other things) invalidates unreasonable fetters on the freedom of workers to move between employers or establish businesses of their own.[18]

The most significant role of the common law, however, is to provide the legal framework for the operation and enforcement of individual employment contracts.[19] The existence of such a contract, whether made verbally or in writing, is usually a prerequisite to the operation of labour standards set by legislation, awards or collective agreements. In other words, these standards only apply to workers considered at common law to be employees. The terms expressly agreed by the parties may also themselves be an important source of rights and obligations, especially (but not solely) for employees not covered by awards or registered collective agreements. Employment contracts often specify what is expected of employees by way of job performance and conduct, a subject less commonly covered by awards, collective agreements or (outside the public

16. Stewart et al. (n. 3) 330-333.
17. *See* Stewart et al. (n. 3) 953-963.
18. *See* Dyson Heydon, *The Restraint of Trade Doctrine* (3rd ed., LexisNexis Butterworths 2008).
19. *See* generally Mark Irving, *The Contract of Employment* (LexisNexis Butterworths 2012); Gordon Anderson, Douglas Brodie & Joellen Riley, *The Common Law Employment Relationship: A Comparative Study* (Edward Elgar 2017).

sector) legislation. That said, many employers who have adopted detailed policies, procedures or codes of conduct now avoid formally incorporating them into individual contracts, for fear of being found liable for not meeting their own commitments as to the fair treatment of employees.[20] Employers who do this can still rely on such documents to inform the scope and content of each employee's general duty to comply with lawful and reasonable instructions as to the performance of their duties.[21]

The common law also plays an important role in supplying default rules for the employment contract, in the form of implied terms. These terms will be taken to be part of each employment contract, unless excluded by, or otherwise inconsistent with, any express terms.[22] For example, if the parties have not agreed on the duration of a job, it will be implied that either party can end the employment by giving reasonable notice.[23] It is also implied that each party will take reasonable care not to cause injury or damage to the other, that they will not disclose or misuse any confidential information belonging to the other party, that employees will perform their duties faithfully and obediently, etc. The recognition of such terms would seem to require a policy decision. But while some courts are prepared to accept that,[24] the High Court in recent years has insisted that new terms will be implied in law only when strictly 'necessary' to make a contract workable. In *Commonwealth Bank of Australia v. Barker*,[25] this narrow view led it to refuse to follow English law in recognising a general duty on both parties – but more especially the employer – to maintain 'mutual trust and confidence' in the employment relationship.

Perhaps surprisingly, Australian labour statutes do not tend to be explicit about the relationship between an employment contract and statutory standards, awards or registered collective agreements.[26] Indeed there has at times

20. For examples of such liability, *see Goldman Sachs JB Were Services Pty Ltd v. Nikolich* (2007) 163 FCR 62; *Romero v. Farstad Shipping (Indian Pacific) Pty Ltd* (2014) 231 FCR 403. Compare *Yousif v. Commonwealth Bank of Australia* (2010) 193 IR 212, where the relevant policies were expressly stated *not* to be incorporated into the employee's contract. Clauses of this kind are now common.
21. *Downe v. Sydney West Area Health Service (No 2)* (2008) 71 NSWLR 633, [342]. Even where such a general duty is not expressed in an employment contract, it will be implied by the common law, as discussed below.
22. *Byrne v. Australian Airlines Ltd* (1995) 185 CLR 410, 449-450. Such default terms are said to be 'implied in law' into all contracts, or all contracts of a particular class. Terms may also be implied 'in fact', to reflect the presumed intentions of the parties to a particular contract or implied to give effect to a custom or usage in a trade or region. But in practice, the tests for such implication are hard to satisfy: *see* Stewart et al. (n. 3) 280-281.
23. Whether such a term can be implied in the face of an award or statutory provision prescribing a minimum period of notice is a matter of some contention: *see Heldberg v. Rand Transport (1986) Pty Ltd* (2018) 280 IR 93, [95]-[106].
24. *See*, e.g., *University of Western Australia v. Gray* (2009) 179 FCR 346, [136]-[142].
25. (2014) 253 CLR 169. For discussion, *see* G. Golding, *Terms Implied by Law into Employment Contracts: Are They Necessary?*, 28 Aust. J. Lab. L., 113 (2015); and the various articles in 32(1) Int. J. Comp. Lab. L. & Indus. Rel. (2016).
26. For limited exceptions, *see* FW Act sections 128, 326.

been extensive debate and uncertainty over this issue.[27] Nevertheless, it is generally understood that while it is unlawful for a contract to provide wages or entitlements that are inferior to the minimum imposed by legislation or an industrial instrument (an award or registered agreement),[28] it is permissible to negotiate higher pay, or other contractual terms which are more beneficial to the employee.[29] It has also been held that the terms of an applicable award or registered agreement will not automatically be treated as part of any contract regulated by that instrument. Hence a breach of the instrument will not normally constitute a breach of contract.[30] An employer and employee may expressly agree that the terms of an instrument will have contractual effect.[31] But such an intent will not usually be inferred merely because a contract states that a worker's employment is 'governed by' or 'subject to' an award or registered collective agreement.[32]

7.2.7 Soft Law

The concept of regulation extends more widely than legally enforceable rules. For example, governments may seek to use their funding or purchasing power to influence employment relations, even in the private sector, by requiring compliance with certain standards. Historically such initiatives were generally associated with a desire to raise conditions. But the most notable recent examples in Australia have had a very different purpose, that of persuading building employers who want to undertake state-funded construction work to push back against both unlawful and (in some cases) lawful attempts by unions to negotiate favourable agreements.[33]

---

27. *See, e.g.*, G. Tolhurst, *Contractual Confusion and Industrial Illusion: A Contract Law Perspective on Awards, Collective Agreements and the Contract of Employment*, 66 Aust. L.J., 705 (1992).
28. *See, e.g.*, *Kronen v. Commercial Motor Industries Pty Ltd* (2008) 171 FCR 521; *Fair Work Ombudsman v. Glasshouse Mountains Tavern Pty Ltd* [2014] FCCA 1115.
29. *Kilminster v. Sun Newspapers Ltd* (1931) 46 CLR 284; *Shop Distributive and Allied Employees' Association v. Karellas Investments Pty Ltd (No 2)* (2007) 166 IR 51. It is less clear, however, whether a contract can derogate from a right granted to an employer by a registered agreement, even if that would be beneficial to the employee: *see* Stewart et al. (n. 3) 292-293, discussing *Visscher v. Giudice* (2009) 239 CLR 361.
30. *Byrne v. Australian Airlines Ltd* (1995) 185 CLR 410; *Soliman v. University of Technology, Sydney* (2009) 191 IR 277.
31. *See, e.g.*, *True v. Amalgamated Collieries of WA Ltd* (1939) 62 CLR 451, 455-456.
32. *See, e.g.*, *Australian Workers Union v. BHP Iron Ore Pty Ltd* (2001) 106 FCR 482; *Gramotnev v. Queensland University of Technology* [2015] QCA 127.
33. *See* A. Forsyth, *'Restoring the Rule of Law' Through Commercial (Dis)incentives: The Code for the Tendering and Performance of Building Work 2016*, 40 Syd. L. Rev., 121 (2018).

7.3 A CHANGING MIX OF SOURCES[34]

In the sections that follow, we trace changes in both the role of different sources and some of the rules governing their interaction, over the course of five distinct federal labour law regimes. In section 7.4 below we go on to summarise some of the more important trends.

7.3.1 The Arbitration System, Pre-1993

Under the arbitration system that operated for the bulk of the twentieth century, pursuant to the Conciliation and Arbitration Act 1904 (Cth) and later the Industrial Relations Act 1988 (Cth), awards were regarded as the primary way of regulating employment conditions. Outside the public sector, few federal statutes directly set minimum standards, although State and Territory laws could and did deal with matters such as long service leave, discrimination, health and safety, workers compensation and training, even for workers covered by federal awards. Indeed their role in that regard has continued and, if anything, increased over the periods described below.

Collective bargaining between trade unions and either employer associations or larger employers was common before 1993, even if formalised agreements were rare. The content of awards was in practice often determined by negotiations between unions and employer representatives, with the tribunal issuing 'consent awards' or arbitrating only on unresolved matters. At the same time, however, those negotiations occurred 'in the shadow' of the tribunal's power to impose an outcome, and also to reject settlements that did not accord with its wages policies or broader view of the 'public interest'. Similarly, while stronger unions could and did directly negotiate 'over-award' payments or conditions with specific employers, such agreements could not conflict with or displace applicable awards. As noted earlier, these unregistered agreements were of uncertain legal status, although they were treated as binding as a matter of practice.

7.3.2 The Industrial Relations Reform Act, 1993-1996

In the late 1980s and early 1990s, key union leaders and the federal Labor government then in office became convinced that a more 'decentralised' approach to the setting of pay and conditions was necessary if Australian businesses were to be more productive and competitive in increasingly globalised markets. This was reflected in the Industrial Relations Reform Act 1993 (Cth),

34. For further details and supporting references for the summaries that follow, *see* Bray & Stewart (n. 4) 27-47.

which amended the 1988 Act to privilege enterprise-level bargaining as the main rule-making process, while retaining vestiges of the arbitral model.

Employers and unions could now apply to have agreements certified by the Australian Industrial Relations Commission (AIRC) if certain criteria were met. The AIRC could still reject a multi-business agreement on the basis that it was contrary to the 'public interest', but no such discretion applied to agreements for the whole or part of a single business. More contentiously, as far as unions were concerned, employers were given a new option of asking a group of their employees to approve an Enterprise Flexibility Agreement (EFA), even without union involvement. This had the same status as a union-negotiated agreement, though it was subject to additional procedural safeguards. For the first time too, employees were given a legal right to take 'protected' industrial action in support of an enterprise-level agreement. Strikes and other work bans had previously been common in practice, but almost invariably unlawful. Awards remained, though their role changed to that of providing a 'safety net' for enterprise bargaining. Although overridden to the extent of inconsistency with a certified agreement or EFA, awards could and did still apply on matters not dealt with by the agreement, as well as applying in full for workers not covered by any agreement. Importantly too, the AIRC had to be satisfied before approving an agreement that it did not disadvantage the affected employees compared to their award entitlements. This 'no-disadvantage test' ensured that if an agreement sought to derogate from certain award conditions, it would usually have to offer some compensating benefit – very often in the form of higher pay.

There was little increase in the role played by legislative standards, although the 1993 Act did introduce the first clear federal protections against unfair dismissal.

7.3.3 The Workplace Relations Act, 1996-2006

In 1996 the conservative LNP government led by John Howard introduced amendments which renamed the 1988 Act as the Workplace Relations Act 1996 (Cth), although it was forced into compromises to secure parliamentary support for its reforms. The agreement-making system was modified, with both non-union and union collective agreements now requiring a majority vote of support from affected employees.[35] An important new option, mentioned earlier, was for employers to make and register individual AWAs. These would entirely exclude the operation of awards and (in some situations) collective agreements, although once again AWAs had to leave employees no worse off overall than they

35. An exception here was that 'greenfields agreements' could be negotiated by employers and unions for a new business or project, in advance of employees being hired. For reasons of space, the following treatment excludes such agreements, which have been widely used for construction projects: *see* Stewart et al. (n. 3) 362-365.

would have been under a relevant award. The content of awards was also narrowed, while restrictions were imposed on the AIRC's power to arbitrate disputes.

It also became apparent, albeit belatedly, that the permissible content of statutory agreements was limited to matters that were considered to directly 'pertain' to the individual employment relationships regulated by the agreement. Narrow court interpretations of what constituted permissible content,[36] coupled with overt restrictions on agreement content later introduced by the 'Work Choices' amendments (*see* section 7.3.4 below), caused a resurgence in the use of unregistered collective agreements, which had largely died out after the 1993 reforms. Some unions used these 'side deals' to maintain what were often long-standing employer commitments on a range of 'non-pertaining' or prohibited content.[37] Their use has continued under the current FW Act, though they are less common because of that Act's slightly more liberal approach to the content of registered agreements.

7.3.4 The 'Work Choices' Regime, 2006-2009

After improving its parliamentary position at the 2004 federal election, the Howard Government introduced the Workplace Relations Amendment (Work Choices) Act 2005 (Cth). This distinctly neo-liberal legislation, which took effect in March 2006, did not abolish either awards or the AIRC but significantly downgraded their roles. The AIRC's general power to arbitrate disputes was removed, and it was tasked with 'rationalising' and simplifying awards through a process triggered and regulated by a formal direction from the Minister for Workplace Relations. Workplace agreements of all kinds, both individual and collective, would now displace the operation of any award – for some purposes with permanent effect, not just while an agreement was in place. Crucially, the no-disadvantage test was removed, so that collective agreements and AWAs could now quite lawfully undercut award standards. Employers could insist on new employees signing an AWA, and such agreements also now excluded the application of collective agreements in all situations.

The safety net role was instead left to the Australian Fair Pay and Conditions Standard, which for the first time at a federal level laid down minimum standards for the employment of all federal system employees, not just those covered by awards.[38] The Standard covered five matters: pay, maximum working hours, annual (recreational) leave, personal leave (including

36. *See*, e.g., *Electrolux Home Products Pty Ltd v. Australian Workers Union* (2004) 221 CLR 309.
37. *See* A. Stewart & J. Riley, *Working Around Work Choices: Collective Bargaining and the Common Law*, 31 Melb. U.L.R., 903 (2007).
38. Similar standards had in fact applied under Schedule 1A of the original Workplace Relations Act 1996, but only for certain workers in the State of Victoria.

sick leave) and parental leave. On wages, the primary entitlement was to any base rate of pay set by a relevant award,[39] or for non-award workers a national minimum wage. There were also separate standards relating to meal breaks, public holidays and notice of termination.

7.3.5 The Fair Work Act 2009

After the defeat of the Howard Government at the 2007 election, Labor moved to undo some, but by no means all, of the Work Choices changes. Under the FW Act, the concept of a statutory safety net for all national system employees was retained, in the form of the National Employment Standards. The process of rationalising (or 'modernising') awards, never actually started by the previous government, was undertaken by the AIRC, before that body's replacement by Fair Work Australia (as the FWC was originally called). The new tribunal was given more extensive authority to facilitate and supervise bargaining, though no general power to arbitrate disputes.

AWAs were abolished, and the primacy of collective agreements (now called enterprise agreements) was restored. The division between union and non-union agreements was removed, with all enterprise agreements now conceived as being made by employers with groups of their employees. In formal terms, the role of unions is no longer to make agreements, but to act as bargaining agents – and even union members can select other bargaining representatives if they wish. There were also still restrictions on the permissible content of agreements, though fewer than under Work Choices. And the safety net role of awards was restored, with enterprise agreements having to pass a 'better off overall test', a successor to the no-disadvantage test abolished by Work Choices. While multiple-enterprise agreements can be made without any special permission from the tribunal, the parties cannot be obliged to bargain in good faith, while industrial action cannot lawfully be taken in support of such an agreement. Furthermore, even if an employer is party to a multiple-enterprise agreement, it can escape that instrument by making a single-enterprise agreement of its own.

7.4 KEY TRENDS

Table 7.1, adapted from earlier work,[40] summarises the changing role and significance of the different sources of federal labour law over the five periods

39. The restriction to base rates of pay meant that the Standard did not cover the higher loadings or allowances typically prescribed for overtime, shift work, evening or weekend work, etc.
40. Bray & Stewart (n. 4) 48. The original table differs from this one, because we were specifically concerned there with processes for making rules to govern employment relationships, rather than general sources of labour law.

identified in section 7.3. Our categorisation of each source as having a limited, moderate or extensive role reflects a qualitative judgment based on the expressed objectives of the legislation at the relevant time, the scope or range of matters typically regulated by that source and the legal priority accorded to that source compared to others. We have omitted for this purpose both constitutional norms and soft law, given their relatively peripheral role, but separated out registered and unregistered collective agreements.

Table 7.1 Relative Importance of Different Sources over Five Regimes

Model/Period	*Legislation*	*Delegated Legislation*	*Collective Agreements (Registered)*	*Collective Agreements (Unreg'd)*	*Statutory Individual Agreements*	*Common Law*
1. Pre-1993	✓	✓✓✓	✓	✓		✓✓
2. 1993-1996	✓	✓✓	✓✓✓			✓
3. 1996-2006	✓✓	✓✓	✓✓	✓	✓✓	✓
4. 2006-2009	✓✓	✓	✓✓	✓✓	✓✓✓	✓
5. 2009- (ongoing)	✓✓✓	✓✓	✓✓	✓	✓	✓

✓ = limited role ✓✓ = moderate role ✓✓✓ = extensive role

It is clear that, over time, legislation has progressively become a more important source of both substantive and procedural regulations. This reflects the introduction of statutory minimum conditions in 2006, but also, starting even before then, a greater level of prescription of tribunal processes, award-making and collective bargaining. Delegated legislation, particularly in the form of awards, has undergone a resurgence following the attempt by Work Choices to downgrade it. But that masks an important change in the character and focus of award regulation, as noted in section 7.5. Collective bargaining, especially of the formal variety, has played a central role since the 1993 reforms. But even though clearly intended by the architects of the FW Act to be the primary way of setting wages and employment conditions, the limited (and indeed falling) coverage of collective agreements makes it difficult to describe them as now having an extensive role. Statutory individual agreements have risen and fallen in significance, while the greater role of legislation and industrial instruments has left less space for the common law to operate.

7.5 THREE DISTINCTIVE FEATURES OF AUSTRALIAN LABOUR LAW

According to some commentators, there has been a convergence towards neo-liberalism in industrial relations institutions among developed countries and, more specifically, a tendency for Australian labour regulation to move closer to the approach taken by other liberal market economies. For example, Colvin and Darbishire suggest that six Anglo-American countries (US, the UK, Ireland, Canada, Australia and New Zealand) have converged towards a common model:

> We have argued that the last three decades have seen the emergence of a new Anglo-American model of employment relations. Whereas prior to 1980 there was substantial divergence across this set of countries, over time there has been growing convergence on a model characterized by two main features. The first aspect is the emphasis on private ordering in labor relations, in which the role of laws and institutions governing collective representation is to support and encourage decentralized determination of the terms and conditions of employment at the organizational level. The second aspect is the emphasis on the role of employment law to establish a minimum basket of standards from which employees and employers can negotiate upward.[41]

There is some merit in this argument, but it overreaches with respect to Australia. On the first point, the decline of delegated regulation in Australia certainly reduced dramatically the 'public' determination of wages and conditions by tribunals and placed them in the 'private' hands of employers, employees and (to a lesser extent) unions. This neglects, however, the growing regulation by statute and tribunals of bargaining processes and the continued importance of awards. Moreover, Colvin and Darbishire's second point fails to take account of the scope and breadth of the statutory rights now granted in Australia to individual employees, in relation to matters such as protection from unfair dismissal, leave entitlements and so on. These far surpass anything generally available to non-unionised workers in the United States. Indeed, leximetric assessments of the 'protective strength' of labour laws in Australia, the UK and New Zealand have found no particular evidence of any convergence towards an Americanised model.[42]

In any event, there are three aspects of the Australian system that continue to distinguish it from its liberal market counterparts and from most national systems around the world: awards, non-union collective agreements and the extensive layering of labour regulation.

7.5.1 The Continuing Role of Awards

The regulation of labour through the creation and enforcement of awards has been an important and distinctive feature of Australian labour regulation since the introduction of the compulsory conciliation and arbitration systems at the

41. A. Colvin & O. Darbishire, *Convergence in Industrial Relations Institutions: The Emerging Anglo-American Model?*, 66 Ind. & Lab. Rel. Rev., 1047, 1073 (2013).
42. P. Gahan, et al., *Economic Globalization and Convergence in Labor Market Regulation: An Empirical Assessment*, 60, Am. J. Comp. L., 703 (2012).

turn of the twentieth century. Despite this long continuity, the function of awards, their form and the processes by which they are made have changed over time. In 1993, for example, awards became part of the 'safety net' of minimum standards underpinning other sources of legal regulation. This was quite different from the central role they had played for many decades in determining the actual wages and working conditions of many workers.

The form of awards has also changed in several ways, including their number, coverage and scope.[43] A key turning point here was a rapid process of 'award modernisation' in 2008–2009 in preparation for the beginning of the Fair Work Act. During this period, a very complicated – if not ramshackle – regime of 'old' awards, comprising an estimated 1560 federal and former State awards that applied to specified industries or occupations, was reduced to just 122 'modern' awards.

Most of the modern awards, which commenced operation in January 2010, cover employees within a specific industry. Together, they effectively provide minimum standards to most nonmanagerial employees in the federal system, which covers around 85% of all employees in Australia. Their scope (i.e., the aspects of the employment relationship they regulate) remains broad and quite prescriptive, in that they include many minimum wage rates but also rules on a wide range of other matters from working hours to leave entitlements, work uniforms and consultation procedures. A novelty, however, compared to the 'old' awards, is that their scope has become relatively standardised across industries. So, the comprehensive coverage and wide scope of modern awards under the FW Act – as well as the exclusive role of industrial tribunals in making and varying them – makes them quite different to the minimum standards in most other countries.

Modern awards, however, also display a characteristic that is more consistent with the broader trend in Australian – and overseas – labour law towards neo-liberalism: namely, they have become essentially codes of individual rights rather than the collectivist regulatory instruments they once were.[44] This transition can be seen in three aspects of awards. First, like 'old' awards, modern awards cover large groups of workers, but where the coverage of awards previously reflected (or at least was strongly influenced by) the organisational choices of trade unions, employees are now covered simply because they fall within a class considered appropriate by the tribunal. Second, the processes by which modern awards are made is predominantly an administrative one, in which the FWC unilaterally determines the minimum standards appropriate for any given industry in which workers are employed. Awards are less often the

43. *See* Mark Bray, *The Distinctiveness of Modern Awards* (Marian Baird, Keith Hancock & Joe Isaac, eds), *Work and Employment Relations: An Era of Change*, 17 (Federation Press 2011).
44. M. Bray & J. Macneil, *Individualism, Collectivism and the Case of Awards in Australia*, 53 J. Indus. Rel., 149 (2011).

result of collective bargaining between employers and unions, although there is still some scope in practice for negotiated provisions to be accepted by the tribunal. Third, the process by which award provisions are enforced when they have been (allegedly) breached is now an individualised one, where either the worker pursues the employer through independent litigation or a government agency (usually the Fair Work Ombudsman) enforces it on their behalf. This stands in contrast with the collectivist past, in which the enforcement of awards was a routine part of union activities.[45]

7.5.2 Non-union Collective Agreements

A second unusual feature of the Australian system is the recognition, if not encouragement, of legally binding collective agreements made without the involvement of trade unions and, potentially, without any genuine bargaining between employers and employees. As previously noted, legislative provisions on such agreements were first introduced in 1993.[46] The most recent incarnation of non-union collective agreements under the FW Act, however, is peculiar. First, the Act has eliminated the separate regulatory streams of earlier regimes, bringing both union and non-union instruments under the same provisions. This means that non-union enterprise agreements are subject to the same procedural provisions and have the same legal effect as those negotiated by unions. Second, workers have the right to be represented in any bargaining over the terms of a new enterprise agreement (union or non-union) and employers are obliged to bargain 'in good faith' with any nominated representative. These rights, however, belong to workers as individuals and there are no representational structures specified in the Act if no representatives are nominated. In a non-union or weakly unionised enterprise, this can mean that employers create the collective agreements they want. Third, the key procedural step in turning a draft collective agreement into a legally binding instrument is the consent of the workers to be covered by the agreement, which is determined by a ballot arranged by the employer. Consent means a favourable majority among those who vote.[47]

It is unclear whether non-union collective agreements under the FW Act represent a new form of (non-union) collectivism, perhaps reminiscent of works councils in Europe, or a 'trojan horse' designed to undermine unionism and

45. Ingrid Landau, Sean Cooney, Tess Hardy & John Howe, *Trade Unions and the Enforcement of Minimum Employment Standards* (Research Report, Centre for Employment and Labour Relations Law, The University of Melbourne 2014).
46. For background and subsequent developments, *see* C. Briggs & R. Cooper, *Between Individualism and Collectivism? Why Employers Choose Non-union Collective Agreements*, 17(2) Lab. & Indus., 1 (2006).
47. K. Walpole, *The Fair Work Act: Encouraging Collective Agreement-Making but Leaving Collective Bargaining to Choice*, 25 Lab. & Indus., 205 (2015).

deepen individualism. Either way, they are almost unique compared to other countries, especially those considered Anglo-American, where collective bargaining and collective agreements are confined to relations between unions and employers.[48]

7.5.3 The Layering of Regulatory Instruments

The diverse instruments that can regulate employment relationships, and the sources of law from which they flow, have meant that Australia's system of labour law has always been very complex. And it still is under the current FW Act, despite some improvements compared to earlier regimes.[49]

There are various dimensions to the complexity of a legal system. But one type is what Shuck has termed 'differentiation' – the number of different instruments or decision-making regimes.[50] Bray and Waring distinguish between 'vertical' and 'horizontal' forms of such complexity in labour regulation.[51] The former involves parallel systems of rules covering different groups of workers within an industry or workplace. In Australia, this was historically the result of multiple unions operating in the same industry and overlapping coverage by federal and State arbitration systems. Such vertical complexity, however, has been reduced over recent years through the centralisation of legislative authority described earlier, and also by concerted efforts to reduce the number of unions.

By contrast, horizontal complexity, which involves the extent to which multiple regulatory instruments operate in a 'layered' way to determine the rules of a single employment relationship, remains very strong in Australia. As we have explained, a national system employee may be subject to rules derived from the FW Act and other legislation, an award, a registered collective agreement, an individual flexibility arrangement, an unregistered collective agreement, expressly agreed contractual terms, terms implied by the common law and organisational policies and procedures. As empirical research has shown, the extent of layering has been reduced somewhat as legislation has come to insist that enterprise agreements replace, rather than supplement, the awards that underpinned them.[52] Nevertheless, it is still necessary to have

48. *See* S. McCrystal & M. Bray, *Non-union Agreement-Making in Australia in Comparative and Historical Context*, Comp. Lab. L. & Pol'y J. (forthcoming).
49. *See* Andrew Stewart, Peter Gahan, Shae McCrystal & Anna Chapman, *Labour Regulation: Is There a Case for Major Reform?*, 23-26 (Submission to the Productivity Commission Inquiry into the Workplace Relations Framework 2015).
50. P. Shuck, *Legal Complexity: Some Causes, Consequences, and Cures*, 42 Duke L.J., 1 (1992). He also identified 'technicality', 'density' and 'uncertainty' as other forms of complexity.
51. M. Bray & P. Waring, *'Complexity' and 'Congruence' in Australian Labour Regulation*, 47 J. Indus. Rel., 1 (2005).
52. C. Sutherland, *Enterprise Bargaining as a Tool to Reduce Regulatory Layering: A Content Analysis Study*, 42 Fed. L. Rev., 559 (2014).

interaction rules that define the relationships between the various regulatory layers.

As explained in section 7.2.6, there remains considerable uncertainty about the relationship between statutory instruments and employment contracts, for lack of explicit interaction rules on that subject. By contrast, far more legislative attention has been devoted to the circumstances in which registered collective agreements can breach the minimum standards set by either legislation or awards. These have involved a series of 'tests' administered by tribunals or other statutory agencies to determine whether agreements (individual or collective) are approved, and thereby gain legal standing. They have been variously called a no-disadvantage test, a fairness test and – the current nomenclature – a better off overall test.[53] Their operation has often been controversial. The Howard Government's attempt in its Work Choices laws to eliminate the test – and remove the safety net role of awards – was a key factor leading to its downfall at the ballot box. More recently, it has been revealed that the FWC had routinely been approving enterprise agreements struck by the shopworkers' union with large retailers and fast-food chains, even though they cut wages for evening and weekend work below award levels. These cuts were supposedly offset by contingent benefits which few employees would in practice access. It was only when an affected worker successfully challenged one of these agreements that the tribunal's failure to properly apply the better off overall test was revealed.[54] The subsequent tightening of the test's administration has not just slowed the process for getting an agreement approved, but induced a number of employers to abandon enterprise bargaining altogether.[55] These events illustrate both the workplace and political consequences of the unusual layering of labour regulation in Australia.

7.6 CONCLUSIONS

The mix of different sources of labour regulation in Australia continues to set it apart from other countries. This is especially true of the recognition of collective

53. *See* Carolyn Sutherland, *Making the 'BOOT' Fit: Reforms to Agreement-Making from Work Choices to Fair Work* (Anthony Forsyth & Andrew Stewart, eds), *Fair Work: The New Workplace Laws and the Work Choices Legacy*, 99, 111-118 (Federation Press 2009). The 'fairness test' operated briefly under the Workplace Relations Amendment (A Stronger Safety Net) Act 2007, introduced by the Howard Government in response to the public concerns noted in the text that follows.
54. *See Hart v. Coles Supermarkets Australia Pty Ltd* [2016] FWCFB 2887; B. Schneiders, N. Toscano & R. Millar, *Sold Out: Quarter of a Million Workers Underpaid in Union Deals* (Sydney Morning Herald 30 August 2016). Even under previous regimes, there had been concerns about how rigorously the no-disadvantage test was being applied to certain agreements: *see* R. Mitchell et al., *What's Going on with the 'No Disadvantage Test'? An Analysis of Outcomes and Processes under the Workplace Relations Act 1996*, 47 J. Indus. Rel., 393 (2005).
55. Pennington (n. 12) 31-32, 71-75.

agreements made without the involvement of a union (or indeed any form of bargaining), and the important role played by industry-level awards – albeit awards are no longer the product of compulsory arbitration. The role played by different sources, and the rules for determining their interaction, have also significantly evolved over the past three decades. Notable developments have included the greater use of legislation to set minimum standards and a rise and fall in the use of both statutory individual agreements and unregistered collective agreements. The relationship between awards and registered collective agreements has both created controversy and exposed the complexity created by the layering of different regulatory instruments.

Australian labour law has been relatively stable over the past decade, with few changes to the FW Act. Although the conservative LNP government first elected in 2013 initiated a review of the workplace relations system by the Productivity Commission, an advisory body staffed principally by economists, the resulting report was largely positive about the current regulatory framework.[56] There has been no sign since of the conservative parties (who retained office after the 2019 election) seeking to revive the Howard Government's plans to wind back award or statutory protections, although the possibility remains. By contrast, the Labor opposition has come to accept that the Act does not go far enough in protecting workers or facilitating collective bargaining. A future Labor government might well make it easier for unions, at least in some sectors, to pursue industry-level agreements. How these agreements would interact with both awards and enterprise-level agreements is an important issue of detail that would need to be worked out.[57] Clearly, however, there is a potential for the Australian system to become even more layered and complex than it already is.

BIBLIOGRAPHY

Gordon Anderson, Douglas Brodie & Joellen Riley, *The Common Law Employment Relationship: A Comparative Study* (Edward Elgar 2017).

M. Bray & A. Stewart, *What Is Distinctive about the Fair Work Regime?*, 26 Aust. J. Lab. L., 20 (2013).

M. Bray & E. Rasmussen, *Developments in Comparative Employment Relations in Australia and New Zealand: Reflecting on 'Accord and Discord'*, 28 Lab. & Indus., 31 (2018).

M. Bray & J. Macneil, *Individualism, Collectivism and the Case of Awards in Australia*, 53 J. Indus. Rel., 149 (2011).

56. Productivity Commission, *Workplace Relations Framework* (Inquiry Report No. 76, Productivity Commission 2015).
57. *See* Andrew Stewart, Jim Stanford & Tess Hardy, *Conclusion: Wages and Inclusive Growth* (Andrew Stewart, Jim Stanford & Tess Hardy, eds), *The Wages Crisis in Australia: What It Is and What to Do about It*, 277, 288-289 (University of Adelaide Press 2018).

M. Bray & P. Waring, *'Complexity' and 'Congruence' in Australian Labour Regulation*, 47 J. Indus. Rel., 1 (2005).

Mark Bray, *The Distinctiveness of Modern Awards* (Marian Baird, Keith Hancock & Joe Isaac, eds), *Work and Employment Relations: An Era of Change*, 17 (Federation Press 2011).

C. Briggs & R. Cooper, *Between Individualism and Collectivism? Why Employers Choose Non-union Collective Agreements*, 17(2) Lab. & Indus., 1 (2006).

A. Colvin & O. Darbishire, *Convergence in Industrial Relations Institutions: The Emerging Anglo-American Model?*, 66 Ind. & Lab. Rel. Rev., 1047-1073 (2013).

A. Forsyth, *Restoring the Rule of Law Through Commercial (Dis)incentives: The Code for the Tendering and Performance of Building Work 2016*, 40 Syd. L. Rev., 121 (2018).

R. Freeman, *Learning from Other Economies: The Unique Institutional and Policy Experiments Down Under*, 82 Econ. Record, 195 (2006).

P. Gahan, R. Mitchell, S. Cooney, A. Stewart & B. Cooper, *Economic Globalization and Convergence in Labor Market Regulation: An Empirical Assessment*, 60, Am. J. Comp. L., 703 (2012).

G. Golding, *Terms Implied by Law into Employment Contracts: Are They Necessary?*, 28 Aust. J. Lab. L., 113 (2015).

Dyson Heydon, *The Restraint of Trade Doctrine* (3rd ed., LexisNexis Butterworths 2008).

Mark Irving, *The Contract of Employment* (LexisNexis Butterworths 2012); Gordon Anderson, Douglas Brodie & Joellen Riley, *The Common Law Employment Relationship: A Comparative Study* (Edward Elgar 2017).

Ingrid Landau, Sean Cooney, Tess Hardy & John Howe, *Trade Unions and the Enforcement of Minimum Employment Standards* (Research Report, Centre for Employment and Labour Relations Law, The University of Melbourne 2014).

S. McCrystal & M. Bray, *Non-union Agreement-Making in Australia in Comparative and Historical Context*, Comp. Lab. L. & Pol'y J. (forthcoming).

Shae McCrystal, Breen Creighton & Anthony Forsyth (eds), *Collective Bargaining under the Fair Work Act* (Federation Press 2018).

R. Mitchell, R. Campbell, A. Barnes, E. Bicknell, K. Creighton, J. Fetter & S. Korman, *What's Going on with the 'No Disadvantage Test'? An Analysis of Outcomes and Processes under the Workplace Relations Act 1996*, 47 J. Indus. Rel., 393 (2005).

Alison Pennington, *On the Brink: The Erosion of Enterprise Agreement Coverage in Australia's Private Sector* (Centre for Future Work 2018).

Ben Schneiders, Nick Toscano & Royce Millar, *Sold Out: Quarter of a Million Workers Underpaid in Union Deals* (Sydney Morning Herald 30 August 2016).

P. Shuck, *Legal Complexity: Some Causes, Consequences, and Cures*, 42 Duke L.J., 1 (1992).

A. Stewart & J. Riley, *Working Around Work Choices: Collective Bargaining and the Common Law*, 31 Melb. U.L.R., 903 (2007).

Andrew Stewart, Jim Stanford & Tess Hardy, *Conclusion: Wages and Inclusive Growth* (Andrew Stewart, Jim Stanford & Tess Hardy, eds), *The Wages Crisis in Australia: What It Is and What to Do About It*, 277, 289 (University of Adelaide Press 2018).

Andrew Stewart, Peter Gahan, Shae McCrystal & Anna Chapman, *Labour Regulation: Is There a Case for Major Reform?*, 23-26 (Submission to the Productivity Commission Inquiry into the Workplace Relations Framework 2015).

C. Sutherland, *Enterprise Bargaining as a Tool to Reduce Regulatory Layering: A Content Analysis Study*, 42 Fed. L. Rev., 559 (2014).

Carolyn Sutherland, *Making the 'BOOT' Fit: Reforms to Agreement-Making from Work Choices to Fair Work* (Anthony Forsyth & Andrew Stewart, eds), *Fair Work: The New Workplace Laws and the Work Choices Legacy*, 99, 111-118 (Federation Press 2009).

G. Tolhurst, *Contractual Confusion and Industrial Illusion: A Contract Law Perspective on Awards, Collective Agreements and the Contract of Employment*, 66 Aust. L.J., 705 (1992).

K. Walpole, *The Fair Work Act: Encouraging Collective Agreement-Making but Leaving Collective Bargaining to Choice*, 25 Lab. & Indus., 205 (2015).

CHAPTER 8

The (Once) Radical Continuities of Brazil Labor Regulation

Jedidiah Kroncke

8.1 THE CORPORATIST FOUNDATIONS OF BRAZILIAN LABOR LAW

The history of Latin American is often told as a history of revolutions. Starting with its independence from Portugal in 1822, Brazil has had its share of formal regime changes. But what is most striking about postcolonial Brazilian history is a noted lack of what some might deem truly revolutionary social change, especially after the formal abolishment of slavery in 1888. Brazilian legal history speaks to this continuity in different ways, but the enduring foundations of modern Brazilian labor law do so with specific force. This endurance in the face of multiple regime changes speaks to the many unresolved tensions at the heart of Brazil's legacy of slavery so enmeshed in its racial and labor politics.

Brazil's first postmonarchial Constitution in 1891 established its lasting transition to a system of governance as a strongly federal, unitary system with the then increasingly common tripartite division of power between executive, legislative and judicial branches—with a relatively permanent tilt toward strong executive power. Today, Brazil has twenty-six states (as well as the capital district of Brasilia) which have few of the shared sovereign powers common under common law federal systems.

In the broadest strokes, Brazil's legal system also still bears the strong mark of its Portuguese civil law ancestry. As such, Brazilian law is grounded in codes with a historical emphasis on legislative production and revision as the primary sources of law. Following this tradition, Brazilian statutory law has been governed by the norms outlined in its foundational code, today called the Statute of Introduction to Brazilian Law (Lei de Introdução às Normas do Direito Brasileiro) and which has gone through several revisions over the past century. Derived from a unitary governmental structure, federal legislation thus predominates, and herein labor law is no exception. Though state legislation on labor topics would come to be allowed by federal statute in more recent decades, so far this influence has been limited and still absent in adjacent areas of law that touch on labor such as criminal law.

Until the late 1930s, formal regulation of labor was primarily based on legislation passed after the enactment of the 1891 Constitution, but such legislation did little to upset the practices of employer dominance that persisted after the formal abolishment of slavery. As labor unrest and protest were an ongoing focal point of Brazilian politics during this era, the formal regulation of labor was far less relevant to almost the entirety of Brazil's working population than were the social realities of power and accountability over which Brazilians struggled.

Herein, following German precedents influencing, Brazilian Constitutions from this time onward would directly regulate key aspects of labor conditions and authorize a system of corporatist bargaining which encompassed the vast majority of formally employed workers. It was not until the rise of what would be called the "New State" (Estado Novo) of Getulio Vargas inaugurated in 1937 that the enduring twentieth-century structure of Brazilian labor law would be firmly entrenched as the formal economy would be fully corporatized to centralize negotiation between labor and industrial group agents.

In creating the structure of the New State, Getulio Vargas and his advisers were influenced by a range of American and European examples and global intellectual trends.[1] Dominant in this era were corporatist conceptions of democracy where bargaining between collective representatives was seen as an effective means to channel growing postindustrial social unrest through a process. While inclusive of any number of social interests, labor was one of the most relevant arenas for corporatist theorization. The essentially group-based logic of corporatism meant that negotiation between labor and employee organizations was meant to supersede and discipline the individual agency of individual workers and employers. The presumed benefit of this system was that standardizing labor conditions, at least among those workers covered by the system, would be both economically efficient and diffuse political instability. While born in a global intellectual current, international legal sources would be marginal until over fifty years after the New State was first created.

1. P. Fontes, A. Fortes & D. Mayer, *Brazilian Labour History: New Perspectives in Global Context*, 62 Int'l Rev. Soc. Hist., 1 (2017). Also see the volume of essays this article introduces for new cosmopolitan histories of Brazilian labor history.

Surviving many constitutional regime changes, the centerpiece of Brazilian labor regulation has long been the federal Consolidated Labor Code (Consolidação das Leis do Trabalho, or CLT) which was first promulgated in 1943. The CLT recognized broad sectoral worker and employee unions who were empowered to bargain over the terms of employment. Some adjacent sources of federal statutory law would always touch on labor-adjacent issues, while state and municipal legislation was generally preempted by the CLT. Employment contracts were traditionally an afterthought following in the process as the collective agreements reached under the CLT system gave them increasingly little space for individual variation over time, especially in contrast to those in common law systems. Under this original model, the system of labor courts created in 1934 sat alongside this system and, in theory, was solely an elaborator rather than a source of law itself.

The struggle over the content of these primary sources of Brazilian labor law, the Constitution and the CLT would form part of the symbolic politics and practical realities of labor regulation from this era onward. Critiques of the corporatist system were also commonly asserted, but even coups and the new regimes they would precipitate would not fundamentally alter this basic structure of labor governance. Instead, change would occur in the extensivity of labor law enshrined in various Constitutions, who was designated as corporatist representatives and the relative impact of the labor courts on shaping labor policy. Until quite recently, the content of individual employment agreements for most workers was relatively marginal—following both civil law theories of contract formation/interpretation and the central role of collective bargaining. The 1988 democratization in Brazil entrenched rather than overturned this system, reflecting the continued persistence of not only the traditional hierarchy of labor sources but also their fundamental logic.

While critics of this system had been at the margins of recent Brazilian legal discourse, there had also been a long-standing critique of Brazilian labor law in the post-1988 era as overly protective.[2] Following standard neoclassical arguments about labor legislation, the argument was made by more conservative elements in Brazil that both the union system and robust individual employment law protections reduced economic growth or induced informal labor contracting. Internationally, Brazil had always been an uncomfortable example for this claim. For while Brazil did still have high levels of informality compared to higher-income countries, for its per capita income, it not only had comparatively low levels of informality but also had actually decreased informality in the last fifteen years while increasing levels of labor protection.[3]

2. J.F. Mayer, *The Limits of Labor Legislation Reforms: Rigidity, Growth, and Employment in Brazil (1995–2010)*, 8 J. Pol. Latin Am., 95 (2016).
3. S. Coslovsky, R. Pires & R. Bignami, *Resilience and Renewal: Labor Unions, Inspectors, Prosecutors and the Enforcement of Labor Laws in Brazil*, 59 Latin Am. Pol. & Soc'y., 77 (2017).

Yet, the impact of the 2013 economic recession, ending a decade of robust economic growth, and a wide-ranging corruption scandal eventually led to the impeachment of President Dilma Rousseff in 2016 and the jailing of former President Lula in 2018 on corruption charges. One of the few legislative successes of the subsequent interim presidency of Michel Temer was a systematic reform of the entire gamut of Brazilian labor legislation in November 2017. Following neoclassical prescriptions, this reform, known as the Reforma Trabalhista, specifically targeted labor provisions in the Constitution, the CLT and the practices of the Labor Court.[4] As such, the relationships of the sources of Brazilian labor law have recently been upturned and have laid the groundwork for a great deal of uncertainty moving forward.

8.2 THE PROGRESSIVE CONSTITUTIONALIZATION OF BRAZILIAN LABOR LAW

Brazilian constitutional revision has been an active part of modern Brazilian legal reform, in no small part due to relatively frequent regime changes and the comparative ease of constitutional amendment. Between 1891 and 1988, multiple regimes took control over Brazilian governance. Some were putatively democratic, others openly authoritarian. Getulio Vargas, architect of the Estado Novo, had emblematically been both a military dictator and democratically elected president.

As noted earlier, from 1891 onward Brazilian Constitutions have specifically addressed a wide-range of labor issues on which its content is legally supreme, enshrining regulatory issues as detailed as a federal minimum wage, vacation time and working hours The formation of the modern Brazilian corporatist state is tied to the 1934 Constitution which went beyond its antecedents in constitutionalizing not only specific substantive labor law content but also the structure of the system of collective bargaining under which the production of subsidiary source of labor law would play out. The 1934 Constitution also laid out the structure of the court system, institutionalizing the role of specialized courts to address labor law following the modern civil law trend. While short-lived, the 1934 Constitution established the continuing precedent of Brazilian Constitutions as the centerpiece of labor law. While significant in many ways, the 1937 constitutional enacted as part of Getulio Vargas' military rule reemphasized corporatist bargaining by centralizing many economic arenas as part of a plan of industrial policy. Brazil would move between democracy and dictatorship in 1946, 1967 and 1988. Throughout the period, all Constitutions

4. J. Renda Leal Fernandes, *Labor Law, CLT and the 2017 Brazilian Labor Reform*, 5 Panorama of Brazilian L., 210 (2017).

recognized collective bargaining and the right to strike, as well as directly laying out the terms of various labor law policies.

This progressive process of increasing constitutionalization continued through the Constitution now in force in Brazil. The 1988 Constitution, known as the Citizen's Constitution (Constituição Cidadã), was created during an era of the global trend toward "transformative constitutionalism," which saw constitutional law as a vehicle for thorough legal change. As a result, the 1988 Constitution greatly expanded the scope and content of constitutionalized social rights, including those related to labor. Five Articles, 7 through 11, of the new Constitution specifically addressed labor issues and the structure of labor law regulation. Herein, the mandatory minimum content of labor law was expanded again to touch on virtually every aspect of working life. These new baselines included a cap on working hours, a higher federal minimum wage, a bonus thirteenth-month salary, increased vacation days and other aspects of a growing system of social welfare provision including universal health and unemployment insurance. Notably, public workers were also finally granted the right to union representation (as well as for-cause firing protections) and, save the military, the right to strike. At least formally, the rights of rural workers were harmonized with those of urban workers.

While without a clear formal place within the Brazilian legal system writ large, the postdemocratization era also saw international law becoming an increasingly important source of law at the constitutional level.[5] This influence could be seen a pattern of constitutional amendment that incorporated the content of the international treaties that Brazil had become a party to. Particular to labor, Brazil signed onto a number of International Labour Organization conventions as well as the American Convention on Human Rights—all of which have strong labor components. The impact of these convention harmonizations has been especially notable in the constitutional implementation of nondiscrimination norms and other issues related to discrimination such as equal pay. These constitutional norms thus directly infused all subordinate federal legislation helped spur continued expansion of constitutional protections for labor, notably the 2012 amendment that extended labor protection to domestic workers.

Given the centrality of the constitutional in modern Brazilian labor law, the sweeping reforms of the recent labor law reforms involved numerous constitutional amendments the content of which is better addressed as it affects the other subordinate sources of labor. Many of these changes are still being litigated in Brazilian courts, but none of which move to de-constitutionalize labor law in any significant manner.

5. Ana Gomes, *The Effects of the ILO's Declaration on Fundamental Principles and Rights at Work on the Evolution of Legal Policy in Brazil: An Analysis of Freedom of Association* (University of Toronto, 2009).

8.3 THE ENDURING CENTRALITY OF THE CLT IN STATUTORY LABOR LAW

From 1891 onward, the content of federal legislation on labor law has varied considerably, as it can touch on any nonconstitutionalized subject and has the capability of enhancing any constitutional minimum. More importantly, federal statutes can establish new minimums which form a new baseline that collective agreements, and in turn employment contracts, could not traditionally reduce.

The most critical piece of Brazilian labor legislation has been the CLT of 1943. As Brazil's modern Labor Code, the CLT has laid off the system of collective bargaining which still gives life to Getulio Vargas' vision of corporatist labor regulation.[6] The original CLT concentrated all existing statutory enactments relating to labor law, including those regarding the organization of employer groups. Most significantly, the CLT laid out the terms by which labor and employer unions would be recognized and subjected their operation and bargaining to growing regulation over time. Prior to 1988, these representatives where recognized unilaterally by the Ministry of Labour, giving a great of power to the central government over whom could bargain under the CLT system.

Prior to the CLT, there has been no overarching structure to labor regulation, and most labor disputes where resolved through individual litigation—when realistically available to a small number of workers. The CLT also enshrined the procedures of the new labor courts which has been increasingly active since 1939 and would also provide increasing greater detail to their operation even as constitutional regimes shifted before 1988. The primary exception to the scope of the CLT was its omission of agricultural and public workers, who were respectively subject to either regular contract law or other statutory enactments.

One would normally expect that a modern democratic revolution would upend the long corporatist legacy of the CLT, emergent from a very different era of Brazilian and global thinking on labor regulation. This expectation was, in fact, all the more anticipated because the authoritarian nature of the traditional system under the CLT was a key rallying cry for the coalition politics that gave rise to the 1988 democratization movement which ended then decades of military dictatorship in Brazil. The Workers Party (Partido dos Trabalhadores, or PT) that emerged out of this movement had close and direct ties to CUT (Central Única dos Trabalhadores) which was formed as a "central trade union" in 1983 outside of the traditional state-dominated CLT system. CUT promoted a "new unionism" for Brazil as a clear break from the past system.[7] Core to CUT's critique of the CLT system was the idea that state-nominated corporatist unions

6. John French, *Drowning in Laws; Labor Law and Brazilian Political Culture* (UNC Press, 2004).
7. Mauricio Barros, *Labour Relations and the New Unionism in Contemporary Brazil* (Palgrave, 1999).

were undemocratic and did little to truly represent the interests of workers and thus called for significant reform to the CLT.

On many levels, the modern democratization of Brazil did lead to several substantial changes in Brazilian labor law. CUT's chief reform aim goal was achieved, as the system of corporatist representation shifted to one of formally private self-regulation. Rather than recognition at the discretion of the Ministry of Labour, unions had to demonstrate worker representation and then petition for recognition by the labor courts. As we will soon see, the centrality of the CLT was not undermined in this process and survived to continue to be the central piece of labor legislation under the Constitution in Brazil. There are still occupational exclusions to scope of the CLT, such as the employment of officers of a company is governed by the contract law elaborated in the Civil Code.

It should also be noted that after 1988, the expansion of other statutory provision touching on labor issues continued to accelerate. Though not part of labor regulation directly, federal statutory law governed the whole host of social welfare provisions workers enjoy, as well as any relevant civil and criminal issues such as harassment or discrimination in the workplace which had received constitutional recognition. The new constitutional mandates for the judiciary and the executive were then fueled by a whole host of new legislative enactments both specifying the implementation of constitutional mandates as well as periodically addressing new issues such as employer patents, intern abuse, profit sharing, maternity leave and disability rights. Most areas of work were given detailed statutory specification, including the traditional professions (doctors, lawyers and engineers) to vocations as varied as journalists, artists and bank workers.

As a result, the post-1988 era saw the empowerment of what could be called the modern Brazilian federal administrative state. Formally emanating from the executive, the Ministry of Labour and Employment (Ministério do Trabalho e Emprego) became a central actor in facilitating the enforcement of labor and social welfare legislation and thus also a new source of law as a key secondary interpreter of legislation. Among many of the independent new public ministries was the Public Labour Ministry (Labor Ministério Público) which was charged with the enforcement of the CLT. Often heralded internationally, the Labour Inspection Secretariat (Secretaria de Inspecao do Trabalho)—which has existed in some form since the beginning of the Estado Novo—was given new life postdemocratization and tasked with proactive workplace level legislation enforcement, and also with overseeing a set of regional offices.[8]

The new breadth and depth of labor legislation, as well as its agents of interpretation, became reflected in the fact that labor law a compulsory subject on the certification exam for Brazilian lawyers, labor law courses constituted the

8. Coslovsky, Pires & Bignami (n. 3) 59.

longest mandatory series in Brazilian legal education and labor law attracted the largest number of law professors specializing in its study.

Again, the labor law reforms of 2017 have significantly altered the content of key provisions of the CLT, as well as other statutory enactments. Yet, as thoroughgoing as these reforms have been, the CLT remains the primary statutory source of law only second to the Constitution in the hierarchy of Brazilian labor law.

8.4 THE NARROWING SCOPE OF COLLECTIVE BARGAINING

The system of collective bargaining enshrined in the CLT has grown in strength and coverage of the Brazilian working population since the 1940s. Given the sectoral nature of this bargaining, the output of this system has traditionally represented the major source of variation in the terms of employment under Brazilian labor law. Under the modern system of formally private union recognition, the collective agreements are reached through employee-employer negotiation that is still highly corporatist in nature. The three core principles of union formation and bargaining established by the CLT were: (1) unicity, or mandatory representation by a single union; (2) union organization by occupational and geographic criteria; and (3) mandatory membership fees paid by workers (and employers). Moreover, there has never been an individual right to strike recognized by the CLT, as all labor action must be legally authorized by a representative union who often is required to give notice to employer unions.[9] Thus, once a union is recognized, it is almost never replaced and rarely bargains for radical changes in the terms of previous agreements.

Moreover, all of these changes did little to modify the basic structure of regulation under the Estado Novo—practically and symbolically surviving in the persistence of the CLT.[10] While CUT and the PT had energized the democratization process with the promise of a newly democratic union system, this promise never materialized. In fact, in the process of negotiating the post-1988 regime CUT entrenched itself and other central unions at the heart of the old corporatist system.[11] While no longer needing formal Ministry of Labour recognition, the basic concepts of unicity and mandatory fee payments meant that unions faced few electoral mechanisms of accountability from workers and were almost impossible to dislodge once legally empowered. At the same time, the legislative regulation of union procedures grew even more detailed when it came

9. C. Mercante, *As Raizes Autoritarias da Atual Lei Greve Brasileira* [*The Authoritarian Roots of Brazil's Current Law on Striking*], 7 Rev. Dir. Mackenzie, 42 (2014).
10. A. Gomes & M. Prado, *Flawed Freedom of Association in Brazil*, 32 Comp. Lab. L. & Pol'y J., 843 (2011).
11. P. Ribeiro, *An Amphibian Party? Organisational Change and Adaptation in the Brazilian Workers' Party, 1980–2012*, 46 J. Latin Am. Stud., 87 (2014).

to striking and almost every aspect of union operation. When the PT came to federal power in 2003, some thought that this might be an opportunity for the "new unionism" reforms to be enacted. But, again, the opposite again occurred. President Luiz Inácio Lula da Silva (popularly known as Lula) demonstrated a preference for greater group consultation and negotiation rather than less. He initiated a National Labour Forum (Forum Nacional do Trabalho) soon after his term began, but this lead to few union reforms and none that improved internal union democracy.[12] Notably, the one ILO convention that Brazil has never signed was the one that recognized an individual right of association to form unions.[13]

The legal output of this bargaining is most commonly a collective convention (convengdo coletiva) that covers the workers in a particular geographic arena within an occupational group. It is possible for agreements to be signed with individual companies by a union (acordo coletivo), but such agreements have been until quite recently rare. Traditionally, the content of these agreements was restricted by the constitutional principle that any collective agreement cannot undermine any constitutional or legislative minimum. As a result, even though the post-1988 Brazilian unions have been quite strong, the actual the scope of bargaining—while not formally as circumscribed as in the American model—is generally compressed by these baselines. The actual degree to which collective agreements represent real bargaining was inversely related to how generous the constitutional and legislative minimums imposed on the process were by various constitutional and legislative revisions.

This progressive narrowing of the scope of collective agreements was dramatically reversed during the 2017 reforms. By amending the Constitution and the CLT, the reforms changed the long-standing principle that collective bargaining could not go below statutory baselines, even if constitutional baselines were still in force. The reform thus introduced a fundamental logic of individuation premised on individual employee-employer negotiation which gave increasing space for employees above a certain income to opt out of the system in its entirety. Indirectly, though with no less impact, the mandatory fees which unions could previously collect were eliminated. This meant that the financial base of unions was severely weakened at the same time as their bargaining position was undercut. Moreover, collective agreements that expired were no longer presumptively valid until renegotiated.

The sum force of these reforms was to leave the future strength of collective agreements in question while shifting their priority in the hierarchy of Brazilian labor law. On the one hand, they could be supplanted by individual agreements,

12. M. Doctor, *Lula's Development Council Neo-Corporatism and Policy Reform in Brazil,* 34 Latin Am. Persp., 131 (2007).
13. Gomes (n. 5).

and, on the other, they could override statutory minimums which were previously supreme.

8.5 THE RISE OF THE LABOR COURT PRECEDENTS

The separate system of specialized labor courts first addressed in the 1934 Constitution traditionally recognized its operation following the general presumptions of civil law adjudication. Guided by the content of the CLT, the labor courts did not produce formal precedents or case law that could be construed as a source of law. Structurally, the Superior Court of Justice (Superior Tribunal de Justiça) oversees the Superior Labor Court (Tribunal Superior do Trabalho, or TST) whose jurisdiction and composition is outlined in the CLT. The TST then oversees regional and trial labor courts whose staffing and operation are also specifically regulated by statute.

Yet, in 1988 the courts were given new life as one facet of the growing power of the Brazilian judiciary meant to carry out the "transformative" ethos of new Constitution. The most prominent outgrowth of this change was that the TST came to periodically produce several "Statements of Precedent" which, though not following any formal doctrine of stare decisis, articulated several powerful pro-employee interpretive and substantive conclusions with presumptive weight throughout the labor court system. The jurisprudence embedded in these statements directly invoked the ethos of constitutional provisions to supplement and interpret the CLT and other relevant statutory sources of law. As a result, these statements have new meaning to the content of individual employment contracts by proactively extending the principles of nonwaivability and continuity into areas of law unaddressed by other sources of law. Importantly, the power of the labor courts was greatly increased by procedural changes which rendered litigation mostly free for employees and thus made judicial remedies a realistic alternative for many Brazilian workers for the first time. Brazilian labor courts of the post-1988 era, in fact, became internationally emblematic of activist labor jurisprudence—handling over three million cases a year by the late 2010s. The jurisprudence of the new court system thus became an important, but contentious, source of law as novel areas of modern employment regulation—notably outsourcing—became completely governed by case law. The heavy case load of the labor courts and the issuance of the Statements shifted in practice, if not in theory, labor courts to the center of Brazilian labor regulation.

The emergence of the labor courts as a source of law was also specifically targeted in the 2017 labor reforms. Specific TST rulings were overturned, as technical as those allowing of uniform changes or commuting to be counted job time. Most notably, outsourcing was authorized. These reforms also directly addressed the interpretive power of labor courts more generally by revising the

Constitution to directly refute the power of the TST to issue Statements of Precedent and legislatively asserted that the labor courts should not restrict employee-employer bargaining or create new obligations unless such was enumerated in legislation. Again, these formal changes were made exponentially more effective by procedural reforms which rendered employee litigation no longer free for most workers, as well as subject to the risk of bad faith penalties for losing parties. At the same time, the reform enabled a far greater role for arbitration in labor disputes with a loser pays fee structure. Initial surveys have estimated that in the time since the reform the labor court system in 2018 decided a third the number of cases as it had in 2017.

8.6 THE EMERGENCE OF INDIVIDUAL CONTRACTING

The mix of significant constitutional and statutory baselines alongside the prominence of collective agreement traditionally left individual Brazilian employment contracts highly standardized since the enactment of the CLT. Moreover, these contracts were subject to the presumption of continuity where once agreed to they were both indefinite and could only be increased in favor of employees. The increasingly generous constitutional and legislative provisions for workers meant that there was even less ground for individual employment contract negotiation than for collective bargaining, and no individual contract could fall below the minimums set in collective agreements.

The terms of who is and is not an employee followed well-understood norms implemented by the labor courts, and, as with many civil law countries, Brazilian law has never permitted franchising or other forms of strategically fragmented employer responsibility. The major deviation from other civil law labor systems was the continued formal persistence of at-will employment, even though termination without cause still requires notice and often carries with its specific employer penalties, while causes for firing are limited to an enumerated set of accepted grounds.

While formally last as a traditional source of labor law in Brazil, it is important to note some very large exceptions to this formal arrangement. Large classes of workers have been excluded from the system, notably agricultural workers and until very recently domestic workers (whose work was designated as "noneconomic"). The structure of Brazilian labor unions also presented obstacles to the organization of certain marginalized groups such as farmworkers, interns and temporary workers who were not regulated under the CLT but separate statutes which granted much fewer baseline rights without the right to union representation, or access to a number of social rights and welfare provisions. As a result, the terms of these workers individual employment agreements were highly variable and thus much more significant than for employees under the CLT. Another significant limit is that a great deal of informality has characterized Brazilian labor markets up until the present, including the persistence of nonnegligible numbers under conditions of forced labor. For these workers, there is often no contract that governs their employment.

In a reversal of previous trends, it is, however, individual employment contracts that have gained the most prominence under the 2017 labor law reforms. The very ethos of the reforms is to give new priority to individual bargaining over the terms of employment and to elevate employment contracts above collective agreements and in some cases statutory sources of law. In an open turn away from the principles of nonwaivability, previously advanced by the TST, employers are now free to seek from employees releases and waivers of a host of employment rights. The nature of this bargaining had also changed, as penalties have been lessened for at-will termination, and bargaining with unions is no longer required for any termination or changes in employment terms due to business reorganizations. The standardization of employment contracts, especially in the structure of working hours, has been significantly reduced. Part-time contracts have become possible, with a spectrum of exemptions allowed to facilitate intermittent working hour arrangements. Employees who meet a relatively low-income threshold are now almost completely free to negotiate every term of employment save those still present in the Constitution.

8.7 THE UNCERTAINTY AHEAD FOR BRAZILIAN LABOR LAW

The story of general continuity in modern Brazilian labor law would have generally ended here but just a few years ago. Debates about reforming the CLT system, from expanding the number of workers it covered to a thorough revamping of its corporatist logic, were popularly made under the presumption of only further constitutionalization and broadening the number of workers covered by the ambit of the CLT. The normative evaluation of this continuation of the corporatist system became the focus of any number of debates in and outside of the labor movement prior to 2017.[14] The systemic gains for Brazilian workers in the last few decades have been impressive on any number of evaluative grounds. What is nonetheless clear is that the pattern of continuity in Brazilian labor regulation had lasted almost a century and survived the most dramatic political regime change to date. Prior to the recession and political scandals of recent years, many had argued that Brazil represented a new developmental model that other countries could emulate. Its international

14. J. Dari Krein & M. de Barros Biavaschi, *Os Movimentos Contraditórios da Regulação do Trabalho no Brasil dos Anos 2000* [*The Contradictory Movements in the Regulation of Work in Brazil in the 2000s*], 32 Cuadernos del Cendes, 48 (2015).

reputation as a successful and worker-friendly state was in part well-earned while also in part concealing its long-simmering class and racial divisions.

The labor reforms initiated by Temer have been met with by some resistance, and some aspects of the reform are still being challenged in court. However, the election of Jair Bolsonaro in 2018 reenergized the cultural and economic politics which had long prioritized the labor reforms initiated by Temer. Bolsonaro's marked hostility to the whole range of PT policies manifested in executive support for deepening the reforms through a number of aggressive provision measures while continuing to undermine the judicial and administrative enforcement of labor rights more generally. Whatever impact international sources of law had in the past are unlikely to continue in the short-term, especially as antidiscrimination norms are a high-profile target for Bolsonaro's regressive cultural politics.

The 2017 reforms have thus presented a significant ongoing challenge to the traditional hierarchy of sources by centering individuated bargaining over the terms of employment and sidelining the force of collective agreements and the precedential case law of the TST. In structural terms, the place of the constitutional at the top of the hierarchy of Brazilian labor law remains untouched. The CLT is still the primary federal source of statutory law which creates the basic structure of union bargaining and employment contracting, but the relationship of legislation and collective agreements to individual employment contracts has been reshaped. The shift in a few basic presumptions about the standard-setting role of these sources of law shows how much a system of labor regulation can be transformed even when the formal hierarchy of its legal sources remained in place.

BIBLIOGRAPHY

A. Gomes & M. Prado, *Flawed Freedom of Association in Brazil*, 32 Comp. Lab. L. & Pol'y J., 843 (2011).

Ana Gomes, *The Effects of the ILO's Declaration on Fundamental Principles and Rights at Work on the Evolution of Legal Policy in Brazil: An Analysis of Freedom of Association* (University of Toronto, 2009).

C. Mercante, *As Raizes Autoritarias da Atual Lei Greve Brasileira* [*The Authoritarian Roots of Brazil's Current Law on Striking*], 7 Rev. Dir. Mackenzie, 42 (2014).

J. Dari Krein & M. de Barros Biavaschi, *Os Movimentos Contraditórios da Regulação do Trabalho no Brasil dos Anos 2000* [*The Contradictory Movements in the Regulation of Work in Brazil in the 2000s*], 32 Cuadernos del Cendes, 48 (2015).

J.F. Mayer, *The Limits of Labor Legislation Reforms: Rigidity, Growth, and Employment in Brazil (1995–2010)*, 8 J. Pol. Latin Am., 95 (2016).

J. Renda Leal Fernandes, *Labor Law, CLT and the 2017 Brazilian Labor Reform*, 5 Panorama of Brazilian L., 210 (2017).

Jeff Sluyter-Beltrao, *Rise and Decline of Brazil's New Unionism* (Peter Lang, 2010).

John French, *Drowning in Laws; Labor Law and Brazilian Political Culture* (UNC Press, 2004).

M. Doctor, *Lula's Development Council Neo-corporatism and Policy Reform in Brazil*, 34 Latin Am. Persp., 131 (2007).

Mauricio Barros, *Labour Relations and the New Unionism in Contemporary Brazil* (Palgrave, 1999).

P. Fontes, A. Fortes & D. Mayer, *Brazilian Labour History: New Perspectives in Global Context*, 62 Int'l Rev. Soc. Hist. 1 (2017).

P. Ribeiro, *An Amphibian Party? Organisational Change and Adaptation in the Brazilian Workers' Party, 1980–2012*, 46 J. Latin Am. Stud., 87 (2014).

S. Coslovsky, R. Pires & R. Bignami, *Resilience and Renewal: Labor Unions, Inspectors, Prosecutors and the Enforcement of Labor Laws in Brazil*, 59 Latin Am. Pol. & Soc'y., 77 (2017).

CHAPTER 9

Multilayers and Complexity of Chinese Labour Laws Sources

Dong Yan

9.1 INTRODUCTION

The sources of labour regulation in the People's Republic of China (PRC) have undergone a rapid expansion between 1994 and 2012, most notably in 2008 when three labour-related laws came into force. One interpretation which has been widely put forward is that the building of a regulatory framework in the field of labour that demonstrates China's efforts towards the establishment of the 'rule of law'.

At the same time, it has been common in China for laws to be associated with a set of implementation rules and interpretations, together with voluntary rules like collective agreements and codes of conduct, to deal with specific problems which are likely to arise in the course of the enforcement of those laws. Thus, without exception, when the new sets of labour regulation came into force in 2008, they were accompanied by a veritable wave of administrative and judicial implementation regulations, together with a horizontal set of voluntary rules, to ensure that those laws reach out to the general public.

On most occasions, the labour-related laws or regulations issued by the National People's Congress (NPC) and State Council sit at the centre of the Chinese labour regulatory framework and therefore are commonly referred to as 'core' sources of laws. Accordingly, their implementation instruments and voluntary agreements generated by the related enforcement agencies and parties are viewed by many as 'peripheral' sources of regulation.

It is suggested that the main attention of most commentators has traditionally been focused on (and currently remains with) the 'core' sources and their statutory text, without sufficient awareness of the 'peripheral-complementary' sources of regulation. The real progress and challenges of Chinese labour legislation, however, remain significantly under-explored, as those 'core' sources fail to provide a 'complete picture' or 'accurate picture' of Chinese labour regulation.[1] In many cases, indeed, the so-called peripheral sources have played an important role in dealing with reality.

This chapter therefore seeks to set out a complete picture of the sources of Chinese labour law, including both the 'core' and the 'peripheral' instruments, along with their internal relations. It is argued that commentators and legal professionals alike need not only to 'read between the lines' of the 'core' regulations but also to take full account of the relevant 'peripheral' instruments before offering advice to policymakers or external readers.

9.2 LABOUR LAWS ISSUED BY THE NPC AND THE STATE COUNCIL: THE 'CORE LAWS'

9.2.1 The Prominent Role of NPC

The National People's Congress is the national legislature of the People's Republic of China. According to the Constitution and the Legislation Law, the NPC is vested with the highest lawmaking powers, but it is only held once a year to discuss the basic laws. The Standing Committee of the NPC is a committee of about 150 NPC members, which is convened between plenary sessions of the NPC. It has the constitutional authority to modify legislation within the limits set by the NPC and thus acts as an important legislative body in the field of labour law.

During the economic reforms that were put into effect after 1978, the Chinese government withdrew from micro-labour management and left room for formal laws, such as Labour Law 1994, to establish the requisite regulatory framework. Previously, under the planned economy, the State had acted as a micro-administrator on labour issues,[2] so that the employment relationship was dealt with primarily by Party policies implemented through 'administrative muscle', rather than through legislation by way of law and enforcement agencies.

In 1982, the NPC amended the Constitution with a view to restoring 'law and order', as well as a legal system, in China. Thus, in order to facilitate the

1. For instance, *see* S. Cooney, *Making Chinese Labor Law Work: The Prospects for Regulatory Innovation in the People's Republic of China*, 30 Fordham International L. J., 30 (2007); R. Brown, *Understanding Labor and Employment Law in China* (1st ed., Cambridge University Press, 2009).
2. B. Taylor, C. Kai & L. Qi, *Industrial Relations in China* (Edward Elgar Publishing, 2003).

recently declared 'Open Door' Policy in the country, a new law – namely, the Foreign-Investment Enterprises Law of the PRC – was enacted to provide managerial autonomy to foreign-investment enterprises, including their personnel/HR management. Later, in 1987, the State proceeded to call for the establishment of individual 'employment contracts' between workers and management in enterprises.[3] Undoubtedly, this marked a clear trend for the State to introduce some sort of law-based 'labour market governance' familiar to many Western countries.[4]

The enactment of Labour Law 1994 demonstrated that the emerging legal system was about to place the labour relationship under the radar. Labour Law 1994 deals with ten areas, each of which is regulated by a separate chapter – covering employment promotion, employment contract, holidays, wages, occupational health and safety, special groups, occupational training, social security, labour-dispute settlement and inspection. One can hardly suggest, seriously, that Labour Law 1994 merely constitutes a symbolic gesture to embrace the 'rule of labour law', given that it not only sets out the legitimate rights and obligations of all the labour market players but also offers a framework for law enforcement, with a dedicated dispute-settlement mechanism and inspection arrangements for labour issues.

As what follows, the Standing Committees of NPC and State Council have enacted or amended a number of labour-related laws and generally 'completed' the picture raised by Labour Law 1994. A common feature that underlines the current PRC policy formulation is the evident endeavour to deliver the promises made by Labour Law 1994 for Chinese citizens. Labour Law 1994 establishes the framework for the labour regulatory framework in China.

The amended Trade Union Law and the Law on the Protection of Rights and Interests of Women further fulfil the promises made by Labour Law 1994. While the enactment of Occupational Disease Prevention Law 2001 and Safe Production Law 2002 was undertaken to assure workers a safe workplace, Social Insurance Law 2010 seeks to offer a secure life. Employment Promotion Law 2008 signals a 'strategic road map' for the role of the State in employment relationships. The relationship between an employer and employee is embedded in the Labour Contract Law, while the Labour Disputes Conciliation and

3. In the early stage of reform, local authorities retained de facto power to influence the employment of State Owned Enterprises (SOEs) even where this was inconsistent with the enforcement of the labour contract system. Before being applied to all enterprises, a labour contract system, which aimed to promote management autonomy of enterprises, was experimented with to replace the labour planned mechanism in the SOEs from 1983. However, according to the call for a labour contract system – the *Interim Provision on Implementing the Labour Contract System* in SOEs 1986 (State Council) – local labour authorities were supposed to cede their labour allocation powers to the SOEs, but 'could guide the SOEs to recruit publicly based on their capacity' (Article 4).
4. A.H.Y. Chen, *An Introduction to the Legal System of the People's Republic of China* (Butterworths Asia, 1992).

Arbitration Law are taking a lead in settling problems arising out of that relationship.

9.2.2 Administrative Regulations of the State Council

The State Council can produce administrative regulations and orders under the provisions of Legislation Law 2000. Historically, notwithstanding disruptions to the legal system from 1958 to 1978, the State Council had continued to issue labour-related rules, but with a slight change in focus. The legislative activity returned to normality in the wake of the economic reforms from 1978 onwards. In particular, Article 56 of Legislation Law 2000, in conjunction with Article 89 of the Constitution 1982, empowers the State Council to issue administrative regulations to implement the laws.[5] In 2001, the State Council enacted its Regulation on the Administrative Regulation-Making Procedure, which addresses the legislative procedure of the State Council in somewhat loose terms.

Indeed, the State Council has issued a set of administrative regulations in the field of labour protection, such as the Labour Protection Inspection Provision 2004. Thus, the State Council may interpret a textual issue arising out of the concrete application of the law in areas other than adjudication and procuratorial work.[6] Such activity is known as administrative or executive interpretation.[7]

9.3 LABOUR REGULATIONS FROM OTHER SOURCES ('PERIPHERAL INSTRUMENTS')

Apart from the top legislatures (namely the NPC, its Standing Committee and the State Council), the ministries, judicial bodies and even local authorities can also produce normative labour rules, particularly in response to the matters arising from implementation. Although those normative regulations produced by lower-level legislatures, formally speaking, may carry lighter legislative weight in accordance with Legislation Law 2000, they are actually crucial in Chinese labour market governance for a threefold reason.

First, those normative rules, as being designed, are either to fill the gap left by the higher regulations or to provide practical guidance to implementing them. In theory, and as indicated in the performance, those normative rules are major

5. The State Council may be specifically authorized to issue an administrative regulation on matters originally under the authority of the NPC or the Standing Committee. Indeed, within the *Constitution 1982* of the State Council, there was no mention of any procedural matters regarding producing an administrative regulation.
6. P. Keller, *Legislation in the People's Republic of China*, 23 University of British Columbia L. R., 3, 633 (1989).
7. Chen (n. 4).

references where law and order enforcement agencies cannot find clear guidance from the major regulations that are often deliberately drafted in abstract terms to give flexibility in labour regulation for China in a large scale.

Second, the scale of lower-level normative rules is not less and covers equal, if not more, range of issues as the core laws do. The lower-level normative rules are designed to provide support for all higher-level regulations, which shall cover all the subject matters therein. Moreover, as to be discussed in the following section, many lower-level normative rules often expand their scope of application to address many new issues.

Third, the normative rules often actually carry more weight than the regulations, as their policymakers often are the direct superiors running the implementation agencies.[8] Therefore, the enforcement officer has to follow the rules of their institute even if they contradict the higher-level regulations.

Therefore, it is worthwhile to lay out the possible normative rules issued by different bodies prior to analysing the internal relationship between regulations under Chinese labour law framework. According to Legislation Law 2000, there are three sorts of normative regulations at lower level, which are ministerial regulations, judicial interpretations and local regulations. In addition, there are other sorts of voluntary rules permitted by labour laws, such as collective agreements and codes of conduct.

9.3.1 Ministerial Regulations

Legislation Law 2000 provides that Ministries can issue substantive Ministerial Regulations within their field of jurisdiction. Along with Legislation Law 2000, the Regulation on the Procedure for the Enactment of Ministerial Regulations 2002 was issued by the State Council in 2001 to govern the Ministerial rule-making procedure. In consequence, the Ministries themselves have the power to launch initiatives and draft a proposal.

Most of the labour-related Ministerial Regulations in China are issued by the Ministry of Human Resource and Social Security (MoHRSS),[9] and these, by and large, are concerned with the issue of the administrative implementation of laws and regulations. Indeed, there are a large number of laws that have been enacted in the form of Ministerial Regulations, dealing with matters ranging from wage payments to labour protection and the management of social security schemes.

It is also necessary to mention that many regulations are not enacted solely by the MoHRSS. Thus, for example, in relation to occupational health and safety

8. R. Peerenboom, *China's Long March Toward Rule of Law* (Cambridge University Press, 2002).
9. It is also worth noting here that the Ministry of Labour and Social Security was separated out from the Ministry of Labour and Personnel in 1987 and was then merged back with the Ministry of Personnel – as the Ministry of Human Resource and Social Security – in 2008.

issues, the MoHRSS very often works in collaboration with the State Administration Bureau of Work Safety and the Ministry of Health to issue health and safety standards and inspection rules. Meanwhile, by reason of the special political arrangements, the All-China Federation of Trade Unions (ACFTU) also plays an interesting role in relation to the issuing of Ministerial Regulations.

Strictly speaking, policy documents of the ACFTU are not considered as regulations, since the ACFTU is not an administrative body. However, in practice, the ACFTU is permitted to issue regulations jointly with other Ministries and enact regulations under joint names. Indeed, although the name of the ACFTU is always listed after any other Ministries, the authoritative nature of the ACFTU cannot be denied.

For instance, on 29 April 2006, the ACFTU along with the State Administration of Work Safety and the State Administration of Coal Mine Safety jointly issued a Notice regarding the launching of a 'Special Campaign for Migrant Worker Safety and Health'. The Notice required trade union branches and work safety bureaux to conduct safety awareness programmes and training for workers and managers in the mining, construction and manufacturing industries, where there is a high concentration of migrant workers. Through such joint legislative methods, therefore, the ACFTU has gained a powerful political status, which enables it to intervene in labour issues as an administrative player rather than as purely one of the 'social partners'.

9.3.2 Judicial Interpretations

In the field of labour law, the Supreme People's Court has the power to interpret certain legal issues arising from the application of the law in the adjudicative work of the courts.[10] The interpretations from the Supreme People's Court are referred to as 'judicial interpretations'. Since 1979, large quantities of interpretative materials have fallen within the category of judicial interpretation. Judicial interpretations issued by the Supreme People's Court have varied dramatically in terms of their titles, length, format and style.

First, the Supreme People's Court may issue a short reply to a specific question of law submitted by a lower court, where that court is in the process of dealing with a case in which that question has arisen. The reply will refer to the

10. The Supreme People's Procurate may also interpret points of law arising from the concrete application of the law in procuratorial work. It should, however, be noted that the involvement of the Supreme People's Procurate in the labour law field is very rare (effectively limited only to where there has been a serious accident raising issues in relation to health and safety at work), and the formality of its juridical interpretation is also similar to that undertaken by the Supreme People's Court. In consequence, therefore, this presentation concentrates more on the role and work of the Supreme People's Court than the Supreme People's Procurate as regards judicial interpretations.

facts of the case or will merely state an abstract proposition of law without any specific reference to the facts.

Second, a document may be drawn up in a 'question-and-answer' format to be used by the Supreme People's Court for responding to various questions that have been posed by different lower courts.

The third type of document will set out a list of opinions on a particular piece of law: something which comes close to 'legislation' in both form and nature. The list of opinions will be used to interpret or elaborate upon legislative provisions, and to supplement, or even fill in gaps in the existing legislation. Thus, for example, the Supreme People's Court issued a Judicial Interpretation in 2006 in relation to settling labour disputes, which not only deals with the procedural matter of labour dispute settlement but also touches upon various other substantive issues of labour law, such as the right to be paid.[11]

9.3.3 Local Regulations

According to Legislation Law 2000, Local People's Congresses and governments are provided with an inherent authority to legislate. Local People's Congresses have the inherent authority to '... in light of the specific conditions and actual needs of their respective administrative areas, formulate local regulations, provided that such regulations do not contradict the Constitution, laws and administrative regulations'.[12] Similarly, the provincial local governments also enjoy a certain degree of legislative power. As Article 73 of the Legislation Law declares: 'Local governments may formulate rules to govern the following matters: (1) matters requiring the formulation of rules to implement the provisions of laws, administrative regulations and local regulations; (2) specific administrative matters pertaining to their respective administrative areas.'

In fact, despite lacking direct powers from Legislation Law 2000, many other local governing bodies enjoy a degree of de facto legislative power through the issuing of directives, guidances and decrees. Thus, local administrative discretion has been granted to local authorities after the economic reforms. It has been suggested, indeed, that local administrative officials need more discretionary powers in order to respond to the demands of a rapidly changing economy.[13] Since most of the implementation power in the labour field is handed over to local labour authorities, it is common for these bodies to issue mandatory 'codes

11. For instance, wage arrears are defined as a labour matter by *Labour Law 1994*. However, this judicial interpretation views wage arrears disputes as civil cases, so that the parties can seek a verdict from the Court, instead of processing their claim through the Labour Arbitration Committee.
12. *See* Article 63 of *Legislation Law 2000*.
13. *See*, for example, Peerenboom (n. 8) 412.

of practice' where the central regulations need to be further clarified in the course of resolving day-to-day issues.

Apart from the administrative branch, local People's Courts – especially the High Courts at the provincial level – very often issue codes of practice or guidances for the lower courts, in response to some specific practical issues arising out of the implementation of national laws and regulations. Indeed, Labour Dispute Conciliation and Arbitration Law 2008 maintains a procedural hybrid for administrative and judicial organs to deal with labour disputes as a labour dispute can go through both administrative arbitration and judicial litigation. Both local authorities and judicial institutions play a greater role regarding the rule-making in the field of labour law than in most other areas – as very often comes across with decrees and guidances from local authorities and courts dealing with labour relations.[14]

9.3.4 Collective Agreements

Labour Contract Law 2008 has dedicated a chapter for collective agreement to ensure its wide range of applicability. As being addressed in Article 51 of the chapter, 'after bargaining on an equal basis, enterprise employees as one party and their employing unit may conclude a collective agreement on such matters as labor remuneration, working hours, rest and leave, labor safety and hygiene, insurance and welfare, etc'. Indeed, the parties of labour relationship are allowed to form their own agreement for every aspect of the workplace.

As a procedural safeguard, there are requirements for employee participation and administrative oversight. First, the draft of the collective agreement shall be presented to the employee representative congress or all the employees for discussion and approval. Second, the concluded collective agreement shall be submitted to the labour administration department. The collective agreement will then become effective upon fifteen days from the date of receipt thereof by the authority, unless any objection to the agreement has been raised.

However, the status of a collective agreement remains uncertain while it has been frequently or widely regarded as a source of labour law. Although, Article 54 of Labour Contract Law 2008 has articulated that if an employer has breached a legitimate collective agreement, the trade union may, in accordance with the law, seek remedy against the employer through labour arbitration or litigation. However, there are some but a very few claims, awards or judgments that refer to the collective agreement. In principle, a collective agreement can

14. As being established by Labour Law 1994 and restated by Labour Dispute Conciliation and Mediation Law 2008, a labour dispute needs to go through arbitration that is run by labour authority before getting into People's Court. In other words, the People's Court only deals with the labour case that is arbitrated by Labour Arbitration Committee and appealed by the parties.

only set the protection above the floor laid by statutory laws (in favour of employees).

9.3.5 Code of Conduct

Both Labour Law 1994 and Labour Contract Law 2008 have admitted to using codes of conduct to deal with the relationship between employer and employees in the workplace. In accordance with Article 4 of Labour Contract Law 2008, the code of conduct can be adopted to set the rules of not only the disciplinary process and actions but also remuneration, welfare, labour protection, working hours, employment training, etc. In essence, the code of conduct is able to cover the specifications of all aspects of work, as long as it does not contradict with existing statutory laws and collective agreements.

In order to ensure that the code of conduct is both legitimate and sensible for all, Labour Contract Law 2008 requires its enactment subject to 'due process', so-called democratic process. Employees, employee representatives and trade unions ought to be involved while drafting a code of conduct. Employers also take the responsibility to notify all their employees of the enacted code of conduct, the manner in which it is rendered as a publicly accessible rule.

It is noteworthy that codes of conduct, in fact, play a rather important role in regulating daily working life. In particular, Article 38 of Labour Contract Law 2008 enlists the violation of company rules as a legitimate reason to dismiss employees. As illustrated by many adjudications, Chinese labour arbitration committees and People's Courts often take the code of conduct of a claiming company as a reference point where a dispute of dismissal has arisen.

9.3.6 Individual Employment Contract

The employment contract system has been formally adopted by Labour Law 1994. It is a mandatory requirement to form an employment contract between the parties, who want to establish an employment relationship. Indeed, Labour Contract Law 2008 has further stipulated the need for a written employment contract within one month of commencing work.[15] Labour Contract Law 2008 has even imposed a penalty on those employers who failed to sign a written employment contract with their employees.[16]

Labour Law 1994 allows parties to set their rights and obligations through an employment contract as long as it does not contradict the existing statutory laws. For instance, the employer and the employee can set any level of remuneration as long as it has exceeded the level of minimum wages. Once an

15. *See* Article 10 of Labour Contract Law 2008.
16. *See* Article 82 of Labour Contract Law 2008.

employment contract has been concluded in accordance with the law, it shall possess legal binding force. Thereafter, the parties involved must fulfil the obligations as stipulated in the employment contract.[17] For those who breach the existing contract, the counterparty has the right to seek a remedy through judicial process.

9.4 HIERARCHY OF CHINESE LABOUR LAWS

The hierarchy of labour laws is also of importance in the context of understanding their status. Where two labour regulations conflict with each other, their respective level of authority will depend on their hierarchical status. Consequently, it is important here to spell out the hierarchical structure of the Chinese labour regulations.

The relative level of authority for labour laws in China always depends on the hierarchical status of the lawmaking body responsible for enacting the particular law. The hierarchy of any lawmaking body is organized (from most to least powerful) as follows: (1) the NPC, (2) the Standing Committee of the NPC, (3) the State Council and the Ministries (equivalent to Provincial Government) and (4) voluntary rules, for example, collective agreements and codes of conduct.[18] No matter what designation is given to a particular piece of legislation, its authoritative status is determined by the hierarchical position of its enacting body. Thus, for example, a regulation released by the State Council will 'outrank' any Ministerial regulation produced by the Ministries.

A related problem concerns the confusion surrounding the same level of lawmaking organs within the system. This problem will particularly arise between normative documents issued by the Ministry and a Provincial Government and between Ministries. For instance, in 2003, both Beijing and Shanghai introduced domestic rules prohibiting migrant workers from accessing certain categories of jobs – provisions which directly conflicted with the MoHRSS' Reply on Applying Labour Laws to Rural Migrant Workers 2003 of the same year, which prohibited such restrictions nationwide.

Yet another problem involves the conflict between administrative rules and a judicial interpretation issued by the Supreme People's Court. Indeed, as regards this particular issue, there is no formal 'ranking system' available in weighing up a measure comparatively as between the Ministries and the Supreme People's Court.

---

17. *See* Article 17 of Labour Law 1994.
18. However, the Provincial People's Congress can, in accordance with *Legislation Law 2000*, draft domestic regulations. Indeed, the hierarchal relationship between the Provincial People's Congress and the Ministry is not specified by *Legislation Law 2000*. Since this law merely focuses on the central legislation, the Provincial People's Congress will not be discussed in detail here.

In relation to the above-mentioned problems, Legislation Law 2000 has established a 'report and review' mechanism. Thus, in terms of the legislative issue arising from two equivalent lawmaking bodies, the general principle is that the matter should be reported to the body which stands above them. For instance, when there is a legislative dispute between Ministries or between a Ministry and a Provincial Government, the matter will be handed over to the State Council to settle.[19] However, if such an issue arises between a Ministry and the Supreme People's Court, the matter has to be reported to an even higher authority – the NPC Standing Committee, which is the legislative governing body for both institutions.

Due to the complexity of such checking procedures on the legislation, the problem of conflicts between normative documents made by institutions at the same level of hierarchical authority becomes an omnipresent reality for the Chinese legal system.

9.5 DEVELOPMENTS AND CHALLENGES ON THE SOURCES OF LABOUR LAW

There is little doubt that the regulatory framework of Chinese labour law is gradually taking a complete shape, contributed to by the legislation from the NPC and the State Council. While Labour Law 1994 sets up the structure of labour governance for Chinese workers, other related laws have been either amended or produced in order to 'flesh out' the areas set out in the law. The efforts to build a wholesome protective infrastructure for Chinese workers have been significant and concrete. Therefore, it is arguable that the emergence of modern labour laws in China represents a further step in the direction of the 'rule of law' as regards legal certainty and clarity.

At the same time, the Ministries, judicial bodies and local authorities responsible for labour-related matters continue to issue interpretations and implementation rules to fill the gaps left by these 'higher' laws. In many ways, the lower normative rules play, if not a more important, certainly an equal role with 'upper' laws, as most law and enforcement branches are required to act in line with their superior authority.

Other players in labour relations are also encouraged to form their voluntary rules to guide the specifications of labour management and cooperation. Together with statutory provisions, collective agreements and codes of conduct have established hybrid normative rules for Chinese workplaces, after four decades of development.

However, the multilayers and complexity of the multilayer complex sources of Chinese labour law have created a challenge for many, as one cannot

19. *See* Article 86 of Legislation Law 2000.

build nationwide, unified presumptions based on national laws without recognizing the variety of labour law sources. These sources include administrative and local regulations, collective agreements and codes of conduct. In theory, the local regulations shall toe the line with central regulations or at least amend themselves to reduce their inconsistency. Ironically, the local regulations may prevail when they conflict with central regulations since law enforcement power has been decentralized and they opt for local development strategy.[20]

It can be a bitter factor for those enterprises which wish setting out single employment management scheme across the country. Many enterprises have opened up branches in different regions of China and involve in frequent transferring or hiring of employees across regions. Regional differences in labour regulations bring difficulties for the companies in setting up a standard practice. Instead, many have to choose segmented human resource practices, which still remain risky, particularly when they transfer employees.

One may draw an inaccurate picture by singling out either administrative or judicial labour regulations, or without recognizing each one's practical importance in dealing with labour disputes. As labour dispute shall go through administrative judication before appealing to litigation, both administrative and judicial rules have an equal impact on guiding practice in the workplace. The conflict between them may create an incomplete picture that leads to a number of particular issues in the field of labour law.

9.6 CONCLUSION

Chinese sources of labour law create a profound system which not only includes the laws issued by the NPC but also integrates the normative rules created by various central and local authorities, and among individual players. The former has received the most attention among the commentators either abroad or in China to decrypt Chinese labour governance. The latter, however, has been barely reviewed by mainstream scholarship.

Indeed, this chapter suggests that, in the field of labour governance, the lower-level sources of labour law play an equally, if not more, important role in forging labour practice in Chinese workplaces. By its own nature, the lower-level regulations and grassroots voluntary rules are more specific and operative than their superior laws, and therefore are more likely to be referenced by the law and order enforcement agency. In those areas that have not been addressed by the higher-level laws, the lower-level regulations and rules might be the only reference for the local authority to adopt. Therefore, it is utterly necessary to throw more light upon the lower-level sources of labour law rather than simply focus on the clauses in the core laws.

20. Z. Qianfan, *The Constitution of China: A Contextual Analysis* (Bloomsbury Publishing, 2012).

BIBLIOGRAPHY

S. Cooney, *Making Chinese Labor Law Work: The Prospects for Regulatory Innovation in the People's Republic of China*, 30 Fordham International L. J., 30 (2007); R. Brown, *Understanding Labor and Employment Law in China* (1st ed., Cambridge University Press, 2009).

P. Keller, *Legislation in the People's Republic of China*, 23 University of British Columbia L. R., 3, 633 (1989).

R. Peerenboom, *China's Long March Toward Rule of Law* (Cambridge University Press, 2002).

B. Taylor, C. Kai & L. Qi, *Industrial Relations in China* (Edward Elgar Publishing, 2003).

Z. Qianfan, *The Constitution of China: A Contextual Analysis* (Bloomsbury Publishing 2012).

CHAPTER 10

The Danish Struggle to Maintain the Primacy of Collective Bargaining

Christian Højer Schjøler

10.1 INTRODUCTION AND RELEVANT SOURCES OF LABOUR LAW

The chapter reflects on the development in the hierarchy of norms in Danish labour law with particular emphasis on the Danish model of voluntarist collective bargaining, which contrary to other European Union (EU) Member States does not give *erga omnes* effect to collective labour agreements (CLAs). After a brief analysis of the historical background of the model and CLAs as a labour norm, the chapter will highlight the struggles the model has had to overcome during the course of time to maintain the prerogative of CLAs and the regulatory powers of the social partners. The introduction of labour norms and fundamental rights by the EU has entailed a restriction on the regulatory framework of the social partners vis-à-vis the rights to free movement of services and workers. The present trend of self-employment over regular employment presents a difficult challenge to the model, which has historically focused on collective rights of employees.

The chapter will focus on the three prevailing sources of labour law in Denmark, which are very much intertwined. They are statutory legislation, CLAs and EU law.

10.1.1 Principles Governing the Hierarchy

Determining the hierarchy of labour law norms involves taking a closer look at the national and international sources of law and on what legal criteria their relationship to each other is built. One quickly discovers a multitude of rule-makers at different levels and no overarching particular ranking of the different sources; the EU unilaterally adopts EU-legislation; the European social partners conclude cross-industry framework agreements; the Danish State unilaterally adopts statutory legislation; national trade unions and their counterpart, the employer organisations, enter into collective bargaining agreements; local employee-representatives and their counterpart, the employer, conclude local agreements at plant level through bargaining; the employees and their counterpart, the employer, conclude employment contracts through individual negotiations; and finally, the employer can unilaterally issue staff policies governing the workplace. They all have different characteristics and very different objectives albeit the unilateral regulation from the EU and the national state legislator primarily serve the purpose of providing the employee with adequate protection in coherence with the paradigm of the worker being the weaker party. Staff policies however are issued by the employer with their prime objective being to serve the interest of the employer. Is it possible to flesh out legal criteria or principles governing the relationship of these comprehensive labour law regulations such as to avoid clashes between them? To some extent yes. The principle of favourability allows the contracting parties to deviate from statutory law or even CLAs if they agree upon more favourable conditions for the employee. The principle is, however, not unconditional, which the chapter will return to. The use of opening clauses also provides guidance when determining the hierarchy between labour law norms, but first it is necessary to understand the historical background behind the development of the primacy of CLAs in Denmark.

10.1.2 Historical Background

Danish labour law is part of the Nordic law family and is structured on the principles of contract law.[1] Labour law not only covers rules on civil law but also to some extent rules on public law as well,[2] especially with regard to public employees, where laws on public administration govern certain aspects of the employment relationship in addition to said principles and labour law.

The history behind the present hierarchy of legal norms within the labour market starts in the early 1800, at the time of industrialisation in Denmark, where there was only little interest in regulating working conditions by law. Due to a very modest interest in governing working conditions by means of legislation, only a few and sporadic statutes existed, which regulated a small number

1. Ole Hasselbalch, *Labour Law in Denmark*, 30 (4th ed. 2016).
2. One example is the rules on health and safety on the workplace, which consists of numerous acts on the working environment, considered public law.

of select groups, for instance seafarers. Instead, working conditions were primarily regulated through individual employment contracts supplemented by custom and craft guilds.[3] The so-called June Constitution brought about a new ideological foundation based on personal liberty and free competition incorporating a range of new freedoms, *inter alia* the freedom of association.[4]

These new freedoms were the backdrop of an emerging organisation of workers. In the late nineteenth century, a system of organisation-based collective bargaining emerged and the idea of CLAs as the dominant legal norm on the labour market was born. At the time, labour was in abundant supply, working conditions were very poor, and the only way for workers to improve working conditions was by gaining bargaining leverage acting in solidarity. This led the local trade unions to unite and form national federations of trade unions utilising strikes and boycotts in order to force employers into concluding CLAs improving working conditions.[5] The movement in the year 1898 lead to the formation of a confederation called the Danish Workers Confederation (now known as FH – the Danish Trade Union Confederation) consisting of most of the national trade unions. The response of the employers to the increasing unified efforts of the trade unions was to establish corresponding employers' federations. In 1896 most of these had unified in a national confederation, the Danish Employers' Confederation (known as DA).[6] The bargaining efforts gave way for an increasing number of conflicts, and in 1899 a particular serious and long nationwide conflict lasting for more than 100 days was finally brought to an end with the historic September Agreement. The September Agreement ended the conflict and laid down namely two fundamental principles – the rules dictating the framework for establishing industrial conflicts and acknowledgement of the employers' managerial authority. Perhaps more importantly, the premises of the agreement later on became subject to interpretation by the Danish Labour Court, whereby the Court created a system of rules comprising the rules of collective labour law.[7] The agreement and its resulting case law obviated the need for statutory legislation on collective labour law.

10.1.3 Collective Agreements and Statutory Legislation as Legal Norms in Labour Law

There is a very strong tradition in Danish labour law that the state entrusts the social partners with legislative-like powers through their formation of rules of

3. Hasselbalch (n. 1) 35.
4. Jens Kristiansen, *The Growing Conflict Between European Uniformity and National Flexibility: The Case of Danish Flexicurity and European Harmonisation of Working Condition*, 24 (Djoef Publishing 2015).
5. Hasselbalch (n. 1) 35.
6. *Ibid.*, p. 26.
7. *Ibid.*, p. 32; Kristiansen (n. 4) 25.

law by conclusion of CLAs with each other. Only in exceptional cases, has it been necessary to issue statutory legislation and only in instances where the aim was to protect certain groups of workers whose organisation had insufficient power to protect their members or were otherwise in need of special protection, and never on the topic of pay.[8] The social partners have played a considerable role in the formation of such legislation and its amendments.[9] One such instance was the need for a general legal framework for white-collar workers (salaried employees), which in 1938 – following a series of failed proposals for similar acts – lead to the introduction of the Act on the legal relationship between employers end salaried employees (Funktionærloven).[10] At that time white-collar workers were a minority compared to blue-collar workers, and many white-collar workers were not covered by CLAs, which has dramatically changed since then. The Salaried Employees' Act regulates certain aspects of the employment conditions in terms of lawful termination and notice periods, but it does not regulate minimum wages or working time.

Hence, there is a mutual understanding between the social partners and the legislator that there should be as little as possible interference by the State in matters concerning pay and working conditions, as these matters are more suitable to be settled by collective bargaining.[11] Naturally, this recognition of CLAs as the primary rule of law is only possible, if the social partners represent a substantive number of employees and employers acting as their representative. The unionisation rate is high in Denmark[12] at 67% (2017)[13] with approx. 74% of workers in the private sector and almost every public employee in the public sector covered by a CLA.[14]

Even though CLAs seem to take precedence over statutory legislation, there is no vertical ordering as such of CLAs towering over statutory legislation, but the aforementioned circumstances have dictated that the Danish parliament has not passed systematic legislation governing employment conditions concerning minimum wages,[15] normal working time,[16] overtime payment, sick leave pay,

8. Hasselbalch (n. 1) 39.
9. Kristiansen (n. 4) 13.
10. Statutory Act No. 1002 of 24/8/2017 on the legal relationship between employers end salaried employees.
11. Hasselbalch (n. 1) 44; Kristiansen (n. 4) 13.
12. In 2008 the average on unionisation in Europe was less than 25%. Kristiansen (n. 4) 45.
13. European Trade Union Institute (ETUI) – *Benchmarking Working Europe 2017*, 44 (ETUI, 2017). The benchmark does, however, show a small decline in the unionisation level from the period 2000-2008 until now.
14. Oktober 2015 Dagpengekommissionen, Det danske arbejdsmarked 22.
15. There are only three minor exceptions: vocational trainees are by statutory legislation ensured a minimum wage equal to the wage in the normal CLA in the trade in question, and the pay of 'crown servants' is ultimately fixed by the Parliament if the organisations do not come to an understanding during the negotiations. And finally, if the job is created as a initiative under the public unemployment scheme, a statutory act requires the pay to be settled according to the CLA within the trade. Hasselbalch (n. 1) 135.
16. Hasselbalch (n. 1) 120.

maternity leave pay, pensions, continuing education or lawful termination of employment.[17] The national legal framework regulating the conclusion of CLAs only consists of the Act on the Labour Court (Arbejdsretsloven)[18] and the Act on a Public Concilitator (Forligmandsloven).[19] However, these do not regulate how the trade unions are organised, the actual content of CLAs or the lawfulness of industrial conflicts.[20] Given the considerable scope awarded to the social partners, it is worth mentioning that their right to collective bargaining is not explicitly protected in the Constitution.[21] The right to form associations with a lawful purpose and the right to assembly and peaceful demonstration are constitutional rights, but neither the right to strike nor the right to join or not to join a trade union is protected by the Constitution.[22]

This framework is referred to as the Danish model,[23] in which the social partners de facto act as the sector-specific legislator overseeing the labour market - the specialised Labour Court and Industrial Arbitration Tribunals serving as the dispute resolution mechanism within the model.[24]

10.2 INTERPLAY AND HIERARCHY BETWEEN LEGISLATION AND COLLECTIVE AGREEMENTS

One cornerstone of the model is a long time understanding between the social partners and Government according to which, the Parliament institutes tripartite negotiations between the social partners and the legislators before passing legislation affecting any area of the labour market.[25] This mechanism is undoubtably an important element in the hierarchy of labour norms, although it is not prescribed in any statutory legislation and hence not binding for the Parliament. The passive role of the Parliament in relation to the formation of labour norms naturally adds to the perceived primacy of CLAs, but it is not as such a strict rule resulting in a hierarchical primacy whereby CLAs cannot be set aside by statutory legislation. It is rather a token of a high degree of voluntarism

17. Kristiansen (n. 4) 31.
18. Statutory Act No. 1003 of 24/08/2017 on the Labour Court and industrial arbitrations. The English version is available at The Labour Court and Industrial Arbitration: Arbejdsretten http://arbejdsretten.dk/generelt/labour-court/labour-court-act.aspx, http://arbejdsretten.dk/generelt/labour-court/labour-court-act.aspx (last accessed 30 August 2019).
19. Statutory Act No. 709 of 20/08/2002 on Conciliation in Collective Disputes.
20. Hasselbalch (n. 1) 51.
21. Jens Kristiansen, *Den kollektive arbejdsret*, 112 (3d ed. Djøf Forlag 2014).
22. Hasselbalch (n. 1) 51.
23. *Ibid.*, p. 44.
24. Hasselbalch (n. 1) 44.
25. There is a continuous dialogue between the parties with the latest agreement being an agreement on continuing training from October 2017 and an agreement on apprenticeships from August 2016. Trepartsaftaler, https://bm.dk/arbejdsomraader/politiske-aftaler-reformer/politiske-aftaler/trepartsaftaler/ (last accessed 30 August 2019).

leaving rights and obligations on the labour market to the social partners to agree upon.

Denmark's membership of the EU and the obligation to implement directives by statutory law has challenged Denmark's pronounced voluntarism by forcing the legislators to play a more active role deviating from their traditional facilitating role.[26] The Parliament sought to mitigate the challenge in 1993 by formally proclaiming their interest in maintaining the Danish model while upholding the obligation to implement directives. The Parliament formally urged the Government to cooperate with the social partners in order to ensure that the social partners are given the opportunity to implement EU's measures with the framework of the Danish model. The manoeuvrability of the social partners in the topics historically reserved for collective bargaining has none the less increasingly been inhibited by harmonisation efforts of the EU thereby challenging the legal hierarchy of norms on the labour market. These circumstances led the Danish parliament and the most influential negotiators in the labour market organisations to issue a unified 'no' as their response to the proposal by the President of the European Commission, Jean-Claude Juncker, in 2014, trying to ensure a minimum wage in all twenty-eight EU Member States.[27]

The EU model of ensuring social rights for employees indirectly poses a challenge for the existence of the Danish model, as it bestows legislative responsibility for implementing EU directives and for adjusting national law in conformity with the Court of Justice of the European Union case law with the State - not the social partners.[28] When legislative power is taken from the social partners their mandate and influence is effectively weakened, which can have an effect on their ability to attract members. One vital factor in the models' sustainability is a high degree of unionisation, because if the social partners, and in this case especially the trade unions, cannot attract members, they will not have the necessary bargaining leverage to exhort pressure on undertakings to conclude CLAs. And if the trade unions are weakened to the point, where they cannot effectively proliferate coverage of CLAs, the basis of their regulatory powers disintegrates, which would force the State to assume more responsibility for the working conditions on the labour market.

Another possible challenge for the importance and precedence of CLAs is the increasing shift in the occupational structure of the labour market from blue-collar jobs to white-collar jobs.[29] The shift entails that an increasing

26. Kristiansen (n. 4) 17.
27. Eurofound, *Denmark: Heated Debate about Introducing Minimum Wage* (Eurofound 2015), https://www.eurofound.europa.eu/publications/article/2015/denmark-heated-debate-about-introducing-minimum-wage (last accessed 30 August 2019).
28. Kristiansen (n. 4) 173.
29. T. Bredgaard & P. Madsen, *Farewell Flexicurity? Danish Flexicurity and the Crisis*, Transfer: Eur. Rev. of Lab. and Res., 8 (2018).

number of workers are protected by the Act on Salaried Employees mentioned above.

10.2.1 The Normative Effect of Collective Agreements Without *Erga Omnes*

In order for a worker to enforce the minimum wage stipulated in a CLA, it needs to be applicable to the employment relationship. If no CLA is applicable, the parties are free to negotiate employment conditions only having to observe the different statutes on employment conditions prohibiting, for instance, unequal treatment of men and women. As mentioned above, none of this statutory legislation concerns the hourly or monthly pay or the number of working hours.[30] However, in case the terms agreed in the employment contract are considered unreasonable, they or even the entire contract can be modified or set aside by the courts according to section 36 in the Act on Contracts of which there - admittedly - are only very few examples in the case law of labour law.[31]

Collective agreements are applicable on the employment relationship only if the employer is a member of an employer association or has concluded a CLA directly with a trade union or a collectivity of workers bearing the characteristics of an organisation in the workplace.[32]

10.2.1.1 Presumption of Normative Effect Regardless of Membership

When the undertaking is bound by a CLA through the membership of an employer organisation, it is perceived as a prerequisite of the sector agreements that they cover all workers performing work within the occupational scope of the agreements, regardless if the workers are members of the trade union party to the sector agreements or not.

Sector agreements usually only describe the scope of the agreement through an occupational approach. Their scope can in theory be limited to members of the signatory trade union, but that option is very rarely utilised by the social partners. The normative effect regardless of membership is not explicitly mentioned in the agreements and not a result of the bargaining process. Instead, it was established through the case law of the Labour Court. This effect is an interesting aspect of the perception of CLAs as a universally binding labour norm because it relies on the contractual background of CLAs to expand the coverage of CLAs onto third parties utilising a rule of assumption.

30. Hasselbalch (n. 1) 135.
31. Statutory Act No. 193 of 2/3/2013 on contracts and other judiciary acts in the area of private law. There is no available translated version of the Act.
32. Kristiansen (n. 4) 40.

Formally the agreement is only binding on the signatories and their members. The employees who are not members of a trade union or are members of a competing union, i.e non-unionised,[33] attain no rights nor obligations themselves under the CLA.[34] However, according to the national case law, an employer bound by a CLA is under the duty to apply the terms of the agreement to all the work and positions which, according to the agreement, falls within the occupational scope of the agreement.

The case law of the Labour Court has provided an assumption entailing that work carried out for an organised employer is organised under the terms and conditions of the CLA due to the obligation of the employer to adhere to the CLA. This, however, leads to an inconsistency between the obligations of the employer and the rights of the non-unionised employee, as they are not necessarily reciprocal vis-à-vis the individual and collective level. In order for non-unionised workers to enforce the rights of the CLA, such as a minimum wage at the individual level, the rights need to be transferred to the employee via referral in the employment contract of the employee,[35] or implicitly by the practice of the parties. If the employment contract refers to the CLA, it becomes an individual right for the non-unionised worker, which the worker can enforce in the civil courts. However, if the employment contract explicitly grants the non-unionised employee less favourable rights than those stipulated in the CLA, the employee has no further rights. This could in theory could undermine the understanding of CLAs as the predominant labour norm given the obvious opportunity for the employer thereby to circumvent the CLA with regard to non-unionised workers.

However, by doing so, the employer thereby treats non-unionised workers less favourable than the provisions in the CLA enabling the trade union party to the agreement to seek action against the employer for violation of the contractual duty towards the union to organise all work under the terms and conditions of the CLA. In such cases, the employer is liable to be imposed a financial penalty according to the Labour Courts Act based on an overall assessment of the cost saving the employer achieved through the less favourable treatment combined with a punitive element to discourage the employer from violating the CLA. The penalty is not explicitly divided into these two parts in the judgment or adjudication. Perhaps surprisingly to some, the entire penalty is paid to the trade union, not to the non-unionised employee, who does not have recourse against the trade union.[36] The trade union can choose to redistribute the savings part of the penalty to the underpaid employee, but it is not obliged to do so.[37] It has been

33. The term non-unionised semantically only suggests non-membership, but for the purposes of this chapter, the term also includes employees that are members of a competing trade union that is not party to the CLA covering the work of the employee.
34. Hasselbalch (n. 1) 251.
35. *Ibid.*
36. Hasselbalch (n. 1) 252.
37. Kristiansen (n. 4) 213.

speculated by some practitioners, whether the part of the penalty related to the underpayment of the employee, despite being characterised a penalty and not being specified in the sentence of the Labour Court, is rightfully the possession of the employee and therefore protected by the protection of property in Article 1 of the first Protocol to the European Convention on Human Rights (ECHR).[38] The question has, however, not been dealt with by the national courts yet, and neither the case law of the European Court on Human Rights (ECtHR) has dealt with the issue before. In the Evaldsson and others v. Sweden case, the ECtHR found that deductions of 1.5% on the employees' wages that were made to cover the monitoring conducted by the trade union deprived the employees of their possessions within the meaning of the second sentence of the first paragraph of Article 1 of Protocol No. 1.[39] According to the Court, the wage monitoring activities lacked the necessary transparency and was thus disproportionate to the legitimate aim in 'the public interest' required to justify the deduction. Hence the Court found there had been a breach of Article 1 of Protocol No. 1 to the Convention. But contrary to the deduction of 1.5% in the Evaldsson case, the proposed possession of the employee is not specified in the sentence of the Labour Court, which could prove to be a crucial difference in the eye of the courts.

10.2.2 The Enforceability of Collective Agreements

If an employer breaches a CLA by underpaying employees, the employer risks being imposed a financial penalty by the Danish Labour Court as mentioned above. The normative effect of CLAs is therefore closely linked to the enforceability of CLAs through the Labour Court. Judicial review of disputes concerning breaches of CLAs rests exclusively with the Labour Court according to section 11(1) of the Act on the Labour Court, which ultimately precludes the civil courts from enforcing the normative effect of CLAs on the collective level. The financial penalty is a cornerstone of the Danish model and pivotal for the trade unions in their endeavours to ensure that their contractual counterpart, the employers, abide by the CLAs. The legal nature of the penalty is, however, debatable since it, on the one hand, encompasses a penal element and, on the other hand, maintains a restitutional aspect. In the original Labour Court Act of 1910, the sanction was meant to act as a special sort of compensation based primarily on the idea of being liable for damages, although the perception of it being a question of liability was later on abandoned.[40]

38. S. Kachchi & J. Sand, *Underbetaling af uorganiserede lønmodtagere*, 12 HR Jura Magasinet, 7-20 (2017).
39. *Case of Evaldsson and Others v. Sweden*, App. No. 75252/01, judgment of the 13 February 2007.
40. Hasselbalch (n. 1) 324; Kristiansen, (n. 4) 617.

It is called a bod which most accurately translates into being a fine even though it was established from a contractual point of origin. Furthermore, it does not have compensation as its primary objective given it can be imposed irrespective of actual losses. It could perhaps most easily be described as a sanction sui generis.[41]

The penal character of the fine has been raised as an issue vis-à-vis Article 6 of the European Convention on Human Rights and Protocol No. 7 to the Convention[42] in conjunction with the fact that there is no appeal against the judgments of the Labour Court.[43] If perceived as a sanction for a criminal offence, Article 2(2) of the protocol requires there to be a right to have the sentences reviewed by a higher tribunal.

The issue was raised by an employer before the Danish Labour Court in 2000,[44] where the Court dismissed the allegation. According to the Court, the requirement of a right to launch an appeal or second judicial review did not apply to civil cases, such as those under the competence of the Labour Court. Moreover, the fine was not a punishment of a criminal law nature. A fine would only be imposed on the initiative of the complainant, who was also entitled to withdraw the request for a fine. The fine is not paid to the Danish State but the complainant, who is also responsible for recovering the amount with the employer. That judgment by the Supreme Court to a large extent brought an end the discussion, until very recently, when the question came up before a lower Italian court in Siracusa, because an Italian employer had been imposed a fine of DKK 14 million (EUR 2 million) by the Danish Labour Court, which the Italian employer refused to pay.

The Danish trade union initiated a procedure to recover the fine in Italy, but Solesi interjected by filing a claim against the trade union with the Italian Court of Siracusa claiming the judgment from the Labour Court could not be enforced due to it being a manifest violation of the Italian ordre public confer Article 45(1)(a) of Regulation No. 1215/2012.[45] Before the Italian court in Siracusa Solesi *inter alia* argued the fine imposed by the Labour Court had the characteristics of a criminal penalty, since the calculation of it was not a based on a restitutional formula, but rather a penal, which led to Solesi to highlight the lack

41. Hasselbalch (n. 1) 325.
42. Protocol No. 7 to the Convention on the Protection of Human Right and Fundamental Freedoms as amended by Protocol 11 of 22/07/1984.
43. Kristiansen (n. 4) 618.
44. Labour Court judgment of 17/11/2000 in case A1996.225.
45. Regulation (EU) No. 1215/2012 of the European Parliament and of the Council of 12 December 2012 on jurisdiction and the recognition and enforcement of judgments in civil and commercial matters.

of second judicial as conflicting with Article 2 in protocol 7 to the ECHR as mentioned above.[46]

In December 2018 the court of Siracusa quite surprisingly ruled in favour of Solesi and refused to recognise and enforce the judgment of the Labour Court. According to the Italian court it was inconsistent with principles underpinning Italian law, EU law and the ECHR such as ordre public and the principle of legality. The judgment has been appealed to the Court of Appeal in Catania, and the decision of the appeal court is not expected until the year 2021. The decision by the Italian court caused uncertainty and anxiety among the social partners in Denmark, *inter alia*, because it threatens the enforceability of Labour Court judgments and indirectly weakens the legal status of CLAs as binding labour norms.

10.3 WHERE DO COLLECTIVE AGREEMENTS FIT INTO THE LEGAL HIERARCHY?

As indicated above there is not just one type of CLA. Instead, working conditions are regulated by way of a multitude of CLAs of a different hierarchical nature. Regardless of their position within the hierarchy, they only have normative effect applicable to members or a designated occupational area as mentioned above.[47]

The lack of an *erga omnes* extension through a legislative act could imply a lower legal dignity compared to statutory legislation, but that is not the case. The collective bargaining autonomy of the social partners is perceived as an almost exclusive legislative power within the confines of the labour market. Allowing the legislator to take part-ownership of CLAs by transforming them into statutory legislation would be interfering with their autonomy. The normative effect hence requires an employer to be bound by the CLA either through a membership of an employer organisation, which in turn is party to an industry-wide agreement, or through an individual agreement with a trade union. Almost all public employers are covered by CLAs, which is a result of an outspoken willingness with the public employers to enter into CLAs if the trade union in question represents the majority of the employees.

10.3.1 Types of Collective Agreements

There are various types of CLAs intertwined into a hierarchy of agreements. The hierarchy is supported by a number of fundamental principles used when

46. N.V. Munkholm, *Self-Regulating Collective Labour Relations: Trends and Responses*, 28 Aarhus U., 21 (2018).
47. Collective Agreement with Erga Omnes Applicability/Eurofound, https://www.eurofound.europa.eu/efemiredictionary/collective-agreement-with-erga-omnes-applicability.

interpreting the agreements. The highest position in the legal hierarchy belongs to the cross-sector main agreements followed by sector agreements and local agreements being of the lowest rank in the hierarchy. The hierarchical structure is governed by rank. Main agreements take precedence over sector agreements, which again take precedence over local agreements unless deviation is allowed through the use of opening clauses. The same hierarchy applies to both the private and public sector, but each sector has its own separate CLAs, which does not apply to the other sector.

Main agreements are typically concluded between the main national organisations, the most important in the private sector being the main agreement between the FH and DA.[48] Main agreements are binding on all member organisations of the national confederations. Main agreements act as the overall framework for the relationship between the main organisations and their members by regulating the lawfulness of strikes and lock-outs, possible limitations on the employer's managerial authority, termination of CLAs and the peace obligation.[49] They do not regulate the material working conditions such as wages or working hours, and they are therefore rarely renegotiated.[50]

The second tier in the hierarchy consists of sectoral agreements. Despite being secondary to main agreements they de facto make out the material labour norms in both sectors and are typically concluded between a national trade union and a national confederation of employers (or one single employer).[51] They regulate the material working conditions such as wages, working hours, overtime pay, rules of termination and often rules concerning union representatives.[52] These agreements cannot be terminated during the period of two-three years in which the agreement is valid. In order to renegotiate sectoral agreements, the parties have to give a notice of termination and await the expiration of the agreement.[53]

The sectoral agreements have a broad material scope and do not have regard for the conditions and circumstances at individual plants, which is why they often contain explicit opening clauses allowing local parties to supplement, and in rare cases to deviate from the agreement. Hence the local management

48. FH is an abbreviation for the name *Fagbevægelsens Hovedorganisation* (previously called LO), the Danish Trade Union Confederation, which is the largest national trade union confederation in Denmark. DA, *Dansk Arbejdsgiverforening*, the Confederation of Danish Employers is the largest national main employers' organisation in Denmark. Their agreement is available in English at http://www.da.dk/bilag/General%20Agreement_net.pdf.
49. Hasselbalch (n. 1) 60.
50. The most recent amendment to the Main agreement between FH and DA was negotiated in 1993.
51. If the employer is not a member of an employer organisation, the employer can accede to the industry-wide agreement by concluded an *adoption agreement* with a national trade union party to such an industry-wide agreement.
52. Hasselbalch (n. 1) 60.
53. Hasselbalch (n. 1) 259.

and a collectivity of employees of an undertaking very often supplement or amend the provisions in the sector agreements through local agreements.[54]

An example of such an opening clause can be found clause 8(1) of the sectoral Industrial Agreement between DI Overenskomst I and CO-industri according to which: 'Local agreements may be entered into between the local parties at the enterprise in respect of employees covered by this Agreement.'[55]

The wording could suggest an almost indefinite scope for departure from the clauses in the agreement. However, clause 8(7) of the sectoral agreement furthermore singles out a number of topics, which, if the local agreement concerns these topics, requires the local agreement to be in writing and only be valid if entered into with a union representative.

10.3.2 The Effect of the Hierarchy on the Relation Between the Agreements

The normative effect and hierarchy of CLAs in many respects resemble that of legislative regulation. The main agreements are comparable to the Constitution providing an overall legal framework. The sectoral agreements resemble statutory acts containing – both contain material provisions but do not regulate in detail. Local agreements regulate the individual plant and often contain detailed provisions of a more technical nature, which is similar to the administrative orders issued by public authorities, typically ministries, on the basis of an authority contained in the statutory acts.[56] Collective agreements of a lower level, such as local agreements, thus respect the clauses of the applicable sectoral agreement, which is also true of the hierarchy of legislative regulation, where statutory acts cannot defer from the Constitution and administrative orders cannot defer from statutory acts. There is, however, the added effect that a local agreement, which does not respect inderogable terms of a sector agreement, besides being null and void, also constitutes a breach of the sector agreement by the employer, even if the employee side has acceded to the local agreement.[57] If a party breaches a CLA, a financial penalty can be imposed on the party by the Labour Court independently of any loss occurred by the other party.

54. Hasselbalch (n. 1) 61.
55. The agreement is available in English here: https://www.danskindustri.dk/globalassets/di-dokumenter-kun-til-dokumentsider-i-radgivningsunivers/for-alle-kraver-ikke-login/overenskomst-fx-io/industrial-agreement-2017-2020.pdf.
56. Hasselbalch (n. 1) 48.
57. Hasselbalch (n. 1) 64. In the case AR2013.0679, judgment of 20 April 2016, the Labour Court imposed an employer a financial penalty of DKK 25,000 and a duty to reimburse the employees their underpayment, because the local agreement, which was met the formal requirement of being concluded by the union representative, awarded the employees a lower rate sick pay, than the inderogable rate of the sector agreement.

Local agreements cannot deviate from the sector agreements unless it is stipulated by opening clauses in the sector agreement as illustrated above. However, recent developments in the bargaining of sector agreements have procured the use of opening clauses allowing local representatives to negotiate wages and other terms of employment to the preferred or specific circumstances of the individual undertaking.[58] The opening clauses even allow for disadvantageous terms for the employees as long as the local representative of the trade union accedes. This tendency of transferring bargaining power to the local parties reflects an increasing demand for CLAs to be flexible towards the needs of different kind of undertakings and different groups of employees. The local parties are still subject to the peace obligation in the sector agreement under which they negotiate, which prevents the local parties from resorting to industrial action if they cannot agree on completing or amending provisions.[59] The local agreements can even be short-term agreements concerning specific production assignments or periods, which is to the benefit of both employees and employers in their efforts to obtain the best agreement at plant level.

10.3.3 The Interplay Between Collective Agreements and Statutory Legislation

Collective agreements are still the preferred way of regulating pay and working conditions, which meant that legislation has been sporadic and piecemeal. More so, when the legislature has seen fit to legislate on labour conditions, the purpose has not been to deregulate CLAs, but rather to extend the well-proven principles and worker protection found in CLAs to persons not covered by a CLA, which bears the characteristics of an *erga omnes* effect.

Two examples of such gap-filling were the adoption of the Salaried Workers' Act (Funktionærloven)[60] and the Holiday Act (Ferieloven)[61] in 1938. Prior to the enactment of the Salaried Workers' Act in 1938, a proposal to the Act was put forth before the Parliament, which intended to cover only those workers, which were not covered by CLAs, since the Parliament acknowledged its tradition of leaving it to the organisations to resolve labour issues through collective bargaining.[62]

The Holiday Act was enacted in the same year but on a slightly different background given the fact that many workers within the private sector did not have a right to annual holiday. In the year 1928, a statistic was produced by a

58. S.J. Kaine, *Decentralised Bargaining in Denmark and Australia: Voluntarism Versus Legal Regulation*, 43 ABL (2017).
59. Kristiansen (n. 4) 32; Kristiansen (n. 4) 310.
60. Statutory Act No. 1002 of 24/8/2017.
61. Statutory Act No. 1177 of 9/10/2015.
62. The proposal was submitted before the Parliament on the 7 May 1937, Parliamentary report, session 1936-1937, appendix A, column 2485.

public authority encompassing a survey on the right to annual holiday of 224,000 workers.[63] Only 85,000 workers had a right to annual holiday through an applicable CLA, but in many cases, the length of the holiday was not stated in the agreement, and within the largest Danish industry at the time, the iron industry, the applicable CLAs typically only awarded workers three-four days of unpaid annual leave per year. The right to annual leave was therefore an important right for the trade unions to improve for their members, which proved difficult to achieve through collective bargaining. The trade unions accomplished a minor breakthrough during the collective bargaining process in 1931, where the major national trade union De Samvirkende Fagforbund, now called FH, and Dansk Arbejdsgiverforening, DA agreed to award the workers one week paid annual leave covering half of the members of the national trade union, which increased in the bargaining process two years later. The trade unions gained even more momentum in 1936, as the International Labour Organisation adopted Convention No. 52.[64] Section 2(1) of the Convention grants every person, to whom the Convention applies, an annual holiday with pay of at least six working days to which they were entitled after one year of continuous service. A social democratic Government rained power in Denmark at the time, and heavily encouraged by suggestions by the trade unions, the Government sought to ratify the Convention, while using the occasion to introduce even more favourable holiday rights than those stipulated in the Convention.

According to the preparatory works of the Holiday Act, the Government viewed the one-year seniority requirement of the Convention as limiting the scope of the Convention too extensively and therefore suggested discarding it in the proposed Holiday Act.[65] Instead, the Act proposed a system according to which the worker would earn one day of paid annual holiday per month, the worker was employed, which would yield the worker a total of twelve days paid annual holiday per year. The right to twelve days paid annual holiday brought Denmark to the forefront of contemporary workers' rights compared to other European countries such as Finland, where workers had the right to seven days of paid annual holiday.[66]

Statutory legislation and CLAs are intertwined in many aspects and there are many cross-references between them. Legislative acts concerning the labour

63. Appendix III to the proposal to a Holiday Act, session 1937-1938, appendix A, column 3746.
64. Convention No. 52 concerning Annual Holidays with Pay. It entered into force the 22 September 1939.
65. The proposal was submitted before the Parliament on the 8 February 1938, Parliamentary report, session 1937-1938, appendix A, column 3722.
66. Column 3762 and onwards, which consists of a comparative report on the holiday acts of several European countries. It illustrates that the Government had its attention on holiday as an international labour norm.

market often encompass opening clauses allowing the social partners to incorporate the provisions of the Act into a CLA, thereby allowing for any interpretation and breach of such provisions to be decided in the industrial tribunal system. The opening clauses do not apply to individual contracts. Some legislative acts even allow the social partners to deviate from the provisions of the Act effectively entrusting the legislative power to the social power, keeping in mind that an option to deviate by CLA does require express legal basis, i.e an explicit opening clause, which provides a limitation for the deviation. Such deviations are allowed for several reasons; given the equal balance between the collective parties, the interests of the employees, which are normally perceived as the weaker party, are adequately looked after by their trade unions. Without an opening clause, CLAs cannot deviate from statutory provisions to the detriment of the employee.[67]

The Holiday Act contains several opening clauses, one of which being section 4(2), which allows the employee to be awarded better rights under CLAs, individual agreements, customary practices, etc. The Holiday Act furthermore allows for a number of provisions to be deviated from by CLA to a varying detrimental degree.[68] Section 5 of the Act provides a threshold for access to these opening clauses in order to protect the employees. It requires a certain level of representation in that the trade union representing the employee must be a national organisation, which is seen as an extra level of security for the employees.

Many statutory acts that are based on EU legislative act use opening clauses, which allow provisions to be deviated from almost limitlessly by CLA as long as the agreement is concluded by the 'most representative' social partners in Denmark, and the agreement is valid within the entire Danish area. This type of opening clause is one of two available alternatives for Members States, which do not have a regulatory system for declaring CLAs universally applicable. The other being to open deviation by CLAs, which are generally applicable to all similar undertakings in the geographical area and in the profession or industry concerned.

These opening clauses were chosen for the right to equal treatment of Temporary Agency Workers,[69] the Statutory Act on Posting of Workers, section 6a(2), the Statutory Act on an Active Employment Social Policy, section 72(1), the (new) Act on Taxi Driving from December 2017 section 10, the Act on

67. In the judgment U.1981.478H by the Supreme Court, a CLA reduced the sick pay of salaried employees who according to section 5 of the Act on Salaried Workers are entitled to receive their normal pay during sickness absence. The Supreme Court found the reduction clause in the agreement to be invalid, because there was no opening clause in the Act allowing such deviation by a CLA. The rest of the CLA was upheld as valid.
68. Current Holiday Act sections 6, 10, 20, 21, 27, 30a, 31 and 40.
69. Statutory Act on Temporary Agency Workers, *Vikarloven*, No. 595 of 12/06/2013, section 3(5).

Vocational Education section 55(2). It was also utilised in the new Holiday Act, which was adopted in January 2018.[70]

Besides being required by the European legislative act, which some of the listed statutory acts are meant to implement, the threshold of 'most representative' is meant to prevent social dumping and seeks to ensure adequate representation for the employees, who due to the deviation can no longer rely on the protection stipulated in the legislative act. By qualification of the employees' representative, it is ensured that these most representative associations have the necessary bargaining leverage needed to negotiate an adequate agreement to the benefit of their members and the employees covered by the agreement by virtue of the rule of assumption mentioned above.

10.4 COLLECTIVE AGREEMENTS AS AN OPT-IN CHOICE FOR THE EMPLOYEE?

In April 2018, 3F, the largest trade union in Denmark (United Federation of Danish Workers) concluded a ground-breaking CLA with a digital platform, Hilfr, which acts as an intermediary between private cleaners and customers.[71] The agreement is an attempt by the social partners to embrace the new forms of non-typical employment emerging from the digitisation of the labour market and rethink CLAs as a labour norm.[72] The agreement represents a new flexible approach to CLAs as binding inderogable labour norms because it provides the platform worker with a choice of opting in or out of the agreement on certain terms.

The agreement assigns the cleaners a default status as freelancers for the first 100 hours of services, after which the status automatically changes to one of 'employee'. From this point on, the agreement applies to the – now – employee. The agreement allows the cleaner the choice to receive 'employee' status before having provided 100 hours of services, or to retain his/her 'freelancer' status after having provided 100 hours of services. Letting the applicability of the agreement be an option for the worker represents a novelty and a departure from CLAs as being indispensable at the individual level.

The platform can refuse a request for 'employee' status from cleaners who have worked less than 100 hours if providing a fair and objective reason for such refusal. Employed cleaning assistants are entitled to an hourly minimum pay corresponding to the sectoral agreement.

70. Statutory Act on Holiday, *Ferieloven*, L 116 2017-18 of 25 January 2018 in force 1 September 2020, http://www.ft.dk/ripdf/samling/20171/lovforslag/l116/20171_l116_som_vedtaget.pdf.
71. https://fho.dk/blog/2018/04/10/historic-agreement-digital-platform-concludes-collective-agreement/ (last accessed 20 August 2019).
72. *See* N.V. Munkholm & C. Højer Schjøler, *Platform Work and the Danish Model: Legal Perspectives*, 1 Nordic J. of Com. L, 31 (2018) for a more in-depth analysis of the trial agreement.

10.4.1 Thoughts on the Novel Approach

The agreement represents a novel approach at solving a number of issues by adapting certain provisions on working conditions to fit persons performing work via digital platforms.

But giving the employees an unrestricted choice to opt in or opt out of the collective agreement goes against a fundamental feature of CLAs on the part of the workers' association – to be binding by nature thereby securing the rights of their members. As mentioned above, CLAs in Denmark have normative effect when applicable, which prevents employers and employees bound by a CLA to reach individual agreements in conflict with the collectively negotiated terms, unless the individual agreement grants the employee more favourable conditions than the CLA.

Allowing an employee, a choice of status is not in the interest of the trade unions, as it allows the employer to exercise coercion on the worker, to opt out of the binding collective provisions and instead negotiate individually. The individual negotiation happens in a setting, where the employee is the weaker party due to the lack of support of the collectivity. This sincerely questions the element of 'free choice' of the worker agreeing to provisions negotiated individually and in the interest of the employer.

The agreement must be admired for its innovative approach, but it does leave a number of questions unanswered concerning the normative effect of such an agreement.

The agreement attempts to resolve the difficult relationship between platform work and regular employment with a novel approach of introducing innovative features. The effects however remain to be seen.

10.5 CONCLUSIONS

The Danish labour market is primarily regulated by CLAs, statutory acts and EU law, and in many cases they overlap. But where the national statutory legislation and the regulatory framework from the EU have a public regulatory background in common, the CLAs instead stem from a contractual background, which makes a difference in terms of enforceability, sanction regime and applicability, even though the hierarchical nature of CLAs resembles that of the legislative acts. CLAs, however, operate on two levels, the collective level which comprises the contractual relationship between the two signatory parties and the individual level, which relates to the relationship between the employer and individual employee at plan level.

CLAs to this day remain the primary tool for regulating the working conditions on the Danish labour market, despite a decline in the unionisation rate. The negative development of the number of members within the (traditional) trade unions could prove critical for the future of the model.[73]

The stream of harmonising EU legislative acts reduces the room available for the social partners to negotiate in, although they are given wide access to implement these acts in their CLAs and even in some cases to deviate from them.

As seen with the trend of decentralised bargaining and the trial agreement on platform work, CLAs as a labour norm is undergoing a, albeit quiet, transformation initiated by the social partners in order to adapt to the changes of the labour market. The question is whether the transformation can suit the needs of the employers or employees, who both seek more flexibility – only time will tell.

BIBLIOGRAPHY

T. Bredgaard & P. Madsen, *Farewell Flexicurity? Danish Flexicurity and the Crisis*, Transfer: Eur. Rev. Lab. Res., 8 (2018).

European Trade Union Institute (ETUI), *Benchmarking Working Europe 2017*, 44 (ETUI, 2017).

European Trade Union Institute (ETUI), *Benchmarking Working Europe 2017* (ETUI, 2017).

Ole Hasselbalch, *Labour Law in Denmark*, 30 (4th ed. 2016).

S. Kachchi & J. Sand, *Underbetaling af uorganiserede lønmodtagere*, 12 HR Jura Magasinet, 7-20 (2017).

S.J. Kaine, *Decentralised Bargaining in Denmark and Australia: Voluntarism Versus Legal Regulation*, 43 ABL (2017).

Jens Kristiansen, *Den kollektive arbejdsret*, 112 (3rd ed., Djøf Forlag 2014).

Jens Kristiansen, *The Growing Conflict Between European Uniformity and National Flexibility: The Case of Danish Flexicurity and European Harmonisation of Working Condition*, 24 (Djoef Publishing 2015).

N.V. Munkholm & C. Højer Schjøler, *Platform Work and the Danish Model: Legal Perspectives*, 1 Nordic J. Com. L., 31 (2018).

N.V. Munkholm, *Self-Regulating Collective Labour Relations: Trends and Responses*, 28 Aarhus U., 21 (2018).

73. *See* European Trade Union Institute (ETUI), *Benchmarking Working Europe 2017* (ETUI, 2017). https://www.etui.org/Publications2/Books/Benchmarking-Working-Europe-2017 (last accessed 20 August 2019) for an analysis on the decline of the unionisation rate.

CHAPTER 11

The Tremendous Upheaval in Sources of Labour Law in France

Isabelle Daugareilh

11.1 INTRODUCTION

Nothing had changed for almost a century in the organisation of sources of French labour law: the fact that legislation took precedence over all other sources and the hierarchy among legal sources. The legal edifice, marked by organised pluralism,[1] was first shaken by the 1982 Auroux laws. The Auroux reforms, based on the idea of corporate citizenship, promoted different forms of worker participation, including collective bargaining at enterprise level. The legislators' risk in responding to a strong call for decentralised norms (democratisation) was minimised by the existence of a more even balance of power between business leaders and trade unions compared to the present situation.

French legislation has thus been engaged in a process of decentralising collective bargaining towards the enterprise level since the 1980s. This movement has also been supported by the Constitutional Court. In a ruling of 29 December 2004, the Constitutional Court established the relationship between law and collective bargaining as follows:

> While the eighth paragraph of the preamble to the Constitution of 27 October 1946 stipulates that 'all workers participate, by the intermediary of their delegates, in

1. According to A. Jeammaud, M. Le Friant & A. Lyon-Caen, *L'ordonnancement des relations de travail*, Dalloz, 359 (1997). In France norms originating from the business world have gradually been recognised as sources of labour law: collective agreements in the law of 23 March 1919, personnel regulations policy in the orders of 6 November 1945 and 4 August 1981, and unilateral commitments, since the Court of Cassation ruling of 4 April 1990 (Soc. 4 avril 1990, Maguin, Bull. civ. V, n°161).

> collective determination of working conditions, as well as corporate management', article 34 of the Constitution specifies that establishing the fundamental principles of labour law falls within the scope of legislation; thus it is the legislators' responsibility to determine the conditions and guarantees of its implementation, in compliance with the principle stated in the 8th paragraph of the preamble; on the basis of these provisions, once the legislators have defined the rights and obligations associated with working conditions and labour relations, they may leave it up to employers and workers, or their representative organisations, to specify the practical arrangements for applying the legislative norms, particularly by means of collective bargaining.[2]

One learned author on constitutional case law considers that one of the main effects of constitutional labour law was to strengthen the position of collective bargaining, starting with the aforementioned 2004 Decision[3] and further reinforced by the laws of 31 January 2007 on the modernisation of social dialogue and 20 August 2008 on the renewal of social democracy. Indeed, since the law of 2007, before introducing any labour-relations reform, the government is under the obligation to submit a policy document to the business and social partners, presenting the intended objectives and key choices in the system envisaged. If the social partners decide to launch national inter-sectoral negotiations on the issue, they inform the government how long they need to conduct this negotiation. The legislative body then adopts the provisions of the negotiated agreement and enacts them into law. The 2008 law on the renewal of social democracy put an end to trade unions representation imposed by decree, replacing it with proven representation.[4]

Since 2013, not a year has gone by in France without a major reform affecting the system of sources of labour law, inexorably reinforcing agreement-based law at the expense of national legislation, with an irreversible trend towards the decentralisation of collective bargaining to enterprise level.[5] No fewer than five legislative texts were thus adopted in the past five years. How can we interpret this legislative frenzy except by recognising that, step by step, it is imposing a reversal of sources in agreement-based law, while legislation remains the decisive factor in this reorganisation of sources?

2. Cons. Const. Déc. 29 avril 2004, n°2004-494 DC.
3. O. Dutheillet de Lamothe, *Existe-t-il un droit constitutionnel du travail?*, 6-7 La Semaine Juridique Social,1050 (2012).
4. For stakeholders involved in collective bargaining to be entitled to sign collective agreements, they must have received at least 10% of the votes cast in the first round of the employee representative elections on company level and 8% on sector and industry level. For a collective agreement to be recognised as valid, it must have been signed on enterprise, sector, or industry level by trade unions that had received at least 30% of the votes cast and not have been opposed by trade unions that had received half of the votes.
5. Loi du 14 juin 2013 sur la sécurisation de l'emploi, loi du 5 mars 2014 sur la formation professionnelle, l'emploi et la démocratie sociale, loi du 17 août 2015 sur le dialogue social et l'emploi, loi du 8 août 2016 sur le travail, la modernisation du dialogue social et la sécurisation des parcours professionnels, et les ordonnances du 22 septembre 2017, ratifiées par la loi du 29 mars 2018.

The present government's ambition is to update labour law as a whole. Be that as it may, the 'Copernican Revolution' announced by President Macron may actually turn out to be the end of a long transformation process that started in 1982, as far as collective bargaining is concerned.[6] One response to criticism of the inefficiency of French labour law and its inadequacy to meet the challenges of globalisation is that it has actually been constantly updated[7] since the turn of the century. However, although it is not explicitly announced, the subtext of the Macron reforms is the idea of reorganising the functions and purposes of labour law to focus on competitiveness, competition, and markets, in short, to replace the central objective of protecting workers - the weaker party to the contract - by that of favouring business. The ambivalence that has always characterised labour law is now leaning towards corporate interests, especially those of small businesses.

The present trend, which started just after the 2008 financial crisis in most European Union (EU) Member States and was strongly supported by the EU, has brought about profound changes in the importance and functions of collective bargaining in regulating labour relations. Its sole aim is to offer greater flexibility to businesses and help them adapt to market demands. Perulli[8] speaks of a trend towards corporatisation[9] of industrial relations systems that has had a significant impact on the traditional organisation of sources of labour law, turning the pyramid of norms upside down and bringing about a radical change in the traditional position of collective bargaining, which was intended to improve the situation of workers and provide a legal framework for innovations to support social advancement.

Today, collective bargaining functions increasingly in derogation mode, not bringing additional benefits to workers, but, on the contrary, reducing the rights or benefits expressed in sectoral collective agreements and even by legislation. In France, the Auroux laws were responsible for authorising enterprise-level derogatory agreements on working hours for the first time. This moved into a second stage with the Aubry I and II laws on the thirty-five-hour workweek in the late 1990s. The process then accelerated with a series of laws during the 2000s.[10]

---

6. *See* G. Géa, *Avant-propos*, Droit social, 996 (2007).
7. Géa (n. 6).
8. A. Perulli, *Observations sur les réformes de la législation du travail en Europe*, Revue du Droit du Travail, 170 (2015).
9. Term used by Perulli (n. 8) to define the movement which tends to give enterprises increasing autonomy, making them a key level in developing new regulations.
10. This was the case of the 2004 Fillon law, giving enterprise-level agreements autonomy from sectoral agreements, the 2007 Larcher law, prescribing negotiations on a national and multi-industry level prior to any reforms in employment and labour law, and the 2008 Bertrand law, which overturned the hierarchy of norms in favour of enterprise-level agreements on working hours.

The laws adopted during this period referred to substantial issues to collective bargaining on industry, sector, or enterprise level. A non-exhaustive list illustrating this tendency includes: working hours, worker savings plans, Sunday work, job and skill management, gender equality, intergenerational contracts, vocational training, mobility, stability of employment, job protection plans, and, since the Macron order of 22 September 2017, fixed-term employment contracts. In addition to that, the proliferation of obligations to negotiate on enterprise or sector level means that hardly any aspects of employment today are excluded from collective bargaining.

However, the problematic issue is not so much this expansion of the areas covered by collective bargaining, but the relationship between different sources of law. Indeed, national regulations are increasingly becoming non-mandatory, leaving the field wide open for agreement-based regulation, and enterprise-level negotiation has, in turn, been freed from legal constraints and the framework of sectoral agreements. The relative positions of sources of law and the historical 'most favourable' principle have, de facto, been seriously challenged.

What are the challenges? The main issue is to establish the legitimacy of labour organisations and their capacity to conduct a social dialogue that does not simply consist of obtaining new benefits for workers, but, on the contrary, obliges them to waive some advantages, make compromises and sometimes painful choices on the issue of wages, in a context of increasing asymmetry, due to unemployment rates, economic difficulties, job scarcity, and, finally, the workers' deep discontent with trade-union organisations as intermediaries in this process. One author considers that one of the tendencies of recent reforms 'is to envision trade-union representation as an increasingly specialised, professional activity, focused entirely on producing enterprise-level norms, integrated in the managerial order' (...) 'this represents a sort of logical conclusion to a highly-reductive concept of trade union action as being subordinate to corporate interests and, in a way, instrumental in applying the logic of financial profitability'.[11]

While, in France, legislation was and, despite recent reforms, still is the key element among the sources of labour law, it has been responsible for releasing collective agreements from a number of constraints and has thus brought about a reorganisation of legal sources, first by introducing agreement-based sources (11.2) and, second, by giving priority to enterprises as the key level and source of labour law (11.3).

11. S. Béroud, *Représentation syndicale, représentativité et négociation*, Droit social, 264 (2018). G. Gourgues & K. Yon, *Démocratie, le fond et la forme: une lecture 'politique' des ordonnances Macron*, Revue de Droit du travail, 625 (2017). L. Willemez, *Le travail dans son droit*, Sociologie historique du droit du travail, LGDJ (2017).

11.2 THE REORGANISATION OF LABOUR LAW AROUND AGREEMENT-BASED SOURCES

The 2016 El Khomri law set the tone: 'Unprecedented importance has been given to collective bargaining. The role of legislation, which remains essential, is refocused on the elements strictly necessary to protect public order (1). Huge opportunities have thus been opened up for professional sectors and enterprises to adapt to business needs. Enterprise-level agreements have thus become the forum for legal norms on working hours.'[12] To give the fullest scope to collective agreements, legislators have also taken action to minimise the capacity for resistance via individual employment contracts and the scope for interpretation in the courts in cases where individuals refuse to give way to the collective norm (2).

11.2.1 The Orchestration of the Legislators' Legal Retreat

On reading Article L.2251-1 of the French Labour Code, which states that: 'a convention or agreement may include stipulations more favourable to employees than the existing legal provisions. They are not authorised to waive provisions that concern public order', it might be possible to consider that nothing had changed in the relationship between legislation and collective agreements in France. However, some commentators consider that the El Khomri law of 8 August 2016 added the final touch to sweeping changes that have been implemented since the 1982 government orders, reorganising the articulation between legislative and agreement-based sources. In 2016, the legislature 'attempted to initiate a process of reducing labour law to agreements'.[13]

The first objective of legislation was to reduce – or return – the role of legislation to stating fundamental principles, according to Article 34 of the French Constitution. This represented, therefore, a narrowing of the scope of legislation by giving agreement-based law the central role: not only were there no longer any issues outside its scope but, furthermore, also it was released from the obligation to be more favourable than the law. It had been granted full, authentic autonomy. It should, however, be remembered that the legislature has

12. Explanatory memorandum on the law.
13. F. Favennec, *La hiérarchie des normes en droit du travail: rupture ou continuité?*, 1742 Semaine Sociale Lamy (2016).

retained exclusive jurisdiction[14] over the definition of the fundamental principles of labour law cited in Article 34 of the Constitution, as well as the implementation of constitutional principles.[15]

It may thus be considered that there has been no inversion of norms between legislation and collective agreements[16]; legislation remains at the top of the pyramid of sources and, above all, the law delegates jurisdiction to collective agreements. Thus, according to Article L.3111-3 of the French Labour Code, there can be no derogatory agreement or non-mandatory law unless expressly authorised by legislation. There are thus the two routes to disengagement of the law: derogatory agreements and the non-mandatory nature of some legal norms.

The non-mandatory nature of the law was supported by the Combrexelle report[17] and widely applied in the El Khomri law on working hours, covering the duration and organisation of working hours; night, part-time, and intermittent work; daily rest periods; public holidays; time-savings accounts; and paid and unpaid leave.

A derogation from legislation via a collective labour agreement challenges the principle of favouring workers which settled conflicts between sources in France until the 2004 law. This principle was developed by the Court of Cassation in a ruling on 18 March 1988 ('in case of competition between collective agreements, more than one benefit with the same purpose or cause may not be granted concurrently, unless otherwise stipulated, but only the most favourable shall be granted'[18]). This decision was confirmed by the ruling of 17 July 1996: 'the fundamental principle, in labour law, according to which, in case of conflict of norms, the one most favourable to the workers shall be applied'.[19]

The 'most favourable' principle is a fundamental principle of labour law, according to Article 34 of the Constitution, although it has no constitutional value, so its content and scope are exclusively determined by legislation.[20] Thus, the legislators are still in charge, as they have the power to define the issues that may be included in derogatory agreements, as well as the restrictions placed on them. By multiplying the opportunities for collective agreements to establish derogations *in peius*, legislation has undermined the 'most favourable' principle that governed the hierarchy of sources. As collective labour agreements are not automatically integrated into employment contracts in France, adopting a derogatory agreement runs the risk that these modifications will be rejected by

14. This exclusive jurisdiction must be fully exercised: Conseil Constitutionnel, 7 août 2008, DC. n° 2008-568, 1008 Dalloz, 2064 (2008).
15. Conseil Constitutionnel, 6 novembre 1996, n° 96-383 DC, Dalloz, 152 (1998).
16. L. Pécaut-Rivolier, *Quel ordonnancement des sources du droit du travail? Les rapports de l'accord collectif avec la loi et le contrat*, Revue Droit Travail, 791 (2016).
17. J.D. Combrexelle, *La négociation collective, le travail et l'emploi*, rapport France Stratégie (2015).
18. Ass.plén. C. Cass, 18 mars 1988, Bull. Ass. plén. n°3, note J.P. Chauchard, Dalloz 221 (1989).
19. Soc. 17 juillet 1996, Bull.ci. V, n297.
20. Conseil Constitutionnel, 29 avril 2004, DC n°2004-494, obs. X. Pretot et D. Chellem, Dalloz 3029 (2004).

the workers. For this reason, the legislature has restricted the possibility of contractual and judicial opposition to collective labour agreements.

11.2.2 Limitations Placed on Employment Contracts and the Courts by Legislation

At a single stroke, the legislature has attenuated the power of contracts, as well as that of the courts that interpret them and express the law.

Under the law dated 11 February 1950, collective labour agreements take precedence over employment contracts, unless the contractual provisions are more favourable. In France, the 1980s marked the rehabilitation of individual employment contracts, especially to provide protection from mass redundancies or contract modifications. The French courts relied on the principle of good faith governing contractual relations as a means of protecting workers from redundancy and obliging employers to look for redeployment solutions before resorting to dismissals.

The very clear weakening of the mandatory force of employment contracts following the reforms of the past twenty years could only be due to the fact that collective agreements met a certain number of legally established conditions concerning content and form. Several laws established the precedence of collective labour agreements on various issues and dealt with dismissal following the refusal of an employee to accept a collective agreement, to prevent any challenge to the scope of the rules resulting from it.

The 2008 Aubry law was the first in a long series to stipulate that an employment contract is not considered to have been modified by the simple application of an agreement to reduce working hours or the implementation of an agreement on variations in working hours. In the case of an employee's refusal, breach of contract would not be based on the rules concerning mass redundancies but those on individual dismissal. Subsequently, while the law of 13 June 2013 on protecting employment gave workers the opportunity to refuse the application of an collective agreement on employment stability or internal mobility when their own contract was more favourable, it nevertheless stipulated that the dismissal following this refusal was 'on economic grounds' and could not be treated as a collective redundancy, even if it involved at least ten employees.

Then the Macron law of 17 August 2015 established that dismissal following a refusal to accept an employment stability agreement was based on 'real and serious grounds', thus ensuring that the terms of dismissal would be favourable to the employer. The 2016 Employment Law continued in the same vein, only imposing the limitation that the employee's monthly salary should not be decreased as a result of implementing the 'offending' clauses in the employment stability agreement. The Employment Law stipulated, in line with the Combrexelle report, that dismissal despite the absence of financial difficulties 'is based on specific reasons that constitute real and serious grounds'.

Once again, the Macron orders completed and radicalised a process that had been ongoing since 2008, by literally removing the last objections on merits and form, while maintaining the principles of precedence, thus dealing a fatal blow to individual employment contracts. Thus, Article L.2254-1 of the French Labour Code continues to affirm that collective norms take precedence over individual norms, as follows: 'when an employer is bound by the clauses of a convention or agreement, these clauses are applicable to employment contracts with that employer, unless the contract provisions are more favourable'.

Without reversing the hierarchy of norms, Article L.2254-2 paved the way for sidelining the 'most favourable' principle and the imperative force of employment contracts in the most liberal way possible. Thus, it provided that: I. 'to respond to necessities related to company operations[21] or with a view to preserving or developing employment, an enterprise-level agreement may modify working hours, salaries, and the conditions for worker mobility' (...) and III. 'The provisions of the agreement automatically replace any contradictory or incompatible clauses in the employment contract, including those concerning working hours, pay, and mobility.' Collective regulations may thus be imposed to the detriment of clauses in individual employment contracts, even if jobs are not at issue – necessities related to company operations are sufficient – and the legislation specifies that 'a dismissal following an employee's refusal is based on specific reasons that constitute real and serious grounds'.

While some authors may have considered that the El Khomri law gave employment contracts some opportunity to resist,[22] this is no longer possible since the change in wording of Article L.2254-2 of the French Labour Code, resulting from the Macron orders. Finally, Macron's latest bold legislative move: according to Article L.2232-21 of the French Labour Code, it is now possible to implement an agreement without collective bargaining. 'The employer may propose a draft agreement on any of the topics open to enterprise-level collective bargaining (...)' intended to, in the terms of Article L.2254-2, 'respond to necessities related to company operations (...)', and its 'provisions automatically replace any contradictory or incompatible clauses in the employment contract'. The Constitutional Court ruling of 20 October 2017 approved the competitiveness agreement system with regard to the right to employment (not necessarily the right to maintain employment).[23]

21. Underlined by the author. Collective agreements negotiated on this basis are also described as 'competitiveness agreements'.
22. L. Pécaut Rivollier (n. 16), 794.
23. Cons. Cont. 20 octobre 2017, n° 2017-665, Dalloz, 2105 (2017).

Of course, these competitiveness agreements may only be implemented with majority approval, i.e., if they are signed by one or more trade-union organisations representing over 50 % of the votes cast in the first round of the last elections to the Works Council or by the single workers' delegation, irrespective of the number of voters. Otherwise, trade unions that received at least 30 % of the votes or the employer may organise a worker consultation. In addition, this type of agreement may be implemented in very small enterprises (under eleven employees), using an extreme derogation mechanism, whereby the draft agreement presented by the employer simply needs to be ratified by a two-thirds majority of workers. Furthermore, this type of agreement, introducing, need I remind you, changes in wages, working hours, or mobility may be unlimited in time, whereas agreements on maintaining or preserving employment, demanding comparable sacrifices from the workers, were only applicable for a defined period.

Collective bargaining was traditionally intended to compensate for the existing imbalance between the parties to the employment contract; it aimed, therefore, to strengthen the employee's contractual position; 'it was, in a way, supposed to support the mandatory force of the contract and not the reverse'.[24] The Macron orders clearly overturned this historical function of collective bargaining. While it is by no means sure that the trade unions will accept the role assigned to them by this law, if only because their representativeness depends on the workers' vote, it is certain, in any case, that, in 2017, the legislators took things much further than the highly controversial El Khomri law of 2016 in unravelling the French Labour Code, without any form of democratic debate.

11.3 THE KEY POSITION OF ENTERPRISE-LEVEL AGREEMENTS IN THE NEW ORGANISATION OF AGREEMENT-BASED SOURCES

The El Khomri law and Macron orders have been responsible for transferring power from sector to enterprise level (1) and ensuring that all enterprises can implement collective bargaining, even the smallest, where there are often no trade-union representatives (2).

24. G. Borenfreund, *Quel ordonnancement des sources du droit du travail? Les rapports de l'accord collectif avec la loi et le droit du travail,* Revue de Droit du Travail, 788 (2016).

11.3.1 The Confrontation Between Enterprise-Level and Sectoral Agreements

11.3.1.1 The End of the 'Most Favourable' Principle

Sectors had been the dominant level in the French labour-relations system since the law of 11 February 1950.[25] Their importance started to decline with the 1982 order on the duration and organisation of working time and the obligation to hold annual negotiations in enterprises. It has taken over thirty-five years to supplant sectors, which still continue to exist, but enterprise-level agreements have become the linchpin of social dialogue and taken their independence from sector-level collective agreements.[26] That was the result of the El Khomri law of 2016 and, above all, the Macron orders of 2017. The El Khomri law created a complete break with the past in the relationship between sectoral and enterprise-level agreements. Until that time, the broadest collective agreement took precedence over agreements with a more restrictive scope. By referring first to enterprise-level agreements and 'otherwise' to sectoral agreements in various scenarios, the law of 8 August 2016 actually modified the hierarchy of agreement-based sources.

The coexistence of several levels of collective bargaining is a potential source of conflicts of norms and rights.[27] This conflict may be settled on a higher level, by legislation, or by applying the 'most favourable' principle, or by derogation. Conflict may be avoided by giving priority to one level over another or even by specifying different roles for each level. The rule governing conflicts remained that of the 'most favourable' principle until 2004. Indeed, the law of 4 May 2004 replaced the 'most favourable' principle with that of the non-mandatory nature of sectoral agreements, which remained applicable only in the absence of an enterprise-level agreement. However, this law had so many exceptions that it was hardly ever applied, and the 'most favourable' principle continued to dominate in settling conflicts between agreement-based norms. By insisting that aspects concerning working hours were handled first by enterprise-level agreements and only 'otherwise' by sectoral agreements or

25. A sector has no legal definition; it corresponds to the scope of application of an agreement-based rule. France has an impressive number of sectors – in the vicinity of 700. Several reports have emphasised the necessity to reduce this number to approximately 200, with a national scope of application, rather than individual regions or départements. Several laws have taken up this theme: 17 August 2015 and 8 August 2016, as well as, finally, order 2017-1385 of 22 September 2017. *See* S. Nadal, *La restructuration des branches professionnelles: réflexions sur une mutation force*, Droit social, 110 (2016).
26. J.F. Cesaro, *L'autonome dans les branches professionnelles et quelques mesures portant sur la négociation collective*, 1306 JCP (2017).
27. H. Tissandier, *Quel ordonnancement des sources du droit du travail? Les rapports entre accords collectifs*, Revue de droit du travail, 794 (2016).

decrees, the law of 20 August 2008 expressly gave precedence to enterprise-level agreements over those negotiated on sectoral level, thus preventing any conflict.

The Macron orders made the precedence of sectoral over enterprise-level agreements a pure formality. Despite the restatement of the principle,[28] analysis of the two articles devoted to this issue makes it clear that enterprise-level agreements take precedence when they offer 'equivalent guarantees' which concerns thirteen areas specified in the law, some of which had already been similarly covered by the 2004 (minimum wages, classification, collective complementary coverage in addition to social security, and pooling in-service training funds), and 2016 laws (gender equality at work). The other topics had already been included in a few provisions of the French Labour Code, for example issues concerning working time and its organisation, as well as probationary periods.

Some authors consider that the wording of Article L.2253-1 of the French Labour Code 'converts what could have been considered a monopoly into simple superiority'.[29] This superiority may be overturned not by more favourable terms, but by equivalent guarantees. Without stating it explicitly, this superiority opens up new areas hitherto managed on sectoral level to enterprise-level negotiation, such as open-ended employment contracts for the duration of a project. Finally, while sectors may ensure that they take precedence in the four areas covered by Article L.2253-2 (the lock-in clauses in the 2004 law), even there, they may be obliged to give way to equivalent guarantees in enterprise-level agreements.

The elimination of any reference to the application of the most favourable norm in case of conflict between agreement-based norms certainly deserved a parliamentary debate, but this was avoided by Mr Macron when he chose the legislative technique of issuing an order. Indeed, the 'most favourable' principle is one of the fundamental principles of labour law and, consequently, comes under the exclusive jurisdiction of legislation, under Article 34 of the Constitution.

Thus, whether this principle stems from legislation or collective agreements themselves, sectoral agreements only take precedence if an enterprise-level agreement does not offer at least equivalent guarantees. How can equivalence be measured? On the same issue or among several different ones? By means of an overall, objective, quantitative evaluation, or a subjective, qualitative assessment? Furthermore, equivalence is a way of circumventing case law from the Court of Cassation, taking into consideration benefits with the same

28. *See* G. Auzero, *Conventions d'entreprise et conventions de branche*, Droit social, 1018 (2017).
29. Cesaro (n. 26) 1306.

cause or purpose to determine whether provisions in an agreement were more favourable to workers or not.[30] This will provide grist for the court's mill.

11.3.1.2 Sectoral Agreements Superseded

Sectors retain seventeen areas of intervention, including thirteen[31] where the provisions of a sectoral agreement 'take precedence over those of any prior or subsequent enterprise-level agreement (...) except when the enterprise-level agreement offers at least equivalent guarantees'.[32] The Macron order withdrew the overall missions entrusted to sectors at a stroke:

(1) The power to define guarantees applicable to employees, especially those concerning minimum wages, classification, collective complementary coverage in addition to social security, pooling in-service training funds, the effects of exposure to work-related risk factors, and gender equality at work.
(2) The option of introducing lock-in clauses, whereby sectoral agreements determine the topics on which enterprise-level agreements cannot be less favourable than sectoral conventions and agreements (with the exclusion of issues where legislation gives precedence to enterprise-level agreements).
(3) The generic function of sectoral agreements: 'to regulate competition between enterprises within its scope of application'. Following Macron order 2017-1385 of 2 September 2017, sectors retain the responsibility for defining working and employment conditions and the guarantees applicable to them on the subjects referred to in Articles L.2253-1 and L.2253-2 of the French Labour Code.[33]

30. Cass. Ass. Plénière du 18 mars 1988, Bull. civ. V, ass. plén. n° 3. *See* Jean Pelissier, Antoine Lyon-Caen, Antoine Jeammaud & Emmanuel Dockès, *Les grands arrêts du droit du travail* (4th ed. Dalloz 2008).
31. According to Article L. 2253-1 of the French Labour Code, this concerns minimum wages at different levels in the organisation, classifications, pooling funding for union-management organisations, pooling in-service training funds, complementary coverage in addition to social security, measures concerning working hours, work schedules, and flexibility; measures concerning fixed-term and temporary employment contracts, open-ended employment contracts for the duration of a project or operation, gender equality at work, the conditions for renewing probationary periods and their permissible duration, arrangements for continuing contracts between two enterprises, provision of temporary workers, and minimum wage for workers using wage portage services.
32. Article L.2253-1 paragraph 2 of the French Labour Code.
33. The following issues are specified in Article L.2253-2 of the French Labour Code: prevention of the effects of exposure to risk factors in the workplace, integrating workers with handicaps into working life and maintaining them in employment, the headcount above which trade-union representatives may be appointed and their number, validation of trade-union experience, and bonuses for hazardous work.

Order n°1385 of 22 September 2017 establishes the precedence of enterprise-level agreements over sectoral agreements in all areas other than the eighteen cited in Article L.2253-1 and 2 of the Labour Code. This precedence is unconditional, i.e., not subject to more favourable or equivalent provisions. This precedence became exclusive and radical starting on 1 January 2018. The application of sectoral agreements in the absence of an enterprise-level agreement became non-mandatory.

The expansion of enterprise-level agreements has, therefore, followed several routes. Besides enterprise-level agreements being given precedence in principle over sectoral agreements, they have also been given new scope, including economic and social adaptation and collective redundancy by mutual consent,[34] and negotiation has been freed from certain constraints. Thus, on this last point, the 2017 order extended the possibility of decentralising negotiation from enterprise to establishment level for all topics covered by mandatory enterprise negotiations. It also extended the maximum term of an enterprise-level agreement from three to four years, specifying the frequency and content of mandatory negotiations.

The 2017 order harmonised competitiveness agreements with collective agreements on employment by establishing a single system for dismissal of a worker who refuses the application of the collective agreement. Above all, the text stipulates that necessities related to company operations are sufficient for an enterprise-level agreement to modify working hours,[35] wages,[36] and professional or geographical mobility[37] of workers within an enterprise. This constitutes a total liberalisation of enterprise-level agreements, which no longer need to rely on the issue of jobs to introduce changes in employment contracts. The stipulations of the agreement "automatically replace any contradictory or incompatible clauses in the employment contract. (...); A worker may refuse a modification to the employment contract (...); but if the employer starts a dismissal procedure (...) 'this dismissal is based on specific reasons that constitute real and serious grounds (...)."[38]

The legislature seems to want to smooth the way for employers to make workers redundant surreptitiously, via individual or collective redundancies on economic grounds. In this way, they have managed to evade judicial review of dismissals, which could be considered contrary to France's international commitments, including ILO convention 158 on dismissal, Article 30 of the EU Charter, and the 1996 revision of Article 24 of the European Social Charter.

---

34. Article L.1237-17 of the French Labour Code.
35. Article L.2254-2, I of the French Labour Code.
36. According to Article L.3221-3, provided it complies with the statutory minimum wage and minimum wages at each level in the organisation, Article L.2254-2-I.
37. Article L.2254-2, I of the French Labour Code.
38. Article L.2254-2, III and V of the French Labour Code.

11.3.2 A New Era for Professional Sources on Enterprise Level

Collective bargaining on enterprise level may not be successful in case of disagreement, or may not take place for lack of negotiators, i.e., trade-union representatives, which is often the case in Small and Medium Enterprise. For this reason, the legislation had to envisage substitution scenarios based on ad hoc representation or even no representation at all, giving free rein to the employer's unilateral power and combining to produce derogatory negotiation procedures.

The law of 12 November 1996 was the first to introduce the idea of derogations to the negotiation procedure, and this measure was approved by the Constitutional Court in a ruling of 6 November 1996. In this context, a sectoral agreement was entitled to authorise negotiations, with either elected worker representatives or workers delegated by one or more representative trade unions to negotiate on that specific issue.

The Aubry II law of 19 January 2000 very clearly favoured this type of delegation; agreements were to be approved by a simple majority vote. The law of 20 August 2008 made possible for elected and delegated workers to negotiate, but only on measures where implementation was subject by law to the existence of a collective agreement. This option was only available to enterprises with under 200 employees. The validity of the agreement was subject to negotiation by titular, elected members of the Works Council or Workers' Delegates representing the majority of the votes cast in the previous elections, as well as approval by the joint sectoral committee. In enterprises with at least 100 employees, the union section representative may be delegated to negotiate on all topics and the agreement is subject to approval by a majority vote of the workers.

The law of 17 August 2015 reformed the negotiation system with a worker representative, opening up this possibility to any enterprise with no union representatives, irrespective of headcount, and creating the new role of elected representative. The law of 8 August 2016 further liberalised derogations to the negotiation procedure by broadening the scope of negotiations open to workers' representatives to include all measures negotiated in enterprise- or establishment-level agreements and eliminated the obligation for the joint sectoral committee to approve the resulting agreement, replacing it with a simple requirement to inform. This increasing flexibility in collective bargaining conditions is solely aimed at supporting the negotiation of derogatory agreements imposed by legislation in many areas and confirming the precedence of enterprise-level over sectoral agreements.

The order dated 22 September 2017 modified the rules on derogatory negotiations. The text retained the system of negotiating without union representatives in enterprises with over fifty employees and authorised alternate delegates to negotiate; agreements no longer need to be transferred to the joint sectoral committee. The emancipation of enterprise-level agreements is thus accompanied by emancipation from even the oversight of the union organisations. In enterprises with under fifty employees, agreements may be negotiated either with one of the workers' delegates, who may or may not be a member of the Social and Economic Committee (ESC), or with one or more members of the ESC, who have not been specifically delegated. Employers may now, therefore, negotiate with a non-delegated elected representative on any issue open to negotiation and not only those specified by the law on derogatory agreements. Delegation is, therefore, no longer a condition and the validity of agreements negotiated by non-delegated elected representatives is no longer subject to a referendum.

The order dated 22 September went even further in enterprises with eleven to twenty employees that have no ESC. In this case, the employer may propose a draft agreement to the workers for consultation on any of the topics listed for negotiation by the Labour Code for a minimum of fifteen days from the date it is communicated to each employee. Is it still legitimate to describe this as an enterprise-level collective agreement, when negotiation and the presence of worker representatives are no longer necessary and a 2/3 majority workers' vote is sufficient to approve the agreement? The Macron order thus eliminated one of the benefits of sectoral agreements under the El Khomri law, which consisted of preparing a standard agreement with provisions for enterprises with under fifty employees.[39]

11.4 CONCLUSION

The company agreement ended up winning all the honours in France, starting with the power to take precedence over branch agreements when offering 'equivalent guarantees'. Furthermore, with the El Komri reforms of 2016 and Macron reforms of 2017, all contractual and judicial opposition to flexible working conditions outlined by collective labour agreements has been eliminated. By associating the forced reduction of social benefits with corporate collective bargaining, including during periods of corporate prosperity, for the sake of performance and competitiveness, the French legislator has diverted collective bargaining from its historical attributes to turn it into a tool benefiting employers. Worse still, they have also radically distorted collective bargaining, which no longer has to be undertaken by representatives of the workers' community, since employers in small businesses (less than twenty employees) have the right to design a draft text that may become a collective agreement if approved by a qualified majority of the company's workers. Is it not the very negation of the conflicts of interest, rights, and logic that prevailed in the

39. Article L.2232-10 of the French Labour Code.

establishment of labour law, which is now being imposed? Beyond this, would these reforms not reflect a contemporary vision of enterprises as institutions?

BIBLIOGRAPHY

G. Auzero, *Conventions d'entreprise et conventions de branche*, Droit social, 1018 (2017).

S. Béroud, *Représentation syndicale, représentativité et négociation*, Droit social, 264 (2018).

G. Borenfreund, *Quel ordonnancement des sources du droit du travail? Les rapports de l'accord collectif avec la loi et le droit du travail*, Revue de Droit du Travail, 788 (2016).

J.F. Cesaro, *L'autonome dans les branches professionnelles et quelques mesures portant sur la négociation collective*, 1306 JCP (2017).

J.D. Combrexelle, *La négociation collective, le travail et l'emploi*, rapport France Stratégie (2015).

O. Dutheillet de Lamothe, *Existe-t-il un droit constitutionnel du travail?*, 6-7 La Semaine Juridique Social, 1050 (2012).

F. Favennec, *La hiérarchie des normes en droit du travail: rupture ou continuité?*, 1742 Semaine Sociale Lamy (2016).

G. Géa, *Avant-propos*, Droit social, 996 (2007).

G. Gourgues & K. Yon, *Démocratie, le fond et la forme: une lecture 'politique' des ordonnances Macron*, Revue de Droit du travail, 625 (2017).

A. Jeammaud, M. Le Friant & A. Lyon-Caen, *L'ordonnancement des relations de travail*, Dalloz, 359 (1997).

L. Pécaut-Rivolier, *Quel ordonnancement des sources du droit du travail? Les rapports de l'accord collectif avec la loi et le contrat*, Revue Droit Travail, 791, (2016).

S. Nadal, *La restructuration des branches professionnelles: réflexions sur une mutation force*, Droit social, 110 (2016).

L. Pécaut-Rivolier, *Quel ordonnancement des sources du droit du travail? Les rapports de l'accord collectif avec la loi et le contrat*, Revue de Droit du Travail, 791 (2016).

Jean Pelissier, Antoine Lyon-Caen, Antoine Jeammaud & Emmanuel Dockès, *Les grands arrêts du droit du travail* (4th ed. Dalloz 2008).

A. Perulli, *Observations sur les réformes de la législation du travail en Europe*, Revue du Droit du Travail, 170 (2015).

H. Tissandier, *Quel ordonnancement des sources du droit du travail? Les rapports entre accords collectifs*, Revue de droit du travail, 794 (2016).

L. Willemez, *Le travail dans son droit*, Sociologie historique du droit du travail, LGDJ (2017).

CHAPTER 12

The Sources of German Labour Law

Manfred Weiss

12.1 INTRODUCTION

The origins of German labour law date back to the nineteenth century. Already then there was not only labour legislation but also first attempts of collective agreements and workers' participation appeared. However, only after World War II at the beginning of the so-called Weimar Republic the top organizations of employers' associations and trade unions formed the so-called Central Commission of Cooperation. In the agreement, on which the Commission was based, the employers' associations guaranteed the trade unions full recognition, and both parties declared collective agreements to become the main instrument to regulate working conditions. In section 159 of the Weimar Constitution, freedom of association was, for the first time in German history, guaranteed without any limitation. The Weimar Era was not only the time when the system of collective bargaining was growing rapidly, but it was also the time when fundamental features of today's labour law were developed. Among these the most important was the Act on Works Councils of 1920, the creation of a specific system of labour courts in 1926.

Interrupted by the fascist system of the Nazis where all the indicated achievements were abolished, the development which started in the Weimar Republic has been continued after World War II in West Germany (FRG) and since the unification of 1990 extended also to East Germany (GDR).

In this chapter, the sources as they have developed in Germany will be sketched (*see* section 12.2) and the problems arose in the recent past will be discussed (*see* section 12.3).

12.2 THE SOURCES

12.2.1 Constitution

At the top of the hierarchy of sources of labour law is the Constitution. It plays a dominant role in labour law. Problems not regulated by the legislator have to be solved by recourse to the Constitution.[1] The first and most important chapter of this Constitution contains a catalogue of fundamental rights. These fundamental rights are the strongest pillar on which Germany is built. The Constitution can be amended by a two-thirds majority in the legislative bodies. But amendments by which the principles guaranteed by the articles on fundamental rights would be affected, are considered to be null and void (Article 79 paragraph 3). This safeguard against the abolishment of fundamental rights (and other pillars of the Constitution) is a reaction to the experience made in the Nazi period where it became clear that majority vote does not prevent the perversion of the rule of law.

The Constitution explicitly only refers to the vertical application in the relationship between citizens and the State. This reflects the traditional understanding of fundamental rights as a defence against State power, thereby guaranteeing the citizens an area of freedom in which the State cannot interfere. In the meantime, this traditional understanding only is considered a starting point. Fundamental rights nowadays in Germany are considered to be the expression of values on which the legal order as a whole is based. Therefore, they no longer can be ignored in the relationship between private actors. Inequality of power is not only a characteristic of the relationship between State and citizens but is a growing phenomenon also between private actors, as for example employers and employees. This insight has led in Germany to the concept of indirect horizontal application of fundamental rights. This is a soft way of introducing the fundamental rights into relationships between private actors. The fundamental rights are not applied strictly the same way as in the relationship between State and citizens. But the law governing private relationships between private actors are to be interpreted in the light of values expressed by the fundamental rights. This, of course, gives the judiciary on all levels a broad leeway of interpretation in adapting the fundamental rights to the specific situation.

1. For a detailed description *see* M. Weiss, *The Interface Between Constitution and Labor Law in Germany*, 26 Comp. Lab. L. & Policy J., 181 (2005).

12.2.2 Statutory Law

Legislation sets minimum standards for all employees, whether or not they are union members. Since the competence to legislate in the field of labour law lies with the federal legislature, it is almost exclusively federal law that counts. Thus, despite a well-developed German federalism (Germany is a federation of sixteen States), a homogeneous pattern of labour law evolved throughout Germany. To the extent that State laws and constitutions conflict with federal law, the latter invariably has priority. There is one area where differences between the States play an important role, i.e., staff representation in the public sector. Here the Federal Act on Staff Representation only sets a framework which is interpreted differently by the acts on staff representation of the various States.

Germany does not have a Labour Code. German statutory labour law consists of a multitude of statutes on specific topics, many of which were enacted at different times. It is difficult even for experts to grasp the whole picture.

To an increasing extent, the legislature delegates the power to regulate specific matters to administrative agencies or other bodies. The Constitution requires that such a delegation be precisely defined so as to avoid the danger of vesting the respective agency or body with undue legislative powers.

12.2.3 Courts Decisions

Since, as already indicated, the Constitution plays a crucial role in German labour law, it goes without saying that the judgments of the Federal Constitutional Court interpreting the Constitution are of utmost importance.

Court decisions by the labour courts[2] play a very important role in the field of labour law. Courts not only interpret the general clauses and general terms of laws but also fill in the gaps left open by the legislature. According to the Labour Courts Act, the Federal Labour Court has exclusive power to develop the law further. In fact, in the field of labour law, the judge made law generated by the Federal Labour Court has become almost as important as activities of the legislature. The labour courts not only interpret the law but also develop the law in the light of the fundamental rights of the Constitution. This for example in the absence of statutory law has led to a whole set of detailed rules on strike.

Not surprisingly, there has been since quite a time a fierce debate over the proper role of the labour courts, compared to that of the legislature. The central question of this debate is whether the actual role of the courts, particularly that of the Federal Labour Court, comports with the principle of separation of

2. For a description of the labour court system *see* M. Weiss, *Labour Dispute Settlement by Labour Courts in Germany*, 15 Indus. L.J. (Johannesburg/South Africa), 1 (1994).

legislative and judicial powers required by the Constitution. But given legislative inertia or the frequent inability of the legislature to generate the necessary votes on specific issues, the courts have little choice but to act on behalf of the legislature. Thus, the allocation of power discussion remains largely academic.

12.2.4 Collective Agreements

Collective agreements in Germany[3] mainly are concluded between a trade union and an employer association for a whole branch of activity or at least a region of it. Collective agreements with a single company are a rarity.

The normative part of collective agreements addressing such core matters as hiring, wages and termination, stands in contrast to the obligatory part which deals with other rights and duties between the contracting parties in that it directly affects the individual employment relationship. In other words, if rights laid down in normative clauses of collective agreements are violated, the individual employee, or the employer to whom these clauses apply, has recourse to the court. In principle, however, such clauses cover only union members being employed by an employer who himself is a member of the employers' association which signed the respective collective agreement.

The relation between legislation and the normative part of collective bargaining agreements is rather complicated. If there is a legislative act which stipulates a minimum standard, the collective agreement cannot fall below, but can only rise above this standard. If the law does not set a minimum standard but only contains non-binding regulations, the collective agreement may disregard these regulations. The problem is that it is often not clear whether the legislature intended to set binding or non-binding standards, and it is left to the courts to decide these cases by interpreting the legislative intent.

For the relationship between collective agreements and court decisions, it has to be distinguished between cases where courts only apply existing legislation and – as indicated above – cases where courts further promote the law. If existing law is applied, court decisions bind the parties of the collective agreements as legislation itself. If, however, judge-made law goes further, the question arises whether the parties to collective agreements have to respect it. In principle, such judge-made law has to be treated as if it would be legislation which means that collective agreements cannot go below the standards set by the courts. However, judge-made law some time only strictly binds the parties to individual employment contracts and to work agreements but allows the parties to collective agreements to fall below these standards. Whether this is the case,

3. For a detailed description of the collective bargaining system *see* M. Weiss & M. Schmidt, *Labour Law and Industrial Relations in Germany*, 180 (4th ed., Kluwer Law International, 2008).

often is not explicitly stated by the court decisions but has to be found out by way of interpretation.

12.2.5 Works Agreements

The works council[4] and the employer in the private sector (or staff representation and employer in the public sector) may sign works agreements containing normative clauses, having basically the same effect on the individual employment relationship as normative clauses of collective agreements. There is an important difference, though: works agreements always cover the entire workforce, whether or not the workers are union members. As already indicated, collective agreements cover only those who are members of the union which signed the respective collective agreement. This basic disparity creates enormous problems of harmonization between the two sources of law. The complicated relationship between collective agreements and works agreements will be discussed in detail below.

12.2.6 The Individual Employment Contract

The individual labour contract is still an important source of law even for those covered by protective laws, collective agreements and/or works agreements. The area dominated by the individual contract in these cases is above the minimum level already regulated by other sources. Thus, the function of the individual employment contract serves mainly to improve the individual working conditions already guaranteed by other sources without any exception.

12.2.7 Custom

Custom may only be a source of law if it favours employees. Under certain conditions, privileges voluntarily granted by the employer cannot simply be withdrawn. The mere fact that they were granted for a certain period may nevertheless entitle employees to claim their continuation. Such a claim is then treated as if it were based on individual contract.

4. For a description of the works council system *see* Weiss & Schmidt (n. 3) 222.

12.3 PROBLEMS AND TRENDS

12.3.1 Failed Attempts to Codification

Since the beginning of the twentieth century, many attempts were made to combine at least the principal rules of individual labour law in one single code. All these attempts failed. When in 1990 FRG and GDR were unified, this idea became a new push. The GDR had a comprehensive Labour Code. According to the GDR delegation negotiating the Unification Treaty (UT), the united Germany had to be achieved by way of a mutual reform of both systems of social protection in the two German states, integrating their positive elements. For labour law, this was supposed to mean that historically grown social standards in both German states are to be maintained, further developed and lifted to a higher level of social protection. Such a strategy was considered to serve as a model for the economic, social, and political integration of a united Europe. Labour law in a united Germany was thus conceived to become a mixture of the better parts of both systems.[5]

It soon became evident, however, that such a strategy would have met strong opposition in the FRG. The FRG was interested in transferring its system, including labour law, to the territory of the former GDR. In the Unification Treaty (UT) the GDR's attempt to rescue GDR labour law turned out to be unsuccessful. The FRG's strategy, stressing the overarching need of having a homogeneous pattern throughout the united Germany, was at the very end accepted. According to Article 8 of the Unification Treaty, all law of the original FRG, including, of course, labour law, was extended to the territory of the former GDR. To avoid depriving the GDR delegation of all hope, however, decisions regarding the character of individual labour law were not finalized in the Treaty. According to Article 30 paragraph 1 of the Treaty, the Parliament of the united Germany is supposed to codify as soon as possible 'the law referring to the individual employment relationship as well as the protective standards referring to working time, work on Sundays and holidays and the specific protection of women'.

Stimulated by Article 30 of the UT, in 1992 a group of labour law professors from east and west presented a draft for a code on employment contract law. It soon turned out that this draft had no chance, but the idea was not given up. Two states presented different drafts to be considered by the Federal legislator. In 2005 the private Bertelsmann Foundation has entrusted two distinguished German scholars with drafting a Code on Individual Labour Law. However, these attempts had the same destiny as all their predecessors. They had no

5. For a detailed description of the whole process *see* M. Weiss, *The Transition of Labor Law and Industrial Relations: The Case of German Unification – A Preliminary Perspective*, 13 Comp. Lab. L.J., 1 (1991).

chance to be realized.[6] After all these experiences it may be predicted that Germany will continue to live with a multitude of Acts on specific problems of labour law. This, after all, has advantages. These acts can be amended and it is easier to, thereby, adapt German labour law to European Union law. If labour law is spread in many single Acts there is no need to maintain a consistent system of a comprehensive Code.

12.3.2 Experimental and Dispositive Statutory Law

Modern societies are becoming more and more complex. Since many factors are interrelated between economic factors and the labour market, it is becoming more and more difficult to foresee the practical impact of legislation. Therefore, it has become risky to legislate at all because the effects might be counterproductive. This has led the legislator to limit the lifetime of legislation. The idea is to abolish the law after a certain time if it does not work or to extend it if it works.

A very illustrative example of such an experimental strategy is the legislation on fixed-term employment contracts. Until the mid-eighties fixed-term employment contracts only were allowed if there was a specific justification for such a limitation. Confronted with massive unemployment the legislator in 1985 tried to fight unemployment by facilitating fixed-term contracts, allowing them to conclude fixed-term contracts without any precondition for the first eighteen months of an employment relationship.[7] Newly established enterprises and employers employing twenty or less employees were even entitled to conclude fixed-term contracts for up to twenty-four months. The idea was to motivate employers to hire more employees since they can be sure to get rid of the employees after the fixed period without facing the obstacles in case of dismissal. However, since the legislator was not sure at all about the effects of the law, it was limited for five years. The law was supposed to be examined and evaluated by experts. The evaluation should decide whether it might be extended. It was extended twice for each time five years. Only then it was slightly modified and transferred into a law for an unlimited period.[8] This example shows very well the legislator's insecurity in reference to the effects of legislation and it also shows the increased need for legitimacy due to the increased complexity of society.

This complexity has also pushed another strategy. The level fixed by legislation might be appropriate in general. But due to the differences between branches of activity or due to the impact of economic cycles, it might be recommendable to deviate not only in favour of the employees but even below

6. For all the different attempts and their failure *see* Enrico Iannone, *Die Kodifizierung des Arbeitsrechts – Ein Jahrhundertprojekt ohne Erfolgsaussicht?* (1st, Peter Lang, 2009).
7. Act on the Promotion of Employment of 1985 (26 April 1985).
8. Act on Part-Time and Fixed Term Employment of 2000 (16 November 2000).

the level fixed in the law. As already indicated, the legislator has the power to entitle the parties to conclude collective agreements accordingly. It is also possible to empower in such a way the parties to works agreements. The more complex the society is and the less predictable the economic development, the more the legislator makes use of this possibility.

Again, an example may illustrate what is meant. The Act on Working Time regulates

the maximum daily working time, the minimum standards for breaks, for shift work and for rest periods between daily working time and the next day, to just list up the main topics. Since the legislator, however, is not sure whether this is compatible with the need for working time flexibility, it allows the parties to collective agreements or the parties to works agreements within a certain frame to deviate from the fixed rules of the law. Thereby they are entitled to extend the maximum daily working time or to lower the minimum standards for breaks, shift work etc.

As the example shows, it is a contribution to flexibility by the legislator. It, however, might be problematic for the trade union or the works council, since it puts pressure on them to make use of those possibilities, which might not necessarily be in the interest of their constituency.

12.3.3 The Erosion of Collective Bargaining

12.3.3.1 Main Reasons for the Erosion

As already indicated, the normal pattern of collective bargaining in Germany is sectoral bargaining for a whole branch of activity. Formerly the coverage of collective agreements in Germany was very high. This has changed dramatically. According to latest estimates, the coverage is around 60%. This is an average figure. The differences between branches are as significant as the differences in reference to the size of companies.

There are several reasons for this development. One is, of course, the decline of membership in the trade unions. The average rate of unionization is now slightly below 20%, but more or less stable since 2011. Only members of the concluding trade union employed by an employer who either concluded a collective agreement or is member of the concluding employers' association are bound by norms of collective agreements, the coverage by collective agreements would be lower if simply the law would be applied. However, this rule does not describe properly the scope of application of collective agreements in actual practice. Employers and non-unionized employees often refer in the individual employment contracts to the collective agreements thereby extending the coverage. However, first there is no guarantee that this de facto coverage happens andsecond it is much easier to change the conditions of an individual employment contract than of a collective agreement. But this possibility of extension of coverage by individual employment contract shows that for coverage of collective agreements in actual practice the decisive element is the rate of membership in the employers' associations.

For a long time, the degree of membership in the employers' associations was very high, which led to a high coverage by collective agreements. This has changed dramatically in two ways. First, the organization rate has significantly decreased.[9] Secondly, the employers' associations developed a new pattern of organization. Many employers did not want to be bound by norms of collective agreements but did not want to give up the other advantages linked to membership in employers' associations (all kind of helpful services). Therefore, in order not to lose these members, the employers' associations created a new type of membership: membership disconnected from coverage by collective agreements. This type became very attractive in the employers' circles. The result is that now within the same employers association there are members covered by collective agreements and members who have nothing to do with collective agreements. The members have the choice between the two types. However, if a collective agreement is already in force it is not possible during the lifetime of the agreement to change from normal membership into the new type of membership. It has to be stressed that the members of the new type, in spite of being disconnected from collective agreements, maintain a significant influence on the internal strategies of the employers association (e.g., by electing the executive board etc.)

Since collective bargaining is the core activity of employers' associations, it was very controversial, whether this new type of membership is lawful at all. The segmentation of functions of an employers association implied by this new type was challenged as a violation of the freedom of association as guaranteed by the Constitution. The supporters of this new type of membership to the contrary were referring to the employers' associations' autonomy to regulate their internal affairs. This controversy came – at least for the time being – to an end by a judgment of 2006 the Federal Labour Court which accepted this new type of membership as being lawful.[10]

9. According to the last available figures, the organization rate in companies between 200 and 499 employees is 49% and in companies above this size 78% on average. The figure of companies below 200 employees is significantly lower.
10. Federal Labour Court judgment of 18 July 2006.

12.3.3.2 *Attempts to Stop the Erosion*

The basic problem is – as already explained – that in Germany only members of the contracting trade union employed by a member of the contracting employers' association are covered by the collective agreements.

The law provides a possibility to extend the coverage of collective agreements to non-organized employers and non-unionized employees by way of a declaration of general binding.[11] At first sight, this declaration of general application of collective agreements may appear to be an adequate instrument to stop the decreasing importance of the industry-wide collective agreements. However, the legislator imposed high hurdles for the use of this instrument. General application of collective agreements could be requested only if a minimum of 50% of employees, falling within the scope of the collective agreement, work for employers with a binding commitment to collective agreements. In addition, a general application of collective agreements can only be enacted by the responsible Federal Ministry only in the event of prior agreement of a committee of three representatives each from the employers and employees umbrella organizations and if it is in the general public interest.

By an amendment of the Collective Agreements Act in 2014, the legislator has facilitated the declaration of general binding by removing the above-described requirement of 50% and by defining the general public interest in a way which makes it easier to pass such a declaration. Now the general public interest is to be assumed if the collective agreement has gained main relevance in the sector for which it is made or if the declaration of general binding is necessary to prevent negative economic consequences. Thereby, the legislator has significantly reduced the discretion of the Federal Ministry.

The trade unions, however, consider this amendment still too weak. The prior agreement of the committee of the umbrella organizations on both sides is seen as too much of an obstacle since the interests of the representatives of the umbrella associations do not necessarily coincide with the interests of the parties in the branch of activity where the collective agreement has been concluded. The main obstacle in their view, however, is the requirement that the collective agreement has gained main relevance in the sector in order to be qualified for a declaration of general binding.

The seriousness of this problem may be illustrated by the caretaking sector. There – for many reasons not easy to be changed – the rate of trade union membership is extremely low. As a consequence, a collective agreement never gains main relevance in the sector and, therefore, does not qualify for a declaration of general binding. But there is no doubt, that particularly in the caretaking sector minimum conditions for all employees regulated by collective

11. For a description of this instrument *see* Weiss & Schmidt (n. 3) 190.

agreements are necessary. Otherwise, the quality of caretaking might suffer and there might not be enough personnel to do the job. The debate on a further reform on the preconditions for a declaration on general binding is going on and a result is not yet in sight.

12.4 RELATIONSHIP BETWEEN DIFFERENT COLLECTIVE AGREEMENTS

The conflict between collective agreements concluded with the same trade union and covering the same topics is not resolved by legislation. However, the judiciary has developed the principle of specialty for this conflict.[12]

Following the logic of this principle, the company collective agreement replaces the sectoral collective agreement. However, the judiciary went even further. Since collective bargaining coverage only applies to the relationship of the members of the contracting trade union with the members of the contracting employer association or the contracting individual employer, it would be possible in principle that different collective agreements concluded with different trade unions apply to different employment relationships in the company. However, the judiciary had rejected collective bargaining plurality and postulated, primarily for practical reasons, the principle of collective bargaining unity. An employer was to be bound by only one collective bargaining agreement.[13] Subsequently, thanks to the combination of the principles of specialty and collective bargaining unity, the company agreement replaced the sector collective agreement even if it had been concluded with another trade union, irrespective of its content, even if the conditions therein were less favourable for the employees. The rule of more favourable conditions did not apply in this context. A co-existence of collective agreements in one and the same business was not tolerated.

In 2010, the Federal Labour Court[14] performed a spectacular U-turn abolishing the principle of collective bargaining unity in favour of collective bargaining plurality. Neither side was amused about this: the employers saw themselves exposed to the potential danger of continuous collective bargaining and strikes, while the trade unions organized within the Confederation of German Trade Unions (DGB) felt threatened by the implied upgrading of the specialized unions representing individual occupational groups. This led to a united approach of the Confederation of German Employers' Associations and the Confederation of DGB, who jointly produced a draft law which was not only to lay down the return to the principle of collective bargaining unity, but also to

12. Federal Labour Court, judgment of 26 January 1994.
13. Federal Labour Court, judgment of 20 March 1991.
14. Federal Labour Court, judgment of 7 July 2010.

replace the principle of specialty by the principle of majority. Hence the trade union, which had more members in the company, was to prevail. Thus, the radius of action of competing trade unions is significantly limited and their possibilities to go on strike largely eliminated. In spite of irritations between the DGB trade unions the DGB continued to support the project. This approach has been fixed by a law of 2015 amending the Act on Collective Agreements. Recently the Federal Constitutional Court has approved it in principle.[15]

12.5 RELATIONSHIP BETWEEN COLLECTIVE AGREEMENTS AND WORKS AGREEMENTS

As already indicated, Germany has a highly elaborated system of works councils representing all employees in an establishment. They enjoy strong participation rights, including co-determination for quite a few important issues. However, the works council is supposed to collaborate with the employer in good faith. Strike as a means of conflict resolution between works council and employer is excluded.

Employers and works councils may conclude so-called works agreements[16] not only in matters in which the works council has a right to co-determination, but in all matters relating to labour-management relations within the establishment. Of course, without co-determination rights for the works council there would be little leverage to induce management to sign such an agreement.

Just as a collective agreement, a works agreement may establish rights and duties between the concluding parties (employer and works council). Furthermore, it may contain normative provisions. Such normative clauses have a direct and mandatory effect on the employment relationships, no matter whether the employees are unionized or not. Works agreements may be concluded for a definite or indefinite period. Unless otherwise agreed upon, works agreements may be terminated on three months' notice, but the parties remain free to agree on different terms.

Works agreements dealing with remuneration or other working conditions are only permitted if the same matter is not already regulated in a collective agreement. A matter is considered 'already regulated' if it is usually regulated in collective agreements in the respective region and branch of activity. In other words, an existing collective agreement that covers the region and the industry branch, excludes a works agreement even if the former does not apply to the specific establishment and to the employment relationships within this establishment. As a result, even in establishments where neither the employer is a member of the employers' association nor the employees are union members,

15. Federal Constitutional Court, judgment of 11 July 2017.
16. For a detailed description *see* Weiss & Schmidt (n. 3) 242.

remuneration or other working conditions cannot be regulated by works agreements.

This rather rigid rule only applies to works agreements on matters in which the works council has no right to co-determination.[17] In these cases, the works council has no power to induce the management to sign such an agreement. The reason for excluding such works agreements in cases of already existing collective agreements is to prevent the works council from competing with trade unions. Such a competition is seen as a threat to the collective bargaining system. Should the system of collective agreements break down, then there would be no adequate substitute at plant level where works agreements cannot be enforced by the works council. Thus, in order to safeguard the strength of the collective bargaining system, the status of collective agreements as exclusive means to regulate working conditions was long left untouched.

This general rule notwithstanding, parties to a collective agreement may authorize that works agreements supplement the collective agreement. This may be done by including a so-called opening-clause into the collective agreement. In the past, few collective agreements contained opening clauses because the unions feared that this device might destroy the homogeneous standards within the branch of activity and undermine the basis for solidarity within the trade union.

The trade unions for a long time refused to include such opening clauses in collective agreements. They did not want the works council to be a competitor in collective bargaining. However, during the period of the 'German economic miracle' in the formative era of the FRG this rule was gravely violated. The collective agreements for a branch of activity had to make sure that marginal companies were not overburdened. As a result, the wage level fixed in collective agreements was far below the possibilities of prospering companies. Therefore,

17. The main topics for co-determination are listed up in section 87 of the Works Constitution Act (25 September 2001): matters relating to order within the establishment and conduct of the employees in the establishment; beginning and termination of daily working hours, including breaks and allocation of working hours over the single days of the week; temporary reduction or extension of the usual working hours in the establishment; time, place, and mode of payment of wages and salaries; establishment of general principles regulating annual vacations, establishment of a vacation schedule, as well as fixing individual employee vacation schedule if employer and employee fail to reach an agreement; introduction and use of technical devices designed to monitor the employees' conduct or performance; regulations for the prevention of work accidents and occupational diseases; form, structure, and administration of social services whose scope is limited to the establishment, to the enterprise, or to the group; assignment and cancellation of rooms, apartments or houses rented to employees in view of their employment relationship, as well as general determination of the conditions of using these facilities; questions relating to remuneration arrangements, including in particular the establishment of principles of remuneration and the introduction and application of new remuneration methods as well as the modification of existing methods; determination of piece-rates, premiums and other comparable payments based on results, including money factors; establishment of principles for the handling of proposals for improvements; principles on the performance of team-work. Other important areas of co-determination refer to restructuring, to in-house training and to job creation.

in those companies after each bargaining round the works council and the employer (who was interested to maintain a skilled workforce) started negotiations for works agreements fixing the wage level significantly above the level fixed in the collective agreement for the branch of activity. These works agreements evidently were null and void but nevertheless executed. Neither the employer nor the works council nor the employees were interested to challenge them in the labour court. And the trade unions did not dare to do it because they were afraid to risk the loss of members in the respective companies. In short: an evidently unlawful situation was tolerated.

Starting in the 1980s, the situation became more dramatic, when due to increased competition companies to an increasing extent were forced to reduce labour costs. The pressure to reduce costs was combined with the employees fear to lose their jobs and end up in unemployment. Confronted with the employers demand to reduce costs, works councils increasingly concluded works agreements in order to save jobs which ignored the minimum standards for remuneration fixed in collective agreements. And they combined it as a trade-off with increased job security for a certain period. Even if such concession agreements were evidently against the law, they again remained unchallenged for the same reasons as explained above.

However, these developments have triggered a heated debate over the future of sectoral collective bargaining. Indeed, since the 1990s, the so-called crisis of sectoral bargaining became the key issue in labour law discourse on how to shape industrial relations. The question was whether the relationship between works agreements and sectoral collective agreements should not be reversed in a way that works agreements should always be allowed and have priority over the collective agreements. Since trade unions as well as employers' associations understood very well that this would have been the end of sectoral bargaining, they both fought this idea as much as possible and, thereby, prevented legislative intervention.

But the debate led to a far-reaching modification of collective bargaining. Trade unions and employers' associations have significantly modified their strategy by using opening clauses and by confining collective agreements essentially to mere framework regulations. Thus, the works council has become increasingly integrated into the structure of collective bargaining. The collective agreements for a branch of activity now have become very flexible instruments, not only containing opening clauses but also options to be chosen by works agreements (so-called cafeteria systems). In short, by radically changing the structure of the collective agreements, trade unions and employers' associations succeeded in elaborating a fair balance between centralized and decentralized bargaining.[18] This development has brought trade unions and works councils even closer together than before.

12.6 THE PRINCIPLE OF MORE FAVOURABLE CONDITIONS

According to the law, the relationship between collective agreements and individual employment contracts is governed by the principle of more favourable conditions. This means that employment contracts cannot undercut the minimum conditions in collective agreements but grant more favourable conditions for the employees. This is uncontested.

The question is what is more favourable? Is it necessary to compare each item in an isolated way or is it possible to compare the whole set of regulations in the collective agreement with the whole set of clauses in the employment contract? Since a comparison of the whole set would be very difficult and, therefore, lead to arbitrary manipulation, it is agreed that in principle each item has to be compared in an isolated way. However, the Federal Labour Court has opened the door for a solution in between: items belonging closely to each other (e.g., duration of leave and supplementary payment for leave) may be put together in a group.[19] This is problematic, since it is unclear what belongs closely to each other (this for example is denied for wage and working time) and how to measure which group is more favourable for the employee (more leave and less supplementary leave payment or the other way around). A certain degree of arbitrariness cannot be excluded.

Recently it was suggested in academic debates to not measure favourability in an objective way but leave it to the subjective estimation of the employee (e.g., to earn less but to increase job security). This suggestion, however, remained to be an unsuccessful episode.

12.7 CONCLUSIONS

On the whole, the system of sources of labour law has proved to remain rather stable. The unresolved problem is the erosion of sectoral bargaining which, nevertheless, plays the dominant role in German labour relations. The new pattern of flexible collective agreements with opening clauses is a success story leading to a fair balance between centralized and decentralized bargaining. Whether the new pattern for the resolution of conflict between competing collective agreements in an establishment will survive, remains to be seen.

18. For this development *see* A. Seifert, *Employment Protection and Employment Promotion as Goals of Collective Bargaining in the Federal Republic of Germany*, 15 Intl J. Comp. L. Indus. Rel., 343 (1999).
19. Initiated by Federal Labour Court, judgment of 24 May 1984.

There the European Court of Human Rights still has to give its view. Another big problem is the fact that in spite of the law in many small companies no works councils are elected and, therefore, no works agreements can be concluded at all.

BIBLIOGRAPHY

E. Iannone, *Die Kodifizierung des Arbeitsrechts – Ein Jahrhundertprojekt ohne Erfolgsaussicht?* (1st, Peter Lang, 2009).

A. Seifert, *Employment Protection and Employment Promotion as Goals of Collective Bargaining in the Federal Republic of Germany*, 15 Intl J. Comp. L. Indus. Rel., 343 (1999).

M. Weiss & M. Schmidt, *Labour Law and Industrial Relations in Germany*, 180 (4th ed., Kluwer Law International, 2008).

M.Weiss, *Labor Law* (Joachim Zekoll & Matthias Reimann, eds), *Introduction into German Law*, 299 (Kluwer Law International 2005).M. Weiss, *Labour Dispute Settlement by Labour Courts in Germany*, 15 Indus. L.J. (Johannesburg/South Africa), 1 (1994).

M. Weiss, *The Interface Between Constitution and Labor Law in Germany*, 26 Comp. Lab. L. & Policy J., 181 (2005).

M. Weiss, *The Transition of Labor Law and Industrial Relations: The Case of German Unification – A Preliminary Perspective*, 13 Comp. Lab. L.J., 1 (1991).

CHAPTER 13

The Hungarian Experiment to Promote Collective Bargaining: Farewell to 'Principle of Favour'

Tamás Gyulavári

13.1 INTRODUCTION

Statutory law has always been and still is the dominant source of Hungarian labour law. Collective agreements have never played an important role in Hungarian regulation of employment, and the agreements of the parties have also had a very limited capacity to form the labour law framework. Accordingly, the Labour Code had a primary function in employment regulation. Statutory employment provisions have allowed derogation for collective agreements and employment contracts in favour of employees since 1992 (1992 Labour Code), with only a few exceptions.

The reform of the Labour Code in 2012 (2012 Labour Code) attempted to extend collective bargaining and in general to reinforce contractual sources of labour law. Therefore, a new hierarchy of sources was introduced, which now allows free derogation for collective agreements and several *in pejius* deviations for employment contracts from statutory minimums.

This provoking experiment to promote collective bargaining will be analysed by outlining (section 13.2) the historical evolution of labour law sources and their hierarchy, respectively (section 13.3) the 2012 reform on collective agreements and (section 13.4) on employment contracts. Finally (section 13.5) the meaning of the more favourable rule and (section 13.6) other sources of labour law will be described. The question is whether the new hierarchy of labour law sources strengthens contractual sources in practice.

13.2 HISTORICAL EVOLUTION OF LABOUR LAW SOURCES

The evolution of Hungarian labour law may be divided into three, very distinct periods. Market-based labour regulation ended shortly after World War II when market economy was replaced by socialist law based on state ownership and an extremely centralized labour regulation. The shift back to market economy and democratic legislation was the result of the political changes in 1990. The first market-oriented Labour Code was passed in 1992 and remained in force for twenty years until the present Labour Code was passed in 2012. I will summarize below the structure and hierarchy of labour law sources in three periods: the beginning (1840s-1948), socialist labour law (1948-1990) and under the 1992 Labour Code (1992-2012). After this historical analysis, I will turn to the present system of labour law sources, based on the 2012 Labour Code.

13.2.1 Before World War II

Statutory regulation of employment started in the 1840s, and later several sectoral Acts determined standards of employment in sectors like commerce, industry and agriculture. Remarkably, several laws passed in the Austro-Hungarian Monarchy before 1918 were still in force during World War II, even if with several amendments. This sector-based elaboration of labour law lacked uniform standards until 1948. The sectoral Acts allowed deviation only in favour of employees.[1] Collective agreements were not regulated, even if several such agreements were concluded in practice. The legal debate stuck at the issue of the legal value of collective agreements, however, without statutory solution.[2] Thus, statutory law played the central role in regulation.

13.2.2 Socialist Labour Law

Socialist law had a fundamental influence on Hungarian labour law and its sources. Socialist labour law was entirely based on the Labour Code (passed first in 1951[3] and the second in 1967[4] based on the soviet sample) and its implementation decrees issued by the government and the minister of labour. As a consequence of these detailed regulations, collective agreements had a very

1. Gusztáv Vincenti, *A munka magánjogi szabályai*, 27, 78 (Grill Károly Könyvkiadóvállalata, Budapest, 1942).
2. G. Berke, *A kollektív szerződés a magyar magánjogi gondolkodásban*, 7 Pécsi Munkajogi Közlemények, 9, 60 (2014).
3. Decree-Law No. 7 of 1951 was the first – soviet type – Labour Code, which was followed by the Labour Codes of 1967, 1992 and finally 2012.
4. Act 2 of 1967.

limited regulatory function. The sectorally organized 'socialist' trade union was fully under state control.

Collective agreements could deviate from the Labour Code and its implementation decrees if it were specifically allowed by the given provision. Thus, statutory law was *ius cogent* as a main rule, and dispositive rules were the rare, although gradually increasing exceptions. The same hierarchy applied to various levels of collective agreements since a lower-level collective agreement was prohibited to regulate the same issue as a higher-level collective agreement. Moreover, the employment contract was a formal part of establishing an employment relationship, as it could not deviate at all from law or collective agreements.[5] Consequently, socialist labour law had a 'cogent' system with the dominance of the Labour Code and its implementation decrees. In this context, socialist labour law strengthened the heritage of 'Act-based' regulation of employment, without a significant contribution of contractual sources.

13.2.3 Collective Agreements Between 1992 and 2012

The first codex in the market economy, the 1992 Labour Code,[6] aimed for an essentially private law-based regulation of employment relationships. It introduced minimum standards in the Labour Code, while more favourable rules for employees could be regulated by collective agreements. There were three kinds of exceptions from the general principle of *in melius* derogations.

First, any alteration from cogent provisions (*ius cogent*) was null and void. Second, the Labour Code exceptionally allowed collective agreements to deviate *in pejius* from a few provisions of the Labour Code.[7] For example, the employee's base wage was the basis for the calculation of wage supplements, 'unless otherwise agreed'. The Supreme Court clarified in 2003 that this clause refers to the possibility of a derogation to the detriment of employees as well.[8] Third, a few statutory provisions allowed for *in pejius* derogations only to a limited extent. The only remarkable change was that harmonization amendments of the Labour Code increased the number of possible derogations from the law to the detriment of employees after 2001.[9] However, these were scarce and individual interventions and did not change the general rule of *in melius* derogation.

5. Gyula Berke, *A munkaviszonyra vonatkozó szabályok*, 70 (György Kiss, Gyula Berke, Zoltán Bankó & Edit Kajtár), *Emlékkönyv Román László születésének 80. évfordulójára* (PTE, Pécs, 2008).
6. Act 22 of 1992 on the Labour Code.
7. *See* especially Act No. 16 of 2001 on the amendment of the 1992 Labour Code concerning transposition of nine Directives.
8. Principled published decision of the Supreme Court: BH 2003/973.
9. *See* especially Act No. 16 of 2001 on the amendment of the 1992 Labour Code concerning transposition of nine Directives.

The objectives of the 1992 Labour Code, such as private law-based regulation with vivid collective bargaining, were only partially realized.[10] Collective agreements remained insignificant instruments in the regulation of employment relationships.[11] In 2009 only 33.9% of all employees were covered by collective agreements. Although the scope of collective agreements could be extended to an entire sector of the economy as well, only 8.6% of employees were covered by this kind of sector-level agreements.[12] Beyond the numbers, the contents of collective agreements were also deficient, as they often merely repeated the Labour Code (parrot clauses),[13] and included meaningless terms.[14]

Depressed collective agreement coverage has traditionally been a decisive characteristic of Hungarian labour law, just like in other post-socialist European Union Member States (except Slovenia and Romania).[15] There are several reasons explaining the weak regulatory function of collective agreements in Hungary, such as mass privatization, vertical disintegration of the 'socialist firm',[16] spread of micro-employers, weak and declining trade unions, low coverage of employers' organizations. In addition, employers were not interested in the conclusion of collective agreements due to the general principle of *in melius* derogations.

The main field of collective bargaining has always been the workplace; thus, sector-level collective agreements traditionally played an extremely limited role in labour law regulation, restricted to agreements with an extended scope. This situation did not change after the detailed regulation of sector-level collective bargaining in 2009. The Act on Sectoral Social Dialogue Committees[17] introduced the possibility for sector-level collective agreements. However, only a few such sectoral agreements have been concluded due to the weak motivation of employers and their infirm associations. Consequently, collective bargaining, irrespective of its level, has been henceforward confined to a limited regulatory role.

10. G. Kiss, *Munkajog a közjog és a magánjog határán – egy új munkajogi politika kialakításának szükségessége*, 63 Jogtudományi Közlöny, 70-81 (2008).
11. J. Radnay, *Munkajogunk helyzetéről*, 18 Gazdaság és Jog 32, 33 (2010).
12. Gábor Kártyás, *Kollektív szerződés*, 477 (Tamás Gyulavári, ed.), *Munkajog* (4th ed., Eötvös Kiadó, Budapest, 2014).
13. József Újvári, *A papagájklauzula esete a munkaszerződéssel*, 427-430, Tanulmányok Dr Veres József egyetemi tanár 70. születésnapjára, Szeged, 1999).
14. G. Kártyás & G. Takács, *Pellengér vagy piedesztál? A kiterjesztett hatályú kollektív szerződések normatani értékelése*, 4 Pécsi Munkajogi Közlemények, 91, 91-111 (2011).
15. European Commission, *Industrial Relations in Europe 2010*, 36 (Luxembourg, 2011).
16. T. Laky, *Az atipikus foglakozásokról*, 14, https://docplayer.hu/932249-Laky-terez-az-atipikus-foglakozasokrol.html (accessed 21 January 2019).
17. Act No. 74 of 2009 on sectoral social dialogue committees and certain issues on medium level social dialogue.

13.3 REFORM ON COLLECTIVE AGREEMENTS IN 2012

The current Labour Code came into effect in 2012 replacing the former codex after twenty years.[18] The 2012 Labour Code, just like the preceding one, defines 'employment regulations' as the sources of labour law and lists the following sources as such: law, collective agreement, works agreement and the binding decision of a conciliation committee.

In fact, the dominant source of labour law is still statutory law. Legal regulation of employment relationships must be elaborated in Acts since they arrange fundamental economic and social matters. The Labour Code has traditionally been the main Act in labour law since 1951. However, several other Acts are also regulating employment in fields like strike,[19] equal treatment,[20] health and safety,[21] procedural law[22] or labour inspection.[23] Certainly, the Constitution is the basis of these Acts with defining fundamental social rights.[24] However, the Constitutional Court has the exclusive authority to the abstract interpretation of the Constitution. Therefore, the courts may only use the rights enlisted by the Constitution to interpret statutory law.

The above-mentioned employment-related Acts apply exclusively to employees, so all other persons (non-employees) work under the scope of the Civil Code,[25] without any employment protection. In addition, the public sector will not be analysed here either, since employment of persons working for the state has been regulated separately and differently in several Acts since 1992.[26]

Lower-level laws, such as decrees of the government and ministers, can only regulate employment, if it is specifically allowed by an Act, above all the Labour Code. The yearly regulation of the minimum wage is the most prominent example for such an authorization by the Labour Code.

Reorganization of the hierarchy of labour law sources and particularly the derogations from law in collective agreements was the central pillar of the 2012 labour law reform since the legislator explained low collective agreement coverage above all by the rigidity of labour law.[27] Since free deviation from the Labour Code is the central measure of the reform, thus, I will discuss this issue in detail. Beyond free deviation from law, two less important reforms have also

18. Act No. 22 of 1992 on the Labour Code came into effect on 1 July 1992.
19. Act 7 of 1989 on strike.
20. Act 125 of 2003 on equal treatment and the promotion of equal opportunities.
21. Act 93 of 1993 on safety at work.
22. Act 130 of 2016 on civil procedural law.
23. Act 75 of 1996 on labour inspection.
24. Basic Law of Hungary (2011), Articles 15, 17.
25. Act 5 of 2013 on the Civil Code.
26. The most important Acts in the public sector are Act 33 of 1992 on public employees and Act 199 of 2011 on civil servants. Service relationships of certain groups of public servants are regulated by individual employment acts, such as soldiers, policemen, judges and prosecutors.
27. This is explained by the ministerial reasoning of the 2012 Labour Code.

been passed, namely potential decentralization of collective bargaining and the new possibility of concluding normative works agreements. In this chapter, I will analyse these three reforms in collective labour law.

13.3.1 Free Deviation from the Law by Collective Agreements

The 2012 Labour Code introduced fundamental changes concerning the relationship between law and collective agreement. The 'main rule' was changed, since collective agreements may derogate since 2012 from most of the rules on individual labour law[28] and on collective labour law[29] also to the detriment of employees.[30] There are over fifty provisions in the Labour Code, which allow both *in melius* and *in pejius* derogations for collective agreements.

There are three exceptions from the general rule (free derogation). First, there are over thirty 'cogent' rules, which do not allow any deviation. Only the second part[31] and the third part of the Labour Code[32] are dispositive, all other parts (Parts 1, 4 and 5)[33] are cogent. Additionally, the chapters within Part 3 of the Labour Code on general provisions of industrial relations and on works councils are also cogent.[34]

Second, only *in melius* derogation is allowed from certain provisions, for example on employer liability for damages. Here the protection of really minimum standards is the dogmatic reason for limited derogation.

Third, there are statutory provisions, which allow for *in pejius* derogation only to a limited extent, for example, extra hours may be up to 250 hours per year, which threshold may be raised to 300 hours in a collective agreement. This system of derogations is rather complicated; thus, the exceptions from the general rule are listed – under the heading 'Derogations by agreements' – at the end of each chapter, within the second and the third part of the Labour Code.[35] Any derogation violating these rules shall be null and void, and anyone may allege the invalidity of an annulled contract without a time limit; moreover, the court observes the nullity of the agreement of its own motion.[36]

28. Part 2, Articles 32-229.
29. Part 3, Articles 230-284.
30. Article 277 of the 2012 Labour Code.
31. The second part is on 'Employment relationship'.
32. The third part is on 'Industrial relations'.
33. These parts deal with general provisions (Part 1), labour disputes (Part 4) and closing provisions (Part 5).
34. Section 277(3) The collective agreement: (a) may not contain derogations from Chapters XIX and XX; and (b) may not contain any restrictions concerning the provisions contained in sections 271-272.
35. *See* also Article 277 on further exceptions.
36. Article 27 of the 2012 Labour Code.

The legislator expected that the aforementioned wide possibility of *in pejius* derogations makes employers interested in concluding collective agreements. Despite this legal incentive, there has been a remarkable decrease in the number of collective agreements since 2012. Although there is only scarce data on collective agreement coverage, it dropped from 33.9% in 2009 to around 20-25% in 2015,[37] which fall was particularly salient in the public sector.[38] It is not an exaggeration, thus, that the reform resulted in the opposite of its original target. Consequently, the legislative strategy of fueling collective bargaining by free derogation apparently did not work.

So the question is more obvious than the answer: why did collective agreement coverage fall despite the legislative reform? The answer must take into account that the legislative strategy was confined to a single measure, namely motivating employers (beyond some further steps analysed below). Along these lines, there are two underlying questions: first, whether this individual measure of motivation is sufficient in itself to reach the ambitious goal, and, second, if employers have really become motivated by the prospect of free derogation.[39]

The obvious answer for the first question is that one simple measure is unable to change the long-standing problem of low collective agreement coverage. On the contrary, a set of complex measures would be necessary to handle the structural problems of collective bargaining, such as increasing the financial, professional and political strength of trade unions and also of employers' organizations. It is evident that there is no efficient bargaining without strong social partners. Unfortunately, the 2012 Labour Code moved to the opposite direction and further weakened trade unions.[40] The motivation of declining trade unions and poorly organized employer organizations seems to be far from a complex, powerful reform. In addition, the lack of sectoral collective bargaining is a fundamental defect of the Hungarian system, which evidently cannot be promoted by the outlined changes.

As for the second question, even the aim of motivating employers was apparently not achieved. Above all, the 2012 Labour Code is very flexible in an

37. Központi Statisztikai Hivatal, *15–64 éves alkalmazottak megyék, nemek és aszerint, hogy van-e a munkahelyen érvényben kollektív szerződés, 2015. II. negyedév,* http://www.ksh.hu/docs/hun/xstadat/xstadat11evkozi/e11szerv911011145.html (accessed 21 January 2019).
38. András Pásztóy, *Nézzünk szembe a szakszervezeti valósággal,* http://ujegyenloseg.hu/nezzunk-szembe-a-szakszervezeti-valosaggal/ (accessed 21 January 2019).
39. *See* in details: Tamás Gyulavári, *Chasing the Holy Grail? Stumbling Collective Bargaining in Eastern Europe and the Hungarian Experiment,* 42-46 (Sylvaine Laulom, ed.), *Collective Bargaining Developments in Times of Crisis* (Wolters Kluwer, Bulletin of Comparative Labour Relations, 99).
40. A trade union will be entitled to conclude a collective agreement if its membership reaches 10% of all employees of a given employer (Article 276 of the 2012 Labour Code).

international comparison;[41] therefore, employers seem to be satisfied with the statutory provisions, and they are not really interested in going below these minimum standards.

There are only a few dispositive provisions, which may surely interest employers. It is still worth stipulating, for instance, thirty-six months for a reference period instead of the statutory four months, which new possibility was introduced by the amendment in 2019. In addition, employers may also achieve a higher minimum (instead of the statutory forty-four workdays) in a collective agreement for using employees at other workplace, employer or task. Therefore, increased motivation of employers is questionable due to the pulled down statutory protection of employees. Thus, the lawmakers' strategy was flawed for both its instrument and the way it was implemented.

13.3.2 Decentralization of Collective Bargaining

As it has been mentioned above, sector-level collective agreements hardly exist in the Hungarian labour market. As an exception to the lack of special provisions on sectoral agreements in the Labour Code, it regulates the relationship between higher (sector) level and lower (workplace) level collective agreements. Hence, a lower-level collective agreement may depart from a collective agreement of a broader scope insofar as it specifies more favourable conditions for employees.

Although the new Labour Code retained this traditional principle on the hierarchy of collective agreements at various levels, however, it added an important exception, opening the door to decentralization of collective bargaining. Accordingly, the higher-level collective agreement may allow the lower-level (typically employer) collective agreement to derogate from its designated provisions to the detriment of employees.[42] This new possibility[43] may weaken the capability of higher-level collective agreements to standardize working conditions in an entire sector,[44] even if it has not been exploited due to the lack of sector-level agreements.

13.3.3 Normative Works Agreement: Auxiliary Channel of Collective Bargaining

The Labour Code defines 'employment regulations' as the sources of law and lists the following sources as such: law, collective agreement, works agreement

41. OECD, *Economic challenges and policy recommendations for the Euro Area*, 27, https://www.oecd.org/about/publishing/Euro11Area11Brochure11EN.pdf (accessed 21 January 2019).
42. Article 277 of the 2012 Labour Code.
43. The 1992 Labour Code prohibited any derogation to the detriment of employees in a lower-level collective agreement.
44. Kártyás (n. 12) 491.

and the binding decision of the conciliation committee. Therefore, works agreements and the binding decisions of the conciliation committee will be analysed below as sources of labour law.

Before 2012, works agreements, concluded by the Works Council and the employer, could regulate only the privileges of a Works Council and its relations with the employer.[45] Nonetheless, the 2012 Labour Code allows works agreements to take over the normative role of collective agreements under certain conditions.[46] This so-called normative works agreement may be concluded, if the employer is not covered by a collective agreement,[47] and there is no representative trade union[48] authorized to conclude a collective agreement.[49]

The primary role of works agreements is still the arrangement of the relationship between the Works Council and the employer.[50] The novelty is that works agreements may also contain provisions on rights and obligations of the parties. This normative part of a works agreement may derogate from law the same way as the normative part of collective agreements. Apparently, the legislator wanted to apply the same rules for collective agreements and normative works agreements, but the explicit legal basis of this interpretation is missing from the Labour Code.[51]

There is only one restriction on the content of normative works agreements, as it cannot derogate from the Labour Code on wages.[52] This exception is problematic since higher wages are usually the compensation for flexible working time and rest period rules in collective agreements. As such a pecuniary compensation is not allowed, a balanced deal may be hindered.

Since the number of collective agreements is still very low, therefore, the aim of normative works agreements is to promote the conclusion of 'auxiliary' collective agreements in medium-sized companies with small trade union membership. A Works Council must be elected if the number of employees is

45. Article 64/A of the 1992 Labour Code, introduced by an amendment of the original text in 1995.
46. The possibility of works agreements replacing collective agreements was already in place, but only for a very short period between 1999 and 2002 (Article 31 of the 1992 Labour Code, amended by Act 19 of 2002).
47. As a result, the employer may conclude a normative works council agreement, in case it falls under the scope of a subsector or sector-level collective agreement.
48. The representativity criteria is quite soft since 10% of employees must be the member of the trade union. Considering the constantly declining membership among all employees (now around 10%), it is a less attainable condition at many workplaces.
49. Article 268 of the 2012 Labour Code.
50. Article 267(1) of the 2012 Labour Code: 'The employer and the works council may conclude a works council agreement for the implementation of the provisions of this Chapter and for promoting their cooperation.'
51. The derogation from the Labour Code by the works agreement is not regulated since Article 268(1) of the 2012 Labour Code arranges only the contents of such normative works agreements.
52. Chapter XII, Articles 136-165.

above fifty at the employer or its establishment.[53] There is usually no trade union at all at this level, as employee organizations are concentrated in large companies, particularly in state-owned (public service, such as railways) and multinational firms (e.g., Tesco, Audi).

As a result, large- and medium-sized firms without a notable trade union have not really had a practice or even an interest in collective bargaining. This situation may somewhat change by this measure, as medium-sized employers may be motivated to conclude a normative works agreement to draw advantages of flexible working time provisions. Unfortunately, there is not any data on such agreements, yet their number seems negligible. So it remains an open question as to how these companies may be engaged in collective bargaining.

Beyond collective agreements and normative works agreements, binding decisions of conciliation committees are also considered as employment regulations, and they function as a collective agreement. These decisions are passed by committees formed by the employer and the Works Council or the trade union, and they may have similar contents as a collective agreement. Consequently, the relationship between a binding decision and the Labour Code should be similar as in case of collective agreements; however, this legal issue is simply neglected by the Labour Code.[54]

13.4 EMPLOYMENT CONTRACT: RISING IN PEJIUS DEROGATIONS

The renewed hierarchy of labour law sources also effects derogations by agreements of the parties, particularly by employment contracts.[55] The main aim of the conceptual change is to enhance the regulatory role of contractual sources, in particular that of collective agreements (collective autonomy), but also that of the contract (individual autonomy). Although, the employment contract is formally not a source of labour law (not an employment regulation), it is indeed a source of rules for the parties.

The 1992 Labour Code allowed employment contracts to derogate from statutory rules and also from collective agreements in favour of employees. There were also three exceptions, just like for collective agreements. First, employment contracts could not deviate from the cogent statutory rules, second they could derogate from a very few provisions to the detriment of the employees as well, and third deviate *in pejius* to a limited extent. Since *in pejius*

53. In principle it is compulsory to elect a Works Council; however, employers must be away from the election, and there is no sanction if employees choose not to elect it (Article 236 of the 2012 Labour Code).
54. Articles 13 and 291 of the 2012 Labour Code.
55. The same rules apply to the employment contract and other agreements of the parties regarding derogations.

exceptions were insignificant, firm restriction of contractual freedom was the underlying concept.

The 'principle of favour' was kept as the main rule by the 2012 Labour Code, however, it remarkably increased the possibility of *in pejius* derogations. The approximation of labour law to civil law served as the dogmatical basis for enhancing contractual freedom. The regulatory function of the employment contract was strengthened by free derogation from a few, however, very important statutory provisions to the detriment of employees. For instance, the parties may agree that: the employee must provide all working conditions; the basis of wage supplements may be lower than base wage; daily working time may be split up in two periods; or a significant part of annual leave may be allocated for the next year.[56]

The new possibilities of *in pejius* derogations from statutory minimums mark fundamental changes compared to the former hierarchy of contract and law. These provisions provide new forms of flexibility for employers, as the weak bargaining position of employees usually does not make a real obstacle of these disadvantageous conditions of employment. This sensitive issue was particularly highlighted by the Labour Code amendment on overtime in 2019.[57] The parties may now agree on 150 extra working hours beyond the statutory maximum of 250 hours per year. Before the amendment, only a collective agreement could increase the annual maximum to 300 hours; however, from now on the parties may increase it to 400 hours.[58] In a working time frame, it may practically mean six working days per week.[59] Thus, the contract may deteriorate the respective provision in the collective agreement. Interestingly, trade unions and some employers make 'agreements' prohibiting derogation from their own collective agreement, but the binding force (legal nature) of such an agreement is quite vague.

Taking into account the unequal position of the parties, the above-mentioned new provisions entail the risk of abuse by the employer. While the strengthened role of the parties' agreement is less important than the changing concept of collective autonomy, it highlights the increasing emphasis on contractual freedom.

56. Articles 51, 100, 123, 139 of the 2012 Labour Code.
57. Act 116 of 2018.
58. Article 109 of the 2012 Labour Code.
59. Another important new amendment is that the employer must notify the employee on the schedule, but it may be changed any time based on the 'employee's request' (Article 97 of the 2012 Labour Code).

13.5 MEANING OF THE 'MORE FAVOURABLE' RULE

The above-described relationship between law, collective agreement and contract requires clarification of what 'more favourable for employee' means. This question was first addressed by the Supreme Court in 1991: the more favourable nature of the provision shall be assessed by the comparison of all provisions (on severance pay in the given case), instead of comparing every single rule separately and individually.[60]

This line of interpretation was first adopted in law by the 2012 Labour Code. This novel statutory provision seems to solve the question by saying that 'derogations for the benefit of employees shall be adjudged by a comparative assessment of related regulations'.[61] Yet, the courts have not clarified the limits of such an interpretation, even though there are at least three rather different interpretations of this sentence.

First, the compared related regulations may belong to different chapters of the Labour Code, in particular to the chapter on working time and the separate chapter on wage, since working time provisions are usually compensated by some sort of extra payment. According to the second interpretation, the rules within the same chapter may be compared (e.g., working time provisions). In accordance with the third, narrowest reading, even the comparison of the provisions of the same chapter shall be rather restricted, for instance only the provisions on severance pay may be compared. This fundamental question remains for the labour courts to respond to.

13.6 OTHER SOURCES OF LABOUR LAW

Beyond employment regulations and agreements, there are also other sources of labour law, such as unilateral statutes of employers and decisions of labour courts.

13.6.1 Unilateral Sources: Company Statutes

In parallel to the growing number of large international companies, unilateral company statutes, codes and by-laws are playing an increasing role in the Hungarian regulation of employment relationships. It is understandable that the 1992 Labour Code was silent on the legal nature and applicable rules of company

60. Resolution No. 147. of the Supreme Court, under the scope of the 1967 Labour Code.
61. Article 277(5) on collective agreements and Article 43(2) of the 2012 Labour Code regarding employment contracts.

statutes; however, the lack of detailed provisions led to problems in practice, for instance regarding termination of employment.[62]

Taking into account the relevance of soft law instruments, the 2012 Labour Code[63] contains a short article on unilateral company statute and workplace practice, declaring both to be a special form of order by the employer, as a unilateral legal statement of the employer.[64] Apparently, company statutes are not a legal source of labour law (not an employment regulation),[65] but rather the normative order of the employer.

Company statutes may regulate employment relationships as long as this is explicitly permitted by a law, collective agreement, or it contains a unilateral commitment made by the employer. As for derogations, the provisions on agreements of the parties shall apply to unilateral acts, including a company statute and workplace practice.[66] If we translate this provision to derogations, company statutes may deviate from dispositive statutory minimums and also from collective agreements only in favour of employees. In addition, the above described *in pejius* derogations available for employment contracts may also be exploited by company statutes. It must be emphasized here that there is no specific provision on the hierarchy of company statutes and employment regulations. Thus, the interpretation above is exclusively based on a single legal reference to agreements.

In addition, the collision between a company statute and workplace practice is also an open legal puzzle, for example if termination of employment is based on the breach of obligations by the employee. Consequently, the new article of the Labour Code on company statutes and workplace practices did not really help clarify the debated issues raised by previous court practice. These issues may be settled by specific provisions of the Labour Code on the establishment, amendment, termination and contents of unilateral sources of employment law.

13.6.2 Court Decisions

The Hungarian legal system does not follow the common law concept of precedents, but uniform court practice is acknowledged. There are several forms

62. Tamás Gyulavári & Attila Kun, *Munkáltatói jogalkotás? A munkáltatói szabályzatok szerpe a munkajogi szabályozásban*, 59 Magyar jog, 157, 160 (2012); György Kiss, *Munkajog*, 79 (2nd ed., Osiris, Budapest, 2005).
63. Article 17 of the 2012 Labour Code.
64. Section 17 '(1): Employers shall be able to implement the legal acts referred to in sections 15-16 by means of internal rules established of their own accord or by way of a procedure formulated unilaterally (hereinafter referred to as "employer's internal policy"). (2) The employer's internal policy shall be considered delivered if published by means considered customary for, and commonly known in, the area.'
65. Article 13 of the 2012 Labour Code.
66. Article 15(3) of the 2012 Labour Code.

of uniform court practice; however, they are mostly not binding for the courts. Uniformity decisions of the Supreme Court are the exceptions, as the highest instance judicial forum has the constitutional duty to harmonize the administration of justice. The Supreme Court renders uniformity decisions in cases raising issues of theoretical importance in order to ensure the uniform application of law. Such decisions are binding on all Hungarian courts.

Published decisions of the Supreme Court are not compulsory for the parties and the courts, but they are usually widely followed as long as a new published decision or the law does not change the legal practice it offered.[67] In the field of labour law, the Labour Law Chamber of the Supreme Court had published resolutions on legal issues of labour law before 1997. The importance of these resolutions is shown by the fact that they are updated by the Supreme Court and still followed by legal practitioners. This also elucidates the relevance of case law in filling in the gaps left by labour law regulation, particularly in topics such as termination of employment, liability for damages, collective agreements and harmonizing EU Directives.

For example, the Supreme Court stated that an '*in melius* derogation' in the collective agreement providing higher severance pay is compulsory for the parties if the employer applies it for a long time even after the expiration of the collective agreement. This collective agreement shall be applied until the amendment of the collective agreement on severance pay.[68] Similarly, the employer cannot refuse a payment at the time of terminating employment based on the argument that the collective agreement was not in force any more, if the employer had applied this collective agreement for years before termination of employment since this behaviour violates the principle of bona fides.[69]

The message of these judgments is that the stable, uninterrupted application of the collective agreement, which is in fact not in force at the time of application, results in the establishment of particular employee rights. However, the legal basis of applying an outdated collective agreement is somewhat unclear in the judgments, although it could have been for instance post-effect of the collective agreement, unilateral commitment by the employer or implied conduct.[70]

67. There are two kinds of published decisions of the Supreme Court: court decisions (BH) and principled court decisions (EBH). The procedure is different, but the outcome is the same in case of BHs and EBHs, since neither of them is obligatory to follow.
68. Published decision of the Supreme Court: BH 1998/97.
69. Published decision of the Supreme Court: BH 2001/191.
70. Gyula Berke, *A kollektív szerződés a magyar munkajogban*, 169 (Utilitates Bt., Pécs, 2014).

13.7 CONCLUSIONS: THE AUTARCHY OF STATUTORY LAW

Hungary is a typical post-socialist EU Member State with a strong tradition of continental law, where employment is dominantly regulated by statutory law. There is a strong, again and again reaffirmed labour law tradition that the law recounts your employment rights. In addition, employment law is centralized in one single codex, the Labour Code. However, certain other Acts also provide important detailed rules in related fields such as strikes, equal treatment or health and safety at work. Consequently, contractual sources of labour law, whether collective or individual, have traditionally played an insignificant role in labour law regulation. Particularly, collective agreements have never achieved the high coverage typical for most of Western Europe.

Therefore, the strengthening of contractual sources, above all collective agreements, was the central objective of the labour law reform in 2012. This aim was supposed to be obtained by motivating employers with free derogation from law. The relationship between the Labour Code and collective agreements has traditionally been based on the principle of favour since 1992. This established regime was essentially reformed, as an absolute freedom of the parties of a collective agreement to derogate from the Labour Code became the general rule.

However, the 2012 reform seems to be a failure. The decline in an otherwise moderate level of collective bargaining may be explained above all by the general strategy of 'flexibilizing' labour standards in fields like working time and rest periods. At the same time, the strengthening of the hardly existing sector-level bargaining was not even mentioned in the legislative strategy. In addition, the freedom of the parties of the employment contract to derogate from several statutory provisions was remarkable and gradually broadened. Certainly, the reformed hierarchy of labour law sources did not manage to strengthen collective bargaining, but it gives some more freedom to the agreement of the employer and the employee.

BIBLIOGRAPHY

Tamás Gyulavári & Gábor Kártyás: *The Hungarian Flexicurity Pathway? New Labour Code after Twenty Years in the Market Economy*, 21-33, https://www.researchgate.net (Pázmány Press, 2015).

Tamás Gyulavári & Nikolett Hős: *The Road to Flexibility? Lessons from the New Hungarian Labour Code. European Labour Law Journal*, 4, 253-270 (2012).

Tamás Gyulavári: *Chasing the Holy Grail? Stumbling Collective Bargaining in Eastern Europe and the Hungarian Experiment* (Sylvaine Laulom) *Collective Bargaining Developments in Times of Crisis* (Sylvaine Laulom), 99, *Bulletin of Comparative Labour Relations*, 29-46 (Wolters Kluwer 2019).György Kiss: *Transition of Contract of Employment: From the Locatio Conductio to the Relational Contract. New Zealand Journal of Employment Relations,* 43(3), 75-90 (2018).

Attila Kun: *How to Operationalize Open Norms in Hard and Soft Laws: Reflections Based on Two Distinct Regulatory Examples. International Journal of Comparative Labour Law & Industrial Relations,* 34, 23-52 (Kluwer Law Online, 2018).

CHAPTER 14

The Precarious Balance among Hierarchy, Coordination and Competition in the Italian System of Labour Law Sources

Iacopo Senatori

14.1 INTRODUCTION AND OUTLINE OF THE CHAPTER

Despite the major political and constitutional discontinuity occurred in Italy in the years 1946-1948, which marked the transition from a dictatorial regime to a democratic republic, one may argue that the Italian system of labour law sources as it currently stands did not undergo a substantive change between the two periods, at least at a first sight. The linkage is represented by the Civil Code, enacted in 1942, at the twilight of the Fascist era, and still in force today. Article 1 of its Introductory Provisions enlists the following sources of law, in a hierarchical order: statutes, administrative regulations, corporative regulations and customary rules.

Indeed, the Civil Code is yet one of the most important normative sources in Italian labour law. It contains the definition of a dependent (or 'subordinate') employee,[1] which represents the basic gateway for the access to the core of labour law, i.e., the provisions that apply to an employment contract, mostly aimed at protecting the weakest part of the employment relationship. It also provides for a number of key rules on pay,[2] on the essential obligations of the employee,[3] and on the legal effects of collective agreements,[4] just to name a few.

1. Article 2094 of the Civil Code (hereinafter C.C.).
2. Article 2099 C.C.
3. Article 2104 C.C. on the duty of diligence; Article 2105 C.C. on the duty of loyalty.
4. Article 2077 C.C.

The Civil Code had once been the pivotal element of the legal system of labour law, with regard to both its substantive provisions and those that shape the hierarchy between the different sources. However, at a closer look, one would find that it is now relegated to a complementary role, although it had not been substantively amended. This is due in particular to two circumstances: the extensive body of special legislation that grew over time since the inauguration of the Republican regime, resulting in amendments, integrations or additions to the provisions of the Civil Code, and, first and foremost, the entry into force of the Constitution on 1 January 1948.

The Constitution, which is self-evidently placed at the highest rank in the hierarchy of the sources, is vigorously focused on employment rights. Its very first statement[5] paves the way, although rhetorically,[6] to a remarkable number of principles and substantive provisions addressed to employment in the main body of the act. As a consequence, it comes with no surprise that those principles and substantive provisions have been capable to carve the interpretation of pre-existing legislation and drive the subsequent law-making action and case law, deeply influenced by the rulings of the Constitutional Court.[7] It is also worth to note that the Constitution provides for the rules of competence that allocate the authority to enact labour law norms between the central State and the Regions.

The branch of labour law which experienced to the greatest extent the consequences of the shift from dictatorship to democracy is collective relations, with a particular regard for the role of collective agreements as a normative source. The Introductory Provisions of the Civil Code enlisted the 'corporative regulations' among the sources of law in a strict sense. In a similar vein, the rules that governed the effects of collective agreements (which formed part of the family of corporative regulations) in respect of the law as well as over individual employment contracts operated in line with a strictly hierarchical principle of coordination. As a consequence, collective agreements were placed under the power of the statutes and above the realm of individual contractual autonomy. With the advent of the Republican Constitution, collective relations have been brought into the domain of civil liberties and contractual freedom. As a consequence of such major change, a different relationship between statutes and collective agreements was established, with the latter still operating as a de facto

5. Article 1: 'Italy is a democratic republic founded on labour'. A semi-official English translation of the Italian Constitution is available at: https://www.senato.it/documenti/repository/istituzione/costituzione_inglese.pdf (accessed 27 April 2019).
6. In the sense that the opening statement is something different from a general principle, and should be preferably interpreted as the expression of a 'spirit' which, while indicating the basic values that inspire the Nation and the legal system, brings together the constitutional principles and ensures the consistency among them: *see* C. Mortati, *Il lavoro nella Costituzione*, I Dir. Lav. 149 (1954).
7. It is interesting to note that two labour law professors currently sit among the fifteen members of the Court: Giulio Prosperetti and Silvana Sciarra.

normative source in the framework of a complex regulatory system, parallel to the State and in a certain sense depictable as autonomous from it.[8] Against such background, the law and collective bargaining have established a close relationship that evolved over time following different patterns, mostly taking the shape of a coordinated role-sharing, but at times hampered by the insurgence of conflicts that brought back to the spotlight the issues of competence and hierarchy.

Similar issues have arisen in the context of collective bargaining, with regard to the criteria that apply to settle antinomies between agreements signed at different levels. In the absence of a general statutory regulation of trade union and collective bargaining matters (such regulation being in place only in the public sector), the solution of such issues has been mainly referred to case law or to the autonomous initiatives of social partners, with the flaws that such solutions entail in terms of effectiveness and legal (un)certainty. Flaws that have been exacerbated by the circumstance that in Italy collective agreements are regulated by the law of contracts, and therefore their effects should be limited, in strictly legal terms, to the employees and employers that are affiliated to the signatory unions and employers' associations.

Statutory law and collective agreements have traditionally worked as sources of mandatory obligations for individual contracts, which in principle can only depart from such provisions to introduce more favourable terms and conditions in the interest of the employees. However, in recent times the law has opened new room for individual autonomy, introducing broader options for employers and employees to draw up tailor-made arrangements on topics such as working time or functional flexibility at the workplace.

Thus, as this introduction has attempted to show, the sources of labour law in Italy are organized into a multi-layered and dynamic system, whose constitutive elements interact over time according to changing patterns that mirror different regulatory strategies, political conditions and the volatility of the coordination criteria set up by the law. The following sections of this chapter will address into detail the issues briefly outlined above, with the aim of shedding light on the mixture of formal and informal solutions that have ensured the preservation of a balanced relationship between the sources, despite a number of interpretative uncertainties. Section 14.2 will briefly summarize the features of the pre-republican system, with a view to illustrating the effects of the constitutional transition and the legacy that the Corporatist era passed on to the Republican regime. Sections 14.3-14.7 will present the main specific sources in their hierarchical order (the Constitution, statutory law, collective agreements), attempting to analyse the intersections among them and the way in which they affect individual autonomy. The status of case law and of customary and

8. Gino Giugni, *Introduzione allo studio dell'autonomia collettiva* (Giuffrè 1960).

unilateral sources will also be briefly addressed, despite the minor systemic role they play in a civil law order characterized by a high density of juridification like Italy.

14.2 BEFORE THE REPUBLIC: THE CORPORATIST ERA

Italian labour law, here meant not as a scholarly field but as the sector of the legal system specifically addressed to the employment relationship, rose during the so-called Liberal period that coincided with the unification of the country, years before Fascism came into power in 1922.[9] However, the legislative framework established by the Fascist lawmakers for the administration of economic and employment affairs is particularly relevant in connection with the topic of this chapter, due to the close ties it holds with the current Republican system, both in chronological and in substantive terms.

The Fascist regulatory machinery was also known as 'Corporatist', since among its pivotal elements stood special public law bodies called 'Corporations'. Those bodies, which brought together representatives of employers, employees and the State, were entrusted with the general representation of economic interests and were equipped with a rule-making authority for that purpose.[10] Such system assumed the full identification of private interests of a social and economic nature with those of the State. In other words, every aspect of social autonomy in employment relations, at both the individual and the collective levels, had to converge towards (or give way to) the higher values and goals pursued by the Nation, as the Government interpreted them.

The implications of this scheme were particularly relevant with regard to the role of collective agreements and their relationship with statutory law. As for the first issue, collective agreements were defined as the inherent expression of solidarity and appeasement between the productive factors and made subject to the superior national interest in 'production'.[11] Against such background, sectoral collective agreements signed by those trade unions and employers' associations which had previously received an official acknowledgement by the Government (only one for each industrial sector) were granted the authority of sources of law in a strict sense. In fact, the law declared those collective agreements applicable to the whole workforce and to all the employers in the

9. The Civil Code of 1865, inspired by a liberal ideology, regulated the lease of works and services. The first sectoral acts that departed from the general law of contracts date back to the second half of 1800.
10. According to the Labour Charter (*Carta del lavoro*) enacted on 21 April 1927, Sixth declaration, Corporations represented wholly and comprehensively the interests of productive forces and, in such capacity, they could establish mandatory provisions on employment issues as well as on the coordination of production.
11. Section IV of the Labour Charter.

industry.[12] The law further stated that sectoral agreements should, in any case, prevail over those signed at the lower levels[13] and that individual contracts should abide by collective provisions unless they provided for more favourable terms and conditions in the interests of employees. Individual clauses in breach of this obligation were to be automatically replaced by those laid down in the collective agreement.[14] Hence, collective agreements were surrounded by a legislative shield that tied them to serve a public purpose. At the same time, the law interfered in the internal structure of collective bargaining, organizing it under a strictly hierarchical criterion.

With regard to the relationship between collective agreements and statutory law, the scheme established a sort of complementarity based on the subject covered by each source, since the law gave collective agreements a general authority to regulate employment issues.[15] This however did not put the statutes and collective agreements on an equal standing among the sources of labour law. In fact, on the one hand, the statutes maintained the power to set terms and conditions of the employment contract: even before the enactment of the Civil Code, which laid down a comprehensive set of employment legislation, a number of sectoral regulations were put in place.[16] On the other hand, collective agreements and trade unions were placed under a strict surveillance and coordination from the law and the executive power, which confirmed and reinforced the supremacy of the State.[17]

14.3 A REPUBLIC FOUNDED ON LABOUR: THE CONSTITUTION AT THE TOP OF THE SYSTEM

The repeal of the legislation which established the Corporations, in the wake of the collapse of the Fascist regime,[18] and the shift from the monarchy to the Republic, which culminated in the entry into force of the Constitution on 1 January 1948, made it possible for the new institutional order to perpetuate the pre-existing broad regulatory structure, at the same time eradicating its authoritarian features.

12. Article 10 of the Act No. 563 of 1926.
13. Article 6 of the Act No. 563 of 1926 granted sectoral trade union federations the power to sanction the peripheral branches which did not comply with the rules set at the higher level.
14. Article 2077 C.C.
15. Michel Martone, *La fase corporativa*, 63 (Mattia Persiani ed., *Le fonti del diritto del lavoro. Trattato di diritto del lavoro diretto da Mattia Persiani e Franco Carinci*, Vol. 1, CEDAM 2010).
16. *See* Royal Law-Decree No. 692 of 1923 on working time; Royal Law-Decree No. 1825 of 1924 on the employment contract of white collars.
17. Article 8 of the Act No. 563 of 1926.
18. *See* Royal Law-Decree No. 721 of 1943 enacted on 9 August 1943, only fifteen days after the removal of the dictator Benito Mussolini on 25 July 1943. The Fascist Trade Unions were suppressed later by the Lieutenant's Decree No. 369 of 1944.

The Constitution offers a wide catalogue of rights and principles addressing specific aspects of the employment relationship, in both the individual and the collective dimensions, starting from the declaration in Article 35 that commits the Republic to protect work 'in all its forms and practices'. It goes beyond the purpose of this chapter to enter into the details of every provision, but mention should be made at least of the principle of equal treatment, affirmed in general terms by Article 3 and translated by Article 37 into a specific right to equal terms and conditions of employment, including pay, between men and women; of the right to work stated in Article 4; of trade union freedom, including the right to collective bargaining, asserted in Article 39, and coupled with the right to strike set out in Article 40; of the right to a just and fair compensation declared in Article 36.

Such a direct focus on employment rights in the primary source could have been interpreted as the announcement of an intense 'social' legislation which actually failed to materialize, at least in the early Republican age.[19] Nonetheless, it would be wrong to underestimate the influence exerted by the Constitution on the lawmakers and the judiciary.

This is true, in particular, for those provisions that have been declared directly applicable to individual litigations, even in the absence of any implementing measure in secondary legislation. The most relevant case is represented by Article 36, which entitles every worker with the right to receive a fair compensation, proportionate to the quantity and quality of the work performed, and in any case sufficient to ensure to the employee and his (or her) family a free and decent life. In fact, the Supreme Court has regularly and consistently declared null and void the clauses of the individual employment contracts which failed to align with those constitutional parameters and replaced them with an equitable appreciation by the judge.[20]

The same has been with the prohibition of discrimination on the grounds of gender affirmed by Article 37, which has led the Supreme Court to tackle the issue even before a specific legislation was enacted, banning the clauses of collective agreements that provided for different terms and conditions of employment to male and female employees.[21]

An ambiguous decision given in 1989 by the Constitutional Court has been interpreted by certain lower courts as if a similar horizontal effect could be attached to the general principle of non-discrimination declared by Article 3, in conjunction with the limitations to the freedom of undertaking laid down in

19. For a review of the options discussed within the Constitutive Congress elected with the mandate to draft the text of the new Constitution *see* Lorenzo Gaeta ed., *Prima di tutto il lavoro. La costruzione di un diritto all'Assemblea Costituente* (Ediesse 2015).
20. Supreme Court 4.7.2018 No. 17421; Supreme Court 23.12.2016 No. 26953.
21. Supreme Court 23.12.1981 No. 6771.

Article 41, section 2.[22] As a consequence of this standing, the employer would be deemed to bear an obligation to grant equal terms and conditions to employees performing the same job in the same company, as a direct application of Article 3 of the Constitution. However, such interpretation of that ambiguous ruling has been in the end rejected by the Supreme Court.

Nevertheless, and despite these ambiguities, it is undisputable that in rare but significant circumstances the priority of the Constitution over the other sources of labour law has manifested itself through the capacity of constitutional provisions to directly command the adjustment of the pre-existing regulatory patterns in private litigations.[23]

In other cases, the constitutional provisions have not exerted such an enhanced strength, but still have influenced the evolution of statutory law, as they served as the legal (and political) ground to uphold the enactment of a certain piece of legislation. A recent example that is worth mentioning is the Legislative Decree No. 150 of 2015, which regulates the organization of Public Employment Services. In fact, Article 1 of the Decree explicitly claims the purpose to enforce the rights to work, vocational training and professional advancement stated by Articles 1, 4, 35 and 37 of the Constitution. The most important of such cases in the history of Italian labour law is certainly the Act No. 300 of 1970, also known as the 'Workers' Statute'. This piece of legislation contains a number of provisions aimed at reinforcing the civil liberties of the employees, such as personal freedom, freedom of expression and the right to form and join a trade union, and for this reason, it has been said to 'bring the Constitution into the workplace'.

Finally, in its (most common) role as the standard-setting source to assess the legitimacy of statutory legislation, the Constitution has also played a major role in shaping modern labour law. For instance, it is owed to the Constitutional Court the removal from the Criminal Code of a number of provisions inherited from the previous regime that punished the exercise of strike (now protected as

22. Constitutional Court 9.3.1989 No. 103, https://www.cortecostituzionale.it/actionPronuncia.do (accessed 27 April 2019). In that circumstance the Court examined a claim brought by a lower court against certain provisions of the Civil Code, concerning the matters of pay and job classification. According to the referring judge, those provisions allowed the employer to pay different wages to employees performing one same job, hence they conflicted with Articles 3 and 41, section 2, of the Italian Constitution (the latter stating that private economic initiatives shall not be carried out against the benefit of the society or in such a way as to harm human safety, freedom and dignity). The Court rejected the claim, suggesting that the limitations to the employer's unilateral power deriving from the constitutional principles, statutory legislation and collective agreements were capable of ensuring the protection of employees' dignity. The statement is ambiguous as it could be interpreted either as affirming the existence of a general principle of equal pay for equal jobs, or as permitting a differentiation within the boundaries of a correct application of the regulatory framework that surrounds the employer's power.

23. *See* Luigi Montuschi, *La Costituzione come fonte regolatrice del lavoro*, 416 (Mattia Persiani ed., *Le fonti del diritto del lavoro. Trattato di diritto del lavoro diretto da Mattia Persiani e Franco Carinci*, Vol. 1, CEDAM 2010).

a right by Article 40 of the Constitution, but harshly restrained under Fascism). The Constitution has also outdated the provisions of the Civil Code which determined authoritatively which sectoral collective agreement employers would be obliged to apply, depending on the economic activity they exercised: such provisions, that are at odds with the right to trade union freedom, are now applied only in marginal cases where it is unclear which collective agreement the parties have autonomously agreed to refer to.[24]

In the same vein, it is worth to point out that the Constitutional Court has contributed to settle the relationship between the competences of the lower regulatory sources (or, one may say, their hierarchy). In fact, the Court has repeatedly stated that the law can limit in scope and time the capacity of collective bargaining to regulate a certain employment-related topic, but cannot prevent or obstruct the bargaining activity on a permanent basis, nor can totally deprive collective agreements of their function of setting terms and condition of employment.[25] Likewise, the Court has conceded that the law can 'promote' the collective agreements signed by representative unions and rely on them to complete and specify the contents of a given legal provision, without infringing the right to trade union freedom.[26]

To summarize and conclude this section, it is thus possible to maintain that the Constitution, as the primary source of labour law, has modelled the whole regulatory system, provided an effective guidance to judges and lawmakers and made it possible to harmonize the pre-existing body of legislation with the new principles and values enshrined in the democratic republic.

14.4 THE DOMAIN OF STATUTORY LEGISLATION: A MULTI-LEVEL REGULATORY PATTERN

Employment legislation in Italy is not assembled into a Labour Code. A specific and comprehensive body of rules is only present in the civil service, a field that pursuant to a reform process started in 1992 has gradually been brought from the realm of public law into private law. Article 2, sections 2 and 3 of the Legislative Decree No. 165 of 2001 ('Consolidated Act on Public Sector Employment') state that the employment relationship of civil servants is regulated by means of contracts under the provisions of the Civil Code and of the other legislation applied to employees in the private sector, unless differently provided for.

In the private sector, the regulation of employment contracts is contained in the Civil Code and in a large set of sectoral legislation which has slowly but

24. Supreme Court 18.12.2014 No. 26742.
25. Constitutional Court 26.3.1991 No. 124; Constitutional Court 23.7.2015 No. 178, https://www.cortecostituzionale.it/actionPronuncia.do (accessed 27 April 2019).
26. Constitutional Court 26.3.2105 No. 51, https://www.cortecostituzionale.it/actionPronuncia.do (accessed 27 April 2019).

relentlessly stratified since the inauguration of the Republican order. Among the most significant steps of such stratification one can mention, in a first period characterized by an expansive social legislation between the 1960s and the 1970s, the Act No. 604 of 1966 on the limitations to individual dismissals and the above-discussed Act No. 300 of 1970 ('Workers' Statute'). In more recent times, after the turn of the Century, mention can be made of the Act No. 276 of 2003, also known as 'Biagi Law', which was mainly focused on the labour market and the regulation of 'atypical' or 'flexible' forms of employment, and of the Act No. 183 of 2014, also known as 'The Jobs Act'. This latter piece of legislation has been later implemented by a series of eight governmental decrees, which embraced a large amount of topics ranging from employment services to social safety nets, atypical contracts, the sanctions for unlawful dismissals and certain aspects of the standard employment relationship such as the power to assign tasks and to monitor the employee's performance.

With regard to the specific topic of this chapter, two issues should be addressed as long as the legislative source is concerned: the relationship between statutory law and collective agreements, and the relationship between the different authorities provided with a law-making power. The first issue will be discussed in the next section. As for the latter, it needs to be emphasized that a constitutional reform took place in 2001,[27] aimed at reshaping the form of government in a 'quasi-federal' fashion. This reform allocated the regulatory competences on employment issues between the central State and the Regions in a highly fragmented way, suggesting a possible evolution of the regulatory system towards a multi-level pattern.

To go more into detail, under the current constitutional framework[28] the State holds the full and exclusive competence to legislate on 'civil law' and on the 'determination of the basic level of benefits relating to civil and social entitlements to be guaranteed throughout the national territory', whereas the Regions can claim the exclusive authority on matters such as 'vocational training'. In-between rest a number of matters for which the competence is shared between the State, that has the power to lay down the general principles, and Regional Laws that can settle the detailed regulation. Among the matters of this latter kind, one can find 'complementary and supplementary social security', 'professions' and, first and foremost, 'employment protection and safety'.

The puzzling terminology used by the Constitution encouraged, in the early comments of the reform, a drastic interpretation of the phrase 'job protection and safety', which envisaged an almost complete 'regionalization' of labour law based on the argument of its mainly protective nature.

27. Constitutional Act No. 3 of 2001.
28. Article 117 of the Italian Constitution, as amended by the Constitutional Act No. 3 of 2001.

Nonetheless, the Constitutional Court has soon rejected the most radical views and reaffirmed the pre-eminence of the State Law as the normative authority in the domain of employment. First, the supreme judges made it clear that the contractual relationship between employers and employees is a branch of civil law, and hence shall be brought back to the exclusive normative authority of the State.[29] Second, the Court could not refrain from pointing out that the rigid allocation of competences between State and Regional legislation outlined in the Constitution can be at odds with the complexity of several topics (for instance: occupational health and safety), whose concrete regulation stems from the overlapping of rules belonging to different subject-matters. As a consequence of such complexity, the judges came to uphold, in practice, the deep intrusion of State Law on topics that undoubtedly fall, at least in part, into the competence of the Regions. This is the case, for instance, with the organization of Public Employment Services, which falls into the shared competence on 'employment protection and safety', or with the apprenticeship contract, whose regulation is the outcome of an entangled mixture between the contract of employment and vocational training, respectively leading to the exclusive authorities of State and Regional Law.

In such circumstances, the Court approved detailed State regulations, either justified by the purpose of dictating the general principles of a certain matter and the basic standards concerning civil and social rights or explained by the unambiguous belonging of the 'core' of a complex piece of legislation to a subject covered by State authority.[30] Moreover, it required that joint State and Regional competences be exercised according to a principle of 'loyal cooperation', meaning in practice that State Law interfering with the regional areas of competence can be upheld provided that the Regions have been duly involved in the decision-making procedures.[31]

Thus, the resemblance of a multi-level law-making system is probably more apparent than real, as the State still holds a firm hand on the statutory sources of labour law.

14.5 COLLECTIVE AGREEMENTS: A PRIVATE SOURCE BETWEEN STATE INTERVENTION AND HORIZONTAL COMPETITION

The description of the sources of labour law as the elements of a multi-level system is only formally true if the observation is limited to the domain of

29. Constitutional Court 28.1.2005 No. 50, https://www.cortecostituzionale.it/actionPronuncia.do (accessed 27 April 2019).
30. *See* for instance Constitutional Court 7.12.2006 No. 406, on Public Employment Services, https://www.cortecostituzionale.it/actionPronuncia.do (accessed 27 April 2019).
31. Constitutional Court 28.1.2005 No. 50, Constitutional Court 28.1.2005 No. 51, https://www.cortecostituzionale.it/actionPronuncia.do (accessed 27 April 2019).

statutory legislation, but certainly more accurate when applied to the relationship between the law and collective agreements. It has already been mentioned that collective agreements (particularly in the private sector) are basically governed by the ordinary law of contracts, therefore labelling them as sources of law in a strict sense might not be appropriate. However, their role goes far beyond the simple perspective of 'social' sources and entails a neat characterization in legal terms. Such characterization has been acknowledged, for instance, by the Civil Procedure Code, which equalizes sectoral collective agreements to the law as long as certain aspects related to the judicial cognizance in employment disputes are concerned.[32]

Indeed, the broad coverage of collective agreements, reaching almost 80% of the national workforce,[33] supports the view of them as a fundamental normative source as much as it was with their ancestors from the Corporatist regime (*see* above, section 14.2), in spite of their different nature and the different institutional framework in which they operate. The Republican Constitution considers collective agreements as a form of exercise of the right to trade union freedom, unsuited to any strict control by the State or assignment of functions in the public interest. As a matter of fact, the Constitution envisages a special legal machinery which grants sectoral collective agreements a general scope of application (erga omnes effect) on the grounds of the signatory parties' representativeness.[34] However, the social partners have traditionally refrained from triggering such mechanism, since the tangible and well-established embeddedness of collective agreements in the regulatory system was considered as a sufficient guarantee of their effective role as de facto sources of labour law. A role that has constantly been reinforced by the judicial propensity to uphold the indirect extension of the scope of collective agreements to non-unionized employees, based on their 'social normativity'.[35]

32. Article 360 of the Civil Procedure Code includes the infringement or erroneous interpretation of sectoral collective agreements among the grounds for challenging before the Supreme Court a decision taken by a lower judicial authority. Article 420-bis of the Civil Procedure Code permits the prejudicial decision on the validity, effectiveness and interpretation on sectoral collective agreements.
33. Data referred to December 2018: *see* ISTAT (National Institute of Statistics), *Contratti collettivi e retribuzioni contrattuali*, 31 January 2019, https://www.istat.it/it/files//2019/01/Comunicato-ottobre-dicembre-2018.pdf (accessed 24 April 2019). The data elaborated by Organisation for Economic Co-operation and Development, more easily accessible by international readers, show the same results, although referred to a less recent period: *see* https://stats.oecd.org/Index.aspx?DataSetCode=CBC (accessed 24 April 2019).
34. Article 39, section 4 of the Constitution.
35. *See* Gaetano Vardaro, *Contrattazione collettiva e sistema giuridico* (Jovene 1984); Carlo Zoli, *Contratto collettivo come fonte e contrattazione collettiva come sistema di produzione di regole*, 487 (Mattia Persiani ed., *Le fonti del diritto del lavoro, Trattato di diritto del lavoro diretto da Mattia Persiani e Franco Carinci*, Vol. 1, CEDAM 2010). It is worth noting that the achievement of such 'social normativity' was also made possible by a strong promotional legislation which was enacted in the early years of the Republic. The Legislative Decree No. 741 of 1959 transposed into law the collective agreements then in force, in order to set up a common level

Against such background, the relationship between collective agreements and statutory law represents a challenging issue which escapes any clear-cut governing criterion, be it given in terms of hierarchy, competence or favourability.

The Constitutional Court has repeatedly paid a high consideration to collective bargaining as the privileged source for the establishment of terms and conditions of employment, starting from the crucial matter of pay which is currently not addressed in statutory law.[36] A special case is represented by the public sector, where collective agreements are considered by the law itself as the mandatory source of regulation of employment and trade union matters, including salaries,[37] although the power of the law to drive and circumscribe the action of collective agreements in the field has been subject to a high degree of variation over the last decade.

However, the Constitutional Court has firmly denied the existence of a reservation of competence in favour of collective agreements, and has conversely affirmed the power of the law to restrict the regulatory action of the social partners, particularly in the face of overwhelming reasons of public interest and provided that such restrictions operate only for limited periods.[38] The experience of the public sector is emblematic in this regard: while the early period of the legislative reform of the sector (1992-2001) was characterized by an almost all-encompassing delegation of the normative authority on terms and conditions of employment to collective agreements, a more recent legislation has brought back a large share of such power into the hands of statutory law.[39]

To summarize the above considerations, it seems possible to assert that the relationship between the law and collective agreements in Italian labour law is not construed in the form of differentiation of competences based on the topic addressed by the regulatory action, as it is the case with the relationship between State and Regional Law. Nor it can be depicted as if it was governed by a strictly hierarchical order, since the hierarchical principle in favour of statutory law, although existing, essentially appears as a weak and residual option. The traditional principle of favourability is also of little help in this respect. In fact, while it is true that often the normative role of collective agreements consists in building on the minimum standards set out by the law to provide for better terms and conditions in the interests of employees, it cannot be neglected that in a

---

playing field of basic terms and conditions of employment and encourage social partners to further engage in collective bargaining.

36. Constitutional Court 26.3.1991 No. 124, https://www.cortecostituzionale.it/actionPronuncia.do (accessed 27 April 2019).
37. *See* in particular Articles 2, 40 and 45 of the Legislative Decree No. 165 of 2001.
38. Constitutional Court 19.12.1962 No. 106, Constitutional Court 7.2.1985, No. 34, https://www.cortecostituzionale.it/actionPronuncia.do (accessed 27 April 2019).
39. The Act No. 15 of 2009 enlisted a number of topics that collective agreements can regulate only within the (rather strict) limits set out by the law itself. Such restrictive approach was softened but not reversed by the Legislative Decree No. 75 of 2017.

remarkable number of circumstances the law itself grants social partners the power to lay down a more complex adaptation of the legislative floor, reflecting a policy trend started in the last two decades of the twentieth Century.

This is the case with the provisions that allow collective agreements to introduce flexible arrangements on working time or on the use of atypical forms of employment, in such a way that it would be complicated to identify which regulatory solution fits better with the interest of the employees.[40] Another outstanding case is represented by the so-called proximity agreement, a special kind of collective agreement established by an act of Parliament in 2011. Proximity agreements can be signed either at the company or at the local levels and enjoy the power to deviate from the clauses of higher level agreements as well as from the legislative standards on a broad range of labour market and individual employment topics. Their prerogatives extend to setting lower levels of protection, the only boundaries being represented by the provisions of the Constitution, international conventions and European Union law.[41]

Thus, the best description of the relationship between the two sources is probably the image of a competition disguised as hierarchy, where the law, claiming its formal prominence, attempts to exert an influence on collective bargaining, whereas the latter, as an expression of contractual autonomy, tends to circumvent any external interference and conform to it only as long as it matches the social partners' will.[42]

An additional feature should also be pointed out to understand the whole picture. State Law has often attempted to establish a cooperation with collective bargaining, relying on it as a complementary asset to tackle circumstances in which a contractual source could prove to be more responsive and adaptable than a rigid piece of legislation. In fact, the delegation of normative powers from the law to collective agreements has been a typical pattern of Italian labour law at least since the 1980s.[43] This method has been used, for instance, to introduce higher degrees of flexibility in atypical employment (e.g., to allow flexible time arrangements in part-time work[44]), to set out the selective criteria for workers involved in collective dismissals,[45] or to stipulate exceptions to the effects of certain legal provisions aimed at protecting employees' rights. An example of the latter kind is the measure of Legislative Decree No. 81 of 2015. It provides for the

40. Legislative Decree No. 66 of 2003 on working time; Articles 19 and 31 of the Legislative Decree No. 81 of 2015, respectively on fixed term work and agency work.
41. Article 8 of the Law-Decree No. 138 of 2011. *See* Giuseppe Antonio Recchia, *Law Pressure on the Industrial Relation System: The Italian Case*, 35 (Adalberto Perulli & Stefano Bellomo eds, *New Industrial Relations in the Era of Globalization*, CEDAM 2019).
42. For instance, the most representative social partners agreed in a joint statement made on 21 September 2011 to make a limited use of proximity agreements and the related regulatory powers.
43. *See* Luigi Mariucci, *Le fonti del diritto del lavoro quindici anni dopo* (2nd ed., Giappichelli 2003).
44. Article 6 of the Legislative Decree No. 81 of 2015.
45. Article 5 of the Legislative Decree No. 223 of 1991.

application of the laws on subordinate employment to independent contractors bound by a particularly close functional dependency with their client, except in circumstances that have been previously regulated by a collective agreement.[46]

In such cases, the statutes follow a 'bargaining in the shadow of the law' approach, providing collective agreements with the power to replace the standard legal provisions that will apply in case social partners decide to refrain from acting. In other cases, the law simply grants collective agreements the power to build on the standard regulation with additional or more analytical provisions.

Whatever the adopted technique, the delegation of power entails the purpose of the law (and to some extent the outcome) of supporting and encouraging collective bargaining. This benefit comes with a side-effect for the social partners, as it may interfere with their autonomous decision making. In fact, depending on the circumstances, the law may either decide to surround such transfer of power with a set of conditions, limitations and guidelines, or opt for a blank delegation. This difference has been particularly evident as long as the State influence on the internal allocation of normative authority between the different levels of collective bargaining is concerned.

Since the signature of a milestone Intersectoral Agreement in 1993, Italian industrial relations have been organized according to a two-tier coordinated system of collective bargaining, whereby the sectoral level keeps the highest authority and secondary bargaining, either at the company/plant or at the local level, is authorized to operate only under the conditions set out by sectoral agreements and in compliance with a no duplication rule (ne bis in idem). Nonetheless, in the absence of a legislative regulation of representation and bargaining issues, the actual balance between the two levels depends on the autonomous arrangements reached by social partners and remains subject over time to their political ability to ensure the effective implementation of the agreements. The current regulatory framework for the manufacture sector,[47] which represents so far the final stage of a reform process started in 1993, has enlarged the room for decentralized bargaining. It provides that, under circumstances related to an economic downturn or to the availability of fresh investments, company agreements can depart from the provisions of sectoral bargaining and even introduce lower standards on a limited range of topics,

46. Article 2 of the Legislative Decree No. 81 of 2015.

47. *See* the Intersectoral Agreement of 10 January 2014 signed by the Employers' association Confindustria and the main Trade Union Confederations CGIL (Confederazione Generale Italiana del Lavoro – Italian General Labour Confederation), CISL (Confederazione Italiana Sindacati Lavoratori – Italian Confederation of Workers' Unions) and UIL (Unione Italiana del Lavoro – Italian Union of Labour) and, more recently, the Intersectoral Agreement signed by the same parties on 9 March 2018. Similar agreements have been signed also in other sectors. For an outline *see* Gaetano Zilio Grandi, *Collective Bargaining*, 301 (Franco Carinci & Emanuele Menegatti eds, *Labour Law and Industrial Relations in Italy. Update to the Jobs Act*, Wolters Kluwer 2015).

encompassing working time and workplace organization, without a prior authorization from the upper level. However, this measure represents an exception in a system which is still based on the firm coordination by the central level.

Against such background, the conventional approach taken by State law has swung between the laissez-faire and a mild support for sectoral bargaining. However, in the past decade the law has moved away from this conventional approach. In fact, the above illustrated 2011 legislation of proximity agreements, with the enhanced legal effects it envisages, represents an unprecedented forcing on social partners in favour of a marked decentralization. Nevertheless, such an approach has been mitigated by the subsequent legislation. The 'Jobs Act', implemented in 2015, marks a return to a fully liberal approach, since the prerogative it entrusts to collective agreements can be exerted at any level and without any requirement for a prior coordination between the levels.[48]

14.6 THE RISE OF INDIVIDUAL ARRANGEMENTS

The mandatory effect of statutory law and collective bargaining provisions over individual arrangements has always represented the fundamental regulatory feature of Italian labour law. As a corollary of such scheme, the former are usually conceived as minimum standard-setting sources whereas individual autonomy is only authorized to introduce better terms and conditions in the interest of the employees.[49]

It is well known, however, that a large share of modern legal theory has challenged the capacity of binding external regulations to protect effectively the interests of employees and pursue the goals of labour law.[50] In this vein, Italian legislation has recently manifested a cautious acknowledgement of the power of individual arrangements to adjust statutory or collective rules, although only in limited and very peculiar situations.

An example that concerns the direct relationship between the law and individual agreements is the reform of the employer's unilateral power to assign tasks to the employees, implemented by the already mentioned 'Jobs Act' in 2015.[51] As a general rule, the law stipulates that an employee can be shifted only among tasks belonging to the same rank of qualification or to a higher rank, and that he or she can be moved to a task classified in the lower rank only under a limited and predetermined number of circumstances (such as an organizational change of the undertaking that affects the position held by the employee, or

48. Article 51 of the Legislative Decree No. 81 of 2015.
49. *See* Article 2077 C.C. with regard to the relationship between collective agreements and individual contracts.
50. *See* for instance Ralf Rogowski, *Reflexive Labour Law in the World Society* (Edward Elgar 2013). A summary of the different opinions is offered by the seminal work of Guy Davidov & Brian Langille eds, *The Idea of Labour Law* (OUP 2011).
51. Article 3 of the Legislative Decree No. 81 of 2015.

other cases identified by collective agreements) and without any loss of pay. Other unilateral orders or agreements aimed at downgrading the employee are in principle null and void. Nevertheless, the current legislation introduced a relevant exception to this rule. In fact, the parties to the individual contract are allowed to agree on a broader modification of the original terms on conditions of employment, entailing the transfer to a lower rank and a proportional reduction of the salary, on the condition that such arrangements are meant to address the employees' interest in safeguarding their employment, gaining a new professional skill or improving their life conditions.

With regard to the situations where the relationship between the law and individual autonomy is usually mediated by collective agreements, in the sense that a special individual arrangement is possible only if authorized by a collectively agreed rule, it is worth mentioning the cases where the law itself has made such mediation not necessary and replaceable by individual agreements. This is, for instance, the case with 'elastic clauses' that permit the employer to unilaterally modify the schedule and/or the duration of the work performance in part-time contracts.[52] Such regulatory patterns, however, do not establish a full equivalence between collective and individual sources. In fact, the individual regulation can be triggered only as long as a collective agreement is missing on that specific issue, hence reaffirming the subsistence of a residual preference for the collective sources.

In all the circumstances outlined above, the law does not neglect the problem of the contractual imbalance between the parties, which represents the main explanation of the extensive use of the technique of mandatory regulation in labour law. A specific mechanism is set out to ensure that such 'flexible' (or 'waiving') arrangements embody an authentic expression of individual autonomy on the employees' side: in fact, individual pacts and clauses of this kind are only valid if overseen and approved by special bodies provided with a public trust authority, such as conciliation and certification commissions.

14.7 THE NEGLECTED SOURCES: COMPANY CUSTOMARY RULES AND WORKPLACE BY-LAWS

The Italian labour law system is characterized by a high degree of juridification in which little room is left to minor sources. Nevertheless, at least two of the latter are worth mentioning because of the importance they exert in practice, although they cannot be defined as sources in a strict sense.

The first category is represented by workplace by-laws, here meant as the unilateral regulations set out by the employer. They are considered as part of the employer's power to organize and oversee the work performance and can either

52. Article 6 of the Legislative Decree No. 81 of 2015.

address specific topics (such as job design, job ranks or codes of discipline) or encompass a broader range of workplace matters. Since the function exerted by such unilateral regulations is comparable to that of collective agreements, a specific problem that may arise concerns the co-existence and the possible conflicts between the two 'sources'. For instance, the lawfulness of an employer's decision to refuse bargaining and impose a unilateral by-law could be challenged as infringing the right to trade union freedom.

The second category is represented by company customary rules. Their definition differs from the 'general' customary rules mentioned by the Civil Code at the bottom of the list of the formal sources of law. In fact, they operate as factual rules stemming from the behaviour of the employer, that complement the contents of the individual employment contract under the general principles of private law. Company customary rules consist of terms and conditions more favourable than those provided for by the law or by collective agreements: typical examples thereof are supplementary compensation or specific working time arrangements. Their constitutive elements are the spontaneity of the behaviour (in the sense that it is not assumed as the fulfilment of an obligation), its reiteration and its application to the whole workplace community.[53] It is disputed in case law whether a posterior collective agreement can be allowed to curtail the content of a company customary rule already in force. Some judges believe that the two sources operate on different levels and therefore collective agreements cannot go against customary rules[54]; others take the opposite view.[55]

14.8 CONCLUSIONS

This chapter has been opened with the description of the path dependency that links the current structure of labour law sources in Italy with the legal order in force during the Fascist regime. Pointing out such linkage helps explain some peculiar patterns of the Republican system, particularly as long as the role and functioning of collective bargaining is concerned. However, it should not raise doubts on its compatibility with the democratic principles. In fact, the differences with the Corporatist period are as important as the continuities. Among the former, it is worth mentioning in particular three elements: the Constitution, with the active role played by the Constitutional Court in bringing about a continuous adaptation of the legal framework to the Republican values; the principle of trade union freedom, that shapes the constitutional role of social

53. Supreme Court 18.1.2016 No. 15995.
54. Supreme Court 13.12.2012. No. 22927.
55. Supreme Court 19.2.2016. No. 3296.

partners as private normative agents; and the existence of a democratically elected Parliament.

Collective agreements hold a central position among the sources of labour law, despite the ambiguities that surround their legal effectiveness as a consequence of their nature of ordinary contracts governed by private law. Their relationship with statutory law over time has essentially been smooth and harmonious. A significant feature in this regard has been the consideration (and the support) granted by the law to collective agreements as 'regulatory resources' that can adapt and specify the statutory standards, of in turn deviate from them, to ensure a more effective regulation of labour issues. Recently, however, a number of attempts by the legislation to reinforce the hierarchical pattern, interfering with the rule-making prerogatives and the operational mechanisms of collective agreements, have been observed. The phenomenon can be partly brought back to a broader political discourse advocating the «disintermediation» of the relationship between the decision-makers and the citizens, and the corresponding marginalization of social partners and other intermediary entities. Nevertheless, the authority of the law to contain the sphere of collective autonomy is limited on constitutional grounds.

Finally, a significant and recent innovation in the system concerns the position of individual contracts. The reference is to the cautious emergence of examples of 'reflexive' regulation, open to an individual adaptation of the normative standards with a view to accommodate personal needs of the workers. Such innovations mirror the acknowledgement of the increased complexity of societal patterns by the lawmakers.

BIBLIOGRAPHY

Giuseppe Antonio Recchia, *Law Pressure on the Industrial Relation System: The Italian Case*, 35 (Adalberto Perulli & Stefano Bellomo eds, *New Industrial Relations in the Era of Globalization*, CEDAM 2019).

Guy Davidov & Brian Langille eds, *The Idea of Labour Law* (OUP 2011).

Lorenzo Gaeta ed., *Prima di tutto il lavoro. La costruzione di un diritto all'Assemblea Costituente* (Ediesse 2015).

Gino Giugni, *Introduzione allo studio dell'autonomia collettiva* (Giuffrè 1960).

Luigi Mariucci, *Le fonti del diritto del lavoro quindici anni dopo* (2nd ed., Giappichelli 2003).

Michel Martone, *La fase corporativa*, 63 (Mattia Persiani ed., *Le fonti del diritto del lavoro. Trattato di diritto del lavoro diretto da Mattia Persiani e Franco Carinci*, Vol. 1, CEDAM 2010).

Luigi Montuschi, *La Costituzione come fonte regolatrice del lavoro*, 416 (Mattia Persiani ed., *Le fonti del diritto del Lavoro. Trattato di diritto del lavoro diretto da Mattia Persiani e Franco Carinci*, Vol. 1, CEDAM 2010).

Costantino Mortati, *Il lavoro nella Costituzione*, I Dir. Lav. 149 (1954).

Ralf Rogowski, *Reflexive Labour Law in the World Society* (Edward Elgar 2013).Gaetano Vardaro, *Contrattazione collettiva e sistema giuridico* (Jovene 1984).

Gaetano Zilio Grandi, *Collective Bargaining*, 301 (Franco Carinci & Emanuele Menegatti eds, *Labour Law and Industrial Relations in Italy. Update to the Jobs Act*, Wolters Kluwer 2015).

Carlo Zoli, *Contratto collettivo come fonte e contrattazione collettiva come sistema di produzione di regole*, 487 (Mattia Persiani ed., *Le fonti del diritto del lavoro. Trattato di diritto del lavoro diretto da Mattia Persiani e Franco Carinci*, Vol. 1, CEDAM 2010).

CHAPTER 15

Collective Bargaining in the Shadow of Legislation: Labour Law Sources in Poland*

Łukasz Pisarczyk

15.1 OPENING REMARKS

This Chapter discusses the sources of labour law in Poland. The starting point is the general description of the Polish legal system. In the following paragraphs the reader will find an analysis of generally binding sources of law and acts of autonomous nature (collective agreements, internal acts issued by employers). The subsequent points refer to the scope of application of labour law sources, and to their hierarchy and functioning mechanism (principle of employee privilege). The system of labour law sources is discussed in a broader perspective, taking into account the specific historic conditions and the current situation of social dialogue. Unlike in Western European countries, collective bargaining in Poland plays a rather limited role (sectoral negotiations are almost non-existent). The employment conditions of large groups of workers are determined by the legislation and employment contracts (in some cases also by acts issued by employers).

15.2 GENERAL FEATURES OF THE SYSTEM OF LABOUR LAW SOURCES IN POLAND

Polish law belongs to continental legal systems of statutory (written) law. In recent decades the system of labour law sources has undergone a significant

* This article is a result of project No. 2018/29/B/HS5/02600 financed by the National Science Centre Poland.

evolution. The main challenge has been the transition from communism and a centrally-planned economy to democracy and a free market economy[1] as well as the adjustment of the Polish law to European Union standards. The initial transformation period was ushered in by the enactment of the Constitution (1997).[2] The Constitution determines the basis of the political, social and economic system; the fundamental rights of individuals (including collective labour rights); the structure and hierarchy of the sources of law; as well as the organisation of state and local authorities.[3]

The Constitution determines a closed catalogue of sources of law created (or authorized) by the state or local authorities (sources of universally binding law): international treaties, statutes (acts of Parliament) and regulations issued by public administration bodies. The sources of universally binding law may regulate the rights and duties of individuals and various entities (also independent from the state and its bodies). At the same time, the Constitution does not exclude autonomous standards created by the interested parties themselves. This phenomenon is confirmed by Article 9 § 1 of the Labour Code[4] which stipulates that for the purposes of the Labour Code, labour law should be understood as the provisions of the statutes as well as the provisions of collective agreements and internal acts issued by the employer[5] as far as they regulate the rights and duties of the parties to the employment relationship.[6] Collective agreements and internal acts issued by employers are referred to as autonomous sources of labour law. The right to create these acts may be derived, *inter alia*, from the freedom of association (collective agreements) or freedom of contract

1. *See* more Michał Seweryński, *Polish Labour Law from Communism to Democracy* (Dom Wydawniczy ABC 1999). One of the most important objectives was the reconstruction of the system of collective agreements.
2. The Constitution was enacted in 1997. The English translation of the Constitution: www.sejm.gov.pl. *See also* W. Sanetra, *Social Dialogue as an Element of Polish Socio-Economic System in the Light of the Constitution of the Republic of Poland*, in *Collective Labour Law*, 60 Studia Iuridica 191 (2015).
3. According to the Constitution, the Republic of Poland shall be a democratic state ruled by law and implementing the principles of social justice (Article 2). The basis of the economic system is a social market economy, based on the freedom of economic activity, private ownership, and solidarity, dialogue and cooperation between social partners (Article 20). Work shall be protected by the Republic of Poland. The State shall exercise supervision over the conditions of work (Article 24).
4. The law of 26 June 1974 – Labour Code (Journal of Laws 2019, item 1040, as amended), hereinafter referred to as 'Labour Code'.
5. The acts that regulate internal structure of specific entities and bodies, e.g., universities or companies. They may regulate the rights and duties of the parties to the employment relationship.
6. It is necessary to stress that the definition of labour law embodied in Article 9 § 1 of the Labour Code has been formulated only for the purposes of the Labour Code. It does not modify the constitutional catalogue of the sources of law. However, it is used in each case where the Labour Code refers to the concept of labour law. As a result, Article 9 § 1 of the Labour Code entails some normative consequences. *See* more e.g., Krzysztof Wojciech Baran, *Outline of Polish Labour Law System*, 89 (Krzysztof Wojciech Baran ed., Wolters Kluwer 2016); Leszek Mitrus (Zbigniew Hajn & Leszek Mitrus, eds), *Poland* (Roger Blainpan, Editor-in-Chief) *International Encyclopaedia of Laws: Labour Law and Industrial Relations*, 31 (Kluwer Law International 2016).

(internal acts issued by the employers). The law may extend their effectiveness (*erga omnes* effect). Alongside the law sensu stricto they shape a polycentric normative order.

Due to the complexity of the sources of labour law it is necessary to determine the relationships between respective acts. The hierarchy of labour law sources, regulated by the Constitution and the Labour Code, is as follows: (1) generally binding sources of law; (2) collective agreements; (3) unilateral acts issued by the employer. The functioning of the system is based on the principle of employee privilege. Acts located lower in the hierarchy cannot be less favourable for employees than acts with a higher position.[7]

15.3 SOURCES OF UNIVERSALLY BINDING LAW AND ITS EVOLUTION

The Constitution enumerates a closed catalogue of the sources of universally binding law. This solution (contrary to the standards existing in the communist period) was intended to protect individuals against arbitrary actions of public authorities. The sources of universally binding law[8] include: the Constitution itself, statutes (acts of Parliament), ratified international treaties, and regulations issued by public administration bodies.[9] The statutes are enacted by the Parliament according to the procedure determined by the Constitution. Regulations are issued by specific state authorities (e.g., the Council of Ministers, the Prime Minister and ministers).

Labour law is treated as a separate branch of law and has been codified. The codification was a result of a long-lasting evolution that began after World War II when the communist party came into the power. Before World War II the basic labour institutions were regulated by the civil law. The construction of the employment contract was the subject of the Obligation Code (1934) while some protective standards, e.g., protection against dismissal, health and safety, and working time, were regulated in separate statutes. The main source of collective labour law was the Law on Collective Agreements (1937). Creating a new socio-economic order required a gradual reconstruction of labour law. However, until the beginning of 1970s, the previous structure of legal acts was maintained. In 1971, following the Soviet example, the preparation of the Labour Code began.[10] Ultimately, the Code was enacted in 1974.[11] Since the communist

7. *See* Article 9 §§ 2 and 3 of the Labour Code.
8. The universally binding law may shape the situation of individuals and private entities.
9. Article 87.1 of the Constitution. According to 87.2 of the Constitution enactments of local law issued by the operation of bodies shall be a source of universally binding law of the Republic of Poland in the territory of the body issuing such enactments.
10. During the 'wave' of codifications in the communist countries.
11. The codification was intended to unify the labour law. It played, to an extent, an ideological role, underlying the position of labour law in communist countries and also reflecting specific

system collapsed, labour legislation has been amended several times to adjust the legal solutions to the changing political and socio-economic environment as well as to the European standards. From the beginning of 2000s, there has been a visible tendency to flexibilise labour law. Subsequent amendments have intended to give more room for the social partners to regulate the employment standards (also to depart in peius from statutory standards).[12]

After thirty years of profound transformation, it has become clear that there is a need to create a new and comprehensive statute (or statutes) regulating labour law issues (the idea of recodification). However, there is a strong conviction that labour law should remain codified (other countries of the region have also chosen this solution, adopting new labour codes). Decodification would be treated as a regress in worker protection (in symbolic as well real-life terms). In 2002 and 2016 the government appointed codification committees. Both committees prepared drafts of separate codes: a Labour Code (individual labour law) and a Collective Labour Law Code.[13] Unfortunately both attempts to recodify the labour law failed, in the latter case due to strong opposition of trade unions.

The structure of labour legislation remains complex. The Labour Code is not exhaustive. Some labour law matters are regulated in separate acts. Other laws regulate, *inter alia*, a large part of collective labour law, including the structure of social partners,[14] collective disputes[15] and collective dismissals.[16]

features of the then prevailing system (a lack of democracy; a centrally-planned economy). There was no room for any real bargaining between management and labour (the state was the main owner and, consequently, employer).

12. Two significant amendments to the Labour Code came into force in 2002 and 2003, which were the legislator's reaction to a very high level of unemployment (almost 20%). For instance, the legislation enabled social partners to temporarily worsen the working conditions (e.g., collective agreements may modify working conditions determined in individual employment contracts) In 2013 working time standards were flexibilised. However, compared to some other countries, the room left for the social partners remains limited.
13. Drafts were published in Polish on the website of the Ministry of Family, Labour and Social Policy (https://archiwum.mpips.gov.pl/prawo-pracy/projekty-kodeksow-pracy/ and https://www.gov.pl/web/rodzina/bip-teksty-projektu-kodeksu-pracy-i-projektu-kodeksu-zbiorowego-prawa-pracy-opracowane-przez-komisje-kodyfikacyjna-prawa-pracy).
14. The Act of 23 May 1991 on Trade Unions, Journal of Laws 2019, item 263, hereinafter referred to as 'TUL'; the Act of 23 May 1991 on Employer Organisations, Journal of Laws 2019, item 1809, as amended. *See also* the Law of 7 April 2006 on Informing and Consulting Employees, Journal of Laws No. 79, item 550, as amended, that regulates the composition and competences of employee councils.
15. The Act of 23 May 1991 on Solving Collective Labour Disputes, Journal of Laws 2019, item 174, as amended.
16. For example the Act of 13 March 2003 on Special Principles Concerning the Termination of Employment for Reasons not Related to Employees (Collective Redundancies), Journal of Laws 2018, item 1969, hereinafter referred to as 'CRL'.

There is also separate legislation concerning the minimum wage,[17] the institutions of the labour market[18] (that can be treated as labour law in a broad sense) as well as anti-crisis solutions.[19] Finally, there are separate legal acts regulating the rights and duties of special groups of employees, e.g., civil servants and teachers. The labour legislation creates a core of rights and duties of the parties to the employment relationship. Due to the weakness of social dialogue, the legislation does play a crucial role in shaping employment standards.

The labour legislation in a strict sense (including the Labour Code) covers, as a rule, employees only (unless otherwise provided). Such a solution has been confronted with an enormous increase in atypical work. According to various statistics, hundreds of thousands of workers are engaged on the basis of civil law contracts (although in many cases they perform work in conditions similar to employees[20]). As a result, alternative protection for non-employees has been provided. For instance, workers (non-employees)have been granted health and safety protection,[21] protection against discrimination and guarantees regarding the minimum hourly rate (2016). On 1 January 2019, an important reform of collective labour law came into force,[22] wherein the personal scope of trade union rights was extended to workers who are not employees. The scope of application of protective standards is varied. In some cases the form of employment is used as the criterion. For instance, the minimum hourly rate is provided for in the case of workers employed on the basis of specific civil law contracts: service contracts (while specific task contracts are excluded).[23] Freedom of association is based on the features of employment. The right to form and join trade unions has been guaranteed to persons who perform work personally, in return for remuneration, do not employ other workers and have collective interests that can be represented by trade unions.[24] The guarantees cover people employed on the basis of various civil law contracts and also self-employed (formal entrepreneurs) if they meet statutory conditions.

---

17. The Law of 10 October 2002 on Minimum Wage, Journal of Laws 2018, item 2177.
18. The Law of 20 April 2004 on Promotion of Employment and Institutions of Labour Market, Journal of Laws 2019, item 1482, as amended.
19. The Law of 1 July 2009 on Mitigation of the Economic Crisis Consequences for Employees and Entrepreneurs and the Law of 6 November 2013 on Special Solutions Concerning the Protection of Workplaces, Journal of Laws 2019, item 669. The laws provided, *inter alia*, the possibility to introduce short-time systems. *See* more L. Mitrus, *Anti-crisis Regulations of Polish Labour Law*, 2 European Labour Law Journal (2010). The practical importance of anti-crisis solutions is rather limited.
20. The Polish law does not provide for an efficient legal mechanism to reclassify the legal basis of employment.
21. Article 304 of the Labour Code.
22. The Law of 5 July 2018 Amending the Law on Trade Unions (Journal of Laws 2018, item 1608).
23. The self-employed (formal entrepreneurs) are not excluded from the guarantees as far as they are parties to service contracts.
24. *See* the Law of 5 July 2018 Amending the Law on Trade Unions (Journal of Laws 2018, item 1608). The law came into force on 1 January 2019 (there are some lesser exceptions).

Court judgments are not treated as sources of labour law since the decisions are effective only between the parties. Some of the judgments of the Supreme Court are treated as principles of law (e.g., resolutions of the full panel of the Court, resolutions of the full panel of the chamber and resolutions of seven judges if they decide to treat their ruling as a legal principle). Even resolutions representing legal principles are binding for the Supreme Court itself (and courts involved in a specific case) but not for other courts and bodies. In practice, however, rulings of the Supreme Court (especially the legal principles) play an important role determining the final interpretation of legal norms. Books of authorities are not sources of law either, although they are used in the interpretation process.

15.4 COLLECTIVE AGREEMENTS

As regards autonomous sources of labour law, their legal nature is deeply influenced by the constitutional position of trade unions and employer organisations. According to the Constitution, social dialogue is one of the fundaments of the socio-economic system (Article 20). The most important instruments of social dialogue include collective bargaining, collective disputes and collective agreements. The Constitution recognises not only the right to form and join trade unions and employer organisations,[25] but also the right to bargain collectively and conclude collective agreements.[26] Trade unions also have the right to organise strikes and other forms of protests.[27]

On the one hand, collective agreements are regulated in the chapter of the Constitution devoted to fundamental rights and they are not referred to as sources of law. This chapter underlines the fundamental difference between the state law and the sources of autonomous nature. On the other hand, constitutional references to collective agreements mean that they cannot be treated as simple contracts binding *inter partes* (in that case, separate guarantees would not be needed). The constitutional regulation can be understood in this sense that the state recognises the *erga omnes* effect of collective agreements that are binding for all the employees engaged in a given establishment.[28] In this interpretation the Constitution confirms the traditional construction of collective agreements in the Polish law (the *erga omnes* effect was provided for already in the Law on collective agreements of 1937).

25. The Republic of Poland shall ensure freedom for the creation and functioning of trade unions, socio-occupational organisations of farmers, societies, citizens' movements, other voluntary associations and foundations (Article 12).
26. *See* more K.W. Baran, *Model of Collective Labour Agreements in the Polish Legal System*, 2 Praca i Zabezpieczenie Społeczne (2019).
27. Article 59.1-4 of the Constitution.
28. It is assumed that the constitutional concepts refer somehow to the legal state that existed at the moment of entry into force of the Constitution.

The Constitution distinguishes between typical and atypical collective agreements. Atypical collective agreements are utilised in extraordinary cases expressly indicated by the legislation (Article 9 § 1 LC).

The Labour Code creates a comprehensive framework for typical collective agreements.[29] They can be concluded by trade unions (only), on the one hand, and employers or their organisations, on the other. The legislator has not extended the right to conclude typical agreements to non-union employee representation (e.g., work councils or ad hoc bodies that are entitled to negotiate some atypical agreements). Typical collective agreements have a broad subject scope: the conditions of work and pay, the rights and duties of the parties to the agreements, social matters.[30] They cannot interfere with the rights of third parties. The Labour Code regulates in detail the parties to the agreement, the procedure of their conclusion as well as the conditions of application. Typical collective agreements are subject to an obligatory registration procedure. The Labour Code distinguishes company-level collective agreements (concluded for one employer, with the exception of collective agreements for a legal person or another organisational unit covering more than one employer: Art. 241^{28} of the Labour Code) and multi-employer collective agreements (concluded for more than one employer).

Atypical collective agreements can be concluded in instances (usually of a special character) expressly indicated by the law.[31] The idea behind atypical collective agreements is to encourage or to allow the social dialogue in extraordinary circumstances when usually there is no room for normal negotiations. As a result, the procedure of their conclusion is less formal than the bargaining process leading to conclusion of typical collective agreements and its registration is not required. However, the subjective scope of atypical collective agreements is limited to the issues determined by law (e.g., collective redundancies).

Some atypical collective agreements are aimed at protecting employees involved in the transfer of undertaking procedures and collective redundancies.[32] A separate category is represented by agreements concluded to settle a collective dispute. Their subjective scope is relatively broad (similar to typical collective agreements). Usually, they are aimed at improving wages and working conditions, trade union rights or social benefits. As a result, they can be treated

29. In Chapter XI of the Labour Code. *See* L. Mitrus, *Relationship Between Statutory Law, Collective Agreement and Employment Contract: Case of Poland*, https://mta-pte.ajk.pte.hu/downloads/leszek_mitrus.pdf, 5-6.
30. In practice the scope of collective agreements remains, however, limited. Compare G. Goździewicz, *Collective Labour Agreements as a Fundamental Tool of Trade Union Operation* in: *Collective Labour Law*, Studia Iuridica Nos 60, 83 (2015).
31. *See*, e.g., K.W. Baran, *The Autonomous Labour Law: De Lege Lata and De Lege Ferenda* in: *Collective Labour Law*, Studia Iuridica No. 60, 18-19 (2015). However, the legal basis for concluding an agreement may result from all the provisions of a given act (*see*, e.g., judgment of the Supreme Court of 22 August 2018, III PK 60/18).
32. Article 3 CRL, Article 26^1 TUL.

as acts of protective nature. They are separated from typical collective agreements because they constitute the result of a special procedure in which it is possible to organise a strike.[33]

Other categories are atypical agreements enabling the flexibilisation of the employment relationship (mainly working time[34]) and collective agreements used to worsen (temporarily) the conditions of work and pay. The social partners may (depending on the situation of the specific employer): suspend the provisions of a collective agreement (even concluded at a multi-employer level), suspend the provisions of other autonomous sources of labour law (e.g., internal acts issued by the employer), as well as worsen the conditions of work and pay arising from individual employment contracts.[35] The suspension or worsening must be justified by the employer's financial situation and these agreements may be concluded for a maximum term of three years.

The majority of atypical collective agreements are negotiated with trade unions and (where there are no trade unions) with employee representatives elected according to the rules adopted in the respective company. The latter solution is disputable due to the relatively weak position of these ad hoc representatives. The law does not provide any legal framework for the election. In practice, the procedure is quite often determined by employers. Jurisprudence requires these rules to be consistent with the standards arising from ILO Convention No. 135. Another problem is the lack of special protection against anti-union behaviour. General anti-discrimination provisions seem insufficient. It may influence the position of representatives and (as a consequence) the results of negotiations (in a way unfavourable for workers).

In some cases, legislation has introduced further requirements or limitations concerning either parties to an agreement or a procedure itself. They are justified by the special nature of the matters negotiated by the social partners. First, a group of atypical collective agreements can be concluded with trade unions only (employee representatives elected according to the rules adopted at a given employer are excluded). Only trade unions can be part of collective disputes. They also have exclusive rights to conclude collective agreements dealing with collective redundancies, the transfer of the undertaking and intermittent work. Second, the law expands the formal requirements concerning

33. The Polish law distinguishes between procedures to negotiate typical collective agreements and procedures to resolve collective disputes. In the latter case, trade unions not only formulate their demands but also inform about the possibility of organising the strike. The procedure is regulated by the Law on Resolving Collective Disputes.
34. Atypical collective agreements may extend the reference period of working time as well as introduce intermittent working time and flexible working hours. *See* Articles 129 § 2, 139 § 3, 140^1 and 150 § 3 of the Labour Code. The social partners may also establish a legal framework for telework (Article 67^6 § 1-2 of the Labour Code).
35. Articles 9^1, 23^1a, 241^{27} of the Labour Code.

the procedure of resolving collective disputes. Two obligatory stages (negotiations and mediation[36]) are required. Each of these stages can lead to the conclusion of a collective agreement.[37]

To recapitulate, the system of collective agreements comprises both typical and atypical ones. Typical collective agreements can be concluded by trade unions and employers (employer organisations) without further authorisation and may regulate a wide variety of issues connected with the employment relationship. Exceptionally the law authorises the social partners to negotiate atypical collective agreements. They are intended to: (1) protect workers (collective disputes, collective redundancies, the transfer of the undertaking); (2) flexibilise the employment relationship (flexible working time, telework); (3) temporarily worsen the conditions of work and pay (suspension of collective agreements, suspension of other autonomous acts, worsening of conditions of work and pay arising from employment contracts).

Finally, it is necessary to stress that the constitutional role of social dialogue is not reflected in its real status.[38] Over the recent years no multi-establishment collective agreement has been concluded (the last was concluded in 2014). The number and scope of application of company-level agreements has also been limited. As a result, the coverage by collective bargaining is one of the lowest in Europe (around 15%).[39]

15.5 INTERNAL ACTS ISSUED BY EMPLOYERS

The next tier of autonomous sources of labour law are unilateral acts issued by the employer.[40] The two main forms are work order regulations and pay regulations. Work order regulations contain organisational rules, e.g., specific working days and working hours, rules of confirming presence at work, rules for justifying absence, and hours of night time. Pay regulations determine remuneration as well as other benefits related to work (e.g., allowances, reimbursement of expenditures, and car policy). Pay regulations are intended to replace

36. The procedure creates a legal framework for a legal strike action.
37. If the collective agreement has not been concluded the trade unions are entitled to initiate the strike procedure.
38. Trade unions are active only in relatively few companies. They are present mainly in bigger enterprises (particularly former state-owned companies). In private sector trade unions are much weaker; in smaller companies almost non-existent. The crisis of trade unions is deepened by the construction company trade union organisation. To be active in a given establishment a trade union must unite at least ten workers (employees or workers who are not employees but have been employed for at least six months). On the situation of collective bargaining in Poland *see* more e.g., Ł. Pisarczyk, *The Crisis of the Collective Bargaining System in Poland*, 35 International Journal of Comparative Labour Law and Industrial Relations, 1, 62 (2019).
39. *See* https: //stats.oecd.org/Index.aspx?DataSetCode = CBC.
40. *See* more e.g., Krzysztof Wojciech Baran, *Outline of Polish Labour Law System*, 106-111 (Wolters Kluwer 2016).

(temporarily) collective agreements. They are binding until a collective agreement comes into force.[41] In practice the regulations supersede collective agreements.

The adoption of internal acts (concerning work order and remuneration) is mandatory for large companies who are not covered by collective agreements and who employ more than fifty employees. Employers with at least twenty employees are obliged to issue the regulations on the demand of a company-level trade union representative. All other companies may adopt these unilateral regulations voluntarily. In practice internal regulations replace collective agreements. Trade unions, if they exist in a given company, are involved in the procedure. The position of the employer remains, however, dominant (particularly in case of work order regulations).

A separate category includes internal statutes that determine the structure of specific entities (e.g., commercial law companies and universities). The internal statutes may regulate selected matters in the field of labour law.

15.6 SCOPE OF APPLICATION AND LEGAL CHARACTER OF AUTONOMOUS SOURCES OF LABOUR LAW

The normative character of autonomous sources of labour law is underlined by the *erga omnes* effect provided for by the legislation. The extended application is provided for not only in the case of collective agreements but also in the case of internal acts issued by employers. The law differentiates, however, groups of workers that are covered by various autonomous sources of labour law. In some cases, these sources cover only employees while other acts are applied to employees as well as to workers engaged outside the employment relationship.

In the past, autonomous sources of labour law applied mainly to employees, which was the consequence of exclusion of other workers from collective rights. The Constitutional Court challenged this solution in 2015. According to the Court, the collective rights should be guaranteed, irrespective of the nature of employment, to all workers who perform personal work for remuneration, whose interests can be protected by trade unions.[42]

Consequently, the Law on Trade Unions was amended by extending collective rights to workers who are not employees.[43] As a result of the enlargement of the personal scope of the freedom of association, the provisions

41. Regulations concerning remuneration (pay) must be agreed with trade unions. But if there are no trade unions or they are unable to work out a common view, the employer issues the regulations unilaterally.
42. Judgment of the Polish Constitutional Court of 2 June 2015, K 1/13, Journal of Laws 2015, item 791.
43. Article 2.1 TUA. The amendment came into force on 1 January 2019. Volunteers, trainees and workers who perform unpaid work are entitled to join trade unions under conditions determined by the union statutes (Article 2.4^1 TUA).

concerning typical collective agreements[44] and resolving collective disputes apply mutatis mutandis to workers (performing paid work) who are not employees.[45] Both procedures are directly rooted in the freedom of association. However, the majority of other collective institutions (including atypical collective agreements and internal acts issued by the employers) retain a pure employee character. Their content is strictly connected with the content of the employment relationship, e.g., they regulate the rights and duties arising from the employment relationship or are derived from the employer's organisational power. Another disputable element is the limitations of the personal scope of collective agreements in public administration.[46] Although the Constitutional Court has not challenged this solution[47] it seems to go too far, at least from the perspective of international standards.[48]

The autonomous sources of labour law (both collective agreements and internal acts) cover, respectively, all the employees or workers employed by a given company unless the act provides otherwise. However, discriminatory provisions are prohibited.

Autonomous sources of labour law influence directly the rights and duties of the parties to the employment relationship (they operate in a manner similar to the sources of universally binding law). The new autonomous standards are applied by virtue of law. There is, however, an important exception concerning collective agreements and internal acts concerning remuneration. If they provide for less favourable conditions than previous collective agreements or internal acts, the new (less favourable) conditions must be implemented to the individual employment relationship (Article 241^{13} § 2 LC).[49] Moreover, the law regulates the relationship between autonomous sources of labour law and

44. Article 21.3 TUA.
45. In the case of those of them who are formally entrepreneurs, there is a potential conflict between social protection and economic freedoms. *See* judgment in *FNV*, EU:C:2014:2411. It is not really enough to apply the criterion of interests that can be protected in a collective manner.
46. They cannot be concluded for: (1) civil servants in governmental administration, (2) employees of State offices employed on the basis of appointment or nomination, (3) employees of local authorities employed on the basis of election, appointment, or nomination and (4) judges, associate judges and prosecutors (Article 239 § 3 of the Labour Code).
47. Judgment of the Polish Constitutional Court of 17 November 2015, K 5/15, Journal of Laws 2015, item 1982.
48. Mainly the ILO Convention No. 151 (Labour Relations (Public Service)) that has been ratified by Poland. Compare, e.g., B. Gernigon, A. Odero & H. Guido, *ILO Principles Concerning Collective Bargaining*, 139(1) International Labour Review, 47-48 (2000), and Z. Góral, *Collective Representation of Public Sector Employees*, in *Collective Labour Law*, 60 Studia Iuridica 102-103 (2015).
49. The Polish law recognises the construction of unilateral amendment of employment standards by the employer with period of notice (Article 42 of the Labour Code). The employee may reject the proposed conditions, but it leads to the termination of the employment contract (with period of notice). The employer has to utilise the procedure to implement less favourable conditions of a new collective agreement or an internal act concerning remuneration. More favourable working conditions arising from collective agreements and internal acts concerning remuneration are applied by virtue of law.

individual employment contracts. Provisions of individual employment contracts cannot be less favourable for employees than the labour law, including the provisions of autonomous sources of labour law (Article 18 § 1 of the Labour Code). Less favourable provisions are null and void and are replaced by appropriate provisions (Article 18 § 2 of the Labour Code).

15.7 THE HIERARCHY OF LABOUR LAW SOURCES

The relationships between the sources of law created by public authorities are regulated by the Constitution, while the relationship between the law in a strict sense and autonomous labour law sources, as well as the relationship between these acts, are subject to the provisions of the Constitution, the Labour Code and other laws.

As regards the sources of law created by public authorities, there are no special rules concerning labour law. The general principles arising from the Constitution should be applied. The top position is occupied by the Constitution, which determines the character and binding force of the rest of the sources of law. In the light of the Constitution, among generally binding sources of law, the first position after the Constitution itself was granted to international treaties ratified with prior consent granted by act of Parliament.[50] The next level is constituted by acts of Parliament (statutes, laws). They are supplemented by regulations (decrees). The regulations (decrees) are issued on the basis of specific authorisation contained in and for the purpose of implementing statutes (laws) by the bodies specified in the Constitution.[51] Below, the generally binding laws are sources of so-called internal law. They are created by state bodies (e.g., Council of Ministers, ministers) but are binding only for these entities that are dependent on an authority (body) that has issued a given act (and not for individuals and other, e.g., private entities). As a rule, acts which are located lower in the hierarchy cannot interfere with acts that occupy a higher position. Acts that contradict this principle may be challenged by the Constitutional Court and declared not binding.[52] The potential conflict between norms located at the same level must be solved by means of general rules of interpretation.

---

50. The agreements may be ratified by various bodies. The Parliament must, however, accept the ratification.
51. The authorisation shall specify the body appropriate to issue a regulation and the scope of matters to be regulated as well as guidelines concerning the provisions of such act. A body authorised to issue a regulation shall not delegate its competence, referred to in paragraph 1 above, to another body.
52. The Constitutional Court shall adjudicate regarding the following matters: (1) the conformity of statutes and international agreements to the Constitution; (2) the conformity of a statute to ratified international treaties whose ratification required prior consent granted by statute; (3) the conformity of legal provisions issued by central State bodies to the Constitution, ratified international treaties and statutes (Article 188 of the Constitution).

The position and hierarchy of autonomous acts has been determined by the Constitution, the Labour Code and other laws. First of all, autonomous acts are dependent on the generally binding sources of law. The law creates a legal framework for autonomous sources and limits the scope of collective bargaining (primarily to protect employees). As regards internal structure of autonomous acts, the Labour Code distinguishes two main tiers: collective agreements and acts created by the employer. Collective agreements, as a result of the social dialogue (rooted in the Constitution), are above the internal acts issued by the employer. In addition, the law regulates the relationship between establishment (company-level) and multi-establishment collective agreements. The multi-establishment agreements have stronger legal standing. The relationship between typical and atypical collective agreements is unclear. Although they are in the same group of autonomous acts (Art. 59.2 of the Constitution, Art. 9 of the Labour Code), the Supreme Court has recently stated that provisions of atypical collective agreements cannot replace more favourable provisions of typical collective agreements that were concluded earlier.[53]

As a result, the hierarchy of labour law sources (based on employee privilege principle) can be summarised as follows: the Constitution, international treaties (ratified by the Parliament), statutes, regulations issued by public authorities, multi-establishment collective agreements, company-level collective agreements; internal acts issued by the employer (including internal statutes).

15.8 PRINCIPLE OF EMPLOYEE PRIVILEGE

The functioning of autonomous labour law sources is based on the principle of employee privilege. This is justified by their traditional goal: the protection of the employee as a weaker party to the employment relationship. It also reflects the usual role of collective agreements that were intended to improve the position of workers. As a result, acts that are located lower in the hierarchy cannot be less favourable for employees than acts that are located higher.

This entails three main consequences. First, autonomous sources of labour law cannot be less favourable for employees than generally binding provisions. Second, collective agreements concluded for one employer cannot be less favourable than those of multi-establishment character. Third, unilateral acts issued by the employer cannot worsen the position of employees in comparison with standards arising from the law and collective agreements. Certain exceptions may be provided at each level.

Over recent years there has been an observable tendency to limit the principle of employee privilege. In numerous countries social partners have been

53. Judgment of the Supreme Court of 22 August 2018, III PK 60/18.

authorised to depart from statutory standards, sometimes in a direction less favourable for employees. Moreover, the role of collective agreements concluded at the company (or even plant) level has been increased. All these solutions are intended to safeguard greater flexibility for employers. They are connected with economic, organisational or even social changes. The tendency to decentralise employment standards has been stimulated by the economic crisis.[54] Countries most affected by the crisis have been encouraged to implement such solutions. The main idea is to enable employers to adjust working conditions to their current situation so as to avoid or overcome economic difficulties. The scale of decentralisation varies from country to country.

Polish law continues to develop areas in which collective agreements may depart in peius from statutory standards. The scope of possible derogations was changed by subsequent anti-crisis legislations (2002, 2009 and 2013). The general rule remained unchanged: autonomous sources of labour law cannot be less favourable for employees than generally binding laws.

However, the list of potential exceptions has been gradually extended. The legislation provides for various techniques of derogations. They reflect the character of matters regulated by the law as well as the position of social partners. In some cases the derogations are allowed only by means of typical collective agreements that are concluded with trade unions and guarantee the highest level of protection.[55]

However, the most common solution nowadays is to allow modifications in peius, not only in typical collective agreements, but also in atypical ones (depending on the social partners' decision). They are concluded with trade unions or (in the absence of trade unions within the establishment) by employee representatives elected according to the rules adopted in a given company. This makes it possible to take the advantage of these instruments for numerous employers that are not covered by trade union organisations. However, the law neither regulates the election nor protects representatives against employer's repressions. As a result, no equilibrium, necessary for collective bargaining, is guaranteed.

Derogations applied in this way are utilised mostly in the sphere of working time. The social partners may extend the reference period of working time up to

54. *See*, e.g., U. Liukunnen, *The Role of Collective Bargaining in Labour Law Regimes. Draft General Report*, XXth Congress of the International Academy of Comparative Law, 2-3 (Fukuoka, Japan 22-28 July 2018) and S. Laulom, *From Decentralisation of Collective Bargaining to De-collectivisation of Industrial Relations Systems?* (Sylvaine Laulom ed.), *Collective Bargaining Developments in Times of Crisis*, 15-28, 99 Bulletin of Comparative Labour Relations (Kluwer Law International 2018).
55. Only typical collective agreements may provide for a payment of remuneration in kind (instead of money).

twelve months and may introduce daily intermittent working[56] time and flexible working hours. Another category comprises agreements adopting short-time work (shorter working hours accompanied by lower remuneration, partially compensated from public funds). Due to restrictive criteria, short-time systems have been applied to a very limited extent.

Finally, social partners may temporarily worsen the conditions of work and pay by means of either suspending autonomous legal acts (Article 9^1 of the Labour Code) or worsening the conditions of work and pay arising from individual employment contracts (Article 23^{1a} of the Labour Code). In the latter case the collective agreement modifies (*in peius*) employment standards, usually remuneration, determined by the parties to the employment relationship.[57]

Derogations by means of collective agreements are based on the consent of employee representatives (either trade unions or other employee representatives). They cannot be applied to unilateral acts issued by the employer. As a result, they may depart from standards determined by the law only in a few (usually organisational) matters. If employees are not covered by a collective agreement, work order regulations may introduce a sixty minute break that is not counted as working time and increase the yearly limit of overtime hours.[58] There are special rules that apply to limiting or liquidating the social fund required to be established by some employers. The liquidation or limitation may be introduced by means of collective agreements or (if there is no collective agreement) by means of pay regulations. However, in the latter case it must be accepted either by trade unions or by employee representatives (if there are no trade unions).

Unlike Western European countries, Poland does not have a problem with deviation from industry-specific (or other multi-establishment) standards at the company level, since industry-specific or sectoral collective agreements are almost non-existent. Over the recent years no multi-employer typical collective agreements have been concluded. According to data published by Ministry of Family, Labour and Social Policy, at the moment only around 200,000 workers are covered by multi-employer (including industry-specific) typical collective agreements[59] (while the total number of workers is around 17 million).

---

56. There are two periods of work with a break (not longer than five hours) which is not included in working time.
57. This solution is highly disputable, perceived as too far-gone interference with the autonomy of the will of the social partners. It applies in case of employers that are neither covered by collective agreements nor obliged to issue internal acts concerning work order and remuneration. The only source of working standards is then the individual employment contract.
58. The statutory number of supplementary hours is 150 per year. The social partners are limited by the maximum number of working hours per week (forty-eight). It gives, taking into account the period of annual leave, 376 or 384 hours per year.
59. http://www.dialog.gov.pl/dialog-krajowy/uklady-zbiorowe-pracy/stan-rejestru-prowadzonego-przez-ministra-rodziny-pracy-i-polityki-spolecznej. *See* more Pisarczyk (n. 38) 63.

In any case, there is a legal mechanism enabling modifications in peius at lower levels (at the moment only theoretical). Employers and company trade unions may suspend provisions of multi-employer collective agreements. The suspension must be justified by the financial situation of the employer. The agreement may be concluded for a term up to three months.[60]

The principle of employee privilege is also applied as regards the relationship between the employment contract and the sources of labour law. Article 18 § 1 of the Labour Code stipulates that the provisions of an individual employment contract cannot be less favourable for employees than the provisions of the labour law (understood according to Article 9 § 1 of the Labour Code).[61] Despite all the ongoing economic, technological and organisational changes, the employee remains a weaker party in the employment relationship (their dependence on the employer is even increasing). So, there are no grounds for releasing the principle of employee privilege. As a rule, the parties to the employment contract cannot depart in peius from the standards established either in the sources of universally-binding law or in autonomous sources of labour law.

15.9 CONCLUSIONS

Polish law provides for a complex and comprehensive system of labour law sources. The Constitution shapes the basis of the socio-economic system as well as safeguarding a number of fundamental rights including collective freedoms and rights. It also regulates the system of generally-binding sources of law: international treaties (ratified with the consent of the Parliament), statutes (laws) and regulations (decrees) issued by public authorities. Further, the law recognises autonomous sources of labour law: collective agreements and internal acts issued by employers (including work order regulations, pay regulations and internal statutes).

To sum up, the sources of labour law may be divided into two categories: sources of the law in a strict (constitutional sense) and autonomous sources of labour law. The first category is composed of the Constitution, ratified international treaties, the statutes (laws) enacted by the Parliament, regulations (decrees), internal law and acts created by local authorities. Autonomous sources of labour law are constituted by collective agreements (typical and atypical ones) and internal acts issued by the employer (e.g., work order and pay regulations) and internal statutes.

60. Article 241^{27} of the Labour Code.

61. According to Article 18 LC less favourable provisions of employment contracts are null and void. Appropriate provisions of the labour law are to be applied instead. The labour law is understood broadly covering not only generally binding norms but also autonomous acts (Article 9 § 1 LC). *See* more L. Mitrus, *Relationship Between Statutory Law, Collective Agreement and Employment Contract: Case of Poland*, https://mta-pte.ajk.pte.hu/downloads/leszek_mitrus.pdf, 1-2.

The functioning of autonomous acts is based on the principle of employee privilege. They cannot provide for solutions less favourable for workers than the law. The same rule applies to the relationship between internal acts issued by the employer and collective agreements. Due to the weakness of social dialogue a very important role is played by statutory standards. The derogations *in peius* from statutory standards are allowed only in cases expressly indicated by the law.

There have also been some visible changes in terms of the functioning of labour law sources. Due to the lack of multi-employer agreements, the legislator did not have to decentralise the system. However, the system has become more flexible. Flexibilisation manifests itself in an increasing role of collective agreements in relation to legislation. More recent are cases in which collective agreements may depart from statutory standards in a way less favourable for workers. The most important area of flexibilisation is working time. Although the list of exceptions has been gradually extended, it remains relatively short.

BIBLIOGRAPHY

K.W. Baran, *Model of Collective Labour Agreements in the Polish Legal System*, 2 Praca i Zabezpieczenie Społeczne (2019).

K.W. Baran, *The Autonomous Labour Law: De Lege Lata and De Lege Ferenda* in: *Collective Labour Law*, Studia Iuridica No. 60, 18-19 (2015).

Z. Góral, *Collective Representation of Public Sector Employees*, in *Collective Labour Law*, 60 Studia Iuridica 102-103 (2015).

G. Goździewicz, *Collective Labour Agreements as a Fundamental Tool of Trade Union Operation* in: *Collective Labour Law*, Studia Iuridica Nos 60, 83 (2015).

Sylvaine Laulom, *From Decentralisation of Collective Bargaining to De-collectivisation of Industrial Relations Systems?* (Sylvaine Laulom ed.), *Collective Bargaining Developments in Times of Crisis*, 15-28, 99 Bulletin of Comparative Labour Relations (Kluwer Law International 2018).

Leszek Mitrus (Zbigniew Hajn & Leszek Mitrus, eds), *Poland* (Roger Blainpan, Editor-in-Chief) *International Encyclopaedia of Laws: Labour Law and Industrial Relations*, 31 (Kluwer Law International 2016).

L. Mitrus, *Anti-crisis Regulations of Polish Labour Law*, 2 European Labour Law Journal, (2010).

Leszek Mitrus, *Relationship between statutory law, collective agreement and employment contract: case of Poland*, https://mta-pte.ajk.pte.hu/downloads/leszek_mitrus.pdf.

Ł. Pisarczyk, *The Crisis of the Collective Bargaining System in Poland*, 35 International Journal of Comparative Labour Law and Industrial Relations, 1, 62 (2019).

W. Sanetra, *Social Dialogue as an Element of Polish Socio-Economic System in the Light of the Constitution of the Republic of Poland*, in *Collective Labour Law*, 60 Studia Iuridica 191 (2015).

Michał Seweryński, *Polish Labour Law from Communism to Democracy* (Dom Wydawniczy ABC 1999).

Krzysztof Wojciech Baran, *Outline of Polish Labour Law System*, 89 and 106-111 (Krzysztof Wojciech Baran ed., Wolters Kluwer 2016).

CHAPTER 16

Law in Transformation: The Evolution of the System of Labour Law Sources in Russia – Tensions and Opportunities

Olga Rymkevich

16.1 INTRODUCTION

In a relatively short period of time in the twentieth and twenty-first centuries,[1] Russian labour law has undergone radical transformations as a result of the changing political regime (the Revolution of 1917 and then *perestroika* with the subsequent transition to the market economy from 1992). These changes have had a profound impact on the national legal system as a whole, as well as on the system of labour law sources.

Russian law belongs to the continental (Romano-Germanic) legal tradition and in addition it is characterised by original features due to its borderline position between East and West, the influence of Byzantine legal traditions, Mongol-Tartar customs, the Russian Revolution and the socialist past.[2] Legal regulation in Russia has traditionally played a central role, while collective

1. Labour law became an independent branch of law only after the adoption of the first Labour Code (LC) of 10 December 1918 (KZoT RSFSR).
2. According to some scholars the law of the Soviet Union which largely influenced contemporary Russian law belonged to the socialist law family. By socialist law they meant 'the law of countries whose governments officially considered the country as being either socialist or moving from capitalism to socialism and which hold a communist society as an ultimate goal'. The specific features of these legal systems have led some scholars to consider socialist law as a 'third family' distinct from common and civil law systems. R. David, *Traité élémentaire du droit civil comparé*, 319 (1950) cited in J. Quigley, *Socialist Law and the Civil Law Tradition*, 37(4) The American Journal of Comparative Law, 781-808 (1989).

bargaining has always played a relatively limited role both in the Soviet Union and in modern Russia, albeit for different reasons.

The Russian labour law system is a complex, hierarchical, codified multi-level system consisting of acts responding to various legal objectives. In comparative terms, labour law remains fairly protective of employees albeit with clear signs of greater flexibility following the transition to the market economy. The need to adapt to the new economic realities has resulted in the expansion of collective and individual employment relations in recent decades with the consequent appearance of new labour law sources and changes in their hierarchy, number, qualitative contents, scope of application and methods of interaction. This paper aims to provide a critical assessment of the current state of the system of labour law sources through the prism of recent historical, social, political and economic developments with the purpose of casting light on the tensions and opportunities in the changing institutional and regulatory setting.

16.2 DEFINITION AND CLASSIFICATION OF THE SOURCES OF LABOUR LAW

There is no single approach in the Russian literature to the definition or classification of labour law sources. The expression 'sources of law' is a polysemantic term. An analysis of numerous points of views on this issue goes far beyond the scope of this paper as it could be an object of a separate monograph. As a result, we will consider mainly the official classification of the sources of labour law (based on legal acts and official doctrine), where necessary outlining diverging opinions.

The most widely used definitions among Soviet and Russian scholars include those of authors who consider sources of law as provisions in which a rule of behaviour (legal norm) is objectivised.[3] Others (and this point of view was predominant in the Soviet period) define them as a kind of State activity aimed at the establishment of social norms. These authors identify labour law sources with labour legislation and legal acts containing labour-related norms.[4] One of the most accepted approaches, even in the Soviet period, concerns the distinction between sources of law in the material sense and the formal juridical sense. In the material sense, they are considered general socio-political and economic conditions of the society in a given period, reflecting the will of the ruling class. In the formal-legal sense, the source of law could be considered as an external form of the expression of the law consisting of legal norms such as legal acts or other normative provisions to which the State assigns an obligatory

3. N. Korkunov, *Lectures on General Theory of Law*, 66 (1909) (in Russian).
4. N. Alexandrov, *Notion of Labour Sources*, 8 Scientific Works. VIUN, 8 (1946) (in Russian).

nature.[5] Such an approach, free from Soviet ideology, exists also today but it is not widely supported.

Among the modern definitions, arguably, a significant one is proposed in labour law manuals that define the sources of labour law as the result of the state bodies rule-making and joint regulation of employers and employees (or their representatives) in the regulation of labour or labour-related relations.[6]

However, it is difficult, if not impossible, to provide a universal definition of the sources of labour law because of their multifaceted and abstract, if not metaphoric nature.[7] Moreover, because they are closely linked to the constantly changing social, economic, cultural and political framework which defines the purposes of legal regulation in a certain historical period reflected in the legal sources.

In this regard, major changes have taken place in Russia since the collapse of the Soviet Union. The centralised method of government has given way to a more decentralised, market-based approach with more space for collective and individual autonomy. New bargaining agents such as employers' organisations have appeared and new methods of cooperation with the State and trade unions have been defined by means of the relevant legislation. Trade unions have undergone major changes linked to the dramatic decline in membership and popularity in comparison with the Soviet era. Moreover, their institutional role has changed, as they no longer act as an ally of the State and Communist Party distributing social and material benefits, but now seek to play a role as an autonomous bargaining agent empowered to represent and defend workers' interests. In addition, the loss of power of the Communist Party has led to changes in the normative and ideological value of the provisions enacted by it in the Soviet era.[8]

At the same time, local governmental bodies at the level of the Subjects of the Russian Federation (RF) have been granted law-making powers within the limits of the powers laid down by legislation. Collective agreements and

5. S. Vilniavsky, *On the Sources of Soviet Law*, 4-5 Problems of Soviet Law, 62 (1939) (in Russian).
6. A. Kurennoy et al., *Labour Law in Russia*, Jurist, 50-51 (2004) (In Russian).
7. Some authors consider labour law sources as a sort of metaphor or a sort of a conventional definition. *See* A. Rubanov, *Meaning of the Source of Law as a Manifestation of a Metaphoric Nature of Legal Culture*, Judicial Practice as a Source of Law, 42 (1997) (in Russian); B. Topornin, *System of Legal Sources: Tendencies of Development*, Judicial Practice as a Source of Law, 16 (2000) (in Russian).
8. Although the decisions and directives of the Communist party did not have legal value and formally cannot be considered to be sources of law, it is necessary to consider them within the specific legal and political framework in which the State and the Communist Party were indistinguishable and governed as a single actor with the Politburo at the top. In this context many decisions and orders of the State bodies were either dictated by or needed the prior approval of the Politburo. In practice the political and ideological directives of the Politburo served as the foundation for official legal acts and by-laws. *See* S. Kodan, *Party Documents in the System of Sources of Studying the History of Soviet Law*, 2 Vestnik of the Legal Academy of Saratov, 109 (2016).

individual employment contracts have taken on an increasingly important role compared to the Soviet period, and this is especially important in the context of the expansion of atypical forms of employment, with employment now highly differentiated compared to the past system of wage setting and the definition of employment conditions.

On the one hand, since many of these changes have taken place as a result of top-down pressure, often as a result of political compromise, the pre-requisites have not always been in place. On the other hand, many emerging issues (such as temporary agency work,[9] distance work[10]) in the absence of a political compromise or due to a lack of attention on the part of the legislator, or intentionally, have remained unregulated for a long time, while others have continued to be regulated by the laws along Soviet lines, partially or entirely inconsistent with the new market economy.

Such inconsistencies have inevitably given rise to numerous gaps and contradictions in terms of the interaction between the legal sources, their status in the hierarchy and their ability to act as fully-fledged sources of law.

One of the particular features of Russian labour law is that the law imposes fairly strong formal employee protection through detailed legislative provisions and collective agreements. However, when it comes to its implementation, the provisions are often watered down, giving rise to a significant gap between the law in the books and the law in real life.

The factors contributing to this phenomenon include weak enforcement mechanisms and the reluctance of workers to seek judicial remedies with the support of trade unions, due to mistrust in the system, as well as the difficult economic situation which forces workers to turn a blind eye to the repeated violations of the rights laid down in labour legislation, collective agreements or individual employment contracts.[11] Last but not least, the national legal culture should be considered. In Russia, traditionally, the severity of the laws has been offset by low levels of compliance, resulting in a sort of legal nihilism. According to some western scholars, in general, the law has traditionally been valued much less in Russia than in Western countries.[12]

For these reasons and due to the uncertainty arising from law enforcement, in practice officially recognised labour law sources do not always perform their functions according to their hierarchical status. As a result, some scholars and

9. The debate on its regulation started in 2004 while the law was adopted only in 2016 (Law 'On temporary agency work' from 1.01.2016) N. 116-FZ.
10. Federal law, 5 April 2013, N. 60-FZ introducing Chapter 49.1 to the LC.
11. V. Gimpelson, R. Kapeliushnikov & A. Lukiyanova, *Employment Protection Legislation in Russia: Regional Enforcement and Labour Market Outcomes*, IZA DP No. 4484 (2009). P. Biysukov, *Individual Labour Conflicts: Can Employees Defend Their Rights Only by Themselves* (2011) (in Russian); P. Biysukov, *Practice of the Regulation of Labour Relations in Terms of Unstable Employment* (2013) (in Russian).
12. H. J. Berman, *The Spirit of Soviet Law*, 23(2) Washington Law Review (1948).

practitioners cast doubt on their normative role or attribute the role of labour law sources to other sources including legal precedent, legal doctrine, judicial interpretation, individual employment contracts and customary law, mainly to fill in the gaps in legislation. This has given rise to a heated debate among legal scholars about what should be classified as labour law sources and what should not.

In addition, socio-political and economic changes influence the priority of certain legal sources over others in any given period, giving rise to further uncertainty about the interaction between the sources with a different hierarchical status and sometimes also of the legal status and application of the *in favorem* principle that will be analysed further in this paper.

16.2.1 The Constitution

The Constitution[13] is the supreme source that is directly applicable, as stated in Article 15(1),[14] defining the system of legal acts regulating labour relations, their scope and competence. From the point of view of labour law, the current provisions are characterised by a strong path dependency in relation to the previous Soviet Constitutions of 1924, 1936, 1977, that were progressive for the time in terms of workers' rights as laid down in the ILO conventions which Russia was among the first countries to ratify.[15] The Constitution of 1993 regulates a number of labour-related issues[16] further specified in the Labour Code (LC) and other legal acts. Among the most important, mention should be made of the right to equal treatment and non-discrimination (Article 19), freedom of association (Article 30), and freedom of labour and labour conditions respecting the principle of non-discrimination, remuneration, health and safety, working hours, holidays, collective rights and the right to collective and individual disputes (Article 37).

Another important change that took place after the collapse of the Soviet Union is the change in the institutional system[17] with the establishment of the

13. The Constitution of the RF was adopted in a national vote on 12 December 1993 coming into force on 25 December 1993.
14. 'The Constitution of the Russian Federation shall have the supreme juridical force, direct action and shall be used on the whole territory of the Russian Federation. Laws and other legal acts adopted in the Russian Federation shall not contradict the Constitution of the Russian Federation'.
15. The Constitution of 1936, Article 118, guaranteed right to work with the salary according its quality and quantity; Article 122 regulated principle of gender equality including labour, remuneration, rest and social insurance.
16. Articles 2, 6, 7, 15, 17, 18, 19, 20, 30, 32, 37, 45, 46, 55, 62, 72, 76.
17. Article 5 of the Constitution.

Federal Government and Subjects of the Russian Federation[18] with the consequent division of powers. Under Article 72 of the Constitution, labour regulation comes under the joint competence of the Federal Government and its Subjects.

Coming closer to the topic at hand, the Constitution lays down a clear hierarchy of legal sources (Article 76) that defines the relation between laws and other normative acts adopted within the competence of the Federal Government, joint competence of Federal Government and the RF Subjects, competence of the Subjects and the hierarchy of the legal sources of the Federal Government and its Subjects.[19]

The hierarchy of the legal sources is further specified in Article 90[20] and Article 115 of the Constitution.[21] Lower-level legal acts (even those adopted by the Subjects of the RF within their legislative competence) cannot be in contrast with the Constitution. In case of contradiction, they will be deemed to be null and void and the constitutional norms will be applied directly.

16.2.2 Labour Code

The LC became effective from 1 February 2002. Like the Constitution, it is characterised by historical and structural path dependency in relation to the Labour Codes of 1918, 1922 and 1971. The LC is a federal law at the highest level in the hierarchy of labour law sources and the main legal act regulating labour relations (as laid down in Article 1 LC).

Formally, the priority of the LC,[22] as well as the hierarchy of labour law sources, is specified in Article 5 LC as follows:

- Constitution;
- federal constitutional laws;
- Labour Code;
- other federal laws and laws of Subjects of the Russian Federation containing labour law norms;
- other normative legal acts[23] containing labour law norms;

18. Subjects of the Federation: http://www.statdata.ru/spisok-regionov-rossii-s-kodamy, the eighty -five Subjects are listed in Article 65 of the Constitution of the RF.
19. More specifically the principles of the division of powers between federal level and the level of the subjects is specified in the Federal law from 06.10.1999 N 184-FZ as amended on 01.05.2019) 'On general principles of organisation of legislative (representative bodies) and executive bodies of the State authority of the Subjects of the Russian Federation'.
20. Regulating presidential decrees and orders.
21. Regulating governmental decisions and orders.
22. Russian legislation does not automatically lay down the priority of the codified normative acts over other legal acts, unless directly laid down in the Code itself, as in case of the LC.
23. A normative act is defined in the legal doctrine as an agreement between two or more parties on mutual recognition of their commitments in the process of joint or unilateral activity which on the basis of agreements between the parties acquire juridical force. In N. Voplenko, *Sources and Forms of Law*, 52 (Volgograd 2004).

- decrees of the RF President;
- decisions of the RF Government and normative legal acts of federal executive governmental bodies;
- normative legal acts of executive governmental bodies of Subjects of the Russian Federation;
- normative legal acts of local self-government bodies.

Finally, it is specified that labour relations and other relations directly related thereto are also regulated by collective agreements, collective contracts and local normative acts containing labour law norms, enabling us to refer to these acts as officially recognised sources of law.

Under the same Article, the labour law norms contained in other federal laws are required to comply with the LC. In the case of conflict between the LC and federal laws containing labour law norms, the LC is applicable. If a new federal law is in contrast with the LC, this law can be implemented only after the necessary amendments to the LC.

This leads to frequent amendments to the LC which can be considered a positive fact, making it possible to preserve the centrality of the Code in the regulation of labour relations. However, frequent amendments risk generating confusion and inconsistency with other normative acts.[24]

16.3 CONSTITUTIONAL FEDERAL LAWS AND FEDERAL LAWS

According to Article 76(1) of the Constitution, there are two kinds of legal acts to be adopted exclusively within the competence of the Federal Government: federal constitutional laws and federal laws having direct effect over the entire RF territory. There is no delimitation of the subject matter (competence, jurisdiction) between federal constitutional laws and federal laws. This distinction is made in the Constitution when it is indicated which kinds of act should be adopted in relation to specific matters. Constitutional laws are intended to regulate the most important spheres of social life where fundamentals of the public and state system are expressed. They comprise the Constitution, federal treaties, acts of referendums and so on.

The President does not have the power to change federal constitutional laws. Article 76(3) of the Constitution lays down a hierarchy between federal constitutional laws and federal laws. Due to their specific nature (as provisions to be adopted on matters directly laid down in the Constitution, with more complex procedures for their enactment, and no provision for presidential veto) federal constitutional laws are assigned a higher rank than federal laws.

24. K. Tomashevsky, *The System of Labour Law Sources, in the States, Members of the Eurasian Union*, Dissertation, 131 (2017) (In Russian).

In Russia, there is a two-tier regulatory system in which the Subjects can legislate on the matters of joint competence listed in Article 72 of the Constitution. Under Article 72(5), laws and other legislative acts of the Subjects of the Russian Federation are required to comply with federal laws adopted pursuant to Article 76(1)-(2) (On the issues under the jurisdiction of the Russian Federation and under joint jurisdiction). In case of an inconsistency between a federal law and a normative act issued on the territory of the Russian Federation, the federal law is to be applied. Under Article 76(6), in case of a contradiction between a federal law and a normative act of a Subject of the Russian Federation adopted according to Article 76(4) (On issues not under the jurisdiction of the Russian Federation and not under joint jurisdiction) the normative legal act of the Subject of the Russian Federation is to be applied.

16.3.1 Federal Laws of Subjects of the Russian Federation

The system of labour law sources of the Subjects of the RF reflects the vertical structure adopted at federal level. The fundamental principle of the division of powers is laid down in Article 6 of the LC and in Federal law 06.10.1999 N. 184-FZ 'On the general principles of the organisation of the law-making (legislative) and executive bodies of power of the Subjects of the RF'.

The LC defines the powers of federal state bodies in the sphere of employment relations. They mainly concern the policies that require the consistent application of provisions concerning fundamental problems including:

- the fundamentals of legal regulation of labour relations and other relations directly associated with them (including the definition of rules, procedures, criteria and standards aimed at preserving the life and health of employees in the course of their employment);
- the level of labour rights, freedoms and safeguards for employees (including additional safeguards for individual categories of employees) ensured by the state;
- procedures for concluding, amending and terminating employment contracts; fundamentals of social partnership, procedures for arranging collective bargaining, concluding and amending collective contracts and agreements; procedures for resolving individual grievances and collective labour disputes;
- principles and procedures for the implementation of state enforcement of and control over observation of the labour legislation and other normative legal acts containing labour law norms, as well as the structure and authority of the federal bodies of state power in charge of enforcement and control;

- procedures for investigation of industrial accidents and occupational diseases;
- the system of, and procedures for, conducting an ascertainment of working conditions, a state expert examination of working conditions, a confirmation of the compliance of labour protection measures with the state labour protection standards;
- procedure and terms of material liability of the parties to the employment contract, including compensation procedure in cases of damage to life and health of the employee in the course of his/her employment;
- types of disciplinary sanctions and procedures for their application; the system of state statistical reporting pertaining to employment and safety issues; particulars of legal regulation of the work of individual categories of employees.

The Subjects of the RF can legislate on issues not regulated in Article 6 LC i.e., not relating to the competence of the Federal Government (Article 6(3) LC). In case of the adoption of the federal law on these matters, the corresponding act of the Subject of the RF must be revised accordingly. The Subjects of the RF can improve labour rights and safeguards for employees compared to those laid down by federal laws and other normative legal acts, but the respective costs must be covered from their own budgets.

In cases in which the normative provisions of the Subjects of the RF reduce the level of labour rights and safeguards for employees specified in the LC or other federal laws, the other federal laws are to be applied.

16.3.2 By-Laws

By-laws are normative provisions adopted in accordance with the law. By-laws may comprise different kinds of normative acts or provisions such as acts adopted by the President, Federal Government and governments and ministries: presidential decrees, presidential orders, governmental regulations, and so on. They may be complex (combining norms from labour law and other branches of law) or ordinary acts (with only labour law norms), as well as acts with a narrower scope of application regulating particular aspects of labour law or a particular category of workers. Their role consists in the further development, concretization and implementation of higher-level normative acts.

16.3.2.1 Decrees of the President of the Russian Federation

These acts are first in the hierarchy of by-laws. They are regulated by Article 90(1) of the Constitution which empowers the President to issue decrees and orders applicable throughout the territory of the Russian Federation. Article 90(3) specifies that they are subordinate to the Constitution.[25]

16.3.2.2 Decrees and Orders of the RF Government

These normative acts are regulated by Article 115 of the Constitution which defines their subordinate nature respect to the Constitution, federal laws and normative decrees of the President. The decrees and orders of the Government are applicable in all parts of the Russian Federation. In case of inconsistency with the above-mentioned acts, they may be repealed by the President. Their peculiarity consists in the fact that they may be adopted only on the basis of federal laws and presidential decrees.[26]

16.3.2.3 Acts of the Ministry of Labour and Social Protection

Ministries and other federal executive bodies may issue decrees, orders, instructions, rulings and explanations within their competence as defined by the federal laws and decrees of the President and the Government. Normally they are issued at the indication of a higher-level body. They are intended to implement higher-level normative acts in relation to a certain industry and ensure appropriate supervisory functions. In certain cases, they may be of general validity for all citizens.[27]

16.4 COLLECTIVE LABOUR REGULATION

For various reasons, collective labour regulation has never played a decisive role in the Soviet Union or modern Russia. Since the beginning of the nineteenth century, it has evolved from a system dominated by the State towards a more autonomous institute regulated by the social partners and the State with an increasingly extensive regulatory scope.

Even if the origins of collective labour regulation can be traced back to the beginning of the twentieth century,[28] collective agreements have always performed a secondary role in relation to legislation. The Labour Code of 1918

25. 'Decrees and orders of the President of the Russian Federation shall not run counter to the Constitution of the Russian Federation and the federal law'. Article 90(3) Constitution of the RF.
26. One of the recent examples is the order of the RF Government of 22 September 2018 N 1129 'On approval of the rules of accreditation of the private employment agencies and recognition of invalidity of some acts of the RF Government'.
27. For example, the decree of the Ministry of Labour of 25 December 1997 N. 66, On the norms of free delivery of special occupational clothing and other means of individual protection for workers.
28. The first collective agreements were concluded in 1904 but in the absence of a legal basis they were rare and occasional initiatives. One of the first normative acts regulating the stipulation of

(KZoT) did not contain a definition of collective agreement. According to Article 7 KZoT, employment conditions in state enterprises were regulated by the tariff agreements approved by Narkomtrud in the Soviet Union. In the absence of an agreement between management and the workers, collective agreements were put forward by trade unions with the further approval of Narkomtrud. The tariff agreements of 1919-1921 regulated salaries, hiring and firing, and contained peremptory norms limiting the possibility of the autonomous regulation by the social partners. As a result, they could not be classified as agreements in the strict sense. In general, during the period of the civil war and military communism (1918-1921) the practice of such agreements was not widespread.

Collective agreements were re-established following the adoption of the new economic policy (NEP)[29] and the Labour Code of 1922 which, together with the law 'On collective agreements'[30] widened the sphere of the collectively negotiated regulation of employment relations and introduced a multilevel system of collective bargaining (sectoral, area and local). The period of relative autonomy of collective bargaining was short-lived as trade unions quickly became part of the State and the Party. In the monopsonist economy, the State was the sole bargaining agent and instead of focusing on employment conditions, collective agreements mainly focused on the obligations to be fulfilled in terms of production targets in the planned economy.

In the 1930s collective bargaining went into decline. Between 1934 and 1947 collective agreements in the Union of Soviet Socialist Republics (USSR) were not concluded because from 1930 all labour conditions were laid down by law. Collective bargaining was permitted only from 1947 onwards in a top-down manner.[31]

In this period, the absence of formal opposition between employers and employees prevented the development of collective bargaining in the classical sense. Consequently, collective agreements could be considered to be not so much a legal source but rather political and economic statements concluded between the State and labour collectives aimed at improving the motivation of workers to perform (and outperform) state production plans.[32]

Serious changes in the regulation of collective agreements occurred after the 1980s with the transition towards the market economy. The first step towards greater recognition of autonomy and reinstatement of the role of

---

collective agreements in the Soviet Russia was the decree of the Peoples' Commissars '*On the Modality of the adoption of collective agreements (tariffs) establishing salary rates and labour conditions*' of 02.06.1918. Following the adoption of KZoT (1922) these matters were regulated by the LCs.

29. The period of the NEP lasted until 1929.
30. Decree of the Council of People Commissars, 23.08.1922.
31. Provision of the Council of Ministers USSR, 04.02.1947.
32. A. Zapesotsky, *Collective Agreement as a Mechanism of Prevention of Social and Labour Conflicts*, 11 Social and Labor Conflicts (2018).

collective agreements was the law 'On collective agreements and contracts' of 11.03.1992 N. 2491-1.[33] The Labour Code of 2001 provided detailed regulation of the legal status of collective agreements. Another important step in the development of collective bargaining was the adoption of the law 'On Trade Unions, their Rights and Guarantees' of 12.01.1996 N. 10-FZ and the Law on 'Employers' Associations' of 27.11.2002 N. 156-FZ. In this way, both trade unions and employers' associations were formally recognised as independent from the State actors.

To further enhance collective bargaining, a special chapter on 'Social partnership' was included in the new LC (section II, Articles 23-55). Under this chapter, collective agreements/contracts may be concluded at six different levels: federal, interregional (at the level of two or more RF Subjects), regional (at the level of one RF Subject), sectoral (intersectoral), territorial (area level) and enterprise levels (Article 26 LC).

Article 27 LC defines the main forms of social partnership including: collective bargaining for the preparation of draft collective agreements and their conclusion; mutual consultations (negotiations) on issues of labour relations and other relations directly connected with them, safeguards for labour rights and the improvement of labour legislation; the participation of employees and their representatives in management; the participation of representatives of employees and employers in the out-of-court settlement of labour disputes. However, these forms are not exhaustive. In practice, other forms are to be found, provided by regional labour laws.

Collective contracts and agreements are the main legal instruments of social partnership. Article 40 of the LC defines a collective contract as 'a legal deed entered between the employee representatives and an employer (or its representatives), regulating the social and labour relations at the enterprise level'.

The definition of a collective agreement is given in Article 45 of the LC: a 'collective agreement is a legal deed that sets out the common regulatory principles underlying the social, economic and labour relations entered between the employee representatives and an employer at federal, interregional, regional, sectoral (intersectoral), territorial (or area level) within the limits of their competences'.

However, this does not presuppose a subordination principle with the lower-level agreement having less legal value than the higher one. Any inconsistencies in this regard should be decided on the basis of the *in favorem* principle (Article 48(6), LC).

33. Abrogated by the Federal Law, 30.06.2006 N. 90-FZ 'On amendments to the Labour Code RF and abrogation of some legal acts of the USSR and RF'.

These agreements can be bilateral or trilateral (with the participation of the State). Article 41 LC provides some recommendations concerning possible provisions of collective agreements/contracts while leaving the parties free to determine them.

The peculiarity of the Russian model of social partnership is that it was introduced as a top-down process. As a result, the enactment of the special legislation has not automatically brought about its smooth functioning. It is based primarily on a tripartite model characterised by the strong presence of the State.

Among the main shortcomings of the modern system of social partnership is the vague nature of obligations laid down in collective agreements. In fact, many of them simply reproduce the provisions of the existing legislation (which lays down only minimum rights and safeguards). The other shortcomings include the failure to comply with collective agreements by the employers and also by the State (often a party to the agreement), insufficient monitoring of performance and extremely modest sanctions imposed on the employers in the case of non-fulfilment of obligations under collective agreements. In fact, the fine for violations of the obligations under the collective agreements established in the Code of Administrative Offences (Article 5.31) amounts only to RUB 3,000-5,000.[34]

In short, the absence of effective mechanisms to ensure the implementation of collective agreements and contracts significantly undermines their role as a fully-fledged and respected source of law.

16.5 LOCAL NORMATIVE ACTS

Local normative acts are regulated by Article 8 LC as acts adopted by administrative bodies in companies intended to implement the higher-level acts in order to adapt them to the internal situation of the organisation. As they are lower in the hierarchy of labour law sources, they cannot contradict federal laws and other superior normative acts, including collective agreements. If the norms of a local normative act have a negative impact on employment conditions compared to the higher-level acts, or if they are adopted without taking into account the opinion of an employee representative body when required (Article 372 LC), the norms of the higher-level acts will be applicable.

Local normative acts may be adopted on the basis of the principle of social partnership following bargaining between the duly authorised representatives of the parties. Alternatively, they may be adopted by the employer, taking into consideration the opinion of the body representing the employee at the level of the organisation, or at the initiative of the employer.

34. EUR 43 and 71 respectively (at the official exchange rate on 24 July 2019).

As a rule, local normative acts include internal regulations, provisions on salaries in the organisation and so on.

16.6 SOURCES OF LAW NOT OFFICIALLY RECOGNISED: INDIVIDUAL EMPLOYMENT CONTRACTS

In formal terms, the LC does not include individual employment contracts among the sources of labour law. However, they may be deemed to be a source of regulation on the basis of Articles 8 and 9 LC which lay down the possibility to regulate employment relations by means of individual employment contracts. Previous LCs gave limited space to individual bargaining (each LC was different in this regard, granting more or less discretion) as almost all the employment conditions were defined at central level. Pay scales were uniformly laid down in the wage agreements, and most conditions were regulated by administrative provisions, while in the period of Revolution and War and afterwards other matters, such as the liability of the employer for violations of labour conditions, and the dismissal of employees, were regulated by the Penal Code.[35] This was especially important during the Second World War when the regulation of employment relations was not based on the LC but on special legislation severely restricting employee rights.

Arguably, before the transition to the market economy, individual employment contracts mainly concerned the administrative aspects of the employment relation (with the indication of information such as the employee's name, place of work, job position, and the starting date), while the main provisions were defined at central level.

The current LC leaves much more room for individual bargaining. Article 57 LC includes information about the employee and employer, while specifying the obligatory conditions to be included, and in the last part leaving room for the optional conditions that are not allowed to worsen employee rights and safeguards compared to labour legislation and other normative provisions, collective agreements and local normative acts. It specifies some additional conditions that can be included but the list remains open.

16.6.1 Court Rulings

In the continental legal system legal precedent or judge-made law is not officially recognised as a source of law. However, considering the important role of the Constitutional and the Supreme Court in ensuring the consistent interpretation and application of the law on the RF territory, there is an ongoing debate among

35. The refusal to take part in obligatory national labour service ceased to be punished under the Penal Code only after the adoption of the new Penal Code of the RSFSR of 1961.

legal scholars who are in favour of considering the rulings of the Constitutional Court and the Supreme Court and their plenums as a source of law.

The rulings of the Constitutional Court are extremely important for law enforcement. According to the federal law 'On the Constitutional Court' of 24 June 1994, the Court not only deals with the issues concerning the constitutional status of legal acts but also provides obligatory interpretations. Acts deemed by the Constitutional Court to be anti-constitutional are struck down. The rulings of the Constitutional Court are immediate, of direct application, and obligatory throughout the territory of the RF; they are subject to official publication and have a high moral value. They are final and can be amended only by the Constitutional Court itself.

The role of the Supreme Court is reflected in Article 126 of the Constitution which empowers it to monitor the activities of the lower courts and provide explanations on procedural matters. However, it does not contain any explicit indication on the obligatory nature of such explanations,[36] thus leaving open the question as to whether or not to consider these acts as a source of law.

In theory, the function of the courts consists of the interpretation and application of legal norms with the aim of ensuring the consistency of law enforcement. They have no powers to 'create law'. However, in practice it is sometimes difficult to find a formal dividing line between where interpretation ends and where judge-made law begins, especially considering the numerous gaps and inconsistencies in the existing legislation.

According to some legal scholars, even if court rulings do not have the status of sources of law de jure, they possess such a status de facto by influencing the decisions of the lower courts. This is also in part due to the tradition inherited from the Soviet Union when the Supreme Court would be unlikely to adopt a line of reasoning contrary to the one it had adopted previously in similar cases. In cases in which its interpretation was not duly considered, there was a high risk that the judgment of the lower court would be quashed or amended. In Russia the quality of justice since the period of the Soviet Union has been measured by a specific metric known as 'judgment stability', i.e., the number of quashed or amended judgments.[37] So even if in formal terms according to the Constitution[38] and the Law 'On the status of judges of the RF' the judiciary is independent, there is an informal mechanism that

36. This explanatory function intended to ensure the uniformity of legislation within the RF territory is reflected in the acts: 31.12.1996 N1-FKZ 'On the judicial system of the RF' Article 19(4), and the Act of 05.02.2014 N3-FKZ 'On the Supreme Court of the RF' Article 2(7). Also, in this case there is no indication about the obligatory nature of these explanations.
37. This fact remains decisive in defining the career and advancement, professional reputation and remunerations of judges who in this way are highly motivated to consider the decisions of the Supreme Courts. A. Burkov, *Status of Decisions of the Plenum of the RF Supreme Court in Legislation and Judicial Practice*, 5 Izvestia Vusov, Pravovedenie (2011).
38. Article 10 of the RF Constitution on the balance of powers.

provides a strong incentive to the Courts to apply the decisions of the Supreme Court in similar cases, in most cases without direct reference to such decisions.

Such a practice has led some scholars to classify these acts as non-traditional sources of law, 'hidden' source of law or 'interpretation precedent' the status of which comes close to the status of federal laws and by-laws aimed at implementing the constitutional norms or norms of the LC.[39]

However, in spite of these legitimate considerations, legal precedent is not at present part of the formally recognised system of labour law sources and in general sources of law as this would be in contrast with the foundations of the RF legal system.

16.6.2 Customary Law

Customary law is not recognised as an official source of labour law. In fact, in the Soviet Union customary law was not recognised as a source of law and was deemed to be a characteristic of capitalist society. None of the LCs of the Soviet Union and the RF contain any reference to customary law. However, considering that labour legislation is still characterised by many gaps, some scholars consider customary law in terms of behaviour approved by the State and argue that it is a potential legal source. In practical terms, customary law could be considered by the courts in the absence of specific legal provisions. As an example, according to well-established judicial practice, in case of the dismissal of a worker at the request of the employee or by mutual agreement between the parties, the employee can be reinstated in case the decision was taken under pressure from the employer or if the employee was in a particularly difficult personal situation. In another case, in the absence of a written employment contract, the employee has the right to an employment contract from the moment when he/she started work.[40]

16.7 CONFLICT BETWEEN NORMATIVE ACTS AND THE IN FAVOREM PRINCIPLE

The conflict of laws in the field of labour law is resolved by applying the in *favorem* principle which presupposes the priority of the more favourable provision for the employee in the case of a conflict between norms. However, this principle is not unequivocal in the RF legislation, which only lays down the prohibition on downgrading employee rights and guarantees by means of lower-level normative acts but does not directly determine the priority of the norms upgrading the conditions of the employee, except for Article 48(6) LC

39. *Ibid.*
40. E. Ershova, *Customs with the Norms of Russian Labour Law*, 3 Labour Law (2008).

which states that when the employee is covered by more than one collective agreement, the most favourable conditions for the employee are to be applied.

In this regard, a logical question concerns the scope of applicability of the in *favorem* principle in employment relations. The attitude of the legislator towards this principle has changed over time on the basis of the economic and political situation in certain periods. For example, Article 5 KZoT 1971 did not allow any contradictions between the law and collective agreements or employment contracts, regardless of whether they were aimed at upgrading or downgrading employment conditions.

At present, it is possible for the lower-level acts to upgrade the level of employee rights and safeguards while any changes in *peius* can be implemented only by means of federal law. This principle is laid down in Article 55(3) of the Constitution and in Article 252 LC which further elaborates this principle stating that the peculiarities of particular kinds of work may be established in labour laws, collective agreements and local normative acts. However, any downgrading of rights and safeguards can be established only by the LC thus giving the Code absolute priority in this regard.

Lower-level acts including acts of the RF Subjects or local normative acts can upgrade the terms and conditions of employment but using their own financial means. Under Article 6 LC, Subjects of the RF adopting the normative acts within their legislative competence can upgrade employee safeguards, but only from their own budgets.

According to Articles 8 and 9 LC, normative acts adopted at the local level cannot downgrade employee conditions compared to the higher-level legislative acts or collective agreements. From this provision, it is possible to deduce that they can upgrade conditions even if it is not directly stated.

Article 41(3) LC allows collective agreements to upgrade rights and safeguards for the employee compared to those defined by law, other normative acts and collective agreements.

However, this possibility may be limited because LC still contains norms from the Soviet era delegating to collective agreement the possibility to regulate certain aspects. For example, Article 147 regulating the employment of workers in difficult and dangerous conditions delegates to collective agreements the power to increase minimum wage. The same provision can be found in Article 152 LC regulating overtime work, Article 153 on holiday work, Article 154 on night work and so on. However, many enterprises do not have collective agreements or contracts as it is not an obligation for the employer. These provisions can undermine the implementation of the in *favorem* principle.

Unlike many other countries where the principle of decentralised bargaining is adopted, in Russia there is no direct legal provision to reduce the level of employee rights and safeguards by means of collective agreement. This can be done only by means of federal law.

Moreover, it is necessary to consider some points already mentioned in this regard. First, the law lays down only a minimum threshold of rights and safeguards and it would be difficult to further reduce them by means of collective agreement. Second, the conclusion of collective agreements is not an obligation for the employer, and where there are no collective agreements and no trade unions, especially in small and medium-sized enterprises, it is sufficient for the employer not to conclude them or not to comply with the existing agreement in order to avoid upgrading employee safeguards. Finally, employers and the State often reproduce the existing legal provisions establishing minimum rights in collective agreements and contracts, or fail to comply with the in *favorem* provisions laid down in the collective agreements. Since the sanctions for non-compliance are modest, this is still a widespread practice that again undermines the implementation of the in *favorem* principle.

16.8 CONCLUSIONS

The system of the sources of labour law is characterised by a strong historical and structural path dependency not only with the Soviet past but in general with the earlier Russian legal traditions. Legal regulation continues to play a central role, but at the same time since the collapse of the Soviet Union the role of the negotiated sources of law such as collective and individual agreements and contracts has significantly increased along with the autonomy of the Subjects of the RF. Such a radical economic and political transformation has logically resulted in the emergence of new labour law sources and changes in their formal hierarchy.

At the same time, this profound transformation has not automatically brought about changes in national legal culture and legal consciousness. Currently, partly due to the gaps and inconsistencies in the existing labour legislation and general weakness of social dialogue, partly because of the tradition of non-compliance with the law, the stakeholders in labour relations, even at the federal level, are not always aware how to use the potential of their collective and individual autonomy. As a result, they tend either to underuse or to abuse it.

Arguably, the sources of labour law, while demonstrating a strong path dependency with the past and reflecting the national characteristics, also represent a constantly changing concept, moving forward with the evolution of society, not always at the same pace, but finding their particular *ubi consistam* in the diversity of the context in which they operate.

BIBLIOGRAPHY

H.J. Berman, *The Spirit of Soviet Law*, 23(2) Washington Law Review (1948).

P. Biysukov, *Individual Labour Conflicts: Can Employees Defend Their Rights Only by Themselves* (2011).

P. Biysukov, *Practice of the Regulation of Labour Relations in Terms of Unstable Employment* (2013).

A. Burkov, *Status of Decisions of the Plenum of the RF Supreme Court in Legislation and Judicial Practice*, 5 Izvestia Vusov, Pravovedenie (2011).

E. Ershova, *Customs with the Norms of Russian Labour Law*, 3 Labour Law (2008).

A. Kurennoy et al., *Labour Law in Russia*, Jurist, 50-51 (2004).

S. Kodan, *Party Documents in the System of Sources of Studying the History of Soviet Law*, 2 Vestnik of the Legal Academy of Saratov, 109 (2016).

J. Quigley, *Socialist Law and the Civil Law Tradition*, 37(4) The American Journal of Comparative Law, 781-808 (1989).

A. Rubanov, *Meaning of the Source of Law as a Manifestation of a Metaphoric Nature of Legal Culture*, Judicial Practice as a Source of Law, 42 (Moscow, 1997).

K. Tomashevsky, *The System of Labour Law Sources, in the States, Members of the Eurasian Union*, Dissertation, 131 (2017).

B. Topornin, *System of Legal Sources: Tendencies of Development*, Judicial Practice as a Source of Law, 16 (2000).

A. Zapesotsky, *Collective Agreement as a Mechanism of Prevention of Social and Labour Conflicts*, 11 Social and labor conflicts (2018).

CHAPTER 17

Spain: A Lasting Struggle about the Boundaries of Statutory Law and Collective Bargaining

José Maria Miranda Boto

17.1 INTRODUCTION

Traditionally, statutory law has been the core of labour law in Spain. The Constitution of 1978 did not greatly change this panorama, although it contains the foundations of the democratic system of industrial relations. The last forty years have seen a legal and political debate about the role of collective bargaining and its articulation with statutory law.

The main labour law reforms have tried to enhance and redefine the role of collective bargaining. However, it is an unfinished task, and the current political situation does not help to establish a stable model. The structure of collective bargaining in Spain is hard to understand, as there are nearly 10.000 collective agreements in force and their organization is not centralized. Thus, there are, on the one hand, company agreements and branch agreements. On the other hand, branch agreements can be either State-level, regional, provincial or even local. Their co-existence has a big importance in the Spanish system.

This paper will deal, in descending hierarchical order, with the different sources of labour law in Spain, pointing out the habitual problems in their relationship and the relevant academic debates.

17.2 HISTORICAL BACKGROUND

1978 marks the division between old and new in Spain, with the passing of the democratic Constitution[1] that nowadays still rules the life of contemporary society. However, some of the traits of the past survive in Spanish Labour Law and are, indeed, some of the most remarkable features of the system.

Labour Law was born in Spain in a traditional, continental way. Conservative governments at the end of the nineteenth century and the beginning of the twentieth, under the influence of the social doctrine of the Catholic Church, created some laws in order to fight the pre-revolutionary workers' movement and resolve the so-called 'social issue'. Statutory law was, from the beginning, the core of Spanish Labour Law and collective bargaining was insignificant. Perhaps the Second Republic (1931-1936) could have been the scenario for a new model of industrial relations, but the Civil War (1936-1939) put an end to this experiment.

Thus, Franco's dictatorial regime (1939-1975) is the immediate antecedent of the current system of industrial relations. Obviously, in an authoritarian, sometimes fascist, right-wing state the initial model of labour law was strongly centralized. Centralization, certainly, could be the general explanation of francoism in many aspects. But the need for political integration in Western Europe in the 1950s led to some opening of the regime. As far as sources of labour law are concerned, that necessity led to the birth of collective bargaining by a 1958 law.[2]

It was obviously not a free, democratic collective bargaining, but a merely corporatist tool within the regime. But the action of anti-regime, clandestine trade unions during the 1960s and 1970s gave the system an unexpected efficacy, and it was used as a model by the democratic legislator in 1980. The general efficacy of collective agreements is the relic of the immediate past.

The Constitution of 1978 transformed Spain, nearly, into the most decentralized State in Europe. Autonomous regions received a huge deal of competences and this issue has marked Spanish politics in the last four decades. However, labour law is one of the areas which has been reserved to the State, since no attempt has ever been made to break the uniformity of labour legislation, in contrast to what has happened with regard to social protection.[3]

1. In this paper, the following abbreviations will be used: Constitución Española - CE (Spanish Constitution of 1978); Estatuto de los Trabajadores - ET (Employees' Statute, main Labour legislation); Sentencia del Tribunal Constitucional - STC (Ruling from the Constitutional Court); Ley Orgánica - LO (Organic Law); Ley - L (Act); Real Decreto - Ley - RD-L (Decree-Law); Ley Orgánica de Libertad Sindical - LOLS (Organic Law on Freedom of association for trade unions). The translation of the text of the Constitution comes from the Boletín Oficial del Estado; all other translations of legal texts and academic doctrine are mine.
2. Law of 24 April 1958 on Collective Agreements.
3. Concerning the sources of Social Security *see* Javier Gárate Castro, *Leyes y reglamentos reguladores de la Seguridad Social española* (José Luis Monereo Pérez, Guillermo Rodríguez Iniesta,

17.3 SOURCES OF LABOUR LAW: AN ENUMERATION

Traditionally, the sources of Law were listed by Article 1.1 of the Civil Code of 1888: statutory law, customs and general principles of Law. The Constitution brought an important change in this scheme, as the interpretation of the term 'law' grew bigger than the original redaction of the Code: 'law' meant more than 'acts of Parliament'. Furthermore, the Constitution enshrined in its Article 9.3 the following: 'The Constitution guarantees the principle of legality, the hierarchy of legal provisions'.

For its part, the Employees' Statute (ET) of 1980 established in Article 3 a revision of the classical rule of the Civil Code, when defining the sources of the labour relationship: (a) legal dispositions and bylaws from the State; (b) collective agreements; (c) the will of the parties, which should not provide less favourable employment conditions than those established by statutory law and collective bargaining; (d) local and professional customs.

The same Article 3 of ET established in an indirect way the principle of hierarchy of these sources and several other principles. Under them, individual autonomy (agreements of the parties) had a little margin, and has never been considered as a source of law, but just as a source of obligations: derogation *in peius* through individual agreements is never possible. Collective agreements can only derogate *in peius* when statutory law includes that possibility.

The doctrine was not satisfied with this enumeration, as many technical flaws were pointed out. Particularly international, European Union (EU) and constitutional sources are missing from this ensemble. Too much history, missing elements, its consideration as a list of sources of the employment relationship and not actually of labour law were all problems that called for a revision of the text.[4] Article 3 of ET has recently been criticized as being 'obsolete, insufficient, ambiguous and unfocused'.[5] The main criticisms point to collective autonomy, as its variety and ways of articulation are not reflected by this article, and to the fact that it is written in terms of conflicts of application of norms, and not on their creation.

Indeed, the principles mentioned in Article 3 of ET are not the same principles mentioned in Article 1.1 of the Civil Code. The latter were conceived

---

Juan Antonio Maldonado Molina & Angel Luis de Val Tena, eds) *Tratado de Derecho de la Seguridad Social*, p. 173 (Laborum, 2017).

4. Joaquín García Murcia, *Constitución y Ley* (Joaquín García Murcia, ed.) *El sistema de fuentes de la relación laboral. Estudios ofrecidos al Profesor Martín Valverde por el Área de Derecho del Trabajo de la Universidad de Oviedo*, p. 22 (Universidad de Oviedo, 2007).
5. Tomás Sala Franco & Eva López Terrada, *La reforma de las fuentes de la relación laboral* (Tomás Sala Franco, ed.) *Propuestas para un debate sobre la reforma laboral*, p. 23 (Francis Lefebvre, 2018). According to them, Spanish Labour Law does not clearly establish the principle of hierarchy in the elaboration of norms, and it is up to the Courts to enforce this principle.

as true sources of law,[6] but those in the ET are, as pointed out beforehand, principles of application. Thus, the principles of the 'more favourable norm' or 'more beneficious condition' in Article 3.3 of ET deal with existing sources of law but do not organize their elaboration. If a Spanish judge has to apply one of two collective agreements, for example, he/she will choose the most favourable one for the worker, in an ensemble evaluation of its contents. Therefore, a choice of singular contents from both of them (cherry-picking) is not allowed. However, derogations *in melius*, coming from employment contracts or individual agreements with the employer, will not be affected by any posterior modification of the source that regulates the issue unless it gives a more beneficious treatment.

Therefore, there have been proposals[7] for the removal of these principles and the simplification of the panorama, leaving only a clear and express consecration of the principle of hierarchy. In my opinion, these proposals are too technical for the current political situation in Spain, so, despite their good load of reason, they are not going to be followed by any future legislator.

17.4 THE CONSTITUTION AS CORNERSTONE OF INDUSTRIAL RELATIONS

One of the landmarks of the text of 1978 was its position as a direct source of law, a situation unknown in Spanish constitutional history.[8] From the point of view of the sources of law, the Constitution must be studied in two dimensions: from the organic point of view, it regulates the sources of law, and in its dogmatic content, it serves as summit of the hierarchy, providing also directly enforceable norms. Thus, constitutional provisions can be intended either as principles, to be respected and/or implemented by the legislature, or as directly enforceable sources (whenever its content is clear and does not need any legislative implementation).

First, as said beforehand, Article 9.3 of the Spanish Constitution of 1978 (CE) establishes the governing principles of legality and hierarchy of norms, among others. In its Third Title, the Constitution regulates the procedures of elaboration of laws, and in its Eighth Title, it develops the competences and powers of state and autonomous regions.

Second, the true innovation of this text is that the Constitution is a material source of law. This general rule has a special relevance when thinking about the

6. Article 1.5: 'General legal principles shall apply in the absence of applicable statute or custom, without prejudice to the fact that they contribute to shape the legal system'.
7. Sala Franco & López Terrada (n. 5) pp. 28-29.
8. Manuel Alonso Olea, *El sistema normativo del Estado y de las Comunidades Autónomas* (Centro de Estudios Políticos y Constitucionales, eds) *Derecho del Trabajo y de la Seguridad Social en la Constitución*, p. 15 (Centro de Estudios Constitucionales, 1979).

labour law content of the Constitution. According to the doctrine,[9] the first goal was the removal of the old legal system, but it evolved into the foundation of a system of industrial relations where dignity and other fundamental rights have their own space.

Trade unions' freedom of association is specifically recognized as a fundamental right, as well as the right to strike.[10] Several other provisions deal with 'simple' rights, such as the right to work, the right to a fair wage, and the right to collective bargaining and industrial action, other than strike. Lastly, in a third category, there are steering principles for public policies, that include for example the provision of social security, employment policy and professional training.

All these principles, establishing a minimum of employment and social protection for workers, have shaped the legal development of labour law heavily. The Constitutional Court has clearly ruled that they must allow the program of different political options, always respecting the essential content of these rights, especially in the field of social security.

The Constitution can be enforced directly by ordinary courts, other than the Constitutional one, as some of its contents do not need any further development, its mandate being clear and direct.[11]

17.5 THE UNDISPUTED CENTRAL ROLE OF STATUTORY LAW

The Constitution reserves the competence on labour law to the state, leaving the autonomous regions only limited possibilities of development and execution.[12] In decentralized Spain, this is nearly an exception and the regulation of the labour market is only nuanced territorially by the developments of regional collective agreements on certain issues.

The formal rank of law includes four types of norms: organic law (a terminology coming from Francoism and the remote past), legislative decree, decree-law, and 'ordinary' law. In respect to the principle of hierarchy, all four of them hold the same rank. The distribution of functions responds to the principle of competence, especially in the contents of organic law.

Organic laws were conceived by the Constitution as state covenants on important issues. The qualified majority needed in Parliament to pass them should reinforce this idea, as their main goal is the development of fundamental rights. In the labour law field, the Organic Law on Freedom of Association for Trade Unions (LOLS[13] is the main text from 1985. It has not been reformed since

9. García Murcia (n. 5), pp. 36-37.
10. Article 28 CE.
11. Alonso Olea (n. 8), p15.
12. Article 149.1.7ª CE.
13. Ley Orgánica de Libertad Sindical.

then, which is remarkable in the restless Spanish legal system. The great missing law is the one on strike, as no Government has ever been able to pass one through Parliament.

The legislative decree is a less interesting type of statutory law. According to the Constitution[14] it can be used to develop delegated legislation, but never on the issues reserved to organic law. It could be used to develop new legislation according to the principles given by the Parliament, or to systemize existing statutory texts. Once and again, the main labour legislation has been the subject of the second formula. For example, the current version of ET is legislative decree 2/2015.

Speaking about real codification, the ET[15] put upon the Government in 1980 the preparation of a Labour Code, containing all sources with legal rank, in a proper order and numeration, in a single text. No Government since that year has made the slightest attempt to perform this task.

The role of decree-law is more open to discussion. Its use implies the assumption of legislative powers by the Government in cases of urgent and extreme need. This vague constitutional definition has been interpreted as meaning the political need to give a quick, immediate answer to situations, either conjunctural or unexpected, that cannot be solved through an ordinary procedure.[16] Among other prohibitions, a decree-law can never deal with fundamental rights. And, paradoxically, the right to strike is ruled by a decree-law from 1977, thus, pre-constitutional and un-constitutional in form, but admitted early by the doctrine[17] and later by the Constitutional Court in one of its very first and finest rulings.[18]

Nonetheless, the real theoretical problem has been the use and abuse of decree-law, by all Government since 1982 to implement labour reforms, as the above said definition has been widely interpreted. The Constitutional Court has repeatedly ruled that they should not be used in this way, the last time in June 2018.[19] No real effect has derived from this case law, as governments, irrespective of their political make-up, have kept on this trend, most recently by RD-L 8/2019 on social protection and labour precariousness. Governments' explanations on urgent and extreme necessity usually fill several paragraphs, but the feeling of the lawyer is the classical '*excusatio non petita, acusatio manifesta*'.

14. Article 82 CE.
15. Additional Disposition 8 of ET (1980).
16. García Murcia (n. 5), p. 59.
17. Alonso Olea (n. 8), p. 22.
18. STC 11/1981.
19. STC 61/2018

As a minority, individual opinion,[20] I have proposed that decree-law should be the right tool to implement EU Law after a procedure under Article 258 TFEU has led to an unfavourable ruling from the European Court of Justice, and even after a prejudicial ruling has pointed out an incompatibility of Spanish Law with EU Law. The Government, on its own, but without any general purpose, used decree-law after the second ruling on dockers' work,[21] modifying a system originating from 1985.[22]

Finally, 'ordinary' laws have no speciality at all. They are the normal way of transposing EU Directives and consolidating labour law reforms implemented through a decree-law. The original versions of the ET and the legislation on employment services, administrative labour infringement, temporary work, posting of workers, labour court procedure, occupational risk prevention are good examples of decree-laws.

As advanced beforehand, statutory law is the cornerstone of Spanish Labour Law. Collective bargaining, under a specific expression of the principle of hierarchy,[23] must respect statutory law, and of course individual autonomy is also subject to it. As for derogations from statutory law, we can distinguish a) 'absolutely' imperative norms, where no derogation by collective bargaining is allowed,[24] and b) 'relatively' imperative norms, where *in melius* derogations are permitted (both as maxima and minima, according to the article).

There is also a third kind of relationship between statutory law and collective bargaining when *in peius* derogation is also allowed. In any case, these episodes of de-legalization must be allowed by the legislation. There are two provisions at present, which specifically allow *in peius* derogations: the length of the probation period[25] and the agreement on maximum hours of overtime for part-time workers.[26] They are nothing but exceptions to the suzerainty of statutory law (absolutely dispositive norms).

The basic rights of workers are established in statutory law and it is a tendency that is going to last.[27] One has just to remember that the ET deals with individual employment relationship, workers' representation and collective bargaining procedure, to understand that one single act regulates most of the working life. This does not mean, however, that stability is a trait of the ET, as it has been modified over fifty times since 1980, according to politics, economy or EU Law.

---

20. José María Miranda Boto, *El control de la recepción del Derecho de la Unión Europea en la legislación laboral española a través del Recurso por incumplimiento*, 113 Documentación laboral (2018).
21. ECLI:EU:C:2017:548.
22. RD-L 8/2017
23. Article 85 ET.
24. Article 35.1 ET.
25. Article 14 ET.
26. Article 12.5 ET.
27. García Murcia (n. 5), pp. 65-66.

17.6 THE LIMITED ROLE OF ADMINISTRATION

The Government exercises statutory authority in accordance with the Constitution and the law, thus, with a general subjection to the hierarchy of norms.[28] Statutory law passed by the administration must respect statutory laws passed by the Parliament.

The most remarkable intervention of the Administration through bylaws, since 1963, (royal decree, being the most common type) is the yearly fixation of the minimum wage, compulsory for all activities. In the last years, politics, rather than social dialogue, have brought momentum to this measure. Thus, during the years of the financial crisis, the conservative Government opted to freeze the minimum wage. However, as one of the main measures from the Socialist Party-Podemos pact, the wage for 2019 was raised by 22%, the biggest increase in history, up to EUR 900 per month. In spite of talks that the measure was going to be passed through a decree. Beyond that, the development of legislation is the main role of bylaws,[29] in respect of the principle of hierarchy. The majority of them deals with details of the individual employment relationship, such as the form of contracts, fixed-term contracts, but also the details of workers representatives' elections, risk prevention and social security.

This subjection, nonetheless, is not absolute, as legislation can establish the power of the Government to regulate certain issues *in peius*. This exception must always be expressed in the legal act, since implicit derogations are not allowed. Working time, is the most important of these situations, giving rise to the RD 1561/1995, on special working times.[30]

One of the most remarkable changes in the transition from francoism to democracy was the shift of the power of regulating working conditions from administration to collective bargaining. Until 1980, the Labour By-laws prepared by the Ministry of Labour were the main tool to regulate this issue, unilaterally, from Madrid.[31] Nowadays, this space of regulation has been occupied by collective agreements and the role of the administration, even concerning public employment, has greatly diminished.

However, theoretically, there is still the possibility of unilateral regulation in the legislation, as the Government has the power to regulate branches of activity, after consultation with the social partners, only if no collective agreement is in place.[32] Nonetheless, this procedure can only be used if the implementation of the special procedure for extension of collective agreements has

28. Article 97 CE.
29. *See* Final Disposition 2 of the *Estatuto:* The Government will make as many norms as necessary to develop this law.
30. As provided for by Article 34.7 ET.
31. *See* Alonso Olea (n. 8), p. 41.
32. Additional Disposition 7 ET.

not been possible.[33] These difficulties have produced no single utilization of it, along with the idea that this is no longer a task for the Government. And no one contemplates it in the immediate future, not even dealing with the gig economy.

Further from this situation, in the early 1980s, the possibility of an autonomous bylaw was the subject of discussion and a lot of scientific literature. It was another remain from the francoist past and this power was thought, nearly unanimously, not fit for a democratic system of industrial relations. The only surviving example is the replacement contract, approved by the Supreme Court in a controversial ruling. Legally, this contract is used to replace an employee who is entitled to a secured leave. The bylaw on it created a different possibility, the hiring of an employee during the procedure of filling a vacancy, up to three months. This possibility in public employment has no time limits and has led to the use and abuse of it by all the Spanish administrations, involving several rulings from the European Court of Justice.[34]

In the end, the administration has lost its key position in the governance of industrial relations. The almighty power of the Ministry of Labour is a forgotten episode of the past.

17.7 CHALLENGES FOR THE SYSTEM OF COLLECTIVE BARGAINING: DECENTRALIZATION AND GENERAL EFFICACY

Article 37.1 CE establishes the binding force of collective agreements. The translation of that constitutional principle into effective detailed rules has been left to statutory Law. The ET made patent that decision in 1980, in its Title III, when it chose to maintain the general efficacy of the francoist collective agreements. The politics behind that choice have been thoroughly studied. It has led to one of the most characteristic traits of Spanish Labour Law. The great reform of 1994, under the Socialist Party, gave a wider space to collective bargaining, releasing subjects formerly reserved to statutory law. The reform of 2012, then under a right-wing Government, was the third milestone in the history of democratic collective bargaining. As it has been pointed out,[35] these thirty years are the story of the permanent construction and renovation of a model, and it is, yet, a work in progress.

33. 'Extension' of collective agreements in Spanish Law has a specific meaning: an administrative procedure to bring the contents of a branch to another, similar branch, where the lack of one of the social partners has made impossible the bargaining of an agreement.
34. De Diego Porras I (ECLI:EU:C:2016:683), Martínez Andrés (ECLI:EU:C:2016:680), De Diego Porras II (ECLI:EU:C:2018:936).
35. Fernando Valdés Dal-Ré, *La negociación colectiva, entre tradición y renovación*, p. 9 (Comares, 2012).

The 1980 legislative decision led, nowadays, to the paradox of one of the highest coverage rates of collective bargaining in Europe (about 80%),[36] with one of the lowest affiliations to trade unions (about 17%). As a collective agreement will be applicable to all employees working in the branch or the company, and closed shop is forbidden, there is no incentive for many employees to join a trade union.[37]

The debate about the general efficacy of collective agreements, thus, can be approached from opposite views. On the one hand, there are liberal academic opinions that ask for a limited, contractual interpretation, on grounds of free market.[38] On the other hand, according to the opinion of some trade unions, never expressed in scientific literature, the end of their general application could bring higher rates of affiliation and a greater commitment to the organizations.

Only agreements bargained according to the rules of Title III of ET (dealing with bargaining agents, contents, procedures etc.) are entitled to general efficacy.[39] All employers and employees under the scope of a collective agreement are bound by working rules established in it. As said beforehand, all the contents of collective agreements must bring an improvement of the minima imposed by statutory legislation, unless *in peius* derogations are expressly allowed by it.

The reality, nonetheless, is more complex, as several collective agreements may regulate at the same time the same employment relations. Traditionally, branch conventions have been the strongest in Spain. And even in this panorama there was a fragmentation, as we can point out the existence of State-level, regional (seventeen regions) and provincial collective agreements (and there are fifty of them).

Here appears the first dimension of decentralization in collective bargaining: State-wide versus regional agreements. Politics have played an important role in the configuration of the balance of powers between these possibilities, as legal reforms have had sometimes their roots in the interest of enhancing the regional spaces of industrial relations, especially dealing with the regions with nationalist governments, such as the Basque Country and Catalonia, and in a lesser way, Galicia. This is a peculiar problem of Spain, where many conflicting interests come together and Courts have not been able to find equilibrium between all those interests.

---

36. 79.5% in 2014, according to J.I. Pérez Infante, *La estadística de convenios colectivos y la medición de la cobertura de la negociación colectiva*, 136 Temas Laborales, p. 163 (2017).
37. One possible counterbalance for this situation was established in Article 11 LOLS. It allows trade unions to collect fees as a canon for the task of collective bargaining. Doubts about its constitutionality were cleared by STC 89/1985, but this measure is never enforced, as it is obviously unpopular, and the Constitutional Court made compulsory the individual agreement of each payer, which leads to a difficult implementation.
38. Jesús Lahera Forteza, *Normas laborales y contratos colectivos* (Reus, 2008).
39. According to Article 82.3 ET.

However, legal rules are not enough to fully understand the articulation of the system of territorial collective bargaining. Article 83.2 of ET gives social partners the power of deciding the structure of collective bargaining, even modifying some statutory rules that will be exposed in the following paragraphs. These are the most political collective agreements, but their real efficacy was severely reduced by the reform of 1994.[40]

At the same time, the social partners in regions have the power to bargain branch collective agreements that can derogate to the State-wide branch sectoral agreements,[41] unless it is forbidden by an agreement passed according to Article 83.2 ET. However, there are several issues that can only be regulated in State-wide agreements, unless, once again, an agreement according to Article 83.2 ET allows the regional regulation. These issues are: probation period, labour contract modalities, professional classification of workers, maximum yearly working time, disciplinary regime, minimal dispositions on occupational risk prevention and geographic mobility.[42]

Quite singular is the position of provincial agreement. Formally they are subordinated to other levels of collective bargaining, no having any formal competence reserved to them. In practice, they have turned out to be the most important collective agreements nowadays.[43] Proximity of bargaining agents, inertia or pure conservatism in the bargaining process have led to the survival of the weakest. Stability[44] is the word to describe the panorama of the practice of collective bargaining in Spain.

The second dimension of decentralization comes from the conflict between branch agreements, of any geographical level, and company agreements. The change in the priority between them is the most recent innovation in collective bargaining, as it appeared shyly in the reforms of 2011,[45] made by the Socialist Party, and again more clearly in 2012[46] made by the Popular Party.

The 2012 reform provisions, which are currently in force, generated a landslide in the equilibrium between collective agreements. The will of the legislator was clear, as this reversal of forces was considered as 'the most radical

40. Fernando Valdés Dal-Ré, *Estructura contractual y concurrencia entre convenios colectivos* (Miguel Rodríguez-Piñero y Bravo-Ferrer & Fernando Valdés Dal-Ré, eds) *La reforma laboral de 2012 en materia de negociación colectiva*, p. 84 (La Ley – Wolters Kluwer, 2012): social partners 'were deprived of the freedom to establish an articulated system of bargaining'.
41. Article 84.3 ET
42. Article 84.4 ET. On the territorial and political problems of the articulation of State-wide and regional agreements, Sala Franco & López Terrada, (n. 5), p. 57.
43. http://www.mitramiss.gob.es/estadisticas/cct/welcome.htm. According to the official statistics from the Ministry, in respect to the agreements signed in 2017, 3.472.290 employees worked under a provincial agreement, 3.170.200 under a State-wide, 1.958.755 under a regional and 704.578 under a company agreement.
44. But not petrification: *See* Valdés Dal-Ré (n. 40), p. 67.
45. RD-L 7/2011.
46. RD-L 3/2012 and L 3/2012.

and devastating reform ever since 1980'.[47] According to the new law, company agreements may derogate *in peius* branch agreements, whatever their territorial scope, for the first time in history.

The list of matters susceptible of derogation is composed by the following subjects:[48] base salary and salary supplements, including overtime and shift work, setting, including those linked to the situation and results of the company; schedule and distribution of working time, shift work regime and annual vacation planning; adaptation to the scope of the company of the system of professional classification of workers; adaptation of the aspects of the employment contract modalities that are attributed by ET to company agreements; and measures to favour the reconciliation of work, family and personal life.

Nonetheless, this list must be understood as closed, a matter of public order, and subject to restrictive interpretation by the courts.[49] Some authors have proposed, in the event of a future reform, making it disposable by the social partners, instead of its derogation.[50] There are some other nuances that must be made to this affirmation. It is a list that can be expanded by the above-mentioned agreements on structure according to Article 83.2 ET. But, however, it cannot be limited by them. This prohibition of modification of the list was seen as a severe attack to the foundations of collective autonomy, as it restricts social partners' self-determination:[51] statutory law has remained the organizer of collective bargaining.

The legislative reform of 2012 brought also an enhancement of a mechanism already existing in the ET: opting out of sectoral collective agreements through a consultation procedure. In short, in case of economic difficulties, an employer together with workers' representatives can decide to change in *peius* the provision coming from a branch agreement. Beforehand, only opting out of salaries' regulation was possible, but after the reform, more subjects have joined the ranks.

It is easy to perceive that the reform of 2012 made a clear bet on the decentralization of the system. Its never-hidden goal was to promote collective bargaining at company level. Collective agreements should be, thus, a tool for cost competitiveness rather than stability. Using the words of the reform: collective bargaining should be a tool and not an obstacle in the management of industrial relations within the company. This philosophy, however, was rejected, of course, by trade unions, but also by many small and middle-sized

47. Miguel Rodríguez-Piñero y Bravo-Ferrer, *Presentación* (Miguel Rodríguez-Piñero y Bravo-Ferrer & Fernando Valdés Dal-Ré, eds) *La reforma laboral de 2012 en materia de negociación colectiva,* p. 17 (La Ley – Wolters Kluwer, 2012).
48. Article 84.2 ET
49. For example, a recent decision established that the priority is only applicable to company-level agreements, not to establishment-level agreements.
50. Sala Franco & López Terrada (n. 5), p. 57.
51. Valdés Dal-Ré (n. 40), p. 59.

companies, that felt that this measure only helped large employers. Statistics show that company agreements have not increased, and that opting outs, apart from the period between 2013 and 2015, have been just painful exceptions.

In the 1980s, there was a great academic discussion about the agreements that did not comply with Title III of ET, either about the majorities needed to pass the agreement or the formal procedure (so-called convenios extraestatutarios). The concern was whether they were lawful[52] or not,[53] and in case they were, what kind of legal force they might have. Nowadays, the legality of this possibility is fully recognized, even with a limited efficacy. However, their status is currently being debated by those who think that they are special sources of law[54] and those that consider them just 'normal' contracts.[55] In any case, the Supreme Court has forbidden this kind of agreements to have any 'appearance of general efficacy': no clause can be written in general terms, for example, and every provision must clearly show its limited scope. They are, in the end, a small minority in legal practice.

As for the future, the challenge is still to foster a better collective bargaining. There is a consensus in the academic doctrine that the model must be improved. Decentralization has translated into deterioration of working conditions. Company agreements are not behaving just as tools of flexible organization, but of cost competitiveness.

In any case, the State must leave its role of principal actor of industrial relations. In this panorama, perhaps the biggest problem is a preliminary one: what is the meaning of 'collective agreement' in Spanish Law? There is no single definition in the legislation, but actually there are many different agreements in ET, suitable for different functions, and with different legal effects. The requisites for their existence are different, as also are their effects. The creation of a hierarchy of collective agreements could improve the system, especially at company level, and bring more legal certainty.

52. Fernando Valdés Dal-Ré, *Configuración y eficacia de los convenios colectivos extraestatutarios* (ACARL, 1988).
53. Alfredo Montoya Melgar, *Sobre la viabilidad legal de convenios colectivos al margen del Estatuto de los Trabajadores* (Alfredo Montoya Melgar, ed.) *Problemas actuales de la negociación colectiva* (CEOE, 1984).
54. Valdés Dal-Ré (n. 35).
55. Antonio Martín Valverde, Fermín Rodríguez-Sañudo Gutiérrez & Joaquín García Murcia, *Derecho del Trabajo* (27th ed., Tecnos, 2018).

	Type of agreement		Characteristics
General Efficacy	'Structure agreement'		83.3 ET: It can modify some rules of priority, normally State-level by main social partners
	Branch	State-level	84.4 ET: Issues reserved, unless agreement based on 83.3 ET.
		Regional	84.3 ET: Can derogate State-level
		Provincial	No priority over any type, but numerically the most important type of agreement
	Company		Priority over any agreement in the issues of art.84.2 ET
	Establishment		No priority over any type, scarce
	Extraestatutario		No general efficacy, cannot derogate any agreement

17.8 THE ROLE OF CASE LAW

As well as other civil law system, Spanish Law has never given to case law the rank of a formal source of law. The Civil Code[56] has established since 1974, that 'case law shall complement the legal system by means of the established jurisprudence of the Supreme Court in its interpretation and application of statutes, customs and general legal principles'.

There is a distinction between 'jurisprudence' and 'courts' doctrine'. The court's doctrine includes any ruling from a court, which does not constitute a binding precedent for other courts. Under the term 'jurisprudence' we include a single decision of the Supreme Court in 'cassation for the unification of doctrine'; two decisions in 'ordinary cassation'; or one decision from the Constitutional Court. The position of the European Court of Human Rights and the European Court of Justice as formal jurisprudence is not clear, yet.[57]

The position of case law as a 'complement' is a well-established idea.[58] It integrates the existing reality of the source, thus developing an active role of collaboration in the normative production. This idea is particularly strong when speaking about the incorporation of the doctrine of the European Court of Justice. As it has been repeatedly pointed out, the lack of activity of the Spanish legislator about unfavourable decisions from the Court is being substituted by the Supreme Court. Its case law is developing itself nowadays as a secondary transposition, which leads to a considerable amount of legal insecurity.

17.9 CONCLUSION

Statutory law will keep on being the core of Spanish Labour Law for many years, despite all its technical flaws. Politics will stop any 'scientific' revision of the ET

56. Article 1.6.
57. On this debate, Yolanda Maneiro Vázquez, *La infracción de la normativa y de la jurisprudencia del Tribunal de Justicia como motivo de acceso a los recursos de suplicación y casación*, 47 Revista General de Derecho del Trabajo y de la Seguridad Social (2017).
58. Antonio Martín Valverde, *Jurisprudencia y casación para unificación de doctrina*, p. 22 (Universidad de Oviedo, 2009).

and will mark the pace of future reforms. The abuse of decree-law will continue and no organic law will be passed in the next years.

In spite of all the reforms, the 'culture' of collective bargaining is not yet firmly established. Lack of mutual confidence between social partners; a crisis that has not yet been fully resolved; a preference for an external solution coming from the State; the absolute absence of a political agreement concerning the model of collective bargaining, are factors leading to continuous reforms and counter-reforms. All these factors concur to make very difficult the creation of a system that satisfies all parties concerned.

BIBLIOGRAPHY

Manuel Alonso Olea, *El sistema normativo del Estado y de las Comunidades Autónomas* (Centro de Estudios Políticos y Constitucionales, eds) *Derecho del Trabajo y de la Seguridad Social en la Constitución* (Centro de Estudios Constitucionales, 1979).

Maravillas Espín Sáez, Adoración Guamán Hernández, Yolanda Maneiro Vázquez & José María Miranda Boto, *Evolution in Labour Law and Social Security in Spain During the Economic and Financial Crisis (2007-2014)* (Martin Stefko, ed.) *Labour Law and Social Security Law at the Crossroads* (Charles University in Prague, 2016).

Javier Gárate Castro, *Leyes y reglamentos reguladores de la Seguridad Social española* (José Luis Monereo Pérez, Guillermo Rodríguez Iniesta, Juan Antonio Maldonado Molina & Angel Luis de Val Tena, eds) *Tratado de Derecho de la Seguridad Social* (Laborum, 2017).

José Ignacio Pérez Infante, *La estadística de convenios colectivos y la medición de la cobertura de la negociación colectiva*, 136 Temas Laborales (2017).

Jesús Lahera Forteza, *Normas laborales y contratos colectivos* (Reus, 2008).

Yolanda. Maneiro Vázquez & José María Miranda Boto, *The Spanish Example*, 99 Bulletin of Comparative Labour Relations (2018).

Yolanda Maneiro Vázquez, *La infracción de la normativa y de la jurisprudencia del Tribunal de Justicia como motivo de acceso a los recursos de suplicación y casación*, 47 Revista General de Derecho del Trabajo y de la Seguridad Social (2017).José María Miranda Boto, *El control de la recepción del Derecho de la Unión Europea en la legislación laboral española a través del Recurso por incumplimiento*, 113 Documentación laboral (2018).

Antonio Martín Valverde, Fermín Rodríguez-Sañudo Gutiérrez & Joaquín García Murcia, *Derecho del Trabajo* (27th ed., Tecnos, 2018).

Antonio Martín Valverde, *Jurisprudencia y casación para unificación de doctrina*, 22 (Universidad de Oviedo, 2009).

Alfredo Montoya Melgar, *Sobre la viabilidad legal de convenios colectivos al margen del Estatuto de los Trabajadores* (Alfredo Montoya Melgar, ed.) *Problemas actuales de la negociación colectiva* (CEOE, 1984).

Ricardo Rodríguez Contreras & José María Miranda Boto, *Spain* (Sylvaine Laulom, Pascale Vielle, Emmanuelle Mazuyer & Marie-Cecile Escande, eds), *Quel Droit social dans une Europe en crise?* (Larcier, 2012)

Miguel Rodríguez-Piñero y Bravo-Ferrer, *Presentación* (Miguel Rodríguez-Piñero y Bravo-Ferrer & Fernando Valdés Dal-Ré, eds) *La reforma laboral de 2012 en materia de negociación colectiva* (La Ley - Wolters Kluwer, 2012).

Tomás Sala Franco & Eva López Terrada, *La reforma de las fuentes de la relación laboral* (Tomás Sala Franco, ed.) *Propuestas para un debate sobre la reforma laboral*(Francis Lefebvre, 2018).

Fernando Valdés Dal-Ré, *Configuración y eficacia de los convenios colectivos extraestatutarios* (ACARL, 1988).

Fernando Valdés Dal-Ré, *Estructura contractual y concurrencia entre convenios colectivos* (Miguel Rodríguez-Piñero y Bravo-Ferrer & Fernando Valdés Dal-Ré, eds) *La reforma laboral de 2012 en materia de negociación olectiva,* (La Ley - Wolters Kluwer, 2012).

Fernando Valdés Dal-Ré, *La negociación colectiva, entre tradición y renovación,* (Comares, 2012).

Helana Ysás Molinero, *Recent Collective Bargaining Articulation Reforms in France and Spain,* 7 Spanish Labour Law and Employment Relations Journal (2013).

CHAPTER 18

Sources of Labour Law in Sweden

Jenny Julén Votinius

18.1 INTRODUCTION

The theme of this chapter is the legal sources and the hierarchy of norms in Swedish labour law. The sources of labour law are discussed in the light of national labour market structure and its historical development, as well as in the light of the European legal context. In Sweden, labour law has developed in close relation to the national industrial relations model. Typical features for this model include powerful social partners who sign nationwide collective agreements; a high degree of unionization; and virtually no state intervention in the negotiation or carrying-out of collective agreements. Following a long period of integration and cooperation with the European countries, Sweden joined the European Economic Area in 1994 and became a member of the European Union (EU) in 1995. Since then, the discourse on the EU level has had significant impact in many ways on the Swedish legislative development in the area of labour law, and over the years, EU law has established its position as an important legal source within the field.

The chapter is structured as follows. Section 18.2 is an introduction to the Swedish labour law and industrial relations system and an overview of the legal sources. The following sections highlight the different sources of law one by one. Thus, section 18.3 deals with international conventions and EU law; Section 18.4 addresses national laws and regulations, section 18.5 deals with collective agreement and section 18.6 with the employment contract, section 18.7 explains the function of preparatory works and section 18.8 deals with precedents of the Swedish Labour Court. Finally, the discussion in section 18.9 concludes the chapter.

18.2 THE STRUCTURE AND SOURCES OF SWEDISH LABOUR LAW

18.2.1 The Swedish Labour Law and Industrial Relations System

Swedish labour law is characterized by the importance of the collective agreement, in the same time that there is a comprehensive body of statutory law.[1] The highly refined interaction between statutory law and collective agreements is an outflow of the significant role of the Swedish labour-market parties in the development of labour relations.

The cornerstones of the national industrial relations system are self-regulation, cooperation between social partners and autonomous collective bargaining. The degree of collective agreement coverage is higher in Sweden than in most other countries, and the labour-market parties have been given – and they themselves have also been taking – a significant responsibility for the development of labour relations and working life.[2] The successive establishment of model for social dialogue often referred to as the Swedish Model, started with the December compromise in 1906 and included the important main agreement *Saltsjöbadsavtalet*, which is still in force. During the greater part of the 1900s, legislation on the area of labour law was very limited. Instead, collective agreements were the primary source of regulation. The relationship between the social parties was marked by collaboration and consensus. The tranquillity in the labour market persisted until the end of the 1960s. From that point, the relations became much more turbulent and conflicted.[3] Eventually, the Government considered that it had reason to intervene by imposing legislation, and in the 1970s Sweden saw what is commonly referred to as a legislative explosion within the area of labour law. Largely, the legislative structure that was shaped around that time still applies.[4]

Today, the body of labour legislation is extensive and detailed and has a uniform scope. It covers areas such as employment protection, workplace health and safety, non-discrimination, working time, co-determination, freedom of association, collective bargaining and collective action. Normally, the same legislation applies to all employees irrespective of labour-market sector, position and duration of employment contract. With the exception of wages, most areas of labour law are statutorily regulated. However, most of the legislation is

1. For a comprehensive introduction to Swedish labour law, *see* Ann Numhauser Henning, *Labour Law* (Bogdan Michael, ed.) *Swedish Legal System* (Norstedts Juridik, 2010).
2. Around 90% of the employees work for an employer with a collective agreement, and about 70% of all employees are members of a union, Swedish National Mediation Office (2018) *Annual Report 2017* (Stockholm).
3. Sofia Murhem, *Turning to Europe, A New Swedish Industrial Relations Regime in the 1990s* (Uppsala University, 2003).
4. Axel Adlercreutz & Birgitta Nyström, *Labour law in Sweden: International Encyclopedia for Labour Law and Industrial Relations*, 47 (Kluwer Law Online, 2015).

semi-mandatory in the sense that otherwise mandatory rules may be deviated from by collective bargaining. As a result, collective agreements regulate the majority of employee's terms and conditions of employment and hold a significant position as a legal source in labour law.

18.2.2 About Legal Sources in Sweden

The concept source of law has an extensive application, and its content is not firmly decided.[5] There is no legal regulation of the sources of law, apart from the constitutional provision in Chapter 1 section 1 of the Instrument of Government stating that all public power is exercised under the laws. For international conventions, Sweden applies a dualistic approach; international legal norms are not applied by the domestic authorities and may not be invoked before domestic courts until they have been transformed into national law.[6]

Constitutional and then statutory laws, which must be interpreted in conformity with EU law, are at the top of the hierarchy of the legal sources. Within the field of labour law, collective agreements also belong to this top-level category, as well as the individual employment contract. Other sources of law; preparatory works, precedents, customs and legal scholarship are combined in the interpretation of what is existing law. As regards these other legal sources, there are different views as to whether there is a strict hierarchy between them, and, if so, what the actual content of this hierarchy should be. Generally, it is common to divide the legal sources into binding and non-binding legal sources, or into sources that the Court has to consider, should consider or may consider.[7] It bears noting that, also for this division, the discourse is marked by somewhat different views as to in which category certain sources belong.

A special note should be made about general principles of law. Such principles hold de facto an important position in legal argumentation and may have a significant impact both on the legislative process and in the reasoning of the courts. However, strictly speaking, general principles of law are not considered a source of law in the Swedish context. The concept general principle of law has no clear definition, and it is applied differently in different legal fields. Within labour law, general principles of contract law normally apply, but there are also general principles particular for labour law. These principles primarily origin from customs and case law. At the very core of the employment relationship are the managerial prerogative, and the principle on subordination,

5. Gunnar Bergholtz & Aleksander Peczenik, *Precedent in Sweden* (D. Neil MacCormick & Robert S. Summers, eds) *Interpreting Precedents: A Comparative Study* (Aldershot, 1997).
6. Göran Melander, *Sweden* (Martin Scheinin, ed.) *International Human Rights Norms in the Nordic and Baltic Countries* (Kluwer Law International, 1995). The State is bound by the Convention already from the time of ratification.
7. Aleksander Peczenik, *Vad är rätt – om demokrati, rättssäkerhet, etik och juridisk argumentation*, 213 (Fritzes, 1995).

including the duty to obey and the duty of loyalty. Other general principles relate to the relationship between the social partners, such as the principle on the normative function of the collective agreement, which will be described in detail below in section 18.5.

In this chapter, most attention will be paid to laws and other regulations, collective agreements, the employment contract, preparatory works, and case law from the Swedish Labour Court. This is a reflection of the fact that these are the legal sources of most practical importance in the field of labour law. It should be noted that considerations of and references to EU law may be necessary for relation to all other sources of law, as national law is always to be interpreted in conformity with EU law.

18.3 EU LAW AND INTERNATIONAL CONVENTIONS

18.3.1 EU Law

The Instrument of Government states that Sweden is a member of the EU, and allows the Parliament to transfer decision-making authority within the framework of EU cooperation.[8] Regulations from the EU and other provisions in EU law that have direct effect are a binding source of law at the top level of the hierarchy of norms. EU directives, however, normally have to be implemented in national law for its content to become binding. Their function as a source of law is as a tool for interpretation of the national legislation through which they have been implemented.

As explained above, national statutory labour law is mainly composed of a framework of semi-mandatory rules, which are to be adjusted and complemented by collective agreements for different sectors. In the negotiations that led up to the Swedish EU membership, there was a promise that this regulative model would be considered as fulfilling the requirements of EU law. However, since then, the Court of Justice of the European Union has rejected collective agreements as sole method of implementation of EU directives. As a consequence, Sweden had to introduce mandatory minimum rules in fields that previously belonged to the autonomy of the social partners, i.e., in the field of working time. Another, famous, example of how EU law may conflict with and triumph over national labour law is the Laval case. Here, national legislation on the right to strike was found to be incompatible with EU law on the free movement of services.[9]

8. Chapter 1 section 10 and Chapter 10 section 6 of the Instrument of Government (1974:152).
9. *Laval un Partneri Ltd v. Svenska Byggnadsarbetareförbundet* (2007) C-341/05.

18.3.2 The European Convention of Human Rights

In 1952, Sweden ratified the European Convention of Human Rights (ECHR), and since 1995 it is incorporated in national legislation. Albeit its formal status as statutory law, the ECHR holds a special position in the Swedish legal system, as Chapter 2 section 23 of the Instrument of Government SFS 1974:152 prohibits legislation that violates the Convention. The Tort Liability Act allows natural or legal persons to obtain damages from the state or a municipality for violations of the ECHR.[10] An action against public authorities pursuant to this provision constitutes a civil law case and must be brought before a general court under the rules for optional proceedings. Beyond what applies in the relationship between the State and the individual, employees in public employment may bring action against their employer regarding violation of ECHR rights in the individual employment relationship. As regards the collective bargaining relationship, the Swedish Labour Court has ruled that a party bound by a collective agreement may set aside a clause in the agreement that violates individual's rights under the ECHR, without risking liability for damages for breach of contract.[11] There is, so far, no case law indicating an obligation for the parties to set aside such a clause, or that the parties could be made liable for damages if a clause in the collective agreement is in contravention with the ECHR.[12] Of most direct relevance for the matter of the status of the ECHR as a legal source is perhaps how its provisions play out at the judiciary level. Here, first, a Court must set aside national labour legislation that is contrary to the Convention. In practice, this will happen only in rare cases, as the State may not adopt legislation that is in contravention with the ECHR. Second, and of most practical importance, the courts must interpret national labour legislation in conformity with the ECHR. As stated by the Supreme Court, this means that in some cases it may be necessary to set aside limitations to the national legislation stipulated in preparatory works, case law or in legal scholarship.[13]

18.3.3 ILO Conventions

Sweden has ratified the majority of the International Labour Organization (ILO) conventions currently up to date and in force, as well as the Revised European

10. Chapter 3 section 4 of the Tort Liability Act (1972:207), Government Bill Prop. 2017/18:7. The provision codifies Swedish Supreme Court judgement 2005 p. 642 and later case law.
11. Swedish Labour Court judgment AD 2012:74.
12. Where a collective agreement violates individuals' rights under the Convention, claims for damages shall be brought against the State and regard the legislative shortcomings which permits collective agreements to violate Convention rights, Case No T 4110-10, 5 June 2013, District Court of Helsingborg, cf. European Court of Human Rights *Evaldsson and others* (No. 75252/01) 13 February 2007, 54 & 63.
13. Swedish Labour Court judgement AD 2017 No. 23; Swedish Supreme Court judgement NJA 2009 p. 463.

Social Charter. The fact that national legislation provides a high level of legal protection for employees, which has made the ratification of many ILO conventions uncomplicated. Sweden has refrained from ratification of conventions and provisions in areas where the social partners regulate with no or almost no interference of the State, such as the area of wages and working time.[14] Both ILO conventions and the Revised European Social Charter allows for ratification through collective agreement. Before the ratification of a convention in the area of labour law, the Government always consults the social partners. The social partners also have representatives in the ILO committee, a public authority regularly serving as a consultative body in the drafting process foregoing a ratification of an ILO Convention. Generally, the social partners discourage ratification on matters that may be subject to collective bargaining.[15]

As international legal norms must be transformed into national law in Sweden before they can be applied by the domestic authorities or be invoked before domestic courts, the role of the ILO conventions as a legal source is limited to that of a tool for interpretation of the national legislation through which they have been implemented. Although the Swedish Labour Court sometimes refer to both the ECHR and, more rarely, ILO conventions, legal scholarship shows that it is very unusual that international conventions have had substantial impact on the outcome of the case.[16] This does not mean that the Court has decided in contravention with the conventions, but simply that the outcome of the cases would have been the same if only national law had been considered.

18.4 CONSTITUTIONAL PROVISIONS AND STATUTORY LEGISLATION

18.4.1 Introduction

Laws and other regulations are the very core of the legal sources.[17] The hierarchically arranged categories of laws and regulations are: constitutional laws, statutory laws, followed by ordinances and statutory instruments. Laws, which form the basis of the regulatory body, are adopted by the Parliament.[18] In a law, the Parliament may authorize the Government, to further specify the content of the legislative text by issuing ordinances. In cases where there is a

14. Government Bill Props. 1991/92:98 and 1997/98:8.
15. Petra Herzfelt Olsson, *Folkrätten i arbetsrätten* (Rebecca Stern & Inger Österdahl, eds) *Folkrätten i svensk rätt,* 206, (Liber, 2012).
16. *Ibid.*, 228.
17. Hans-Heinrich Vogel, *Sources of Swedish Law* (Bogdan Michael, ed.) *Swedish Legal System* (Norstedts Juridik, 2010).
18. Chapter 8 section 1 of the Instrument of Government SFS 1974:152, as amended by SFS 2010:1408.

need for even more detailed rules, the Government may authorize a public authority to issue statutory instruments. In the area of labour law, statutory instruments exist regarding health and safety matters.[19] The following section will focus on the laws, starting with the constitutional laws. Ordinances and statutory instruments will not be further discussed in the following.

18.4.2 Constitutional Provisions

The Swedish constitution is formed by four constitutional laws: the Instrument of Government, the Act of Succession, the Freedom of the Press Act and the Fundamental Law on Freedom of Expression. For the area of labour law, the Instrument of Government (1974:152) is of most interest. The main part of this law is devoted to matters of governance including the distribution of decisive and executive powers, but Chapter 2 of this law contains rules on fundamental rights and freedoms; for instance freedom of expression, freedom to demonstrate, freedom of worship, protection against discrimination and right to industrial action. Some of the rights are absolute and others may be limited by law.[20] Apart from the right to industrial action, which concerns the relationship between parties in an industrial conflict, the rules on fundamental rights and freedoms regulate the relationship between the individual and the State.[21] Thus, in its capacity as a source of labour law, Chapter 2 of the Instrument of Government can only be applied in matters regarding public employment. Regarding employment or promotion decisions for posts within public employment, there is also a constitutional requirement that only objective factors shall be taken into account.[22] This provision is primarily aiming to prevent nepotism, but in practice, it also has the effect of excluding discriminatory considerations in public employment recruitments.

18.4.3 Statutory Law: Mandatory and Semi-Mandatory

There is no Labour Code in Sweden. Instead, within the area of labour law, legislation has the form of separate laws. The same laws apply more or less

19. The statutory instruments are issued by the Swedish Work Environment Authority, based on authorizations in the Ordinance on Work Environment (1977:1166).
20. Chapter 2 section 2 of the Instrument of Government. *See* further Government Bill Prop. 2009/10:80, 150ff.
21. Chapter 2 section 14 of the Instrument of Government, protecting trade unions, employers' organizations and individual employers. On the employee side, only trade unions may take to industrial action, not individual employees.
22. Chapter 12 section 5 of the Instrument of Government. Cf section 4 of the Public Employment Act SFS 1994:260. This provision only applies in the state sector. However, with reference to the abovementioned policy provision in Chapter 1 section 2 of the Instrument of Government, the same demands for objective grounds – skills and merits – applies also for employment decisions in the municipality sector.

uniformly to all employees, although still some limitations to the right to strike apply for certain groups in the public sector. In addition, contrary to employees in the private sector, public employees may invoke Chapter 2 of the Instrument of Government and the ECHR against the State or municipality in its capacity as employer.

The body of labour legislation is comprehensive and covers virtually all aspects of the employment relation except wages, which are regulated in collective agreements. Of crucial importance is the Employment Protection Act (1982:80) on temporary employment, just cause for dismissal, notice periods and, in cases of redundancy, rules on seniority and preferential right to re-employment. In the area of collective labour law, the Co-Determination in the Workplace Act (1976:580) is key; it regulates freedom of association, collective bargaining negotiations, information and consultation, along with industrial action. The Discrimination Act (2008:567) prohibits discrimination on a number of grounds in many areas of society, including working life. Other important laws are the Work Environment Act (1977:1160) and the Working Time Act (1982:673).

A typical feature of Swedish labour law is that only a limited number of provisions are mandatory; basically, rules that safeguard the industrial relations model and protect the employee in fundamental areas such as employment protection, working time, leave of absence, non-discrimination etc. However, most of the legislation is semi-mandatory; the social partners are permitted to deviate from them through collective bargaining. Each law specifies if, and to what extent, the social partners are permitted to deviate from the provisions of that particular law. Should the matter of a semi-mandatory provision be covered by an EU-directive, the law will prohibit the social partners to deviate from the directive in question; in these cases, the law is described as semi-mandatory with an EU-barrier.

In practice, the collective agreement normally replaces most semi-mandatory statutory provisions, regulate almost all terms and conditions of employment, and is an important source of law. There is no procedure to extend collective agreements to apply erga omnes. Nevertheless, collective agreements regulate virtually the entire labour market.

18.5 COLLECTIVE AGREEMENTS

The industrial relations system operates on three levels – the national intersectoral level, the sectoral level and the local, workplace, level.[23] Collective

23. Sweden applies a so-called *single-channel* system; the employees are represented by their unions alone, with essentially no parallel forms of representation through systems within the company, such as work councils. *See* Marco Biagi & Michele Tiraboschi, *Forms of Employee Representational Participation* (Roger Blanpain, ed.) *Comparative Labour Law and Industrial Relations in*

agreements are concluded on all three levels. Today, collective agreements on national intersectoral level are few in number, but of crucial importance as they provide the outer framework for the cooperation between the social partners and for collective bargaining. Thus, these agreements form the very base in the structure of industrial relations structure. Industry-wide sectoral collective agreements cover all sectors in the Swedish economy and sets the framework for the negotiations on the local, workplace, level.[24] The sectoral level agreements often delegate to the local level to decide on derogations from semi-mandatory legislation. However, in certain questions, some sectoral agreements require that local level agreements are approved on industry level in order to be valid. In a conflict between collective agreements on different levels, a sectoral agreement will precede over a local one. Normally, an employer is bound only by one single collective agreement (or one collective agreement for blue-collar workers and another collective agreement for white-collar workers). Should the employer have signed more than one collective agreement, the first agreement will apply before the more recent one.

A collective agreement is defined by law as 'an agreement in writing between an organization of employers or an employer and an organization of employees about conditions of employment or otherwise about the relationship between employers and employees'.[25] The collective agreement is a private law contract. It binds the signatory parties, but it is equally binding for members of the signatory trade union and, when applicable, the signatory employers' organization. With regard to employees who are members of the signatory union, this principle means that clauses in the individual employment contract that contradict the collective agreement are void. Instead, the corresponding clause of the collective agreement is applied. section 27 of the Co-Determination in the Workplace Act (1976:580).

Employers bound by a collective agreement are obliged to the signatory trade union to apply the collective agreement for all employees, regardless of whether or not they are members of the trade union with whom the employer has the collective agreement. The obligation to apply the collective agreement also to employees who are non-unionized or members of a different trade union follows from the principle on the normative function of the collective agreement, which is considered a tacit clause in all collective agreements. The normative function of the collective agreement cannot be invoked by a non-unionized

---

Industrialized Market Economies, 525 (Wolters Kluwer, 2010); Greg J. Bamber & Russell D. Lansbury, *An Introduction to International and Comparative Employment Relations* (Greg J. Bamber & Russell D. Lansbury, eds) *International and Comparative Employment Relations. A Study of Industrialised Market Economies* (Revised Edition, Sage, 1998).

24. Reinhold Fahlbeck, *Employee Participation in Sweden: Union Paradise and Employer Hell Or?*, 14 (Juristförlaget, 2008).
25. Section 23 of the Co-determination Act (1976:580).

employee to claim certain rights under the collective agreement.[26] Instead, a failure to apply the collective agreement to all employees in the workplace constitutes a breach of the collective agreement, and the employer becomes liable for damages to the signatory trade union. Many times, however, the individual employment contract refers to the collective agreement at the workplace. In these cases, the content of the collective agreement is part of the individual employment contract.

Around 90% of the employees work for an employee who has signed a collective agreement.[27] In the relatively few workplaces where no collective agreement is in force, terms in the industry agreement may still be applied as a source of law. Here, the collective agreement works as the expression of established custom and practice.[28]

In the interpretation of collective agreements, general principles for interpretation of contracts apply. There are different opinions within legal scholarship as to whether interpretation of collective agreements deviates from the interpretation of other contracts.[29] In case law from the Swedish Labour Court, special importance is attached to the intention of the contracting parties at the time of the conclusion of the collective agreement. When a joint intention of the parties cannot be decided, the Court tends to rely mainly on the wording of the collective agreement. In the case law, emphasis is also put on deciding which of the parties that should bear the responsibility for any unclear terms in the agreement. Other aspects that are of importance for the interpretation are customs between the disputing parties, the purpose of the agreement, and reasonableness if the interpretation.[30]

18.6 THE EMPLOYMENT CONTRACT

In contrast to the collective agreement, the individual employment contract does not have to be in writing or meet any other formal requirements.

The freedom of contract of the parties in an employment contract is limited by law and, in relevant cases, collective agreement. With few exceptions, labour law legislation is mandatory or semi-mandatory, and may thus normally not be deviated from – or deviated from to the detriment of the employee – in an

26. Swedish Labour Court judgement AD 1983 No. 184.
27. Swedish National Mediation Office (2018) 224.
28. Olof Bergqvist, Lars Lunning & Gudmund Toijer, *Medbestämmandelagen: lagtext med kommentarer*, 310 (Norstedts, 1997); Jonas Malmberg, *Anställningsavtalet. Om anställningsförhållandets individuella reglering*, 144 (Iustus, 1997).
29. Folke Schmidt, *Typfall, partsavsikt och partsculpa – riktpunkter för avtalstolkning*, Svensk juristtidning, 497-520, (1959); Mikael Hansson, *Kollektivavtalsrätten* (Iustus förlag, 2010); Bert Lehrberg, *Avtalstolkning: tolkning av avtal och andra rättshandlingar på förmögenhetsrättens område* (Iusté, 2014).
30. Hansson (n. 29).

individual employment contract.[31] Detrimental clauses do not render the employment contract void, instead, the clause shall be disregarded and replaced by the statutory provision. In cases where an employment contract provides for both better and worse employment conditions that what is required by law, the better conditions shall continue to apply, whereas the worse conditions shall be replaced in accordance with the statutory requirements.[32]

In addition to statutory law, the collective agreement that applies in the workplace sets limits for the content of the individual employment contract. If the employee is a member of the signatory trade union, both the employer and the employee are bound by the collective agreement and may not agree upon terms that are in contravention with the collective agreement. As explained above, such terms are void, and the corresponding clause of the collective agreement must be applied instead.

For employees who are not members of the signatory union, freedom of contract applies irrespective of the collective agreement. Clauses in the employment contract that are in contravention with the collective agreement are valid. To the extent that the employment contract does not regulate certain conditions, the collective agreement has a complementary function.[33]

The previous sections have dealt with sources of labour law at the top of the normative hierarchy: laws and regulations, the collective agreement and the employment contract. In relation to the statutory legislation, another legal source is of great significance come into play: the preparatory works, which is the theme of the following section.

18.7 PREPARATORY WORKS

In the Swedish legal system, the *travaux préparatoires* or preparatory works are key to the interpretation and application of the law. The function of the preparatory works has been described as complementary, but necessary, to give the legislation full force.[34]

The importance given to the preparatory works as a source of law is related to the structure of the legislative process. Legislation is adopted by the Parliament, normally at the initiative of the Government but sometimes at the initiative of a member of Parliament. The legislative process is extensive and which involves a number of different bodies. The very first step is that the

31. Malmberg (n. 28), 100.
32. Government Bill Prop. 1938:286 p. 217, Swedish Labour Court judgement AD 1977 No. 24.
33. Malmberg (n. 28), 158. Swedish Labour Court judgement AD 2001 No. 9.
34. Aleksander Peczenik & Gunnar Bergholtz, *Statutory Interpretation in Sweden* (D. Neil MacCormick & Robert S. Summers, eds) *Interpreting Statutes: A Comparative Study*, 298 (Aldershot, 1991). The importance attached to preparatory works can be seen also in the other Nordic countries, Jacob Sundberg, *Från Eddan till Ekelöf: repetitorium om rättskällor i Norden*, 232 (Studentlitteratur, 1978).

Government appoints an inquiry chair – or, sometimes, a group appointed internally within the ministry – to investigate the matter and propose legislation. The inquiry chair delivers a report that is referred for consultation to a large number of authorities, agencies, municipalities and organizations. Also, stakeholders who have not received the report for consultation may deliver their comments. After the consultation round, the Government prepares a draft for a legislative proposal which is referred to the Council on Legislation for a judicial preview of legislative proposals and a non-binding but authoritative opinion on the legal validity of the proposed legislation. The Government then develops the draft into a final legislative proposal (proposition), which is presented before the Parliament. The parliamentary committee in charge of the matter examines the proposal and give its opinion before the vote in the Parliament. If the Parliament approves to the proposal, the law is adopted and will be published in the Swedish Code of Statutes.

The final legislative proposal shall be guiding in the interpretation of a law. The proposal consists of a comprehensive part presenting the general background and arguments for the law and the proposed provisions, along with a concentred part called the special motivation, which addresses the separate provisions one by one. The special motivation gives more or less detailed explanations of the content of each provision and indicates the intentions of the legislator as regards its interpretation and application.

There is no statutory provision regarding the requirement to consider preparatory works when interpreting the legislative acts. Instead, the legal base for acknowledging the preparatory works status as a source of law is the customs established by the courts in their adjudicative activities. The preparatory works are not binding but guiding. They may only be deviated from where there are reasonable grounds to do so. To the extent that a preparatory work is in contravention with international conventions, EU law or general principles of law, the Court must disregard it. Preparatory works are also set aside when they are too old, or insofar as that they are contradictory or contain typographic mistakes.[35]

18.8 PRECEDENTS OF THE SWEDISH LABOUR COURT

The Swedish Labour Court was established through the 1928 Collective Agreements Act. Originally, it had jurisdiction as a single instance in matters of interpretation and application of collective agreements, whereas all labour disputes that concerned matters outside the application of collective agreements were to be settled in general courts. Through the adoption of the Labour

35. Ola Svensson, *Att avvika från lagmotiven. Några tankar om bevisbördans placering*, Juridisk Tidskrift, 741-753 (2016).

Disputes Act (1974:371), in order to promote a more coherent jurisprudential development, the distribution of disputes between the Swedish Labour Court and the general courts changed.[36] The Swedish Labour Court was given exclusive jurisdiction for virtually all labour disputes in the organized part of the labour market and also became appellate instance to the district court in disputes between non-unionized parties. With the exception of some adjustments, this order still prevails.[37] The majority of the members in the Swedish Labour Court are appointed by the labour-market organizations. Normally, the Court convenes with seven members, including two professional judges (the chairperson and the vice chairperson), one neutral expert on the labour market, and two members representing the interests of the employer and the employee interests, respectively.[38]

Generally, the function of precedents as a source of law has been much debated in legal scholarship.[39] It is clear that precedents are not binding de jure, but it is also clear that the courts de facto regularly follow precedents.[40] It may thus be more relevant to address precedents as a source of law in terms of presumption than in terms of boundness. In line with this, the role of the precedent as a legal source has been described as 'limiting and restraining'.[41] The lower court must actively take note of every relevant precedent and make an assessment as to whether it should be followed. This has sometimes been referred to as conditioned boundness; the precedent should be followed unless there are reasonable grounds against it.[42]

In labour law, the role of precedents must be understood in the light of the dispute resolution model that applies in the labour market, which reflects the strong position of the social partners. The overwhelming majority of labour-market disputes are settled in grievance negotiations.[43] The number of judgments delivered by the Swedish Labour Court is very limited, and in the last ten

36. Government Bill Prop. 1974/77.
37. Court proceedings must be preceded by grievance negotiations between the employer and the trade union and, effectively, the negotiation procedure functions as a first instance in most labour disputes. In cases where the employee is not represented by a trade union (or the Equality Ombudsman), or in the less common situation that the employer is not bound by a collective agreement, action must be brought before a local district court in first instance.
38. The Court may also convene with only three members, or, on the contrary determine the case in a plenary session. In all settings, the representatives of the social partners are in the majority. A particular composition applies in cases on discrimination, where the social partners' representatives are *not* in the majority, Chapter 3 section 9 of the Labour Disputes Act (1974:371) and Chapter 6 section 1 and Chapter 3 section 6 a of the Discrimination Act (2008:567).
39. Ola Svensson, *Christina Ramberg, Prejudikat som rättskälla inom förmögenhetsrätten*, 1 Juridisk Tidskrift, 194 (2018).
40. Bergholtz & Peczenik (n. 5).
41. Christina Ramberg, *Prejudikat som rättskälla i förmögenhetsrätten*, 55 (Wolters Kluwer, 2017).
42. Svensson (n. 39).
43. Out of all legal disputes in the organized part of the labour market, more than 90% – and maybe as many as 98% – are resolved in grievance negotiations and thus never reach the Court, Government Report SOU 2012:62, 74.

to fifteen years, the number has declined.[44] The few precedents coming from the Swedish Labour Court has a significant impact on the content of labour law. It may thus be that precedents have a stronger position in labour law than in some other areas of law.

18.9 CONCLUSIONS AND TRENDS

The most prominent characteristic of Swedish labour law as regards the legal sources is the importance of collective agreements, which cover almost all employees and regulate the major part of the employment conditions. A collective agreement in force in a workplace replaces semi-mandatory statutory rules and functions within the framework of the mandatory statutory regulation.

Besides the high impact of the collective agreements, the structure of legal sources in Sweden is also characterized by the importance as a legal source attached to the preparatory works. In recent years, a general trend in certain areas of private law is, however, the increasing significance of precedents as a legal source. This development was anticipated already when Sweden became a member of the EU, and recent legal scholarship argues that this prediction has been confirmed.[45] In the hierarchy of norms as it traditionally has been conceptualized, preparatory works come second after laws and regulations. Only after the preparatory works, the precedents follow, and after that comes customs and legal scholarship.[46] There are voices today, however, that points to a tendency that precedents are gaining ground on the expense of the preparatory work. In this respect, the hierarchy of norms is somewhat blurred. It might be too much to say that a rule created by a precedent always applies before a rule expressed in a preparatory work.[47] It has been suggested, however, that a precedent may be applicable even if it is contrary to a rule expressed in a preparatory work, as long as the precedent presents a reasonable ground.[48] In relation to precedents, and their significance as a source of law, it is noteworthy that the number of judgments from the Swedish Labour Court has decreased continuously since 2005. The downward trend was broken in 2018, but the number of cases is still at a very low level.

In comparison with many other countries, constitutional aspects are of limited importance in the Swedish labour law system. However, the trend towards a constitutionalization of labour rights in Europe noted by many

44. In 2005, the Swedish Labour Court ruled in 131 cases. Since then, an ever smaller number of judgements have been delivered. In 2017 the Court only ruled in 66 cases. The decline can partly be explained by the requirement for leave to appeal that was introduced in 2008, Government Bill Prop. 2007/08:72. In 2018, the number of judgements increased to 81.
45. Bergholtz & Peczenik (n. 5), 298; Ramberg (n. 41), 330.
46. Bergholtz & Peczenik (n. 5),
47. Ramberg (n. 41), 330.
48. Svensson (n. 39).

scholars can be seen also in Sweden.[49] This is an expression of a wider development towards an increased internationalization and europeanization also in relation to the legal sources. References in legal argumentation to EU law and to the ECHR are more frequent, and constitutional arguments, especially as regards fundamental rights and freedoms are raised more often and with more emphasis than before.[50]

BIBLIOGRAPHY

Axel Adlercreutz & Birgitta Nyström, *Labour Law in Sweden. International Encyclopedia for Labour Law and Industrial Relations*, 47 (Kluwer Law Online, 2015).

Gunnar Bergholtz & Aleksander Peczenik, *Precedent in Sweden* (D. Neil MacCormick & Robert S. Summers, eds) *Interpreting Precedents: A Comparative Study* (Aldershot, 1997).

Marco Biagi & Michele Tiraboschi, *Forms of Employee Representational Participation* (Roger Blanpain, ed.) *Comparative Labour Law and Industrial Relations in Industrialized Market Economies*, 525 (Wolters Kluwer, 2010).

Reinhold Fahlbeck, *Employee Participation in Sweden: Union Paradise and Employer Hell Or?*, 14 (Juristförlaget, 2008).

Greg J. Bamber & Russell D. Lansbury, *An Introduction to International and Comparative Employment Relations* (Greg J., Bamber & Russell D. Lansbury, eds) *International and Comparative Employment Relations: A Study of Industrialised Market Economies* (Revised Edition, Sage, 1998).

Göran Melander, *Sweden* (Martin Scheinin, ed.) *International Human Rights Norms in the Nordic and Baltic Countries* (Kluwer Law International, 1995).

Sofia Murhem, *Turning to Europe, A New Swedish Industrial Relations Regime in the 1990s* (Uppsala University, 2003).

Ann Numhauser Henning, *Labour Law* (Bogdan Michael, ed.) *Swedish Legal System*, (Norstedts Juridik, 2010).

Aleksander Peczenik & Gunnar Bergholtz, *Statutory Interpretation in Sweden* (D. Neil MacCormick & Robert S. Summers, eds) *Interpreting Statutes: A Comparative Study*, 298 (Aldershot, 1991).

49. *See*, for instance, Judy Fudge, *Constitutionalizing Labour Rights in Europe* (Tom Campbell, K.D. Ewing & Adam Tomkins, eds) *The Legal Protection of Human Rights: Sceptical Essays* (OUP, 2011); Dagmar Schiek, *Economic and Social Integration: The Challenge for EU Constitutional Law*, 94 (Edward Elgar, 2012).
50. Mia Rönnmar, *Fundamental Rights and Swedish Labour Law* (Janice Bellace & Beryl ter Haar, eds) *Research Handbook Labour, Business and Human Rights Law* (Edward Elgar: 2019).

Mia Rönnmar, *Fundamental Rights and Swedish Labour Law* (Janice Bellace & Beryl ter Haar, eds) *Research Handbook Labour, Business and Human Rights Law* (Edward Elgar: 2019).
Hans-Heinrich Vogel, *Sources of Swedish Law* (Bogdan Michael, ed.), *Swedish Legal System* (Norstedts Juridik, 2010).

CHAPTER 19

Collective Agreements on the Crest of the Legislative Wave, but the Common Law Still Making Ripples: The Sources of Labour Law in South Africa

Rochelle Le Roux

19.1 INTRODUCTION

This chapter examines the sources of labour law in South Africa. In the context of this book, the term 'sources of labour law' is understood as the instruments that litigants would turn to in order to establish and enforce their rights. The brief is to consider the hierarchy of sources at a horizontal level and to disregard the relationship between national and supra-national sources. However, in the case of South Africa, international law is firmly established as a source of labour law, even at the horizontal level. It will therefore be necessary to engage with international law in order to explain its position and relevance as a source of labour law. Further, the significance of some of the current sources of South African labour law can only be understood against the backdrop of South Africa's history and the evolution of labour regulation in South Africa. Section 19.2 provides an overview of the evolution of labour law from 1652 until 1994 when South Africa became a constitutional state. In section 19.3 the reach of the Constitution of the Republic of South Africa, 1996 (the Constitution)[1] in labour matters is explained and a short synopsis of labour legislation passed with the advent of constitutionalism is provided. Section 19.4 deliberates the continued

1. The Constitution replaced the Constitution of the Republic of South Africa, 1993, Act 200 of 1993, often referred to as the interim Constitution.

significance of precedent as a source of labour law in light of the labour dispute resolution structure established in 1995. Section 19.5 explains the continued, but perhaps waning, role of the common law and the contract of employment. In section 19.6 the levels of collective bargaining and the permeating role of collective agreements as sources of labour law are discussed. Section 19.7 explains the role of international law as a horizontal source of labour law. The conclusion in section 19.8 argues that the sources of South African labour law are now firmly embedded in a sophisticated legislative web. However, all of this must be understood against the backdrop of South Africa's unemployment rate hovering at 25% and above for a number of years, poor education and skill levels, and poor institutional support for some of the legislative structures.

19.2 HISTORICAL EVOLUTION OF LABOUR LAW IN SOUTH AFRICA (1652-1994)

South Africa has its origins in the establishment of a Dutch replenishment station at the Cape of Good Hope in 1652, but was occupied by Britain, first in 1795, and finally in 1806. From here expansion occurred northwards, with further colonisation and the establishment of a number of independent republics. The current boundaries were more or less established in 1910 with the unification of some of the different colonies and republics into the Union of South Africa. The Union of South Africa remained a British colony until 1962, when South Africa became a republic.

Even after the final British occupation, Roman-Dutch law, previously introduced by the Dutch, was retained and remains part of the South African common law. This pre-dated the codification of Dutch law and it is thus Roman-Dutch law in its purist iteration that informs the South African common law. Nonetheless, in areas of Roman-Dutch law that were not well developed, the courts turned to English law for guidance. As employment was not an autonomous institution in Roman-Dutch law and seen as a species of letting and hiring, employment is one area where the courts often turned to English law for guidance, with vicarious liability probably being the most germane example.[2]

As slaves met the labour demand, there was no significant labour regulation at the time of the final British occupation of the Cape. This only occurred after the abolition of slavery and with the introduction of the first Master and Servant laws in 1841, which remained in place in various forms until 1974.[3] From the start of the twentieth century and as South Africa emerged as a mining giant, more workers were covered by industrial relations legislation, but it was also at this point that labour regulation took on a distinctly racial dimension. The

2. R. le Rox, *The Evolution of the Contract of Employment in South Africa*, 39 I.L.J. 139, 152 (2010).
3. *Ibid.*, 144-145.

various iterations of industrial relations legislation prior to 1995 were premised on voluntary centralised collective bargaining and the possibility of extending this to non-parties within the area or industry, a feature that survived and remains part of current legislation. However, black workers – initially only men, but later also women – were excluded from the statutory system, although various legislative devices were available to extend minimum wage rates and hours to black workers, not for their protection, but rather to protect white workers from being replaced by cheaper black labour.[4] In the 1970s, black workers responded by joining unregistered unions. These unions could not operate within the statutory system and focused their energies on plant-level agreements. This led to a dual system of industrial relations: white unions within the statutory system and black unions outside it.[5] The dual system of labour regulation, however, was not limited to industrial relations. In respect of wage labour, the Master and Servant laws, essentially the regulation of employment relationships through the criminal justice system, continued to be applied in the non-industrialised sectors, primarily agriculture and domestic service.[6] However, for higher-earning servants in these sectors – mostly white – the common law was applied.[7] As these sectors were dominated by black workers, this represented another racial divide in labour relations and continued until the repeal of the Master and Servant laws in 1974.[8]

Following a number of strikes by black trade unions in the 1970s, the Wiehahn Commission of Inquiry into Labour Legislation was established and, as a result of its recommendations in 1979, a number of amendments were made to the Industrial Relations Act 28 of 1956. Apart from changing its name to the Labour Relations Act (LRA 1956), the statute was deracialised and an Industrial Court (IC) with jurisdiction to adjudicate unfair labour practices was established,[9] for the first time opening the door for individuals to litigate under the Act.[10] The definition of an 'unfair labour practice' was very broad;[11] nonetheless, the outlines of a coherent body of labour law as well as an understanding of the right to fair labour practices began to emerge from the jurisprudence of the IC.[12] With the emergence of the post-apartheid constitutional state, the right to

4. Darcy du Toit, et al., *Labour Relations Law: A Comprehensive Guide*, Chapter I, §2.1 (6th ed., LexisNexis 2015).
5. *Ibid.*, §2.2.
6. Le Roux (n. 2), 143-144.
7. *Jamieson v. Elsworth*, 115 S.A. 118 (A.D. 1915).
8. The Master and Servant laws were bolstered by prosecutions under pass laws. Le Roux (n. 2) 143-145.
9. Du Toit et al. (n. 4), Chapter I, §2.1.
10. Le Roux (n. 2), 160.
11. M.J.D. Wallis, *Labour and Employment Law* Chapter 1, §4 (Service Issue 5, Butterworths 1995). The definition was amended to include specific acts constituting unfair labour practices, but eventually the open-ended definition was reverted to.
12. *Ibid.*

fair labour practices was elevated to a constitutional right[13] and is one of the cornerstones of the Labour Relations Act 66 of 1995, which is the centrepiece of post-apartheid labour legislation. In developing its jurisprudence, the IC often turned to the common law, but in giving content to the meaning of unfair labour practices, it relied heavily on the 1982 International Labour Organisation (ILO) Convention 158 on Termination of Employment.[14] This Convention has never been ratified by South Africa, but the IC's reliance on it is an early illustration of the important role that international law would come to play in modern South African labour law, not only from a policy perspective but, as will be illustrated later, as a primary source of law.

The only other significant statutes that spoke to individual conditions of employment before 1995 were the Wage Act 5 of 1957 and the Basic Conditions of Employment Act 3 of 1983 (BCEA).[15] The former regulated wages in industries and areas with no industrial council agreement coverage and the latter prescribed minimum conditions of employment in the private sector. Both statues were criticised for their inflexibility, limited reach, poor enforcement mechanisms and the lack of protection for the most vulnerable workers: for instance, while the BCEA applied to farmworkers (from 1993) and to domestic workers (from 1994), the Wage Act never applied to them.[16] In the public sector, labour relations were regulated by the Public Service Labour Relations Proclamation 105 of 1994 and the Education Labour Relations Act 146 of 1993.

From the above, it should be clear that, by 1995, when the current LRA was passed, the sources of labour law were rather eclectic. While it is true that a spectrum of labour law-specific sources were emerging, there was no clarity about their hierarchy: the common law certainly maintained a central role; collective agreements still suffered from the legacy of the dual system of regulation, were uneven, and lacked a clear legal basis for their incorporation into individual contracts of employment; the IC was a tribunal and not a court and could not establish firm precedent; reliance on international law was sporadic rather than principled; legislation provided very little guidance on the hierarchy of sources; and separate legal frameworks existed for public sector and private sector employees. This changed with the adoption of the Constitution, the fundamental status given to the right to fair labour practices,[17] the guidance that the Constitution offers on the sources of law in general, and also by the suite of labour legislation passed after the adoption of the Constitution.

13. Section 23 of the Constitution.
14. *See*, e.g., *NUMSA v. Atlantis Diesel Engines (Pty) Ltd*, 14 I.L.J. 642 (L.A.C. 1993).
15. This Act replaced the Shops and Offices Act 75 of 1964 and the Factories, Machinery and Building Work Act 22 of 1941 which regulated minimum conditions in confined sectors.
16. Du Toit et al. (n. 4), Chapter X §2.1; Wallis (n. 11) Chapter 1, §13.
17. Section 23 of the Constitution.

19.3 THE CONSTITUTION AND THE LEGISLATIVE LANDSCAPE

The Constitution, which contains a Bill of Rights in Chapter 2, is the supreme source of law in all areas of law in South Africa. In terms of labour relations, the most significant rights in the Bill of Rights are, first and foremost, the right to fair labour practices in section 23, but also the right to freedom of association,[18] the right to demonstrate and picket,[19] and the right to equality,[20] all of which are significant in areas beyond labour relations. The right to fair labour practices is an unusual right and its fundamental status a novelty, but an acknowledgement of the role that trade unions played in ending apartheid.[21] While it remains an open-ended right with huge potential to accommodate new forms of work,[22] it is clear that it at least encompasses an individual right to form and join trade unions,[23] an individual right to strike,[24] a collective right to organise,[25] and a collective right to bargain collectively.[26] By 1995, the labour legislation in force could not adequately give effect to these fundamental rights and a major overhaul of the labour legislative landscape was required. The task of negotiating the new labour legislation was given to the National Economic, Development and Labour Council (NEDLAC).[27] The primary function of NEDLAC, a tripartite body not dissimilar to the ILO, is to seek consensus between government, organised labour and organised business in respect of labour, economic and development-related legislation before such legislation goes to Parliament for enactment. Although the labour-related legislation passed immediately after the advent of the Constitution is arguably its greatest achievement, NEDLAC continues to play a brokering role, as is seen with the amendments to labour legislation passed from time to time. However, the envisaged role of NEDLAC as a promotor of a national accord amongst its constituencies never came to fruition and hence there is no form of national-level bargaining in South Africa.[28]

The most important statutes passed to give effect to the labour-related fundamental rights were a new LRA, a new Basic Conditions of Employment Act 75 of 1997 (BCEA) and the Employment Equity Act 55 of 1998 (EEA). This legislation applied to all employees, whether employed in the public sector or

18. Section 18 of the Constitution.
19. Section 17 of the Constitution.
20. Section 9 of the Constitution.
21. Rochelle le Roux, *The New Unfair Labour Practice*, 41 (Rochelle le Roux & Alan Rycroft), *Reinventing Labour Law*, 41 (Juta 2012).
22. *Ibid.*, 54-57.
23. Section 23(2)(*a*) and (*b*) of the Constitution.
24. Section 23(2)(*c*) of the Constitution.
25. Section 23(4)(*b*) of the Constitution.
26. Section 23(5) of the Constitution.
27. Established in terms of the NEDLAC Act 35 of 1994.
28. Shane Godfrey, Johann Maree, Darcy du Toit & Jan Theron, *Collective Bargaining in South Africa*, 227-228 (Juta 2010).

private sector.[29] The three statutes share the same definition of an employee, which specifically excludes an independent contractor, thereby endorsing a contractual model of employment. Nonetheless, through the subsequent introduction of a presumption as to who is an employee,[30] deeming provisions,[31] and the amendment of the definition of dismissal to refer to the termination of employment rather than the termination of the contract of employment,[32] the exclusionary effect of the contractual model has been blunted.

The LRA has three broad aspects to it: the establishment of a labour dispute resolution structure; the regulation of collective bargaining and its agents; and the definition and regulation of unfair dismissal and unfair labour practices. The BCEA accommodates regulated flexibility by providing for minimum conditions of employment (such as working time, leave and notice periods) and tools for the downward variation of some of these conditions, but not below a certain level. Unfortunately, the enforcement of the BCEA has been poor, due to a poorly resourced labour inspectorate. The EEA is charged with the elimination of unfair discrimination and the implementation of affirmative action in the workplace.[33] Today the labour arena is regulated by a complex web of statutes (and codes of good practice and regulations) with the Constitution at the apex:[34] apart from section 39(2) of the Constitution requiring legislation to be interpreted so that it promotes the spirit, purport and objects of the Constitution, legislation must comply with the Constitution.[35] However, despite the supremacy of the Constitution, it is seldom the immediate source of a remedy for a litigant: where a statute is passed to give effect to a constitutional right, a litigant who claims that the statute is deficient in this regard must first contest the constitutionality of the legislation before relying directly on the Constitution for a cause of action.[36] The Constitution aside, the LRA and the EEA can generally be regarded as the principal sources of labour law. This is so because of section 210 of the LRA and section 63 of the EEA, which provide that, if there is a conflict between the provisions of the LRA or the EEA and 'any other law', except the Constitution, the provisions of the LRA or the EEA, as the case may be, will apply. However, a later statute with a similar provision will overrule the older statute, and it is for this reason that the EEA takes precedence over the LRA as it is a later

29. P. Ndlovu J. in *Chirwa v. Transnet Ltd*, 4 S.A. 367, paragraph 102 (C.C. 2008).
30. Section 200A of the LRA and section 83A of the BCEA.
31. Sections 198(2) and 198A-D of the LRA.
32. Section 186(2) of the LRA as amended by section 30 of the Labour Relations Amendment Act 12 of 2002.
33. Section 2 of the EEA.
34. A. Rycroft & R. le Roux, *Decolonising the Labour Law Curriculum*, 38 I.L.J. 1473, fns 9 and 10, 1476 (2017). These lists do not include mining legislation.
35. This is a general principle of constitutional interpretation, but also *see* section 3(*b*) of the LRA and section 3(*a*) of the EEA.
36. *Minister of Health v. New Clicks SA (Pty) Ltd*, 1 B.C.L.R. 1, paragraph 439 (C.C. 2006).

enactment.[37] Since the phrase 'any other law', it is suggested, not only refers to another statute, but also to delegated legislation, the common law, judicial precedent and international law, these two provisions in effect generally peg either the LRA or the EEA as the principal source of labour law beyond the Constitution. The LRA would therefore usually be the starting place for establishing labour rights outside workplace discrimination matters. Indeed, this has been confirmed by the Constitutional Court (CC) when it commented on section 210 of the LRA: 'This section heralds the LRA as the pre-eminent legislation in labour matters that are dealt with by that Act. Only the Constitution itself or a statute that expressly amends the LRA can take precedence in application to such labour matters.'[38]

Almost all the post-constitutional labour legislation provides for the publication of Codes of Good Practice that must be taken into account by a person interpreting or applying that particular statute.[39] While these Codes provide guidelines and are not capable of supporting independent rights, it is mandatory to consider them and to show good reason when deviating from them.[40]

Legislation (and its derivatives), however, can seldom solve all labour disputes. It can provide minimum standards (i.e., the BCEA) or regulate processes (i.e., collective bargaining) within which to nurture minimum standards, but it cannot rule on its own application or interpretation. Unless provision is made for dedicated labour dispute resolution bodies, the civil courts will usually be called upon to do this. In the case of South Africa, 'a one-stop shop dispute-resolution structure',[41] in the form of the Commission for Conciliation Mediation and Arbitration (CCMA), a Labour Court (LC) and a Labour Appeal Court (LAC), has been established by the LRA. Beyond the legislation that these structures are required to apply or interpret, they can turn to three additional aides for guidance: the common law, stare decisis and, perhaps unusually, international law. The following paragraphs will focus on these.

19.4 THE COURTS AND STARE DECISIS

The virtues of stare decisis or the doctrine of precedent are widely acknowledged and the doctrine has been accepted as part of South African law since at least 1880.[42] The doctrine not only binds lower courts but also binds courts of final

37. There is no similar provision in the BCEA and, in the event of a conflict, the LRA or the EEA will overrule the BCEA.
38. P. Skweyiya J. in *Chirwa v. Transnet Ltd*, 4 S.A. 367, paragraph 50 (C.C. 2008).
39. Section 203 of the LRA; section 87 of the BCEA and section 54 read with section 3(c) of the EEA.
40. *Moropane v. Gilbeys Distillers & Vintners*, 19 I.L.J. 635, 640I (L.C. 1998). Rycroft & Le Roux (n. 34) fn 10, 1476.
41. P. Skweyiya J. in *Chirwa v. Transnet Ltd*, 4 S.A. 367, paragraph 54 (C.C. 2008).
42. Herman Robert Hahlo & Ellison Kahn, *The South African Legal System and Its Background*, 214, 240 (Juta 1968).

jurisdiction to their own decisions; the latter can depart from previous decisions of their own only when they are satisfied that the previous decisions are clearly wrong.

The advent of constitutionalism did not change this, and the doctrine continues to apply, even in respect of pre-constitutional judgments, save when a judgment is in conflict with the Constitution or was based on *boni mores* that do not reflect constitutional values.[43]

The IC, established in 1979, was a tribunal, not a court, and did not create precedent. Its jurisdiction was premised on the perpetration of an unfair labour practice that was coached in very broad terms, i.e., 'any labour practice which in the opinion of the industrial court is an unfair labour practice'. The IC seldom engaged with the definition of an unfair labour practice and its principal function was to determine whether the industrial relations conduct brought before it was unfair – rather than unlawful – and, if so, whether the conduct constituted an unfair labour practice.[44] Since matters were decided on the factual circumstances before the court, decisions were not of general application.[45] Nonetheless, general principles emerged from similar cases and, by the time the IC was dissolved in 1995, sufficient clarity had developed about conduct that would typically constitute an unfair labour practice to inform the definition of an unfair labour practice in the LRA. Initially, there was no right of appeal against a decision of the IC, but in 1998 a LAC with a similar status as that of a High Court[46] was established.[47] Whereas stare decisis did not apply to the IC, it did apply to the then LAC and henceforth the IC would have been bound by the decisions of the LAC. In that way, the LAC would have played some role in developing the meaning of an unfair labour practice. Because of the relatively short lifespan of this LAC – it was dissolved with the repeal in 1995 of the LRA 1956 – it was probably less influential than the IC in shaping the meaning of an unfair labour practice. Nonetheless, because of the application of stare decisis, its judgments remain valid precedent to the extent that they had not become obsolete because of the repeal of the underlying legislation. It is not unusual for the current LC and LAC to refer to these judgments when engaging with general notions such as fairness and equity.

The current LC was established as a court of law and equity and with the same status as a division of the High Court.[48] It has exclusive jurisdiction in

43. Section 39(2) of the Constitution. Also *see Afrox Healthcare Bpk v. Strydom*, 6 S.A. 21, paragraphs 27-30 (S.C.A. 2002) and *Camps Bay Ratepayers' and Residents' Association v. Harrison*, 4 S.A. 42, paragraphs 28-30 (C.C. 2011).
44. Wallis (n. 11) Chapter 1, § 4.
45. *Ibid.*
46. The current High Court was then called the Supreme Court. Today the superior civil courts consist of various divisions of the High Court, the SCA and the CC.
47. Labour Relations Amendment Act 83 of 1988.
48. Section 151(1) of the LRA. Also *see* section 77(3) of the BCEA.

respect of most statutory employment-related issues, but in respect of a small number of issues it has concurrent jurisdiction with the High Court (e.g., the contract of employment and violations of fundamental rights, other than labour rights, arising from employment or labour relations).[49] The LAC, also established as a court of law and equity and having similar status to the Supreme Court of Appeal (SCA),[50] is the final Court of Appeal in labour-related matters, except in those matters raising constitutional issues, which may be appealed to the CC.[51] The LC is bound by stare decisis and must follow a judgment of the LAC even if it is of the view that it is wrong. The application of stare decisis is very much a consequence of the common law, but is reinforced by section 182 of the LRA, which provides that a judgment of the LAC is binding on the LC. The application of the general principle of stare decisis in its common-law guise further means that the LC is bound by another judgment of the LC unless it is of the view that the judgment is clearly wrong.[52] Both the LC and the LAC are bound by the judgments of the CC. In respect of the issues where there is concurrent jurisdiction with the High Court, the LC would be bound by a judgment of a High Court of higher standing or a judgment of a High Court with similar standing, unless it is of the view that the latter is clearly wrong, and the same would apply to the LAC in respect of the SCA. It is not quite certain what the designation of the LC and the LAC as courts of equity implies and has seldom been debated in the courts. It has been suggested that this description should be repealed as it adds nothing to the jurisdiction of the court,[53] but it might point to considerations that would inform fairness and would ordinarily not be relevant in disputes of a purely commercial nature.[54]

While the LC continues to adjudicate the unlawfulness of contractual disputes, applying principles of common law, it is, unlike the civil courts, firmly charged with the fairness of employment conduct. However, the LC does not have jurisdiction over matters covered by a collective agreement.[55] Disputes about the interpretation and application of collective agreements must be resolved through a process provided for in the agreement or, failing this, by the CCMA.[56]

The CCMA is the primary dispute resolution body established by the LRA and generally all non-contractual disputes, whether of a collective or individual nature, must first be referred to the CCMA for conciliation before being referred

49. Section 157(1) and (2) of the LRA.
50. Section 167(1) and (2) of the LRA.
51. Section 167(3) of the LRA. Also *see* the Constitution Seventeenth Amendment Act of 2012.
52. *Tiger Wheels Babelegi (Pty) Ltd t/a TSW International v. NUMSA*, 1 B.L.L.R 66 (L.C. 1999).
53. *3M SA (Pty) Ltd v. SACCAWU*, 5 B.L.L.R. 483, paragraph 17 (L.A.C. 2001).
54. *Transman v. SAPO*, 8 B.L.L.R. 834, paragraph 15 (L.C. 2005).
55. Section 24 read with section 157(5) of the LRA.
56. Section 24 of the LRA.

for arbitration or adjudication, depending on the nature of the dispute.[57] Conciliation proceedings are not published, but arbitration awards are published and widely accessible. Although arbitration awards might have some persuasive value, they are not subject to the doctrine of stare decisis and are not binding.

19.5 THE COMMON LAW AND THE CONTRACT OF EMPLOYMENT

The common-law contract of employment remains an important source of labour law. Of course, the presence of a contract of employment is the clearest indication that a worker is an employee and entitled to statutory labour protection. However, in recent years, mostly to protect vulnerable workers, statutory protection has been extended to workers even in cases where it is not obvious that a contract of employment has been concluded in common-law terms.[58] This is not to say that the courts are disregarding the need for an underlying contract. Indeed, the courts continue to examine contractual arrangements between parties to discern the true nature of the relationship between parties and do not hesitate to find that there is no employment if there is no contract at all or if, in the absence of a sham, the contract does not suggest employment: In a matter where the relationship between a priest and a church was at issue, the LAC found that the presumption as to who is an employee presupposes a 'legally enforceable agreement or some contractual working arrangement' and that 'an employment relationship presupposes a working arrangement of a contractual nature between two or more persons, in circumstances where the rights, duties and obligations *inter partes* are legally enforceable'.[59] More recently, the LC found that the concession by drivers that there was no contract (of any kind) between them and Uber SA – the entity that they choose to sue – was fatal to their claim that they were employees of Uber SA.[60]

The common-law contract of employment, even without statutory intervention, has never been a static institution and, through the jurisprudential development of the common law, a number of terms have been implied into the contract of employment.[61] This stemmed from the courts' inherent jurisdiction to develop the common law,[62] but this is now reinforced by section 8(3) of the Constitution which requires courts, when applying a provision of Bill of Rights, to develop the common law to the extent that legislation does not give effect to

57. Bargaining councils, if accredited, can perform some of the dispute resolution functions of the CCMA. *See* sections 51-52 of the LRA.
58. Section 200A of the LRA.
59. *Universal Church of The Kingdom of God v. Myeni*, 36 I.L.J. 2832, paragraphs 40 and 51 (L.A.C. 2015).
60. *Uber SA Technology Services (Pty) Ltd v. NUPSAW*, 39 I.L.J. 903, paragraph 73 (L.C. 2018). Also *see Phaka v. Bracks NO*, 36 I.L.J. 1541 (L.A.C. 2015).
61. *SA Maritime Safety Authority v. McKenzie*, 3 S.A. 601, paragraph 11 (S.C.A. 2010).
62. *Afrox Healthcare Bpk v. Strydom*, 6 S.A. 21, paragraph 29 (S.C.A. 2002).

that provision.[63] Although there have been attempts, relying on section 23 in the Bill of Rights, to develop the common law so that a right to fair dealing and, more specifically, a right to a pre-dismissal hearing, can be implied into the contract of employment, the courts have resisted this. They have done so on the basis that legislation in the form of the LRA is giving effect to these rights, but the SCA still indicated that in the narrow instances where the LRA does not apply - e.g., the armed forces - such a development might be necessary.[64] However, even for employees covered by labour legislation, it is conceivable that where the legislation is not giving proper effect to the constitutional right to fair labour practices, it might become necessary for the courts to develop implied terms through development of the common law. Nonetheless, it is far more likely that terms would be implied by the operation of law rather than through the development of the common law.

Hence, once employment is established, either because there is clearly a contract of employment in place or because one is imputed through legislative or jurisprudential fiat, the actual terms and conditions of employment will need to be constructed from whatever express or tacit terms might have been agreed to by the parties, terms implied by the common law, and, as will be shown below, by legislation and/or relevant collective agreements. The rest of this paragraph will focus on terms implied by statute and collective agreements.

The provisions of the BCEA constitute terms of any contract of employment unless the actual terms of the contract are more favourable, another law provides more favourable terms, or the provisions have been varied in a manner permitted by the BCEA.[65] These variations can be achieved in a number of ways, but a collective agreement is one such permitted method of variation.[66] In line with the statute's aim of regulated flexibility, the variation may, subject to the statutory floors, also be downward. The BCEA does not apply universally: some provisions apply only to employees who earn above a threshold,[67] work a certain number of hours,[68] or occupy a certain position.[69] It is also not possible to contract out of the provisions of the BCEA.[70] Although wages are central to employment, the BCEA has never prescribed minimum wages, but provides for the publication of sectoral determinations - another permissible means of varying the BCEA - typically in sectors without a strong collective bargaining tradition.[71] Until recently, this was the only means of setting minimum wages for

63. When developing the common law, courts must promote the spirit, purport and objects of the Bill of Rights. Section 39(2) of the Constitution.
64. *SA Maritime Safety Authority v. McKenzie,* 3 S.A. 601, paragraph 54 (S.C.A. 2010).
65. Section 4 of the BCEA.
66. For example sections 12 and 49 of the BCEA.
67. For example section 6(3) of the BCEA.
68. For example section 19(1) of the BCEA.
69. For example sections 3 and 6(1) of the BCEA.
70. Section 5 of the BCEA.
71. Section 51 of the BCEA.

a particular sector. This has now changed after the recent promulgation of the Minimum Wage Act 8 of 2018, which applies to all workers,[72] regardless of the sector in which they work and which replaces wage determinations made under the BCEA if the latter are below the new statutory minimum wage.

It is not only the provisions of the BCEA, and now minimum wage legislation, that can reshape the agreed terms of the contract of employment. Apart from varying the BCEA via a collective agreement, the terms of a collective agreement generally trump a contract of employment. Under the LRA 1956, the courts struggled to find a legal basis that could explain the variation of a contract of employment by a collective agreement, but this is now addressed by sections 23 and 199 of the LRA.

Section 23(3) provides that a collective agreement varies the contract of employment if the employer and the employee are both bound by the collective agreement.[73] Section 199 provides that a contract of employment entered into before or after the coming into effect of a collective agreement may not permit an employee to receive lesser remuneration, benefits or treatment than provided by a collective agreement binding the parties, and it is not possible for the parties to contract out of this scheme.[74] The combined effect of these two provisions is that a legal basis is provided for the incorporation of the collective agreement into the contract of employment and a floor of minimum conditions are established below which a contract of employment may not go. Thus, when a collective agreement prescribes not actual, but minimum, terms and conditions, more beneficial contracts of employment will be unaffected, as are matters not covered by the collective agreement. Where the collective agreement provides for actual conditions of employment, these are deemed to be incorporated into the contract even if the parties have agreed to more favourable terms. This is so in order not to undermine the supremacy of collective bargaining.[75]

The earnings threshold determined in terms of the BCEA is occasionally also used to determine the application of other legislation. The provisions on non-standard employment in the LRA, introduced in 2015, are an important example.[76] These provisions apply to employees earning below the threshold and who are placed with a client by a labour broker; employed on a fixed-term contract for longer than three months where the use of a fixed-term contract

72. The statute has wider application than traditional labour legislation as it applies to workers and not employees. A worker is defined without reference to a contract and as any person who works for another and who receives, or is entitled to receive, any payment for that work, whether in money or in kind.
73. This is discussed in §6.
74. Section 199(2) of the LRA.
75. Du Toit et al. (n. 4) *see* Chapter V, § 5.2 and fn. 282.
76. Section 198A-D of the LRA.

cannot be justified; and part-time employees. The provisions provide for employment to be on similar terms and conditions as those that apply to comparable permanent employees at that workplace and, where applicable, for employment to become indefinite. These provisions are another clear illustration of the legislature's ability to reshape the contract of employment without the consensus of the parties, in order to bring their terms and conditions into line with whatever norm applies to those in indefinite employment at the workplace in question. These norms, in turn, might have their origin in contract, legislation and/or collective agreements.

The above illustrates that the contract of employment has, in varying degrees and depending on whether an individual earns below or above the earnings threshold, become a morphed institution and in many ways it is simply a fiction: 'something' with terms resembling a contract of employment, which is constructed from legislative provisions, collective agreements and/or the norm at the workplace, without the parties ever reaching consensus on those terms or having reached consensus on completely opposite terms.

19.6 COLLECTIVE BARGAINING AND COLLECTIVE AGREEMENTS

In the previous section, the legal basis for the variation of contracts of employment by collective agreement was explained. This paragraph highlights more fully the profound reach of collective agreements by clarifying when such variation may occur.

The right to engage in collective bargaining is entrenched in the Bill of Rights and is one of the cornerstones of the LRA which, in turn, is informed by three principles: majoritarianism, voluntarism and sectoral bargaining.[77] The supremacy of collective bargaining is demonstrated by the fact that the right to strike – another fundamental right – can be limited by collective agreements[78] and, further, by the LC not having jurisdiction over disputes concerning the application or interpretation of collective agreements.[79] It should therefore come as no surprise, as shown in section 19.5, that collective agreements generally trump individual contractual arrangements where the employer and the employee are both bound by a collective agreement.

Bargaining councils are the platform preferred by the LRA for the delivery of centralised bargaining and can be established for a sector[80] and an area. However, not all sectors in South Africa are covered by bargaining councils. For

77. Debbie Collier, et al., *Labour Law in South Africa: Context and Principles*, 332 (D. Collier, E. Fergus) (Oxford 2018).
78. Section 65(1)(*a*) of the LRA.
79. Section 24 read with section 157(5) of the LRA.
80. A sector means a service or an industry. *See* section 213 of the LRA.

instance, the services, mining, manufacturing and domestic sectors – all numerically significant sectors – are not organised into bargaining councils. This is partly a consequence of voluntarism, the fact that some sectors are simply not suited to central collective bargaining,[81] or a lack of effective organisation. In these sectors collective bargaining is either accommodated through private central structures (e.g., mining), limited to plant-level bargaining (e.g., services) or covered by sectoral determinations under the BCEA (e.g., domestic workers) as a surrogate for collective bargaining.

Despite the LRA's support for sectoral bargaining, it was always envisaged that multi-level bargaining will continue with sectoral agreements the site for the conclusion of minimum conditions, and actual conditions negotiated at plant level. Workplace forums were envisaged to be the primary structure for negotiations at plant level.[82] However, employers have generally resisted multi-level bargaining and trade unions, fearing the erosion of their power, have not supported the establishment of workplace forums, with very few in existence.[83] Consequently, sectoral agreements have by and large set actual conditions of employment, leaving little scope for either trade unions functioning at plant level, or individuals, to negotiate improved conditions of employment.[84] However, where a sectoral agreement does not prohibit plant-level bargaining on a topic covered by that sectoral agreement, a workplace agreement concluded will usually provide for improved conditions of employment or address workplace-specific matters not covered by the sectoral agreement.

Section 23(3) addressed the lacuna in previous legislation, which did not provide a clear legal basis for the incorporation of collective agreements into individual contracts, but also prescribes the moment when such variation will occur, namely *when both the employee and the employer are bound by the collective agreement*.

The LRA, almost intuitively, provides that collective agreements are binding on the parties to the agreement and, depending on the context, also the members of the parties (e.g., a trade union member) to the collective agreement.[85] Such binding effect is for the duration of the collective agreement.[86] Even if a member resigns from a trade union during the currency of the collective agreement, or joins the trade union party after the conclusion of the collective agreement, the member will be bound by it.[87] However, less intuitively, collective agreements can also be binding beyond the parties or members of a party to a collective agreement. The LRA provides a mechanism for the

81. Also *see* Godfrey et al. (n. 28), 188-189.
82. Godfrey et al. (n. 28), 226-229.
83. *Ibid.*
84. C. Todd, *Collective Bargaining Law*, 94 (Siber Ink 2004).
85. Sections 31 and 23(1)(*a*)-(*c*) of the LRA.
86. Section 23(2) of the LRA.
87. Section 23(2) of the LRA.

obligatory extension by the Minister of Labour of collective agreements concluded in the bargaining council to non-parties when the trade unions and employers' organisations voting for the extension represent the interests of the majority of employees represented in the council (and gives the Minister a discretion to do so if these parties are sufficiently representative).[88] The LRA's preference for majoritarianism is further illustrated by its provision for the extension of any collective agreements in a workplace to non-parties if the trade union party has as its members the majority of the employer's employees in that workplace.[89] The effect of these provisions is profound because such extensions not only limit the right to strike off the non-parties but also vary their contracts of employment. The constitutionality and legality of these expressions of majoritarianism in the LRA have been subjected to a number of court challenges, but have been found not to offend the Constitution, primarily because they advance orderly collective bargaining.[90] Whatever the criticism against the foundational principles of the LRA, the provisions providing for extensions are an illustration of the importance of collective agreements as a source of labour law in South Africa. Indeed, their quasi-judicial nature has been confirmed by the CC when it commented that 'invoking s 23(1)*(d)* is not simply a private matter between private parties. It affects the public. The rationale for the power and its exercise is the public interest in improving workers' conditions through collectively agreed bargains. What is more, the decision to conclude and extend the agreement is rooted in parliament's exercise of its legislative power: it is licensed by legislation.'[91]

19.7 INTERNATIONAL LAW

When the IC was given jurisdiction over unfair labour practices, the meaning of an unfair labour practice was by no means clear. Although the nomenclature probably had its origins in the United States, it was clear that the South African hybrid was aimed, not only at employer and trade union relations but also at the employment relationship itself. Being something of a phantom, the IC often turned to ILO instruments for guidance in order to flesh out the meaning of an unfair labour practice. The use of international law as a source of labour law was therefore a practice that was well entrenched by the time the LRA was passed. However, both the Constitution and the trilogy of major labour statutes passed

88. Section 32 of the LRA.
89. Section 23(1)(*d*) of the LRA.
90. *AMCU v. Chamber of Mines of South Africa*, 3 S.A. 242 (C.C. 2017); *Free Market Foundation v. Minister of Labour* 37 I.L.J. 1638 (G.P. 2016); *Confederation of Associations in the Private Employment Sector v. Motor Industry Bargaining Council*, 36 I.L.J. 137 (G.P. 2015).
91. *AMCU v. Chamber of Mines of SA*, 38 I.L.J. 831, paragraph 79 (C.C. 2017).

at the time promoted the use of international law from a practice to a compulsion.

The Constitution provides that customary international law is law in South Africa,[92] but also entreats courts, when interpreting legislation, to prefer an interpretation that is consistent with international law over an interpretation that is inconsistent with international law.[93] Given that international conventions, whether they have been ratified or not, are regarded as a source of customary international law, courts in labour matters are obliged to interpret labour legislation with due regard to ILO Conventions.[94] The eminence of international law is reinforced by a constitutional instruction that, when interpreting the Bill of Rights, a court, tribunal or forum *must consider international law* and may consider foreign law[95] and by labour legislation underscoring the role of international law in their interpretation, whether ILO conventions specifically, or international conventions more generally.[96] This implies that international law not only informs the broad sentiments underlying labour legislation, but can also vividly determine the minutiae of disputes where legislation leaves doubt: the right of a minority union to strike,[97] the definition of employee in the context of migrants,[98] severance pay for retrenched employees,[99] the jurisdiction of the LC when both parties are *peregrines*,[100] and procedural fairness in the case of dismissal[101] are all examples of issues where the outcome was either finally determined or at least significantly influenced by international law and/or foreign law.[102]

19.8 CONCLUSION

Labour regulation in South Africa, and hence the sources of labour law, can be divided into roughly four periods. The first wave of labour regulation started after slavery was abolished and lasted from 1841 until the early 1900s. During this period the Master and Servant laws, and to a lesser extent, the common law, were the predominant sources of labour law. The second wave started with the introduction of industrial relations legislation and continued until 1979, when

92. Section 232 of the Constitution.
93. Section 233 of the Constitution.
94. Halton Cheadle, *Reception of International Standards in Common-Law Legal Systems*, 256 in Le Roux & Rycroft (n. 21) 248. Also *see S v. Makwanyane*, 3 S.A. 391 (C.C. 1995).
95. Section 39(1) of the Constitution.
96. Section 1(*b*) of the LRA; Section 2(*b*) of the BCEA and section 3(*d*) of the EEA.
97. *NUMSA v. Bader Bop (Pty) Ltd*, 3 S.A. 513 (C.C. 2003).
98. *Discovery Health Ltd v. CCMA*, 29 I.L.J. 1480 (L.C. 2008).
99. *Irvin & Johnson Ltd v. CCMA*, 27 I.L.J. 935 (L.A.C. 2006); *Rogers v. Exactocraft (Pty) Ltd*, 36 I.L.J. 277 (L.C. 2015).
100. *Moslemany v. Unilever Plc*, 27 I.L.J. 2656 (L.C. 2006).
101. *Avril Elizabeth Home for the Mentally Handicapped v. CCMA*, 27 I.L.J. 1644 (L.C. 2006).
102. Collier & Fergus (n. 77), 60-64.

major amendments were made to the LRA 1956. During this period the main sources of labour law were sectoral agreements, the common law and the waning Master and Servant laws. It was also during this period that labour regulation took on a distinctly racial character since labour regulation was organised along racial lines. The third wave started in 1979 with the deracialisation of industrial relations laws and the introduction of the unfair labour practice concept. While the common law still informed decision-making, unfairness began to compete with unlawfulness as the central notion of labour law, and collective agreements assumed a more pervasive role in industrial relations. It was during this time that labour law became recognised as an autonomous discipline and taught as a subject in South African universities. The current (fourth) wave took off in the mid-1990s when the right to fair labour practices, the right to bargain collectively and the right to strike were given fundamental status by the Constitution, augmented by the LRA, the BCEA and the EEA. Backed by a comprehensive dispute resolution structure in the form of the CCMA, the LC and the LAC, unfairness displaced unlawfulness as the lodestar of decision-making. This is not to say that the common law is obsolete: it continues to play a significant role in matters such as restraint of trade and vicarious liability and where lawfulness is in dispute, but in many ways the contract of employment is simply a nominal notion on which to peg the definition of employee and the terms and conditions of employment, whether originating from the BCEA or collective agreements. While they are not always concluded as centrally as originally envisaged, collective agreements are powerful quasi-legislative instruments that can suspend the right to strike and their tentacles reach far beyond the parties to the agreements.

Today a sophisticated web of legislation (with the Constitution at the apex) is the dominant source of South African labour law. Given the significant reach of collective agreements and their symbiotic relationship with legislation, they are probably the penultimate source of South African labour law. The common law is a constitutionally endorsed source of law and lives on in certain pockets of the labour arena, but has by and large been reduced to a notional framework hosting the rights originating from a combination of statutes and collective agreements. Precedent is at best a secondary source of labour law, but remains a key vehicle for certainty and consistency. International law is a constitutionally recognised source of law and has played cameo roles in settling doubtful issues, but is not a front-line source of labour law. It is hard to see this hierarchy changing in the foreseeable future. Given the dawn of the Fourth Industrial Revolution, the erosion of employment, and the fact that trade unions and collective bargaining are under threat, a decline in the significance of collective agreements as a source of law might be on the cards. However, given South Africa's continued high levels of unemployment and poor education and skill levels, it is difficult to see the return of the common-law contract of employment, which assumes equal bargaining power, as a major source of law. It is more likely that legislation will continue to be the leading source of labour law: whether it will provide effective protection depends on its enforcement mechanisms and its understanding of the definition of employee. Herein, it is suggested, lie the seeds for the next wave of labour regulation.

BIBLIOGRAPHY

Debbie Collier, et al., *Labour Law in South Africa: Context and Principles* (Debbie Collier & Emma Fergus) (Oxford 2018).

Darcy du Toit, et al., *Labour Relations Law: A Comprehensive Guide* (6th ed., LexisNexis 2015).

Shane Godfrey, Johann Maree, Darcy du Toit & Jan Theron, *Collective Bargaining in South Africa* (Juta 2010).

Rochelle le Roux & Alan Rycroft, *Reinventing Labour Law* (Juta 2012).

R. le Roux, *The Evolution of the Contract of Employment in South Africa*, 39 I.L.J. 139, 152 (2010).

Rochelle le Roux, *The New Unfair Labour Practice*, 41 (Rochelle le Roux & Alan Rycroft), *Reinventing Labour Law* (Juta 2012).

Herman Robert Hahlo & Ellison Kahn, *The South African Legal System and Its Background*, 214, 240 (Juta 1968).

A. Rycroft & R. le Roux, *Decolonising the Labour Law Curriculum*, 38 I.L.J. 1473 (2017).

Chris Todd, *Collective Bargaining Law* (Siber Ink 2004).

M.J.D. Wallis, *Labour and Employment Law* (Service Issue 5, Butterworths 1995).

CHAPTER 20

The Informing Ethos Behind the Sources of UK National Labour Law

Michael Doherty & David Mangan

20.1 INTRODUCTION

The sources of United Kingdom (UK) national labour law[1] will likely continue to be a fascinating area of study as the UK removes itself from the European Union (EU); setting out on the 'British Way'[2] when the country establishes itself as an individual trading partner (separate from the EU). Still, Lord Wedderburn's summary of labour law in the UK remains apt: 'It is a place where law, politics and social assumptions meet in a person'.[3]

Unlike other jurisdictions considered in this volume, the UK does not operate under a written constitutional system. Rather, it employs an unwritten Constitution which places the government in a pivotal role of directing the sources of national labour law. As we will see, the government influence, certainly since the 1980s, has resulted in a predominantly economic approach to labour law regulation.[4] Statutes have been the primary source of national labour law in the UK; with case law supplementing these provisions. There have been two distinct models since the period beginning immediately after the Second

1. The discussion here focuses on labour law in England and Wales; there are some distinctions in the relevant law of Northern Ireland and Scotland.
2. M. Taylor, *Good Work: The Taylor Review of Modern Working Practices*, 7 (2017).
3. L. Wedderburn, *The Worker and the Law*, 835 (3rd ed. Pelican, 1986).
4. The focus here is on the economic emphasis of labour regulation. This is not to overlook that social impacts also remain, notably during the time of exiting the EU. For further discussion, *see* M. Doherty, *Through the Looking Glass: Brexit, Free Movement and the Future*, 27 KLJ 375 (2016).

World War;[5] the period of collective laissez-faire, and the more recent deregulatory, interventionist approach. Political will to support or change the model has been pivotal. Underlying each perspective has been the private law principles of obligations (primarily contract law). The political (and increasingly economic) influences on labour law regulation complicate this study. The intermingling may be somewhat challenging to follow.[6] Nevertheless, this chapter will outline, in an abbreviated space, how UK labour law has evolved since World War II in a manner that is strongly shaped by the prevailing political perceptions. To that end, a historical rendering of signposts will be utilised.

The two separate systems used since the Second World War speak to two different outlooks within the UK. With collective laissez-faire, discussed in section 20.2 below, the parties largely negotiated particular arrangements fitting their circumstances. The collective laissez-faire period has been described as one of government abstention from legislating. This may give an incorrect impression that the state left matters exclusively to the social partners. Rather, the state did regulate but in a manner that subtly supported a collective bargaining/collective agreement framework. Flexibility, though, has been a persistent hallmark of UK labour law which, perhaps paradoxically, meant that this collective framework may not necessarily be legally binding. Collective bargaining in the UK generally occurs at the company level. However, collective agreements, as a general principle, have not been legally enforceable for several decades[7] and they are usually not binding.[8] Despite this, the term-setting aspect of collective agreements can become legally effective through the incorporation of terms into individual contracts.[9] As fervour for greater national intervention increased (expressed by government legislation), the collective laissez-faire approach faded. Labour relations became a matter of national importance as concern about increasing levels of industrial action across the country mounted. The dominant focus was on curbing the power of trade unions; whether it be their political influence or their effectiveness in collective bargaining. In 1979, the Conservative Government marked the start of a neoliberal deregulation era, as outlined in section 20.3 below. The 1980s saw legislative interventions that sought to diminish the role of trade unions. Unionisation rates started to gradually decline; in the early twenty-first century approximately 23.4% of employees are trade union members, with the majority of those working in the

5. For a summary of the framework before the end of World War II, *see* K. Ewing & J. Hendy, *New Perspectives on Collective Labour Law: Trade Union Recognition and Collective Bargaining*, 46 ILJ 23 (2017).
6. Davies put forward a compelling overview of the area in A.C.L. Davies, *Perspectives on Labour Law* (Cambridge: CUP, 2003). *See* especially Chapter 1.
7. *Ford v. AUEF* [1969] 2 QB 303.
8. S. Deakin & G.S. Morris, *Labour Law*, 9-26 (6th ed Hart, 2012).
9. Deakin & Morris (n. 8).

public sector.[10] With the election of a Labour Government in 1997 (after close to two decades of Conservative leadership), some hoped for a union resurgence. However, the optimism was quickly dashed. The 'New Labour' government largely followed the deregulatory approach of its Conservative predecessors. Criticism of this era of British Government centred around its (at least perceived) endorsement of neoliberalism; something that would philosophically stand out for a trade union-based political party. The ensuing governments (the Coalition (between the Conservative and Liberal Democrat parties) and the Conservative majority of 2015) left the path set in the 1980s relatively undisturbed; though in the later period it rekindled the more aggressive legislative agenda of the 1980s. The sum effect has been a withering of workers' protection (and a facsimile of 1970s labour unions).

The austerity measures employed by the government at the time of the economic crisis post-2008 illustrate, amongst other points, how employment regulation has been subsumed by economics. Productivity levels have been a focal point and, at this time, lower production has been used to justify austerity steps.[11] The measurement was based on comparison with the highpoint of 2007 Quarter 4 figures.[12] The danger in looking at the predicament as one of low labour productivity was that it easily fell into a theme that in England has a long history – worker lethargy and its associated ills. The outlook ignores that both productivity and wages over the last forty years have increased and data from July 2014 showed that productivity had surpassed real wages (keeping in mind a figure of 87% inflation during that period).[13] The fall in wages has been used to explain why UK employment was not more negatively affected during the recession.[14] According to the Governor of the Bank of England, workers during the crisis seemed to have 'effectively priced themselves into low-productivity

10. Department for Business, Energy and Industrial Strategy, *Trade Union Membership Statistics 2018* (30 May 2019). Within the public and private sectors, unionisation sat at 52.5% and 13.2% respectively. In figures, the peak was around 1979 with 13 million members with the figure as of May 2018 sitting at around 6.23 million: (sources respectively) Department of Trade and Industry, *Labour Market Trends* (2009) 329-330; Trade Unions Congress, '*Trade Union Membership Is Growing, but There's Still Work to Do*' (2018) https://www.tuc.org.uk/blogs/trade-union-membership-growing-there's-still-work-do (Last accessed August 2019).
11. Private sector per hour labour productivity was at about 8% below its pre-crisis peak as of August 2013: Bank of England, *Inflation Report August 2013*, 26 (2013).
12. N. Oulton & M. Sebastia-Barriel, *Long and Short-Term Effects of the Financial Crisis on Labour Productivity, Capital and Output*, Bank of England Working Paper No. 470 (2013). It should be noted that the data supporting a finding of lower productivity (such as the 2007 Q4 information) is not beyond query. The Bank of England questioned the sustainability of the financial services sector's productivity prior to the recession: Bank of England, *Inflation Report August 2013* (2013).
13. Office for National Statistics, *UK Wages over the Past Four Decades – 2014* (3 July 2014). *WERS 2011* has also noted a fall in real terms of average earnings. The recession, however, does not explain away a troubling trend.
14. B. Van Wanrooy, et al., *The 2011 Workplace Employment Relations Study: First Findings* 121 (BIS, 2013).

work at a time of weak demand.'[15] This is not to cast aside positives. For example, lower wages may have contributed to keeping employment levels higher during trying economic times. Also, maintaining some level of employment helps workers retain and develop new skills.[16] These positive points do not obfuscate the fact that lower productivity figures precipitated concerns which the government believed required austerity measures.

Since the 1970s the traditional suspicion of labour towards the courts has seemingly dissipated in favour of accessing courts in order to enforce rights. Section 20.4 below outlines this shift. In a 1987 article, Lord Wedderburn[17] argued passionately for the autonomy of labour law: its separation from the common law courts. The time is now different. In this period of the UK leaving the EU, worker advocates are turning to the common law courts in order to establish or entrench employment protections. This more recent appeal to the common law underscores the muted force of collective labour relations in the UK of the twenty-first century. Moreover, reliance upon, and resort to, common law redress continues the individuating process initiated in the 1980s. Workers appeal to the courts now in order to mitigate government intervention. The UK Supreme Court's 2017 decision in *R (on the application of UNISON) v. Lord Chancellor*[18] buoys the current optimism in common law redress.

With the many uncertainties facing the country, there is evidence of pessimism, tinged with pockets of hope, regarding labour law in the UK. Contemplating a slowing economy in the coming years (as forecast by the Organisation for Economic Co-operation and Development (OECD) in 2017[19] and a Discussion Paper from the Bank of England[20]), UK labour law will likely continue to be steered by governments focusing on economic competitiveness. Legislative efforts show little sign of shifting away from that point. Redress through the common law courts has reallocated efforts to the legal route. Still, the dual efforts of legal redress through the common law courts coupled with political/public efforts to effect positive legislative change are necessarily intermingled.

15. Bank of England, *Remarks by Given by Mark Carney, Governor of the Bank of England*, Davos CBI British Business Leaders Lunch (24 January 2014), 7.
16. *Ibid.*, 8.
17. L. Wedderburn, *Labour Law: From Here to Autonomy?*, 16 ILJ 1 (1987). *See also* D. Howarth, *The Autonomy of Labour Law: A Response to Professor Wedderburn*, 17 ILJ 11 (1988).
18. [2017] UKSC 51.
19. OECD, 'United Kingdom – Economic forecast summary (November 2017)' http://www.oecd.org/unitedkingdom/united-kingdom-economic-forecast-summary.htm (Last accessed 30 July 2019).
20. Bank of England (External Monetary Policy Unit), *The Brexit Vote, Productivity Growth and Macroeconomic Adjustments in the United Kingdom*, Discussion Paper No. 51 (2019).

20.2 COLLECTIVE LAISSEZ-FAIRE: THE SOURCES OF NATIONAL LABOUR LAW POST-1945

Sir Otto Kahn-Freund QC famously characterised the UK after World War II as a locale for 'collective laissez-faire' labour relations.[21] He perceived labour law's role being 'to regulate, to support and to restrain the power of management and the power of organised labour' and 'to redress any disequilibrium of power'.[22] While the description no longer applied by the 1980s, the points that would bring about its end started in the 1960s.

Collective laissez-faire was a time of strong liberalism (in a more classical sense). Davies and Freedland (who chronicled this period through to the deregulatory time in the 1980s) characterised the period as 'doubly abstentionist' because the government largely remained outside of industrial relations. Through the collective bargaining process, employers and trade unions voluntarily set the terms and conditions of employment: the parties were the 'source of control both of the procedures and, at least equally significantly, the outcomes of collective bargaining'.[23] In relying upon the potential for a system of voluntary collective bargaining, a regulatory approach had been adopted by successive governments to effect 'a particular set of positive normative outcomes'.[24] A qualification is necessary here. Abstention had not been equivalent to an absence of legislative efforts by sitting governments. Rather, especially compared to the current era of labour regulation, governments had been neither so prolific nor so detailed in their legislation. The effect had been subtle support for the collective bargaining framework.

And yet, collective agreements remained largely unenforceable in courts[25] (a fact that continues today). This may be astonishing for those unfamiliar with UK labour law. As noted above, however, while parties usually do not bind themselves to a collective agreement,[26] the term-setting aspect of collective agreements can find effect by incorporation of terms into individual contracts.[27] If a term of a collective agreement is incorporated into the employment contract, any breach of the term will amount to a breach of contract. Terms of collective agreements can be incorporated into the employment contract in three ways.

---

21. O. Kahn-Freund, *Labour Law* (Morris Ginsberg, ed.) *Law and Opinion in England in the 20th Century* 224 (Stevens, 1959). The voluntarist, abstentionist collective laissez-faire characterisation of the State's role in labour law has been questioned in Ewing & Hendy (n. 5) 23.
22. O. Kahn-Freund, *Labour and the Law* 291 (3rd ed. Stevens, 1983). This view has been challenged by H.A. Clegg, *Otto Kahn-Freund and British Industrial Relations* (Lord Wedderburn, Roy Lewis & Jon Clark, eds) *Labour Law and Industrial Relations: Building on Kahn-Freund* 14-28 (Clarendon Press, 1983).
23. P. Davies & M. Freedland, *Labour Legislation and Public Policy* 642 (OUP, 1993).
24. P. Davies & M. Freedland, *Towards a Flexible Labour Market*, 2 (OUP, 2007).
25. As established in *Ford v. AUEF* [1969] 2 QB 303.
26. Deakin & Morris (n. 8) Chapter 9.
27. Deakin & Morris (n. 8) Chapter 4.

First, they may be incorporated by the trade union reaching an agreement with the employer while acting as an agent of the employees. Second, terms may be expressly incorporated by agreement between the parties. Third, such terms can be incorporated by way of implication on the part of a Court. Incorporation by implication of a court is very rare; only occurring where terms of the collective agreement are clear and unambiguous, and, in the opinion of the court, intended to be legally binding by the parties. The legislation noted here contributes to that term-setting dimension of employment contracts.

Although the endpoint for collective laissez-faire has been identified with the Conservative Government (of Margaret Thatcher) coming into office in 1979, a trajectory for increasing intervention had been laid much earlier. In a step that underscored the growing intervention and departure from collective laissez-faire, the 1968 Report of the Royal Commission on Trade Unions and Employers' Associations (known as the Donovan Commission)[28] cemented the place of industrial tribunals within the employment law dispute resolution framework,[29] so that parties were provided 'with an easily accessible, speedy, informal and inexpensive procedure for the settlement of their disputes, and for this purpose to remove the present multiplicity of jurisdictions.'[30] These tribunals were venues for all matters 'arising from the contract of employment and from statutory rights arising from the employment relationship.'[31] The Donovan Commission also unequivocally endorsed collective bargaining (and implicitly labour law) within the parameters of the national interest (such as strike reduction[32]): 'properly conducted, collective bargaining is the most effective means of giving workers the right to representation in decisions affecting their working lives, a right which is or should be the prerogative of every worker in a democratic society'.[33] However, the legislative framework for such a whole-hearted endorsement did not materialise. The most proximate came with the Labour Government of the mid-1970s (identified in the next paragraph).[34] Still, the Donovan Commission's form of intervention[35] was modest when compared with the government of the 1980s.

28. T. Donovan, *Report of the Royal Commission on Trade Unions and Employers' Associations* (Cmnd 3623) (HMSO, 1968).
29. Employment law is used here to mark a more individualised approach coming into focus.
30. Donovan (n. 28).
31. Donovan (n. 28).
32. R. Lewis, *The Role of Law in Employment Relations* (Roy Lewis, ed.) *Labour Law in Britain*, 32 (Blackwell, 1986).
33. Donovan (n. 28) 212.
34. Other instances of legislative interjections included the Sex Discrimination Act 1975 and the Equal Pay Act 1970 (which came into effect in 1975).
35. 'advocating a series of legislative measures and ... strongly emphasising the need for managerial and economic efficiency, a strand of industrial relations policy which was closely linked with the requirements of incomes policy': *see* Lewis (n. 32).

Following a general election, a Labour Government was installed in 1974. Its strategy to address the prevalence of strike action was the Social Contract: an unofficial agreement with the trade unions that the Labour Government would pass labour protection legislation in exchange for a decline in industrial action. One significant example was the passage of the Employment Protection Act 1975[36] which abandoned the regulatory approach of the Industrial Relations Act 1971 and instead focused upon supporting collective bargaining.[37] This approach did not survive the monumental shift of the 1980s largely due to the 'Winter of Discontent' of 1978-1979 when there was a marked increase in high-profile strike actions. The discontented winter led to a spring election win for the Conservative Government that (to this point) set UK labour law on a distinct path that continues today.

Another legacy from the mid-1970s remains in place, the independent Advisory, Conciliation and Arbitration Service (ACAS). Outside of mediation and conciliation, ACAS' role continues to include the 'improvement of industrial relations'[38] and related to that charge it provides industrial relations advice to all parties (upon request or through the publication of general advice on industrial relations)[39] as well as inquiring 'into any question relating to industrial relations generally or to industrial relations in any particular industry or in any particular undertaking or part of an undertaking.'[40] ACAS may establish Codes of Practice, but they are subject to a consultation process and approval of the Secretary of State.[41] Currently, ACAS has published five Codes of Practice.[42] These Codes may be admitted into evidence before employment tribunals and the Central Arbitration Committee (CAC) (discussed below), but not courts.[43] How determinative these Codes may be in proceedings seems limited because a failure to

36. The Industrial Relations Act 1971 introduced (by the Conservative Government of the early 1970s) unfair dismissal as a statutory protection. Unlike the enforceability of collective agreements, the Labour Government preserved this right in the Trade Union and Labour Relations Act 1974 and built upon it in the Employment Protection Act 1975.
37. Section 1(2) emphasised that the 'general duty' of ACAS included 'in particular of encouraging the extension of collective bargaining and the development and, where necessary, reform of collective bargaining machinery'.
38. Section 209 of Trade Union and Labour Relations (Consolidation) Act 1992 (TULRCA). This was part of the original mandate in the Employment Protection Act 1975, as noted above, but now does not include the encouragement of collective bargaining.
39. Section 213 of TULRCA. Section 4 of the Employment Protection Act 1975 contained a non-exclusive list of items which ACAS may advise.
40. Section 214 of TULRCA. This provision has remained similar to the original provision in section 5 of the Employment Protection Act 1975.
41. Section 200 of TULRCA. This process must also be followed for revisions to the published Codes (section 201) and revocation of a Code (section 202).
42. The latest (Code 5) was: *Handling in a Reasonable Manner Requests to Work Flexibly* (TSO, 2014).
43. Section 207 of TULRCA.

follow the Codes 'shall not of itself render [an employer] liable to any proceedings.'[44] The Secretary of State may also publish Codes of Practice (pursuant to section 203 of the Trade Union and Labour Relations (Consolidation) Act 1992 (TULRCA)), but this power has yet to be used. As will be noted later, ACAS' role was expanded through legislative reforms in 2013.

Two other administrative agencies were first set up by the Employment Relations Act 1975. These related exclusively to collective labour relations. The CAC was also established by the Employment Protection Act 1975.[45] The CAC draws its resources (such as staff and accommodation) from ACAS.[46] The CAC's responsibility includes the following areas of dispute: statutory recognition of trade unions; disclosure of information for collective bargaining; applications and complaints related to information and consultation arrangements.[47] It also offers voluntary arbitration in collective disputes. Similar to the CAC, the position of Certification Officer was first appointed under the Employment Protection Act 1975 and it, too, draws its resources from ACAS.[48] The Certification Officer's role, discussed below, was expanded in 2016.

20.3 NEOLIBERAL DEREGULATION: EMPLOYMENT REGULATION AS A TOOL FOR ECONOMIC STIMULUS, FROM 1979 ONWARDS

Collective laissez-faire officially ended with the election of a Conservative Government (lead by Margaret Thatcher) in 1979.[49] Her entry into office did not instantly bring change.[50] Rather, it is in retrospect that 1979 marked the start of a period of monumental change to the sources of English labour law. This movement carried the regulatory approach to labour law away from collective laissez-faire (as noted, a change that had been developing prior to 1979) towards labour market regulation conducted 'in the interests of a free market economy'.[51] This ethos continues to shape national labour law. Legislation constituted the primary method by which this shift had been effected. The

44. Section 207(1) of TULRCA.
45. Employment Protection Act 1975, section 10. *See* now sections 259 ff. of TULRCA.
46. Section 259(3) of TULRCA.
47. CAC, 'About Us' https://www.gov.uk/government/organisations/central-arbitration-committee/about.
48. Section 254(5) of TULRCA.
49. Margaret Thatcher served as Prime Minister until 1990 when she was replaced by John Major. The Conservative party continued in government until its defeat in 1997 by the Labour party. Due to space considerations, Thatcher's legislative reforms are focused upon as the Major period continued the path set by Thatcher in labour law.
50. This is not to overlook the swift action taken by the government upon taking power. Rather, the emphasis is upon the accumulation of efforts during the approximate decade in power, expressed through legislation such as the Employment Acts of 1980 and 1982, and the Trade Union Act of 1984.
51. Davies & Freedland (n. 24), 5.

outcome moved employment regulation closer to common law courts' interpretation of employment contracts; a change that had been warned against.[52]

20.3.1 The 1980s: Aligning Employment Regulation with Economic Stimulus

Upon taking office, the Conservative government placed primary importance on improving the economy. The method selected, monetarism, required abandoning collective laissez-faire because it was viewed as a root cause of a lacking economy.[53] The new policy changed the sources of national labour law from largely one of the contracts between the parties to one steered by legislation (and policy) situating employment regulation as a support for the national economy.[54] Since then, regulation in labour law has focused on economic liberalism: enabling commerce by minimising or removing (perceived) restrictions on the competitiveness of businesses. Employment regulation has been drafted into a 'proactive role as an engine for trade'.[55] Criticism arises when freedoms are viewed as workplace protections that (arguably) attenuate commercial competitiveness. The free market system requires as few encumbrances as possible. Second, liberalism also spoke to individual freedoms. The state could intervene so that there were equal opportunities.[56] This version of liberalism developed more overtly during the period of the Labour Government at the turn of the twenty-first century.

The UK legislative agenda from the 1980s illustrated not only a notable shift away from collective labour law, but also the embedding of employment regulation within macro-economic policies. On the former point, inspiration was drawn from Friedrich von Hayek. He believed trade unions 'operated as uniquely privileged institutions to which the general rules of law do not apply'.[57] von Hayek's objection centred around the coercive force of trade unions regarding their membership.[58] The Government passed the Employment Act of 1980 which withdrew protections for trade union members participating in

52. *See*, for example, Wedderburn (n. 17) 1.
53. *See* F. A. von Hayek, *The Constitution of Liberty*, Chapter 18 (University of Chicago Press, 2011). von Hayek was a guiding voice for the Conservative Government of the 1980s.
54. 'Analyses that centred on market competitiveness and monetarist economics have put in issue not only such institutions as employment protection legislation but, much more profoundly, the collective base of labour relations': Wedderburn (n. 3) 838.
55. Lord Irvine's comment on the nature of commercial law is not isolated to that discipline: 'the law ... assumed a proactive role as an engine for trade': L. Irvine, *The Law: An Engine for Trade*, 64 Mod. L. Rev. 333 (2001). Lord Irvine was the first Lord Chancellor of the Labour Government coming to power in 1997. His work is noted here as a foreshadowing of philosophical alignment between the two governments of different parties.
56. This point was taken up in the UK through the Third Way and controversially Tony Blair's 'New' Labour. *See* for example, A. Giddens, *The Third Way and Its Critics* 86-89 (Polity Press, 2000).
57. von Hayek (n. 53) 384.
58. *Ibid.*, Chapter 18.

secondary picketing, and narrowed the definition of a trade dispute, thereby expanding the exposure of strikers to legal sanctions. The Employment Act 1982[59] further weakened the immunities[60] for trade unions regarding industrial action and no limitation on the quantum of damages against a union was set by the Act.

While employment regulation had been reconfigured to support macro-economic aims, it may be surprising that the legislative changes during the 1980s did not themselves precipitate a marked economic improvement[61] This outcome has been familiar in labour law where belief has often trumped evidence.[62] Although the certainty that trade unions had held the country back was challenged, the conviction remained.

20.3.2 'New Labour' and a Third Way

With the election of a Labour Government in 1997, a new approach to the reform of labour laws would have been a welcome if not anticipated outcome. Whether it is called the 'Third Way' or 'New Labour', the period of Tony Blair's time as the first Labour Prime Minister since the 1970s has been (critically) discussed as predominantly staying the course set by Margaret Thatcher[63] or, perhaps more charitably, a 're-convergence of objectives'.[64] This assessment remains sound,[65] but there are important themes which originate during this time. The first matter to discuss is the Third Way. Illustrating the continuation of intervention by way of legislation, the next sub-section discusses some of the more important and lasting legislative changes.

59. *See* von Hayek (n. 57), Chapters 15-16.
60. In the UK, the law does not provide a positive right to strike. Rather, 'immunities' are provided, insulating those who undertake valid strike action from civil or criminal liability. Strike action can constitute (amongst other things) an inducement to breach a contract creating a situation of civil liability in tort: *Taff Vale Railway v. Amalgamated Society of Railway Servants* [1901] AC 426 (HL). For further discussion *see*, Tonia Novitz & Pascale Lorber, *Industrial Conflict in the UK*, Chapter 5 (Interstentia, 2012).
61. K.D. Ewing, *Economics and Labour Law in Britain: Thatcher's Radical Experiment*, 28 Alberta L. Rev. 632, 645-647 (1990).
62. For an elaboration of this critique, *see* S. Slinn, *The Limitations of Pieces of Paper: A Role for Social Science in Labour Law*, 12 CLELJ 291 (2006).
63. One critic characterised 'New' Labour's 'Third Way' as neoliberalism 'by stealth': *See* S. Fredman, *The Ideology of New Labour Law* (Catherine Barnard, Simon Deakin & Gillian Morris, eds) *The Future of Labour Law: Liber Amicorum Bob Hepple Q.C.*, 9-10 (Hart, 2004).
64. Davies & Freedland (n. 24) 42. The authors (page 43) contended: 'Our analysis will suggest that there was at least a partial sense in which a new way was found, though perhaps more at the level of methodology than at the underlying objectives'.
65. Drawing from H. Collins, *Regulating the Employment Relation for Competitiveness*, 30 ILJ 17 (2001) in which he discussed 'flexible employment', Davies & Freedland argued that the over-arching aim of Labour during this time had been establishing 'managerial flexibility': 'the capacity of, and the propensity for, employing enterprises to engage in job re-structuring and institutional re-structuring': Davies & Freedland (n. 24) 21.

20.3.2.1 The Third Way

The 'Third Way', the approach closely associated with the Labour Government at the turn of the twenty-first century, originated with Anthony (now Lord) Giddens in *The Third Way: The Renewal of Social Democracy*.[66] Giddens later delivered a restatement of the 'Third Way', addressing the criticism of this political theory.[67] In this later work, Giddens responded vigorously in a pointed explanation: '[The Third Way] is concerned with restructuring social democratic doctrines to respond to the twin revolutions of globalization and the knowledge economy. Third way politics is not, as it is so often portrayed, a capitulation to neoliberalism.'[68] Giddens endeavoured to distinguish the Third Way from (and as an alternative to[69]) neoliberalism. Influenced by the 'Third Way', the Labour Government sought to balance social and economic factors in the employment portfolio.[70]

20.3.2.2 'New Labour' Legislating for Fairness at Work

First, the Labour Government brought into force legislation deriving from the EU, which had been passed by the Conservatives. Most notably, Labour quickly brought into force in the UK the EU working time directive through The Working Time Regulations 1998.[71] This was significant because of the opposition by the preceding Conservative Government to this and other regulations of EU origin.

The National Minimum Wage Act 1998 had been introduced in *Fairness at Work* as a measure to 'ensure greater fairness at work and [to] remove the worst exploitation. It will promote competitiveness by encouraging firms to compete on quality rather than simply on labour costs and price'.[72] At the time, the Act had been heralded as 'the most radical and far-reaching reform of employment rights made by the 1997 Labour government'.[73] The minimum wage remains in

66. A. Giddens, *The Third Way: The Renewal of Social Democracy* (Cambridge: Polity Press, 1998).
67. Giddens (n. 56).
68. *Ibid.*, 163.
69. *Ibid.*, 32.
70. The following statement from the Government's White Paper *Fairness at Work* (*President of the Board of Trade, Fairness at Work* (Cmd 3968), 2-13 (TSO, 1998) offers one translation of the Third Way into government aims: 'The keys to securing efficiency and fairness are employability and flexibility. Employability means ensuring that people are well prepared, trained and supported, both initially as they enter the labour market, and throughout their working lives. Flexibility means businesses being able to adapt quickly to changing demand, technology and competition. By enabling business success, flexibility promotes employment and prosperity'.
71. SI 1998/1833. The success of the measure has been critically engaged in C. Barnard, S. Deakin & R. Hobbs, *Opting Out of the 48-Hour Week: Employer Necessity or Individual Choice? An Empirical Study of the Operation of Article 18(1)(b) of the Working Time Directive in the UK*, 32 ILJ 223 (2003).
72. *Fairness at Work* [3.2].
73. B. Simpson, *A Milestone in the Legal Regulation of Pay: The National Minimum Wage Act 1998*, 28 ILJ 1 1 (1999). Perhaps underscoring the moment, this Act was entirely domestic in origin due

place and had even been raised by the Conservative Government elected in 2015.

The passage of the Human Rights Act 1998 early in Blair's premiership ostensibly strengthened the aspirations of a worker-friendly labour law in the UK.[74] However, these hopes were soon diminished, as more general contract law principles[75] seemed to close off the opportunity to provide a foundation for a claim. At best, there seemed to be a remote opportunity to bring a claim against a private sector employer based upon the Human Rights Act 1998.[76]

The Labour Government only brought in modest changes to collective labour law. Statutory trade union recognition stood out as one of the most important for unions. The Employment Relations Act 1999 introduced Schedule A1 into the TULRCA to effect the discrete aim of providing 'for representation and recognition where a majority of the relevant workforce wants it ... to offer greater protection and security at work for the vulnerable.'[77] As with the 1970s and 1980s, concern over industrial action remained to the point that this tiered statutory procedure had been introduced both as 'a means of settling disputes without industrial action'[78] and also to 'complement and enhance competitiveness, prosperity and growth.'[79]

Although it remained likely it would not suggest such proximity with its emphasis on 'managerial flexibility', the Labour Government until 2010 largely continued the policy and practice of the preceding Conservative Governments. And yet, it established a foundation that is now being relied upon; that is, the concept of a floor of rights in the workplace that is not entirely dependent upon legislation. Looking at the UK as a non-EU Member State, the Human Rights Act grounds the discussion of workplace rights, with normative ambitions for labour law.

20.3.3 Back to the 1980s: Economic Stimulus Redux

Whether it is based upon austerity, globalisation, or something else, employment regulation has been a malleable tool for governments since the 1980s. The

to the EU's lack of competence to regulate in the area of pay due to EC Treaty Article 137(5) now Treaty on the Functioning of the European Union (TFEU), Article 153(5).

74. The Human Rights Act is largely directed towards the State, and its various emanations. There had been discussion (early in the life of the Human Rights Act 1998) that there could be spill-over effect to private sector instances. Keith Ewing had written of a potential spill-over effect of the Human Rights Act 1998 in regard to the potential for passage of legislation of more general application: K.D. Ewing, *The Human Rights Act and Labour Law*, 27 ILJ 275-284 (1998). The path was mooted in *X v. Y* [2004] EWCA Civ 662, [59], but has yet to be proven successful.
75. G.S. Morris, *The Human Rights Act and the Public/Private Divide in Employment Law*, ILJ 293-298 (1998).
76. G.S. Morris, *Fundamental Rights: Exclusion by Agreement?*, 30 ILJ 49-58 (2001).
77. *Fairness at Work* [4.11].
78. *Ibid.* [4.16].
79. *Ibid.* [4.17].

Conservative-Liberal Democrat Coalition of 2010-2015 passed a number of employment law reforms as austerity measures in response to the economic crisis beginning in 2007-2008. Consistent with about one-third of OECD countries between 2008-2013, the Coalition set about further liberalising employment regulation.[80] For example, it halved the minimum 90-day consultation period for dismissals of 100 or more workers. For labour rights advocates, the UK was travelling a similar path to the EU itself, which seemed to 'take an increasingly neo-liberal turn'[81] when EU institutions made decreasing the role of collective bargaining of the financial assistance provided to Greece, Portugal and Ireland.[82]

Underlying these changes was a noted unease for the small-to-medium sized employer (SME). SMEs are employing enterprises with between 1 and 249 workers.[83] This concern was expressed in a variety of forms, including the levying of fees to bring a claim to an employment tribunal, and the institution of an early conciliation scheme, administered by ACAS. Both emerged as a response to a growing concern over 'frivolous' employment claims.

Around the same time, the Government expanded the range of employment contracts employers could offer to include the new 'Workers Shareholder' status. A controversial provision,[84] it added section 205A to the Employment Rights Act 1996 and permitted workers to sign away[85] a range of employment protections[86] for shares in their employing company (up to GBP 2,000 worth, fully paid). The Act provides protection against dismissal on the basis of refusal to agree to become an employee shareholder[87] or any detriment.[88] This situation

80. OECD, *Employment Outlook 2013* http://www.oecd-ilibrary.org/employment/oecd-employment-outlook-2013/protecting-jobs-enhancing-flexibility-a-new-look-at-employment-protection-legislation_empl_outlook-2013-6-en.
81. Doherty (n. 4) 380.
82. E. Achtsioglou & M. Doherty, *There Must Be Some Way Out of Here ... The Crisis, Labour Rights and Member States in the Eye of the Storm*, 20 Eur. Law J. 219 (2014).
83. EU Recommendation 2003/361, OJ L 124/38, 20.5.2003, 'Concerning the definition of micro, small and medium-sized enterprises'.
84. As an example of the disquiet this section instigated, the option was labelled an 'attack on long-standing employment law': D. Renton & A. Macey, *Justice Deferred: A Critical Guide to the Coalition's Employment Tribunal Reforms*, 41 (Institute of Employment Rights, 2013).
85. This is not automatic as the agreement is valid only upon the employee having carried out the actions in section 205A(6): 'Agreement between a company and an individual that the individual is to become an employee shareholder is of no effect unless, before the agreement is made - (a)the individual, having been given the statement referred to in subsection (1)(c), receives advice from a relevant independent adviser as to the terms and effect of the proposed agreement, and; (b)seven days have passed since the day on which the individual receives the advice'.
86. An employee shareholder does not have the following rights pursuant to section 205A(2): '(a)the right to make an application under section 63D (request to undertake study or training); (b)the right to make an application under section 80F (request for flexible working); (c)the right under section 94 not to be unfairly dismissed, or; (d)the right under section 135 to a redundancy payment.' These are limited by section 205A(9),(10).
87. An employee is unfairly dismissed if terminated because s/he refuses to become an employee shareholder (Employment Rights Act 1996, section 104G.).
88. Section 47G of the Employment Rights Act 1996.

is reminiscent of the *Wilson and NUJ v. UK*[89] litigation. The National Union of Journalists took their case to the European Court of Human Rights when the employer offered financial incentives for members to refrain from joining the union. The ECtHR ruled there was a violation of the members' Article 11 (freedom of association) rights. With the Worker Shareholder status, however, the worker is offered the opportunity to sign away certain statutory protections.

After winning the 2015 general election, the Conservative Government (no longer in partnership with the Liberal Democrats) returned to the hobby horse of the 1980s, legislation to weaken the power of trade unions, with the Trade Union Act 2016.[90] For example, it modified the ballot threshold for industrial action, expanded the role of Certification Officers, and political funds in trade unions, requiring trade unions to meet a 50% threshold of members voting in favour of industrial action in order for the action to be legal.[91] The 40% turnout threshold for 'important public services'[92] added to the hurdles for industrial action in high union density areas. The meaning of the 40% threshold is that of all members eligible to vote at least 40% of them must have voted in favour of industrial action. The anomalous phrase 'important public services' as opposed to the more well-known essential services remains a matter to be defined.[93] This legislation simply provided more 'fertile ground'[94] for employers seeking injunctions. The Trade Union Act 2016 signified a return to government intervention into trade union activities, but at a time that trade unions arguably had a muted impact as a result of the legislation of the 1980s.

20.4 DEVELOPING A COMMON LAW RESPONSE TO DEREGULATION

Recall mention was made above of a 1987 article by Lord Wedderburn[95] in which he unequivocally argued for the separation of labour law from the common law courts. It is something of a statement on how things change that, about thirty years later, the common law courts are now seen as a viable venue for redress. Not so long ago, the courts were intervening in a manner that undercut labour protections (events which shaped Wedderburn's assessment).

89. [2002] IRLR 568 (ECtHR).
90. For a history of procedural reforms to industrial disputes, *see* J. Elgar & B. Simpson, *The Impact of the Law on Industrial Disputes Revisited*, 46 ILJ 6 (2017).
91. Trade Union Act 2016, section 2.
92. Trade Union Act 2016, section 3.
93. Pursuant to section 3(2) of the Act, the phrase was further outlined by specific regulations in the following service areas: medical, transportation, firefighting and border control. Each of the regulations contained the general heading of the Industrial Action (Important Public Services) Regulations 2017. These were discussed in: Department for Business, Energy & Industrial Strategy, *Important Public Services Regulations 2017* (January 2017).
94. Elgar & Simpson (n. 90) 16.
95. Wedderburn (n. 3) 1. *See also* Howarth (n. 17) 11.

In the early part of the twenty-first century, English courts are being asked to intervene and to preclude government legislative action. A focal point for this optimism has been the exercise of common law courts' residual power to enforce rights as demonstrated in the Supreme Court's decision in *R (on the application of UNISON) v. Lord Chancellor.*[96]

In this section, the basis for pursuing the common law is critically explored. The contention is that common law redress should be pursued in conjunction with continued pressing of the political case for workplace protections in order to address the limitations of common law.

20.4.1 Why Common Law Redress in the Workplace?

Lord Wedderburn's pessimism regarding the common law has faced a few instances in which common law courts have brought the matter to question. These instances have buoyed the recent optimism of the potential for the common law. Foremost amongst these instances is the House of Lords' decision in *Malik v. BCCI.*[97]

In *Malik,* the court recognised an implied term of mutual trust and confidence that may be breached when employers' conduct destroys the relationship of mutual trust and confidence between it and its employees. As a result, employees may claim damages for this breach. Lord Steyn wrote of the recognition of this implied term: 'It is expressed to impose an obligation that the employer shall not: without reasonable and proper cause, conduct itself in a manner calculated and likely to destroy or seriously damage the relationship of confidence and trust between an employer and employee'.[98]

More recently, UK appellate courts have elaborated upon the horizontal direct effect of rights. While these cases do not necessarily establish a concrete rule, they invite further consideration of the topic. The Court of Appeal in *Benkharbouche & Anor v. Embassy of the Republic of Sudan*[99] outlined the horizontal direct effect of Article 47 of the Charter of Fundamental Rights of the EU 2004 (effective remedy for a violation of a right). The *Benkharbouche* Court

96. (n.18). The argument seems to be a common law focused one of a potential spill-over effect of *Unison* to other instances. Keith Ewing had written of a potential spill-over effect of the Human Rights Act 1998 in regard to the potential for passage of legislation of more general application: Ewing (n. 74) 275-284.
97. [1998] AC 20 (HL).
98. This phrase was later interpreted to mean 'calculated or likely to destroy': *Baldwin v. Brighton and Hove City Council* [2007] ICR 680 (EAT), [35].
99. [2015] EWCA Civ 33. The Supreme Court dismissed the appeal against the Court of Appeal's decision, [2017] UKSC 62. The Supreme Court engaged little with Article 47, unlike the Court of Appeal.

ruled that Article 47 was 'enshrined ... as a general principle of Union law'[100] based upon the aforementioned Court of Justice decisions coupled with explanations accompanying the Charter.[101] It may be contended that this decision is of limited value once the UK departs the EU.

Within this context arose the Supreme Court's recognition of a 'common law right of access to courts' for workers bringing employment tribunal claims in 2017.

20.4.1.1 The Common Law Challenge

The trade union, Unison, first challenged tribunal fees in 2014[102] and this litigation concluded with the UKSC's 2017 decision in UNISON. The Supreme Court situated its decision within the notion of a right of access to courts (or here tribunals). The 'common law right of access to justice' where courts administer justice promptly and fairly is one that has a long history, dating to Chapter 40 of the Magna Carta, 1215.[103] On the source of the right, the Court made note that it is not grounded in EU law, but in fact, predated accession.[104]

In finding the fees order to be unlawful, the Court assessed the nature of the interference with the right of access to courts. Interference can be unlawful for the reason that it is insurmountable[105] or that it fails to be justifiable as reasonably necessary for a legitimate objective. Expanding on this disconnect, the court wrote: 'the degree of intrusion must not be greater than is justified by the objectives which the measure is intended to serve.'[106] Insurmountable as a threshold seems to be 'if there is a real risk that persons will effectively be prevented from having access to justice'.[107]

Of further interest here is that the Supreme Court did not write of access to conciliation as satisfying access to justice. Rather, interference with the path to employment tribunals was firmly set as the measurement.

However, while there might be some value in a focus on the potential in the common law, reasons remain for viewing the *Unison* decision as one of narrow application. It arose within a particular, instructive context which recalls some of the criticisms of the initial reconfiguration of UK labour law in the 1980s. Coming out of both the 1980s reforms as well as the period of austerity

100. *Ibid.* The arguments here do not depend upon the finding that the Lisbon Treaty accorded the Charter of Fundamental Rights with the same status as a treaty [78]. Contesting this point, J. Folkard, *Privacy and Conflicts in the Court of Appeal,* 132 LQR 31 (2016).
101. O.J. 2007 C303, 17.
102. *UNISON v. Lord Chancellor* [2014] EWHC 218 (Admin) [*Unison No. 1*].
103. *Unison* [74].
104. *Ibid.* [64].
105. *Ibid.* [87].
106. *Ibid.* [88].
107. *Ibid.* [87].

immediately after the crisis post-2008, there had not been a sense that the preceding sacrifices had yielded an improved economy that benefitted workers.[108] Restraint to and limitations on employment rights had to precipitate a tangible outcome for the UK workforce and this was found to be lacking. And so, the common law has been called upon to establish (or re-assert in some cases) workplace protections. A moment should be observed for this shift. It marks a statement about the muted force of collective labour relations in the UK of the twenty-first century. By extension, reliance upon and resort to common law redress continues the individuating process that restores 'common law rule over collective industrial relations'.[109]

Pertinent to the present collection on national sources of labour law, Unison will likely underpin arguments regarding developing the common law rights of workers. Discussion of 'common law fundamental rights'[110] has been infused with a new vigour.[111] Praise for this decision includes how it provided superior protection than EU law because 'the rule of law recognised in Unison combined with the common law right of access to the courts ... provide a clearer and higher level protection'.[112] The extent to which the rule of law may be the source of redress for employment law issues stands out as the contested point here. Recall that von Hayek, whose writing influenced the Conservative Government of the 1980s, believed trade unions 'operated as uniquely privileged institutions to which the general rules of law do not apply'.[113] The content of the rule of law is not necessarily uniform and will be subject to differing opinions. It remains shaped by external influences and, in the employment area, government economic policy has a significant force. While there remains scope for the common law to recognise rights (either giving greater weight to existing ones or setting out analogical extensions of current rights), it must also be admitted that a corollary to this potential is the limitations of what courts can do. And so, the political dimension of labour law, that has been noted above throughout the different periods since World War II, remains a pivotal component of the national sources of labour law.

The imbalance of bargaining power between parties recognised at common law, as noted in recent Supreme Court decisions,[114] has set out one parameter to

108. For comments on the 1980s *see* Ewing (n. 61) 647, Wedderburn (n. 17) Chapter10.
109. The quotation being from Lord Wedderburn's assessment in 1986: Wedderburn (n. 3), 842.
110. *See* A. Bogg, *Common Law and Statute in the Law of Employment*, 69 CLP 67 (2016).
111. *See* M. Ford, *Employment Tribunal Fees and the Rule of Law: R (Unison) v. Lord Chancellor in the Supreme Court*, 47 ILJ 1 (2018), as well as A. Bogg, *The Common Law Constitution at Work: R (on the application of UNISON) v. Lord Chancellor*, 81 MLR 509 (2018).
112. Ford, 3. Passing mention may be made to the European Pillar of Social Rights (Chapter II, 7, b) which outlines a 'right to access to effective and impartial dispute resolution and, in case of unjustified dismissal, a right to redress, including adequate compensation'; though, the Pillar is not currently a legally enforceable instrument.
113. von Hayek (n. 54) 384.
114. *Autoclenz v. Belcher* [2011] UKSC 41, [35]; *Unison* (UKSC) [21], [24].

adjudication. And yet, there is a question as to the extent of the courts' role. Courts remain better equipped to dissect rights as concepts rather than the precise details of these concepts. Rogers, writing from a United States (US) perspective, argued, using the example of Uber, that the question of when employment duties should be imposed is not one that can be left simply to the courts: 'litigation is time-consuming and expensive, and individual cases are an imperfect vehicle for addressing broader considerations of distribution and social equality ... legislatures should strongly consider socializing employment-related benefits and imposing employment duties on an industry specific basis.'[115] To this, the question of constitutionalising rights, and what that means, may be added. When deliberating on this query, it is valuable to bear in mind that precarity has become an issue because of the quest for flexible work arrangements in operating businesses.[116] Entrenching labour rights within a constitutional framework may well be a way to address deepening precarity. However, it must also be wondered how viable that occurrence may be if perceived rigidities have been replaced with flexibility for economic imperatives.

20.5 CONCLUSION

A legitimate response to the prospect of weakening existing employment regulation has been that the UK is already a remarkably flexible economy (with only the US and Canada being rated by the OECD as higher).[117] There may still be a move to liberalise employment regulation and underlying much of that discussion of economic stimulus will be mention of small-to-medium-sized enterprises (SME). There is no critique here of regulating in ways that can effectively assist SMEs. Rather, actions should be more nuanced and thoughtful so that these aims may be realistically met. Seeing this as a broader regulatory focus is instructive: it is a one-size-fits-all framework, complicated by certain factors. SMEs prefer an informal work environment.[118] And so, on one side, there is a preference for as little regulation as possible. Moreover, this cohort as a whole has not necessarily signalled that regulatory change will create the desired effect (increased employment): the number of workers they employ has been decreasing over time.[119] And so, a framework catering to SMEs may not entirely serve stated goals.

115. B. Rogers, *Employment Rights in the Platform Economy: Getting Back to Basics*, 10 Harv. L. & Pol'y Rev. 479-510 (2016).
116. For more pointed criticism on the point *see* Ewing & Hendy (n. 5) 23.
117. This argument can be found in a number of sources such as, Centre for Economic Performance, *The Consequences of Brexit for UK Trade and Living Standards*, 9 (2016).
118. M. Gibbons, *Better Dispute Resolution: A Review of Employment Dispute Resolution in Great Britain* (Department of Trade and Industry, 2007).
119. Department for Business Innovation & Skills, *SME Business Barometer February 2014* (2014).

On the collective side of labour law, Ewing and Hendy have boldly advocated for a return to more extensive collective bargaining coverage. To restore the collective bargaining apparatus, they focus upon 'the role of law in building the structures necessary'.[120] To the extent that they argue for a reinvigoration of the political and public efforts to press the case for greater workplace protections, Ewing and Hendy have expressed a compelling plan. The critique noted above is the seemingly single-stop reliance upon the common law courts to recalibrate the deepening precarity in which workers are placed through government liberalisation of workplace protections. The courts, absent legislation to guide deliberations, are better suited to dealing with 'broad stroke' labour issues than being a full service venue for all workplace matters, and, especially, for the vindication of worker rights.

BIBLIOGRAPHY

E. Achtsioglou & M. Doherty, *There Must Be Some Way Out of Here ... The Crisis, Labour Rights and Member States in the Eye of the Storm*, 20 Eur. Law J. 219 (2014).

F. August von Hayek, *The Constitution of Liberty*, Chapter 18 (University of Chicago Press, 2011).

Bank of England (External Monetary Policy Unit), The Brexit Vote, Productivity Growth and Macroeconomic Adjustments in the United Kingdom, Discussion Paper No. 51 (2019).

A. Bogg, *Common Law and Statute in the Law of Employment*, 69 CLP 67 (2016).

A. Bogg, *The Common Law Constitution at Work: R (on the Application of UNISON) v. Lord Chancellor*, 81 MLR 509 (2018).

H.A. Clegg, *Otto Kahn-Freund and British Industrial Relations* (Lord Wedderburn, Roy Lewis & Jon Clark, eds) *Labour Law and Industrial Relations: Building on Kahn-Freund* 14-28 (Clarendon Press, 1983).

H. Collins, *Regulating the Employment Relation for Competitiveness*, 30 ILJ 17 (2001).

P. Davies & M. Freedland, *Labour Legislation and Public Policy*, 642 (OUP, 1993).

P. Davies & M. Freedland, *Towards a Flexible Labour Market*, 2 (OUP, 2007).

A. C. L. Davies, *Perspectives on Labour Law* (CUP, 2003).

S. Deakin, G.S. Morris, *Labour Law*, 9-26 (6th ed. Hart, 2012).

M. Doherty, *Through the Looking Glass: Brexit, Free Movement and the Future*, 27 KLJ 375 (2016).

T. Donovan, *Report of Royal Commission on Trade Unions and Employers' Associations* (Cmnd 3623) (HMSO, 1968).

120. Ewing & Hendy (n. 5) 24.

J. Elgar & B. Simpson, *The Impact of the Law on Industrial Disputes Revisited*, 46 ILJ 6 (2017).

K. Ewing & J. Hendy, *New Perspectives on Collective Labour Law: Trade Union Recognition and Collective Bargaining*, 46 ILJ 23 (2017).

K.D. Ewing, *The Human Rights Act and Labour Law*, 27 ILJ 275-284 (1998).

J. Folkard, *Privacy and Conflicts in the Court of Appeal*, 132 LQR 31 (2016).

M. Ford, *Employment Tribunal Fees and the Rule of Law: R (Unison) v. Lord Chancellor in the Supreme Court*, 47 ILJ 1 (2018).

S. Fredman, *The Ideology of New Labour Law* (Catherine Barnard, Simon Deakin & Gillian Morris, eds) *The Future of Labour Law: Liber Amicorum Bob Hepple Q.C.*, 9-10 (Hart, 2004).

M. Gibbons, *Better Dispute Resolution: A Review of Employment Dispute Resolution in Great Britain* (Department of Trade and Industry, 2007).

A. Giddens, *The Third Way and Its Critics* 86-89 (Polity Press, 2000).

A. Giddens, *The Third Way: The Renewal of Social Democracy* (Polity Press, 1998).

D. Howarth, *The Autonomy of Labour Law: A Response to Professor Wedderburn*, 17 ILJ 11 (1988).

L. Irvine, *The Law: An Engine for Trade*, 64 Mod. L. Rev. 333 (2001).

O. Kahn-Freund, *Labour and the Law*, 291 (3rd ed. Stevens, 1983).

O. Kahn-Freund, *Labour Law* (Morris Ginsberg, ed.) *Law and Opinion in England in the 20th Century*, 224 (Stevens, 1959).

R. Lewis, *The Role of Law in Employment Relations* (Roy Lewis, ed.) *Labour Law in Britain*, 32 (Blackwell, 1986).

T. Novitz & P. Lorber, *Industrial Conflict in the UK*, Chapter 5 (Interstentia, 2012).

D. Renton & A. Macey, *Justice Deferred: A Critical Guide to the Coalition's Employment Tribunal Reforms*, 41 (Institute of Employment Rights, 2013).

B. Rogers, *Employment Rights in the Platform Economy: Getting Back to Basics*, 10 Harv. L. & Pol'y Rev. 479-510 (2016).

B. Simpson, *A Milestone in the Legal Regulation of Pay: The National Minimum Wage Act 1998*, 28 ILJ 1, 1 (1999).

M. Taylor, *Good Work: The Taylor Review of Modern Working Practices*, (Department for Gibbo Business, Energy & Industrial Strategy, 2017).

Brigid Van Wanrooy, Helen Bewlen, Alex Bryson, John Forth, Stephaine Freeth, Lucy Stokes & Stephen Wood, The 2011 Workplace Employment Relations Study: First Findings 121 (BIS, 2013).

L. Wedderburn, *Labour Law: From Here to Autonomy?*, 16 ILJ 1 (1987).

L. Wedderburn, *The Worker and the Law*, 835 (3rd ed. Pelican, 1986).

CHAPTER 21

Sources of Labor Law in the United States: Contract Supra Omnis

Paul Secunda

21.1 INTRODUCTION[1]

The fact that many U.S. employees are currently facing harsh labor conditions can be directly related to the unusual hierarchy of labor law sources in the United States. Although the normal hierarchy would place constitutional rights over statutory/regulatory rights, and statutory and regulatory rights over common law/collective agreement/contract rights, U.S. labor law has caused employees to increasingly face the predicament of their earlier-day counterparts who also lacked basic legal protections in the workplace because of the power of employer-dominated contractual conditions. In other words, contractual rights (as even opposed to collective rights) currently appears more important than statutory or constitutional labor rights in the United States. The lack of collective agreement power is both because of the low union density in the United States, as well as the fact that trade unions quickly cede members' rights to contractual arbitration provisions. Indeed, it is not too much of a stretch to say the United States has come full circle from being victimized by one form of contract-based employer power to another. During the early twentieth century, labor law and employment contracts were mostly anti-union in orientation and the United States Supreme Court struck down much worker-protective legislation based on the Lochnerian concept of "liberty of contract." In 1935, the tide began to turn with the addition of statutory workplace protections in the form of the promotion

1. Many thanks to Kylie Owens, Marquette Law School Class of 2020, for her exceptional research and writing assistance on this chapter. All errors or omissions are mine alone.

of collective bargaining through the federal Wagner Act. In the 1950s and 1960s, union density reached its apogee in the United States, coming close to 35% of the workforce. Under this state of affairs, individual contracts were superseded by contrary rights found in collective agreements.

While these statutory protections (and additional common law protections) were helpful to employees, union membership began to decline in the 1970s and 1980s. It appears U.S. employees gained a false sense of security from these very same common law and statutory protections. In the meantime, employers, who were unhappy with expanded employee protections, began relying more on individual employment arbitration (outside of the trade union context) to settle workplace disputes, rather than in the courts. Now, in light of the United States Supreme Court's May 2018 decision in *Epic Sys. Corp. v. Lewis*,[2] a new type of "liberty of contract" has taken hold, where employers can force employees into unequal, individual employment arbitrations, with the consequence that workers are having a more difficult time vindicating their workplace rights. At the same time, even where collective agreements exist in about 10% of the U.S. workforce, unions have ceded statutory rights to contractual arbitration provisions in collective agreements, causing contractual to also be at the top of the hierarchy of labor law sources.

This chapter illustrates how U.S. labor and employment law has become contract-based in a way that unfairly favors employers and undermines fundamental workplace rights of employees in both the union and nonunion workplace. Section 21.2 provides a brief overview of the history of U.S. labor and employment law. Section 21.3 turns to an overview of common law protections granted to employees under contract law, tort law, and under the concept of good faith and fair dealing. Section 21.3 then continues by examining statutory employment law protections by looking at three pieces of representative legislation in approximately thirty-year increments (1935, 1938, and 1993). Lastly, section 21.4 turns to U.S. labor and employment law today, which reflects an alarming return to placing disproportionate power into adhesive employment contracts either in individual employment relations (most of the United States) or in collective agreement that permits such an upside-down hierarchy to exist.

21.2 HISTORICAL DEVELOPMENT OF LABOR & EMPLOYMENT LAW

Labor and employment law has been in a constant state of flux in the United States since its early beginnings shaped by many social, economic, and political forces. In early U.S. history, organized labor was viewed as a criminal or civil

2. *Epic Sys. Corp. v. Lewis*, 138 S. Ct. 1612 (2018).

conspiracy and such organizations were often found to be unlawful.[3] Labor law had not changed much by the late nineteenth and early twentieth centuries during the so-called *Lochner* era. The *Lochner* era refers to Supreme Court decisions from the early 1900s to the beginning of the New Deal in the mid-1930s, when the United States Supreme Court struck down many state workplace protective legislation under the guise of a constitutional form of "liberty of contract" between employer and employee.[4] Courts during the *Lochner* era struck down over 150 pieces of protective workplace legislation, finding they were unconstitutional. Some prominent examples of the time which elevated freedom of contract in employment include: *Adair v. United States* (1908) (striking down federal law prohibiting the firing of workers merely for joining a union); *Coppage v. Kansas* (1915) (invalidating state law prohibiting yellow dog contracts); and *Hitchman Coal & Coke Co. v. Mitchell* (1917) (noting employer's refusal to engage in collective bargaining, firing of employees who join a union, and insistence on having employees sign yellow dog contracts is "a part of the constitutional rights of personal liberty and private property").

The many cases throughout the *Lochner* era make clear that the debate between employers and employees centered around the meaning of the term "liberty." Employers maintained that liberty of contract meant the freedom of businesses to have "at-will" employees that they could fire for any reason. Supporters of unions believed that liberty of contract meant the right to organize without fear of retaliation. Further, supporters of unions argued that liberty of contract was a fiction due to the grossly unequal bargaining power between employers and individual employees in the workplace.

The *Lochner* era coincided with the industrial revolution occurring in the United States, where new types of labor were being practiced, often to the detriment of workers. Such jobs featured dangerous work conditions, little pay, and excessive work hours. As a result, employees sought to organize through unions to have a better opportunity to bargain collectively over the terms and conditions of their employment.

In the midst of significant labor unrest during the Great Depression, Congress passed the National Labor Relations Act (NLRA or Wagner Act) of 1935.[5] Section 7, referred to as the heart of the NLRA, makes clear that the broad intention of the legislation was to guarantee employees[6] had "the right to self-organization, to form, join, or assist labor organizations, to bargain collectively through representatives of their own choosing, and to engage in other

---

3. The very first labor case in United States history held that striking for higher wages was an illegal conspiracy. *Commonwealth v. Pullis*, 3 Commons & Gilmore 59 (Mayor's Court 1806). *See also* P.M. Secunda et al., *Mastering Labor Law*, 8-9 (Carolina Academic Press, 2014).
4. *Lochner v. New York*, 198 U.S. 45 (1905).
5. 29 U.S.C. §§ 151-169 (1935).
6. Note that the language uses the term "employees" not "unionized employees," meaning these rights were granted to all employees no matter their union status.

concerted activities for the purpose of collective bargaining or other mutual aid or protection."[7] Section 8 of the NLRA[8] ensured that all unfair labor practices (ULPs), involving retaliation, intimidation, or restraint of employees' rights under section 7, were prohibited. An example of an ULP would be an employer threatening an employee with termination if they engaged in union activity. Moreover, the NLRA created the National Labor Relations Board, which served to prevent ULPs that were statutorily defined in the NLRA and to regulate the election of unions to represent groups of workers.

Along with the creation of the NLRA and other labor and employment law statutory protections (discussed in Part III), union membership reached its height in 1954. In 1954, 34.8% of the workforce in America was a member of a union. Compare that to 1983 when the union membership rate was 20.1% and in 2017 when the union membership rate is 10.7%.[9] The reduction in union membership and collective bargaining in the United States resulted from two major causes: (1) hostility and anti-union conduct by the American government and employers (including the holding of captive audience meetings)[10] and (2) the introduction of federal and state statutory law and increasing common law protection in the workplace, which made many employees feel that union protections were no longer necessary. It is to this second cause: the rise of workplace common law and statutory protections that the paper now turns.

21.3 COMMON LAW AND STATUTORY EMPLOYMENT PROTECTIONS

Employment-at-will has been the default rule in the United States since the late nineteenth century when Horace G. Wood published a treatise on the topic.[11] The employment-at-will doctrine states that employment may be terminated by either employer or employee for any reason or no reason at all. Essentially, at-will contracts create indefinite employee contracts, as opposed to contracts of specific duration. Employment-at-will is the baseline rule and an employee who wishes to object to their termination must find a legal exception to the rule. There are common-law exceptions to at-will contracts that have been created through judicial decisions and statutory exceptions created through federal and

7. 29 U.S.C. § 157.
8. *Ibid.*, § 158.
9. Bureau of Labor Statistics, "Union Members Summary". https://www.bls.gov/news.release/union2.nr0.htm accessed 15 August 2018.
10. For and in-depth discussion on the limitations of the NLRA and the concerted effort against it. P.M. Secunda, *The Wagner Model of Labour Law Is Dead—Long Live Labour Law!*, 38, Queens L.J. 545, 555-561 (2013).
11. No longer well-respected, many believe the caselaw Wood relied upon does not support the concept of employment-at-will. Either way, courts began relying upon it to justify employment-at-will. H.G. Wood, *A Treatise on the Law of Master and Servant* (J.D. Parsons, Jr., 1877).

state legislation to protect certain groups of employees. Common-law exceptions will be discussed, followed by statutory exceptions.

21.3.1 Common Law

Although the employment-at-will doctrine was applied purely and harshly during the first parts of the twentieth century, state courts began carving out exceptions to the default rule after World War II to avoid anomalous and unfair employee outcomes. These common-law erosions to the employment-at-will doctrine have created other means for employees to be able to challenge their terminations. However, contract, tort, and good faith erosions those have been established by the courts are limited.

21.3.1.1 Contract Erosions

Because employment-at-will is a default rule, an employment contract can change the nature of the employment by simply specifying that change in the contract. An express contract, when the employment contract specifies in writing the changes to be made, is the simplest way to do this. An example of this would be an employment contract specifying (in writing) that the employee will be employed for one year. In that example, a "just cause" standard is implied, meaning that the employee cannot be let go in less than one year, except for just cause. Another example of an express contract is when a collective bargaining agreement is created between a union and an employer. This would be written into the employment contracts of bargaining unit employees and would provide protection for employees by disallowing firings for anything less than just cause.

The more complicated task the courts face is determining what gives rise to an implied contract between the employer and the employee. The courts have found that employer conduct may rise to the level of an implied contract, which would protect the employee. For example, if an employment manual lays out a policy of termination in their employee manual and does not follow that policy in the termination of an employee, the employee will likely prevail in court because they can claim that there was an implied contract between the parties.[12] An implied contract may also exist when an implied promise between an employer and employee can be shown. For example, in one case, a long-time employee was fired without explanation even though he had received no

12. Even if a disclaimer is in the employee manual, an implied contract may still exist. A manager relied on an employee manual that stated that employees working for the company for more than ten years would not be terminated unless "senior corporate management" had reviewed their termination. The court held that if an employee reasonably expects the employer to follow its own procedure in the employee manual, an implied contract may exist. *Zaccardi v. Zale Corp.*, 856 F.2d 1473, 1476 (10th Cir. 1988).

criticism on his work.[13] Because the employer had been known to only fire employees when there was good cause to and because the employee was told if he remained loyal to the company, his job would be secure, the court found that an implied promise existed between the parties. This meant that the employee's firing violated the employment contract.

21.3.1.2 Tort Erosions

Along with the contract erosions, courts have eroded the default employment-at-will rule by allowing employees to circumvent the rule through public policy exceptions present in tort doctrines. If an employee can show that the employer "was motivated by bad faith, malice, or retaliation" and demonstrate "that [they] were discharged because they performed an act that public policy would encourage or refuse to do something that public policy would condemn," they may prevail in a wrongful termination suit.[14]

The concept behind the public policy exception is that some grounds for employee termination are contrary to public policy because they would have a negative effect on society as a whole, so they should be prevented. One example of an employee termination that would qualify for the public policy exception is if an employee was fired for refusing to break the law at their employer's insistence.[15] Another example would be if an employer fired an employee for participating in jury duty.[16]

21.3.1.3 Good Faith Erosions

There is a division between many courts in the United States as to whether there exists an implied covenant of good faith and fair dealing in employment contracts. Some courts in the United States have held that the implied covenant of good faith is not applicable in employment-at-will contracts. The implied covenant of good faith states that every contract "imposes an obligation of good faith in its performance or enforcement."[17] This means that every contract entered into presupposes that each party will act in good faith towards the other and will engage in fair dealings with one another.

However, other courts in the United States have implied the covenant of good faith and fair dealing into employment-at-will contracts. For example, the

13. *Pugh v. See's Candies*, Inc., 250 Cal.Rptr. 195, (Cal.App. 1 Dist.,1988).
14. *Vandergrift v. American Brands* Corp., 572 F. Supp. 496 (D.N.H. 1983).
15. An employee was fired for refusing to commit perjury at his employer's request. *Petermann v. Int'l Broth. of Teamsters, Chauffeurs, Warehousemen and Helpers of Am.*, Local 396, 174 Cal.App.2d 184 (1959).
16. *Nees v. Hocks*, 272 Or. 210 (1975).
17. U.C.C. Section 1-203.

Massachusetts Supreme Court held that the implied covenant of good faith protects benefits previously earned by an employee.[18] There, the employer fired and rehired an employee to prevent the employee from receiving a large sales commission he had earned. The court reasoned that since sales commissions are to be paid for work performed, "the employer's decision to terminate its at-will employee should [have been] made in good faith."[19] Because the court found that the decision to terminate the employer was made to frustrate the employee's legitimate expectations, the court found for the employee.

Courts have also held that the implied covenant of good faith also requires fairness. In one case, after an employee took necessary accrued sick leave, her employer reduced her hours drastically, causing the employee to resign.[20] The Idaho Supreme Court found that there was a legitimate claim of breach of contract due to the implied covenant of good faith and fair dealing. The court reasoned that "[a]ny action by either party which violates, nullifies, or significantly impairs any benefit of the employment contract is a violation of the implied-in-law covenant."[21] Whether an employee will be successful in a good faith contract breach suit, will be dependent on their jurisdiction. This means that the possible protection of this implied covenant is not available to every employee and is limited in its strength.

21.3.2 Statutory

Just like common law protections discussed above, federal and state legislatures have increasingly passed statutes to provide nonunion employees protections in the workplace. With regard to federal versus state law, federal law supersedes state law to the extent there is a conflict under the federal Constitution's supremacy clause. This means that state legislation only plays a role where federal law does not occupy the field of legislation (as in employee benefits law and traditional law). State law, outside of the common law mentioned above, involved topics like unemployment compensation, workers compensation, and certain types of wage and hours laws. Here, for purposes of this chapter, three *federal* statutory protections are discussed below to illustrate the nature and scope of such protections.[22]

---

18. *Fortune v. Nat'l Cash Register Co.*, 373 Mass. 96 (1977).
19. *Ibid.*, at 102.
20. *Metcalf v. Intermountain Gas Co.*, 116 Idaho 622 (1989).
21. *Ibid.*, at 749.
22. Parallel and complementary state law protections are also available for employees in areas such as employment discrimination and wage and hour law.

21.3.2.1 Fair Labor Standards Act

The Fair Labor Standards Act (FLSA) of 1938 was enacted right after the cessation of the *Lochner* era as a response to the Great Depression.[23] Congress' purpose was to combat the negative economic consequences caused by "labor conditions detrimental to the maintenance of the minimum standard of living necessary for health, efficiency, and general well-being of workers."[24] Congress sought to meet that objective by creating a minimum wage, restricting child labor, and prescribing overtime work rules.[25]

In 1938, when the FLSA was enacted, the minimum wage was set to 25 cents per hour. Today, the minimum wage is USD 7.25,[26] but it has not been raised now for over a decade. States may choose to set their own minimum wage, as long as it is above the federal minimum wage. For example, Washington D.C. has set the highest minimum wage at USD 12.50 and Washington state has the second-highest at USD 11.50. The FLSA also restricts "oppressive child labor" by preventing children under fourteen from being employed (except by their parents) and preventing children from fourteen through seventeen from working in particularly hazardous conditions, during certain times of the day, and without work permits or licenses.[27] The FLSA also addresses overtime work. Unless employees fall under a listed minimum wage or overtime exemption (e.g., for being a white-collar executive, professional, or administrator), when they work more than forty hours in a workweek they must be paid "a rate not less than one and one-half times the regular rate at which he is employed."[28] The "regular rate" is pay plus other forms of includable times of compensations like certain types of commissions and bonuses. As with Title VII and the Family and Medical Leave Act (FMLA), the FLSA is a federal statutory law and thus, is superior to common law provisions and state provisions that are contrary. However, none of these federal laws occupy the field, so they act as floors to labor standards, as opposed to ceilings, and thus, state law and contracts can be more generous that what the federal law provides. However, as with all such laws, the problem with truly placing such federal laws in any hierarchy may be the practical difficulty individual workers have in bringing actions under such laws and finding attorneys willing taking such cases if the stakes are not too high.

23. 29 U.S.C. §§ 201-219.
24. *Ibid.*, § 202(a).
25. The United States does not have "maximum hours" laws, but they do require premium pay after forty hours of work in a workweek by an individual employee in order to spread the work to additional employees.
26. U.S. Troop Readiness, Veterans' Care, Katrina Recovery, and Iraq Accountability Appropriations Act, 2007.
27. 29 U.S.C. §§ 212 & 203.
28. *Ibid.*, § 207(a)(1).

21.3.2.2 Title VII

Title VII of the Civil Rights Act ("Title VII") of 1964 protects employees from being discriminated against on the basis of race, color, national origin, sex, or religion.[29] Title VII prevents discrimination of these protected classes, in the hiring and firing of employees, as well as with regard to other terms and conditions.[30] Title VII was created to ensure that employees would have legal recourse if they faced discrimination in the workplace and the Equal Employment Opportunity Commission was created to administer and implement those ends.

An employment practice may be found discriminatory if it can be shown that intentional disparate treatment has occurred or there is nonintentional disparate impact[31] on a protected class under Title VII. Disparate treatment is the most basic—and the most common—type of Title VII discrimination claim. In order for an employee to be successful in a single-motive disparate treatment claim, she must show that she was treated differently because of her status in a protected class under the statute. For example, if an employee could prove that she was not hired because she was black, the burden of production would then shift to the employer to articulate a legitimate, nondiscriminatory reason for the adverse employment decision. If the employer meets this burden, the burden of proof is on the employee to show that the employer's reason is pretextual and the real reason is discrimination. Remedies for unlawful employment discrimination include reinstatement, back pay, limited compensatory and punitive damages, and attorney fees of the employee being paid by the employer.[32]

21.3.2.3 Family and Medical Leave Act

The FMLA of 1993 was created to help protect employees from being fired or losing their benefits if they took leave for the birth of their child or for their own or family health emergencies.[33] The FMLA seeks to promote equal employment between men and women because the burden of care often falls on women when a family member requires medical attention. The law requires that employers (with fifty or more employees) must provide an employee up to twelve weeks of

---

29. 42 U.S.C. §§ 2000e -2000e-17.
30. *Ibid.*, § 2000e-2.
31. Disparate impact is beyond the scope of this chapter, but is fully discussed in P.M. Secunda & J.M. Hirsch, *Mastering Employment Discrimination Law* (Carolina Academic Press, 2010).
32. A more complicated, mixed-motive claim also exists. Because most employment issue involve many factors (some legitimate and some discriminatory), mixed-motive claims can be very complicated, and a successful "same decision" employer defense can also limit damages. Under a mixed-motive claim an employee may be successful if they are able to show that discrimination was a "motivating factor" in the result, even if other factors were present. 42 U.S.C. § 2000e-2(m); 42 U.S.C. § 2000e-5(g)(2)(B).
33. 29 U.S.C. §§ 2601-2654.

job-protected, unpaid leave if there is a birth (or adoption), if the employee needs to care for a baby (through birth, adoption, or foster care), a family member with a serious health condition, or if an employee is unable to work because of a serious health condition. Such protection only applies to employees who have worked for covered employers for at least one year and over 1,250 hours (more than part-time) in that previous year. There are notice and certification provisions that apply to both employer and employee to let the other know of the need for FMLA leave.

Although the FMLA contains far less protections that are far less extensive than all European countries, the Act still protects many workers from being fired for taking appropriate medical leave. While on medical leave, an employee cannot lose any accrued benefits, most importantly health care. That being said, such leave is unpaid, and employers can make employees use whatever vacation pay, sick pay, other paid time off they might have during the FMLA leave period.

In short, statutory and common law protections discussed above provide some protection for employees in the United States, but leave a glaring deficit when compared to the more comprehensive protections of a union collective bargaining agreement, especially with its just cause protections. Additionally, as will be seen below, unions help level the playing field between employers and employees in a way that employees seeking to arbitrate employment issues with their employer cannot. So although there have been statutory and common law protections created for employees in the United States over many decades, many employees are now not able to have their day in court before a jury of their peers because many employers require their employees to sign pre-employment arbitration agreements with class-action waiver provisions. It is to this new form of employer-dominated "liberty of contract" that this article now turns.

21.4 ARBITRATION

With the rise of federal and state statutory protections and common law tort and contract rights that were pro-employee, employers began creating and requiring employees to sign pre-dispute, compulsory arbitration agreements. That is, at the beginning of employment, without really knowing what they were signing, employees are waiving their rights to a judicial forum and a jury trial. Historically, under the common law, courts were hostile towards arbitration. However, in 1925, Congress enacted the Federal Arbitration Act (FAA) with the intent of providing a legal basis for enforcing commercial arbitration agreements.[34] In the 1990s and early 2000s, the U.S. Supreme Court extended the FAA to the employment context and since then, a conservative, business-friendly United

34. 9 U.S.C. §§ 1-307.

States Supreme Court has vigorously upheld the use of arbitration in nonunion employment matters.

In the context of employment law (as opposed to union-based arbitration),[35] arbitration is the process by which parties, subject to an employment contract, agree to resolve disputes through a third-party arbitrator instead of the traditional litigation method. Both parties agree that any decisions made during the arbitration process are final and binding, with very limited appeal rights. While there are many differences between arbitration and traditional litigation, three main variations stand out: (1) arbitration takes place in a conference room, instead of a courtroom; (2) the conventional rules of procedure and evidence are relaxed and applied loosely; (3) the traditional discovery process and motion practice are limited and there is no reasoned decision.

Since the United States Supreme Court ruling in *Gilmer v. Interstate/Johnson Lane Corp.* in 1991, mandatory arbitration agreements have become more common.[36] In 1992 only 2.1% of employees were subject to a mandatory arbitration agreement; today, 56.2% of nonunionized workers are subject to a mandatory arbitration.[37] Further, 23.1% have waived their right to a class-action lawsuit, requiring employees to resolve issues with their employers individually through arbitration.[38] This is a problem with regard to not allowing class-action treatment in the arbitration setting, as some cases are not worth the expense to bring on an individual basis and so are never brought. The percentage is anticipated to increase substantially due to the 2018 Supreme Court ruling in *Epic Sys. Corp. v. Lewis,* because it held that such class-action waivers in arbitration do not run afoul of union or nonunion employees' rights to act concertedly to improve their workplace terms and conditions under the NLRA.[39] It is also important to note that these arbitration practices are more common in low-wage workplaces and, therefore, impact industries that are made up of higher numbers of women and people of color who tend to have less economic power and leverage to resist these one-sided arbitration arrangements.

---

35. Although § 301 of the Labor Management Relations Act grants federal courts jurisdiction over disputes relating to collective bargaining agreements between employers and unions, the Supreme Court has made clear that arbitration is also an acceptable way of resolving such cases. 29 U.S.C. § 185; *Steelworks Trilogy* cases: *United Steelworkers of Am. v. Warrior & Gulf Nav. Co.*, 363 U.S. 574 (1960), *United Steelworkers of Am. v. Warrior & Gulf Nav. Co.*, 363 U.S. 574 (1960), *United Steelworkers of Am. v. Enter. Wheel & Car Corp.*, 363 U.S. 593 (1960) (holding that the arbitrator's function is to determine if a contract is subject to arbitration, the scope of that arbitration and that the court must defer to the arbitrator's interpretation of the collective bargaining agreement in most cases.) Later, the Supreme Court held collective bargaining agreements made between employers and unions are enforceable as long as the arbitration agreement stated which statute is subject to the waiver. *14 Penn Plaza LLC v. Pyett*, 556 U.S. 247 (2009). For more information, Secunda (n. 3), 57-66.
36. *Gilmer v. Interstate/Johnson Lane Corp.*, 500 U.S. 20 (1991).
37. A.J.S. Colvin, *The Growing Use of Mandatory Arbitration* (Economic Policy Institute, 2018).
38. *Ibid.*
39. *Epic Sys. Corp. v. Lewis*, 138 S. Ct. 1612 (2018).

21.4.1 Advantages and Disadvantages of Arbitration

Like most forms of dispute resolution, there are advantages as well as disadvantages to arbitration. However, most of the advantages benefit the employer and most of the disadvantages detrimentally impact the employee. The most commonly cited advantage is that arbitration is economical and efficient. It is far less expensive than traditional litigation because less lawyer-time is needed (if there is any legal representation at all for employees), resulting in an average of 50% savings to the parties.[40] Arbitration is also much faster than civil litigation. The Federal Judicial Center found that, on average, employment litigation takes almost two years to complete. In contrast, arbitration cases are resolved in around eight to nine months.[41] Other advantages of arbitration are that it is private because it is out of the public record and it is also less formal with regard to rules of evidence, procedure, and not requiring a written award or decision.

While these advantages appear beneficial to both parties, the disadvantages reveal grave impediments to the employee. The employee win rate in arbitration cases is only 21.4%, lower than employee win rates in litigation trials.[42] Further, when employees resolve disputes through arbitration, the mean award amount is substantially lower than award amounts in traditional litigation.[43] When the FAA was created, it was in the context of commercial arbitration agreements where each party had equal or similar bargaining power. Moreover, when the FAA was extended to employment contracts, union membership was higher than it is today; meaning there was also a healthier balance of bargaining power between employees and their employer. Many critics argue that arbitration agreements today are coercive because of the drastic differences in bargaining power between a single employee and an employer. Often employees do not realize they are signing such detrimental clauses at the beginning of employment and because arbitration agreements are usually mandatory, employees feel they have no choice but to sign them or else lose their jobs.

Another stark disadvantage to employees is that employers have a built-in advantage in disputes settled by arbitration because employers are "repeat players" and know the arbitration process. Also, judicial review is extremely limited and arbitration awards are final and binding except for very rare circumstances. All of these disadvantages raise two very worrisome concerns.

---

40. M. Halvordson, *Employment Arbitration: A Closer Look* (This article examines the problems with the current system used to resolve workplace disputes, the legal developments that have made pre-dispute mandatory arbitration a viable option), 64 J. Mo. B. 174 (2008).
41. L.L. Maltby, *Private Justice: Employment Arbitration and Civil Rights*, 30, Colum. Hum. Rts. L. Rev. 29, 55 (1998).
42. A. Colvin, *An Empirical Study of Employment Arbitration: Case Outcomes & Processes*, 8 J. Emp. Leg. Studies 1 (2011).
43. *Ibid.*

First, they reveal the involuntary nature of pre-dispute employment arbitration. Second, they create inequitable agreements that end up placing more burdens on employees to seek a remedy and, thus, discourage employees from making potential claims in the first place.[44]

21.4.2 Arbitration in the Nonunionized Workplaces[45]

In the years following pro-arbitration rulings and Congress granting more statutory rights to employees, U.S. employers have become increasingly more likely to require nonunionized employees to sign arbitration agreements as a condition of employment to enforce statutory rights.[46] The Supreme Court ruled on the enforceability of these agreements in *Gilmer v. Interstate/Johnson Lane Corp.* in a nonemployment case because it arose under a registration agreement by the trade association in the securities industries for stockbrokers.[47] There, the employee believed his employer fired him because of his age. He tried to initiate a lawsuit under the Age Discrimination in Employment Act, a statute created to prevent age discrimination in the workforce. However, because the employee had signed an arbitration agreement through his registration agreement with the securities trade association, the Supreme Court held that even if an arbitration agreement waived statutory rights granted to an employee, the arbitration agreement would be upheld since there was no Congressional intent to the contrary.

After *Gilmer v. Interstate/Johnson Lane Corp.*, it was uncertain whether the holding from the case applied only to employment claims. In 2001, *Circuit City v. Adams* resolved that uncertainty when it held that the courts would enforce arbitration agreements under other employment statutes, as long as transportation employees were not involved. From there, a steady stream of Supreme Court cases has further eroded employment-based statutory rights.[48]

In the class-action context, under which many employment claims are brought in the United States, the Supreme Court held that any state law that sought to make arbitration agreements unenforceable was preempted by the FAA. Specifically, at issue in *AT&T Mobility LLC v. Concepcion*[49] was a California state law which required that arbitration agreements that prohibited class-action suits were unenforceable. More recently, the Supreme Court addressed class-action arbitration waivers in the context of employment in *Epic Sys. Corp. v.*

44. J.M. Hirsch et al., *Understanding Employment Law*, 28 (2d ed., LexisNexis, 2013).
45. Because 84% of employees in the U.S. are in the private sector and in the private sector, only 6.5% are unionized, arbitration in unionized workplaces is not discussed here. For more information on arbitration in the union setting, *see* generally Secunda (n. 3) 57-66.
46. *Ibid.*, at 291.
47. *Gilmer v. Interstate/Johnson Lane Corp.*, 500 U.S. 20 (1991).
48. *Circuit City Stores, Inc. v. Adams*, 532 U.S. 105 (2001).
49. *AT&T Mobility LLC v. Concepcion*, 563 U.S. 333 (2011).

Lewis.[50] There, the employers required employees to enter into an arbitration agreement in which individualized arbitration was mandatory if a dispute arose between the parties. Employees sought to litigate both labor law and wage and hour class-action lawsuits in federal court. The Supreme Court ruled 5-4 in favor of the employers' individualized arbitration agreement and held that an arbitration agreement which precludes the employees from bringing their claims in a class-action are enforceable and do not violate section 7 of the NLRA, which give all employees the right to work in tandem to improve the conditions of their workplace.[51]

The debate between Justice Gorsuch, who wrote the majority opinion in *Epic Systems*, and Justice Ginsburg, who wrote the dissent, reveals that both sides of the political spectrum believe *Lochner* era reasoning is present in their opponents' arguments. As discussed in Part II, the *Lochner* era refers to Supreme Court decisions from the early 1900s to the mid-1930s when many federal and state workplace protective legislation was struck down under the guise of a constitutional form of "liberty to contract" between employer and employee. In her dissent, Ginsburg argued that this language and the legislative history of the NLRA make clear that Congress intended to protect employees from contracts that prevented them from engaging in class-action suits. Moreover, she argues that the FAA's legislative history reveals that Congress did not intend the statute to be used in employment contracts at all. For his part, Gorsuch's majority opinion directly accuses Ginsburg of engaging in *Lochner* era reasoning. His argument ends by stating: "This Court is not free to substitute its preferred economic policies for those chosen by the people's representatives. That, we had always understood, was *Lochner*'s sins."[52] Gorsuch's reasoning rests on the idea that the NLRA should be interpreted on its face rather than by looking at legislative intent.

Regardless of Gorsuch's explanation, many U.S. labor law advocates argue that the United States is in a new *Lochner* era, again marked with a pro-business Supreme Court that impedes employees from vindicating workplace rights under the theory of economic liberty for employers.[53] However, rather than striking down workplace protective legislation on constitutional grounds, this Lochner era features adhesive employment contracts being implemented above all other contrary employment laws, policies, and practices.

50. *Epic Sys. Corp. v. Lewis*, 138 S. Ct. 1612 (2018).
51. Section 7 of the NLRA guarantees that employees have "the right to self-organization, to form, join, or assist labour organizations, to bargain collectively through representatives of their own choosing, and to engage in other concerted activities for the purpose of collective bargaining or other mutual aid or protection." 29 U.S.C. § 157.
52. Epic Sys Corp. 138 S. Ct. at 1630.
53. K.A. Sabbeth & D.C. Vladeck, *Contracting (Out) Rights*, 36 Fordham Urb. L. J. 803 (2009). *See also* S.A. Plass, *Mandatory Arbitration as an Employer's Contractual Prerogative: The Efficiency Challenge to Equal Employment Opportunity*, 33 Cardozo L. Rev. 195, 208 (2011).

21.5 CONCLUSION

While many might argue that progress has been made in the area of both labor and employment law in the United States with regard to employee rights, many U.S. employees find themselves in a situation where they have little control over the terms and conditions of their employment. Not only are more employers requiring employees to sign pre-dispute arbitration agreements as a prerequisite to employment but employees are also being forced to sign away their ability to initiate employment-related class-action lawsuits. Along with the decline in union membership, employees have been left with little power over their employment in the United States.

All of these developments indicate that the state of labor and employment law in the United States is similar to that during the *Lochner* era in the early part of the twentieth century, where workers' rights were ignored or abused without consequence. This dynamic is due in no small part to the decrease in union membership, which in turn is based on employees having a false sense of security in common law and statutory protections. Instead of workers being able to rely on constitutional, statutory or common law labor and employment rights in a judicial forum with a jury right, they are left reliant on one-sided contractual provisions that force them to individually arbitrate their employment rights in an unfair forum.

BIBLIOGRAPHY

R.A. Bales, J.M. Hirsch & P.M. Secunda, *Understanding Employment Law*, 28 (LexisNexis, 2007).

Bureau of Labor Statistics, "Union Members Summary," https://www.bls.gov/news.release/union2.nr0.htm accessed 15 August 2018.

A.J.S. Colvin, *An Empirical Study of Employment Arbitration: Case Outcomes & Processes*, 8 J. Emp. Leg. Studies 1 (2011).

A.J.S. Colvin, *The Growing Use of Mandatory Arbitration*, Econ. Policy Inst. (2018).

M. Halvordson, *Employment Arbitration: A Closer Look*, 64 J. Mo. B. 174 (2008).

L.L. Maltby, *Private Justice: Employment Arbitration and Civil Rights*, 30 Colum. Hum. Rts. L. Rev. 29, 55 (1998).

S.A. Plass, *Mandatory Arbitration as an Employer's Contractual Prerogative: The Efficiency Challenge to Equal Employment Opportunity*, 33 Cardozo L. Rev. 195, 208 (2011).

K.A. Sabbeth & D.C. Vladeck, *Contracting (Out) Rights*, 36 Fordham Urb. L.J. 803 (2009).

P.M. Secunda, *The Wagner Model of Labour Law Is Dead—Long Live Labour Law!*, 38 Queens L.J. 545, 555-561 (2013).

P.M. Secunda & J.M. Hirsch, *Mastering Employment Discrimination Law,* (1st ed., Carolina Academic Press, 2010).

P.M. Secunda, A.M. Lofaso, J.E. Slater & J.M. Hirsch, *Mastering Labor Law* 8-9 (Carolina Academic Press, 2014).

H.G. Wood, *A Treatise on the Law of Master and Servant* (J.D. Parsons, Jr., 1877).

STUDIES IN EMPLOYMENT AND SOCIAL POLICY

1. W. Beck, L. van der Maesen & A. Walker (eds), *The Social Quality of Europe*, 1997 (ISBN 90-411-0456-9).
2. R. Blanpain, M. Colucci, C. Engels, F. Hendrickx, L. Salas & E. De Smyter, *Institutional Changes and European Social Policies after the Treaty of Amsterdam*, 1998 (ISBN 90-411-1018-6).
3. V. Lo: *Law and Industrial Relations: China and Japan after World War II*, 1998 (ISBN 90-411-1075-5).
4. A. Den Exter & H. Hermans (eds), *The Right to Health Care in Several European Countries*, 1998 (ISBN 90-411-1087-9).
5. M. Biagi (ed.), *Job Creation and Labour Law from Protection towards Pro- Action*, 2000 (ISBN 90-411-1432-7).
6. W. Beck, L. van der Maesen, F. Thomése & A. Walker (eds), *Social Quality: A Vision for Europe*, 2000 (ISBN 90-411-1523-4).
7. F. Pennings, *Introduction to European Social Law*, 3rd ed., 2001 (ISBN 90-411-1628-1).
8. J. Murray, *Transnational Labour Regulation: The ILO and EC Compared*, 2001 (ISBN 90-411-1583-8).
9. R. Blanpain & C. Engels (eds), *The ILO and Social Challenges of the 21st Century*, 2001 (ISBN 90-411-1572-2).
10. M. Biagi (ed.), *Towards a European Model of Industrial Relations? Building on the First Report of the European Commission*, 2001 (ISBN 90-411-1653-2).
11. J. Clasen (ed.), *What Future for Social Security? Debates and Reforms in National and Cross-National Perspective*, 2001 (ISBN 90-411-1671-0).
12. A. Numhauser-Henning (ed.), *Legal Perspectives on Equal Treatment and Non-Discrimination*, 2001 (ISBN 90-411-1665-6).
13. R. Blanpain (ed.), *Labour Law, Human Rights and Social Justice* 2001 (ISBN 90-411-1697-4).
14. M.-C. Kuo, H.F. Zacher & H.-S. Chan (eds), *Reform and Perspectives on Social Insurance: Lessons from the East and West*, 2002 (ISBN 90-411-1819-5).
15. P. Foubert, *The Legal Protection of the Pregnant Worker in the European Community*, 2002 (ISBN 90-411-1842-X).
16. M. Biagi (ed.), *Quality of Work and Employee Involvement in Europe*, 2002 (ISBN 90-411-1885-3).
17. F. Pennings, *Dutch Social Security Law in an International Context*, 2002 (ISBN 90-411-1887-X).

18. T. Carney & G. Ramia, *From Rights to Management: Contract, New Public Management and Employment Services*, 2002 (ISBN 90-411-1889-6).
19. R. Blanpain & M. Colucci, *European Labour and Social Security Law, Glossary*, 2002 (ISBN 90-411-1905-1).
20. I.U. Zeytinoglu (ed.), *Flexible Work Arrangements: Conceptualizations and International Experiences*, 2002 (ISBN 90-411-1947-7).
21. J. Berghman, A. Nagelkerke, M. Boos, R. Doeschot & G. Vonk (eds), *Social Security in Transition*, 2002 (ISBN 90-411-1969-8).
22. R. Blanpain, *The Legal Status of Sportsmen and Sportswomen under International, European and Belgian National and Regional Law*, 2003 (ISBN 90-411-1980-9).
23. R. Blanpain & M. Weiss (eds), *Changing Industrial Relations & Modernisation of Labour Law, Liber Amicorum in Honour of Professor Marco Biagi*, 2003 (ISBN 90-411-2008-4).
24. J. Malmberg (ed.), *Effective Enforcement of EC Labour Law*, 2003 (ISBN 90-411-2160-9).
25. M. De Vos (ed.), *A Decade Beyond Maastricht: The European Social Dialogue Revisited*, 2003 (ISBN 90-411-2163-3).
26. M. Sewerynski (ed.), *Collective Agreements and Individual Contracts of Employment*, 2003 (ISBN 90-411-2190-0).
27. R. Blanpain & M. Van Gestel, *Use and Monitoring of E-Mail, Intranet and Internet Facilities at Work: Law and Practice*, 2004 (ISBN 90-411-22-66-4).
28. A. C. Neal (ed.), *The Changing Face of European Labour Law and Social Policy*, 2004 (ISBN 90-411-2312-1).
29. E. Sol & M. Westerveld (eds), *Contractualism in Employment Services: A New Form of Welfare State Governance*, 2005 (ISBN 90-411-2405-5).
30. F. Pennings (ed.), *Between Soft and Hard Law – The Impact of International Social Security Standards on National Social Security Law*, 2006 (ISBN 978-90-411-2491-3).
31. L. Dickens & A. C. Neal (eds), *The Changing Institutional Face of British Employment Relations*, 2006 (ISBN 978-90-411-2541-5).
32. G. Sebardt, *Redundancy and the Swedish Model in an International Context*, 2006 (ISBN 978-90-411-2503-3).
33. A.M. Swiatkowski, *Charter of Social Rights of the Council of Europe*, 2007 (ISBN 978-90-411-2608-5).
34. M. Sargeant (ed.), *The Law on Age Discrimination in the EU*, 2008 (ISBN 978-90-411-2522-4).
35. G. Di Domenico & S. Spattini (eds), *New European Approaches to Long- Term Unemployment: What Role for Public Employment Services and What Market for Private Stakeholders?*, 2008 (ISBN 978-90-411-2614-6.)
36. C. Welz, *The European Social Dialogue under Articles 138 and 139 of the EC Treaty: Actors, Processes, Outcomes*, 2008 (ISBN 978-90-411-2744-0).
37. M. Rönnmar (ed.), *EU Industrial Relations v. National Industrial Relations: Comparative and Interdisciplinary Perspectives*, 2008 (ISBN 978-90-411- 2770-9).

38. F. Pennings, Y. Konijn & A. Veldman (eds), *Social Responsibility in Labour Relations: European and Comparative Perspectives*, 2008 (ISBN 978-90- 411-2783-9).
39. F. Pennings & C. Bosse (eds), *The Protection of Working Relationships: A Comparative Study*, 2011 (ISBN 978-90-411-3289-5).
40. S. Devetzi & S. Stendahl (eds), *Too Sick to Work?: Social Security Reference in Europe for Persons with Reduced Earnings Capacity*, 2011 (ISBN 978-90- 411-3426-4).
41. Ulrich Becker, Frans Pennings & Tineke Dijkhoff (eds), *International Standard Setting and Innovations in Social Security*, 2013 (ISBN 978-90-411-3233-8).
42. E. Ales (ed.), *Health and Safety at Work: European and Comparative Perspective*, 2013 (ISBN 978-90-411-4661-8).
43. F. Pennings, T. Erhag & S. Stendahl (eds), *Non-public Actors in Social Security Administration: A Comparative Study*, 2013 (ISBN 978-90-411-4917-6).
44. A. Neal (ed.), *Cross-Currents in Modern Chinese Labour Law*, 2014 (ISBN 978-90-411-4763-9).
45. B. Waas (ed.), *The Right to Strike: A Comparative View*, 2014 (ISBN 978-90-411-5007-3).
46. A. Ojeda-Avilés, *Transnational Labour Law*, 2015 (ISBN 978-90-411-5858-1).
47. A. Numhauser-Henning & M. Rönnmar, *Age Discrimination and Labour-Law: Comparative and Conceptual Perspectives in the EU and Beyond*, 2015 (ISBN 978-90-411-4979-4).
48. A. Perulli & T. Treu (eds), *Enterprise and Social Rights*, 2017 (ISBN 978-90-411-8234-0).
49. Dr F.C.A. van Haasteren, *Decent Flexibility: The Impact of ILO Convention 181 and the Regulation on Temporary Agency Work*, 2017 (ISBN 978-90-411-9236-3).
50. T. Dijkhoff & L.G. Mpedi (eds), *Recommendation on Social Protection Floors: Basic Principles for Innovative Solutions*, 2018 (ISBN 978-90-411-8623-2).
51. A. Perulli & T. Treu (eds), *Sustainable Development, Global Trade and Social Rights*, 2018 (ISBN 978-90-411-9235-6).
52. M. Mironi & M. Schlachter (eds), *Regulating Strikes in Essential Services: A Comparative 'Law in Action' Perspective*, 2019 (ISBN 978-90-411-8997-4).
53. A. Perulli & T. Treu (eds), *The Role of the State and Industrial Relations*, 2019 (ISBN 978-94-035-0661-6).
54. T. Gyulavári & E. Menegatti (eds), *The Sources of Labour Law*, 2020 (ISBN 978-94-035-0284-7).

www.ingramcontent.com/pod-product-compliance
Ingram Content Group UK Ltd.
Pitfield, Milton Keynes, MK11 3LW, UK
UKHW020229290926
15470UKWH00001B/432

9 789403 50284